D0782358

*Tobacco Use by Native North Americans*

The Civilization of the American Indian Series

# Tobacco Use by Native North Americans

## Sacred Smoke and Silent Killer

EDITED BY

Joseph C. Winter

University of Oklahoma Press : Norman

Samford University Library

Text design by Emmy Ezzell.
Composed by C. F. Graphics, Inc.

Library of Congress Cataloging-in-Publication Data

Tobacco use by Native North Americans : sacred smoke and silent killer / edited by Joseph C. Winter.
    p.  cm. — (The civilization of the American Indians series; v. 236)
    Includes bibliographical references and index.
    ISBN 0-8061-3262-0 (cloth: alk. paper)
    1. Indians of North America—Tobacco use.  2. Indians of North America—Religion.  3. Indians of North America—Health and hygiene.  4. Tobacco—United States—History.  I. Winter, Joseph C.  II. Series.
E98.T6 .T63  2000
362.29'6'08997—dc21          99-087201

*Tobacco Use by Native North Americans: Sacred Smoke and Silent Killer* is Volume 236 in the The Civilization of the American Indian Series.

The paper in this book meets the guidelines for permanence and durability of the Committee on Production Guidelines for Book Longevity of the Council on Library Resources, Inc. ∞

Copyright © 2000 by the University of Oklahoma Press, Norman, Publishing Division of the University. All rights reserved. Manufactured in the U.S.A.

1  2  3  4  5  6  7  8  9  10

# Contents

E
98
.T6
T63
2000

∿

List of Illustrations     vii
List of Tables     xiii
Preface     xv

*Part One*: Traditional Uses of Tobacco by Native Americans

1.  Introduction to the North American Tobacco Species     3
     *Joseph C. Winter*
2.  Traditional Uses of Tobacco by Native Americans     9
     *Joseph C. Winter*
3.  North American Indigenous *Nicotiana* Use and Tobacco Shamanism:
     The Early Documentary Record, 1520–1660     59
     *Alexander von Gernet*
4.  Ethnobotanical Notes from Zuni Pueblo     81
     *Carol B. Brandt*

*Part Two*: Description of the North American Tobaccos

5.  Botanical Description of the North American Tobacco Species     87
     *Joseph C. Winter*
6.  Out of California: Cultural Geography of Western North American Tobacco     128
     *Julia E. Hammett*

*Part Three*: The Archaeobotanical Study of Tobacco

7.  Tobacco Use, Ecology, and Manipulation in the Prehistoric and
     Historic Southwestern United States     143
     *Karen R. Adams* and *Mollie S. Toll*
8.  Tobacco on the Plains: Historical Use, Ethnographic Accounts,
     and Archaeological Evidence     171
     *Mary J. Adair*
9.  Tobacco in Prehistoric Eastern North America     185
     *Gail E. Wagner*

*Part Four*: The Identification of Tobacco Pollen

10. Prehistoric Tobacco Pollen in Southwestern Colorado:
        Distribution and Possible Contamination                          205
     *Linda Scott Cummings*
11. Morphological Studies of New Mexico Solanaceae Pollen                211
     *Richard G. Holloway* and *Glenna Dean*
12. Morphological Distinctiveness of *Nicotiana* Pollen and the
        Potential for Identifying Prehistoric Southwest Tobacco Use
        through Pollen Analysis                                          223
     *Jannifer W. Gish*

*Part Five*: Evolution of the Use of Tobacco by Native Americans

13. From Earth Mother to Snake Woman: The Role of Tobacco in the
        Evolution of Native American Religious Organization             265
     *Joseph C. Winter*
14. Food of the Gods: Biochemistry, Addiction, and the Development of
        Native American Tobacco Use                                     305
     *Joseph C. Winter*

*Part Six*: The Negative Health Effects of Tobacco Use

15. Health Effects of Tobacco Use by Native Americans: Past and Present  331
     *Jonathan M. Samet*
16. The Huichol Indians, Tobacco, and Pesticides                        342
     *Patricia Díaz-Romo* and *Samuel Salinas Alvarez*
17. Native Americans and Tobacco: Deer Person's Gift or Columbus's Curse? 353
     *Joseph C. Winter, Glenn W. Solomon, Robert F. Hill,*
        *Christina M. Pego,* and *Suzanne E. Victoria*
18. Tricky Tokes, Those Coyote Smokes: How Coyote Learned
        the True Power of Tobacco                                       382
     *Lawrence A. Shorty*

     References                                                         387
     List of Contributors                                              435
     Index                                                              439

# Illustrations

## Photographs

1. *Nicotiana rustica*, type known as *punche de mexicano*  5
2. Huichol Indian child harvesting commercial *N. tabacum*  6
3. *N. quadrivalvis* var. *wallacei*  6
4. Navajo man pruning mountain tobacco (*N. attenuata*)  7
5. Coyote's tobacco, *N. trigonophylla*  7
6. Seed pods and flowers of tree tobacco (*N. glauca*)  7
7. Eskimo woman smoking a traditional pipe  12
8. Cree Indians and Hudson's Bay Company workers with tobacco "carrot"  13
9. *N. rustica* patch on the Tonawanda Seneca Reservation, 1995  14
10. Seneca Chief Cornplanter's tobacco, *N. rustica*  17
11. Arikara man with seven calumets  23
12. Tlingit hunter smoking a pipe, 1899  27
13. Phoebe Maddux wearing a Karuk hat of a type also used
    as a tobacco basket, 1928  32
14. Southern Ute men with Plains-style pipes and pipe bags  40
15. *N. rustica* at Jemez Pueblo, New Mexico, 1936  45
16. *N. rustica* drying at Jemez Pueblo, New Mexico, 1936  45
17. *N. rustica* field at San Juan Pueblo Agricultural Cooperative,
    New Mexico, 1994  46
18. Navajo herbalist with a freshly picked bunch of *N. attenuata*  46
19. Lacandon Maya woman smoking an *N. tabacum* cigar  47
20. Tarahumara *N. tabacum*, Chihuahua, Mexico, 1953  53
21. Mopan Maya *N. tabacum*  93
22. Mexican *N. tabacum*, with Huichol Indian child laborers  94
23. *N. rustica* grown from seed from Santo Domingo Pueblo, New Mexico  102
24. *N. rustica* var. *pavonii*  102
25. Large-leafed Iroquois *N. rustica*  103
26. Blossom variations among tobacco species used by Native Americans  106
27. Micrographs of seeds of various tobacco taxa  107
28. *N. glauca* (tree tobacco)  109
29. *N. attenuata* grown from seed from a Navajo family  112
30. *N. trigonophylla* grown from seed from old Kumeyaay village, California  124

31. Type specimen of *N. quadrivalvis* var. *multivalvis* collected by
     Meriwether Lewis                                                      129

32. *N. quadrivalvis* var. *multivalvis* grown from seeds collected by
     David Douglas, 1825                                                   130

33. *N. quadrivalvis* var. *multivalvis* grown from seeds collected by
     Elihu Hall, 1871                                                      132

34. Seeds of seven southwestern U.S. *Nicotiana* species                   146

35. Seeds of four native southwestern U.S. *Nicotiana* species             147

36. Seeds of two domesticated and one likely introduced *Nicotiana* species  148

37. Dottle residue from a sandstone pipe                                    180

38. Examples of New Mexico Solanaceae pollen grains                         212

39. Scanning electron microscope (SEM) and light microscope (LM) photographs:
     *Datura quercifolia, D. innoxia, D. meteloides*                       229

40. SEM and LM photos: *Nicandra physalodes, Hyoscyamus niger*             230

41. SEM and LM photos: *Saracha procumbens, Capsicum annuum*               231

42. SEM and LM photos: *Capsicum baccatum, Physalis acutifolia*            232

43. SEM and LM photos: *Physalis hederaefolia, Solanum douglasii, S. jamesii*  233

44. SEM and LM photos: *Solanum fendleri, Chamaesaracha conioides*         234

45. SEM and LM photos: *Chamaesaracha coronopus, Margaranthus solanaceus,*
     *Salpichroa organifolia*                                              235

46. SEM and LM photos: *Cestrum flavescens, Petunia parviflora*            236

47. SEM and LM photos: *Lycium andersonii, L. pallidum, L. torreyi*        237

48. SEM and LM photos: *L. pallidum, L. torreyi*                           238

49. SEM and LM photos: *Nicotiana attenuata*                               239

50. SEM and LM photos: *N. trigonophylla*                                  240

51. SEM and LM photos: *N. trigonophylla, N. rustica*                      241

52. SEM and LM photos: *N. rustica*                                        242

53. SEM and LM photos: *N. rustica*                                        243

54. SEM and LM photos: *N. rustica, N. tabacum*                            244

55. SEM and LM photos: *N. tabacum*                                        245

56. SEM and LM photos: *N. tabacum*                                        246

57. SEM and LM photos: *N. bigelovii*                                      247

58. SEM and LM photos: *N. bigelovii, N. multivalvis*                      248

59. SEM and LM photos: *N. multivalvis, N. quadrivalvis*                   249

60. SEM and LM photos: *N. quadrivalvis*                                   250

61. SEM and LM photos: *N. glauca*                                         251

62. SEM and LM photos: *N. acuminata, N. clevelandii*                      252

63. SEM and LM photos: *N. palmeri, N. sylvestris*                         253

64. Mountain tobacco growing in front of a Navajo hogan                    272

65. Huichol Indian child laborer drinking water from a pesticide container 276

66. Grandfather Fire, in a yarn painting by Mariano Valadez                278

67. Crow Indian tobacco garden                                             287

68. Martha Bad Warrior holding the White Buffalo Calf Pipe of the Lakota   292

69. Captain John, at the Hupa village of Medildin                          294

70. Huichol family offering tobacco and prayers at the ocean               342

71. Yarn *tabla* by José Benítez Sánchez and Tutukila Carrillo             344

| | | |
|---|---|---|
| 72. | Herbicide containers in a Huichol community | 347 |
| 73. | Huichol woman stringing tobacco leaves in lines | 348 |
| 74. | Huichol family cooking in the tobacco fields | 350 |
| 75. | Navajo herbalist collecting *N. attenuata* for use in a ceremony. | 353 |
| 76. | Kuna Indian smoking tobacco during a girl's puberty ceremony | 353 |
| 77. | California Indian smoking a commercial cigarette | 354 |
| 78. | Inuit woman smoking a commercial cigarette, 1979 | 354 |

## Maps

| | | |
|---|---|---|
| 1. | Native North American groups using tobacco | 10 |
| 2. | Natural distribution of the three subgenera of wild tobacco | 91 |
| 3. | Evolutionary geography of the cultivated tobaccos | 96 |
| 4. | Areas of native North American use of *N. tabacum* | 98 |
| 5. | Areas of native North American use of *N. rustica* | 104 |
| 6. | Areas of native North American use of *N. glauca* | 111 |
| 7. | Areas of native North American use of *N. attenuata* | 113 |
| 8. | Areas of native North American use of *N. quadrivalvis* | 119 |
| 9. | Natural range of *N. clevelandii* | 123 |
| 10. | Natural range of *N. trigonophylla* | 125 |
| 11. | Geographic distribution of *N. quadrivalvis* vars. *bigelovii* and *wallacei* | 132 |
| 12. | Geographic distribution of *N. attenuata* | 133 |
| 13. | Geographic distribution of *N. clevelandii* and *N. trigonophylla* | 134 |
| 14. | Geographic distribution of *N. glauca* and *N. acuminata* | 135 |
| 15. | Archaic and Basketmaker sites with *Nicotiana* remains | 153 |
| 16. | Pueblo I sites with *Nicotiana* remains | 156 |
| 17. | Pueblo II–III sites with *Nicotiana* remains | 159 |
| 18. | Late Pueblo sites with *Nicotiana* remains | 164 |
| 19. | Historic sites with *Nicotiana* remains | 166 |
| 20. | Distribution of aboriginal tobacco on the Great Plains | 173 |
| 21. | Great Plains sites with archaeological tobacco | 178 |
| 22. | Distribution of archaeological tobacco across eastern North America | 189 |
| 23. | Distribution of archaeological tobacco in the confluence area | 190 |
| 24. | Distribution of Solanaceae species in Arizona | 257 |
| 25. | Distribution of Solanaceae species in Colorado | 258 |
| 26. | Distribution of Solanaceae species in New Mexico | 259 |
| 27. | Distribution of Solanaceae species in Utah | 260 |
| 28. | Ranges of wild and domesticated Native American tobaccos in North America | 311 |
| 29. | Number of tobacco taxa used by native North Americans | 313 |
| 30. | Sequence of development of native North American use of tobacco | 323 |

## Figures

| | | |
|---|---|---|
| 1. | Masked member of the Haudenosaunee False Face society standing in a patch of *Nicotiana rustica* | 14 |

2. Zuni man smoking a ceremonial cigarette 82
3. Phylogeny of tobacco species used by native North Americans 88
4. Chloroplast DNA relationships of six species of tobacco 88
5. Subfamilies, tribes, and genera in the Solanaceae family 89
6. *Nicotiana tabacum* 92
7. *N. rustica* var. *brasilia* 99
8. *N. glauca* 109
9. *N. attenuata* 112
10. *N. quadrivalvis* var. *bigelovii* 118
11. *N. quadrivalvis* var. *multivalvis* 121
12. *N. clevelandii* 122
13. *N. trigonophylla* 124
14. Drawing of *N. multivalvis* 130
15. Floor distribution of *Zea mays* pollen 206
16. Floor distribution of *Cleome* pollen 206
17. Floor distribution of *Nicotiana* pollen 207
18. Pollen recovered from an unburned cigarette and from chewing tobacco 208
19. Polar length of Solanaceae pollen in micrometers 214
20. Equatorial width of Solanaceae pollen in micrometers 215
21. P/E index for Solanaceae pollen 216
22. Polar area measurements for Solanaceae pollen 217
23. Polar area index for Solanaceae pollen 218
24. Results of cluster analysis for the New Mexico Solanaceae 220
25. Navajo Sky Father and Earth Mother with sacred plants 269
26. The first tobacco growing from the grave of Sky Woman's daughter 282
27. Cihuacoatl, the Aztec earth goddess 299
28. Nicotine frequencies of native North American tobacco taxa 316
29. A Huichol priest's tobacco gourd 345
30. Pesticide- and tobacco-intoxicated Huichols, 1995 351
31. Canadian First Nations smoking rates 355
32. Canadian smoking rates, 1994–1995 356
33. Native American smoking rates in the United States 356
34. Smoking rates in the United States, whites and all races combined 357
35. Use of traditional tobacco by Native American prison inmates 363
36. Association of cardinal directions with other features in Navajo religion 367
37. Native American lung cancer mortality in the United States, 1958–1992 370
38. Male and female lung cancer rates, 1970 U.S. population 371
39. Lung cancer mortality rates for Native Americans in selected states 372
40. Lung cancer mortality rates for Native Americans by
    Indian Health Service area 373
41. Mortality rates for selected smoking-related causes of death 374
42. Native American cigarette smoking among adults 375
43. Alaskan Native American smoking rates 375
44. Smoking rates of Native Americans in Washington, Oregon, and Idaho 376
45. Smoking rates of Native Americans in the western, north-central, and
    south-central United States 377

46. Smoking rates for Native Americans in Montana, the Great Plains, and the northern Great Plains     378
47. Overall smoking rates for California Native Americans     379
48. Smoking rates for California Native Americans by tribe     380
49. Youth smoking rates for southwestern Native Americans     381
50. Coyote smoking tobacco stolen from Mountain Sheep     384

# Tables

| | | |
|---|---|---:|
| 1. | Early history of the use of tobacco | 2 |
| 2. | Tobacco species used by native North Americans | 5 |
| 3. | Arctic Native American groups using tobacco | 11 |
| 4. | Subarctic Native American groups using tobacco | 12 |
| 5. | Eastern woodland Native American groups using tobacco | 15 |
| 6. | Plains Native American groups using tobacco | 21 |
| 7. | Northwest Coast and interior plateau Native American groups using tobacco | 25 |
| 8. | California Native American groups using tobacco | 28 |
| 9. | Traditional species of tobacco used by native Californians | 30 |
| 10. | Great Basin Native American groups using tobacco | 38 |
| 11. | Southwestern Native American groups using tobacco | 42 |
| 12. | Traditional tobacco species used by Native Americans in the Southwest | 43 |
| 13. | Mesoamerican Native American groups using tobacco | 48 |
| 14. | Traditional tobacco species raised or gathered by Mesoamerican groups | 50 |
| 15. | Names of Mexican tobacco species | 51 |
| 16. | Caribbean Native American groups using tobacco | 56 |
| 17. | Documentary sources on tobacco in pre-1660 North America | 60 |
| 18. | References to tobacco cultivation in pre-1660 North America | 67 |
| 19. | References to tobacco preparation in pre-1660 North America | 71 |
| 20. | References to tobacco invocations in pre-1660 North America | 72 |
| 21. | Documentary evidence of Native American tobacco addiction in pre-1660 North America | 75 |
| 22. | *Nicotiana tabacum* in the NAPC seed bank | 95 |
| 23. | South American tribes using *N. tabacum* | 97 |
| 24. | Types of *N. rustica* raised by native North Americans | 100 |
| 25. | *N. attenuata* in the NAPC seed bank | 116 |
| 26. | *N. quadrivalvis* in the NAPC seed bank | 117 |
| 27. | *N. trigonophylla* in the NAPC seed bank | 126 |
| 28. | *Nicotiana* species native to western North America | 128 |
| 29. | Herbarium specimens of *N. quadrivalvis* native to western North America | 131 |
| 30. | General features of southwestern *Nicotiana* seeds | 148 |
| 31. | Sizes of southwestern tobacco seeds | 149 |
| 32. | *Nicotiana* in Archaic to late Basketmaker sites | 154 |
| 33. | *Nicotiana* in early Pueblo sites | 157 |
| 34. | *Nicotiana* in Pueblo II to III sites | 160 |

35. *Nicotiana* in late Pueblo and late Classic Hohokam sites  165
36. *Nicotiana* in historic sites  167
37. Archaeological tobacco on the Great Plains  179
38. Descriptions of *Nicotiana* and *Solanum* seeds  187
39. Sizes of charred prehistoric eastern tobacco seeds  188
40. Archaeological tobacco in eastern North America  191
41. Archaeological contexts and associations for eastern U.S. tobacco seeds  197
42. Discriminant index scores by six and seven variables  219
43. Morphological key to genera of Solanaceae  221
44. Distribution of Solanaceae species in the greater Southwest  224
45. Pollen key  256
46. Non-*Nicotiana* species used as tobacco by the Navajo  274
47. Examples of how native North American spirits crave tobacco  309
48. Nicotine, nornicotine, and anabasine in tobacco species used by native North Americans  318
49. Nicotine and alkaloids in North American tobacco species not used by Native Americans  320
50. Alkaloids in domesticated tobacco species  321
51. Nicotine and alkaloids by rank for native North American tobacco species  321
52. Risks of major disease categories causally related to cigarettes  333
53. Selected surveys of cigarette smoking among American Indians  335
54. Mortality rates for smoking-related causes of death, 1986–1988  336
55. Mortality rates for respiratory causes of death, American Indians and Alaska Natives, 1984–1988  337
56. Mortality rates for cancers, American Indians and Alaska Natives, 1984–1988  338
57. Average annual cancer incidence rates, 1978–1981  339
58. Pesticides used in Mexican tobacco fields  351
59. Diffusion of "trade tobacco" to North American tribes, 1603–1743  359
60. Sources of Native Americans' tobacco in the eastern woodlands  361

# Preface

Tobacco—whether you love it or hate it, crave it or fear it, worship with it or do everything in your power to avoid it, everyone has an opinion about this powerful plant. To most people, tobacco is a mood-altering drug available in cigarette, cigar, pipe, chewing, and snuff forms. Many people use it for pleasure and so-called recreational purposes; most others consider it a foul-smelling, addictive killer. For the Navajo Indians of North America, the creation of the universe could not occur until Sky Father and Earth Mother had smoked sacred tobacco. Other traditional native North Americans have similar beliefs, and the use of small amounts of traditional tobacco forms a central part of their religious systems. In some instances it represents a food of the gods; at times it is a spirit itself. Morning Star, one of the principal Crow Indian deities, fell from the sky and turned into the first tobacco plant. Pulekukwerek, one of the Yurok creator spirits, grew from a tobacco plant. White Buffalo Calf Woman, daughter of the sun and the moon, brought the Lakota their first tobacco, along with their seven most important ceremonies.

Few people realize it, but tobacco grows wild throughout western North America. One day in 1995, I stood with a companion on a low hill above the dry, dusty expanse of Escavada Wash, one of the main tributaries of the equally dry and dusty Chaco Wash in northwestern New Mexico. We were only ten miles from Pueblo Bonito and the other magnificent ruins in Chaco Canyon, but we were a thousand years away in time. For the man I was with was Diné—a

Navajo—a prominent member of the Nageezi ("little pumpkin") community, whereas the ruins were ancestral Pueblo. We were looking at his sacred tobacco, 40 or 50 plants of it, small delicate specimens of wild mountain tobacco (*Nicotiana attenuata*) that looked nothing like the giant commercial tobacco plants grown in Virginia.

I had first met this man about 15 years earlier, when he worked as a translator on one of my projects. Later he served on several others, and slowly a bond of trust had grown between us, until he felt comfortable enough to show me his sacred plants. Even his neighbors didn't know about them, for he was concerned that someone might take them—other Indians or, worse yet, "New Agers" or other *bilagaana* who would steal them for their power.

"*Dzil nat'oh*," he said, as he gently touched a pink-tinged white flower. "That's what we call them in Navajo—*dzil nat'oh*—mountain tobacco. My grandfather planted them here, over 70 years ago. He brought the seeds down from the La Plata Mountains in Colorado, and they've been growing here ever since."

"They're beautiful," I responded. "Do they grow back every year, or do you have to replant them?"

"They grow on their own," he answered. "Every year they reappear from new seeds, to give me power. They are *diyin*—holy people—holy spirits, like *ye'ii*, with great medicine. And they're very dangerous. You have to use them with respect, as prayers and offerings in ceremonies, so they'll reward you. But if you use them without respect, if you smoke them like cigarettes, their power will kill you."

It took me a long time to understand this simple statement and to realize that it explains perfectly why so many people—half a million here in the United States and three, four, or five times that number in the rest of the world—die each year from tobacco. First I had to learn how the power that gives tobacco its sanctity and spiritual value for Native Americans is the same power that causes addiction, illness, and death among natives and non-natives alike—power in the form of nicotine and the other deadly alkaloids in the leaves and flowers of this beautiful plant.

This book presents the results of 20 years of research into the origins, history, and contemporary use of tobacco by native North Americans. My search for knowledge about tobacco took me into the deserts of Arizona and New Mexico, into the dark forests of Maine and Quebec, into the isolated mountains of western Mexico and the even more isolated and distant waters of the upper Amazon in Peru. It was there, in Peru, among the Shipibo, Yagua, and Capa-Nagua Indians on the Ucayali River, that I learned the hard way that both forms of power—the spiritual and the chemical—contain the very power of the sun. Both belong to the Sun and the Hawk. Both are produced by the tobacco plant's amazing ability to create nicotine, to use the miracle of photosynthesis to convert pure sunlight into positive spiritual and negative chemical power. Into sacred smoke and silent killer.

Originally intended as a North American complement to Johannes Wilbert's *Tobacco and Shamanism in South America*, this book provides information about how and why Native Americans use tobacco, how they created the domesticated species of the plant, and how they are affected by its positive religious values and negative health consequences. It describes the various species of wild and domesticated tobacco and examines the ways in which different species can be identified. Many North American Indian

practices and beliefs are analyzed, including the concept that tobacco is so potent and sacred that the spirits themselves are addicted to it.

The book also presents detailed archaeological and ethnographic evidence for a pervasive, continent-wide system of tobacco cultivation, ingestion, and veneration. My colleagues and I discuss information from scores of archaeological assemblages and hundreds of tribal groups. I propose that potent wild tobacco was one of the first plants domesticated by humans in the New World and that its addictive properties and hallucinogenic powers figured prominently in this process. I also suggest that as soon as early Native Americans harnessed its power through domestication (and were in turn ensnared by its nicotine), they used this newfound knowledge of plant cultivation to domesticate corn, potatoes, and other food plants.

In addition, this book presents detailed data about the positive religious and negative health effects of tobacco. When used with respect in small amounts in prayers and ceremonies, traditional tobacco is a life-affirming sacramental substance that confers enormous power on the people using it. When used without respect in cigarettes and other commercial products, tobacco is a deadly killer, regardless of race or religion.

This book is about an extremely important plant that affects our society in more ways than most of us realize. It examines the complex symbiotic and often deadly relationships between humans and the plants we cultivate and whose ranges and natures we forever change. It describes an extremely powerful drug plant at the very heart of an unfolding, daily drama pitting personal rights against the public welfare. This drama involves the clash of national politics, the tobacco industry, and the United States health system.

This book is also about the scientific process. It demonstrates how researchers in a number of different fields—archaeology, cultural anthropology, palynology, archaeobotany, ethnobiology, environmental health research, and medical science—have come together to share their findings, thereby discovering how tiny seeds, beautiful flowers, cross-cultural religious patterns, and Native American health data can all be used to understand an amazing plant.

Finally, this book describes the clash of values between Native Americans and non-Indians regarding the importance and meaning of tobacco. My search for the meaning of tobacco took me to many places, among them some of the worst prisons in the country, where Native American men and women are fighting for the simple right to use traditional tobacco in prayers and ceremonies. Most native inmates do not have this right, and even when they do, the sacred tobacco is strictly controlled and often withheld as punishment for minor infractions. It was there, in the stark gray prison yards surrounded by chain-link fences topped by razor-tipped wire, that I learned the most humbling and wondrous lesson of all about tobacco and its power—that its greatest strength lies in the simple act of giving and sharing, among the poorest of the poor, a few dried leaves of an ancient plant that opens the mind's eye, even in the confinement of prison, to "the spirit that moves, to *Winiya*—The Life Force—to *Wakan Tanka*—the Great Spirit" (Bartlett 1998:3).

"We call this the *Red Road*, or the *Beauty Road*," wrote one inmate of the maximum security unit at the Penitentiary of New Mexico, near Santa Fe. "When we walk the Black Road (i.e., the dark road of alcohol, drug, or tobacco abuse), we are slowly drained of life, our spirit becomes silent and death follows quickly on our heels. When we make a conscious decision to walk in the spirit (the Red Road or Beauty Road) our life is changed and the Great Spirit fills us with a greater portion of life than we've previously experienced" (Bartlett 1998:3).

Thousands of people far too numerous to name have helped me find my way to the point where I could distinguish the fork between the Red Road of positive tobacco use and the Dark Road of tobacco abuse. First I would like to thank the many hundreds of Native Americans

in the United States, Canada, Mexico, and Peru who have shared a little of their precious knowledge and at times the seeds and leaves of their most powerful plant. Many of these men and women are incarcerated, and while they were unable to provide seeds or leaves, they shared their knowledge, sometimes in the form of beautiful pictures drawn on envelopes and scraps of paper that they sent to me in return for the few leaves I was able to provide. Others have asked that I not use their names, so none of the many seed and leaf donors is listed here. You know who you are. You know how the power of tobacco has given you far more than I can ever do, with a few poor words in a book. Perhaps Coyote said it best, in the Crow Indian creation story: "From now on, all people will have this plant. Take it in the spring and raise it. It is the stars up above that have come down like this. They will take care of the people. Take care of this plant. It will be the means of your living" (Lopez 1977:5–6).

In addition to the many individual donors, a number of organizations provided traditional tobacco seeds and support and/or were instrumental in helping me to grow tobacco and to prepare this book. They include Native Seeds/SEARCH, the Eastern Native Seeds Conservancy, the San Juan Pueblo Agricultural Cooperative, the Santa Fe Natural Tobacco Company, the High Desert Conservancy/Sun Farms de las Placitas, El Rancho de las Golindrinas, the Santa Ana Pueblo Native Plant Nursery, the University of New Mexico (UNM) Landscape Department and Greenhouse, the Office of Contract Archeology at UNM, the ". . . Of the Jungle" ethnobotanical seed company, the J. L. Hudson Seed Company, Tionantati—the People of Tobacco, and the botany program at Prescott College.

I also want to thank the various reviewers of this book, including David Brugge, Richard Yarnell, and Jan Timbrook, and the people who accompanied me on my collecting trips to Mexico and South America, including John Roney, Herman Agoyo, Lucille Stilwell, Chris

Toya, Jay Fikes, Tim Baugh, Kelley Klein, Mike Ridomi, and Susan Leopold. I am grateful to the people of the Shipibo village of Canaan in Peru, the people of Tyendinaga in Ontario, the Huichol community of Santa Catarina in Mexico, and the Navajo community of Nageezi in New Mexico. Thanks are also due to the Native American Tobacco Control Network, the American Indian Science and Engineering Society and its journal, *Winds of Change*, and a number of herbaria and gardens, including Rancho Santa Ana, UCLA Herbarium, UC Riverside Herbarium, UC Berkeley Herbarium and Botanical Gardens, Santa Barbara Botanical Gardens, the Oneida Iroquois Agricultural Cooperative, Harvard University Herbarium, Bailey Hortorium at Cornell University, Berkshire Botanical Garden, Plimouth Plantation, the U.S. Tobacco Germplasm Collection, Chullachaquia Ethnobotanical Garden and Sacha Mama Ethnobotanical Garden in Peru, and a number of European herbaria that are mentioned by Jannifer Gish in her acknowledgments for chapter 12. In addition, the National Science Foundation and the Research Allocation Committee at UNM provided some of the funds for my collecting trips.

Equally important, I would like to thank Johannes Wilbert, who agreed when I proposed that this book be published as a North American counterpart to his excellent book *Tobacco and Shamanism in South America* (1987). I also want to thank Richard Evans Schultes and Robert Raffauf, who generously offered to publish the book in their Yale University Press series, *Psychoactive Plants of the World*, which also included Wilbert's book. Both men, however, retired as editors of the series before the book could be published at Yale. I am therefore deeply indebted to John Drayton, Ursula Daly, and Randolph Lewis at the University of Oklahoma Press, who agreed to publish the book in the press's prestigious Civilization of the American Indian Series. I also very much appreciate the editing efforts of Jane Kepp and the beautiful maps by Ron Stauber and drawings by Daniel Burgevin, Ray Allen Hernandez, Bridgette Kludt, and Ronnie Vilas.

Finally, I want to thank the authors of various of the chapters in this book not only for their important contributions but also for their patience and understanding. Most of them presented the first versions of their chapters at a symposium on tobacco that Karen Adams and I co-organized at the 1991 annual meeting of the Society for American Archaeology in New Orleans: Mary Adair, Karen Adams, Linda Scott Cummings, Glenna Dean, Jan Gish, Rick Holloway, Jonathan Samet, Mollie Toll, Alexander von Gernet, and Gail Wagner. The other authors were asked to contribute chapters after I learned of their work: Carol Brandt, Patricia Díaz-Romo, Julia Hammett, Robert Hill, Christina Pego, Lawrence Shorty, Glenn Solomon, and Suzanne Victoria. Last but certainly not least, I want to thank my family, who supported me throughout, even when they did not understand what I was doing with this deadly yet magnificent plant.

JOSEPH C. WINTER
*Albuquerque, New Mexico*

# PART ONE

# Traditional Uses of Tobacco by Native Americans

Table 1: Early History of Native American and Euro-American Use of Tobacco

| Year[a] | Event |
| --- | --- |
| 1492 | Columbus and his men learn of tobacco from Taino Indians on Hispaniola, Cuba, and Bahamas. |
| 1493–1496 | Fray Ramón Pane accompanies Columbus on his second voyage and observes Indians on Hispaniola grinding powdered tobacco, then inhaling it through their noses.[b] |
| 1502 | Natives in Costa Rica are observed chewing tobacco mixed with lime from crushed mussel shells.[b] |
| 1518 | Fray Ramón Pane takes tobacco seeds from Hispaniola to Spain.[c] |
| 1519 | Hernán Cortés describes the importance of tobacco in Yucatán. Tobacco is taken to Germany. |
| 1534 | Jacques Cartier is given tobacco in Canada. |
| 1535 | Spanish tobacco plantations are established in Santo Domingo, Trinidad, Cuba, Mexico, and the Philippines. Yucatán becomes an important producer of tobacco seeds. |
| 1545 | Iroquois in Canada are observed smoking tobacco. |
| 1554 | *N. rustica* is decribed in Holland. |
| 1556 | Tobacco first appears in France. |
| 1558 or 1559 | Tobacco is cultivated in Lisbon, Portugal, by a Dutch physician.[b] |
| 1560 | Jean Nicot takes tobacco seeds from the physician's garden in Portugal to Paris.[b] Tobacco seeds are taken to Rome and propagated. The Portuguese take tobacco to East Africa and India. |
| 1565 | Sir John Hawkins takes *N. rustica* seeds from Florida to England. |
| 1573 | The Portuguese carry tobacco seeds to Japan. China starts raising tobacco. Sir Francis Drake carries *N. tabacum* to England. |
| 1585 | Sir Richard Grenville and Ralph Lane describe tobacco use by Virginia Indians. |
| 1600 | Tobacco is introduced into Russia. The Portuguese begin production in Brazil. |
| 1600–1605 | Spanish sailors and merchants introduce tobacco throughout Africa. |
| 1608 | The English introduce tobacco in Constantinople. |
| 1612 | John Rolfe starts cultivating tobacco in the English colony at Jamestown. |
| 1615 | The Dutch grow tobacco in Utrecht.[b] |
| 1616 | Jamestown colonists ship 20,000 pounds of tobacco to England. Tobacco is used in Sweden by now, if not earlier.[b] |
| 1620 | Tobacco is cultivated in Gambia, Africa. |
| 1631 | Maryland begins to cultivate tobacco. The Dutch in New Amsterdam begin to raise tobacco. |
| 1650 | Germans spread the use and cultivation of tobacco in Hungary and Switzerland. |
| 1652 | The Portuguese introduce *N. rustica* into West Africa. |
| 1700 | The area that is now Turkey becomes the second largest producer of tobacco in the world. |

a  Unless otherwise noted, all dates are from TABAMEX (1989).

b  From Loewe (1988).

c  Feinhandler, Fleming, and Monahon (1979) offer a somewhat different sequence for the introduction of tobacco into Europe and its diffusion around the world. They also discuss the possibility of precontact use by Australian Aborigines, who definitely used indigenous Australian tobacco in historic times (O'Connell, Latz, and Barnett 1983:97).

# Introduction to the
# North American Tobacco Species

Joseph C. Winter

These two Christians met many [Native American] people on the road, men and women, and the men always with a firebrand in their hands, and certain herbs to take their smokes, which are some dry herbs put in a certain leaf, dry also, after the fashion of a *musket* made of paper. . . . [These are] lit at one end, and at the other they chew or suck and take in with their breath that smoke which dulls their flesh and as it were intoxicates and so they say that they do not feel weariness. Those *muskets*, or whatever we call them, they call *tobacos*.

—adapted by Bartolomé de las Casas
from Christopher Columbus's journal entry of November 6, 1492,
as quoted by Jerome E. Brooks, *Tobacco: Its History*, vol. 1

Now known and used daily by hundreds of millions of people throughout the world, tobacco was first introduced to Europeans shortly after Christopher Columbus's momentous landfall on October 12, 1492. For thousands of years before that, its use was restricted to the Indians of North and South America, but after its "discovery" by Europeans in 1492, it was rapidly taken around the world (table 1). In 1518, tobacco seeds were carried to Spain. A year later tobacco was introduced into Germany. Filipinos were raising it in 1535. The plant was cultivated in Portugal in 1558, and in 1560 the Portuguese took it to East Africa and India. By 1600 it was being used throughout the world—in Eygpt, China, Japan, Turkey, and many other locations.

In 1612, the colony of Virginia shipped 20,000 pounds of tobacco to England. By 1992, 1.7 billion pounds of tobacco leaf were being produced in the United States alone. The rest of the world produced ten times that amount.

Native Americans still use tobacco, and although many of them smoke, chew, and otherwise ingest it in the same manner as most non-Indians—that is, as a dangerous recreational drug—a large number of Indians revere tobacco as a sacred plant, a life-affirming force, a food of the spirits, a god itself. From northern Canada to Panama, native North Americans use *Nicotiana tabacum*, *N. rustica*, and other species of tobacco as a narcostimulant—a psychotropic, mind-altering substance that serves as a medium between the ordinary world of humans and the superordinary world of the spirits. Tobacco leaves were and are smoked in pipes, cigars, and cigarettes. Leaves are also chewed (often with lime) and sometimes eaten. Resin and concentrates are licked. An infusion is drunk, occasionally with datura (jimsonweed) or other drugs. Tobacco powder is snuffed. Tobacco smoke is blown on the body and into the air. Tobacco juice is painted on the body and used medically as a poultice. Tobacco incense is burned. Tobacco offerings are buried and are cast onto the ground, into the air, onto the water.

Tobacco is a recreational drug, a mood-altering, addictive substance, a deadly carcinogen, and a sacred, vision-producing force that links the user with the spirit world. It is a metaphor for life and death; it provides a balance between the worlds of humans and spirits; it is a supernatural agent during life-crisis ceremonies; it is the food of the gods.

Tobacco is also an addictive killer. In the United States alone, one out of every six deaths (or about 420,000 a year) is due to the direct effects of tobacco. Another 6,000 deaths (some estimates run as high as 45,000) reportedly occur among nonusers, from years of inhaling passive smoke. More than 50 million Americans (or 26.5 percent of the population over 17 years old) regularly use tobacco, and another 50 million did formerly. Smoking is the single most important cause of chronic disease in the world. The negative health effects of commercial tobacco use and the debilitating effects the industry has on migrant Indian laborers in tobacco plantations in Mexico are discussed in chapters 15–17.

Like other Americans, Native Americans suffer from the adverse health effects of tobacco. Indeed, it is possible that addiction to (or at least the habitual use of) wild forms of tobacco was a major factor leading to the domestication of *Nicotiana rustica* and *N. tabacum.* Tobacco may have been the first plant to have been domesticated in the New World. As its use spread throughout the Americas, the domestication process might then have been applied to corn, beans, and other food plants.

This book explores the prehistoric, historic, and contemporary uses of tobacco by native North Americans. It also describes the methods used to identify seeds, pollen, and other archaeological remains of tobacco, and it presents medical evidence which indicates that tobacco-related diseases were, until recently, less common among traditional Native Americans than among the general population. For most native groups in North America, there were (and to some degree still are) ritual proscriptions against abuse, and it has been only in recent decades, as commerical use has replaced traditional use, that lung cancer and other tobacco-related diseases have become serious problems for Native Americans.

At last count there were 95 known tobacco species in the genus *Nicotiana*, which, along with 95 other genera, belongs to the Solanaceae family of plants (D'Arcy 1991). This large and important family has given humanity dozens of useful plants in addition to tobacco, such as potatoes, tomatoes, chile peppers, eggplants, petunias, jimsonweed, henbane, mandrake, belladona, and many other edible fruits, vegetables, and tubers, as well as ornamentals, drugs, and medicinal plants. Within the genus *Nicotiana*, seven species are used by native North Americans (table 2). Each species and its archaeological record is discussed in some detail in chapter 4. Here I briefly describe them and summarize their uses by Native Americans.

*Nicotiana rustica* L. (photo 1) is one of two domesticated tobacco species. *N. rustica* was (and to some degree still is) widely used by Indians throughout eastern North America, as well as in the southwestern United States, Mexico, and elsewhere in Latin America. It was probably domesticated many thousands of years ago in South America, then slowly carried north from one Indian campsite to another through Central America and Mexico all the way to the eastern woodlands of North America, where it arrived by about A.D. 160.[1] It appears to have been introduced into the southwestern United States by A.D. 720, if not earlier. Seeds of what is probably this very important species have been discovered throughout the eastern woodlands, as well as in the U.S. Southwest and Mexico. It is mainly smoked in pipes and corn-husk cigarettes. The plant grows from about 1.0 to 1.5 meter high and has large fleshy leaves and pale yellow flowers.

*Nicotiana tabacum* L., the other domesticated species, grows to about 3 meters high and is the basis of the worldwide tobacco industry (photo 2). This species is grown by Native Americans throughout much of northern South America and Mesoamerica, as well as in parts of the Southwest. It was probably the tobacco grown by Indians in the Caribbean before they were almost totally exterminated by Columbus

Table 2: North American Tobacco Species Used by Native North Americans[a]

| Species | Regions of Use |
| --- | --- |
| **DOMESTICATED[b]** | |
| *Nicotiana rustica* L. | Eastern U.S. and Canadian woodlands, Mesoamerica, portions of U.S. Southwest, possibly Caribbean |
| *Nicotiana tabacum* L. | Mesoamerica, parts of U.S. Southwest, probably Caribbean |
| **WILD[b]** | |
| *Nicotiana attenuata* Torr. | U.S. Southwest, Great Basin, California, extreme northern Mexico, U.S. Northwest, southwestern Canada |
| *Nicotiana quadrivalvis* Pursh. | |
| var. *bigelovii* | California to Washington |
| var. *wallacei* | Southern California |
| var. *quadrivalvis* | Missouri River valley |
| var. *multivalvis* | Upper Missouri River valley, northern Canadian plains, extreme southern Alaska panhandle, upper Columbia River valley |
| *Nicotiana clevelandii* Gray | Northwest Mexico, possibly southern California |
| *Nicotiana glauca* Grah. | Mexico, California, western Arizona |
| *Nicotiana trigonophylla* Dun. | U.S. Southwest, southern California, Mexico |

a  Exclusive of commercial tobacco, Euro-American trade tobacco, and very recent introductions.

b  Often there is no clearcut line between wild and domesticated species. "Domesticated" generally means that the plants in question cannot survive and/or reproduce without human help, in contrast to truly "wild" species, which generally thrive on their own. "Weeds" fall somewhere in between—they grow best in roadsides, backyards, fallow fields, and other locations disturbed by humans, but they can also grow on their own. *Nicotiana rustica* is considered a domesticate, though feral stands have been noted near former fields where it was previously grown. The *N. quadrivalvis* varieties *quadrivalvis* and *multivalvis* have been observed growing only under cultivation. The other *N. quadrivalvis* varieties (*wallacei* and *bigelovii*) are truly wild.

Photo 1. *Nicotiana rustica* of the type known as *punche de mexicano*, a Mexican Indian variety brought north to New Mexico by early Spanish colonists. Placitas, New Mexico. Height of plant approximately 1 m. Photo by Joseph Winter. JCWSP1.

and the Europeans who followed him. *N. tabacum* was also domesticated in South America, but probably more recently than *N. rustica*. Until recently it was never grown by Native Americans north of southern Arizona or east of Texas, except for the Caribbean. The leaves are thinner than those of *N. rustica* but much larger. Native North Americans ingest this species by smoking the dried leaves in cigars, cigarettes, and pipes, chewing them mixed with lime, and sometimes snuffing powdered leaves through tubes made of bone or other material.

Photo 2. Huichol Indian child laborer harvesting commercial *Nicotiana tabacum* Burley in Nayarit, Mexico. Photo courtesy of José Hernández-Claire, Mexico. HC B/N-8.

Photo 3. *Nicotiana quadrivalvis* var. *wallacei*. Grown from seeds collected from Los Coyotes Cahuilla Indian Reservation, California. Height of plant 0.223 m. Photo by Joseph Winter. JCWSP70.

*Nicotiana quadrivalvis* Pursh (photo 3) is a cultivated tobacco that still has a number of wild varieties, which are gathered and sometimes grown by Native Americans in California and along the Northwest Coast. Botanists disagree over its name; some researchers separate it into two species, *N. quadrivalvis* and *N. multivalvis*, whereas others call it a single species, either *N. bigelovii* or *N. quadrivalvis*. I follow Gordon DeWolf (1957) and others by using the taxonomic term *N. quadrivalvis*. It has four important varieties: *N. quadrivalvis* vars. *bigelovii*, *wallacei*, *quadrivalvis*, and *multivalvis*. The last two are known only in cultivation, primarily along the upper Missouri River valley, where the Crow, Mandan, Hidatsa, and other northern plains tribes use them for ceremonial purposes. The species was also grown by Native Americans as far north along the Pacific coast as the southern end of the Alaska panhandle, where the Haida and Tlingit raised it in pro-

tected locations. The plants grow to 2 meters high; they have narrow leaves up to 15 centimeters long and large white flowers that are pale and viriscent (or that sometimes have a violet blush), opening in the evening. Only a few archaeological sites have yielded its seeds.

*Nicotiana attenuata* Torr. (photo 4), one of the most popular of the wild tobaccos, is gathered by Native Americans between 1,000 and 2,600 meters above sea level throughout the Southwest and the Great Basin, in Washington, Oregon, and Idaho, and in parts of California, extreme northern Mexico, and western Canada. The range of *N. attenuata* has been expanded by Native Americans, who sometimes grow it and who often burn the old plants in the fall to improve the following year's harvest. It grows to about 1.5 meter high, and its leaves are somewhat fleshy but much smaller than those of the domesticated species, growing to only about 10 centimeters long. The flowers, which open in the

Photo 4. Navajo man pruning mountain tobacco (*Nicotiana attenuata*) in his tobacco garden near Nageezi, New Mexico. Photo by Joseph Winter. JCWSP18.

Photo 5. Coyote's tobacco, *Nicotiana trigonophylla*. Albuquerque, New Mexico. Height of plant 0.719 m. Photo by Joseph Winter. JCWSP35.

Photo 6. Seed pods and flowers of tree tobacco (*Nicotiana glauca*). Alpine, California. Photo by Joseph Winter. JCWSP68.

evening, are pale green to yellow or white, with a slight pink blush. Native Americans usually smoke it in corn-husk and cane cigarettes and pipes, though it is sometimes chewed or snuffed. Its seeds are fairly common in prehistoric archaeological sites in the Southwest.

*Nicotiana trigonophylla* Dun. (photo 5) is gathered and sometimes grown by Native Americans between sea level and about 2,300 meters in deserts and other arid areas throughout New Mexico, Arizona, southern California, and most of Mexico. Called "Coyote's tobacco," the plant is usually shorter than *N. attenuata* (up to only 1 meter high), but its leaves are longer—up to 20 centimeters—and the flower is pale green or cream colored. It is used in the same manner as *N. attenuata* but is less preferred. Its seeds have been found in only a few archaeological sites in the U.S. Southwest.

*Nicotiana glauca* Grah. (photo 6) is a wild South American species that was probably introduced into North America in the historic period, though its use by the Tarahumara, Yokuts, Cahuilla, and several other tribes in Mexico and California suggests that it could have been introduced in late prehistoric times. Fast-growing with a woody stem, it sometimes grows up to 10 meters high and is therefore called "tree tobacco." The leaves are pale gray-green, thick, and rubbery, growing to 25 centimeters long. The flower is usually yellow. Generally *N. glauca* is used when the domesticated and other wild species are unavailable, because it lacks nicotine, though it does have anabasine, a nearly identical alkaloid.

*Nicotiana clevelandii* Gray is a diminutive version of *N. quadrivalvis* that may have been used by one or two southern Californian groups. The Seri in northwestern Mexico definitely used it. The species is similar to *N. quadrivalvis* except that its flowers are slightly different and the plant is smaller. It grows to 6 decimeters high with leaves up to 19 centimeters long and white flowers that open in the evening.

In addition to the seven species just described, there are a number of other, recently introduced species that Native Americans occasionally use. *Nicotiana sylvestris*, for example, is a beautiful flowering plant from South America that is becoming popular in flower beds in parts of the United States and Canada. I know one Native American in Ontario who raises it both for the flowers and for use in prayers, and at least one other Native American raises the popular ornamental *Nicotiana alata* for religious use. Owing to the very recent introduction of these and several other species of tobacco, however, they are not discussed in detail in this book.

Notes

1. Tobacco seeds are difficult to identify at the species level, especially after carbonization. Some archaeobotanists believe that the various species cannot be identified using seed size and morphology, whereas others have concluded that they can. I am among the latter.

# 2

# Traditional Uses of Tobacco by Native Americans

Joseph C. Winter

From Alaska to Panama and the Caribbean Islands, many native North Americans revere tobacco as a sacred and powerful substance that is used only in ceremonies and prayers. Unfortunately, many other American Indians and Alaskan Natives misuse tobacco in the form of cigarettes, snuff, and other commercial products. More than 55 percent of indigenous people in Canada and up to 45 percent of natives in the United States regularly use commercial tobacco. This chapter summarizes the traditional uses of tobacco by Native Americans in ten regions of North America: the Arctic, the subarctic, the eastern woodlands, the Great Plains, the Northwest Coast and interior plateau, California, the Great Basin, the Southwest, Mesoamerica, and the Caribbean. Descriptions of Native Americans' so-called recreational uses of commercial tobacco are given in chapter 17.

I want to emphasize that the following summaries are not intended to offer a complete list of every North American native group that uses or used tobacco, nor do they describe all of the uses by any one group. The published literature on North American Indian use of tobacco is much too vast to be summarized in one book, but these descriptions provide, I hope, a fairly representative sample of how most groups use tobacco. I mention more than 300 groups in this chapter; their locations are shown on map 1 and their names are listed in tables throughout the chapter. References are also listed in the tables and are not repeated in the text, except in the case of direct quotations. Many of the groups no longer use native tobacco; some are extinct; some others use native tobacco much less intensively than they did in the past. Verb tenses therefore change frequently throughout this section. Some readers may have more up-to-date information on the status of tobacco use by a particular group, and some may object to the names I use for certain groups. Many Native Americans now prefer to use their own native terms for themselves (such as Lakota) instead of the more common name that Europeans learned from other tribes or otherwise assigned to them (such as Sioux). Whenever possible, I have tried to use both terms, so that non-native as well as native readers can recognize the group.

## The Arctic

Almost without exception, native groups in North America and on its nearby islands used tobacco, and in varying degrees continue to use it, for recreational and religious purposes. Even the Inuit (Eskimo) who live along the frozen shores of the Arctic Ocean and the Bering Sea smoke tobacco, as do the Aleuts and subarctic Indians. None of these far-flung northern groups raises or harvests tobacco, since their bitterly cold, windswept environment is inhospitable even to the hardier species of this highly adaptable plant. All of them, however, obtain it through purchase, trade, and other means, and some may even have received it indirectly by trade in prehistoric times, from the Haudenosaunee (Iroquois), Huron, Siksika (Blackfoot), Tlingit, and other northernmost tobacco growers far to

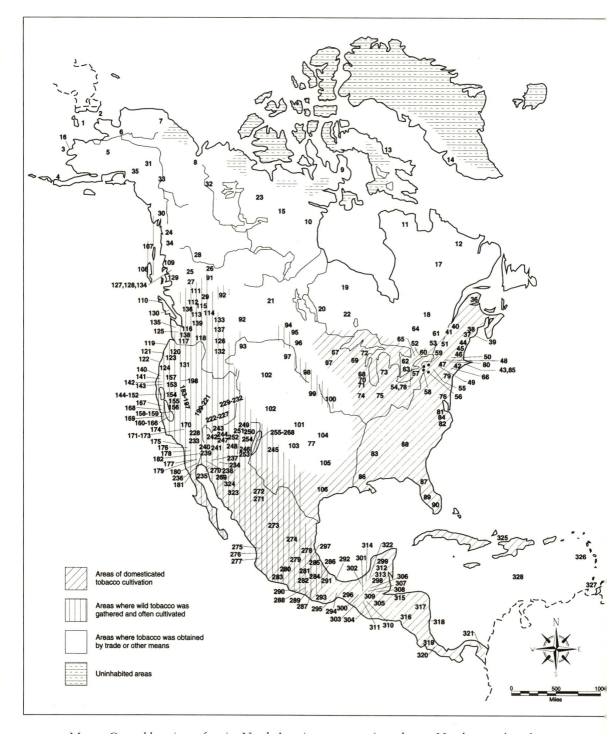

Map 1. General locations of native North American groups using tobacco. Numbers are keyed to accompanying tables.

Areas of domesticated tobacco cultivation

Areas where wild tobacco was gathered and often cultivated

Areas where tobacco was obtained by trade or other means

Uninhabited areas

the south. Separated as they are from the tobacco-growing Indians by hundreds (and at times thousands) of kilometers of deep forest, frozen muskeg, and high mountain passes, the Inuit still covet tobacco and have incorporated it, to some degree, into their religious system (table 3).

The Saint Lawrence Island Inuit in the Bering Sea, for example, sacrificed tobacco, reindeer fat, and spring greens in a ritual emphasizing the importance of whaling. The powerful Inuit shamans living in nearby eastern Siberia wore special tobacco pouches. Inuit whaling-boat captains near Point Barrow in northern Alaska still provide their men with tobacco, food, and ammunition, and dying natives on Baffin Island far to the east were sometimes given tobacco to take to their dead relatives.

Aside from these and a few other brief notes about the role of tobacco in Inuit religion, there is no mention of the plant in Inuit mythology, and none of the rich symbolism, tobacco shamanism, and tobacco deities that are found to the south occurs in Inuit culture. As a consequence, Inuit shamans do not appear to use tobacco at all to help themselves enter trances, communicate with the spirits, or cure the sick, in contrast to the tobacco-gathering and -growing Indians to the south, who regularly use tobacco in shamanistic and other religious activities.

Nevertheless, tobacco was and is an extremely important commodity to the Inuit, so much so that by A.D. 1700 it was traded throughout the Arctic, along with tin for making pipes, iron and copper kettles, and other precious items that soon became essential to the Inuit economy. Some of this tobacco may have come from the south through the vast Indian trade network, but most of it came from Asia, North America, and Europe via Siberian natives, Russian fur trappers, English and American whalers, and Danish colonists in Greenland.

Although tobacco originated in the Americas, it was introduced into Asia and Russia by about 1650, and within a short time the Siberian natives had access to it. Russians were for-

### Table 3: Arctic Native American Groups Using Tobacco

| No. on Map 1 | Group | Reference |
|---|---|---|
| 1 | Saint Lawrence Island Inuit | Hughes 1984a:274 |
| 2 | Siberian Inuit | Chance 1966:16; Hughes 1984b:255–256; Pierce 1988:120; Spencer et al. 1965:491 |
| 3 | Nunivak Inuit | Lantis 1984:216 |
| 4 | Aleut | Fair 1985:133; Pierce 1988:120 |
| 5 | Norton Sound Inuit | Chance 1966:33 |
| 6 | Noatuk and Kobuk Inuit | Chance 1966:33 |
| 7 | Point Barrow Inuit | Chance 1966:16, 33, 40, 47 |
| 8 | MacKenzie Delta Inuit | D. Smith 1984:349, 352 |
| 9 | Iglulik Inuit | Mary-Rousseliere 1984:443 |
| 10 | Caribou Inuit (Ihalmiut) | Arima 1984:452; Mowat 1975:78, 79, 127, 236, 269 |
| 11 | Tarramiut and Siqinirmiut Inuit | D'Anglure 1984:478, 500, 501 |
| 12 | Labrador Inuit | Taylor 1984:517 |
| 13 | Baffin Island Inuit | Boas 1888:59, 205 |
| 14 | Greenland Inuit | Gad 1984:561, 1988:112; Kleivan 1984:609 |
| 15 | Inuktitut (Canadian) Inuit | M. Wilson 1978:180–196 |
| 16 | Nelson Island Inuit | Ager and Price 1980:26–48 |

bidden to trade alcohol and tobacco to the natives, yet the Siberian Inuit were still able to obtain Asian and Russian trade tobacco. They brought it across the Bering Sea to Cape Prince of Wales in extreme western Alaska, where it was traded to the Norton Sound Inuit. From there it was taken to Kotzebue, where the inland Inuit of the Noatuk and Kobuk rivers obtained it and passed it on to the Point Barrow Inuit. Inland Indian groups such as the Gwich'in procured it from the Arctic Ocean Inuit. Pewter and wood pipes patterned after Japanese and Chinese opium pipes also circulated throughout the Arctic trade system, with the western Inuit carving ivory pipes that they traded to whalers for English and American tobacco. Pipes were also made of steatite and wood. Decorated wolverine skin bags were used to carry the tobacco, pipes, flint, steel, and tinder. Tobacco was smoked, snuffed, and chewed.

The eastern Inuit also obtained tobacco through trade with the Greenland colonists and as payment for work, meat, and skins. Many colonists from Denmark married Inuit women who acquired the tobacco habit and then passed it on to their families. Today the Inuit are avid tobacco users, purchasing it in stores, cooperatives, and trading posts scattered throughout the Arctic.

Photo 7 shows an Inuit smoking a pipe. Native Americans are shown with pipes throughout this book, and although tobacco is the most common substance smoked in pipes, many other plants are also used, either alone or as additives to tobacco. Only a few of these are mentioned in this chapter.

Photo 7. Eskimo woman smoking a traditional pipe. Courtesy of the Alaska and Polar Regions Department Archives, Edith Fish Collection, University of Alaska, Fairbanks.

## The Subarctic

Until recently, the Athapaskans, Algonkians, and other Indians in northern Canada and central Alaska also lacked ready access to domesticated or even wild tobacco. Nevertheless, many of them obtained the valuable leaf first from native tobacco growers to the south and later from Inuit and Hudson's Bay Company traders (table 4). Their religious systems incorporated more tobacco symbolism than did those of the Inuit to the north, although the subarctic groups, too, lacked the tobacco deities and intense tobacco shamanism of Indians to the south.

Table 4: Subarctic Native American Groups Using Tobacco

| No. on Map 1 | Group | Reference |
|---|---|---|
| 17 | Montagnais-Naskapi | Rogers and Leacock 1981:170, 175, 185. |
| 18 | Attikamek (Tête de Boule) | McNulty and Gilbert 1981:208 |
| 19 | West Main Cree, Cree | Beardsley 1941:485; Honigmann 1981:224; Leighton 1985:29, 36; Linton 1924:9, 10; Robicsek 1978:10 |
| 20 | Saulteaux (northern Ojibwa or Chippewa) | Ritzenthaler 1978; Steinbring 1981:248, 251 |
| 21 | Chippewa | Densmore 1928:376, 377 |
| 22 | Ojibwa | H. Smith 1932:414, 399, 398 |
| 23 | Yellowknife | Gillespie 1981:288 |
| 24 | Tagish | McClellan 1981a:488; 1981b:391 |
| 25 | Tahltan | MacLachlan 1981:459; McClellan 1981b:391 |
| 26 | Sekani | McClellan 1981b:391 |
| 27 | Carrier | Carrier Linguistic Committee 1973:71; Hocking 1949:12; McClellan 1981b:391 |
| 28 | Kaska | McClellan 1981b:391 |
| 29 | Chilcotin | McClellan 1981b:391; Meilleur 1979:101 |
| 30 | Tutchone | McClellan 1981b:391 |
| 31 | Gwich'in | McClellan 1981b:391; R. Nelson 1983:8, 49, 52 |
| 32 | Hare | Saviskinsky and Hara 1981:316 |
| 33 | Han | McClellan 1981b:391 |
| 34 | Inland Tlingit | McClellan 1981b:391 |
| 35 | Upper Tanana | Kari 1985:4–5 |

Photo 8. Cree Indians and Hudson's Bay Company workers at Fort Pitt, Northwest Territories, about 1885. The company man sitting on the ground is holding a tobacco "carrot." Courtesy of the National Archives of Canada. PA-118768.

The Montagnais-Naskapi of northeastern Canada, for example, received tobacco in trade from the Huron and Iroquois in exchange for moose skins and other pelts. Tobacco and the stone pipes it was smoked in were important elements of a hunter's spiritual equipment, which was used for luck. The Attikamek (Tête de Boule) to the southwest of the Montagnais-Naskapi also appear to have obtained tobacco from the Huron in prehistoric times, while the Saulteaux (northern Ojibway or Chippewa) to the west may have procured it from the southwestern Chippewa. Saulteaux boys went on vision quests to obtain guardian spirits who were later summoned throughout a man's life by offerings of tobacco.

Various northern Rocky Mountain tribes such as the Chilcotin, Carrier, Sekani, Kaska, Tahltan, inland Tlingit, Tagish, Tutchone, Han, and even Alaskan Gwich'in and Tanana may have smoked or chewed tobacco in prehistoric times. Their sources were the tobacco-growing Haida and Tlingit on the Pacific coast and perhaps even the Sarsi and Siksika (Blackfoot) on the northern Great Plains. The southernmost of these tribes—the Chilcotin—live in or very close to the northernmost range of wild *Nicotiana attenuata*, so it is possible that they gathered or grew it. Tobacco is still smoked at Tagish funerals to ensure that the dead ancestors will have it in the other world. The Tahltan received ornate tobacco pipes in trade from the coastal Tlingit. The interior Alaskan Gwich'in also received dentalium shells (and perhaps tobacco) from the Northwest Coast, and they probably received tobacco through the Inuit trading system mentioned earlier. The Gwich'in traveled as far north as the Arctic Ocean, where the Inuit provided them with Siberian and Russian goods.

Beginning in 1670, the Hudson's Bay Company established a series of trading posts on the shores of Hudson and James bays, and later throughout much of northern Canada, so that the rich resources of the region could be exploited. Within a short time tobacco became an extremely important item of trade with the Cree, Hare, Yellowknife, Gwich'in, and other subarctic Indians. Especially valued were "tobacco carrots"—high-quality Brazilian tobacco wrapped in cloth and twine (photo 8). The Imperial Tobacco Company of England produced the carrots, which sometimes weighed up to 15 pounds. Tobacco carrots were passed from one tribe to another as far south as the Cheyenne. In the mid-1800s the Hudson's Bay Company tried to save money by switching to lower-grade U.S. tobacco, but the Indians considered it unacceptable, so the company had to go back to the better Brazilian product (Grinnell 1924, 2:248; Helm, Rogers, and Smith 1981; Ray 1988).

Trade between Indians and Hudson's Bay Company personnel always began with a gift-giving ceremony in which small amounts of clothing, tobacco, and at times alcohol were given to the Indians before the hard bargaining began.

## The Eastern Woodlands

The heart of Indian tobacco-growing country in North America was and is in the eastern woodlands, especially in Connecticut, New York, Virginia, the Carolinas, and the fertile zone between lakes Huron and Ontario. This was also one of the regions where tobacco shamanism and tobacco-using religious societies (such as the Iroquois False Face society) took hold, as described later in this book. From the Passamaquoddy and Penobscot in Maine to the Timucua and Seminole in Florida, tobacco was planted and is still smoked and revered by dozens of tribal groups (table 5). It is likely that the only tobacco that could grow east of the Missouri River (at least until the Virginia colonists introduced *Nicotiana tabacum*) was *Nicotiana rustica*, one of two domesticated species that originated thousands of kilometers to the south, in South America. Most groups raised it in small gardens such as the Haudenosaunee tobacco patches shown in photo 9 and figure 1.[1]

Photo 9. *Nicotiana rustica* patch on the Tonawanda Seneca Iroquois (Haudenosaunee) Reservation, New York, 1995. Photo by Joseph Winter. JCWSP196

Figure 1. Masked member of the Haudenosaunee False Face society standing in a patch of *Nicotiana rustica*. Drawing by Ray Allen Hernandez, based on plate A in Fenton 1987:330.

## Table 5: Eastern Woodland Native American Groups Using Tobacco

| No. on Map 1 | Group | Reference |
|---|---|---|
| 36 | Micmac | Chandler et al. 1979:58; Speck 1917:317; Speck and Dexter 1951:258; von Gernet 1988:86–131 |
| 37 | Penobscot | Speck 1917:309; von Gernet 1988:86–131 |
| 38 | Western Abenaki | Day 1978:153 |
| 39 | Passamaquoddy | Winter 1995a |
| 40 | Odanak Abenaki | Winter 1995a |
| 41 | Madawaska Maliseet | Winter 1995a |
| 42 | Southern New England and eastern Long Island Algonkian | Salwen 1978:163; von Gernet 1988:86–131; West 1934:53 |
| 43 | Montauk | Carr and Westey 1945:120 |
| 44 | Wampanoag | Weinstein-Farson 1989; Winter 1995a |
| 45 | Mahican | McCashion 1994; Setchell 1921:pl. 3 |
| 46 | Mohegan | Carr and Westey 1945:120 |
| 47 | Haudenosaunee (Iroquois) | Bruchac 1985; Fenton 1937, 1941, 1949:235, 1953:81–82, 146–147, 1978:299, 1987:315; Herrick 1977:430; Keppler 1941; Parker 1909:170, 1910:36–37, 161–167; Rousseau 1945:57; Skinner 1925a; Tooker 1994:105, 133; von Gernet 1988:86–131, 1989a, 1989c; Wallace 1972:78–98; Waugh 1916:4, 30; |
| 48 | Oneida | McCashion 1994; Winter 1995a |
| 49 | Onondaga | Winter 1995a |
| 50 | Mohawk | McCashion 1994 |
| 51 | Akwesasne Mohawk | Winter 1995a |
| 52 | Teyindinaga Mohawk | Winter 1995a |
| 53 | Kahnawake Mohawk | Winter 1995a |
| 54 | Six Nations Reserve Cayuga | von Gernet 1995 |
| 55 | Seneca | Fenton 1953:132; Linton 1924:3–4; Skinner 1925a:128 |
| 56 | Tonawanda Seneca | Winter 1995a |
| 57 | Cattaraugus Seneca | Winter 1995a |
| 58 | Allegany Seneca | Winter 1995a |
| 59 | Tuscarora | Winter 1995a |
| 60 | Huron | Fenton 1978:299; Heidenreich 1978:381, 385; Trigger 1969:27, 29, 36, 91, 96, 97, 116; von Gernet 1988:86–131, 1989a, 1989c |
| 61 | Wendake Huron | Winter 1995a |
| 62 | Khionontaternon (Petun or Tobacco Nation) | Fenton 1978:299; Garrad and Heidenreich 1978:395–396; Heidenreich 1978:381, 385; Trigger 1969:27, 36; von Gernet 1988:86–131, 1989a, 1989c |
| 63 | Neutral | Fenton 1978:299; Heidenreich 1978:381, 385; von Gernet 1988:86–131, 1989a, 1989c |
| 64 | Ottawa and other nearby Algonkian | Heidenreich 1978:385 |
| 65 | Mississaugua Anishinabe | Winter 1995a |
| 66 | Catskill | McCashion 1994 |
| 67 | Southwest Anishinabe | Ritzenthaler 1978:754 |
| 68 | Winnebago | Gilmore 1919:11, 113, 1977:62; Radin 1970:68; Snake 1996:35, 214, 228, 256 |
| 69 | Fox (Meskwaki) | Callender 1978:643; Setchell 1921:pl. 3; H. Smith 1928:273 |
| 70 | Sauk | Skinner 1925b:139; West 1934:56; Yarnell 1964:86 |
| 71 | Kickapoo | Latorre and Latorre 1976; Robicsek 1978:53; Skinner 1926:286–287; West 1934:57 |
| 72 | Menominee | Robicsek 1978:30; H. Smith 1923:80; Yarnell 1964:86 |
| 73 | Potawatomi | Skinner 1926:286–287; H. Smith 1933:116, 118, 123; West 1934:56; Yarnell 1964:86 |

Table 5: Eastern Woodland Native American Groups Using Tobacco (continued)

| No. on Map 1 | Group | Reference |
|---|---|---|
| 74 | Illinois | Setchell 1921:pl. 3 |
| 75 | Miami-Mascouten | Hickerson 1970:62 |
| 76 | Leni Lenape (Delaware in Pennsylvania) | Goddard 1978:226; Siegel et al. 1977:19; Speck 1937:28, 91–92; von Gernet 1988:86–131 |
| 77 | Leni Lenape (Delaware in Oklahoma) | Speck 1937; Tantaquidgeon 1995 |
| 78 | Leni Lenape (Delaware in Canada) | Tantaquidgeon 1995 |
| 79 | Nanticoke | Tantaquidgeon 1995 |
| 80 | Schaghticoke | McCashion 1994 |
| 81 | Powhaten, Roanoke, and other Virginia Algonkian | Feest 1978a:258; Robicsek 1978:38; Setchell 1921:pl. 3 |
| 82 | Secotan and other North Carolina Algonkian | Feest 1978b:273, 278; von Gernet 1988:86–131 |
| 83 | Choctaw | Usner 1988:393; Wright 1986:34 |
| 84 | Rappahannock | Carr and Westey 1945:120 |
| 85 | Shinnecock | Carr and Westey 1945:120 |
| 86 | Natchez and other Louisiana tribes | Robicsek 1978:46; Swagerty 1988:357 |
| 87 | Timuca | von Gernet 1988:86–131 |
| 88 | Cherokee | Hamel and Chiltoskey 1975; L. Taylor 1940; Vogel 1969:379 |
| 89 | Seminole and/or Creek | Robicsek 1978:30; Sturtevant 1954:480; Swanton 1928:659; Wright 1986:22–23 |
| 90 | Apalachee | Hann 1986:97 |

Tobacco is so important in the woodlands that the Seneca, Cayuga, Onondaga, Oneida, and Mohawk of the Haudenosaunee, or Iroquois Nation, depend upon it for their very spiritual and cultural survival, as do their linguistic relatives the Huron, Neutral, and Khionontaternon (the Petun or Tobacco Nation). Tobacco permeates almost every facet of Haudenosaunee society, from offerings at sacred ceremonies and everyday social events to the carving of so-called False Face (ga-go-sa) masks and the curing of the sick by shamans and members of the False Face society. Tobacco even figures in the Haudenosaunee creation story, in which the False Faces and the spirits they represent crave tobacco and require it for life. The role of tobacco in Haudenosaunee shamanism and in the False Face society is discussed in more detail in a later chapter.

Tobacco's role in the Haudenosaunee culture and its value to the families that carry the culture from generation to generation was brought home to me by an Allegany Seneca family descended from Chief Cornplanter, who led the Seneca against the American rebels in the Revolutionary War. In 1994, I visited a number of university herbaria, where I obtained N. *rustica* seeds that had been grown from seeds that one of the Cornplanter chiefs had provided in 1915. I was able to grow new plants and then in 1995 to give both the family and the Seneca Tribal Museum in Salamanca New York new seeds, which they now use to produce the sacred tobacco that is so necessary for their ceremonies (photo 10).[2]

To the north and northwest of the Haudenosaunee, between lakes Huron and Ontario, live the Huron, old enemies of the Iroquois, and to the west of them, the Huron's relatives and allies, the Neutral and the Tobacco Nation. Huronia is at the northernmost edge of tobacco-growing country, and although the Huron were able to raise small patches near their longhouses and in other protected locations, most of their ceremonial tobacco had to be imported from the west and southwest, where the Tobacco Nation and Neutral grew it in abundance. Both groups were renowned tobacco growers, so

Photo 10. Cornplanter's tobacco, *Nicotiana rustica*, grown in 1995 from seeds produced in 1921, which in turn were grown from seeds provided by Seneca Chief Cornplanter in 1915. Height of plant 1.229 m. Photo by Joseph Winter. JCWSP98.

much so that the French named the Khionontateron the "Petun" or Tobacco Nation after a Brazilian Indian term for tobacco. In the past they were able to provide the Huron with so much tobacco that it not only met the Huron's own immense needs but also enabled them to pass some of it along to the Ottawa and other Algonkian hunters to the north, who lived beyond the range of *N. rustica* husbandry.

As it is for the Haudenosaunee, tobacco was and is central to the lives of the Huron. Shamans control the weather by instructing Huron farmers to burn tobacco in their corn fields to honor the Sky, the most important deity. Certain large rocks are the homes of other spirits, and the Huron leave offerings of tobacco in cracks in the rocks or throw it into campfires and nearby rivers in order to protect their homes and make their trading ventures successful. Tobacco, furs, and other precious items are also given to the sick and those threatened with sickness during the *ononharia* ("upsetting of the brain"), the main Huron winter festival, performed when many people or someone especially important is sick. The Huron additionally attempt to avoid or cure sickness by satisfying their "soul desire," often with large amounts of tobacco.

The southwestern Anishinabe (Chippewa or Ojibway) to the west of the Huron also consider tobacco to be of supreme significance, as do the Narragansett, Wampanoag, Massachusett, Paugusset, Nipmuck, Montauk, Shinnecok, and other Algonkian tribes far to the east in southern New England and eastern Long Island. The *manitou*s (gods) of the Fox desire tobacco above all else. The Miami-Mascouten, Illinois, Potawatomi, Menominee, Winnebago, and other tribes to the south of the Great Lakes use it in medicine bundles, often cultivate it, and bury their dead with it. The Mascouten plant pumpkins with tobacco, and although the Menominee probably do not cultivate it, they may obtain it in exchange for the wild rice they harvest. They also place offerings of tobacco in the holes left when they pull up medicinal herbs and roots, after which they sing a song or recite a prayer in honor of Earth Grandmother, whose hair the roots and plants represent.

The Wampanoag in eastern Massachusetts still grow tobacco, which they offer to visitors in friendship and hospitality. This practice was observed by the very first European visitors who contacted them in 1602 and who wrote: "We saw manie Indians . . . They gave us of their fish readie boiled, whereof did we eat and judged them to be fresh water fish: they gave us also of their Tabacco, which they drinke [smoke] greene, but dried into powder, very strong and pleasant" (quoted in Weinstein-Farson 1989:25).

The Leni Lenape (Delaware) in Pennsylvania and Oklahoma offer tobacco to Fire, Thunder, and the other *manitous*. They also combine tobacco with sumac leaves and then smoke the mixture for pleasure and relaxation. The distinctive smell is considered a territorial marker. In the feast in honor of Fire, the Leni Lenape offer tobacco by throwing it on 12 stones representing the 12 *manitous*. Their prayer to avert thunder entails the smoking of a pipe filled with Grandfather Tobacco as a sacrifice to Grandfather Thunder.

Gladys Tantaquidgeon (1995) provides many details about Delaware, Mohegan, and Nanticoke uses of tobacco in her study of Delaware folk medicine. Oklahoma Delaware healers are given tobacco when they accept a case. Then one of the first things they do—after they find the proper medicinal plant—is to bury a small amount of "Our Grandfather" or "real tobacco" (*N. rustica*) at the base of the second plant of the same species that they encounter (they leave the first plant to continue growing). Next the healer lights his pipe, smokes, and offers a prayer to the Creator and the spirits of vegetation: "Grandfather, I come now for medical treatment. Your grandson needs your aid. He is giving you a smoke-offering here of tobacco. He implores you that he will get well because he, your child, is pitiful. . . . Hear now him our Grandfather tobacco. I beg of him that he help me when we plead with earnest heart that you will take pity on your grandchild" (Tantaquidgeon 1995:13).

Oklahoma Delaware "love doctors" also offer the spirits some of the tobacco given to them by petitioners, as healers do when they are making medicine such as a mixture of angelica and tobacco for stomach disorders. Likewise, Oklahoma Delaware midwives are provided with tobacco, and a hunter who dreams of his game animal "sacrifices a pinch of tobacco in his camp fire" when he wakes up in the morning (Tantaquidgeon 1995:51). The hunter will also sacrifice tobacco when he starts out on his hunt. And if a witch lights his pipe before starting out on an evil task, he has to return before the tobacco is totally consumed.

The Nanticoke of Delaware and the Canadian Delaware at Six Nations Reserve in Ontario have many of the same tobacco beliefs and practices, as well as additional ones. For example, the Nanticoke blow tobacco smoke into a child's mouth to cure colic, into the ear for earaches, and into a cup of water which is then imbibed to relieve a stomachache. The Canadian Delaware have retained many of these beliefs, despite living on the same reservation as thousands of Haudenosaunee. The Oklahoma and Canadian Delaware and the closely related Nanticoke recognize the power of tobacco and in fact equate it with the Creator and other Grandfathers who control plants, animals, and people.

The Powhatan, Secotan, and other Algonkian speakers in Virginia and the Carolinas also raise or raised tobacco, as did the Choctaw, Natchez, Cherokee, Timucua, Creek-Seminole, and Apalachee well to the south. All of the eastern woodland Indians raised and to some degree still raise the potent *Nicotiana rustica*, which was probably brought into the region no later than the second or third century A.D.

At least two eastern groups—the Tsalagi (Cherokee) and Kickapoo—switched to *N. tabacum* when they were forced to move to the dry plains of Oklahoma and the Texas-Mexican border, where *N. rustica* is difficult to grow. Different varieties of this species are still grown by Native Americans throughout Central America and as far north as the Texas-Mexican border, where the Kickapoo obtained it and apparently passed it on to the Tsalagi in Oklahoma. Also, some of the Tsalagi established commercial tobacco factories in the 1860s, so their *N. tabacum* could have come from a number of sources.

The Kickapoo illustrate how the beliefs and activities associated with *N. rustica* remained the same after the tribe was forced out of the woodlands, ending up far to the south in northern Mexico.[3] The species they now use (*N. tabacum*) and the manner in which they obtain it have changed considerably, but the underlying core of values and beliefs appears to have remained the same. Indeed, Kickapoo tobacco is still considered a *manitou*—a powerful spirit that is offered to the other *manitou*s. Fire is an extremely powerful *manitou*, and tobacco is regularly offered to it by throwing a pinch into the flames. Another *manitou* is Grandmother Earth, who lives by eating the bodies of the dead that are buried within her. Before a Kickapoo plants corn, beans, or squash, he or she offers tobacco to Grandmother Earth. Tobacco is also offered to the *manitou*s of the one-seeded juniper in early spring.

Still other *manitou*s are the Thunderers, who are offered tobacco when storms approach, to dispell them. Evil *manitou*s include witches, centipedes, and rattlesnakes, which can all be appeased with tobacco.

All ceremonies have tobacco offerings. The Adoption ceremony, for example, includes ritual deer hunts in which tobacco is offered to the *manitou*s of the deer, to ask for succcess. Before anyone can eat at an adoption feast, tobacco is offered to the spirit of the adoptee's deceased relative, then burned in a fire. During a New House ceremony, tobacco is offered to Kitzihiat, the main Kickapoo *manitou*. When a clan leader discovers that the supply of tobacco in his medicine bundle is low, a ceremony is held to borrow more tobacco from everyone in the tribe. Tobacco is taken from the bundle and offered to the bundle and to fire during the Rain ceremony, to ask the water *manitou*s to help the Kickapoo during drought. When conventional cures fail, tobacco is offered to the *manitou*s of water, and the patient bathes on four consecutive days in the nearest river. The misuse of tobacco can result in death or insanity. There are four kinds of tobacco: a small-leafed type used in prayers and ceremonies; a type used for curing; one given as gifts to Indian visitors; and ordinary smoking tobacco. The only one identified in Latorre and Latorre's detailed study

(see note 3) is *Nicotiana tabacum*—"Indian tobacco."

Up until the early 1970s, most Kickapoo tobacco was raised by the clan leaders, who held tobacco planting ceremonies before they planted the seeds in March or April. The leaders performed a ritual to communicate with Kitzihiat and the tobacco *manitou*, served a feast of puppy meat or venison and purple corn, and then selected a secluded, easily watered location in which to raise their plants. The plot was fenced, cultivated, and sprinkled with ashes, and the plants were irrigated by hand until they were mature. Tobacco is so important to the life of the clan and the tribe that the leader guarded the plants day and night, even sleeping next to them in a temporary shelter to make certain that women did not approach, because the slightest whiff of a woman wilts the plants. Mexican men and women kill the plants by casting the evil eye on them.

Because of the constant danger of Mexicans killing their plants, most Kickapoo clan leaders have stopped planting tobacco and instead obtain it from clan leaders in Oklahoma. Tobacco is still the soul and heart of the Kickapoo tribe, but the Kickapoo did not always have it:

> Kitzihiat, taking pity upon his children and wanting to send them a gift, called one of the Kickapoos from the spirit world and said, "Go to my children, the Kickapoos, but take care you do not frighten them with your appearance; explain to them that I send a gift, a piece of my heart, and show them how to raise the plant and how to use the plant which grows from my heart." The Kickapoo swallowed a piece of Kitzihiat's heart and went to see his people.
>
> When he appeared, the people were greatly startled at seeing him return to this world, but he reassured them that he was bearing a gift from Kitzihiat and began to vomit and retch the seeds of tobacco. Immediately, a gentle rain came down upon the seeds and they began to grow. At the same time, a voice was heard from the four

corners of the world which said, "Look at me; care for me; water me!" The messenger instructed his people in the uses of this plant: it was to be employed for good and not for evil. With this, he returned to the spirit world. The Kickapoos added this plant to their pantheon of grandfathers—those *manitou*s who take special interest in their welfare and serve to carry their supplications to Kitzihiat. (Latorre and Latorre 1976:353)

Many other eastern woodland tribes have similar beliefs and practices concerning tobacco. In the late summer of 1995, I collected tobacco and associated information from many tribes and bands in New York, Maine, New Brunswick, Quebec, and Ontario. Tribes whose members graciously provided tobacco samples and/or information about the tobacco they grow included the Oneida, Onondaga, Teyindinaga Mohawk, Tonawanda Seneca, Allegany Seneca, Tuscarora, Wendake Huron, Assinot Wampanoag, and Passamaquoddy. Information about the tobacco grown by the Kahnawake Mohawk, Akwesasne Mohawk, and Cattaraugus Seneca was obtained from other sources. Groups that still use traditional tobacco but obtain it from other sources include the Madawaska Maliseet (who obtain it from the Kahnawake Iroquois or use commercial pipe tobacco in their ceremonies); the Odanak Abenaki (who sometimes use trade tobacco but more often than not smoke red willow bark); and the Mississaugua Anishinabe (who obtain *Nicotiana tabacum* from nearby commercial tobacco growers and greenhouse owners). The Wolinak Abenaki and Houlton Maliseet do not appear to use traditional tobacco at all.

## The Great Plains

Wild tobacco cannot grow on its own in the vast grasslands and fertile river valleys of the plains to the west of the Mississippi River, nor can the domesticated *Nicotiana rustica* nor-

mally be grown there. Nevertheless, the Crow, Siksika (Blackfoot), Tsuu T'ina (Sarsi), Arikara, Mandan, Hidatsa, Omaha-Ponca, and Pawnee Indians (table 6) were able to grow two special varieties of *N. quadrivalvis*, whose natural range is far to the west in Oregon and California. The Santee cultivated *N. rustica* in the woodlands of Wisconsin and Minnesota before they moved out onto the plains to become the Lakota, or Sioux. In contrast to the Crow, the Lakota gave up tobacco cultivation, though its use remained important to them, with the smoke of tobacco still serving as the tangible presence of Whope—the Beautiful One—the daughter of the Sun and the Moon. The Lakota obtained their tobacco from the Hidatsa. They called it *pana'nitachani*, or "Ree's tobacco" (Wilson 1987:125).

The Tonkawa just to the south of the Great Plains near the Texas coast appear to have grown *N. rustica*, whereas other south Texas tribes may have grown the domesticated *N. tabacum*, which was raised by Native Americans throughout Mexico, South America, and the Caribbean. The complex and confusing relationships of all of the North American tobacco species are discussed in a later chapter.

Most plains tribes had to obtain tobacco indirectly, through trading expeditions, raids, and other means, from the Crow and other tobacco-growing Plains Indians or from Mexican settlers and Pueblo Indians in the Southwest, who grow and gather several tobacco species. The two varieties of *N. quadrivalvis* grown by the Crow and other Missouri River tribes were especially important trade items; even the eastern woodlands Indians were eager to acquire them, though the plains tribes jealously guarded their seeds. Of all the eastern tribes, only the Winnebago appear to have raised *N. quadrivalvis*.

The Comanche and Kiowa of the southern plains obtained their tobacco from Mexicans and probably Pueblos. At one time the Kiowa lived far to the north in the Black Hills, where they received tobacco in trade from the Mandan, Arikara, and Hidatsa. Traditionally they mixed tobacco with lichens to produce a mildly sopor-

## Table 6: Plains Native American Groups Using Tobacco

| No. on Map 1 | Group | Reference |
|---|---|---|
| 91 | Tsuu T'ina (Sarsi) | Haberman 1984:270, 276; Lowie 1920:112; Meilleur 1979:102 |
| 92 | Siksika (Blackfoot) | Goodspeed 1954:427–430; Haberman 1984:270, 276; Hart 1992:28; Hellson and Gadd 1974; Johnston 1970:319, 1987:52; McClintock 1909:277; Meilleur 1979:102; Setchell 1921:411; West 1934:57 |
| 93 | Crow | Blankenship 1905:12; Goodspeed 1954:453; Haberman 1984:270, 276; Hart 1992:24; Lowie 1920, 1935:xiii–xiv, xvi, 3–4, 238, 1954:27–29; Meilleur 1979:102; Setchell 1921:403; Simms 1904:331–335; Yarnell 1977:871 |
| 94 | Mandan | Bowers 1965:339; Cutright 1989; Goodspeed 1954:449; Haberman 1984:269; La Vérendrye 1941:254; Wilson 1987:7 |
| 95 | Hidatsa | Bowers 1965:300–302; Cutright 1989; Goodspeed 1954:449; Haberman 1984:269; Harrington 1932:42; Setchell 1921; Wilson 1987:121–127 |
| 96 | Arikara | Cutright 1989; Goodspeed 1954:449; Haberman 1984:269; Harrington 1932:42; Moulton 1987:461 |
| 97 | Santee-Lakota, Lakota, Sioux, Teton Sioux | Cutright 1989; Harrick 1964:207; Hart 1992:28; Kraft 1990; Linton 1924:9–10; Robicsek 1978:10; D. Rogers 1980:44; Setchell 1921:pl. 3; H. Smith 1932:417; Wilson 1987:125 |
| 98 | Omaha-Ponca | Bradbury 1819:77; Gilmore 1913:113, 328, 330, 1919:85, 331, 1922:481; Howard 1965:47 |
| 99 | Pawnee | Gilmore 1919:85; Yarnell 1977:871 |
| 100 | Oto | La Barre 1989; Robicsek 1978:53 |
| 101 | Kiowa | La Barre 1989; Robicsek 1978:53; Vestal and Schultes 1939:7, 12, 38, 40 |
| 102 | Cheyenne | Goggin 1938; Grinnell 1924, 1:29, 1972:180, 183; Hart 1981:14; Hoebel 1960:6–7, 16–17, 31, 85 |
| 103 | Comanche | Carlson and Jones 1940:534; Hoebel 1960:16, 23, 40–42 |
| 104 | Osage | La Barre 1989; Robicsek 1978:53 |
| 105 | Caddo | La Barre 1989; Robicsek 1978:53 |
| 106 | Tonkawa | Setchell 1921:pl. 3; West 1934:58 |

ific effect. They also smoked tobacco mixed with smooth upland sumac leaves to purify the body so that peyote could cure tuberculosis. Both the Kiowa and the Comanche still smoke tobacco mixed with lemonade sumac. The Kiowa use corn husks to make cigarettes for their peyote ceremony.

Neither the Comanche nor the Kiowa seem ever to have raised tobacco, yet it was (and is) an important part of their culture, entering deeply into their religious systems. A slain Comanche's father or other close relative would offer a warrior a pipe full of tobacco to smoke, and if the warrior accepted it, he was bound to lead a war party to avenge the man's death. Elderly Comanche men, too old to fight, spent their evenings in the smoking lodge, where they puffed their pipes and talked. When the band was on the move they set up a temporary smoke circle, but whether it was in the lodge or the circle, the evening's session began with the ritualistic lighting of a large communal pipe. The pipe was held to the sky with an offering made to the sun; then a pinch of tobacco was taken from the bowl and placed on the ground as an offering to the earth. Next the pipe was passed around and carefully smoked until all of the tobacco was burned.

Originally the Cheyenne raised tobacco, but as they left the Missouri River valley and moved west toward the Black Hills, they stopped raising it and instead obtained it through trade and raids. Even Hudson's Bay Company tobacco "carrots" somehow made it into the hands of the Cheyenne, probably originating in northern Canada and passing from tribe to tribe all the way south. When Lewis and Clark visited their territory in 1804, the Cheyenne had corn and tobacco fields near the mouth of the White River. Like the Pawnee, they left their crops and villages in the summer to hunt buffalo on the plains. By the late 1800s, however, they had stopped farming altogether.

The Cheyenne used (and continue to use) tobacco for numerous ceremonies, rituals, and everyday occurrences. The most important Cheyenne ceremony is the Renewal of Sacred Arrows, which symbolizes and ensures the collective existence of the tribe. Sacred tobacco is used in the ceremony, just as it is in the Sun Dance and the Massaum (Contrary) or Animal Dance, the other two principal Cheyenne ceremonies. In all three ceremonies there are many ritual movements that involve lighting pipes, smoking them, and sharing them with others.

Not everything that is smoked in pipes is tobacco. Various other medicinal and sacred plants are smoked, including red willow bark. In his detailed description of Ogalala Lakota life, Black Elk mentioned pipe smoking on numerous occasions, but the few times that he named a plant, it was red willow bark (Brown 1953).

Pipes, as well as the tobacco burned in them, are very sacred to Plains Indians. The Calumet ceremony originated on the plains and was later adopted by the Indians of the Midwest, East, and Southeast.[4] The calumet, or pipe, formed the principal part of a ritual that made temporary friends out of deadly foes and gave warring enemies a respite of peace. Father Marquette described the ceremony in 1673:

> There remains no more, except to speak of the Calumet. There is nothing more mysterious or more respected among them. Less honor is paid to the Crowns and scepters of Kings than the Savages bestow upon this. It seems to be the God of peace and war, the Arbiter of life and of death.

It has but to be carried upon one's person, and displayed, to enable one to walk safely through the midst of Enemies—who, in the hottest of the Fight, lay down Their arms when it is shown. For That Reason, the Illinois gave me one, to serve as a safeguard among all the Nations whom I had to pass during my voyage. (Thwaites 1896–1901, 59:129, 131).

The semisedentary Arikara, Hidatsa, and Mandan lived in agricultural villages in the upper Missouri Valley, where they planted *N. quadrivalvis* var. *quadrivalvis* for use in their calumets (photo 11).[5] To the northwest, in Canada, the nomadic Tsuu T'ina (Sarsi) and Siksika (Blackfoot) raised a different variety—*N. quadrivalvis* var. *multivalvis*—as did the Crow on the uppermost reaches of the Missouri.

No group better exemplifies the Plains Indian use of tobacco than the Crow. Details of the pervasiveness of tobacco in Crow culture and religion, such as the development of the Crow tobacco society, are presented in a later chapter.

The Mandan also use tobacco in many ways. When Lewis and Clark visited them in 1804, they were raising "an immense quantity of corn, beans, squash, tobacco" (quoted in Bowers 1965:339). The Mandan believe that all of their crops were brought up from a former underworld by their ancestors and that corn's magical power brings the moisture that keeps tobacco and the other crops alive.

The nearby Arikara raised so much tobacco that Lewis characterized Arikara women as "the gardeners of the Soues [Lakota]." He added that the Arikara had "a partial trade with their oppressors the Tetons [another Sioux or Lakota group], to whom they barter . . . corn, beans, and a species of tobacco."[6]

The Mandan, Hidatsa (called Mintaris by the Mandan), and Arikara are three closely related tribes now known as the Three Affiliated Tribes. At one time the Hidatsa and Crow belonged to the same tribe, which had a tobacco society. In the Hidatsa creation myth, First Creator ordered

Photo 11. "In the Arikara Medicine Lodge." Edward S. Curtis photograph of a man with seven calumets. Courtesy of the Boston Public Library, Department of Rare Books and Manuscripts. From Curtis 1909. See note 5, this chapter.

Male Buffalo to produce tobacco for Lone Man, who carried a pipe but did not know what to do with it. Later, Thunderbird threatened to destroy a village unless Hungry Wolf gave High Bird tobacco. High Bird sent his mother to Hungry Wolf four times for tobacco, and "each time he refused, so the people of the Mourners Camp dug deep holes in which to protect themselves from the celestial flames. Each morning the mourners would go to Hungry Wolf's camp to sing under the direction of seven singers. They sang the Tobacco Songs" (Bowers 1965:300–302). When the flames finally came, the tobacco singers and tobacco rites were saved, but later a quarrel developed over the division of a buffalo, and the seven tobacco singers moved away. That is why the Hidatsa no longer have a tobacco society, in contrast to the singers and other Indians who moved away and whose descendants are now known as the Crow.

The strong variety of tobacco used by the Hidatsa is planted away from their corn, because of tobacco's powerful smell. Young men do not smoke it, because it prevents them from running by causing shortness of breath. The Hidatsa harvest the blossoms, stems, and leaves, then treat them with buffalo fat before storing them.

In *Buffalo Bird Woman's Garden*, Gilbert Wilson (1987 [1917]) provided a detailed description of the Hidatsa use of tobacco. Born in about 1839 in a village that was probably one of the three Hidatsa villages described by Lewis and Clark 35 years earlier, Maxidiwiac (Buffalo Bird Woman) remembered many details of traditional Hidatsa agriculture when Wilson interviewed her in 1906. Rather than repeating the full text of her delightful description of Hidatsa tobacco, which can be found on pages 121–127 of Wilson's monograph, I quote only the opening passages here to demonstrate how the Hidatsa were fully aware of the dangers and debilitating powers of tobacco:

> Tobacco was cultivated in my tribe only by old men. Our young men did not smoke much; a few did, but most of them used little tobacco, or almost none. They were taught that smoking would injure their lungs and make them short winded so that they would be poor runners. But when a man got to be about sixty years of age we thought it right for him to smoke as much as he liked. His war days and hunting days were over. Old men smoked quite a good deal.
>
> Young men who used tobacco could run; but in a short time they became short of breath, and water, thick like syrup, came up into the mouth. A young man who smoked a great deal, if chased by enemies, could not run to escape from them, and so got killed.

For this reason all the young men of my tribe were taught that they should not smoke.

> Things have changed greatly since those good days; and now young and old, boys and men, all smoke. They seem to think that the new ways of the white men are right; but I do not. In olden days, we Hidatsas took good care of our bodies, as is not done now. (Wilson 1987 [1917]:121)

The Siksika (Blackfoot) and Tsuu T'ina (Sarsi) also have tobacco societies. A northern Siksika tobacco society was raising *N. quadrivalvis* var. *multivalvis* as recently as 1971 (Hellson and Gadd 1974). It has also been suggested that the Siksika use *N. attenuata* and/or *N. quadrivalvis* var. *quadrivalvis* (Johnston 1970).

Within the past century, tobacco has become an important element in peyote rituals for a number of plains tribes, as well as for the pan-Indian Native American Church. The Kiowa, Oto, Cheyenne, Caddo, Osage, and Kickapoo use tobacco and offer smoke prayers at peyote meetings, and the Osage and Kiowa smoke cornhusk cigarettes during the rites. Even commercial tobacco is sometimes used in peyote ceremonies, as is shown by John Goggin's (1938) description of a Cheyenne peyote meeting in which corn-husk cigarettes were filled with Bull Durham. The Cheyenne peyote chief presented four peyote buttons and one cigarette to each person. The cigarette was smoked while the person chewed the buttons, and then one cigarette was smoked with each of any additional buttons that were ingested.

## The Northwest Coast and Interior Plateau

One of the most fascinating of the many intriguing facts about North American Indian use of tobacco is that a variety of *Nicotiana quadrivalvis* (var. *multivalvis*) was cultivated as far north along the Pacific coast as the territory of the Haida and Tlingit Indians in the panhandle of southern Alaska (table 7). The Siksika,

## Table 7: Northwest Coast and Interior Plateau Native American Groups Using Tobacco

| No. on Map 1 | Group | Reference |
|---|---|---|
| 107 | Tlingit | De Laguna 1990:212, 220; Drucker 1955:179; Krause 1956:285; Meilleur 1979; Swanton 1905, 1909; Turner and Taylor 1972:251–253 |
| 108 | Haida | Meilleur 1979; Turner and Taylor 1972 |
| 109 | Tsimshian | Compton 1993:350; Turner and Taylor 1972 |
| 110 | Kwakiutl | Turner and Bell 1973:292 |
| 111 | Shuswap | Meilleur 1979:101; Palmer 1975:61, 62, 69 |
| 112 | Lillooet | Meilleur 1979:101 |
| 113 | Okanagan | Meilleur 1979:101 |
| 114 | Kootenay | Turner and Taylor 1972:252; Winter 1996 |
| 115 | Thompson River Salish | Perry 1952:39; Steedman 1928:46, 467, 495; Turner and Taylor 1972:249; Turner et al. 1990:211, 288; West 1934:64 |
| 116 | Coast Salish | Elmendorf 1960:245, 247; Suttles and Lane 1990:495–496; Turner and Bell 1971:81, 82; Turner and Taylor 1972:252 |
| 117 | Chinook | Drucker 1955:105; J. Gibson 1988:376; Silverstein 1990:537 |
| 118 | Upper Columbia Chinook | Cutright 1989; Douglas 1904–1905; Harrington 1932:43; Setchell 1921 |
| 119 | Tillamook | Meilleur 1979:102 |
| 120 | Kalapuya | Meilleur 1979:102; Zenk 1990a:548 |
| 121 | Suislaw | Zenk 1990b:573 |
| 122 | Coosan | Zenk 1990b:573 |
| 123 | Takelma | Harrington 1932:30; Kendall 1990:590 |
| 124 | Southwest Oregon Athapaskans | Kendall 1990:590; Miller and Seaburg 1990:582 |
| 125 | Clallam/Klallam | Fleisher 1980:199; Gunther 1973:16 |
| 126 | Flathead | Hart 1992:52 |
| 127 | Haisla | Compton 1993:291 |
| 128 | Hanaksiala | Compton 1993:291 |
| 129 | Heiltzuk | Compton 1993:239 |
| 130 | Hesquiat | Turner and Efrat 1982:64, 76 |
| 131 | Klamath | Colville 1897:102, 104 |
| 132 | Nez Perce | Hart 1992:26 |
| 133 | Okanagan-Colville | Perry 1952:39; Turner, Bouchard, and Kennedy 1980:64, 96, 101, 140 |
| 134 | Owukeno | Compton 1993:118 |
| 135 | Samish | Gunther 1973:16 |
| 136 | Salish (Other) | Teit 1928:294 |
| 137 | Interior Salish | Winter 1996 |
| 138 | Skagit | Theodoratus 1989:42 |
| 139 | Swinomish | Gunther 1973:16 |

Tsuu T'ina, and Crow Indians of the northern plains continue to cultivate this sacred variety, and in the past it also appears to have been taken west across the Rocky Mountains to the Northwest Coast, where the Haida, Tlingit, and perhaps the Tsimshian grew it in early contact (and probably late prehistoric) times. Farther south, in Washington and Oregon, various coastal and interior tribes also raised *N. quadrivalvis*, probably the variety now known as *bigelovii*. The sacred *multivalvis* variety may also have been grown in Oregon and Washington; it was first collected by David Douglas in 1825 at the great falls of the Columbia (Cutright 1989).[7] He learned that the local Chinook-speaking Indians planted it in soil mixed with ashes in order to make the plants very large.

Anthropologists have long been puzzled by the cultivation of tobacco by the otherwise non-agricultural, fishing and sea-mammal-hunting

Tlingit and Haida Indians. It is unknown when the practice started, and it has been many generations since this sacred plant was grown along the fog-shrouded, forest-covered coast of the northern Pacific. Indeed, after I mentioned this custom at a conference in 1974, a Tlingit man in the audience went home to ask his elderly relatives about it. They told him they had never heard of the custom. Nevertheless, it is fairly certain that the Haida and Tlingit once grew tobacco, as is discussed in detail by Nancy Turner and Roy Taylor (1972) and by Brien Meilleur (1979). Moreover, as is shown by the distribution of tobacco-growing tribes in map 1 and table 7, it is perfectly logical, at least from a geographical perspective, for tobacco to have been grown in the Pacific Northwest. Not only do the Pawnee, Omaha-Ponca, Crow, Hidatsa, Mandan, Arikara, Siksika, and Tsuu T'ina represent a continuum of tobacco-growing cultures up the Missouri River and on into the northern plains of Canada, but also a number of interior plateau and mountain tribes between the Tsuu T'ina and the Haida and Tlingit, such as the Shuswap, Lillooet, Okanagan, Chilcotin, and Kootenay, use tobacco, though it is the wild *N. attenuata* species rather than the cultivated variety of *N. quadrivalvis*. In addition, a nearly solid line of tobacco-using and at times tobacco-growing tribes stretches to the south through Washington and Oregon, as represented by the Coast Salish, Chinook, Tillamook, Kalapuya, Suislaw, and related groups, then on through the Tolowa and Yurok area into California, and from there all the way south into Mexico, Central America, and South America.

The cultivation of tobacco in this far northern region and its incorporation into myth and religion is exemplified by the Haida, who raised the plants in protected locations, harvested and dried the leaves, and mixed rotten wood into the soil to enrich it for the following year's crop. The leaves were pulverized in special stone mortars, and a wad of the tobacco was placed in a person's mouth. Lime made from burned and crushed seashells was inserted into the wad to

stop it from burning the mouth. The mixture was often chewed for hours, and old people sometimes kept it in their mouth overnight. The practice of mixing lime with tobacco is widespread in the Americas; many tribes in California, Mexico, and South America also follow it.

By 1850, dried tobacco plants were an important Haida trade item. Five bundles of plants could be exchanged for a blanket worth $5.00. The importance of native tobacco in trade and for other uses is evident in Haida myths, in which a number of heroes and spirits, including Old Man Great Blue Heron, Sounding-Gambling Sticks, and even Raven, the primary deity, create tobacco, bribe each other with tobacco seeds, and otherwise use it.

The Haida's cultivation of tobacco may represent an ancient practice, but we know little about how the Northwest Coast Indians actually grew and used *N. quadrivalvis* var. *multivalvis*, since it was rapidly replaced by trade tobacco after Russian, British, and American traders and other visitors introduced commercial smoking tobacco. For the Tlingit, supplying tobacco was and is an important element in all kinds of feasts, with guests outdoing each other in smoking, "even to the point of reaching a stage similar to intoxication" (Krause 1956 [1885]). The Tlingit had a Tobacco Feast of Mourning, when the husband of a dead woman said, "Yes, yes my grandfather, we remember you are mourning. We are not smoking this tobacco for which you have invited us. These long dead uncles of ours and our mothers are the ones who smoke it" (Turner and Taylor 1972:252, citing Swanton 1909).

In Tlingit myth, Raven created tobacco. In the Tsimshian myth "The Stars," a sky-being was bribed with tobacco and "began to swell" when he used it. Haida, Tlingit, and Tsimshian myths suggest that the introduction of tobacco into their cultures occurred so long ago that Raven—the ulimate transformer—was intimately associated with the plant. One version of the Haida myth is found in the adventures of He-who-was-born-from-his-mother's-side, a reincarnation of Raven:

Photo 12. "Hoonah Sealers." One Tlingit hunter is smoking a pipe. Photograph from the Alaska Harriman Expedition, 1899. Courtesy of the Bancroft Library, University of California, Berkeley.

Raven was travelling along and came to a group of people shooting leaves off a tall tree and eating the leaves which fell. "That was tobacco," they say. Raven shot at the tree near the base and caused it to fall, making the supernatural beings rejoice. He then said, "Take care of its eggs [seeds]. I will let my cousin, Cloud-woman, take off the head [of the seeds]." Then they sent for her, and she came by canoe. She took all of its eggs, and began to plant them. Cloud-woman, being Raven's cousin, was of the Eagle clan, therefore tobacco was originally the property of the Eagles. (Turner and Taylor 1972:253, citing Swanton 1905).

In addition to smoking it (photo 12), the Tlingit also chewed tobacco in pellets mixed with lime, yellow cedar, and spruce or cedar gum. When clay and other trade pipes were introduced in the late 1700s, the Tlingit began to make elaborately carved pipes for smoking at

funerals. The Haida made beautiful argillite panel pipes that they sold to traders and whalers. Tlingit women continued using snuff pellets until about 1900, though the men gave it up much earlier. Tobacco is still used at memorial potlatches, where guests are entertained at smoking feasts in which tobacco is offered to all of the dead of the host clan.

The nearby Kwakiutl also used tobacco, but it does not appear to have been the native, cultivated variety. Rather, they received wild *N. attenuata*, as well as the introduced commercial *N. tabacum*, in trade from interior Indians. Packets of whole leaves were purchased for use in steam baths and as poultices for sores, lumps, and cuts.

Little is known about the use of the wild *N. attenuata* by the interior Shuswap, Lillooet, Salish, Kootenay, and Okanagan Indians. At one time the interior Salish and Kootenay of Montana grew it at a place called Tobacco

Plains, whereas the Thompson River Salish gathered it wild. To the south, the Coast Salish around Seattle smoked mainly for pleasure. The older people, especially shamans, smoked more than the younger tribal members. Both native and trade tobaccos were highly prized by the Chinook of the lower Columbia, who traded native tobacco with other tribes at The Dalles, a major fishing and trading location.

*Nicotiana quadrivalvis* was cultivated along the coast of Oregon by the Tillamook and inland by the Kalapuya of the Willamette Valley. The latter planted the seeds in small gardens fertilized with ash. The Suislaw and Coosan farther down the Oregon coast also cultivated tobacco, as did the Tutuni, Galice, and Upper Coquille Athapaskans of southwest Oregon, who burned over and fenced in areas where they grew it. Much farther inland, along the Snake and Lemhi rivers, the Shoshone and other Great Basin Indians also used tobacco, thereby forming a continuum

with the interior plateau, just as the Yurok and Tolowa form a continuum of tobacco-using and tobacco-growing Indians into California.

## California

The Indians of California represent a bewildering array of mostly nonagricultural tribes, tribelets, bands, and distinct language groups (table 8), with one of the most varied and densely packed settlement systems on the continent. Their range of tobacco use was also quite varied; among other methods, they ingested nicotine by smoking tobacco, chewing it with lime, and drinking it. Seven different varieties and species were used (and for some groups still are), linking California with the Southwest, Mexico, and the rest of Latin America, where an equally large number of *Nicotiana* taxa are still used (table 9).

## Table 8: California Native American Groups Using Tobacco

| No. on Map 1 | Group | Reference |
|---|---|---|
| **NORTHWEST** | | |
| 140 | Tolowa | Baker 1981; Gould 1978:130; Kroeber 1925:826 |
| 141 | Yurok | Bean and Lawton 1993:43–44; Bean and Vane 1978:664–665; Buckley 1992:123, 137, 160; Gibson 1988:376; Kroeber 1925:74, 88–89, 826, 1960a:245, 1976:114–127; Lang 1996; Sisk-Franco 1996:37–38 |
| 142 | Karok | Baker 1981:58; Balls 1972:81–84; Bean and Lawton 1976:36–37, 1993:43–44; Bean and Vane 1978:664–665; Davis 1974:24; Harrington 1932; Kroeber 1925:104–105; Lang 1996; Lewis 1993:87–89; Merriam 1966:209; Norton 1992:235–238; Palmer 1980; Schenck and Gifford 1952:392; USDA n.d.; Wilbert 1987:183; Winter 1994a |
| 143 | Hupa | Bean and Lawton 1993:43–44; Davis 1974:28; Goodspeed 1954:449; Kroeber 1925:826, 1960:24; Lang 1996; Wallace 1978a:173; Winter 1994a |
| 144 | Chilula | Wallace 1978a:173 |
| 145 | Whilkut | Wallace 1978a:173 |
| 146 | Wiyot | Davis 1974:28; Elsasser 1978a:160; Kroeber 1925:826; Lang 1996 |
| 147 | Chimariko | Silver 1978a:208–209 |
| 148 | Mattole | Davis 1974:28; Elsasser 1978b:198 |
| 149 | Nongatl | Elsasser 1978b:198–199 |
| 150 | Sinkyone | Elsasser 1978b:198–199 |
| 151 | Lassik | Elsasser 1978b:198–199 |
| 152 | Wailaki | Elsasser 1978b:198–199 |
| **NORTHEAST** | | |
| 153 | Wintu | Bean and Lawton 1976:36–37, 1993:43–44; Kroeber 1925:826, 1960b:24; Lapena 1978:331, 325; Redding 1960:286; Setchell 1921:pl. 3; Shepard 1992:192–193 |

Table 8: California Native American Groups Using Tobacco (continued)

| No. on Map I | Group | Reference |
|---|---|---|
| 154 | Patwin | P. Johnson 1978:355; Kroeber 1925:826 |
| 155 | Yana | J. Johnson 1978:364 |
| 156 | Yahi | Kroeber 1925:826, 1960b:24 |
| 157 | Shasta | Davis 1974:24; Setchell 1921:pl. 3; Silver 1978b:214–215, 217 |
| 158 | Atsugewi | Garth 1978:241; Kroeber 1925:826 |
| 159 | Achumawii | Olmsted and Stewart 1978:228, 232 |

**NORTH-CENTRAL**

| 160 | Maidu | Bean and Lawton 1976:36–37, 1993:43–44; Buckskin 1992:240; Garth 1978:241; J. Johnson 1978:364; Kroeber 1925:419, 1960b:24; Merriam 1966:319; Olmsted and Stewart 1978:228, 232; Powers 1877:33, 38; Riddell 1978:379, 383; Strike 1994:97; West 1934:63 |
|---|---|---|
| 161 | Yuki | Chesnut 1902:378; Davis 1974:18; Kroeber 1925:214; Lang 1996; V. Miller 1978:252, 255; Setchell 1921:pl. 3 |
| 162 | Huchnom | V. Miller 1978:252 |
| 163 | Kato | Davis 1974:18; J. Myers 1978:246; Setchell 1921:pl. 3 |
| 164 | Nomlaki | Goldschmidt 1978:346 |
| 165 | Pomo | Barrett 1952:116–118; Chesnut 1902:378, 386–387, 401; Gifford and Kroeber 1937:146, 287; Goodrich and Lawson 1980:115; Goodspeed 1954:449; Harrington 1932:18; Lang 1996, 1997; McLendon and Lowy 1978:317; Setchell 1921:pl. 3; Strike 1994:96; Winter 1994a |
| 166 | Miwok | Bates 1992:110; Bean and Lawton 1976:36–37, 1993:43–44; Callaghan 1978:269–271; Davis 1974:18, 20; Kelly 1978:417; Levy 1978a:403; Lewis 1993:91; Merriam 1966:356; Setchell 1921:pl. 3; West 1934:64 |

**CENTRAL COAST**

| 167 | Costanoan | Bean and Lawton 1993:44; Bocek 1984:14, 253; Harrington 1942:28, 37; Heizer 1974; Kroeber 1925:469, 548, 826; Levy 1978b:489; Parkman 1992:169; Strike 1994:95–96 |
|---|---|---|
| 168 | Esselen | Kroeber 1925:548 |
| 169 | Salinan | Harrington 1942:28, 37; Kroeber 1925:548 |

**CENTRAL VALLEY AND MOUNTAINS**

| 170 | Yokuts | Applegate 1978:34, 48, 50, 67, 80; Bean and Lawton 1976:36–37, 1993:43–44; Davis 1974:20; Gayton 1976a:82–83, 1976b:176, 196; Gayton and Newman 1940:33; Kroeber 1925:502, 509–510, 516, 538, 627, 826, 865, 1960b:24; Powers 1877:384, 386–389, 415, 428; Wallace 1978b:456, 459; Winter 1994a |
|---|---|---|
| 171 | Kitanemek | Blackburn and Bean 1978:565–567; Kroeber 1960b:24 |
| 172 | Western Mono | Davis 1974:20 |
| 173 | Tubatulabal | Applegate 1978:35; Davis 1974:20; Goodspeed 1954:430, 451; Kroeber 1925:627, 826; C. Smith 1978:441, 444; Voegelin 1938:36–38, 68 |

**SOUTHERN COAST**

| 174 | Chumash | Blackburn 1975; Grant 1978:511–512; Harrington 1942:28; Phil Holmes, pers. comm., 1994; Timbrook 1987:175–176, 1990:252 |
|---|---|---|
| 127 | Gabrielino | Harrington 1942:28; Holmes, pers. comm., 1994; Kroeber 1925:826; Strike 1994:95 |
| 176 | Luiseño | Bean and Shipek 1978:552; Harrington 1942:37; Kroeber 1925:674; Setchell 1921:pl. 3; Sparkman 1908:229 |
| 177 | Serrano | Harrington 1942:28; Kroeber 1925:613, 826 |

Table 8: California Native American Groups Using Tobacco (continued)

| No. on Map I | Group | Reference |
|---|---|---|
| **SOUTHERN DESERT AND BAJA CALIFORNIA** | | |
| 178 | Diegueño/Kumeyaay | Bean and Lawton 1976:36–37, 1993:43–44; Davis 1974:24; Goodpeed 1954:427–430; Hedges 1986; Kroeber 1925:997; Setchell 1921:411; Shipek 1992:90; West 1934:64; Winter 1994a |
| 179 | Cahuilla | Barrows 1900:74–75; Bean and Lawton 1993:43–44; Bean and Saubel 1972:91–94, 207; Goodspeed 1954:427–430; Setchell 1921:411; West 1934:64; Winter 1994a |
| 180 | Tipai-Ipai | Luomala 1978:600, 603 |
| 181 | Paipai | Ford 1983:127 |
| 182 | Kamia | Davis 1974:24 |

Table 9: Traditional Species and Varieties of Tobacco Used by Native Californians

| Group | N. attenuata | N. quadrivalvis | N. quad. var. bigelovii | N. quad. var. wallacei | N. clevelandii | N. glauca | N. trigonophylla | Other |
|---|---|---|---|---|---|---|---|---|
| Tolowa | | X | | | | | | |
| Karuk | X | X | | | | | | |
| Hupa | X | | X | | | | | |
| Shasta | | | X | | | | | |
| S. Maidu | | | | | | | | X[a] |
| Maidu | X | | | | | | | |
| Yuki | | X | | | | | | |
| Pomo | | | | | | X | | |
| Clear Lake Pomo | | | X | | | | | |
| Yokia Pomo | | X | | | | | | |
| Kashaya Pomo | | X | | | | | | |
| E. Miwok | X | X | | | | | | |
| Miwok | | X | | | | | | |
| Costanoan | | X | | | | | | |
| Yokuts | | | | | | X | | X[b] |
| Tubatulabal | X | | | X | | | | |
| Luiseño | | | | | | | ? | |
| Gabrieleno | X | X | | | | X | | |
| Chumash | X | X | | | | X | | |
| Kumeyaay | X | | | | | | ? | |
| Diegueño | X | | | | | | | |
| Barona Diegueño | | | | | | | X | |
| Cahuilla | X | | | | ? | X | X | |
| Los Coyotes Cahuilla | X | | | X | | | | |
| Agua Caliente Cahuilla | | | | | | | ? | |
| Morongo Cahuilla | | | | | | ? | | |

a   *Nicotiana plumbaginifolia*, according to Powers (1877:426); probably a misidentification of *N. quadrivalvis*.

b   *Nicotiana rustica* from the Southwest may have been recently introduced via Native Seeds/SEARCH.

In addition to tobacco, hallucinogenic datura (jimsonweed) was also used in central and southern California, at the far northern end of an extremely long chain of hallucinogenic drug use that stretches all the way from San Francisco Bay through the Southwest, Mexico, and on into Panama and South America. Datura is a much stronger drug than tobacco, but the latter plant has a much more extensive range of use (probably because it is safer to use, at least in the short run), and it serves as a mildly narcotic-like hallucinogen. Tobacco is also the only plant that most California tribes grew, at least until relatively recently. Twenty-two California groups also burned old stands of tobacco plants in the fall to stimulate their growth the following year (Lewis 1993).

Information concerning tobacco use in California is vast, varied, and often contradictory. Because of the large number of tobacco-using groups in California, in this section I divide the state into seven geocultural regions: northwest, northeast, north-central, central coast, central valley and adjacent mountains, south coast, and interior southern desert and Baja California.

## Northwest California

The shamanistic use of tobacco is well developed throughout California, especially along the northern coast and up the rugged, forest-covered Klamath and Trinity river valleys, where the Yurok, Karok, Hupa, Chilula, Whilkut, and a number of other groups grew it. The Yurok in particular were "passionate" smokers. One of their creators, Pulekukwerek, grew from a tobacco plant before he gave it to humans. The Yurok supplied tobacco up and down the California coast and continue to use it for religious as well as recreational and medicinal purposes, such as to induce sleep. The Yurok are also a tribe in which tobacco-using shamanism has evolved into a more organized religion. Their World Renewal priests offer and ingest tobacco as a symbol of the yearly transformation and rebirth of the whole of creation.

The Hupa in the Trinity Valley grew, continue to gather, and probably continue to grow the *bigelovii* variety of *N. quadrivalvis*. The neighboring Karok along the Klamath River also grow tobacco. Like the Yurok and Hupa, they rarely gather it wild, in case it is growing on a grave and therefore is contaminated. John P. Harrington (1932), Henry Lewis (1993), and several other anthropologists have described how the Karok sow the seeds of *N. quadrivalvis* and *N. attenuata* in burned-over areas. When the plants are mature, the leaves are gathered, packed in fern fronds and Douglas fir twigs, and dried. Only the men and a few female shamans use traditional tobacco, to induce drowsiness, as an offering to the mountain spirits, for earaches and toothaches, and in many contexts in the World Renewal ceremony and the associated White Deerskin and Jump dances.

Harrington's 1932 description of Karok tobacco use contains 284 pages of extremely detailed observations and photographs supporting his contention that no other substance is of such immense value to the Karok and their gods (photo 13). It is absolutely essential for the World Renewal ceremony, which sets the world right again, year after year. Without tobacco, the ceremony could not be held, which means that existence would cease.

Gary Palmer's 1980 evaluation of the significance of Karok World Renewal locations and associated villages also contains considerable information about the necessity of tobacco for rituals, and Lewis (1993) adds more recent data on everyday use. Together these three sources (especially Harrington 1932) provide the most complete ethnogeographic description ever written of a Native American tribe's complex relationship with this powerful plant.

Other northwest California groups that used (and generally planted) tobacco were the Chilula, Whilkut, Wiyot, Chimariko, Mattole, Nongatl, Sinkyone, Lassik, and Wailaki. Chimariko sucking shamans received power through tobacco; Wiyot homes of the dead were purified with tobacco; Mattole shamans cured with

Photo 13. "Upriver Women's Hats." Hats such as this one, worn in 1928 by Mrs. Phoebe Maddux, a Karuk woman, were often used as tobacco baskets. Mrs. Maddux is also shown picking tobacco in photo 10 in Harrington 1932. Photo by John P. Harrington. Courtesy of the National Anthropology Archives of the National Museum of Natural History, Smithsonian Institution. Negative no. S.I.2868–B.

tobacco; and the Nongatl owned private tobacco plots.

### Northeast and North-Central California

Many of the same uses of tobacco were and are practiced by the many small, scattered tribes of northeastern and north-central California, where *N. attenuata* and *N. quadrivalvis* were gathered wild and often grown. Wintu men smoked and prayed with tobacco every morning and evening and then blew smoke "over the world." Wintu shamans smoked and swallowed tobacco to induce trances. As translated by Alice Shepard (1992:192–193), a Wintu described how a shaman smoked tobacco for quite a while, then fell into a trance. "Look at me," he said [to the patient]. "I smoke a pipe in your company because I want you to be healthy, so that I can be healthy in the same way."

Shasta boys went on vision quests for success in hunting, gambling, and other activities. When they received a vision, they smoked tobacco. The Shasta also burned plots of *N. quadrivalvis* to encourage better crops, owned the plots for a single season, gathered the tobacco wild and sometimes sowed its seeds, thinned and pruned the plants, and watered them by hand when necesary.

Yana shamans smoked tobacco in pipes. Atsugewi shamans had their assistants blow tobacco smoke over them when they were in trances. Achumawii shamans smoked during curing seances. When they succeeded in curing someone, they had to dispose of the poison, sickness, or power that had caused the illness. Sometimes they vomited it out and then covered it before sprinkling tobacco on it.

Maidu shamans also grew tobacco. They smoked it as offerings and during periods of drought. Nomlaki shamans entered trances induced partly by tobacco. Nomlaki shamans continue to smoke tobacco as part of the Bole-

Maru cult, which is similar to the old Ghost Dance, except that it stresses the end of the world, whereas the Ghost Dance emphasized the return of the dead.

Another California religion that uses tobacco is that of the Kuksu, a secret men's society characterized by Kuksu or "Big-Head" dances. In the Pomo version, a bear appears, turns into a man smoking a pipe, and then prays for the health of the people. *Nicotiana quadrivalvis* var. *bigelovii* is used by the Pomo as medicine and offerings. It is very important for the older men and is smoked in the ceremony opening the food-gathering season in the spring.

The Pomo also appear to have used *N. glauca*, and I recently collected *N. quadrivalvis* (probably the variety *bigelovii*) in the yard of a Clear Lake Pomo man in the Big Valley Rancheria near Kelseyville.[8] The elderly man calls tobacco *sa xa*, and when he smokes it, he puffs it out, without inhaling, as an offering to the spirits. He said that the eastern Pomo were created around Clear Lake, where they still use straight wooden pipes with enlarged bowls. *Nicotiana quadrivalvis* grows as weeds around houses, in gardens, and along creeks, as well as on old Pomo villages. Three different people in the Big Valley Rancheria told me that they know where it grows, so it is probably relatively common around Clear Lake. It is still used at ceremonies. Pipes are filled with it and then passed around, and everyone—including children—puffs the smoke out of his or her mouth as an offering. Wild tobacco is very harsh, however, so the gentleman I interviewed mixes it with commercial tobacco.

The nearly identical term *sa-ka'* was used for *N. quadrivalvis* by the Yokia Pomo to the west, around present-day Ukiah. The Yokia prized tobacco leaves for smoking and chewing, as did the Yuki to the north in Round Valley. The Yuki used to gather wild tobacco in large quantities in the summer, when they worked in the hop fields near Ukiah and in the Sacramento Valley. They also smoked it in straight wooden pipes, similar to the ones used today by the eastern

Pomo around Clear Lake. The Pomo crushed dried tobacco leaves and rubbed them on their bodies to cure fevers. The Indians of Mendocino County also used *N. quadrivalvis* to treat illnesses of the brain.

The Yokia Pomo smoked tobacco at bedtime, and their shamans smoked it in pipes as offerings and for curing. The Habenapo (rock people) Pomo of the Big Valley near Clear Lake also used tobacco as offerings, as do their contemporary Kelseyville descendants. Their shamans smoked it in pipes when calling for a spirit's aid. The Yokia singing shamans to the west offered tobacco and shell beads by throwing them in the six cardinal directions. Tobacco was given to a shaman when he treated the sick. In turn, he gave it to his friends. Habenapo Pomo men made tobacco offerings in sweat-house fires for their dead male relatives. The offerings allowed them to forget about the deceased and helped them to stop dreaming about the dead. Habenapo Pomo men also burned tobacco offerings in their assembly-house fires if eagles or hawks flew close over the structures. Then they prayed that the Pomo people would be happy and live long, without sickness or trouble.

Lake Miwok shamans also smoked tobacco before singing the tobacco song. The coast Miwok gathered a strong, heavy tobacco along creek banks, and the eastern Miwok collected *N. attenuata* and *N. quadrivalvis* wild and sometimes planted seeds to produce plants with bigger leaves and better flavor.

Today, tobacco offerings are a standard Miwok practice. Around 1970, some Miwok adopted a new religion when Paiute shamans visiting from Nevada introduced canvas-covered sweat lodges along with Plains Indian catlinite pipes. The new religion, which emphasized Indianness, brotherhood, and kindness, was rapidly accepted.

## The Central California Coast

Three related tribes, the Costanoan, Esselen, and Salinan, living along the California coast to the south of San Francisco Bay used tobacco and *toloache* (datura). *Toloache* was taken for vision quests and to initiate boys into manhood. Tobacco was gathered wild, smoked at bedtime, smoked, eaten, and drunk mixed with lime, used as an offering, and offered to the sun and sky. The Costanoans from San Francisco Bay south to Monterey Bay blew mouthfuls of tobacco to the sky while praying to the sun. Mission San Carlos Costanoans blew smoke to the sun, moon, and sky spirits, saying: "Ah, this wisp of smoke is blown that you may give me a favorable day tomorrow" (Heizer 1974:47). Costanoan men at Mission Santa Cruz would meet secretly in an isolated location, where they erected a high pole, crowned it with a wreath of tobacco leaves or other vegetation, and danced around it.

Father Junípero Serra set aside a section of garden for tobacco at Mission Carmel in 1774. He was prompted to do so by the fact that mission Indians from Monterey to San Diego begged him for Spanish tobacco.

Sir Francis Drake wrote what is probably the first European description of Costanoan tobacco use, during his visit to the California coast beween June 17 and July 23, 1579: "... bringing with them, as before had been done, feathers and bagges of Tobah for presents, or rather indeed for sacrifices, vpon this perswasion that we were gods" (Harrington 1932:18).

The Costanoans used *N. quadrivalvis* for many medical purposes, including the curing of toothaches, earaches, stomachaches, and skin sores. It was also a sedative, an emetic, a stimulant, a cathartic, a hallucinogen, and a psychological aid. Tobacco mixed with lime from pulverized seashells was eaten or drunk with water as a general cure-all.

Tciplitcu, an Ohlone Costanoan from Pleasanton, took the Ghost Dance to the central Miwok around 1872. He was told in his dreams that no one should smoke while he danced. If he saw anyone smoking, he danced up to him, took his pipe, and threw it in the fire.

## The Central California Valley and Mountains

The Yokuts and Kitanemek in and around the San Joaquin Valley of central California used both tobacco and datura as part of the *toloache* cult, an initiation rite in which boys were given the two drugs in order to obtain supernatural power from an animal helper. Throughout the rest of their lives, many Yokuts men (and some older women) received power from their helpers by taking datura or tobacco during dream quests. The Yokuts grew tobacco (and continue to grow it), smoked it in cane cigarettes and pipes, ate it moistened with lime, drank it mixed with water or lime, and ingested it to produce vomiting, which imparted supernatural powers such as the ability to detect wizards.

Kitanemuk boys were rendered unconscious for one to two days by datura. Upon awakening, they were given lumps of tobacco to hold in their mouths, which knocked them out again. The next day they offered tobacco, beads, down, and seeds at a shrine.

Most Kitanemuk used datura and tobacco for curing. The tobacco was pounded into a fine powder and mixed with lime, then eaten to induce a temporary intoxication (probably with hallucinations) along with vomiting. The *toloache*-tobacco cult was well developed among the Kitanemuk, who kept sacred sentient stones wrapped with tobacco and other offerings. The stones protected them from storms or were placed in water that was taken as medicine. The Kitanemuk offered tobacco whenever they passed certain shrines, as did people using the shrines during the summer and winter solstices. The Yokuts and Kitanemuk also used tobacco and toloache to obtain dream helpers and to stimulate visions.

The Yokuts origin myth illustrates the importance of tobacco. In the beginning there was only water, along with the deities Crow and Hawk. After a while they created other birds, including a duck that dove down to the bottom of the ocean, filled its beak with mud, swam back to the surface, and died. Hawk and Crow made the mountains from the dirt, but Crow stole some of Hawk's soil to make his mountains bigger. "Then the hawk went and got some Indian tobacco and chewed it, and it made him exceedingly wise, so he took hold of the mountains and turned them around in a circle, putting his range in place of the crow's" (Powers 1877: 384).

Tobacco was the only food that Hawk ate. In one Kitanemuk myth, datura appears as one of the First People, a powerful old woman who eats only tobacco and is very wise. In one Yokuts myth, Tobacco says, "I'm good for eating at a celebration, or at any time to make you dream any kind of dream. One thing: anyone can smoke me, anyone, and I'll help him" (Applegate 1978:34, citing Gayton and Newman 1940).

After attaining a vision or a dream, the Yokuts smoked a little tobacco as an offering to their animal helper. The Kitanemuk also offered a little tobacco to their helper after a drug-induced vision. Even if a Yokuts rejected the message in a dream, he still had to smoke tobacco as an offering to thank the helper. Without such respect, a helper could make a person ill. Even today, powerful Yokuts shamans communicate with their helpers any time they want by smoking a little tobacco. In difficult curing cases, they also smoke while singing and dancing.

Tobacco figures prominently in the Yokuts' Dance for the Dead, their most important ceremony. As observed by Stephen Powers in the late 1870s, the ceremony begins when a herald calls out to make ready the offerings. "Get ready the tobacco," he calls. "Let us chew the tobacco." Then the Yokuts eat the tobacco, which is prepared by compressing it into solid balls after beating it into very fine powder and adding water. The tobacco acts as an emetic, inducing vomiting during the ceremony. Large numbers of cigarettes (probably commercial) were also smoked during the ceremony observed by Powers (1877:386–389, 428).

During the winter months, most Yokuts men and women gathered together at dusk to drink the lime and tobacco emetic. Then they returned home to dream and to obtain supernatural benefits, for the emetic and fasting helped them to dream of supernatural beings. They hoped that Eagle, Mountain Lion, and other beings would appear in their dreams to help them in hunting, gambling, and other endeavors.

The Tule River Yokuts near Porterville continue to use and grow tobacco. Tree tobacco (*N. glauca*) is collected wild, and one man grows an unidentified taxon (probably *N. rustica*) obtained from the organization Native Seeds/ SEARCH in Tucson.

To the east of the Central Valley, in their mountain stronghold in the Sierras, the Tubatulabal used both *N. quadrivalvis* var. *wallacei* and *N. attenuata* as an emetic before bedtime to ensure dreamless sleep (they believed that the soul left the body during dreams and was vulnerable to attack by malicious shamans). The men mixed it with lime and water and chewed, snuffed, ate, drank, and smoked it. Only very old women smoked it. The Tubatulabal also went on long trading expeditions all the way to the Pacific coast, where they exchanged balls of tobacco for shell disks. The Tubatulabal do not appear to have planted tobacco, but they encouraged the growth of the two wild species by, for example, suckering them—pinching off the flowers and then cutting off the shoots that sprouted from the stems. The women pruned the leaves three times in the summer to produce greater leaf growth. Tubatulabal youths fasted before eating a small ball of tobacco and lime that helped them to secure the assistance of an animal "pet" or helper.

## The Southern California Coast

The *toloache* cult was also present among Indians living along the coast around Los Angeles, such as the Chumash, Luiseño, Gabrielino, and Serrano. The Chumash and Gabrielino still use tobacco in ceremonies, though it is the introduced *N. glauca* rather than one of the local indigenous species. In the old days they smoked tobacco at funerals, chewed it mixed with lime for strength, smoked it at bedtime, drank it as an emetic to cure fever, used it as an offering, and ate it socially. The native tobacco that they gathered appears to have been *N. attenuata* and *N. quadrivalvis*. In Chumash myths, spirits with exceptional supernatural powers are often said to eat only tobacco. Details concerning Chumash tobacco use can be found in Jan Timbrook's 1987 article, "Virtuous Herbs."

Luiseño girls swallowed tobacco balls during their initiation ceremony; only the virtuous were able to stomach the material without throwing up. The Luiseño also used tobacco (possibly *N. clevelandii*) and datura together for medicine and for sacred rituals.

The Serrano smoked tobacco and ate it with lime and water to relieve fatigue. They, too, had the *toloache* cult. They gathered tobacco wild, used it at bedtime, and offered it religiously.

### The Southern Desert and Baja California

Most of the Indians living in the deserts of far southern California and northern Baja California did not have the *toloache* cult, though the Cahuilla drank datura on an individual basis to see the future and to acquire wealth. Only Diegueño boys were initiated into the *toloache* cult, but Diegueño girls ate tobacco during their initiation rites. The Diegueño planted *N. attenuata* (called coyote tobacco) in burned-over areas.

Today most of the Diegueño prefer to be called Kumeyaay. As I recently observed, the Manzanita Kumeyaay still know where *N. attenuata* grows. The Barona Diegueño use *N. glauca* (tree tobacco), which grows on one of their old village sites. One Barona elder told me that his father used tree tobacco when he was a little boy, so the elder considers it the group's traditional tobacco. When I showed a Viejas Kumeyaay elder a number of different pressed tobacco specimens, the man identified *N. glauca*, *N. quadrivalvis* var. *wallacei*, and *N. trigonophylla* as Kumeyaay types.

Other desert dwellers in southern California include the Tipai-Ipai on the United States–Mexico border, where women planted and transplanted wild tobacco. Men smoked it in pipes, and girls drank purifying tobacco during their "roasting" puberty rites. The Paipai and Kamia supplied tobacco to the Cocopa and Yuma.

The Cahuilla's use of tobacco is well documented in an extensive ethnobotany by Lowell Bean and Katherine Saubel (1972). Tobacco was one of the first things created by the deity Mukat, who drew both the plant and the first pipe from his heart. Then he created the sun to light the pipe, but the sun escaped from his grasp, so he used the western light instead. Temaiyawit, his brother god, helped him smoke tobacco ceremonially. Now it is part of every Cahuilla ritual, and songs telling about its first use by the gods are sung at the most important ceremonies. Tobacco figures prominently in Cahuilla oral literature, where it is often associated with power, gaming, and the human soul. Having enough tobacco to give to guests at feasts is just as important as having enough food. Both virtues contribute to the flight of the soul to the land of the dead after the host dies.

David Barrows (1900) described the Cahuilla use of *N. attenuata*. Contemporary Cahuillas told Bean and Saubel that *N. trigonophylla* and *N. glauca* were still used, and I was recently directed to large stands of *N. attenuata* and *N. quadrivalvis* (probably the *wallacei* variety) on the Los Coyotes Cahuilla Reservation. I also collected *N. trigonophylla* in Palm Canyon on the Agua Caliente Cahuilla Reservation and the ubiquitous tree tobacco on the Morongo Cahuilla Reservation. Bean and Saubel suggested that the Cahuilla also used *N. clevelandii*, so this widely scattered group of desert hunters, gatherers, and occasional farmers may have used as many as five different species.

## Contemporary Use of Tobacco by California Native Americans

Tobacco has been and continues to be an important source of spiritual power for the Native Americans of California. The use of as many as five different species by the Cahuilla, and of two and perhaps three by other groups, suggests a relatively long history of tobacco ingestion in the region. The near-domestication of *N. quadrivalvis* occurred here, and perhaps even the evolution of a number of other species as a direct result of human activity.

For traditional California Indians, tobacco is a power "conduit" that should be used only at proper times and in proper places, following set procedures for the power act of smoking or eating this vision- and dream-inducing plant (Bean 1992:25). One of the ways to attain supernatural power is the vision quest and the creation of ecstasy, which allows the dreamer to receive the animal helper or other spirit that confers the power. Throughout North America, and especially in California, the most common, frequent, and safest (at least in the short run) way to induce ecstasy is the ingestion of tobacco. Other potent psychoactive plants, such as *toloache* (datura), can be used but are much more dangerous than tobacco and can produce insanity and death even when used in minute quantities.

All supernatural power is dangerous because it is an amoral force. It has the potential for both good and bad effects and is unpredictable, particularly when used by untrained persons who are ignorant of the full range of its effects. Both tobacco and *toloache* have the ability to grant visions of dream helpers and other spirits, yet both are lethal in excessive doses and must be used carefully. They are also venerated and feared. At times they are deities themselves, and they combine power and danger in the powerful drugs they contain.

This recognition of the danger, power, and sanctity of tobacco is manifested today by the beliefs and actions of many Native Americans in California. One group, the American Indian Tobacco Education Network (AITEN), recognizes that in the use of tobacco, a balance should be attained between abuse and sacred use and between negative health effects and positive religious rewards. AITEN was established in 1990, after the 1988 passage of the California State Tobacco Tax Act, with the primary purpose of educating Native Americans about both aspects of this amazing plant. Run by the California Rural Indian Health Board with tax-generated funds supplied by the Tobacco Control Section of the State of California and the California Department of Health Services, AITEN demonstrates how the power of tobacco continues to be a major force in Indian society, even in the late twentieth century with its technological advances, state-based revenue sources, and complex bureaucracies.

## The Great Basin

Of all the native groups in North America, the Paiute, Goshute, Shoshone, Washo, Kawaiisu, and Ute of the Great Basin best represent the ancient substratum of tobacco-using shamanism that evolved elsewhere into the *toloache* cult, tobacco societies, the World Renewal rite, and other, more complex tobacco-using religious systems. Of the 50 Great Basin groups summarized in table 10, only one—the Kawaiisu at the southwestern edge of the basin—had the *toloache* cult for the initiation of boys and girls, and no group had tobacco societies or other, more complex religious organizations. Since the Kawaiisu live near the Serrano and Yokuts in eastern California, they probably adopted the *toloache* cult from them.

Otherwise, the Great Basin Paiute, Shoshone, and other groups were organized into many small, widely scattered foraging bands that added maize horticulture in the historic period. Several of the groups may also have had corn farming in the late prehistoric period, but for the most part the Great Basin peoples were

Table 10: Great Basin Native American Groups Using Tobacco

| No. on Map 1 | Group | Reference |
|---|---|---|
| 183 | Paiute, northern Paiute | Fowler 1986:93, 1989:129; Steward 1938; Train et al. 1941:10, 106; Winter and Hogan 1986 |
| 184 | Fish Springs northern Paiute | Fowler 1986:93; Steward 1938; Winter and Hogan 1986 |
| 185 | Owens Valley northern Paiute | Clemmer and Stewart 1986:537; Davis 1974:20; Fowler 1986:94; Steward 1933:319, 1938; Winter and Hogan 1986 |
| 186 | Fish Springs northern Paiute | Fowler 1986:93; Steward 1938; Winter and Hogan 1986 |
| 187 | Soda Springs northern Paiute | Fowler 1986:93; Steward 1938; Winter and Hogan 1986 |
| 188 | Pyramid Lake northern Paiute | Fowler 1986:93; Steward 1938; Winter and Hogan 1986 |
| 189 | Reno northern Paiute | Fowler 1986:93; Steward 1938; Winter and Hogan 1986 |
| 190 | Carson River northern Paiute | Fowler 1986:93; Steward 1938; Winter and Hogan 1986 |
| 191 | Humboldt Sink northern Paiute | Fowler 1986:93; Steward 1938; Winter and Hogan 1986 |
| 192 | Mill City northern Paiute | Fowler 1986:93; Steward 1938; Winter and Hogan 1986 |
| 193 | Winnemuca northern Paiute | Fowler 1986:93; Steward 1938; Winter and Hogan 1986 |
| 194 | Quinn River northern Paiute | Fowler 1986:93; Steward 1938; Winter and Hogan 1986 |
| 195 | Surprise Valley northern Paiute | Fowler 1986:93; Steward 1938; Winter and Hogan 1986 |
| 196 | Malheur Lake northern Paiute | Fowler 1986:93; Steward 1938; Winter and Hogan 1986 |
| 197 | Warm Springs northern Paiute | Mahar 1953:108 |
| 198 | Washo | D'Azevado 1986:476; Fowler 1986:93; Goodspeed 1954:427–430; Handelman 1976:389, 391–392; Setchell 1921:pl. 3; West 1934:64 |
| 199 | Shoshone | Fowler 1986:93; Merriam 1966:446; Murphey 1959; Shimkin 1986:326; Siegel et al. 1977:19; Steward 1938; Train et al. 1941:10, 14, 106, 145; Winter and Hogan 1986 |
| 200 | Koso Panamint Shoshone | Bean and Lawton 1976:36–37; Fowler 1986:93; Steward 1938; Winter and Hogan 1986 |
| 201 | Death Valley Panamint Shoshone | Fowler 1986:93, 1994; Steward 1938; Winter and Hogan 1986 |
| 202 | Beatty Shoshone | Fowler 1986:93; Steward 1938; Winter and Hogan 1986 |
| 203 | Lida Shoshone | Fowler 1986:93; Steward 1938; Winter and Hogan 1986 |
| 204 | Smith Creek Shoshone | Fowler 1986:93; Steward 1938; Winter and Hogan 1986 |
| 205 | Ione Valley Shoshone | Fowler 1986:93; Steward 1938; Winter and Hogan 1986 |
| 206 | Reese River Shoshone | Fowler 1986:93; Steward 1938; Winter and Hogan 1986 |
| 207 | Great Smokey Shoshone | Fowler 1986:93; Steward 1938; Winter and Hogan 1986 |
| 208 | Little Smokey Shoshone | Fowler 1986:93; Steward 1938; Winter and Hogan 1986 |
| 209 | Elko Shoshone | Fowler 1986:93; Steward 1938; Winter and Hogan 1986 |
| 210 | Ruby Valley Shoshone | Fowler 1986:93; Steward 1938; Winter and Hogan 1986 |
| 211 | Eggan Shoshone | Fowler 1986:93; Steward 1938; Winter and Hogan 1986 |
| 212 | Hamilton Shoshone | Fowler 1986:93; Steward 1938; Winter and Hogan 1986 |
| 213 | Morey Shoshone | Fowler 1986:93; Steward 1938; Winter and Hogan 1986 |
| 214 | Ely Shoshone | Fowler 1986:93; Steward 1938; Winter and Hogan 1986 |
| 215 | Spring Valley Shoshone | Fowler 1986:93; Steward 1938; Winter and Hogan 1986 |
| 216 | Grouse Creek Shoshone | Fowler 1986:93; Steward 1938; Winter and Hogan 1986 |
| 217 | Snake Valley Shoshone | Fowler 1986:93; Steward 1938; Winter and Hogan 1986 |
| 218 | Snake River/Lemhi Shoshone | Cutright 1989; Fowler 1986:93; Goodspeed 1954:453; Meilleur 1979:102; Setchell 1921:pl. 3 |
| 219 | Goshiute | Chamberlain 1911:375; Fowler 1986:93; Goodspeed 1954:427–430; Setchell 1921:403; Steward 1938; West 1934:64; Winter and Hogan 1986 |
| 220 | Skull Valley Goshiute | Fowler 1986:93; Steward 1938; Winter and Hogan 1986 |
| 221 | Deep Creek Goshiute | Fowler 1986:93; Steward 1938; Winter and Hogan 1986 |
| 222 | Southern Paiute | Bye 1972:98; Fowler 1986:93; Kelly and Fowler 1986:371; Liljeblad 1986:649; Steward 1938; Winter and Hogan 1986 |
| 223 | Ash Meadows southern Paiute | Fowler 1986:93; Steward 1938; Winter and Hogan 1986 |

Table 10: Great Basin Native American Groups Using Tobacco (continued)

| No. on Map I | Group | Reference |
|---|---|---|
| 224 | Moapa southern Paiute | Bye 1972:95; Fowler 1986:93; Steward 1938; Winter and Hogan 1986 |
| 225 | Shivwits southern Paiute | Fowler 1986:93; Steward 1938; Winter and Hogan 1986 |
| 226 | Kaibab southern Paiute | Fowler 1986:93; Steward 1938; Winter and Hogan 1986 |
| 227 | Kaiparowits southern Paiute | Fowler 1986:93; Steward 1938; Winter and Hogan 1986 |
| 228 | Chemehuevi southern Paiute | Fowler 1986:93; Laird 1976:38–40, 44 |
| 229 | Ute | Callaway et al. 1986:343; Fowler 1986:93; Goodspeed 1954:427–430; Setchell 1921:411; Steward 1938; Winter and Hogan 1986 |
| 230 | Moanunts Ute | Callaway et al. 1986:343; Fowler 1986:93; Steward 1938; Winter and Hogan 1986 |
| 231 | Pahvant Ute | Callaway et al. 1986:343; Fowler 1986:93; Steward 1938; Winter and Hogan 1986 |
| 232 | Timpanogos Ute | Callaway et al. 1986:343; Fowler 1986:93; Steward 1938; Winter and Hogan 1986 |
| 233 | Kawaiisu | Fowler 1986:94–95, 97; Kroeber 1925:604; Steward 1938; Winter and Hogan 1986; Zigmond 1981, 1986:399, 402–403, 408 |

hunters and gatherers with a heavy reliance on burning, encouraging, and sometimes irrigating and sowing wild plants, especially *N. attenuata* and *N. quadrivalvis.*

Buffalo hunting and other Plains Indian traits were adopted by some of the tribes in and near the Great Basin, such as the southern Ute (photo 14). The northern and eastern Shoshone also developed many Plains Indian traits and even smoked the same tobacco that the Mandan, Hidatsa, and Arikara used. Lewis and Clark observed the Snake Indians, a northern Shoshone group, using this tobacco, which they obtained "from the Rocky Mountain Indians and some of their own nation who lived further south" (Meriweather Lewis, quoted in Cutright 1989:189).

As Patrick Hogan and I (Winter and Hogan 1986) summarized in our review of plant husbandry in the Great Basin, and as discussed by James Downs (1966), Catherine Fowler (1986), and other authors, almost every Great Basin band burned old tobacco plants in the autumn to encourage the following year's growth. At least six groups sowed wild tobacco, one band irrigated it, and two groups pruned it. The Owens Valley Paiute sowed, irrigated, and burned wild tobacco, thereby producing a large enough surplus to exchange tobacco with the western Mono, Yokuts, and central and southern Miwok on the other side of the Sierra Nevadas in California. They also burned a number of wild food plants to improve their productivity, and irrigated them as well. About a dozen other Great Basin groups also irrigated wild food plants such as shadscale (*Atriplex argentea*) and goosefoot (*Chenopodium* spp.), and most of the tribes in the basin burned wild food plants. This complex of wild tobacco and wild food plant burning, irrigating, and sowing may represent an extremely ancient pre-agricultural adaptation that could have started when the earliest Indians in North America first encountered wild tobacco and attempted to control it for its vision-producing powers.

Shamanism was well developed in the Great Basin, and tobacco was a key ingredient in this basic, individualistic religious complex. Every one of the groups listed in table 10 had shamans, including the Chemehuevi, an offshoot of the southern Paiute who adopted agriculture from their Yuman-speaking neighbors in the Southwest. The Chemehuevi used datura on an individual basis to provide visions and dreams,

Photo 14. Buckskin Charley (seated) and other southern Ute men with Plains-style pipes and pipe bags. Photo by Pennington. Courtesy of the Maxwell Museum of Anthropology, University of New Mexico. 92.1.67 4.U.16. See note 5, this chapter.

though the *toloache* cult was absent. They offered tobacco to the spirits of sacred caves. When the Ghost Dance was sweeping the continent, its pipe came down from the north, and the Chemehuevi smoked it before passing it on to other tribes. About a year later, after the Ghost Dance songs arrived, the Chemehuevi began to dance.

The southern Paiute also chewed and ate datura seeds, again on an individual basis, but tobacco was more important to them because it served as an essential element of a sucking shaman's paraphernalia. The southern Paiute also appeased whirlwinds (ghosts) with offerings of tobacco smoke, and tobacco is mentioned in a southern Paiute Round Dance song: "The tobacco plant is standing where the babbling water runs on the side of the mountain" (Liljeblad 1986:649).

Kawaiisu shamans used tobacco to contact the spirits and to cure the sick. Most Kawaiisu men smoked tobacco in reed-cane cigarettes or in buckwheat-stem pipes. The women ate powdered tobacco mixed with crushed lime. Both sexes used tobacco as an emetic and a soporific. It was also applied externally to relieve pain, to stop bleeding and itching, and to ease parturition. It was blown into the air and tossed on a stone to drive away *inipi* and other malevolent spirits, and it was one of the four primary medicines (along with datura, nettles, and red ants) given to mankind at the beginning of time. All four medicines were taken to induce dreams that were interpreted literally.

*Inipi* were the most common supernatural beings, and everyone had one. Sometimes an *inipi* carried out the evil designs of a witch who controlled it. When an *inipi* was heard approaching at night, it could be frightened off by blowing tobacco powder in the air.

Catherine Fowler (1986) and Maurice Zigmond (1986) each provide excellent descriptions of how the Kawaiisu sowed wild tobacco seeds, burned old tobacco plants, and pruned young plants. *Nicotiana quadrivalvis* var. *wallacei* was preferred over *N. attenuata*, which was considered a poor, weak substitute. The Kawaiisu pruned and weeded the wild plants three times in the late summer, at one-week intervals, in order to achieve hardier plants with bigger leaves. They also irrigated and cultivated the plants. After the third pruning, the leaves were picked, dried, ground into powder, moistened by boiling them with pine nuts and the leaves of bush poppies, and molded into cakes and plugs. Tobacco in all of its forms was used for numerous medicinal purposes and was recognized as an extremely potent magical force—so much so that supernatural beings were afraid of it. As discussed by Zigmond, it was also employed for many other reasons, including infanticide and suicide (by overdosing) and killing rattlesnakes with the plant's spiritual power.

Washo shamans still use tobacco, primarily for curing. Don Handelman (1976:389, 391–392) described how two Washo shamans utilized the drug:

> Traditional Washo curing rituals required a shaman to work for three consecutive nights from dusk to midnight, and a fourth night until dawn. In the course of the ritual, repeated every night, Henry used tobacco, water, a rattle, a whistle, and eagle feathers. He began by smoking, praying, washing the patient's face with cold water, and sprinkling all of his paraphernalia with cold water. He then blew smoke on the patient and prayed to come into contact with water.

For years Henry suffered from rheumatism and from broken ribs that did not heal properly. He went to his uncle, Welewkushkush, to be cured, but his uncle merely gave him a warning:

> He didn't work on me long. He just blew smoke on me, and we talked. He said: "The thing that is causing it is right here in your head, and you will forget all about your stiff joint; you don't have rheumatism. You might be very sick and your mind will go into the White people's world, and I can't go there and bring you back." He blew smoke on my forehead; that thing traveled in the smoke out of me, and I got well. The thing he drew out was a piece of printed matter. I didn't see it; he wouldn't show it to me. It was what I had in my head from studying books.

## The Southwest

The deserts, plateaus, and mountains of the southwestern United States are home to no fewer than 35 tobacco-using groups who smoke and otherwise ingest the greatest variety of domesticated and wild tobacco species of any Native Americans on the continent (tables 11 and 12). The Akimel O'odham (Pima) of southern Arizona grew both of the domesticated species (*N. tabacum* and *N. rustica*) and gathered and sometimes grew three wild taxa (*N. attenuata*, *N. trigonophylla*, and *N. quadrivalvis*). With the possible exception of the Cahuilla to the west in the deserts of southern California, no other tribal group in North America used so many different species, although the closely related, neighboring Tohono O'odham (Papago) grew the two domesticated species and gathered two of the wild taxa (*N. attenuata* and *N. trigonophylla*). The seeds of all four of these species have been reported from prehistoric Hohokam (ancestral Pima) sites in the same region, though the identification of the *N. tabacum* material is questionable (see chapter 5). *N. tabacum* and *N. rustica* and several of the wild species are still used by Native Americans in northern Mexico, so it is clear that the general region was and is a major center of tobacco cultivation and diversity of considerable antiquity. Indeed, it is possible that the diverse species utilized, with their long archaeological record, represent one of the oldest tobacco-growing and tobacco-gathering complexes on the continent, with roots that reach

Table 11: Southwestern Native American Groups Using Tobacco

| No. on Map 1 | Group | Reference |
|---|---|---|
| **LOWER COLORADO RIVER** | | |
| 234 | Akimel O'odham (Pima) | Castetter 1943:322–323; Castetter and Bell 1942:108–109, 1951; Castetter and Underhill 1935:27; Ford 1983:713; Lamphere 1983:762–763; Rea 1997: passim; Russell 1975:118–119, 221, 206, 224, 232, 260, 266, 336–337, 340, 347, 359–360, 363; Switzer 1969:15 |
| 235 | Tohono O'odham (Papago) | Castetter and Bell 1942:108–109, 211, 1951:119; Castetter and Underhill 1935:27; Nabhan 1979b:254; Russell 1975:119; Switzer 1969:15 |
| 236 | Maricopa | Castetter and Bell 1942:109, 1951:115; Ford 1983:713; Spier 1933:43, 333–334 |
| 237 | Cocopa | Castetter and Bell 1951; Ford 1983:713 |
| 238 | Yuma (Quechan) | Castetter and Bell 1942:109, 1951:119–120; Davis 1974:24; Ford 1983:713; Goodspeed 1954:385–386; Kroeber 1925:793; Setchell 1921:413; Spier 1933:159, 332–333; W. Wallace 1953:193 |
| 239 | Halchidoma | Davis 1974:22; Ford 1983:713; Spier 1933:43, 333 |
| 240 | Mohave | Castetter and Bell 1951:119–120; Kroeber 1925:708, 793; W. Wallace 1953:193–195, 197–201 |
| **UPLAND PAI** | | |
| 241 | Yavapai | Drucker 1941; Gifford 1936; Jorgenson 1983:689; Switzer 1969:56 |
| 242 | Walapai | Kroeber 1925:793; Switzer 1969:15 |
| 243 | Havasupai | Castetter and Bell 1942:109; Ford 1983:713; Goodspeed 1954:385–386; Setchell 1921:413; Spier 1928:105; Switzer 1969:15; Weber and Seaman 1985:95–96, 239–240 |
| 244 | Hualapai | Watahomigie 1982:54 |
| **ATHABASCAN** | | |
| 245 | Mescalero Apache | Castetter and Opler 1936:23 |
| 246 | Chiricahua Apache | Castetter and Opler 1936:23 |
| 247 | White Mt. Apache | Reagan 1929:158 |
| 248 | Western Apache | Gifford 1940 |
| 249 | Navajo (Diné) | Brugge, pers. comm. 1990; Brugge and Frisbie 1982:97; Elmore 1944:74–75, 102; Faris 1990:41; Franciscan Fathers 1910; Gifford 1940; Hill 1938:20; Kelley and Francis 1994:66; Kluckhohn and Wyman 1940:29; Knight 1982:680; W. Matthews 1902:308–309n2; Reichard 1950; Setchell 1921:411; Stewart 1942; Switzer 1969:34; Underhill 1953; Vestal 1952; Winter 1994b; Wyman 1987; Wyman and Harris 1941, 1951:41, 61; Young and Morgan 1987:1044 Hocking 1956; Santa Fe Natural Tobacco Company 1993; Tschopic 1941:57, 63 |
| **PUEBLO** | | |
| 250 | Pueblos | Kroeber 1925:793; Lamphere 1983:762–763; Switzer 1969:34; Tyler 1991:99–100 |
| 251 | Hopi | Colton 1974:336–337; Fewkes 1896:19; Ford 1983:713; Hack 1942; Hough 1897:38; Robbins et al. 1916:105; Stephen 1936:172, 599; Vestal 1940:166; Whiting 1939:16–17, 90 |
| 252 | Zuni | Kroeber 1925:793; Setchell 1921:117; Spier 1928:119; Stevenson 1915:54, 86, 95; Tedlock 1979 |
| 253 | Laguna | Boas 1928:12–13; Swank 1932 |
| 254 | Acoma | Castetter 1943:322; Swank 1932:54; Tyler 1991:100 |
| 255 | Eastern Keres | Castetter 1943:322; Ford 1983:713; White 1945 |
| 256 | Santo Domingo | Castetter 1943:322; White 1942 |
| 257 | Cochiti | Boas 1928:12–13; Castetter 1943:322; Lange 1968:95–97; Tyler 1991:101–102; UNM herbarium records; White 1942 |

| No. on Map 1 | Group | Reference |
|---|---|---|
| 258 | Santa Ana | Castetter 1943:322; Switzer 1969:14; White 1941:65; Winter 1994b |
| 259 | Isleta | Castetter 1943:322; Jones 1930; Switzer 1969:14 |
| 260 | Taos | Castetter 1943:322; Ford 1983:713 |
| 261 | Picuris | Castetter 1943:322; Ford 1983:713 |
| 262 | Jemez | Castetter 1943:322; Cook 1930:2; UNM herbarium records; White 1942 |
| 263 | Tewa | Ford 1983:713; Robbins et al. 1916:103–106; Robicsek 1978:30 |
| 264 | San Juan | Robbins et al. 1916:104; Switzer 1969:14; Winter 1994b |
| 265 | San Ildefonso | Gifford 1940; Robicsek 1978:30 |
| 266 | Santa Clara | Robbins et al. 1916:104; Switzer 1969:14 |
| 267 | Tesuque | Gifford 1940 |
| 268 | Hano | Dozier 1966:89, 95; Robbins et al. 1916:105 |

Table 12: Traditional Tobacco Species Used By Native Americans in the Southwest

| Group | *N. rustica* | *N. tabacum* | *N. trigonophylla* | *N. attenuata* | *N. quadrivalvis* | *N. glauca* |
|---|---|---|---|---|---|---|
| Akimel O'odham (Pima) | X | X | X | X | X | |
| Tohono O'odham (Papago) | X | X | X | X | | |
| Yuma | | | X | | | |
| Mohave | | | X | X | | |
| Yavapai | | | | X | | |
| Havasupai | | | X | X | | |
| Hualapai | | | X | | | |
| Navajo (Diné) | | | X | X | | |
| White Mt. Apache | | | | X | | |
| Hopi | ? | | X | X | | |
| Zuni | | | | X | | |
| Acoma | X | | | | | |
| Santo Domingo | X | | | | | |
| Cochiti | X | | | | | |
| Santa Ana | X | | | X | | |
| Isleta | X | | | X | | |
| Taos | X | | | X | | |
| Picuris | X | | | X | | |
| Jemez | X | | | | | |
| San Juan | X | X | | ? | | |
| San Ildefonso | | | | X | | |
| Santa Clara | X | | | | | |
| Tesuque | X | | | X | | |
| Total | 13-14 | 3 | 8 | 15-16 | 1 | 1? |

back to well before the arrival of cultivated food plants in the region.

This diversity and possible antiquity are also reflected in the tobacco-related religious beliefs and medical practices of the various cultures in the region, which vary from the individualistic curing systems of the Diné (Navajo), Apache, and Yavapai to the highly organized religious societies, kiva groups, priesthoods, and kachina cult of the Pueblos. Yuma shamans use both tobacco and datura. The organized *toloache* initiation cult is absent in the Southwest, but most groups use datura on a person-by-person basis, sometimes with tobacco, and Yuma shamans take it to stimulate dreams. Tobacco smoke helps Yuma shamans see evil substances in their patients. Smoke is offered with a prayer: "When I puff out, I think of someone I want helped, and I pray that I may linger for some years more" (Spier 1933:332).

The nearby Mohave Indians of the lower Colorado River valley also raise and gather tobacco. They smoke to keep bad spirits away while sleeping, for good dreams, and as a sedative. Their shamans use both tobacco and datura. The tobacco helps them cure the sick, bring back lost souls, drive away evil spirits, and prevent colds. Datura is taken to stimulate dreams.

Along with several other southwestern peoples, the Akimel O'odham (Pima) equate smoking with rain and fertility, use tobacco during rainmaking ceremonies, and administer it to cure illness. Tobacco also appears in numerous Pima myths, stories, and songs, including the creation story, which is even called "Smoking Tobacco." Earth Doctor is the first primordial being. He unites the male sky and female earth, and Elder Brother is born as a result of the union. After Elder Brother kills an evil female monster, an old woman steals some of the monster's blood and then is killed. The original tobacco plant grows from her grave. Elder Brother instructs the first people how to use it—rolled in cornhusk cigarettes and smoked.

Tobacco also appears in Akimel O'odham myths about Coyote and Mountain Lion and in many old songs and speeches, such as the Tie song (which was sung after a raid against Apaches), the Scalp song, and the speech in which Elder Brother restores himself to life, blows cigarette smoke over magic sticks, and creates magical power. A ceremonial cigarette is smoked at the beginning of the Rain ceremony, and in the ceremony's origin story, Blue Gopher lights a cigarette and puffs smoke toward the east in a great white arch that forms a shadow over the earth. A grassy carpet grows across the earth as Blue Gopher scatters seeds and causes corn to grow.

The Akimel O'odham emphasis on growing and using tobacco as a way to create growth and fertility appears in many other beliefs and practices, just as it does in the religions and cultures of the Hopi, Zuni, Cochiti, San Juan, and other Pueblo Indians of Arizona and New Mexico. The Acoma Mother Goddess or Corn Goddess hid herself because the people mocked her and because something was lacking in their ceremonies. Hummingbird Man, however, loved the nectar in tobacco blossoms. He realized that both the kachinas and the *kopishtaiya* (the collectivity of all spirits) smoked tobacco, so it was decided that the missing element in the ceremonies was a tobacco pipe.

In the Cochiti Pueblo version of this myth, the Corn Goddess tells Hummingbird Man and Fly to ask Turkey Buzzard to purify the earth, the village, and the thunderclouds. They go to Buzzard's house, but their offerings are incomplete because there is no tobacco. Then the Corn Goddess tells them to go to a hill where Tobacco Caterpillar lives. He gives them tobacco, which they take to Buzzard, who agrees to purify the town. "Then he smoked to the north, to the west, to the south, and to the east. He smoked to his mothers the chiefs. . . . Then everything could become clear all around; storm clouds, crops and happiness there around was spread. Then was renewed the food" (Boas 1928:12–13).

For the Pueblos in general, the ceremonial use of tobacco brings fog, clouds, and rain, gives

Photo 15. Pueblo Indian *Nicotiana rustica* at Jemez Pueblo, New Mexico, 1936. From the Soil Conservation Service Collection at the Maxwell Museum of Anthropology, University of New Mexico. 87.45.472.

Photo 16. *Nicotiana rustica* drying at Jemez Pueblo, New Mexico, 1936. From the Soil Conservation Service Collection at the Maxwell Museum of Anthropology, University of New Mexico. 87.45.482.

luck for ceremonies, and heals and nourishes people. Tobacco is used during initiation ceremonies and at political meetings, and it induces the growth of flowers, crops, and other forms of food. The cloudlike puffs of smoke appeal to the clouds, producing rain and fertility. Hopi "cloud tobacco" is a mixture of wild tobacco, corn pollen, yellow feathers, and other plants. The Hopi gather and occasionally grow the wild *N. attenuata* and *N. trigonophylla*, and the Zuni gather and sometimes grow *N. attenuata*. The Hopi may also have started to grow *N. rustica*. Carol Brandt provides details of Zuni tobacco use in chapter 4. Smoking is still one of the most important features of Shalako and other Zuni ceremonies. Tobacco is smoked in the Zuni kivas and other religious chambers. Medicine men blow smoke over their patients' bodies, and they blow smoke to the six cardinal directions so that the rain-makers will not withhold their misty breath.

Descriptions of tobacco use by the eastern Pueblos can be found in the many references listed in table 11. The domesticated *N. rustica* is (or was) grown by many of the pueblos along the Rio Grande and its tributaries, including Acoma, Santa Domingo, Cochiti, Santa Ana, Isleta, Taos, Picuris, Tesuque, Jemez, San Juan, and Santa Clara (photos 15 and 16). I collected specimens of *N. rustica* at Santa Ana Pueblo in 1994. I also obtained seeds and other specimens of *N. rustica* from San Juan, Santo Domingo, Jemez, Cochiti, Isleta, and Tesuque pueblos, as well as from a local Hispanic source. The Spanish *N. rustica* (called *punche de mexicano*) was brought north from Mexico many hundreds of years ago by the first Spanish colonists. The dwarf pumila variety of *N. rustica* may be the one grown at Santa Ana, whereas the other Pueblo villages appear to grow at least one other variety. Some Pueblo groups also gather and at times cultivate *N. attenuata*.

The people of San Juan Pueblo gather the leaves of wild tobacco in the Jemez Mountains to the southwest of their village. A year's supply is gathered at one time, the leaves are dried and

Photo 17. *Nicotiana rustica* field at San Juan Pueblo Agricultural Cooperative, New Mexico, 1994. Photo by Joseph Winter. JCWSP37.

pulverized, and the powder is mixed with moist strands of Bull Durham or other commercial tobacco. Commercial tobacco is sometimes used by itself in ceremonies, and about 15 years ago a local seed bank introduced *N. tabacum*, which was grown for a while around the reservation. A San Juan Pueblo tribal member told me how teenagers are now starting to smoke much earlier in life and in much larger quantities. He also said that each pueblo has its own tobacco-gathering area. In 1994, San Juan Pueblo received a contract to raise several acres of *N. rustica* for the Santa Fe Natural Tobacco Company. The pueblo's agricultural cooperative raised the tobacco, but the plants and quantities were not large enough to make the project economically viable (photo 17).

The Athabaskan-speaking Diné (Navajo) and Apache also use and at times cultivate tobacco. Mescalero and Chiricahua Apache shamans smoke native tobacco during curing rites after they have been offered tobacco and asked to perform the ceremony. Tobacco is so important that the Diné consider it one of the four sacred plants given to humans by the deities. Details on how tobacco is used in the Blessingway, Nightway (*yei bicheii*), and other Diné chantways are provided in a later chapter. Photo 18

Photo 18. Diné (Navajo) herbalist from northwestern New Mexico with a freshly picked bunch of *dzil nat'oh*, or mountain tobacco (*Nicotiana attenuata*). Photo by Joseph Winter. JCWSP5.

shows a Diné man gathering *N. attenuata* from his private patch.

## Mesoamerica

For the contemporary Lacandon Maya of the Yucatán Peninsula, the bearded, white-haired Lords of Rain and Thunder love to smoke cigars. Comets and meteorites are produced by this passion when the lords throw glowing cigars into the night sky. The Yucatec Maya have

Photo 19. Lacandon Maya woman smoking a *Nicotiana tabacum* cigar. Photo by Gertrude Duby Blom. Courtesy of Francis Robicsek (from Robicsek 1978).

similar beliefs; the Balams—the Gods of the Winds and Four Directions—light their cigars with sparks produced by pounding huge rocks together, which also creates thunder and lightning. The very word "cigar" is probably from the Mayan word *sigar* (photo 19).

References to meteorological and other natural phenomena associated with tobacco use by man and god alike abound in the southernmost part of North America (table 13). Forming a natural land bridge between North and South America, Mesoamerica provided an ancient route along which the ancestral wild tobacco species slowly migrated north from South America to Mexico, California, the Great Basin, and other parts of western North America. Mesoamerica also served as a route along which

prehistoric Indians carried the two domesticated species to the north, where they were used in the southwestern United States and the eastern woodlands.

Mesoamerica's funnel-like shape may be one reason why its northern edge in Mexico and the adjacent deserts of the southwestern United States support the greatest variety of tobacco species used by Native Americans—the Akimel O'odham (Pima) raise and gather five species, the Tohono O'odham (Papago) four, the Pima Bajo and Tepehuan three, and the Tarahumara four (table 14). The ways in which tobacco is ingested are similar on both sides of the border, and the individualistic use of tobacco for divination and curing is popular among a large number of corn-raising tribes that probably evolved

Table 13: Mesoamerican Native American Groups Using Tobacco

| No. on Map I | Group | Reference |
|---|---|---|
| 269 | Pima Bajo | Pennington 1980:167, 174, 176, 268, 275, 276, 357 |
| 270 | Yaqui | Bennett and Zingg 1935:end table; Setchell 1921:pl. 3; Spicer 1980:109, 259 |
| 271 | Warihio (Guarijio) | Gentry 1942:64, 232; Nabhan 1977a:261; Native Seeds/SEARCH 1994; TABAMEX 1989 |
| 272 | Tarahumara | Bennett and Zingg 1935:45, 138–139, 169, 259, 276, 278, 292–293, 338; Bye 1979; Nabhan 1977a:261; Ott 1993:374; Pennington 1963:68–69, 232, 1969:261, 1983a:280; Switzer 1969:56 |
| 273 | Tepehuan | Pennington 1969:91–92, 261, 344, 1983b:308 |
| 274 | Zocatec | *Relacion de Nuchistlan*, cited in Robicsek 1978:44 |
| 275 | Huichol | Bauml 1989:7, 9, 1994:250; Bennett and Zingg 1935:end table; Dutton 1962:5–6, 42–43; Fikes 1985:314; Furst 1968:35; Grimes and Hinton 1969:797, 806–811; Lemaistre 1996:315; Lumholtz 1902, 2:31, 127, 130–132, 165, 169; . . . Of the Jungle 1993; Preuss 1996:125, 131; Robicsek 1978:30; Schaefer 1996a:140, 154–155, 167, 1996b:349; Schaefer and Furst 1996:19; Sedlak 1975:15; Seeds of Change n.d.; Siegel et al. 1977:16–18, 22; Valadez 1989:31; Weigand 1972:43; Winter 1995a |
| 276 | Cora | Bennett and Zingg 1935:end table; Grimes and Hinton 1969:797,809 |
| 277 | Tepecano | Bennett and Zingg 1935:end table |
| 278 | Huastec | Alcorn 1984:58–59, 62, 156, 187, 196–200, 227, 712–713; Laughlin 1969a:306; Robicsek 1978:23 |
| 279 | Otomi | Manrique 1969:695, 715, 720–721 |
| 280 | Tarascan | Gorenstein and Pollard 1983:102, 115; Loven 1935:697 |
| 281 | Aztec (Mexica) | Acosta 1591, cited in Brooks 1938:310; Anderson and Dibble 1954, 1970, 1981; Blaffer 1972:93; Brundage 1979:187, 204; Caso 1958:56; Coe and Whittaker 1982:36, 114; De Solis 1724, cited in McGuire 1897:372; Dibble and Anderson 1957, 1959, 1961, 1963, 1969; Martínez 1991; Miller and Taube 1993; Nicholson 1971:437; Robicsek 1978:4–5, 21, 28–30, 37–38, 44, 46, 53; Thompson 1970b:112, 118, 121; Vogel 1969:381 |
| 282 | Nahua | O. Lewis 1960:58, 84 |
| 283 | Cuicatec (Cuitlatec?) | Drucker et al. 1969:567, 572; TABAMEX 1989:100–101; Weitlaner 1969:445 |
| 284 | Popoluca | Foster 1969:475; Hoppe et al. 1969:497 |
| 285 | Totonac | Harvey and Kelly 1969:672, 675; TABAMEX 1989:100–101 |
| 286 | Mazatec | Harrison 1998; Munn 1973:105; Robicsek 1978:30; TABAMEX 1989:100–101; Thompson 1970b:111, 120; Weitlaner 1969:445; Weitlaner and Hoppe 1969:518, 520–521 |
| 287 | Chocho | Hoppe and Weitlaner 1969a:514 |
| 288 | Mixtec | Ravicz and Romney 1969a:381, 396–397; Spores 1965:985 |
| 289 | Ichcatec | Hoppe and Weitlaner 1969b:499 |
| 290 | Amuzgo | Ravicz and Romney 1969b:421, 424, 432; TABAMEX 1989:100–101 |
| 291 | Chinantec | TABAMEX 1989:100–101; Thompson 1970b:120; Weitlaner and Cline 1969:533, 540 |
| 292 | Olmec (region) | Scholes and Warren 1965:786 |
| 293 | Zapotec | Flannery et al. 1981:68; Nader 1969:355; Spores 1965:970, 972, 977 |
| 294 | Mixe | Beals 1973:46; Foster 1969:475 |
| 295 | Tequistlatec | Olmsted 1969:558 |
| 296 | Zoque | Foster 1969:475 |
| 297 | Tlaxcalan | Robicsek 1978:29–30; Thompson 1970b:116 |
| 298 | Maya | Fuentes y Guzmán 1882; Landa, cited in Thompson 1970b:120; Martínez 1991; Miller and Taube 1993:169; Orellana 1987; Robicsek 1978:9, 14, 16, 42, 202; TABAMEX 1989:100–1012; Thompson 1970b:135; Vogel 1969:217 |

| No. on Map I | Group | Reference |
|---|---|---|
| 299 | Yucatec Maya | Robicsek 1978:11, 14, 31, 43; Rojas 1969:252; Roys 1967:97; Thompson 1970b:117–118 |
| 300 | Tzotzil Maya | Blaffer 1972:6, 82n, 91–93, 96, table 13, 134; Laughlin 1969b:185, 187; Robicsek 1978:21, 33; Thompson 1970b:110, 116–117; Vogt 1969:25 |
| 301 | Tzeltal Maya | Berlin et al. 1974:444–445; Robicsek 1978:21, 33, 43; Thompson 1970b:110, 113 |
| 302 | Lacandon Maya | Duby and Blom 1969:281; Robicsek 1978:31, 33, various photos; TABAMEX 1989:100–101; Thompson 1970b:112; Tozzer 1907:142–143 |
| 303 | Cakchequel Maya | Blaffer 1972:82n |
| 304 | Quiché Maya | Robicsek 1978:14; Thompson 1970b:108 |
| 305 | Chorti Maya | Reina 1969:126, 129; Robicsek 1978:20–21, 35–36 |
| 306 | Chiapas Maya | Robicsek 1978:42–43 |
| 307 | Chan Kom Maya | Redfield and Rojas 1962:46, 69, 155, 158, 173, 186, 193 |
| 308 | Jacalteca Maya | Robicsek 1978:21 |
| 309 | Petén Maya | Robicsek 1978:43 |
| 310 | Pokoman Maya | Thompson 1970b:121 |
| 311 | Mam Maya | Thompson 1970b:118 |
| 312 | Zutuhil Maya | Thompson 1970b:110 |
| 313 | Mopan Maya | Thompson 1970b:118 |
| 314 | Tixcacaltuyub Maya | Rico-Gray et al. 1990:484 |
| 315 | Jicaque (Xicaque) | Lentz 1986:212; Thompson 1970b:112 |
| 316 | Chorotega | Stone 1966:221 |
| 317 | Sumu | Conzemius 1932:91–92, 123–124 |
| 318 | Miskito | Conzemius 1932:91–92, 123–124 |
| 319 | Boruca | Stone 1949:11 |
| 320 | Talamanca | Stone 1949:11 |
| 321 | Cuna | Duke 1975:290; Wilbert 1987 |
| 322 | Chontal Maya | Martínez 1991 |
| 323 | Opata | TABAMEX 1989:100–101 |
| 324 | Seri | Felger and Moser 1985:165, 369; Lowell 1970:149 |

from the same ancient hunting-and-gathering "Archaic" base. The use of tobacco is very old in this region, where almost all of the available wild species are gathered, encouraged, and sometimes grown by native peoples. Table 15 lists many of the names given to the different species in Mexico by Indian and mestizo alike.

The Pima Bajo of Sonora, for example, raise *N. tabacum* and collect *N. trigonophylla* and *N. glauca* when the domesticated tobacco is not available in stores or gardens. *N. tabacum* seeds are sown in small beds or broken ollas, and the seedlings are moved to irrigated plots near the river when the plants are about 20 centimeters

(8 inches) high. The Tarahumara in the Sierra Madres of northwest Mexico also raise *N. tabacum* and *N. rustica*, and they collect *N. glauca* and *N. trigonophylla*. The nearby Warijio (Guarijio) raise both domesticated species, as do the Huichol in the mountains to the south. No public or private Tarahumara ceremony is complete without the smoking of tobacco, and many religious beliefs and medical practices emphasize the importance of smoke. Sometimes during foot races smoke is blown toward the opposing runners to make them sleepy. Smoke can also be used to ward off rattlesnakes, scorpions, and centipedes. *Nicotiana glauca* leaves

Table 14: Traditional Tobacco Species Raised or Gathered by Various Mesoamerican Groups

| Group | N. clevelandii | N. glauca | N. rustica | N. tabacum | N. trigonophylla |
|---|---|---|---|---|---|
| Aztec | | | X | X | |
| Chinantec | | | | X | |
| Chontal Maya | | X | | X | |
| Cora | | | | X | |
| Cuitlatec | | | X | X | |
| Cuna | | | | X | |
| Huastec | | | | X | |
| Huichol | | | X | X | |
| Jicaque | | | | X | |
| Lacandon Maya | | | | X | |
| Maya | | | X | X | |
| Mazatec | | | | X | |
| Miskito | | | | ? | |
| Mixe | | | | X | |
| Mopan Maya | | | | X | |
| Pima Bajo | | X | | X | X |
| Popoluca | | | | X | |
| Quiche Maya | | | | X | |
| Seri | X | ? | | ? | X |
| Sumu | | | | ? | |
| Tarahumara | | X | X | X | X |
| Tarascan | | X | | X | |
| Tepehuan | | X | | X | |
| Tixc. Maya | | | | X | |
| Totonac | | | | X | |
| Tzeltal Maya | | | | X | |
| Warihio | | | X | X | |
| Yaqui | | | | X | |
| Zapotec | | | | X | |
| Zoque | | | | X | |

are applied to the head for headaches, and all corn-beer drinking fiestas involve the smoking of large quantities of tobacco in corn-husk cigarettes. The Tarahumara sometimes offer cigarettes to peyote and use cigarettes during peyote ceremonies. Tarahumara sucking shamans use tobacco as well.

The Tarahumara call all of these tobacco species *wipaka*, whereas the local mestizos call *N. tabacum* "papanti," *N. trigonophylla* "tabaco de coyote" or "macuchi de coyote," and *N. glauca* "corneton" (Pennington 1963:68). Robert Bye's records for voucher specimens 3989, 3345, and 5733 at the Harvard Botanical Museum herbarium indicate that other Tarahumara names for tobacco are *wiuraka* and *makuchi*

(*N. rustica*) and *wipanto* (*N. tabacum*).[9] The Tarahumara consider tobacco second in importance only to *hikuri* (peyote), with even more power than *dekuba* or datura (photo 20).

The closely related Warijio also raise a variety of *N. rustica* that they call *makuchi*, as do the Huichol several hundred miles to the south. The Huichol have been known to smoke enormous quantities of *makuchi*, some shamans smoking continuously for up to four days. Huichol tobacco shamanism is explored in more detail in a later chapter.

Most North American shamans use tobacco to help them divine and cure, but the Huichol represent the northernmost contemporary occurrence of full-blown tobacco shamanism, which

Table 15: Names of Mexican Tobacco Species

| Name | Language | Location |
|------|----------|----------|
| **N. CLEVELANDII** | | |
| Tabaco de perro | | Baja California |
| Alamo loco | | Rio Baviste, northeast Sonora |
| **N. GLAUCA** | | |
| Buena moza | | Querétaro |
| Corneton | | Sonora |
| Don Juan | | Alamos, Sonora |
| Maraquiana | | Alamos, Sonora |
| Gigante | | Aguascaliente; Sinaloa; San Luis Potosí |
| Gretano | | Oaxaca |
| Mostaza montes | | Oaxaca |
| Hierba del gigante | | |
| Hoja de cerra | | Campeche |
| Levantate de don Juan | | La Paz, Baja California |
| Me-he-kek | Chontal | Oaxaca |
| Tabaco | | |
| Tabacón-Durango | | Virgin, Durango |
| Palo virgin | | Durango |
| Tacote | | Durango |
| Tabaco amarillo | | Jalisco |
| Tabaco cimarrón | | Mexico D.F. |
| Tabaquillo | | Mexico, Oaxaca |
| Tronadora de Espana | | Guanajuato |
| Tzinyacua | Tarascan | Michoacan |
| Virginio | | Chihuahua; Durango |
| Xiutecuitlanextli | Aztec | — |
| **N. IPOMOPSIFLORA**[a] | | |
| Tabaco cimarrón | | Sonora; Nuevo León; San Luis Potosí; Guanajuato; Baja California; Sinaloa; Coahuila; etc. |
| Tabaco coyote | | Baja California |
| Tabaco de papanta | | Sinaloa |
| Tabaquillo | | Durango |
| **N. MEXICANA**[b] | | |
| Tabaco cimarrón | | Oaxaca; Aguascalientes; Veracruz |
| Tabaquillo | | Durango |
| Tlapacoyote | | Oaxaca |
| **N. PILOSA**[b] | | |
| Tabaco cimarrón | | |
| **N. PLUMBAGINIFOLIA** | | |
| Tabaquillo | | Tabasco |
| **N. PUSILLA**[b] | | |
| Tabaco cimarrón | | Aguascalientes; Veracruz |
| **N. RUSTICA** | | |
| Andumucua | (Tarascan?) | Michoacán |
| Macuche | (Huichol?) | Nayarit |

Table 15: Names of Mexican Tobacco Species (continued)

| Name | Language | Location |
| --- | --- | --- |
| Nohol-x'-i-K'uts | Maya | Yucatán |
| Picietl | (Aztec?) | |
| Tabasco macuche | | Sinaloa |
| Teneshil | Aztec | |
| Tenepete | | Southern Guerrero |
| **N. TABACUM** | | |
| Andumucua | Tarascan | Michoacán |
| Tabaco | | |
| Apuga | Cuicatlecan | Totolapa, Guerrero |
| A'xcu't | Totonac | Northern Puebla |
| Ayic | Popoluca | Sayula, Veracruz |
| Cuauhyetl, Cuayetl | Aztec | |
| Cutz | Lacandon Maya | Monte Libano, Chiapas |
| K'uts', Kuutz, Kuuts | Maya | Yucatán |
| Gueeza, Guexa | Zapotec | Oaxaca |
| Huepa, Huepaca, Huipa | Tarahumara | Chihuahua |
| Iyatl | (Aztec origin?) | Veracruz |
| Ju'uikill | Mixe | San Lucas Camotlan, Oaxaca |
| May | Huastec | Southeast San Luis Potosí |
| Me-e | Chontal Maya | Oaxaca |
| Otzi | Zoque | Tapala, Chiapas |
| Picietl | Aztec | |
| Ro-hu, ro-u | Chinanteca | Comaltepic, Chiltepec, Oaxaca |
| Uipa | Guarigia (Warihio) | Sonora; Chihuahua |
| Ya | Huichol, Chontal(?) | Jalisco; Oaxaca |
| Yana | Cora | Nayarit |
| Hapis copxot | Seri | Sonora |
| **N. TRIGONOPHYLLA** | | |
| Tabaco de coyote | | Sonora |
| Tabaco papanta | | Conitaca, Sinaloa |

Source: Martínez (1991).

a    Probably *N. trigonophylla*, according to Goodspeed (1954).
b    *N. tabacum*, according to Goodspeed (1954).

is common in the lowlands of South America. Tobacco shamans ingest enormous quantities of extremely potent tobacco to place them in contact with the spirit world by means of drug-induced trances and visions. Tobacco is often considered a deity, or at least a spirit helper. Several other North American groups, such as the Sumu and Miskito in Nicaragua, the Talamanca in Costa Rica, and the Cuna in Panama, also practice fully developed tobacco shamanism. Many other tribes may once have practiced it; their present use of lower doses of nicotine to divine and to cure may be a vestige of a once pervasive practice.

Sumu *sukya* (shamans) ingest N. *tabacum* in order to enter a condition of wild ecstasy that enables them to contact friendly spirits who reveal the causes and cures of illnessess. Miskito *sukya* do the same with unspecified tobacco, as do Talamanca *sukia*. Cuna female shamans smoke tobacco in order to commune with the spirits who predict the future, as well as to cure

Photo 20. Tarahumara *wipanto* (*Nicotiana tabacum*) at the ranchito of Teneria, 1953, Chihuahua, Mexico. Courtesy of David Brugge.

patients. The Cuna of Panama chew tobacco, smoke it in pipes and cigars, and have boys blow tobacco into their faces during council meetings and other public occasions. They also use tobacco at childbirth, fumigate women with tobacco smoke before marriage, and combat botfly larvae by blowing smoke from a pipe. The inland Cuna raise enough *N. tabacum* to export it to the island Cuna, as well as to the Yaviza. Nearby groups in South America also practice tobacco shamanisim, as Johannes Wilbert discussed in his comprehensive study *Tobacco and Shamanism in South America* (1987).

Although they do not practice tobacco shamanism, the Seri of the Pacific coast in northwest Mexico are an excellent example of how shamans often use tobacco and how the wild species are (or were) intensively collected. Both

N. *trigonophylla* and N. *clevelandii* were smoked. N. *glauca* was also recognized and named ("hummingbird-what-it-sucks out"), but there is no evidence that it was used. As recorded by Richard Felger and Mary Moser (1985:165), "smoking was for personal rather than ceremonial or ritual purposes. However, a shaman sometimes blew smoke over a patient as part of a curing procedure."

The Seri smoked the dried leaves of tobacco in clay, stone, or reed-cane pipes, as well as in tube-worm shells. Wild tobacco is still considered important, but it has been replaced by commerical tobacco. *Nicotiana clevelandii* is called xeezej islitx—"badger's inner ear." *Nicotiana trigonophylla* is *hapis casa*—"what is smoked putrid," "putrid tobacco," "tabaco del coyote," and "desert tobacco" (Felger and Moser 1985:369; Lowell 1970:149).

Despite its strong smell, N. *trigonophylla* leaves were preferred over the smaller leaves of N. *clevelandii*, and some men made special trips to desirable stands in order to bring back large quantities of leaves. One special stand was at Hapis Ihoom ("what-is-smoked where-it-is" or "where tobacco occurs"), where the plants were very potent and much prized.

Tobacco use was also important for the Aztec and Maya, and it is still an essential aspect of the cultures of various groups in Mexico, Guatamala, and other Mesoamerican countries. The Huastec—linguistic relatives of the Maya—believe that one of the *maam* godpowers who bring rain is associated with tobacco. A miraculous boy named Thipaak was born to save the Huastec and to give them maize, but before he could do so he had to destroy the bloodthirsty Aach-Eagle Grandmother, who demanded child sacrifice. Thipaak hid in a drop of tobacco juice under the lip of a tobacco gourd belonging to the kubi-birds. The Aach slurped up the drop and chewed it vigorously but failed to kill Thipaak, who eventually destroyed her.

The Huastec use tobacco for both good and evil. It has a bad effect on newborns, and some people smoke it in their presence in order to show their strength and power over the infants' parents. *Brujos* (witches) leave tobacco along a trail to harm someone who steps on it, but the evil can backfire and kill the *brujo* if the intended victim sees the tobacco and throws it in water.

Offerings to godpowers are a necessary part of everyday Huastec life—they protect babies, new homes, marriages, cornfields, and many other things. Cigarettes are often provided as offerings, then ritually distributed and smoked. Cigarettes are also given to curers when they are asked to treat a patient.

The Huastec recognize the wild *Nicotiana repanda* but do not use it. Instead, they raise *N. tabacum* for their own use and for sale. This domesticated species is used to treat hemorrhoids, snakebites, and edema; it is rubbed on the body for strength; it is ground and drunk with water to induce vomiting of poison and blood; and it is smoked to scare away snakes and other dangerous animals along a trail at night. It is also used to trap and cripple evil beings, and it is chewed, smoked in corn-husk and commercial cigarettes, exchanged among friends, and grown to decorate patios.

The contemporary Maya use both *N. rustica* and *N. tabacum*, as did the Aztecs, who incorporated both species into their highly organized, state-level theocracy. Details about Aztec use of this plant are presented in a later chapter.

Tobacco is still used for many social and religious situations by the descendants of the ancient Maya and Aztec, as it is by the Yaqui, Cora, Tepecano, Cuicatec, Totonac, Mazatec, Ichcatec, Zapotec, Jicaque, Boruca, and others. Tobacco (*piciete*) is a Mazatec cash crop. Their shamans use it to combat (as well as bring on) tiredness, sorcery, and witchcraft, and the Mazatec believe that the different varieties of *N. tabacum* are San Pedro and other saints with great magical and medicinal power. The Mazatec always carry powdered green tobacco leaves in little gourds to relieve fatigue and to use in witchcraft. A shaman makes a pregnant woman invulnerable to sorcery by rubbing her with tobacco.

Zapotec tobacco ingestion is also widespread, occurring in varying degrees in many different situations, such as fiestas, weddings, markets, funerals, and rituals. At the time of Spanish contact the Zapotec worshipped the god Coquebila, and during the 40- or 80-day fast honoring him, they ingested a quantity of *picietl* (tobacco) once every four days. Tobacco leaf was mixed with lime and chewed all day to fortify the body and maintain strength, to combat colds and cure asthma, and to treat earaches, headaches, and hay fever.

The contemporary Maya are inveterate smokers of both *N. rustica* and the milder *N. tabacum*. Tobacco is one of their most important cultigens, with *N. tabacum* growing to just under 2 meters high. They use it for personal consumption, trade, and sale to nearby Ladinos as well as to other Indians. Considerable amounts of tobacco are grown in the Maya lowlands and then traded widely, not only to the highland Maya but beyond, to other Indians. In *The Smoking Gods* (1978), Francis Robicsek offers many details about present and past Maya uses of tobacco, including its power to ward off evil; to treat insect bites and stings, earaches, chills, lung, kidney, and eye diseases, abdominal pains, heart pain, loss of speech, pox, buboes, and urinary problems; and to dispel seizures and convulsions.

The Yucatec Maya assign world directional colors to tobacco, with red, white, and black tobacco being used to treat asthma. They treat chills, fevers, convulsions, sore eyes, bowel problems, skin diseases, nervous disorders, urinary infections, bites and stings, eruptions, "snake pulsations," tooth worm, beef worm, and placenta problems with this magical plant.

The Tzotzil Maya in Zinacantan and nearby towns smoke, chew, lick, and drink tobacco in order to protect themselves against the gods of the underworld, who haunt isolated crossroads at night. The Tzotzil sometimes rub tobacco on the lips of newborn babies. It is also used to combat a variety of demons, including the Blackman, the Charcoal-cruncher, and the Split-faced man. When a person is frequently molested by the Black-man, tobacco and holy water should be left at his door to keep the demon away and to "civilize" him. Tobacco acts to seal off the demon's transformation from its human form. For example, the Charcoal-cruncher might possess a woman who then detaches her head so that it can roam the forest at night, eating charcoal. The demon is supposedly trapped by putting tobacco, garlic, and salt (all "civilized" creations of mankind) on her severed head. Another local demon, the Split-faced man, can be killed only when he is thoroughly saturated three times with tobacco, salt, and other ingredients.

For the Tzotzil, tobacco is *ankel*—a term used to describe the rain and mountain deity and the protection of mankind, because tobacco cares for our bodies. Some people chew powdered tobacco all day long, from the moment they wake up, keeping it in little gourd bottles at the heads of their beds. When they hear thunder they put some in their cheeks so that the thunder won't be too loud. Tobacco defends people when they die and protects them from being killed by the lightning *ankel*. It is also a cure for sickness caused by black magic. Even the death gods cannot come near a person annointed with it, because of their aversion to it. Tobacco protects the Tzotzil from being seized by the dead. Citsil Bac—Noisy Bones, a death god—stripped off his flesh and wandered off as a skeleton. One man who found the piled-up skin urinated on it and threw powdered tobacco on it, so that the god could not crawl back inside it. Many Tzotzil Maya chew tobacco mixed with lime.

Additional information about the use of tobacco by the Tzotzil Maya, Tzeltal Maya, Lacandon Maya, Quiché Maya, Chorti Maya, and many other groups can be found in the references in table 13. Even Ladino villagers and city dwellers who have lost much of their Indian heritage—for example, the peasants in Tepoztlan—retain a few tobacco traditions, such as when they provide cigarettes at funerals.

The Popoluca and Chocho also provide cigarettes at funerals, and Mixe and Popoluca go-betweens are given cigarettes by young men to take to their future brides' homes. Another Mixe tradition is for the groom and his parents to offer cigarettes to neighbors when asking them to help grind corn for the wedding feast. These related customs are probably the last vestiges of aboriginal tobacco use among the western Mixe. Two to three cartons of cigarettes are part of a Tequistlatic bride price; most of the cigarettes are given away at the wedding feast.

The Otomí are an excellent example of how Mesoamerican Indians are blending new tobacco uses with old customs. Factory-made cigars are commonly smoked, though some people buy tobacco leaves that they tear up and roll in corn-husk cigarettes. Corn, cigarettes, and other presents are offered to saints and other Catholic supernatural beings that are identified with pre-Hispanic deities. Gifts of cigarettes abound at weddings and funerals.

Tobacco is also an invariable part of Mixtec and Totonac fiestas. Mixtec hosts offer cigars or cigarettes to everyone present at almost every occasion. Mixtec workers are given tobacco while they make candles for saint's-day observances. The Totonac believe that tobacco protects them from snakes and spirits of the dead, and they offer tobacco to the supernatural spirits of the forest. Although Totonac men smoke sparingly, they usually smoke local leaf tobacco rather than commercial cigarettes. Most of the other groups listed in table 13 also use commercial tobacco for recreational and some religious purposes, despite the fact that they may have lost much of their Indian heritage, including the knowledge needed to grow the domesticated species or to gather wild *picietl*. Many Indians also work for the Mexican tobacco industry, which produces numerous brands of cigarettes and cigars. The *Atlas del Tabaco en Mexico*, published by the organization TABAMEX (1989), gives an excellent overview of the history of this industry all the way back to the conquest by Cortés. This detailed atlas of the various tobacco species, types, climate zones, soil zones, and other relevant data is a superb source of information concerning how Meso-american Indians grew, and continue to grow, this amazing plant.

## The Caribbean

Europeans were first introduced to tobacco by the Taino Arawak Indians in the Caribbean when Columbus made his landfall at Guanahami (San Salvador) in the Bahamas on October 12, 1492. Several weeks later, two of his men provided the first report of Taino Indians smoking cigars on Cuba, as later recorded by Bartolomé de las Casas around 1527. Before leaving for Europe, Columbus established the tiny settlement of La Navidad on the north coast of Española (Hispaniola), but when he returned on his second voyage in 1494, he discovered that the settlement had been burned and its 39 men killed. At that point there were about one million Taino on Hispaniola, Cuba, Jamaica, Puerto Rico, and the Bahamas. Within 30 years they had been annihilated and became all but extinct.

Despite the Taino's rapid disappearance, there are a number of early records of their tobacco use, as listed in table 16. Wilbert (1987) has also described how their Arawak relatives in northern South America still utilize tobacco. The Caribbean Taino grew tobacco around their houses, chewed and smoked it, and snuffed it in both nostrils through forked, Y-shaped tubes. The tubes were also used to inhale the smoke of burning tobacco leaves, but most people smoked large cigars rolled in tree leaves and corn shucks, tied with a thread.

The tobacco used by the Taino could have been either *N. tabacum* or *N. rustica*, or perhaps both species were ingested. In his multivolume study of tobacco, Jerome Brooks (1937–1952, 1:19, 82, 204) concluded that *N. rustica* was the basic Taino tobacco, with *N. tabacum* introduced from Yucatán by the Spaniards around 1535. Today *N. tabacum*

## Table 16: Caribbean Native American Groups Using Tobacco

| No. on Map 1 | Group | Reference |
|---|---|---|
| 325 | Taino (Cuba and Hispaniola) | Brooks 1937–1952, 1:19, 82, 204, 226; Loven 1935:387–388, 391, 394, 396, 571, 575, 670; Robicsek 1978:4; Rouse 1992:12; Safford 1916a, 1916b:408, 1924:170; Stevens-Arroyo 1988:41, 104–105, 117–118, 188; Wilbert 1987:9, 17–18 |
| 326 | Carib (Lesser Antilles) | Gullick 1985:32, 55–57, 67–68; Harvard Botanical Museum records; Loven 1935:388-389, 391, 394, 670; Wilbert 1987:50, 189 |
| 327 | Inyeri (Trinidad) | Loven 1935:388; Wilbert 1987:50 |
| 328 | No Specific Group | Brooks 1938:249; Cooper 1949:527, 534, 626; McGuire 1897:405; Wilbert 1987:199 |

var. *havanensis* is the basis of the Cuban cigar industry.[10]

In addition to the popular smoking of cigars for pleasure by the general Taino population, the medicine men or shamans (*behiques, bohutios,* and *piaies*) snuffed hallucinogenic *cahoba* powder through the forked tubes. *Cahoba* may have been powdered tobacco (Loven 1935:387; Wilbert 19:17), though William Safford (1916b) has argued that it was a derivation of *Anadenanthera peregrina*. Most likely it was a combination of a number of plants, including powdered tobacco prepared from unfermented tobacco leaves mixed with saltwater and lime. The shamans snuffed *cahoba* to the point of intoxication in order to induce trances, visions, and communication with their personal spirit helpers (*zemis*), as well as to foretell the future, treat diseases, and otherwise help their people. The initial effect of *cahoba* was a strong sneeze thought to magically cleanse the nose, followed by the trance, which often led to stupefaction and unconsciousness for up to a full day or night. Shamans also blew tobacco smoke onto their patients' bodies and rubbed *cahoba* on the images of their *zemis*.

Two versions of the Taino creation myth mention tobacco (Loven 1935:571; Stevens-Arroyo 1988:117–118). Both involve four sons of the Taino earth goddess Itiba Cahubaba. In one version, the brothers (who might represent the four cardinal directions) provide the first Taino with cassava and tobacco. In the other, *cahoba* mixed with *guanquaya* (the spittle produced by chewing raw tobacco) is snuffed through the nose.

The Caribs of Dominica, St. Vincent, and the other islands in the Lesser Antilles have a similar myth, in which two brothers go to the House of the Giant Boa, where they burn powdered tobacco before him on the blade of a paddle. He responds by creating arrowroot (Gullick 1985:32).

There are still some 2,000 Caribs living on St. Vincent, and another group on Dominica. The Caribs continue to raise *N. tabacum*, or at least they did in 1942, when they grew it on the Dominica Carib Reserve.[11] C. J. M. R. Gullick (1985:68) analyzed a number of Carib myths and some observations concerning tobacco dating to the period between A.D. 1530 and 1763. At the end of 10 or 12 months following the birth of his first child or first male child, a Carib father was scarified with an agouti tooth, then rubbed with tobacco juice, pepper seeds, and roucou leaves. This hot, energy-giving substance increased the valor of the infant. If the child was destined to become a *boye* (shaman), he was apprenticed before puberty and trained in the use of tobacco infusions. At the end of five moons, his shaman instructor smoked a cigar and sang a magic song when the cigar was finished. Then the shaman's *eochiere* (spirit helper) entered the hut, and the boy experienced his first trance and spirit flight.

Shamans were called upon when home cures failed. The *boye* entered the dark hut with his glowing cigar. He put the cigar in his mouth, blew smoke five or six times in the air, and rubbed the cigar into powder which he scat-tered in the air. Then the spirit materialized to help him. Tobacco was used in an identical manner when the shaman wanted to forecast the weather.

The Island Caribs added white ashes to dried tobacco leaves softened with sea water, kneaded the mixture into rolls, and chewed them. They also used them as currency. It took only one quid to make a man pale and intoxicated. Only the Carib *boyes* or *piayes* (shamans) smoked cigars, whose pleasing aroma attracted the *zemis*.

The Arawakan Inyeri of Trinidad also appear to have snuffed tobacco. Unspecified groups in the West Indies smoked gigantic cigars to fumigate patients, see visions, predict the future, and deceive the "devil." Tobacco was used for any hurt and in surgery, as well as for various hedonistic pleasures. It was also smoked and blown against approaching storms and clouds.

It is evident from these observations that fully developed tobacco shamanism was practiced throughout the Caribbean, where shamans ingested tobacco snuff (probably mixed with other drugs) to achieve hallucinogenic visions that enabled them to communicate with the spirit world. Similar uses of tobacco, datura, and other drug plants are common in the Amazon basin and elsewhere in northern South America, as well as in several places in Mesoamerica. Later chapters discuss tobacco shamanism and more organized forms of tobacco use, such as tobacco societies and tobacco priesthoods, in more detail.

Notes

1. Some readers may object to the publication of figure 1, since it illustrates a *ga-go-sa* mask, which is considered so sacred that it should never be sold or exhibited in museums. In 1993, the Grand Council of Chiefs of the Haudeno-saunee called for the return of all *ga-go-sa* masks from museums, private collections, stores, shops, and other locations. It is precisely because of this deep religious value, and the equally important

sacred association of the tobacco plants that are also illustrated in the drawing, that this and similar illustrations are reproduced in this book—not to demean or exploit them but to illustrate to non–Native American readers the utmost sanctity of this association and the religious values that it represents. I am convinced that the only way many readers can be reached, and their appreciation of and sensitivity to Native American values increased, is by showing these articles and plants, then discussing them and describing their sanctity in a respectful manner. Many non–Native Americans simply do not understand that Native Americans are still alive and well all across the continent and that their religions, sacred masks, and traditions should be respected and left alone, not turned into museum pieces, sports logos, or advertising symbols.

2. Seeds of the old heirloom varieties of tobacco once raised by many Native Americans or collected by them in the wild can be obtained at no charge from the Native American Plant Cooperative (NAPC) in Albuquerque, New Mexico, so long as the request is made by a Native American or a person of mixed blood who intends to use the resulting tobacco *only* for prayers, offerings, ceremonies, and other traditional purposes, and not for "recreational" purposes.

3. See Latorre and Latorre 1976 for many details about Kickapoo uses of tobacco.

4. The history of the calumet is traced in Brown 1989.

5. The same caution that was expressed in note 1 is repeated here, this time concerning the sacredness of pipes and the substances smoked in them. Photographs of sacred pipes are included in this book to emphasize the utmost sanctity of traditional tobacco, the ceremonial pipes in which it is used, and the values associated with them that are still alive and worthy of respect.

6. Cutright 1989 also contains information about Lewis and Clark's visit to the Arikara.

7. Chapter 6 of this book contains a photograph (photo 32) of the voucher specimen of tobacco grown from seeds collected by David Douglas.

8. The *N. glauca* reference is in Harrington 1932. I visited the Pomo during a collecting trip in 1994 (Winter, field notes, California tribes, 1994).

9. David Brugge, who provided photo 20, was told that Tarahumara *Nicotiana tabacum* is called *wipanto* (personal communication).

10. Cuban tobacco is briefly described in Esquivel and Hammer 1991.

11. Harvard Botanical Museum Herbarium notes for a specimen of *Nicotiana tabacum* collected on the Carib Reserve in 1942.

## 3

# *North American Indigenous* Nicotiana *Use and Tobacco Shamanism*

## The Early Documentary Record, 1520–1660

### Alexander von Gernet

The purpose of this chapter is to identify and organize the rich corpus of ethnohistoric accounts for North America and to scan them for clues that might help our understanding of the prehistoric origins and diffusion of the North American tobacco complex, especially as it relates to tobacco shamanism.[1] The temporal frame of 1520 to 1660 is not entirely arbitrary. Although the first indisputable reference to pipe smoking may be found in Jacques Cartier's account of 1535–1536 (Biggar 1924:183–185), vague allusions to the North American habit were made by various eyewitnesses during the 1520s (for example, Cabeza de Vaca 1966:138; MacNutt 1912, 2:265; Wroth 1970:83, 137, 139–140). A terminal date in the mid-seventeenth century was chosen because this is generally regarded as the end of the Woodland period in eastern North America, the beginning of significant native population movements in the Great Lakes theater, and the launching of intensive European exploration in the interior of the continent. It also coincides with the discovery of American Indian calumet ceremonialism by the French. As an elaborate manifestation of the smoking complex, the calumet pipe generated a wealth of primary literature that has been the subject of numerous studies.[2]

The period under consideration is the era during which European explorers, traders, and missionaries first discovered tobacco and made important observations on the North American smoking complex. At the beginning of the period, Europeans penned awkward, circumlocutory descriptions of a strange habit that was unprecedented in what to them was the Old World. By the end of the period, they had not only appropriated the custom and integrated it into their own cultures on a massive scale but also had established numerous New World "tobacco colonies" to feed smokers in Europe and had begun bringing quantities of the leaf back to the Americas to trade to native peoples. I have detailed this remarkable study in diffusion and transculturation elsewhere (von Gernet 1988, 1995).

A total of 343 passages by nearly 100 eyewitnesses describing tobacco, smoking, or both among 50 different aboriginal groups has been identified. Table 17 lists these groups in alphabetical order, together with the date(s) of observation and the most accessible primary sources. The following is a brief summary of some of the evidence contained in these passages.

### Description and Identification of Tobacco

Sixteenth-century observers commonly compared the seeds of tobacco to a species of *Origanum* or *Majorana*. In a garbled interpolation of Cartier's account of St. Lawrence Iroquoian smoking, André Thevet noted that the "fine little seed" resembled that of "marjoram" (Schlesinger and Stabler 1986:10–11, 47–48). Similarly, William Harrison observed that the tobacco imported into England by the 1570s had seeds reminiscent of marjoram seeds (Dickson 1954:45).

Table 17: Documentary Sources on Tobacco, Pipes, or Smoking in pre-1660 North America

| Cultural Group | Date | Primary Source |
|---|---|---|
| Algonkian | | |
|   Keinouche | 1613 | Biggar 1922–36, 2:275 |
|   Kichesipirini | 1613 | Biggar 1922–36, 2:282–284, 301–302; Lescarbot 1907–14, 3:31–33 |
| | 1623–24 | Sagard 1866, 3:747, 1939:199 |
| | 1646 | Thwaites 1896–1901, 28:299 |
|   Onontchataronon | 1609 | Biggar 1922–36, 2:69, 86 |
| | 1644 | Thwaites 1896–1901, 25:123–125 |
|   Otaguottouemin | 1615 | Biggar 1922–36, 3:38–39 |
|   Weskarini | 1613 | Biggar 1922–36, 2:301–302; Lescarbot 1907–14, 3:32–33 |
| | 1623–24 | Sagard 1866, 3:747 |
|   Unspecified | 1623–24 | Butterfield 1898:173–174; Sagard 1866, 3:752–754, 1939:266 |
| | 1626 | Thwaites 1896–1901, 4:207 |
| | 1633 | Thwaites 1896–1901, 5:131 |
| | 1634 | Thwaites 1896–1901, 6:273 |
| | 1636 | Thwaites 1896–1901, 9:23 |
| | 1640 | Thwaites 1896–1901, 18:187 |
| | 1641 | Thwaites 1896–1901, 20:185–187 |
| | 1642–43 | Thwaites 1896–1901, 24:137 |
| | 1644 | Thwaites 1896–1901, 26:157, 161, 163 |
| | 1645 | Thwaites 1896–1901, 27:157, 285, 301 |
| | 1646 | Thwaites 1896–1901, 29:157 |
| | 1647–48 | Thwaites 1896–1901, 32:229–230, 271 |
| Attikamek | 1642–43 | Thwaites 1896–1901, 24:89 |
| Beothuk | 1597 | Quinn 1979, 4:120 |
| Coast Miwok | 1579 | Quinn 1979, 1:465, 470–473 |
| Cocopa | 1540 | Hammond and Rey 1940:130, 139 |
| Conoy | 1634 | Hall 1910:45 |
| | 1640 | Hall 1910:134 |
| Delaware | 1609 | Jameson 1909:18–21, 24, 48–49; Levermore 1912, 2:410–415, 418 |
| | 1626–28 | Jameson 1909:109 |
| | 1632 | Myers 1912:16–17 |
| | 1633 | Jameson 1909:57 |
| | 1638 | O'Callaghan 1856–1887, 1:598, 12:36–37 |
| | 1639 | R. Bolton 1920:300 |
| | 1642–48 | Holm 1834:121–122, 130, 148, 150 |
| | 1654–55 | Holm 1834:46, 119–120; Johnson 1925:195–197, 221 |
| Eastern Abenaki | | |
|   Kennebec | 1605 | Burrage 1906:367–368, 370, 372–373, 375–376, 380–381, 385, 394; Levermore 1912, 1:323–324, 326, 329, 331–333, 337–338, 342, 351; Quinn and Quinn 1983:267–268, 272, 275–276, 279–281, 308, 310 |
| | 1607 | Strachey 1953:170–171 |
| | 1646 | Thwaites 1896–1901, 28:215 |
|   Penobscot | 1604 | Biggar 1922–36, 1:283–284, 295 |
| | 1605 | Burrage 1906:367–368, 370, 372–373, 375–376, 380–381; 385, 394; Levermore 1912, 1:323–324, 326, 329, 331–333, 337–338, 342, 351; Quinn and Quinn 1983:267–268, 272, 275–276, 279–281, 308, 310 |

Table 17: Documentary Sources on Tobacco, Pipes, or Smoking in pre-1660 North America (cont.)

| Cultural Group | Date | Primary Source |
|---|---|---|
| Huron | | |
|   Arendarhonon | 1609 | Biggar 1922–36, 2:69, 86 |
|   Attignawantan | 1623–24 | Butterfield 1898:173–174; Sagard 1865; Sagard 1866, 1:182, 222–223, 253, 3:604, 747, 752–754; Sagard 1939:62, 85, 88, 96, 98–99, 102, 112–113, 121, 150, 171, 189, 197–198, 203, 266 |
| | 1636 | Thwaites 1896–1901, 10:173, 203, 209, 219, 249, 301, 13:31–33, 55, 141, 157, 171, 203, 219 |
| | 1637 | Du Creux 1951–52, 1:247; Thwaites 1896–1901, 13:259–267, 15:27, 79 |
| | 1638 | Thwaites 1896–1901, 17:81–83 |
| | 1639 | Du Creux 1951–52, 1:261; Thwaites 1896–1901, 17:95, 127, 165, 171–173, 205 |
| | 1640 | Thwaites 1896–1901, 19:87, 173 |
| | 1641 | Du Creux 1951–52, 1:356–357; Thwaites 1896–1901, 23:55 |
|   Attigneenongnahac | 1634 | Thwaites 1896–1901, 7:217 |
|   Unspecified | 1615 | Biggar 1922–36, 3:38–39 |
| | 1615–24 | Le Clercq 1881, 1:216–218 |
| | 1616 | Biggar 1922–36, 3:164–165 |
| | 1634 | Thwaites 1896–1901, 6:273 |
| | 1636 | Thwaites 1896–1901, 9:273, 10:159, 165–167, 11:7 |
| | 1637 | Thwaites 1896–1901, 12:117 |
| | 1637–41 | Boucher 1883:47–48, 55, 59 |
| | 1638 | Thwaites 1896–1901, 14:269 |
| | 1638–39 | Thwaites 1896–1901, 15:155 |
| | 1643 | Thwaites 1896–1901, 26:309–311 |
| | 1645 | Thwaites 1896–1901, 29:249–251 |
| | 1645–49 | Du Creux 1951–52, 1:117; Thwaites 1896–1901, 38:253, 39:13 |
| | 1646 | Thwaites 1896–1901, 28:167 |
| | 1647–48 | Thwaites 1896–1901, 32:229–230 |
| Karankawa | 1528–36 | Cabeza de Vaca 1966:138 |
| Khionontateronon (Petun) | 1616 | Biggar 1922–36, 3:94–95 |
| | 1632 | Biggar 1922–36, 6:248 |
| | 1639 | Thwaites 1896–1901, 17:165, 171–173 |
| | 1640 | Thwaites 1896–1901, 20:43, 51 |
| | 1645–49 | Thwaites 1896–1901, 38:235 |
| Mahican | 1609 | Jameson 1909:21, 23–24; Levermore 1912, 2:415–418 |
| | 1633 | Jameson 1909:57 |
| Maliseet-Passamaquoddy | 1606–7 | Lescarbot 1907–14, 3:176–177, 204 |
| Manahoac | 1608 | Arber 1910, 2:429; Barbour 1986, 2:177; Bushnell 1935:5, 44 |
| Massawomek | 1608 | Arber 1910, 1:72, 367; Barbour 1969, 2:361; Barbour 1986, 1:166, 2:119; Strachey 1953:108 |
| Micmac | 1606 | Biggar 1922–36, 1:443–445; Lescarbot 1907–14, 2:325, 3:279 |
| | 1606–7 | Lescarbot 1907–14, 3:98–99, 123–124, 164, 176–177, 190, 194, 204, 252–254, 266 |
| | 1611 | Thwaites 1896–1901, 1:177; 3:117 |
| | 1632–72 | Denys 1908:419, 424–425, 445 |
| | 1642–43 | Thwaites 1896–1901, 24:151 |
| Mohawk | 1633 | Jameson 1909:57 |

| Cultural Group | Date | Primary Source |
| --- | --- | --- |
| | 1634 | Jameson 1909:141, 143, 145, 161; Gehring and Starna 1988:4, 6, 8–9, 59–60 |
| | 1636–43 | Williams 1973:126–127 |
| | 1641 | Jameson 1909:169; Thwaites 1896–1901, 21:47 |
| | 1642 | Thwaites 1896–1901, 24:281 |
| | 1642–44 | Jameson 1909:177 |
| | 1644 | Thwaites 1896–1901, 26:43; 39:65 |
| | 1645 | Du Creux 1951–52, 2:412, 414; Thwaites 1896–1901, 27:249, 255–257, 271, 285, 301, 29:249–251 |
| | 1646 | Le Clercq 1881, 1:126–127, 2:436; Thwaites 1896–1901, 28:293–295 |
| Montagnais | 1603 | Biggar 1922–36, 1:98–101, 114–115; Lescarbot 1907–14, 2:85–86, 90–91; Sagard 1939:168–169 |
| | 1609 | Biggar 1922–36, 2:86 |
| | 1615–24 | Le Clercq 1881, 1:217–218 |
| | 1623–24 | Butterfield 1898:173–174; Sagard 1939:266 |
| | 1626 | Thwaites 1896–1901, 4:207 |
| | 1633 | Du Creux 1951–52, 1:141; Thwaites 1896–1901, 5:111–113, 131, 159–161 |
| | 1634 | Du Creux 1951–52, 1:166–167; Thwaites 1896–1901, 6:173, 273, 7:23, 123–125, 137–139, 163, 175 |
| | 1640 | Thwaites 1896–1901, 18:187 |
| | 1641 | Thwaites 1896–1901, 20:185–187 |
| | 1642 | Thwaites 1896–1901, 22:237 |
| | 1642–43 | Thwaites 1896–1901, 24:39–41, 137 |
| | 1645 | Thwaites 1896–1901, 27:157 |
| | 1647–48 | Thwaites 1896–1901, 32:229–230 |
| Nadouessis | 1641 | Thwaites 1896–1901, 23:225 |
| Neutral | 1616 | Biggar 1922–36, 3:99 |
| | 1623–24 | Sagard 1939:158 |
| North Carolina Algonkians | 1585–86 | Alexander 1976:74, 79, 83–84; Hulton 1984:31, 79, pl. 49, 117, fig. 15, 122, fig. 20, 126, fig. 24, 179, 180, 182, 189, 190–191; Hulton and Quinn 1964, 1:90–92, 100, 111–112, 2:plates 48, 127b, 131, 135; Quinn 1955, 1:344–346, 420–422 |
| | 1587 | Burrage 1906:292; Quinn 1955, 2:530–531 |
| | 1597 | Dickson 1954:42–43 |
| | 1602 | Quinn and Quinn 1983:198 |
| | 1605 | Brooks 1937–52, 1:417–418; Quinn 1955, 1:345–346 |
| | 1615 | Brooks 1937–52, 2:156 |
| Oneida | 1634 | Jameson 1909:143; Gehring and Starna 1988:6 |
| Ottawa | 1623–24 | Sagard 1939:102 |
| Patuxent | 1634 | Hall 1910:45 |
| Pocomoke | 1524 | Wroth 1970:83, 137 |
| Pueblos (Piro) | 1582–83 | Bolton 1908:178; Hammond and Rey 1966:220 |
| Saint Lawrence Iroquoians | 1535–36 | Biggar 1924:183–185, 245; Schlesinger and Stabler 1986:10–11, 47–48 |
| South Carolina Siouans | 1521–26 | MacNutt 1912, 2:265 |
| Southern New England Algonkians Massachusett | 1603 | Burrage 1906:347–349; Levermore 1912, 1:63–64; Quinn and Quinn 1983:220–223 |

Table 17: Documentary Sources on Tobacco, Pipes, or Smoking in pre-1660 North America (cont.)

| Cultural Group | Date | Primary Source |
| --- | --- | --- |
| | 1629–33 | Wood 1898:75 |
| | 1631 | Hosmer 1959, 1:59 |
| | 1638 | Josselyn 1865:61, 107, 111 |
| Narragansett | 1524 | Wroth 1970:139–140 |
| | 1602 | Levermore 1912, 1:50; Quinn and Quinn 1983:130–131 |
| | 1629–33 | Wood 1898:65 |
| | 1636–43 | Williams 1973:103, 126–127, 134, 150, 187, 244 |
| Pawtucket | 1605 | Biggar 1922–36, 1:327–328 |
| | 1606 | Lescarbot 1907–14, 2:325, 327; Levermore 1912, 1:263, 265 |
| Pokanoket | 1524 | Wroth 1970:139–140 |
| | 1602 | Burrage 1906:333, 339; Levermore 1912, 1:34–35, 40, 42, 46, 48, 50, 54; Quinn and Quinn 1983:122, 125, 130–131, 137, 150, 160 |
| | 1603 | Burrage 1906:347–349; Levermore 1912, 1:63–65; Quinn and Quinn 1983:220–222 |
| | 1605 | Biggar 1922–36, 1:351, 357 |
| | 1606 | Biggar 1922–36, 1:427–428; Lescarbot 1907–14, 2:338; Levermore 1912, 1:275–276 |
| | 1609 | Levermore 1912, 2:398 |
| | 1611 | Bushnell 1911:237; Quinn and Quinn 1983:479–480 |
| | 1620 | Young 1844:145 |
| | 1621 | Young 1844:186–188, 194–196, 210–213, 221 |
| | 1621–23 | Young 1844:363 |
| | 1623 | Young 1844:307 |
| | 1629–33 | Wood 1898:75 |
| Unspecified | 1606–7 | Lescarbot 1907–14, 3:98–99 |
| | 1622 | Brooks 1937–52, 2:90; von Gernet 1988:279 |
| | 1629–33 | Wood 1898:105, 107 |
| Susquehannock | 1608 | Arber 1910, 1:53–54, 118, 350, 2:423; Barbour 1969, 2:342–343, 408; Barbour 1986, 1:149, 2:106, 171; Strachey 1953:48 |
| | 1642–48 | Holm 1834:159 |
| Timucua (Saturiwa) | 1564–65 | Alexander 1976:37; Brooks 1937–52:1:320, 322, 324 |
| | 1565 | Alexander 1976:206; Brooks 1937–52, 1:241; Burrage 1906:125–126 |
| | 1570 | Monardes 1577:45 |
| | 1572 | Bowen 1938:360; Brooks 1937–52, 1:256 |
| | 1578 | Brooks 1937–52, 1:288–289 |
| Virginia Algonkians | | |
| Appamatuck | 1607 | Arber 1910, 1:lxv–lxvi; Barbour 1969, 1:137–138; Tyler 1930:14 |
| Arrohateck | 1607 | Arber 1910, 1:xliii; Barbour 1969, 1:84 |
| Chickahominy | 1614 | Wright 1965:230–231 |
| Kecoughtan | 1607 | Arber 1910, 1:lxiii–lxiv; Barbour 1969, 1:135–136; Tyler 1930:12 |
| | 1610 | Quinn 1979, 5:297 |
| Pamunkey | 1607 | Arber 1910, 1:21–22; Barbour 1969, 1:188; Barbour 1986, 1:59; Tyler 1930:51 |
| Paspahegh | 1607 | Arber 1910, 1:lxvii–lxviii; Barbour 1969, 1:140; Tyler 1930:16 |

Table 17: Documentary Sources on Tobacco, Pipes, or Smoking in pre-1660 North America (cont.)

| Cultural Group | Date | Primary Source |
|---|---|---|
| Powhatan | 1607 | Arber 1910, 1:xliii, 2:385; Barbour 1969, 1:85, 140 |
| | 1614 | Arber 1910, 2:518; Barbour 1986, 2:248–249; Brooks 1937–52, 1:526; Tyler 1930:314 |
| Quiyoughcohannock | 1607 | Arber 1910, 1:lxv, lxxi, lxxiii; Barbour 1969, 1:104, 137, 143, 145–146; Strachey 1953:97–98; Tyler 1930:13–14, 20, 23 |
| | 1607–9 | Arber 1910, 1:78, 374; Barbour 1969, 1:149–150, 2:368–369; Barbour 1986, 1:172, 2:125; Tyler 1930:112–113 |
| Werowocomoco | 1607 | Arber 1910, 2:385; Barbour 1986, 1:140 |
| Unspecified | 1607 | Arber 1910, 1:22; Barbour 1969, 1:101, 189; Barbour 1986, 1:59; Tyler 1930:51 |
| | 1607–9 | Arber 1910, 1:44, 77, 372–373, 381; Barbour 1969, 2:331–332, 367; Barbour 1986, 1:137, 171, 2:123–124, 130; Strachey 1953:97–98; Tyler 1930:78, 111 |
| | 1610–11 | Strachey 1953:39, 79, 94, 122–123, 174–204 |
| | 1615 | Brooks 1937–52, 2:6–7 |

These descriptions compare favorably with those of modern researchers, who have observed that each of a tobacco plant's capsules or pods can contain several thousand seeds (Goodspeed 1954:89). Most are less than one millimeter in size, and hence it is possible to have more than 10,000 seeds per gram of weight (Tso 1972:11). Despite their abundance, the seeds' microscopic diameter meant that most casual observers failed to notice them. There are, in fact, only two seventeenth-century allusions to tobacco seeds in aboriginal North America. In November 1620, 30 men from the *Mayflower* looted a Pokanoket (Wampanoag) cabin and found, among other things, "a little tobacco seed" (Young 1844:145). Sixteen years later a Jesuit missionary, apparently endowed with exceptional eyesight, identified a single specimen in the vomit of a sick Huron (Thwaites 1896–1901, 13:157).

Theodore de Bry's (1591) composite depiction of a North Carolina Algonkian village clearly shows tobacco plants. Contrary to assertions by Paul Hulton and David Quinn (1964: 92), however, the de Bry engraving lacks the detail necessary to permit identification at the species level. Depictions of "yellow henbane" (*Hyoscyamus luteus*), the first of which was published by Rembert Dodoens in 1553, offer much better illustrations of the tobacco plant used by native peoples of eastern North America during the sixteenth century. The common association of tobacco with henbane seemed appropriate, not only because of morphological similarities but also because of the powerful odor and narcotic effects that characterize both solanaceous plants (Schleiffer 1979:166–175; Schultes and Hofmann 1979:45, 86–88; von Gernet 1992a:176–177). While the origin of the particular specimen depicted by Dodoens remains unclear, it was this same species that John Gerard later identified as having been brought to England from North Carolina or New England (Dickson 1954:42–43).

Independent eyewitness reports by explorers in the early seventeenth century offer remarkably consistent estimates of the height of the tobacco plants found in North America. On June 2, 1605, the eastern Abenaki indicated to James Rosier that the plant then growing near their settlements "was growen yet but a foot above ground, and would be above a yard high, with a leafe as broad as both their hands" (Burrage 1906:375–376). The following year, Marc Lescarbot (1907–1914 [1618], 3:252–254) reported that among the Micmac, the plant reached the proportions of "*Consolida major*" (the common comfrey now known as *Symphytum officinale*), a species with a mature height of one meter. In 1611, William Strachey (1953 [1612]:122–123) noted that the indigenous species growing among the Virginia Algonkians was "not fully a yard above grownd." It bore "a little yellow flower like to henn-bane" and had leaves that were short, thick, and rounded at the upper end. John Josselyn (1865:61) also observed a "small round leafed tobacco" harvested by the southern New England Algonkians in 1638 but offered no other details.

The illustrations of "yellow henbane," as well as the ethnohistoric reports, are in accord with the composite characterization of a highly polymorphic species known as *Nicotiana rustica*, as given in the eighteenth century by Linnaeus, who apparently worked with a specimen from a North American type locality (Goodspeed 1954:351–356). William A. Setchell not only found Strachey's description convincing but was able to grow *N. rustica* plants from seed furnished by the Onondaga and the Winnebago sometime prior to 1921. He also noted the existence of "spontaneous plants of *Nicotiana rustica*" in Connecticut, New York, Wisconsin, Illinois, Minnesota, and Texas, which appeared to be "remnants of earlier Indian cultivation" (Setchell 1921:402–403). Setchell's work has been corroborated in more recent times. In 1980 I discovered two feral tobacco plants growing on an undisturbed, prehistoric Iroquoian midden in southern Ontario; these turned out to be *N. rustica* (von Gernet 1992a:177). Seeds I obtained from the Cayuga hereditary chief Jacob Thomas in 1993 have also been identified as *N. rustica*.

Overall, the weight of evidence makes it tempting to surmise that all references to indigenous tobacco in the pre-1660 literature refer to one or more varieties of *N. rustica*. The only obvious exception may be Francis Drake's observations among the coast Miwok of California in 1579 (Heizer 1947), which have generated considerable debate but probably refer to one of the California "desert" tobaccos.[3]

## Distribution

Mapping the distribution of *N. rustica* at the time of first European contact in North America is complicated by the peculiar history of tobacco diffusion. It must be kept in mind that tobacco is unique as the only sixteenth- and seventeenth-century commodity that crossed the Atlantic in both directions and had sources and markets on both sides of the ocean. *N. rustica* (known at the time as "yellow henbane" or "English tabaco") was growing in herbal gardens in Europe by the 1550s and was one of the tobaccos that contributed to the extraordinary smoking rage that had spread throughout England by the end of the century. This rage, which was generated partly by the humoral theory of European medicine and partly by a desire for recreational altered states of consciousness, even stimulated a modest domestic tobacco industry. Once the English learned to smoke, tobacco routinely accompanied them on voyages to the New World, where it was used as a trade good. Only after 1611, when West Indies *N. tabacum* was introduced into Virginia and became the economic lifeline of the first permanent English settlement in North America, did *N. rustica* begin to lose popularity in England. Moreover, England was not the only nation with opportunities to bring nicotian products to America. As early as 1597, Basque sailors were offering tobacco to the Beothuk of Newfoundland, and in 1604 Champlain was handing it out to the eastern Abenaki. By 1615, native peoples living as far inland as Ontario were canoeing hundreds of kilometers through the interior of Quebec to obtain European tobacco from French traders anchored at Tadoussac on the St. Lawrence. The tobacco (*petun*) available to the French at the time was usually imported from Brazil and may have been *N. rustica* (von Gernet 1988; 1995:74–80).

In light of these facts, it is not beyond the realm of possibility that the North American distribution of *N. rustica* was affected by an English and French presence. This makes a careful scrutiny of the ethnohistoric record and the timing of culture contact all the more important. Having examined the evidence, and with the aforementioned caveats in mind, I remain convinced that at the time of initial contact, *N. rustica* was already being utilized by native peoples living along much of the eastern seaboard from Florida to Nova Scotia and as far into the interior as southwestern Ontario. One source (relating to an unspecified Siouan people the French called "Nadouessis") may extend this distribution at least to the western end of Lake Superior (Thwaites 1896–1901, 23:326, 51:53).

Setchell's map showing the distribution of *N. rustica* use in aboriginal North America has often been reproduced by modern authorities (Gilmore 1922:480; Haberman 1984:274; Malefijt 1974:174–179), even though Setchell made errors in locating native groups, drew boundaries based on Clark Wissler's now-obsolete "culture areas," and extrapolated vast distributions from a few scattered ethnohistoric and ethnographic descriptions. As Setchell himself admitted, the western extent of the distribution is particularly problematic.

Evidence for *N. rustica* among the Pueblo peoples has been a matter of controversy. Some scholars have suggested that this species was cultivated in the Southwest in prehistoric times, whereas others insist it was introduced in the twentieth century, and still others believe it was introduced by the Spanish.[4] The ethnobotanist Volney Jones (1944) was unable to find references to tobacco or smoking in the testimony of early Spanish explorations in the Southwest, but it seems he missed one important source in the records of the *entradas* of 1581–1583. Antonio de Espejo stated unequivocally that the

Piro pueblos had "fields of maize, beans, gourds, and *piciete* in large quantities, which they cultivate like the Mexicans" (Bolton 1908:453). Unfamiliarity with the term *piciete* has buried this important passage, and it is absent from a recent list of historic references to tobacco cultivation in the Southwest (Adams 1990a:133). In his summary of the Piro in the *Handbook of North American Indians*, Albert Schroeder (1979:236) equated picietes with "medicinal herbs." This does not correspond to sixteenth-century Spanish usage and masks the fact that the term designates a particular species of *Nicotiana*. In his famous work on tobacco, the Seville physician Nicolás Monardes (1577:folio 34) noted that "the proper name of it amongst the Indians is *Pecielt*." That *picietl* (or *piciete*) was the Nahuatl term for *N. rustica* was confirmed by Bernardino de Sahagún and other sixteenth-century Spanish writers.[5]

The entradas of the 1580s were among the earliest Spanish penetrations into this region (Quinn 1977:492–493). It seems highly unlikely that Europeans introduced *N. rustica* to the Piro before Espejo's arrival and, indeed, doubtful that such opportunities arose until after the establishment of a colony and introduction of new crops later in the century (Eggan 1979: 224). The most reasonable explanation is that these indigenous inhabitants of New Mexico harvested *N. rustica* prior to European contact and that the tentative identifications of seeds of this species by southwestern archaeologists are at least as credible as those made in eastern North America (Adams 1990a:126; and various chapters in this book).

## Cultivation

Although de Bry's famous engraving of a North Carolina Algonkian village is the first to show North American tobacco plants growing in gardens, its value is diminished by the fact that these plants were the engraver's addition to John White's original watercolor (Hulton 1984:

66, plate 36; Hulton and Quinn 1964, 1:90–91). More useful are the written accounts of individuals who were actually there. References to tobacco cultivation in pre-1660 North America are summarized in table 18. It is obvious from the descriptions furnished by the eyewitnesses that in many cases tobacco was "cultivated" in "fields" or "gardens," together with subsistence cultigens such as corn, beans, and squash. There are, however, several reasons why one should not assume a correlation between *N. rustica* and a horticultural mode of subsistence.

Table 18: References to Tobacco Cultivation in pre-1660 North America

| Cultural Group | Date | Primary Source | Description |
| --- | --- | --- | --- |
| Delaware | 1642–48 | Holm 1834:122 | [Tobacco] "grows in their country in great abundance." |
| Huron | 1636 | Thwaites 1896–1901, 11:7 | "They cultivate the fields, from which they gather Indian corn, —the grain which some call Turkish,—abundance of excellent pumpkins, and also tobacco." |
| | 1637 | Thwaites 1896–1901, 15:79 | [A man] "annually makes a small garden [of tobacco] near his cabin." |
| | 1637–41 | Boucher 1883:47–48 | [The Indians raise corn, beans, pumpkins, sunflower] "and a plant from which they make their tobacco." |
| | 1636–41 | Boucher 1883:55 | [It is the men] "also who cultivate the fields of tobacco." |
| Khionontateronon | 1640 | Thwaites 1896–1901, 20:43 | [The Khionontateronon are called Tobacco or Petun] "from the abundance of that plant there." |
| | 1645–49 | Thwaites 1896–1901, 38:235 | "The nation which we called 'Tobacco,' because this plant was produced there in abundance...." |
| Micmac | 1606–7 | Lescarbot 1907–14, 3:252–54 | [The Indians] "plant great store of tobacco." |
| Nadouessis | 1641 | Thwaites 1896–1901, 23:225 | "These Peoples till the soil ... and harvest Indian corn and Tobacco." |
| Narragansett | 1636–43 | Williams 1973:103 | [Tobacco] "is commonly the only plant which men labour in; the women managing all the rest." |
| | 1636–43 | Williams 1973:126–127 | "The men plant [tobacco] themselves." |
| Neutral | 1616 | Biggar 1922–36, 3:99 | [The Indians] "produce a great quantity of tobacco." |
| | 1623–24 | Sagard 1939:158 | [In their country] "is grown a large quantity of very good tobacco." |
| North Carolina Algonkians | 1585–86 | Dickson 1954:135 | "[Tobacco is] sowed a part by it selfe." |
| | 1585–86 | Hulton 1984:126, fig. 24 | [Theodore de Bry's enhancement to John White's watercolor of the village of Secota shows separate tobacco gardens.] |

| Cultural Group | Date | Primary Source | Description |
|---|---|---|---|
| | 1587 | Burrage 1906:292 | [Fleeing Indians] "left all their corne, Tabacco, and Pompions standing." |
| Pawtucket | 1605 | Biggar 1922–36, 1:327–328 | [In fields on the banks of the river] "we saw there many squashes, pumpkins, and tobacco, which they likewise cultivate." |
| Pokanoket or Massachusett | 1603 | Burrage 1906:349 | [Not far from the houses] "we beheld their Gardens and one among the rest of an Acre of ground, and in the same was sowne Tobacco, pompions, cowcumbers and such like; and some of the people had Maiz or Indian Wheate among them." |
| Pokanoket | 1605 | Biggar 1922–36, 1:351 | [In a field on the way to the village] "we saw an abundance of Brazilian beans, many edible squashes of various sizes, tobacco, and roots which they cultivate." |
| | 1611 | Bushnell 1911:237 | "They are plentifull in Corne and Tobacco." |
| Pueblos (Piro) | 1582–83 | Bolton 1908:178 | "Fields of maize, beans, gourds, and [tobacco] in large quantities, which they cultivate like the Mexicans." |
| Paspahegh | 1607 | Barbour 1969, 1:140 | [One of the Indians] "brought us on the way to the Wood side, where there was a Garden of Tobacco, and other fruits and herbes." |
| Powhatan | 1607 | Barbour 1969, 1:85 | [Between his habitation and the water is a plain] "12. score over, whereon he sowes his wheate, beane, peaze, tobacco, pompions, gowrdes, Hempe, flaxe &c." |
| Saint Lawrence Iroquoians | 1535–36 | Biggar 1924:183–185 | "A large supply [of tobacco] is collected in summer." |
| Virginia Algonkians | 1610–11 | Strachey 1953:79 | About their howses, they have commonly square plotts of cleered grownd, which serve them for gardeins, some 100. some 200. foote square, wherein they sowe their Tobacco, pumpeons, and a fruit like unto a musk–million." |
| | 1610–11 | Strachey 1953:122–123 | "There is here great store of Tobacco." |

First, there are hints that tobacco was not always planted in the horticultural fields surrounding villages. For example, in 1607 the Paspahegh led George Percy "on the way to the wood side, where there was a garden of tobacco, and other fruits and herbes" (Barbour 1969, 1:140). A missionary among the Huron observed that every year a man made a small garden of tobacco near his cabin (Thwaites 1896–1901, 15:79). It is conceivable that other small plots were located in clearings in the woods.

Second, Thomas Hariot noted that among the North Carolina Algonkians, tobacco was "an herbe which is sowed a part by it selfe" (Dickson 1954:135). While this may indicate that the plant was raised independently of other horticultural products, at least one modernized edition has rendered this phrase "an herb . . . which sows itself" (Lorant 1946:246)—an interpretation that also seems plausible. Gerard noted that the N. rustica brought to England in the late sixteenth century "doth prosper exceedingly, insomuch that it cannot be destroied where it hath once sowen itself" (Dickson 1954:42–43). In the mid-1920s, Alanson Skinner (1925a:128) obtained tobacco seeds from the Seneca and added that his informants did not know whether tobacco was ever cultivated; "instead it was claimed that the seeds were merely cast out in the dooryard to survive or perish, as the case might be." An Algonkian shaman interviewed in the 1960s recalled that tobacco

grows wild under the branches of big trees, particularly in maple forests. We find a lot of tobacco growing in among willow bogs and along the brooks. . . . They like the sandy soil and it won't grow decently at all in good deep loam. Wild tobacco, as any tobacco man can tell you, is mighty strong. It is cured by nature. It grows in the summer, it drys on the stalk in the fall, and it is cured throughout the winter by frost and defrost. When you find these 14-inch-high plants in the spring they are almost black. If you want it to cure really good you pick the leaves and lay them on a flat rock,

otherwise you put it in a bag and let it cure even more. You have to watch for dampness growth in your tobacco though. . . . After the natural winter curing we used to go into the woods with a thing that looked like a lacrosse stick, only smaller, and swat the tobacco pods. The kids used to do this, and this was the way of spreading the seed all around the forest. (Goodwin 1969:34, 45)

Cayuga Chief Thomas (personal communication, 1993) recalls that his grandfather did not even bother seeding and that the plant seemed to perpetuate itself. The recovery of feral *N. rustica*, as mentioned earlier, tends to support such claims and undermines the assumption that this species "is certain to perish unless fostered by human care" (Berlin 1905:109).

Third, it appears that significantly more native groups were using tobacco than were cultivating it (compare tables 17 and 18). This should come as no surprise, since tobacco use was not restricted to horticulturalists. I have, in fact, recovered carbonized tobacco seeds from a remote protohistoric hunting camp on the Canadian Shield, in an area frequented by Algonkian bands of the upper Ottawa Valley (von Gernet 1992b:76). These bands were primarily nomadic foragers who lived at the northernmost penetration of a marginally horticultural economy and grew a few cultigens wherever and whenever soil and climate made it possible (Day and Trigger 1978:795). There is no evidence that they cultivated tobacco in fields or gardens, although table 17 gives numerous references under "Algonkian."

An even better example are the Montagnais of eastern Quebec and the Labrador Peninsula. Although they were exclusively hunter-gatherers (Rogers and Leacock 1981:169, 174–175), the information in table 17 suggests that they had a significant preoccupation with tobacco. Although the leaf may have been reintroduced to these subarctic peoples by Europeans at a later time (Seig 19:34; N. Smith 1957:77; Speck 1977 [1935]:225), the primary sources listed in table

17 indicate that they already had an elaborate pipe-smoking complex, were infatuated with tobacco, and were obtaining it from the Huron at the time they were first contacted by French explorers and missionaries.

The most telling case involves the Micmac, who lived in what is now Nova Scotia and New Brunswick. Like the Montagnais, these people were hunter-gatherers and fishermen who cultivated no subsistence crops (Bock 1978:109). Their use of tobacco is well documented, however, and there is unequivocal evidence that they harvested their own plants and did not depend on trade with their horticultural neighbors to the south. Marc Lescarbot (1907–1914 [1618], 3:252–254) observed that they "plant great store of tobacco," which they would later gather and dry in the shade.

Finally, in the horticultural societies of eastern North America, it was the women who labored in the fields of corn, beans, and squash. There is no evidence whatsoever that they also planted, tended, and harvested tobacco. Indeed, several independent observers among the Huron and Narragansett noted that this was exclusively a male activity (Boucher 1883:55; Thwaites 1896–1901, 15:79; Williams 1973:103, 126–127). This sexual division of labor suggests an Amerindian taxonomy that classified tobacco not in the same category as subsistence cultigens but rather as a symbolically distinct product.

Because the propagation of *N. rustica* required a minimum of human intervention, it seems unlikely that intensive horticultural preparation was necessary for a successful harvest. In any case, the literature from this early period says nothing about seeding methods, cropping systems, plant spacing, weeding, and other activities normally associated with a domesticated plant. What we do know is that *N. rustica* was harvested by horticulturalists, incipient horticulturalists, and hunter-gatherers. The Micmac case is perhaps the clearest evidence we have that the diffusion of *N. rustica* may have had a historical trajectory different from that of the spread of subsistence cultigens. Indeed, provided ecological conditions were favorable, almost any hunter-gatherer or forager group could have harvested the species (Knight 1975: 126). All that is required is a seasonal round involving annual or semiannual visits to a specific locale, rather than the wholesale adaptive shift demanded of those peoples who depended on maize and bean agriculture.

## Preparation

Table 19 summarizes the available data on native preparation of tobacco. Strachey (1953 [1612]:122–123) observed that the Virginia Algonkians crumbled into powder the "Stalkes, leaves, and all" after drying the plant. While Europeans developed elaborate systems for processing tobacco in an effort to render it a palatable smoking substance, there is no evidence that the Amerindian product was subjected to complex curing methods. Indeed, James Rosier felt that "the simple leaf without any composition" he was given by the Penobscot was a refreshing change from the adulterated material available in England (Burrage 1906:372–373). Nevertheless, some form of curing appears to have been essential, and reports suggest that this was accomplished simply by drying the leaves in either sun or shade or by hanging them over a fire. Numerous explorers, reporting from a diversity of geographic settings, noted that the native *N. rustica* retained its green color even after processing (an attribute not found in the European product, which turned yellow, brown, or black). This fact has helped efforts to distinguish indigenous from European tobacco in the ethnohistoric record. In most cases the dried leaf was reduced to powder or pressed into "cakes" of compressed leaf-mass for easy transport, trade, and use. There is no indication that tobacco required significantly more preparation than most of the other numerous wild plants consumed by Amerindians.

Table 19: References to Tobacco Preparation in pre-1660 North America

| Cultural Group | Date | Primary Source | Description |
|---|---|---|---|
| Delaware | 1609 | Jameson 1909:18, 48 | "Greene Tabacco" |
| Huron | 1636 | Thwaites 1896–1901, 10:173, 249 | "Cakes" |
| | 1637 | Thwaites 1896–1901, 13:259–267, 15:27 | "Cakes" |
| | 1637–41 | Boucher 1883:59 | "Plug" [*pain* or "cake"] |
| | 1639 | Thwaites 1896–1901, 17:95, 171–173 | "Cakes" |
| | 1640 | Thwaites 1896–1901, 29:87 | "Cakes" |
| Micmac | 1606–7 | Lescarbot 1907–14, 3:252–254 | "They dry it in the shade." |
| | 1632–72 | Denys 1908:419 | "A certain green tobacco.... They dried it, and made it into a loaf, in the form of a cake, four inches thick." |
| Montagnais | 1642 | Thwaites 1896–1901, 22:237 | "Cakes" |
| North Carolina Algonkians | 1585–86 | Arber 1895:85–86 | "The leaves thereof being dried and brought into powder ..." |
| Oneida | 1634 | Gehring and Starna 1988:6 | "Green tobacco" |
| Penobscot or Kennebec | 1605 | Burrage 1906:372–373 | "The simple leafe without any composition" |
| Pokanoket | 1602 | Burrage 1906:333 | "Their Tabacco, which they drinke [i.e., smoke] greene, but dried into powder ..." |
| | 1605 | Biggar 1922–36, 1:357 | "Tobacco, which they dry and then reduce to powder ..." |
| | 1609 | Levermore 1912, 2:398 | "Greene Tabacco" |
| Quiyoughcohannock | 1607 | Barbour 1969, 1:143 | "Dried" |
| Saint Lawrence Iroquoians | 1535–36 | Biggar 1924:183–185 | "After drying it in the sun" |
| | 1535–36 | Schlesinger and Stabler 1986:10–11 | "They dry it in the sun after collecting heaps of it ... a piece of this dried plant, which, having rolled it between their hands [they smoke]." |
| | 1535–36 | Schlesinger and Stabler 1986:47–48 | "They gather it in piles and dry it in the sun, and then when it is dry they pulverize it." |
| Timucua (Saturiwa) | 1564–65 | Brooks 1937–52, 1:322, 324 | "The leaves of this plant, properly dried ..." |
| | 1565 | Burrage 1906:125–126 | "Dried" |
| Virginia Algonkians | 1610–11 | Strachey 1953:122–123 | "Dry the leaves of this [tobacco] over the fier, and sometymes in the Sun, and Crumble yt into Powlder, Stalkes, leaves, and all." |

## Tobacco Invocations

Tobacco use among native peoples of North America may be divided into the general categories of invocation and internal consumption. It is conceivable that as much *Nicotiana* was cast into fires, water, and rock crevices during tobacco invocations as was consumed by smoking (table 20). The reason for depositing tremendous quantities of the leaf in various places was linked to the belief that even inanimate objects had souls and that spirits inhabited all awe-inspiring natural features. Moreover, humans were thought to live in a social world where there was a perpetual obligation to fulfil contractual obligations. Spirit beings were particularly fond of tobacco and hence were offered the precious substance at every opportunity. The gifts were sent either directly to the spirits beings' terrestrial and underwater dwellings or indirectly to the skyworld in the form of smoke. In return for these gratuities, which invariably were accompanied by invocatory prayers, the spirit beings were expected to provide certain favors. The remarkable continuity of this animistic belief system and associated practice, from the Quebec Montagnais to the North Carolina Algonkians, points to considerable antiquity (von Gernet 1992a:172, 1995:70). It is again noteworthy that this practice was common to both foragers and horticulturalists.

## Internal Consumption

There is evidence that tobacco was eaten, either in dry leaf form or as a juice that was added as an ingredient in cornbread; however, such consumption appears to have been limited to times of hunger or fasting (Holm 1834 [1702]: 121; Sagard 1865, 1939:199; Thwaites 1896–1901, 10:203, 13:147). Although the active ingredients contained in tobacco may be ingested directly into the gastrointestinal system, a more efficient absorption occurs after combustion and inhalation. Moreover, transforming a leaf into smoke had unparalleled symbolic importance; not only could both interior and exterior parts of a body be exposed to an empowering

Table 20: References to Tobacco Invocations in pre-1660 North America

| Cultural Group | Tobacco Thrown into or on | | | | Primary Source |
|---|---|---|---|---|---|
| | Fire | Water | Air | Ground | |
| Algonkian | | + | | | Biggar 1922–37, 2:301–302; Lescarbot 1907–14, 3:32–33 |
| Huron | + | + | | + | Du Creux 1951–52, 1:117, 356–357; Le Clercq 1881, 1:216; Sagard 1866, 3:747; Sagard 1939:171, 189, 197–198; Thwaites 1896–1901, 10:159, 165–167; 13:31–33, 203, 259–267, 19:87, 23:55, 26:309, 39:13 |
| Khionontateronon | + | | | | Thwaites 1896–1901, 20:51 |
| Micmac | + | | | | Biggar 1922–36, 1:443–445; Lescarbot 1907–14, 3:279 |
| Montagnais | + | | | | Thwaites 1896–1901, 22:237 |
| North Carolina Algonkians | + | + | + | | Quinn 1955, 1:344–346 |
| Virginia Algonkians | + | + | | + | Arber 1910, 1:21–22, 77, 372–373; Barbour 1969, 1:104, 143, 145–146; Brooks 1937–52, 2:6–7; Strachey 1953:97–98 |

substance, but the smoke could also reach the lofty and normally inaccessible realms where many of the spirit beings resided. It is, perhaps, for these reasons that smoking became the most popular form of tobacco consumption.

There are no references to cigars in the early literature on continental North America. Cartier, who visited the St. Lawrence Iroquoians in 1535–1536, was the first to describe smoking through a "cornet de pierre, ou de boys" (cornet or cone of stone or wood), and André Thevet recognized that this differed from the predominant practice he had seen in Brazil (Biggar 1924:183–195; Schlesinger and Stabler 1986:10–11, 47–48). The earliest illustration of a North American Indian smoking tobacco in a pipe was based on eyewitness observations among the Saturiwa eastern Timucua in 1564–1565 by Jacques Le Moyne de Morgues, a member of the Huguenot colony at La Caroline in present-day Florida. Pipes are alluded to so frequently in the early ethnohistoric literature that it is reasonable to assume that all groups listed in table 17 employed such devices during and shortly before European contact. Moreover, pipes are a salient feature of the North American archaeological record, in which they appear in high numbers, including more than 4,000 fragments of ceramic and stone smoking devices recovered at a single prehistoric Iroquoian site (von Gernet 1982, 1985).

The early sources allude to pipes made not only from pottery, stone, and bone but also from wood, reeds, and even lobster claws. Because some of these materials rarely survive for many years, both the spatial and temporal extents of the pipe complex are probably not fully represented by the archaeological record. The first nonperishable smoking implements in eastern North America are tubular in form and date to the Late Archaic period. The resemblance of these implements to shamans' sucking tubes cannot be fortuitous, and I have suggested that the two were once symbolically and functionally equivalent. It is not difficult to imagine an ideational homology between sucking and

blowing "medicine" and the inhaling and exhaling of smoke, since both practices involved the transfer of spiritual power. Whether emerging through an internal evolution of shamanistic practices or stimulated by diffusion, the pipe complex underwent a florescence during the Early and Middle Woodland periods, particularly among the Adena and Hopewell peoples (von Gernet 1992a:178).

Some of the more specific traits associated with this complex have a surprising continuity over time and throughout much of the continent. An example is the association between pipes and the skin of an extinct species of North American parakeet (*Conuropis carolinensis*). This association, which I have documented in various Amerindian cultures living over a period of millennia, is a subset of the even more common association between tobacco paraphernalia and birds, which occurs in both North and South America. Elsewhere I have linked this association to the ornithomorphic accoutrements of ecstatic shamanism, altered states of consciousness, Amerindian dream and soul theory, and the use of psychoactive substances. Furthermore, I have argued that the specific association was not spread through diffusion but emerged independently from the ideological substratum that gives all Amerindians in the New World a culture-historical unity (von Gernet and Timmins 1987:35–42).

By the time of European contact, the pipe complex had been elaborated into a variety of nontubular forms, and although the formal link with sucking tubes was often lost, shamanic associations continued, such as in the iconography of Iroquoian effigy pipes (Mathews 1976), the Conoy or Patuxent practice of blowing tobacco smoke on various parts of the body (Hall 1910), and the "suck doctors" of the California Karuk, who held tobacco smoke in their mouths while simultaneously sucking their patients (Harrington 1932:227–229).

Contrary to assertions made by Jordan Paper (1988:113), native peoples of North America did not practice a "pipe-centered religion." The remarkable consistency in aboriginal belief systems and symbolic structures throughout much of the continent is the result of the constraining influence of an animistic Weltanschauung with roots deep in prehistory (von Gernet 1990:1041, 1995:69). It was not the pipe but the substance(s) it contained that empowered individuals with a sense of the supernatural and offered a means of communicating with other-than-human potencies.

## Psychoactive Effects

The indigenous peoples of North America were aware of virtually the entire inventory of their local botanical environment. They also had a proclivity for altered states of consciousness, which they achieved by a variety of means, including the adjustment of body chemistry through the ingestion of pharmacological agents. Iroquoians, for example, occasionally drank infusions containing plants known to have hallucinogenic and other mind-altering effects. Hence, it stands to reason that at least some of the more than 60 different species of plants known to have been smoked in eastern North America had psychoactive properties. Indeed, of the 14 identifiable plant species smoked by Iroquoians, 4 are strongly suspected of having mind-altering ingredients (von Gernet 1992a:173–176). The most widely used was, of course, tobacco.

The early documentary sources contain numerous allusions to the psychoactive effects of *N. rustica*. Since I have described these in detail elsewhere (von Gernet 1992a), it suffices to say that there is abundant evidence to reject any opinion that the use of tobacco to produce major dissociative states was confined to South America and Mesoamerica. With few exceptions, those Europeans who had prior experience with smoking characterized the native product as very strong. Moreover, observers frequently compared tobacco to wine and alluded to a variety of effects, including dizziness, vertigo, inebriation, intoxication, loss of reason, coma,

and (what they interpreted as) insanity. Tobacco produced or enhanced visions and, according to some native smokers, enabled one to see clearly, thereby providing enlightenment and intelligence during thoughtful deliberations. This documentary evidence is supported by ethnographic observations, chemical analyses, and experimental studies (von Gernet 1992a).

Since the use of tobacco to produce altered states of consciousness is reported for the Micmac (Lescarbot 1907–1914 [1618], 3:177, 153, 398, 439) and even the subarctic Naskapi (Speck 1977 [1935]:226), it is clear that it was not confined to horticultural societies. In light of the known effects of *N. rustica* on humans and the shamanistic worldview of New World hunter-gatherers, this is not unexpected.

## Addiction

There is no question that tobacco and pipes played a prominent role in the rich religious life of aboriginal North America. This has led to a popular impression that native tobacco use was restricted to profoundly spiritual or ceremonial occasions and that frequent smoking and tobacco addiction only occurred long after European contact. Table 21 offers conclusive proof that this impression is unfounded and should be dispelled.

Time and time again, early observers expressed their astonishment at the tobacco addiction of many of the Indians they met. Various peoples belonging to both the Iroquoian and Algonkian language families were seen with pipes in their mouths at all hours of the day and night, and tobacco figured prominently in the dreams they recalled. Not only was the leaf greatly prized, but some individuals appeared sooner to dispense with eating than with smoking. Occasionally, the natives themselves admitted that there was nothing in the world they loved more than tobacco. Pipes were included as essential grave goods, for even the souls who traveled to the land of the dead were dedicated smokers.

Table 21: Documentary Evidence of Native American Tobacco Addiction in pre-1660 North America

| Cultural Group | Date | Primary Source | Description |
|---|---|---|---|
| Algonkian | 1645 | Thwaites 1896–1901, 27:157 | "This same man was singularly addicted to smoking." |
| | 1647–48 | Thwaites 1896–1901, 32:229–30 | [An Indian] "who prefers tobacco to food and drink . . ." |
| Huron | 1623–24 | Sagard 1939:62 | "Smoking [tobacco] quite often during the day deadened their hunger." |
| | 1623–24 | Sagard 1866, 1:182 | "Smoking [tobacco] quite often during the day consoled and fortified them, and deadened their hunger." |
| | 1623–24 | Sagard 1939:85 | "They also used to ask us for tobacco to smoke, and most frequently in order to spare what they had in their own pouch, for they are never without it. But as the crowd was often so great that we scarcely had room in our hut we could not supply it to all, and    made our excuses by saying that they themselves had traded to us the little which we had." |
| | 1623–24 | Sagard 1866, 1:222–223 | "They often asked us for something to smoke, to save the tobacco they had in their pouch, for it was never depleted. But as the crowd was great and they appeared to be greedy, we could not give some to everyone, and excused ourselves by saying that they themselves had traded to us the little which we had, and this reason would satisfy them. Nevertheless, those who surmised we had enough for all, were attracted to our cabin, for tobacco is their honey and sugar, and their most delicious food." |
| | 1623–24 | Sagard 1939:88 | "But as I had never wished to become habituated to tobacco I used to thank them but not take it, at which they were at first all astonished, because there is nobody in all those countries who does not take it and use it." |
| | 1623–24 | Sagard 1939:121 | [Sexual modesty is attributed] "partly to their habitual use of tobacco." |

| Cultural Group | Date | Primary Source | Description |
|---|---|---|---|
| | 1623–24 | Sagard 1939:96 | [Their spare time] "they pass in idleness, gambling, sleeping, singing, dancing, smoking." |
| | 1636 | Thwaites 1896–1901, 9:273 | "They adore" [tobacco]. |
| | 1637–41 | Boucher 1883:47–48 | [They] "are great smokers, and cannot do without tobacco." |
| | 1638 | Thwaites 1896–1901, 17:81–83 | [The Indians] "would as soon dispense with eating as with smoking." |
| | 1639 | Thwaites 1896–1901, 17:127 | "You will find some of them anxious to know if there will be tobacco [in Heaven], saying that they cannot dispense with it." |
| | 1645–49 | Thwaites 1896–1901, 38:253 | "Tobacco which they smoke perpetually,—at the assemblies, and everywhere ..." |
| Micmac | 1606–7 | Lescarbot 1907–14, 3:164 | [Sexual modesty is attributed] "partly to their frequent use of tobacco." |
| | 1606–7 | Lescarbot 1907–14, 3:176–177 | [Tobacco] "the smoke of which they inhale almost every hour ..." |
| | 1606–7 | Lescarbot 1907–14, 3:252–254 | "They will sometimes endure hunger five or six days with the aid of that [tobacco] smoke." |
| | 1606–7 | Lescarbot 1907–14, 3:252–254 | "I shall add that this [tobacco] is so sweet to them that the children sometimes suck in the smoke that their fathers send out of their nostrils, to the end that nothing be lost." |
| | 1611 | Thwaites 1896–1901, 3:117 | "Many ills arise from [tobacco], on account of its excessive use" [among the Indians]. |
| | 1611 | Thwaites 1896–1901, 3:117 | "All their talks, treaties, welcomes, and endearments are made under the fumes of this tobacco. They gather around the fire, chatting and passing the pipe from hand to hand, enjoying themselves in this way for several hours." |
| Montagnais | 1633 | Thwaites 1896–1901, 5:111–13 | [The Indians] "love it to madness." |
| | 1634 | Thwaites 1896–1901, 7:137–39 | "The fondness they have for this herb is beyond all belief. They go to sleep with their reed pipes in their mouths, they sometimes get up in the night to smoke; they often stop in their journeys for the same purpose, and it is the |

| Cultural Group | Date | Primary Source | Description |
| --- | --- | --- | --- |
| | | | first thing they do when they re-enter their cabins. I have lighted tinder, so as to allow them to smoke while paddling a canoe; I have often seen them gnaw the stems of their pipes when they had no more tobacco, I have seen them scrape and pulverize a wooden pipe to smoke it. Let us say with compassion that they pass their lives in smoke, and at death fall into the fire. I brought some tobacco with me, but not for myself, as I do not use it. I have given liberally, according to my store, to several Savages, saving some to draw from the Apostate a few words of his language, for he would not say a word if I did not pay him with this money. When our people had consumed what I had given them, and what they had of their own, I had no more peace. The Sorcerer was so annoying in his demands for it, that I could not endure him; and all the others acted as if they wanted to eat me, when I refused them. In vain I told them that they had no consideration, that I had given them more than three times as much as I had reserved for myself.... It was impossible to resist their teasing, and I had to draw out the last bit, not without astonishment at seeing people so passionately fond of smoke." |
| | 1640 | Thwaites 1896–1901, 18:187 | "Those who know what a mania the Savages and some Frenchmen have for smoking tobacco, will admire this abstinence [in a convert to Christianity]. Intemperate drinkers are not so fond of wine as the Savages are of tobacco." |
| | 1641 | Thwaites 1896–1901, 20:185–87 | "Tobacco, to which the Savages are devoted beyond all that can be said ..." |
| Mohawk | 1645 | Thwaites 1896–1901, 27:271 | [Mohawk response to French gift of tobacco and pipe:] "Only our |

| Cultural Group | Date | Primary Source | Description |
| --- | --- | --- | --- |
| | | | mouth remained free and you have filled it with a fine calumet and have gladdened it with the flavor of a plant that is very pleasing to us." |
| Narragansett | 1636–43 | Williams 1973:126–127 | "Some doe not [smoke tobacco], but they are rare Birds; for generally all the men throughout the Countrey have a Tobacco–bag, with a pipe in it, hanging at their back." |
| Penobscot | 1605 | Burrage 1906:375–376 | [Their tobacco pipe is so large that it] "will hold ten of our pipes full" [and they do not have surplus tobacco to trade] "for they spend a great quantity yeerely by their continuall" [smoking]. |
| St. Lawrence Iroquois | 1535–36 | Biggar 1924:183–185 | [They hold tobacco] "in high esteem," [smoke] "at frequent intervals," [and] "never go about without" [pipes]. |
| | 1535–36 | Schlesinger and Stabler 1986:10–11 | [The Indians smoke] "at all hours of the day." |
| | 1535–36 | Schlesinger and Stabler 1986:47–48 | [Tobacco] "is much esteemed among them"; [they often smoke] "all day." |
| Virginia Algonkians | 1615 | Brooks 1937–52, 2:6–7 | [These Indians] "esteeme [tobacco] exceedingly, and so doe the rest." |

Paul Le Jeune reported that the fondness the Montagnais had for tobacco was "beyond belief." They went to sleep with their pipes in their mouths, got up at night to smoke, interrupted their journeys to do the same, and even scraped and pulverized nicotine-saturated wooden pipes to obtain more smoking material. Five years later, Jérôme Lalemant found the Huron anxious to know whether tobacco was available in heaven, claiming that they could not dispense with it in the Christian afterlife. Indeed, the Jesuits soon regarded abstention from smoking as the most heroic act to be expected of any neophyte.

These sources suggest that in many cases tobacco use had already become what, from a Western perspective, may best be described as secularized. It must be recalled, however, that much of everyday life in native North America was imbued with a sense of sacredness. Hence, this was not merely a profanation generated by the addictive properties of Nicotiana's major alkaloid. It was, in a sense, part of what I have elsewhere referred to as a democratized shamanism (von Gernet 1992a:178, 1995:73–74), in which all members of an egalitarian society had the potential to "dream" and acquire spiritual power for themselves and their community. At the same time, shamans continued to use tobacco, and the leaf was still held in high esteem as the most important gift any human could offer to spirit beings throughout the cosmos.

## Tobacco Shamanism

In my review of Johannes Wilbert's *Tobacco and Shamanism in South America* (von Gernet 1998b:713), I noted that I was left with a nagging question. Wilbert (1987:149–150) suggested that paleo-Indian hunters practiced a "drug-free" shamanism and that the use of tobacco (and, indeed, psychoactive plants in general) originated with "neo-Indian farmers" who developed slash-and-burn agriculture. This seems to contradict the widely accepted belief that the original immigrants who peopled the New World carried with them ideological baggage that included a cultural predisposition for the use of psychoactive plants to attain the altered states of consciousness and visions so important in the religion of hunter-gatherers (Dobkin de Rios 1984:6–7; Furst 1972:ix, 1976:2–6; LaBarre 1970; Schultes and Hofmann 1979:27–30; von Gernet 1992a:173, 1995:68). If the New World psychotropic complex is an archaic residue from Mesolithic Asia, how can the use of psychotropics, including tobacco, be "of relatively late standing?" (Wilbert 1987:150).

Wilbert's argument appears to be based on the observation that in postcontact South America, stimulants and narcotics were confined to horticultural peoples; this knowledge is then projected back into prehistory through what is commonly known as the direct historical approach. I have defended similar forms of analogical reasoning on the grounds that there are some Amerindian culture traits that resist change and exhibit remarkable temporal continuity (von Gernet 1992c, 1993a:68–69). Using the same logic, however, it can be argued that the harvesting of *N. rustica* among foraging societies such as the Micmac indicates that tobacco *preceded* the spread of a horticultural mode of subsistence. The argument is fortified by the fact that other hunter-gatherers, such as the Crow of Montana, had elaborate tobacco-planting ceremonies (Lowie 1920). It is further strengthened by ethnolinguistic evidence that tobacco became part of Iroquoian culture prior

to the adoption of corn and other crops (von Gernet 1992a:179). As Furst (1976:27) notes, there is "no reason why the first cultigens should not have been intended to feed the spirit rather than the stomach."

The most instructive ethnographic analog for a prehistoric diffusion of smoking is the case of the Inuit (or "Eskimo" as they are still often called in the United States). The Inuit received pipes and tobacco not from their Amerindian neighbors to the south but from Russian fur traders in Asia. By the nineteenth century, tobacco had completely circumnavigated the world on European ships and was reintroduced into the New World from the west. This paradox offers us a unique opportunity to see what happened when a New World culture was first exposed to tobacco. Interestingly, the early reports speak of giddiness, intoxication, and prostration in Inuit smokers, suggesting that the habit was easily adapted to the cataleptic trances of an extant ecstatic shamanism (Sherman 1972:49–51; von Gernet 1995:80).

I propose, as a working hypothesis, that the earliest use of tobacco in the New World was generated by the same shamanistic predisposition to seek altered states of consciousness that led to the development of other hallucinogenic plant use. The tobaccos were among the plants that provided empirical support for symbolic power and communication with spirit beings, and hence they were added to an existing repertoire of similar substances. *N. rustica* underwent an artificial selection process by human foragers who frequented sites of wild growth during seasonal rounds. This process may have affected the species' alkaloid content and geographic distribution but had relatively little impact on its overall ability to survive without human intervention. The adoption of a food-producing economy and a concomitant trend toward a more sedentary life were independent and later developments that afforded opportunities for intensifying the production of *N. rustica* at the same time that rising population densities necessitated an increased supply.

Meanwhile, the development of a democratized shamanism meant that tobacco use, originally reserved for the blowing and sucking rituals of the medico-religious specialist, became popular among all those who circumvented the hegemony of the shaman and sought their own direct communication with spirit beings during vision quests. The rampant addiction documented in the early historic record was, in a sense, an indigenous secularization of the habit, augmented by the addition of European imports. Nevertheless, vestiges of a shamanistic origin lingered in the form of pipe ceremonialism, bird associations, and the ubiquitous tobacco invocation.

It is unlikely that any further work on the ethnohistoric and ethnographic literature will enable the testing of these propositions or furnish definitive answers about the timing and chronology of the events. This will come only through the kinds of detailed archaeological investigations that are currently under way in North America but are unfortunately lacking on the southern continent.

## Notes

1. Johannes Wilbert (1987:150) defines tobacco shamanism as the use of tobacco by a shaman "who uses tobacco, whether exclusively or not, to be ordained, to officiate, and to achieve altered states of consciousness." This concept, as well as related ones such as "tobacco societies" and "tobacco priesthoods," is discussed in detail in chapter 13 of this book.

2. For example, see Blakeslee 1981; Brown 1989; Hafner 1962; R. Hall 1983; Le Sueur 1952; Paper 1988; M. Schroeder 1989; Springer 1981; Turnbaugh 1979, 1984.

3. See Brooks 1937–1952, 2:30; Burrage 1906:159; Dickson 1954:133; Harrington 1932:17–18; Heizer 1947:261–262; Porter 1979:184; Setchell 1921:405; von Gernet 1988:124–125; Wright 1965:287.

4. This is discussed in detail in chapter 5 of this book. Also see Adams 1990a:133; Beinhart 1941; Castetter 1943:322–323; Haberman 1984:275; Lowery 1911:33; Spinden 1950:89, 94–95; Switzer 1969:10, 49, 51; White 1941, 1942, 1943.

5. There are many sources for this confirmation, including the following: Brooks 1937–1952, 1:247, 530, 4:400; Dickson 1954:29, 31, 59, 84, 102; Dixon 1921:32–33; Elferink 1983: 112–113; Furst 1976:23, 25; Liberman and Liberman 1975:18–19; M. Porter 1948:142–143; Richter 1928:443; Robicsek 1978:37, 44, 46–47, 58; Spinden 1950:37, 88–89; Thompson 1970b:111–112; von Gernet 1988:91; Wilbert 1987:6.

# 4

# Ethnobotanical Notes from Zuni Pueblo

Carol B. Brandt

## Editor's Introduction

This chapter consists of field notes made by Carol Brandt at the Pueblo of Zuni in the summer of 1995. Originally Brandt did not intend them to serve as a chapter, but when I read them, I asked if they might be included in this book because they serve as an excellent example of how ethnobotanists collect their information. Also, they demonstrate how difficult it can be to collect Native American tobacco. After two unsuccessful attempts to do so, Mr. PL, a member of the *Ne we 'kwe* medicine society at Zuni Pueblo, was finally able to find it, and later he gave it to Carol. He also explained how the Zuni Indians still use wild tobacco, as their grandfathers did many years ago. Figure 2, from Cushing's book *Zuni Breadstuff*, illustrates how one of his grandfathers might have used it.

## Interview with PL while Hiking in the Zuni Reservation, August 20, 1994

PL and I hiked together to an old sheep corral on the east side of the large mesa, Dowa Yalanne, where I've found wild tobacco (*Nicotiana attenuata*) in previous years. We didn't find anything this year, since the summer rains were late and the landscape was still brown and dry. We checked one more corral along the Zuni River with no luck. During our hiking, however, we were able to talk about tobacco.

According to PL, tobacco at Zuni is not the property of any one medicine group or kiva. Tobacco is used exclusively by men and is smoked in the kivas and medicine lodges, as well as during hunting.

Tobacco is picked when it is still green and flowering. The whole plant is collected and hung upside down in a cool, dark place to dry. Only the leaves are used, and they are often ground or crushed on a metate. If someone runs out of tobacco he can borrow it from other kiva groups or medicine societies.

There are no taboos concerning tobacco or growing it in a part of a yard or garden, but no one seems to cultivate it in Zuni.

Tobacco is used by hunters when they make a kill. The hunter brings the deer home, where he and his family "smoke it," or offer a blessing by exhaling smoke on the deer. The hunter and his family lay the deer out on the floor of their living room upon arriving at home and dress it in a woman's traditional manta or a man's kilt, depending on the sex of the deer. Then the hunter smokes a cigarette of wild tobacco and blows the smoke over the deer. In this way they "feed the ancestors" of the deer.

Tobacco is also smoked when men go to collect Douglas fir (*Psuedotsuga menziesii*) branches for the kachinas' costumes as part of the night dances. The men say a prayer and smoke tobacco before taking branches.

I did not ask whether commercial cigarettes were used as a substitute when no traditional tobacco could be found. I find this an inter-

Figure 2. Zuni man smoking a ceremonial cigarette. From Cushing 1920, courtesy of AMS Press.

esting question since at Shalako, one of the most important winter ceremonies, many of the priests who accompany the Council of the Gods smoke commercial cigarettes.

### Interview with PL at Zuni Pueblo, September 3, 1994

PL and I had hoped to continue our search for wild tobacco growing in old, abandoned sheep corrals, but the weather did not cooperate today. While the rain kept us inside we continued our discussion about tobacco.

Generally ceremonial "cigarettes" are dried reed-grass (*Phragmites communis*) stems that are packed with dried, crushed tobacco (*N. attenuata*). These cigarettes with the reed-grass stems are used only during the night dances at Zuni that occur in the late winter and early spring. Ceremonial cigarettes for other occasions

are made from dried inner corn husks, in which the dried, crushed tobacco is rolled. The smoke from these cigarettes is used to bless Douglas fir branches that are used by kachina dancers or to bless yucca (*Yucca baccata*) leaves that are used as wands by kachinas. The cigarettes are lit and the smoke exhaled on the objects to be used by the kachinas in ceremonial activities.

The stems of wild tobacco are never used; only the leaves are picked from the dried plant. Some of the flowers and seeds are inadvertently collected when the leaves are removed and crushed. The whole plant is collected when flowering in the late summer and hung by the roots in a dark place until dried. Then the leaves are removed and crushed by hand or on a metate and stored in an old commercial tobacco tin or in a glass jar.

The Zuni term for smoke is *boli k'ya*. The command or request to bless someone or an object with smoke from tobacco is *aboli k'ya*.

The Zuni word for tobacco is *ana* or *ana'de*. The Zuni term for leaves is *hi ya' chiwe*; singular is *hiya' chinne*.

When tobacco is collected, a person must "pay to the plant." A Zuni man will give an offering with cornmeal, sprinkling the plant and the ground around it with the cornmeal and saying a prayer as payment. Sometimes men also "fix a lunch and feed the plant." That is, a small portion of food such as bread is left on the ground near where the plant is growing.

Only men collect tobacco, and only men at Zuni smoke wild tobacco. The prayers for the use of tobacco at Zuni are known only by men. Tobacco is only used in ceremonial settings and not in any social settings. PL views tobacco that is collected as entirely different from commercial cigarettes.

Tobacco is also used medicinally for skin irritations. Finely ground, dried tobacco leaves are mixed with water to form a paste and applied to the irritation. Some people apply this paste to bald spots on their head to make hair grow.

Tobacco at Zuni is not intentionally propagated, cultivated, or encouraged in any way. Men look for tobacco at abandoned sheep corrals, where it tends to grow in soil rich with sheep manure. During my plant collecting trips I have noted that other members of the Solanaceae family are also found in this context.

When asked, "How do you identify tobacco; what do you look for that tells you this plant is tobacco?" PL replied that the pungent odor of the plant, along with the yellow tubular flowers, was the characteristic that he used for identification.

PL says that he is not aware of any changes in the use of traditional tobacco in his lifetime. He says that his grandfathers used it exactly the way he and other Zuni men are using it today.

# PART TWO

# Description of the
# North American Tobaccos

# 5

## Botanical Description of the
## North American Tobacco Species

Joseph C. Winter

In Yurok Indian mythology, Pulekukwerek is a small humanoid *woge* (immortal) with horns on his buttocks who survives a number of harrowing tests, slays a variety of terrible monsters, and helps create the world. Pulekukwerek grows from a tobacco plant and then gives this powerful drug to the first people:

At first tobacco was not used. People took pepperwood [California bay] leaves, dried them, and smoked them as tobacco. Many were killed by that, it was so strong. Then Pulekukwerek . . . threw away the pepperwood tobacco, [and] he said, "I will give you seeds so you can raise it for yourselves." Then they planted it, grew it, and smoked it after it was dry.

But some tobacco was still too strong. People smoking it fell over and died. Then Pulekukwerek, where he lived (at the) downriver (end of the world), heard that this tobacco was even worse than the other and killed more people. So he came upriver again. All along they were raising tobacco. He came to Rekwoi. There he began to smoke. He said, "No one will be killed by this," and he blew tobacco out from his hand. Then he went up along the river to other places.

At Kenek, he heard, the Earthquakes [called the strong-tobacco brothers] lived, ten of them, and it was a bad place to smoke. That is why he went to Kenek, because the ten Earthquake brothers killed people there with their tobacco. When they saw anyone coming, one of them immediately gave him to smoke. When he had

finished, another one came to give him smoke. Sometimes when six men had given him their pipes, he was dead; sometimes seven killed him. . . .

Pulekukwerek came into the sweathouse. He saw much tobacco hanging in baskets in the sweathouse, drying. He said, "That is what I want: I like to smoke." Then he smoked (with them). He smoked seven pipes. He was talking as if he did not feel anything: they saw him act like this. When he had smoked nine pipes, they saw that he was feeling it. When he had smoked ten, he fell over. They carried him out and threw him in the bush.

[After he came back to life] He said, "This tobacco will kill no one any more. Anyone can smoke it." So it is that no one is killed by tobacco, because Pulekukwerek stopped them from killing people there. "Even," said Pulekukwerek, "though there is some tobacco which they will feel a little, nevertheless it will not kill them." (Kroeber 1976:367–368)

The actual history of the evolution of tobacco and the relationships among its many species are almost as complex as Pulekukwerek's heroic attempts to make it safe. Figures 3 and 4 show two researchers' versions of the phylogeny of the seven species used by native North Americans. The first is the basic taxonomy developed by Thomas Goodspeed (1954:1–2), with certain refinements at the generic and higher levels by William D'Arcy (1991:table 6.1). The second is a chloroplast (cp) DNA genome study of six of the species by Richard Olmstead and Jeffrey

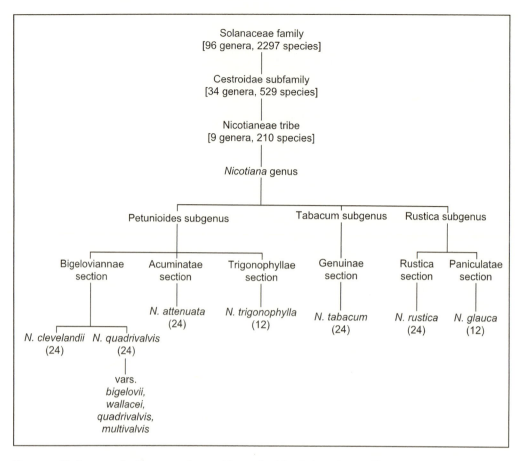

Figure 3. Phylogeny of tobacco species used by native North Americans. Chromosome numbers are in parentheses. After Goodspeed 1954:1–2; D'Arcy 1991:table 6.1.

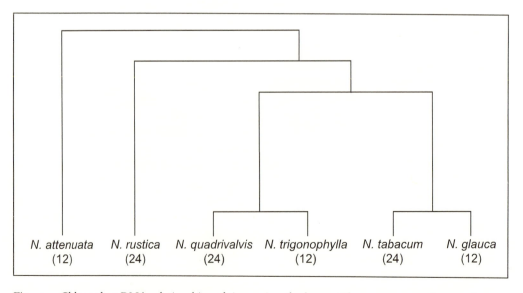

Figure 4. Chloroplast DNA relationships of six species of tobacco. Chromosome numbers are in parentheses. After Olmstead and Palmer 1991: fig. 9.3. N. *clevelandii* was not in their study.

Palmer (1991:fig. 9.3). The recent cp DNA results are more accurate, but Goodspeed's basic phylogeny is still accepted as the standard by most botanists, ethnobiologists, archaeologists, and other researchers interested in tobacco. Both are used in the following descriptions of the various species ingested by native North Americans.

As shown by figure 3, the tobacco genus belongs to the Solanaceae family, which includes 96 genera with 2,297 species (D'Arcy 1991). Relevant subdivisions in this family are the Cestroidae subfamily (which has 34 genera with 529 species), and the Nicotianeae tribe (9 genera with 210 species). Figure 5 illustrates the relationships of these and other taxa in the family. Important genera in the related subfamilies and tribes that are used for medicine, food, and landscaping (and that are mentioned in this book) include *Datura* (toloache or jimsonweed), *Lycium* (wolfberry), *Capsicum* (pepper), *Solanum* (potato), *Lycopersicon* (tomato), *Physalis* (groundcherry), *Hyoscyamus* (henbane), *Mandragora* (mandrake), *Atropa* (belladonna), *Chamaesaracha, Margaranthus,* and *Petunia.*

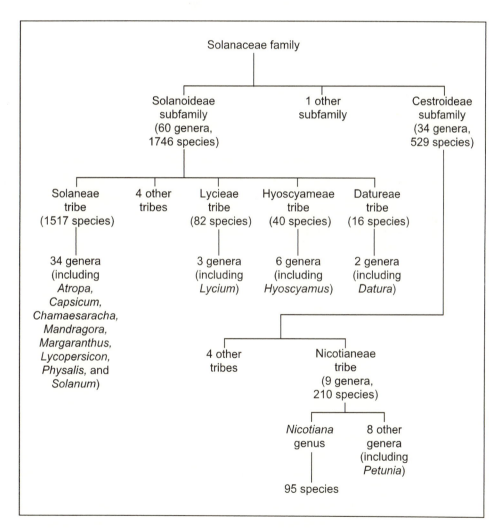

Figure 5. Subfamilies, tribes, and relevant genera in the Solanaceae family. After D'Arcy 1991:table 6.1.

There are 95 species of tobacco. Twenty are in Australia and Polynesia, one is in Africa, and the remainder are in the Americas, with most of the latter in South America, considered the homeland of the genus. The one African species has a distinctive morphology; D'Arcy (1991:92) considers it recent "noise" that has nothing to do with its home range, whereas several other authors propose that it is a very old, endemic relict (Merxmüller and Buttler 1975; H. Smith 1979). "Long distance dispersal from the western Pacific to South Africa seems as unlikely as from South America. The time and method of arrival of this restricted African species remains a tantalising subject" (Symon 1991:143).

Various authors have different opinions about the route and timing of the movement of *Nicotiana* from South America to Australia. Goodspeed (1954) proposed that it occurred when Australia, Antarctica, and South America were joined, before they began to break up about 150 million years ago (mya). D'Arcy (1991: 104) agreed that the ancestral tobacco probably migrated to Australia before the large landmass began to break up. D. E. Symon concurred that the migration took place long ago, but probably after the breakup of the continent. Olmstead and Palmer (1991), in contrast, argue for a relatively recent colonization, on the basis of a lack of cp DNA divergence among the Australian species.

Despite this disagreement, there is no question that the aborigines of Australia used wild tobacco, probably well back into prehistory. The Alyawara of central Australia still ingest up to five *Nicotiana* species for religious and medicinal purposes (O'Connell, Latz, and Barnett 1983:97).

Neither is there any disagreement about the ancestral homeland of all tobacco species: South America. Many of the Solanaceae genera (probably including *Nicotiana*) certainly evolved in South America by the end of the Cretaceous geological period, some 65 mya. The overlapping present-day distribution of the wild species of the three *Nicotiana* subgenera (*Petunioides*, *Rustica*,

and *Tabacum*) in the uplands of western South America suggests that this was the area of ultimate origin (map 2). Wild species of the more primitive *Rustica* and *Tabacum* subgenera are restricted to the southern temperate and upland tropical zones, and although the more advanced subgenus *Petunioides* occurs elsewhere, in North America, Africa, and Australia, certain of its species also grow in the upland South American zone, where it probably originated (D'Arcy 1991:104; Goodspeed 1954:3). According to D'Arcy (1991:104): "Present climates confine the diverse Solanaceae of temperate South America and western Peru to the localities where they are now found, but in the past there were alternating periods of wet and dry, some wet periods being very wet and some dry periods very dry. . . . These should have permitted the migration outwards to eastern temperate South America or to the tropical uplands in the north."

The evolution of the two domesticated tobacco species (*N. tabacum* and *N. rustica*) is discussed later in this chapter, along with their human-aided movement to North America. The ancestral wild species in the subgenus *Petunioides* migrated north to Mexico no earlier than the Upper Pliocene or Early Pleistocene and no later than the Late Pleistocene, at least as envisioned by Goodspeed (1954). According to Goodspeed's model, the ancestral species of the desert and upland North American species (*N. attenuata*, *N. trigonophylla*, *N. quadrivalvis*, and *N. clevelandii*) could not have entered Central America prior to the Upper Pliocene or Early Pleistocene, because tropical conditions before that time (and after the Late Pleistocene) would not have allowed these dryland species to survive in Central America. It was only during the Upper Pliocene and Pleistocene that desert conditions pushed south from Mexico into Panama, linking the environments of North and South America and thereby allowing the ancestral dryland species to move north. The later replacement of the Pleistocene pluvial conditions with more arid environments after 10,000 years before present (B.P.) in northern Mexico and the

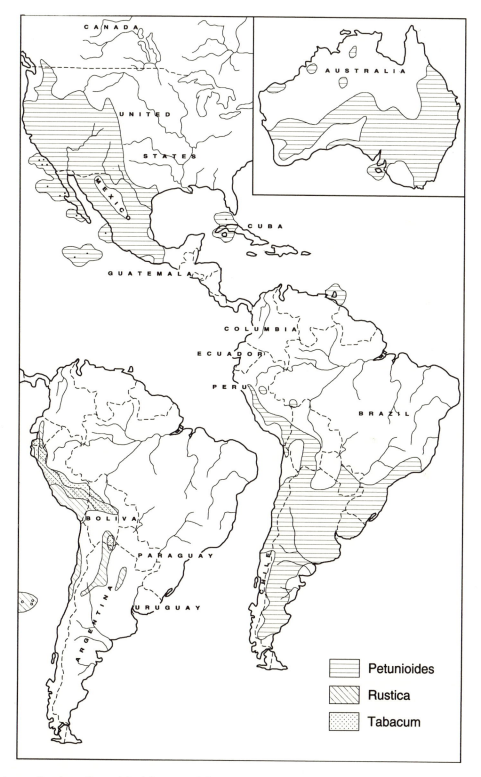

Map 2. Goodspeed's model of the natural distribution of the three subgenera of wild tobacco (Goodspeed 1954:fig. 3).

southwestern United States then allowed *N. attenuata* and the other species (or their ancestors) to migrate even farther north, eventually reaching northern California and the Great Basin. From there, prehistoric Indian encouragement extended them even farther to the north, all the way to the Alaska panhandle and interior Canada. As discussed in a later chapter, prehistoric Indians could even have aided the species' earliest movements into northern Mexico and the Southwest.

Following is a description of each of the seven species, along with a short review of its archaeological record. Detailed descriptions of each species can be found in Goodspeed's definitive book (1954), which is long out of print. Relevant portions of his decriptions are quoted here, following his organization by subgenera.

but occasionally obconic. Limb 10 to 15 mm wide, lobed or pentagonal, white, pink or red. Stamens inserted on base of corolla throat, erect, oriented to upper side of flower or evenly spaced, anthers of two longer pairs near mouth of corolla or slightly exserted, fifth stamen shorter than either pair. Capsule narrowly elliptic, ovoid or orbicular, acute or blunt, exserted or included, 15 to 20 mm long. Seeds spherical or broadly elliptic, *ca.* 0.5 mm long, brown, ridges fluted. Embryo straight. Chromosome number, 24 pairs. (Goodspeed 1954:372–375)

*Nicotiana tabacum* (fig. 6) is the most important tobacco species in modern agriculture and international trade. Estimated worldwide pro-

## Nicotiana tabacum

SUBGENUS *Tabacum* (Don) Goodspeed (1945: 337)
Section *Genuinae* Goodspeed (1945:338)
*Nicotiana tabacum* Linnaeus, Sp. Pl. 1 (1753) 180

Stout viscid annual or limited perennial 1 to 3 m high. Stem thick, erect branches few, rapidly ascending. Leaves decurrent, the largest at least 5 dm long, ovate, elliptic or lanceolate, base tapering or winged-subpetiolate, apex acuminate. Panicle with distinct rachis, several branches, branches usually compound, commonly shorter than rachis. Pedicels 5 to 10 (15) mm long, later 10 to 20 (25) mm. Floral calyx cylindric to cylindric-campanulate, 12 to 20 (25) mm long, viscid, teeth triangular-acuminate, shorter than or equaling calyx tube, unequal. Corolla little if at all curved, outer surface puberulent, tube proper (7) 10 to 15 mm long, 2.5 to 3 mm wide, throat (23) 25 to 40 mm long, lower half cylindric, 3 to 5 mm wide, pale greenish cream, upper half similar in color or pink to red commonly abruptly expanded into deep cup 7 to 12 mm wide,

Figure 6. *Nicotiana tabacum* Linnaeus ("Machu Picchu"). Inflorescence, 1/4X; entire flower, tubular part, limb, capsule, and stamen insertion, 1X; leaf, 3/8X. From Goodspeed 1954:fig. 74; Wilbert 1987:fig. 2.

duction in 1992 was 18 billion pounds (USBC 1993:665, 699), and the species was grown across the globe, except in the Arctic and sub-arctic zones. Less than 10 percent of the world-wide production was in the United States. Though semitropical in origin, from the eastern Andes of South America, *N. tabacum* is culti-vated in Russia to about 50 degrees N latitude and in Australia and New Zealand to about 40 degrees S. It requires a frost-free period of between 100 and 130 days from the date of transplanting to maturity (McMurtrey 1981: 464). It sometimes escapes from cultivation and grows for a generation or two as a weed, but it has never been found as a truly wild plant, and there are no wild varieties (Heiser 1992:54).

As discussed in chapter 2, *Nicotiana tabacum* was and to some degree still is grown by Native Americans in South America and in the south-ern part of North America—that is, in Meso-america, the Caribbean, southern Arizona, and south Texas (photos 21 and 22). When Spanish colonies were established in the Caribbean and Mesoamerica in the late 1400s and early 1500s, Spaniards began raising the *N. tabacum* vari-eties that the Taino, Maya, and other local In-dians grew. Within a short time they established tobacco plantations throughout the region, as far south as Venezuela.

*N. tabacum* has considerable variation, be-cause Native Americans, Spaniards, and other Euro-Americans created numerous morpho-logically distinct types. Portuguese and Spanish sailors took seeds of *N. tabacum* around the world, and English planters at Jamestown in Virginia had adopted it by 1612. Previously the planters had grown the local *N. rustica*, but the English settlers found its powerful smoke harsh and irritating, so John Rolfe obtained *N. tabacum* var. *Orinoco* seeds from Spanish col-onists in Trinidad and Caracas and began plant-ing that species. The first shipment of Rolfe's tobacco sailed to England in 1613, and the pro-duct found a rapidly expanding market through-out Europe and many parts of Asia (Gerstel 1976:273; Tobacco Institute n.d.:3).

Photo 21. Mopan Maya *Nicotiana tabacum* from Guatamala, raised in Albuquerque, New Mexico. Height of plant 1.251 m. Photo by Joseph Winter. JCWSP24.

Thousands of commercial and native types of *N. tabacum* have been developed. As William Setchell (Setchell 1921:3) observed, this species includes as varied an assemblage "of varieties, forms and suspected hybrids as ever were brought together under one specific name." The 1993–1994 U.S. Tobacco Germplasm Catalog lists no fewer than 2,358 cultivars (varieties), 617 of

Photo 22. Mexican *Nicotiana tabacum* Burley, with Huichol Indian child laborers. Courtesy of José Hernández-Claire, Mexico.

which are grown in the U.S. and the rest introduced from elsewhere.

*N. tabacum* varieties that are relevant to this book include the Mopan Maya type illustrated in photo 21 and the *Undulata* variety that is probably grown in southern Arizona by the Akimel O'odham and Tohono O'odham (Pima and Papago) and Yaqui. Other possible varieties

that I have collected (both directly and indirectly) from the Zapotec, Cherokee, Yumbo, Shipibo, and other Native American groups are listed in table 22.

As illustrated by photo 21, Native American varieties generally have smaller leaves than the commercial types and are not as tall. Most Indians leave their plants "untopped" (that is,

Table 22: Examples of Native American *Nicotiana tabacum* seeds in the Native American Plant Cooperative (NAPC) in Albuquerque, New Mexico

| Specimen No. | Group | Type Name | Origin |
|---|---|---|---|
| 14, 24, 56 | Mopan Maya | ? | Petén, Guatamala |
| 15, 22 | Yumbo | ? | Amazonian Ecuador |
| 33 | Zapotec | *Tabaco rosa* | Southern Oaxaca, Mexico |
| 34 | Zapotec | *Tabaco blanco* | Southern Oaxaca, Mexico |
| 147[a] | Huichol/mestizo | ? | Cantilez, Nayarit, Mexico |
| 13B | Cherokee | ? | Oklahoma? |
| 53 | Archidona | ? | Tutakano River, Amazonian Ecuador |
| 55 | Huatla Mazatec | ? | Oaxaca, Mexico |
| 48[b] | ? | *Rosado* | Oaxaca, Mexico |
| 181, 215 | Inca? | *Machu-Picchu* | Old terraces at Machu-Picchu, Peru |
| 179[c] | Yaqui | *Yuaqui* | Southern Arizona |
| 180 | Ika | ? | Valley of Donachui, Columbia |
| 184, 185 | Kofan | *K'iumba* | Near Dureno and Napa, Ecuador |
| 182, 183 | Tarahumara | *Wipaku, wipanto* | Chihuahua, Mexico |
| 186[b] | ? | *Piciete* | Oaxaca, Mexico |
| 187 | Jamamadi | ? | Río Purus, Brazilian Amazon |
| 242 | Shipibo | *Rome* | Río Ucayali, Peruvian Amazon |

a  Reportedly from a mixed Huichol/mestizo community. The author also observed *N. tabacum* growing at the Huichol village of Nueva Colonia.

b  Unknown whether Indian or not.

c  Reported as *N. tabacum* var. *undulatum*.

they do not pinch off the flower buds) so that they can collect the seeds and admire the flowers, which means that the leaves and plants are smaller. Also, commercial types have been bred for 500 years for larger leaves, so even an un-topped commercial variety has larger leaves than most Native American types.

The nicotine content of some of the Native American varieties, as well as the content of several commercial varieties, is discussed in a later chapter. The many varieties differ in chemical, morphological, and physical characteristics. Certain types have specific commercial uses. For example, there are flue-cured, aromatic types that mainly go into blends for cigarettes; burley, which is used for cigarette and some pipe tobacco; and fermented types, often used in cigars (Gerstel 1976:273–274; TABAMEX 1989).

Because of its commercial value, *N. tabacum* is the most extensively studied tobacco species, with its entire chloroplast (cp) genome sequence mapped out (Olmstead and Palmer 1991). Its ancestry is very complex, and there is considerable disagreement over its exact relationship with other species. One thing that is certain is that it is amphidiploid—that is, it combines the 24 chromosomes of two ancestral species (each with 12 chromosomes) that hybridized at some point in the past.

Map 3 shows the locations of some of the presumed ancestral species. Most authors agree that *Nicotiana sylvestris* represents the maternal lineage of *N. tabacum*, but they disagree on the paternal species. Possibilities include *N. glutinosa*, *N. tomentosiformis*, and *N. otophora*, or a form antecedent to them (Gerstel 1976:274; Goodspeed 1954:1–3; Olmstead and Palmer 1991:163).

Today, *N. tabacum* is unknown in the wild, and its range of cultivation (by Native Americans) is to the east of the Andes, as well as in Mesoamerica and southern Arizona and formerly in the Caribbean and south Texas. Richard Schultes and Robert Raffauf (1990), along with Johannes Wilbert (1987), describe its many uses

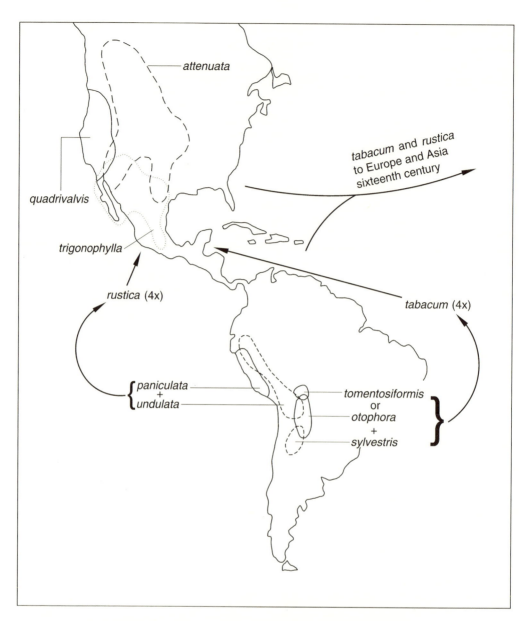

Map 3. Gerstel's model of the evolutionary geography of the cultivated tobaccos (Gerstel 1976:fig. 79.1).

in South America. Table 23 lists some of the many South American tribes that grow *N. tabacum*, as recorded by Schultes and Raffauf and others.

Map 4 illustrates the areas of traditional Native American use of *N. tabacum* in North America. Only two archaeological sites may have produced it, though both identifications are questionable and probably unfounded. Nevertheless, it is entirely possible that *N. tabacum* was used by prehistoric Native Americans at the sites, since historic groups in the same regions are known to have grown it. One of the identified specimens came from Double Butte Cave, a Classic Hohokam (ancestral Pima) archaeological site dating between A.D. 1100

## Table 23: South American Tribes Using *Nicotiana tabacum*

| Group | Native Term for Tobacco |
|---|---|
| Aguaruna | — |
| Amahuaca[a] | Romu |
| Amuesha[a] | Yeats |
| Baniwa | E'li |
| Barasana | — |
| Bare | A'li |
| Bora | — |
| Boras | — |
| Campa[a] | Sheri |
| Caqueta | — |
| Cocamas | — |
| Coto | — |
| Culina[a] | Ssina |
| Deni[a] | Tsina |
| Desano | Mu-lu', pagari-mule |
| Ika[b] | — |
| Inambari[a] | Shahuano |
| Ingano | — |
| Jamamadi[c] | — |
| Jivaro | — |
| Kofan | Kherm'ba, K'iumba[d] |
| Kubeo | — |
| Machiguenga[a] | Seri |
| Makuna | — |
| Mirana | — |
| Muinane | — |
| Nonoyu | — |
| Omagua | — |
| Omurana | — |
| Piro[a] | Yiri |
| Putumayo | — |
| Shipibo[e] | Rome |
| Siona | — |
| Taninuka | — |
| Tariana | Ye'-ma |
| Tikuna | — |
| Tukano | — |
| Waika | — |
| Witoto | De'oo-we |
| Yakuna | Lukux-ri |
| Yamamadi[a] | Shina |
| Zaparo | — |

Source: Schultes and Raffauf 1990:432–436 unless otherwise noted.
a  From Rutter 1990:159, 229.
b  Specimens in Harvard University Herbarium and Botanical Museum of Stockholm.
c  Specimen in Harvard University Herbarium.
d  *Kherm'ba* is the term given in Schultes and Raffauf 1990. K'iumba is the term used on the voucher specimen at Harvard University Herbarium.
e  From Arevalo Valera 1994; Winter 1995c.

and 1400, where material from cane cigarettes was identified as *N. tabacum* (Haury 1945:194). The second sample was pollen from the Rio Sanate Abajo contact-period Taino site on the island of Hispaniola (Fortuna 1978). Later chapters demonstrate how identifications of tobacco species based on pollen are all but impossible.

Elsewhere, unspecified tobacco appears to have been identified from an archaeological site along the north-central coast of Peru, in a pre-ceramic Period VI component dating between 2500 and 1800 B.C. (Lanning 1967:60; Pearsall 1992:178). This material could represent early *N. tabacum*, *N. rustica*, or a local wild species. *N. tabacum* was undoubtedly present in South America in prehistoric times, since it was domesticated there prior to European contact, and it has been collected growing on old terraces at the ruins of Machu Picchu. But without the use of advanced flotation techniques to recover its tiny seeds, tobacco is very difficult to identify in archaeological contexts.

## *Nicotiana rustica*

SUBGENUS *Rustica* (Don) Goodspeed (1945: 336)
Section *Rusticae* Goodspeed (1945:337)
*Nicotiana rustica* Linnaeus, Sp. Pl. 1 (1753) 180
    Coarse annual 0.5 to 1.5 m high. Stems one, less commonly several, erect, rather thick, moist- to viscid-pubescent, branches more slender. Leaves fleshy, minutely puberulent or viscid-puberulent; blade 10 to 15 (30) cm long, ovate, elliptic or cordate, sometimes elliptic-lanceolate or subrotund, base often unequal; petiole much shorter than blade. Panicles narrow and compact or broad and loose, central axis distinct, branches acute. Pedicels 3 to 4 mm long, later 5 to 7 mm. Floral calyx 8 to 15 mm long, poculiform to cylindric, pubescent, membranes narrow, longish, teeth (broadly triangular, acute, one much longer). Corolla greenish yellow, 12 to 17 mm long exclusive of limb, puberulent

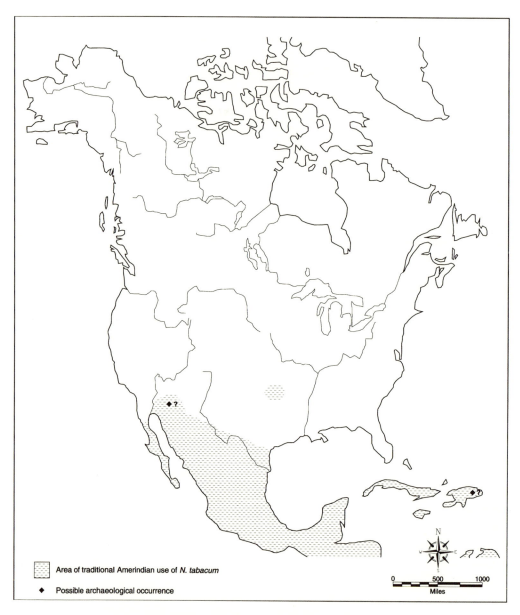

Map 4. Areas of traditional native North American use of *Nicotiana tabacum*.

exteriorly, tube proper commonly 3 mm long, 2 mm wide, throat *ca.* 3 X as long, 6 to 8 mm wide, broadly obconic with slight contraction at mouth, limb 3 to 6 mm wide, lobes very short, obtuse, entire or apiculate. Stamens white-pilose for *ca.* 2 mm above insertion on base of corolla throat, 4 extending nearly to mouth, sigmoidly erect, 5th shorter. Capsule elliptic-ovoid to subglobose, 7 to 16 mm long, included or nearly. Seeds elliptic, oval or angular, 0.7 to 1.1 mm long, dusky brown, surface fluted-reticulate. Embryo straight or bent. Chromosome number, 24 pairs. (Goodspeed 1954:351–353)

The second domesticated tobacco species utilized by Native Americans is *N. rustica* (fig. 7), which is still used throughout the eastern wood-

lands and parts of the U.S. Southwest for ceremonial purposes, as well as in Mesoamerica
and perhaps in South America. Another highly
polymorphic species (table 24), *N. rustica* may
have been domesticated long before *N. tabacum*,
judging from its widespread use throughout
parts of North America and the fact that it
probably originated many thousands of miles
to the south, in the eastern Andes in South
America. Only one possible wild variety (*N.
rustica* var. *pavonii* [Dun] Good.) has been identified—in southwest Ecuador, southern Peru,
and northern Bolivia (Goodspeed 1954:353).
Many other varieties are cultivated, though they
frequently "escape" to the wild and grow for
several generations on their own. The 1993–
1994 U.S. Tobacco Germplasm Catalog lists 80
cultivated varieties and 5 wild types (*pavonii*,
*brasilia*, and three kinds of *pumila*), but it is
likely that only *pavonii* is truly wild.

This was the first tobacco encountered by the
English colonists at Jamestown, in 1607, the
one they found "poore and weake, and of a
byting taste" (Tobacco Institute n.d.:3). Actually,
there is nothing weak about it, as it is stronger,
with a higher nicotine content, than *N. tabacum*,
the species the English adopted from Spanish
colonists in Trinidad and Venezuela. In addition
to its use by Native Americans, *N. rustica* is
cultivated by peasants in eastern Europe and
Asia Minor for smoking and other forms of
ingestion and in the United States and elsewhere
for insecticide (Heiser 1969:175; Siegel, Collings, and Diaz 1977:16). Because of its high
nicotine content, this species has also been used
to produce visions and other altered states of
consciousness so that shamans can communicate with the spirits, diagnose and treat illnesses, and otherwise deal with the supernatural.

Only one native North American variety of
*N. rustica* has previously been defined in the
literature, but there are many Indian types of
this highly variable species, as I have observed
and as listed in table 24. Goodspeed identified
samples of cultivated *N. rustica* collected from
the Pueblo Indian villages of Cochiti, Jemez,

Figure 7. *Nicotiana rustica* var. *brasilia* Schrank.
Inflorescence, 3/8X; entire flower, tubular part,
limb, and capsule, 2X; leaf, 1/2X. From
Goodspeed 1954:fig. 67.

and Santo Domingo as closely resembling the
*pumila* variety, which is the lowest-growing of
the many described varieties (Goodspeed, personal communication, cited in White 1942:59–
60). Later he provided the following description
of the *pumila* variety:

Plant 6 to 8 dm high; stems several from the
ground level, fastigate, viscid throughout
but more so above; leaves plane, blade
oblong-elliptic or ovate-elliptic, base oblique,
apex very obtuse to distinctly acute or even
mucronate; inflorescences loosely brushy;
calyx broadly tubular, *ca.* 13 mm long and
8 mm broad, one segment much larger;
corolla 15 mm long, throat at most 7 mm
wide, limb 5 mm wide, lobes very short,

Table 24: Types of *Nicotiana rustica* Raised by Native North Americans

| Group | Type Name | Specimen No.[a] | Publication/Other Source |
|---|---|---|---|
| Jemez Pueblo | Cf. *pumila; punche* | 236 | Castetter 1943:322; University of New Mexico (UNM) Herbarium records; White 1942 |
| Picuris Pueblo | *Punche* | — | Castetter 1943:322 |
| Cochiti Pueblo | Cf. *pumila; punche;* old time Cochiti | 10 | Castetter 1943:322; Cochiti Pueblo, via Native Seeds/SEARCH 1994; UNM Herbarium records; White 1942 |
| | *Ponche mexicano* | 237 | |
| Santo Domingo Pueblo | Cf. *pumila; punche;* Santo Domingo ceremonial tobacco | 11, 23 | Castetter 1943:322; Santo Domingo Pueblo, via Native Seeds/SEARCH; White 1942 |
| Taos Pueblo | *Punche* | — | Castetter 1943:322 |
| Santa Ana Pueblo | *Ponche; pumila* | 2, 232 | Castetter 1943:322; Santa Ana Native Plant Nursery; UNM Herbarium records; White 1942 |
| Isleta Pueblo | *Punche; pumila* | 16, 37, 62 | Castetter 1943:322; Isleta Pueblo, via Native Seeds/SEARCH 1994; Isleta family |
| Acoma Pueblo | *Punche* | — | Castetter 1943:322 |
| San Juan Pueblo | San Juan Pueblo | 7, 8, 25 | San Juan Pueblo, via Native Seeds/SEARCH 1994 |
| Tesuque Pueblo | Tesuque Pueblo | 29 | Tesuque Pueblo, via Santa Fe Natural Tobacco Company |
| Seneca[b] | Cf. *N. rustica* var. *texana;* Cornplanter's sacred Indian tobacco | 98, 191, 218, 218A | Botanical Museum of Stockholm; Chief Cornplanter, of Lawton, N.Y., via Rancho Santa Ana Botanic Garden; Harvard University Herbarium; University of Copenhagen |
| Seneca | Tonawanda Seneca tobacco | 196 | Tonawanda Seneca Indian Reservation, N.Y. |
| Seneca[c] | Seneca(?) tobacco; | 211 | Cattaraugus Indian Reservation, via Bailey Hortorium at Cornell University |
| Mohawk | Akwesasne Mohawk tobacco | 58, 245 | St. Regis Mohawk Reservation, via . . . Of the Jungle, Eastern Native Seed Conservancy |
| Mohawk | Kahnawage Mohawk tobacco | 169 | Kahnawage Mohawk Reserve, Montreal, via Eastern Native Seed Conservancy |
| Mohawk | Kahnawage Mohawk tobacco | 296 | Kahnawage Mohwak Reserve, Montreal, via First Nations man in Ontario |
| Oneida | Oneida tobacco | 164 | Oneida Agricultural Cooperative |
| Onondaga | Onondaga tobacco | 244 | Onondaga Reservation, via Eastern Native Seed Conservancy |
| Mohawk | Tyendinaga tobacco | 193, 194, 277 | Tyendinaga Mohawk Reserve, Ontario |
| Cayuga | Cayuga tobacco | 148 | Six Nations Reserve, Brantford, Canada, via A. von Gernet |

Table 24: Types of *Nicotiana rustica* Raised by Native North Americans (continued)

| Group | Type Name | Specimen No.[a] | Publication/Other Source |
|---|---|---|---|
| Tuscarora-Mohawk | Tuscarora-Mohawk tobacco | 195 | Tuscarora man of Mohawk ancestry, Tuscarora Reservation, N.Y. |
| Wampanoag(?)[d] | Wampanoag tobacco (?) | 171, 172 | Wampanoag Indian garden at Plimouth Plantation |
| Delaware | Delaware tobacco/ *leni kwshatay* | 246 | Oklahoma, via Eastern Native Seed Conservancy |
| Midwest Algonkian | *Medewiwin* sacred tobacco | 247 | Midwestern Algonkian, via Eastern Native Seed Conservancy |
| Pokagon Potawatomi | *Mede* tobacco | 307 | Cultural Program of Pokagon Potawatomi; seeds originally from archaeological site |
| Winnebago | Winnebago tobacco | 294 | Winnebago, via Native American man in Michigan |
| Cree | Cree tobacco | 300 | Cree |
| Cherokee | Cherokee tobacco | 13A | Oklahoma? via Native Seeds/SEARCH |
| Tarahumara | Tarahumara *el cuervo* | 239 | Botopilas Canyon, Chihuahua, Mexico, via Native Seeds/SEARCH 1994 |
| Tarahumara | *Makuchi* | 189 | Chihuahua, Mexico, via Harvard University Herbarium |
| Tarahumara | *Wiuraka* | 190 | Chihuahua, Mexico, via Harvard University Herbarium |
| Tepehuan | Tepehuan tobacco | 276 | Tepehuan, via Native Seeds/SEARCH 1997 |
| Warihio | *Makuchi* | 6 | Warihio, via Native Seeds/SEARCH 1994 |
| Huichol | *Makuchi* | 36 | Siegel et al. 1977; Huichol Indians, via Santa Fe Natural Tobacco Co. |

a   Specimen numbers are those of the Native American Plant Cooperative (NAPC), Albuquerque, New Mexico.

b   Voucher records indicate that this plant is similar to *Nicotiana rustica* var. *texana*. The seed was obtained from Chief Cornplanter of Lawton, New York, in 1915, then cultivated in 1921 at the University of California at Berkeley. Seeds and voucher specimens from the 1921 plants were sent to a number of institutions, including Rancho Santa Ana Botanic Gardens, the Botanical Museum of Stockholm, the University of Copenhagen, and Harvard University. The author raised specimens in 1994-1995 from the Rancho Santa Ana seeds. He also has seeds from the other institutions.

c   The Cornell University Bailey Hortorium voucher specimen label reads "Cattaraugus Reservation," which implies Seneca (although Cayuga is also possible).

d   Grown by Wampanoag employees at Plimouth Plantation. The original seed source is unknown.

broad, obtuse, faintly apiculate; capsule 13 to 15 mm long, exserted, rotund-oval, indehiscent or dehiscent by narrow slit, valves entire. Embryo bent. (Goodspeed 1954:356)

In 1994, I raised very similar, short specimens of *N. rustica* from seeds and seedlings collected in the Pueblo Indian villages of Santa Ana, Isleta, Santo Domingo, and San Juan. The tobacco at San Juan had been grown from Isleta seed by the San Juan Pueblo Agricultural Cooperative, under contract with the Santa Fe Natural Tobacco Company. I also collected and grew a number of much larger specimens of *N. rustica* from the Pueblo villages of Cochiti, Santo Domingo, San Juan, Isleta, and Tesuque (photo 23).

Previously, at Santa Ana Pueblo in 1936, Edward Castetter had collected a specimen of *N. rustica*, which he called "ponche" (University of New Mexico Herbarium specimen voucher no. 3599). Castetter also observed *N. rustica* "punche" at the Pueblo villages of Jemez, Picuris, Cochiti, Santo Domingo, Taos, Isleta, and Acoma. The Indians told him they had been cultivating it for at least 80 years (Castetter 1943:322). At Cochiti, Castetter collected seeds of "Ponche Mexicano" (University of New Mexico Herbarium, Edward Castetter Seed Collection, "Ponchi Mexicano," Celeniano).

Photo 1 in chapter 1 illustrates the *punche de Mexicano* grown by local Hispanics in the Rio Grande Valley. By way of comparison, photo 24 shows the *pavonii* variety, which is much shorter than most types of *N. rustica*, with smaller leaves and flowers. Photo 25 shows a large-leafed Iroquois specimen of *N. rustica*.

Leslie White (1943) concluded that *punche* had been introduced by Spaniards, and he suggested that the word *punche* had evolved from the Spanish word *pumila* (meaning low or short), rather than meaning "punch," as is commonly asssumed. Judging from my own research as well as that of Edward Castetter and Native Seeds/SEARCH (1994), there is no question that at least one type of *punche*—"punche de Mexicano"—was introduced into the Rio Grande

Photo 23. Tall, lanky *Nicotiana rustica* grown in Albuquerque, New Mexico, from seed from Santo Domingo Pueblo, New Mexico. Height of plant 1.732 m. Photo by Joseph Winter. JCWSP23.

Photo 24. *Nicotiana rustica* var. *pavonii*, grown in Albuquerque, New Mexico. Height of plant above ground surface is 0.863 m. Photo by Joseph Winter. JCWSP66.

Photo 25. Large-leafed Haudenosaunee (Iroquois) *Nicotiana rustica*. Grown from seeds from Akwesasne (St. Regis) Mohawk Reservation. Height of plant 0.976 m. Photo by Joseph Winter. JCWSP58.

Valley by early Spanish settlers. The "ponche Mexicano" at Cochiti Pueblo is also probably from this stock, while the "old time Cochiti" may represent the local indigenous variety. One or more indigenous varieties of *N. rustica* may have been grown by prehistoric Puebloans in New Mexico, so it is possible that there have been at least two sources of this powerful drug. One author adds that non-Hispanic whites additionally introduced a commercial variety of *N. rustica* in 1925 (Beinhart 1941:538–539).

All of this evidence suggests that at least three traditional types of this tobacco are still grown by the Indians and Hispanics of the Rio Grande Valley, possibly along with a fourth, commercial variety. All may be called *punche*, but there are important differences. The smallest type is *N. rustica* variety *pumila*, which Castetter collected at Santa Ana in the 1940s and which I observed there and at Isleta and San Juan in the 1990s. This diminutive type shares a number of similarities with the only variety of *N. rustica* still growing in the wild—variety *pavonii*, in South America—and it may be that it represents a very primitive type that was introduced into New Mexico at least a thousand years ago from Mexico and ultimately South America.

The second type is *punche de Mexicano*—a very large-leafed, bushy, and hardy tobacco of moderate height and with a multitude of stems and leaves. It is likely that this type originated in Mexico in prehistoric times, then was adopted by the Spaniards and brought north by the earliest New Mexican settlers, who arrived in 1598.

The third traditional type is a much taller, large-leafed variety grown at some of the pueblos, including Cochiti, Santo Domingo, San Juan, Isleta, and Tesuque. Native Seeds/SEARCH (1994) gives at least two names to this type—old time Cochiti and Santo Domingo ceremonial tobacco. This type could also date to prehistoric times.

Still other types of *N. rustica* are grown by other native North Americans, including the Mohawk, Cayuga, Tuscarora, Oneida, Onondaga, and Seneca Iroquois (Haudenosaunee) in New York and Canada. One of the Iroquois types—Cornplanter's sacred Indian tobacco—has been described as being close to *N. rustica* variety *texana* (see table 24, note *b*, and photo 10 in chapter 2).

Whatever it is called, the ancestors of this very powerful tobacco are generally accepted to have been *N. paniculata* and *N. undulata* or their predecessors (Gerstel 1976:275; Goodspeed 1954:355; Heiser 1992:54). The ranges of these closely related wild species in the *Paniculatae* section of the *Rustica* subgenus and the *Undulatae* section of the *Petunioides* subgenus are shown on map 3. *N. rustica* probably evolved in north-central Peru or northwest Argentina, then was taken north, perhaps as an encouraged but still wild species, to Mexico, where it may have been domesticated (Heiser 1969:177; Mangelsdorf, MacNeish, and Willey 1964:508). From there it was taken farther north to the southwestern U.S., and beyond to the eastern woodlands. It may not even have been domesticated when it reached the Southwest and eastern woodlands but might instead have been a "weedy form . . . no more domesticated than the 'quasi-cultigen' crops" (Yarnell 1989:52).

The one remaining wild variety (*N. rustica* var. *pavonii*) grows in disturbed locations in the Andes from Chile to Ecuador. Like other wild tobaccos, this variety has dehiscent seed cap-

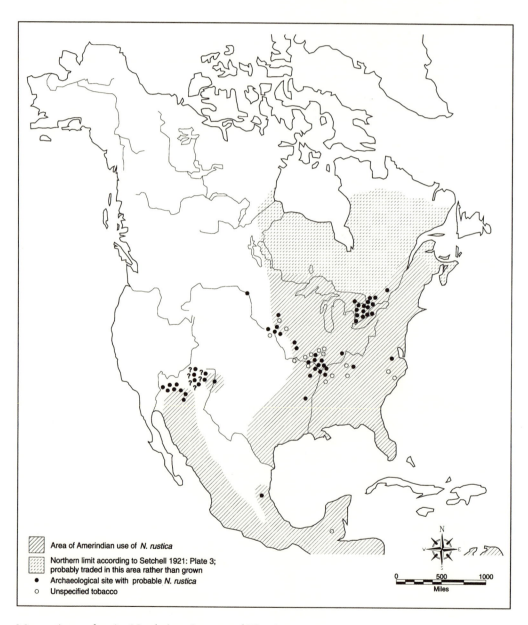

Map 5. Areas of native North American use of *Nicotiana rustica*.

sules (that is, they split open to release their seeds), but it is unknown whether it is still used by any native groups. Because its distribution overlaps with the ranges of *N. paniculata* and *N. undulata*, it is entirely possible that it represents the ancestral wild type that was ultimately domesticated.

Elsewhere in South America, the Indian use of *N. rustica* appears restricted to Colombia and Ecuador (Gerstel 1961:16; Heiser 1992:54). Jonathan Ott (1993) proposed that this species was one of the most common ingredients in the psychoactive *ayahuasca* mixture in eastern Peru, but there are no ethnographic references to the use of *N. rustica* in this hallucinogenic liquid. Rather, *N. tabacum* is the tobacco of choice in the Amazon (Schultes 1945; Schultes and Raffauf 1990). Other tobacco species that are used for various purposes in the Peruvian Amazon include *N. undulata, benavidesii, glauca, knightiana, paniculata,* and *pulmonariodies* (Rutter 1990: 159, 229).

Based on archaeological and ethnographic data, the map 5 shows the range of this species in North America. It is fairly common in the eastern woodlands, where no other tobacco was gathered or grown by Native Americans, at least until English settlers introduced *N. tabacum*. This yellow-flowered species needs less attention than the rose-blossomed *N. tabacum* (photo 26); it has a shorter growing season (*N. tabacum* takes 100 to 130 days from date of transplanting to maturity in the field); and it is grown by the Huron Indians as far north as the northern shore of Lake Ontario and perhaps even farther north by the Cree. It also has the ability to reseed itself for a year or two after the initial planting, so it sometimes appears to be growing wild, though after a few years it must be replanted.

Archaeological evidence suggests that *N. rustica* was used much more extensively and much earlier than *N. tabacum*, at least in North America. The prehistory of this species is fairly well known, though it is not without controversy. A number of authors have concluded that it is possible to distinguish the seeds of *N.*

*rustica* from those of the other tobacco species, on the basis of differences in seed size and form.[1] Other researchers, in contrast, argue that the geographical location of the archaeological collection is the only basis from which to infer the possible species identification, because there is too much variability within species and overlap among species in seed sizes and forms to allow the identification of the separate species (photo 27) (Asch 1995; Asch and Asch 1985a: 195–196; Ford 1985; Richard A. Yarnell, review of a draft of this book, 1996). They nevertheless conclude that "on the basis of the geographic distribution of tobaccos raised by historic Indians, it is most probable that the archaeological seeds from west-central Illinois [and elsewhere in the eastern woodlands] are *N. rustica*" (Asch and Asch 1985a:195–196).

Still other authors take a middle ground.[2] Julia Hammett, for example, believes that it is impossible to identify exact species but that groups of two or three possible species can be identified, with one or two being more likely than the other. Adams and Toll, Adair, and Wagner discuss these approaches later in this book.

The earliest apparent *N. rustica* seeds identified in the eastern woodlands and on the North American continent are from the Middle-Woodland-period Smiling Dan site in Illinois, which has a radiocarbon date of A.D. 180 ± 80 (Asch and Asch 1985a). Even earlier collections may have come from Newt Kash Rockshelter, a multicomponent, Late-Archaic-through-Mississippian-period site that produced apparent *N. rustica* remains, but in undated contexts. The main component at the site dates to Late Archaic–Early Woodland times, with radiocarbon dates of 3400 B.P. to 2600 B.P. (Griffin 1952; Jones 1936; Smith and Cowan 1987). Salts Cave—another Early-Woodland-period site dating from 1540 ± 110 B.C. to 290 ± 200 B.C.—produced questionable *Nicotiana* material. Bennett Young (1910) described the Salts Cave tobacco as having been identified by "experienced judges of tobacco," and Nels C. Nelson (1917:31) listed catalog number 20.0-5763-5778 as including

Photo 26. Blossom variations among tobacco species used by Native Americans. *a, N. glauca* at Barona Diegueño Reservation, California; *b, N. tabacum* Quichua Yumbo from South America; *c, N. quadrivalvis* var. *wallacei* from Los Coyotes Cahuilla Reservation, California; *d, N. attenuata*, Navajo, from Nageezi, New Mexico; *e, N. trigonophylla* from Agua Caliente Cahuilla Reservation, California; *f, N. rustica* from Oaxaca (group unknown). All specimens except *a* were grown in Albuquerque, New Mexico. All photographs by Joseph Winter. JCWSP68, 15, 70, 5, 76, 47.

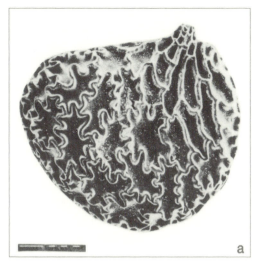

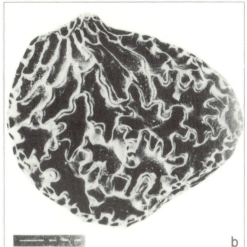

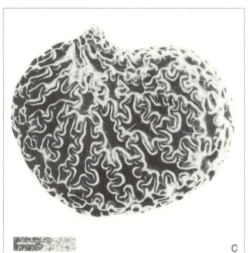

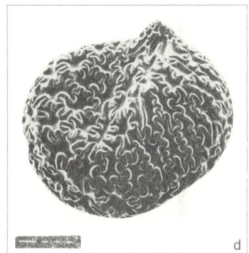

Photo 27. Micrographs of the seeds of various tobacco taxa, from Haberman 1984:figs. 2–3. *a, N. rustica* from the 1921 Cornplanter Seneca collection, at University of California, Berkeley; *b, N. rustica* from Durango, Mexico; *c, N. quadrivalvis* var. *quadrivalvis* from Hoopa Valley, California; *d, N. quadrivalvis* var. *multivalvis* grown at UC Berkeley from David Douglas's 1825 Columbia River seed; *e, N. attenuata* from Nevada. Courtesy of the Society for American Archaeology. Longest line in each scale is 100 microns.

"Tobacco leaf," but in 1936 Volney Jones concluded that the material was definitely not tobacco. At first Richard Yarnell (1964) accepted it as tobacco, but in 1990 (personal communication) he concluded that it was *Gerardia*. Whether it is tobacco or not, and whether the Newt Kash *Nicotiana* dates to Early Woodland times or later, it is entirely possible that tobacco was present in the eastern woodlands in the Early Woodland period (that is, before A.D. 1), and it may have been there much earlier, in the preagricultural Archaic period. Its route of arrival could have been through northeastern Mexico, where the Tamaulipas caves have yielded apparent *N. rustica* dating between A.D. 300 and 800 (Mangelsdorf, MacNeish, and Willey 1964).

Beginning around A.D. 300, tobacco began to appear at numerous Late Woodland sites in the American Bottoms along the Mississippi River floodplain in southern Illinois, where it is also found in later Mississippian-period sites. It appeared slightly later in Plains Woodland then in Middle Missouri sites in northwest Iowa, although Thomas Haberman (1984:272, 280) has suggested that the Middle Missouri Iowa material is *N. quadrivalvis* var. *quadrivalvis* rather than *N. rustica*. The latter may have been present in Ontario by A.D. 700, and it was certainly there by protohistoric times. Fort Ancient Aspect Mississippian sites in Ohio and Indiana have also produced possible *N. rustica* seeds. In addition, seeds identified as *N. rustica* have been recovered in Middle Missouri and protohistoric Hidatsa sites in South and North Dakota. (Again, in 1984, Haberman concluded that the seeds could be *N. quadrivalvis* var. *quadrivalvis* instead of *N. rustica*). Unspecified tobacco that is presumably *N. rustica* has been found in Late Woodland sites in North Carolina and Missouri. These and other finds are discussed in more detail in later chapters.

Some of the most interesting collections of apparent *N. rustica* seeds have been found in prehistoric Hohokam (ancestral Akimel O'odham or Pima) contexts in southern Arizona dating between A.D. 950 and 1200. Charles

Miksicek has identified this species there along with *N. trigonophylla*.[3] *N. rustica* has also been identified at an early historic Pueblo site in New Mexico, although Richard Ford (1985) concluded that this and the more recent *N. rustica* at Cochiti, Santa Ana, and the other Pueblo villages was introduced by Spaniards. Leslie White (1941:64–65, 1942) and E. G. Beinhart (1941) each reached similar conclusions. Edward Castetter (1943), Volney Jones (1944), and Ronald Switzer (1969), in contrast, all argued that *N. rustica* was present in the Southwest in the prehistoric period, which Micsicek's data seems to confirm. Julia Hammett (1993) has also concluded that probable *N. rustica* was used at several Anasazi (ancestral Pueblo) sites in northwestern New Mexico and northeastern Arizona, beginning sometime before A.D. 720 and running through the thirteenth century. The carbonized and unburned seeds could also represent the wild *N. attenuata*, but Hammett proposes that they are more likely *N. rustica*.

Historic and contemporary groups that raise or raised *N. rustica* include the Huron, Petun, Neutral, Haudenosaunee, and Mahigan in Canada and New York; the Winnebago, Ojibway, Illinois, and Sauk-Fox in the Midwest; the Powhaten and Cherokee in the Southeast; the Tonkawa in Texas; various Pueblo groups in New Mexico; the O'odham in Arizona; and the Tarahumara and Huichol, among others, in Mexico (see chapter 2). *N. rustica* is still grown by many of these groups for ritual purposes, although *N. tabacum* cigarettes, snuff, and other forms of commercial tobacco have replaced it for secular smoking. In the Southwest it also appears to have an important complimentary relationship with some of the wild species, such as *N. attenuata*, especially among the Pueblos of New Mexico (Ford 1985:359).

## Nicotiana glauca

SUBGENUS *Rustica* (Don) Goodspeed (1945: 336)

Section *Paniculatae* Goodspeed (1945:336)
*Nicotiana glauca* Grahm.

Rapidly growing, soft-woody, loosely branched shrub or short-lived small tree 3 to 6 (10) m high. Stem in younger parts glabrous, glaucous, greenish or blue-purplish, becoming reddish brown superficially as cork begins to form, then grey. Leaves thickish, rubbery, glabrous, glaucous, blade 5 to 25 cm long, cordate-ovate, ovate, elliptic, or lanceolate, *ca.* twice as long as petiole. Panicles short, flat, ± brush-like by greater elongation of lower branches. Pedicels 3 to 10 mm long, later markedly thickened upright hooks 7 to 12 mm long. Floral calyx 10 to 15 mm long, cylindric, glabrous or minutely pubescent, membranes lacking or nearly, teeth triangular, sharp, much shorter than tube. Corolla 30 to 35 (25–45) mm long exclusive of limb, tube proper 5 to 8 mm long, *ca.* 3 mm wide, throat 3 to 6 X as long, cylindric to clavate, in maximum diameter 6 to 8 mm, commonly yellow, glabrous or green in bud, later greenish or yellow. Stamens subequal, extending almost to mouth, filaments glabrous, shortly kneed immediately above insertion on base of corolla throat. Capsule 7 to 15 mm long, broadly elliptic, included. Seeds longer than broad, truncately angular, laterally compressed, *ca.* 05 mm long, brown, surface honeycombed-reticulate. Embryo straight. Chromosome number, 12 pairs. (Goodspeed 1954:336)

*Nicotiana glauca*, or tree tobacco (fig. 8, photo 28), is native to northwestern and central Argentina and common in many warm temperate

Figure 8. *Nicotiana glauca* Graham.
Inflorescence, 1/2X; entire flower, tubular part, limb, and capsule, 1 1/2X; stamen insertion and leaf, 1X. From Goodspeed 1954:fig. 59.

Photo 28. *Nicotiana glauca* (tree tobacco), near Alpine, California. Photo by Joseph Winter. JCWSP68.

climates, such as those of Brazil, Venezuela, El Salvador, and the West Indies, as well as in Mexico and parts of California and Arizona. Goodspeed considered it a species recently introduced in California, perhaps brought there by Mexicans. Elsewhere, it "has widely colonized in temperate regions of the world where it often has become a permanent and sometimes an aggressive and undesirable element of vegetation" (Goodspeed 1954:11, 336). Michael Moore (1979) suggested that it was "naturally from Peru and apparently first introduced from a botanical garden in Los Angeles during the last century." Richard Schultes and William Davis (1992) recognized several ecological variants (in contrast to true cultural varieties).

In Mexico, N. glauca is used by the Tarahumara, Tepehuan, and Pima Bajo Indians (map 6). The Seri Indians in northwestern Mexico recognize it and have given it a name, but they do not appear to use it. Tree tobacco is common around Guadalajara and in many of the canyons and valleys of Huichol territory, yet the Huichol do not use it, either. They do recognize that it is a weed that has followed the roads up into their country. The Chontal have a distinct name for it (author's field notes, 1995; Felger and Moser 1985; Martínez 1991).

In California, the Pomo may have used it along with N. quadrivalvis. Several groups in southern California still use it—for example, the Barona band of the Diegueño (Kumeyaay) Indians. They consider it a traditional form of tobacco that has been growing on a large abandoned village site since the 1920s or 1930s, when a tribal elder's grandfather used it. This elder still visits the site to gather and use it (see photo 26a).

Other southern California tribes who use N. glauca and consider it a traditional form of tobacco are the Yokuts, Gabrieleno, Chumash, and probably the Cahuilla.[4] Some of the western Navajo in Arizona reportedly smoke it along with more traditional species such as N. attenuata and N. trigonophylla. Vernon Mayes and James Rominger (1994:31) identified it in voucher collections from the western Navajo reservation, and the 1995 ethnobotanical catalog of the plant supply company ". . . Of the Jungle" states that "Navajo elders prize this particular wild tobacco for ritual use during peyote prayers and other ceremonies."

Nicotiana glauca has not been recovered from any prehistoric archaeological sites in North America, although probable tree tobacco seeds have been found at a late-nineteenth-century gold-mining town in western Arizona (Hammett 1993). Goodspeed may therefore have been correct when he stated that it was introduced relatively recently into Mexico and the United States. Nevertheless, the very interesting pockets of native use in the mountains and nearby deserts of northwestern Mexico, as well as in the deserts of southern California and western Arizona, raise the possibility of early historic introduction. The use of it by the Pomo much farther to the north is probably the result of recent introduction, but the other occurrences cannot be explained away so easily—though Pat Hall (1985:71) has attempted to do just that, on the basis of her analysis of 184 herbaria specimens collected in California over a 100-year period (1880–1980) and 193 specimens from adjacent areas: "Nicotiana glauca entered California in two broad coastal areas prior to 1880: the San Francisco Monterey Bay area and southern California. . . . Except for an apparently recent invasion of Tulare, Kern, and Calaveras counties, maps for N. glauca indicate that it has not extended beyond the area attained during the years 1920 to 1939."

W. L. Jepson first collected N. glauca in 1887. Later he noted that it was not mentioned in any of the California floras before 1894 (Jepson 1943:451). He did state, however, that S. B. Parish had concluded that it was introduced into southern California from Mexico during the mission period (1769–1839), undoubtedly as a garden shrub.

### Nicotiana attenuata

SUBGENUS Petunioides (Don) Goodspeed (1945: 339)

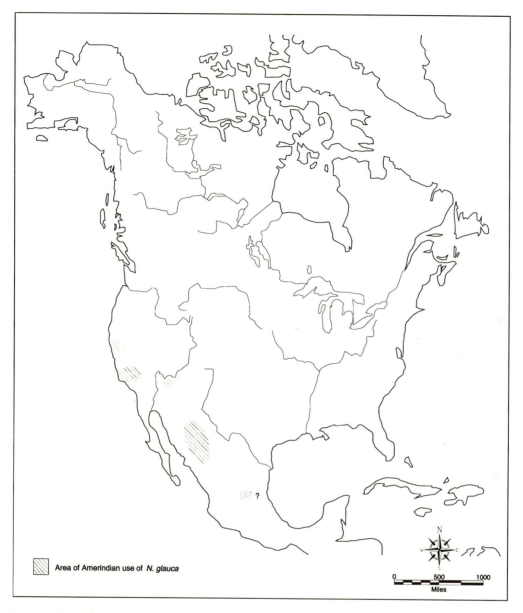

Map 6. Areas of native North American use of *Nicotiana glauca*.

Legend: Area of Amerindian use of *N. glauca*

Section *Acuminatae* Goodspeed (1945:341)
*Nicotiana attenuata* Torrey ex Watson in King
(1871:276)

Erect, one- to several-stemmed annual 0.5 to 1.5 m high, the central axis usually best developed, herbage viscid or nearly glabrous except for scattered, swollen-based hairs. Radical leaves rosulate, somewhat fleshy, blade 5 to 10 cm long, elliptic, ovate-elliptic or elliptic-oblong, obtuse or barely acute, petiole commonly about one half as long as blade, cauline leaves progressively shorter-petioled, blade narrower, lanceolate to linear-lanceolate, apex acute. Inflorescences shortly racemose or narrowly paniculate, branches ± strict. Pedicels 2 to 4 mm long, later 4 to 7 mm. Flowers vespertine. Floral calyx 7 to 10 mm long, elliptic or with elliptic tube, membranes long, swollen-based hairs conspicuous, teeth usually unequal, shorter than tube, acute, sometimes very narrow. Corolla 20 to 27 (32) mm long exclusive of limb, tube proper *ca.* 5 mm long, 1.5 to 2 mm wide, throat usually slightly less than twice the tube proper in width, nearly cylindric, a little asymmetrically dilated apically, outer surface puberulent, pale virescent with slightly pinkish blush. Limb 4 to 6 mm wide, white within, shallowly lobed, the lobes obtuse or barely acute, often three upper lobes slightly reflexed, two lower slightly assurgent. Stamen filaments faintly curved immediately above insertion on base of corolla throat, puberulent there, longest pair with anthers at mouth of corolla, shorter pair with anthers distinctly included, fifth stamen shorter than either pair. Capsule oval, acute, 8 to 12 mm long, usually exerted. Seeds ± reniform or angular-reniform, *ca.* .07 mm long, dull grey-brown, surface fluted-reticulate. Embryo hemicyclic. Chromosome number, 12 pairs. (Goodspeed 1954:429)

*Nicotiana attenuata* (fig. 9, photo 29) is widely used by Native Americans throughout western North America, and it has a long record of prehistoric use in the Southwest (map 7). It grows from northernmost Mexico to southern Canada and from the coast of California to the lower Rocky Mountains. Although it is not a commonly occurring plant, *N. attenuata* can sometimes be found along roadsides, in arroyos and

Figure 9. *Nicotiana attenuata* Torrey ex Watson. Inflorescence: center, 1/2X; right, 2/3X. Entire flower, tubular part, limb, capsule, and stamen insertion, 2X. Leaves (right, radical; left, cauline), 3/4X. From Goodspeed 1954:fig. 94.

Photo 29. *Nicotiana attenuata* grown in Albuquerque, New Mexico, from seed from a Nageezi Navajo family. Height of plant 0.441 m. Photo by Joseph Winter. JCWSP5.

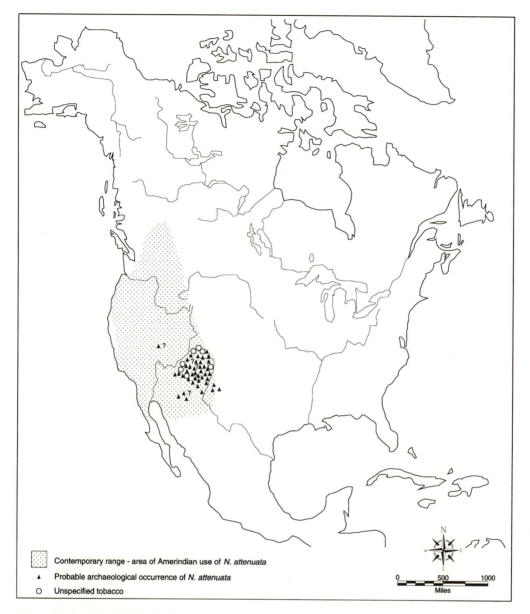

Map 7. Areas of native North American use of *Nicotiana attenuata*.

recently burned locations, and in other disturbed areas in semidesert environments between 1,000 and 2,600 meters in elevation. The higher forested areas of the Rocky Mountains and the lower grasslands of the Great Plains have moisture balances unfavorable to this species, thereby serving as natural barriers.

Native American use has definitely expanded the range of *N. attenuata*, especially to the north, where it appears to grow mainly under cultivation—for example, in southwestern Canada. Elsewhere it grows wild, but as discussed by Goodspeed (1954), Wells (1959), and others, its range has been affected by human use. Some researchers—including Yarnell (1977) and Jones and Morris (1960)—suggest that it was introduced into the Southwest in prehistoric times, then dispersed northward by human actions.

This fascinating proposal is evaluated in a later chapter.

As was illustrated by chapter 2, many Native American groups have used this species, and a number of them encouraged its growth by burning old plants, pruning the leaves, irrigating the plants, and even broadcast sowing its seeds. This type of manipulation is especially prevalent in the Great Basin, where it may have a long history of use. One archaeological site in Nevada has produced probable *N. attenuata* seeds dating to about A.D. 1200 (Winter and Hogan 1986; Julia Hammett, personal communication).

Numerous prehistoric archaeological sites in the southwestern United States contain the burned and sometimes unburned seeds of what is probably this species. Palynological studies have also revealed apparent tobacco pollen that could be *N. attenuata*, judging from its range. Chapters 11 and 12 discuss the difficulties in identifying tobacco pollen.

The earliest tobacco seeds ever found on the continent (and in the world, for that matter) are from AZ:BB:13:425, a buried Late Archaic village near Tucson, Arizona, with a calibrated radiocarbon date of 387 to 205 B.C. Although the species has not been definitely identified, there is no question that the seeds are tobacco, and their size and morphology suggest that they are probably *N. attenuata* (Huckell 1995, and personal communication). Another fairly early tobacco-bearing site is in northwestern New Mexico, where possible tobacco pollen has been recovered from a site that dates between 87 B.C. and A.D. 208 (Gish 1993). If in fact this pollen is tobacco, then it represents the second earliest *Nicotiana* found, not only in the Southwest but in all of North and South America. Tobacco was undoubtedly present earlier, but this and the AZ:BB:13:425 seeds are the earliest so far discovered by archaeologists.

Beginning around A.D. 300 to 400, apparent *N. attenuata* seeds rapidly became common at Anasazi (pre-Pueblo) archaeological sites in New Mexico, Arizona, and Colorado. Some of the sites were very rich in tobacco remains,

particularly the Prayer Rock, Arizona, Basketmaker III caves, dated at A.D. 621–630, which contained tobacco stems, leaves, flower corollas, capsules, and seeds in a pottery vessel; tobacco seeds and bits of capsules in chewed yucca quids; and nicotine and nicotonic acid in dottles in the bowls of clay pipes (Gager, Johnson, and Holmes 1960; Jones and Morris 1960).

Another fairly early site with probable *N. attenuata* seeds is a Basketmaker III pithouse hamlet on the Hopi mesas in Arizona dated at A.D. 800 to 830, where *Datura* species seeds and ceramic pipes were also found. This association of the two powerful drug plants could be the earliest evidence yet of tobacco and datura ceremonialism in North America (Sebastian 1985:172). Elsewhere, early seeds that may be *N. attenuata* have been recovered from Tularosa Cave in southern New Mexico, in levels dated at A.D. 500 to 700, and in the Dolores River valley of southwestern Colorado, in Basketmaker III–Early Pueblo I sites dated at A.D. 600 to 700, as well as in later Pueblo I–II sites dated at A.D. 800 to 1125. There are no fewer than 13 Basketmaker III, Pueblo I, and Pueblo II sites in the Dolores area that have yielded burned and unburned seeds that have been identified as *N. attenuata*, leading Meredith Matthews to conclude that tobacco may have been an encouraged weed, or at least a tolerated one, growing around the villages in much the same way it still grows around houses in the Hopi village of Walpi.[5]

Linda Scott Cummings has also recovered large amounts of apparent tobacco pollen from one of the Dolores sites (Cummings, this volume; Scott 1983:83, 86, 1986). Anne Woosley (1977) had previously identified possible *Nicotiana* pollen at Hovenweep in southwestern Colorado, but Cummings was the first researcher to identify it in well-provenienced samples and to carry out tests to ensure that contamination by tobacco-using archaeologists was not responsible for its presence. As is discussed in chapter 10, she determined that the smoking of fresh cigarettes and the dipping of snuff can contaminate archaeological soils with modern tobacco pollen. However, she also demonstrated that the absence of exotic pollens that are contained in the cigarettes and snuff ruled out contamination at Dolores.

Cummings's research was extremely significant in that it opened up a whole new approach—that of palynology—to the identification of tobacco. Tobacco seeds are so small that they are almost always missed by field screening and often by flotation; they are less than 1 mm in maximum length and so small that it takes approximately 300,000 of them to make an ounce (Haberman 1984:273; Heiser 1969:173). Because palynology has so much potential, several teams of researchers at the University of New Mexico have independently tested Cummings's approach. Their results are presented in chapters 11 and 12.

What are probably *N. attenuata* seeds have also been found in many Pueblo I–III sites in northwestern New Mexico, Pueblo III–IV sites in central New Mexico, Mogollon and/or Pueblo sites in northeastern and southeastern Arizona, Late Classic Hohokam sites in southern Arizona, and a Spanish colonial–U.S. territorial-period site in northwestern New Mexico. A northwestern New Mexico early Navajo site dating from A.D. 1500 to 1600 has also yielded *Nicotiana* seeds. A prehistoric Sinagua site near Flagstaff, Arizona, dating between A.D. 600 and 800, contained possible *N. attenuata* seeds, with a slightly later Sinagua site producing possible *Nicotiana* pollen. Chapter 7 summarizes many of these discoveries.

In historic and modern times, *N. attenuata* was and still is gathered and often raised or at least encouraged by the Hopi, Zuni, Isleta, Santa Ana, and Tewa Pueblos in New Mexico and Arizona; the Havasupai, Yavapai, Mohave, Akimel and Tohono O'odham, and Navajo Indians in Arizona and New Mexico; the southern Paiute, northern Paiute, Gosiute, Ute, Shoshone, and Kawaiisu in the Great Basin; the Tubatulabal, southern Diegueño, Cahuilla, Washo, Maidu, and Miwok in California; and

the Thompson River Salish, Kutenai, Shuswap, Lillooet, Okanagan, and Chilcotin in British Columbia. Many other native North American groups also use this species.

Table 25 is a list of *N. attenuata* specimens collected from Native Americans in New Mexico, Utah, Arizona, and California. Although the species has been identified in archaeological collections from Colorado, New Mexico, and Arizona, its seeds have yet to be discovered in samples from California. Hall (1985), however, on the basis of her examination of herbarium specimens collected between 1880 and 1979, concluded that it was cultivated by Native Americans in the central and southern Sierra Nevada mountains and foothills, as well as in northeastern California. She suggested that it was introduced into California from west-central Nevada after the last glacial retreat and that its regression in range over the past 130 years was "due to the cessation of cultivation practices that served to maintain the species in climatically unfavorable areas" (Hall 1985:82–83).

## Nicotiana quadrivalvis

SUBGENUS *Petunioides* (Don) Goodspeed (1945: 339)
Section *Bigelovianae* Goodspeed (1945)
*Nicotiana quadrivalvis* Pursh.

Annual .3 to 2 m high, of loose or compact habit. Stems or basal branches one to many, clothed with evident patent, moist to viscid hairs. Radical leaves rosulate, somewhat fleshy, commonly glabrate on upper surface, sparsely pilose on lower, blade 10 to 15 cm long, rotund-elliptic to elliptic-ovate, petiole less than half as long as blade, cauline leaves gradually shorter, narrower, blade ovate-lanceolate to lanceolate, petiole short or lacking. Floral region leafy to bracteate, the axis simple or later pinnately branched. Pedicels 4 to 10 mm long, later 7 to 15 mm. Flowers vespertine. Floral calyx 15 to 20 (9 to 35) mm long, elliptic, 10-ridged, hispidulous, mem-

Table 25: Examples of *Nicotiana attenuata* in the Native American Plant Cooperative (NAPC), Albuquerque, New Mexico

| Specimen No. | Group | Type Name | Source |
|---|---|---|---|
| 5, 18 | Navajo | *Dzil nat'oh,* mountain tobacco | Two Navajo families near Nageezi, N.M. |
| 199 | Navajo | Navajo tobacco | San Juan County, Utah; Bailey Hortorium, Cornell University[a] |
| 178 | Navajo | Navajo tobacco | Carrizo Mountains, Ariz., via Harvard University Herbarium |
| 234 | Navajo | Coyote tobacco | Klagetoh, Ariz., via University of New Mexico Herbarium |
| 235 | Navajo | Navajo tobacco | Ya Ta Hey, N.M., via University of New Mexico Herbarium |
| 286 | Navajo | White-tipped tobacco | Navajo herbalist, Shiprock, N.M., 1997 |
| 284 | Hopi | Hopi tobacco | Hopi Mesas, via Native Seeds/SEARCH 1997 |
| 177 | Hopi | *Pi-bu,* Ho-pi tobacco | Hopi region; Harvard University Herbarium |
| 231 | Hopi | *Pi-va,* Hopi tobacco | San Francisco Mts., Ariz., via University of New Mexico Herbarium |
| 63 | Zuni | *Ana', ana'de,* Zuni tobacco | Near Zuni N.M., via Carol Brandt |
| 214, 214A | Zuni | "Tuni" (Zuni) tobacco | Zuni, N.M., via Bailey Hortorium, Cornell University |
| 176 | Paiute | Pah-Ute wild tobacco | Paragonah, Utah, via Harvard University Herbarium |
| 69, 71 | Cahuilla | Cahuilla tobacco | Los Coyotes Cahuilla Indian Reservation, Calif. |
| 73 | Kumeyaay | Kumeyaay tobacco | Manzanita Kumeyaay Indian Reservation, Calif. |
| 138 | Hupa-Karuk | — | Annie Lake, Nevada: tobacco paid to a Hupa-Karuk medicine man in California |
| 282 | Anasazi-Pueblo?[b] | — | Natural Bridges National Monument, Utah |
| 302 | Anasazi-Pueblo?[b] | — | Mesa Verde National Park, Colo. |
| 303 | Anasazi-Pueblo?[b] | — | Mesa Verde National Park, Colo. |

a   Location collected by author and provenience of original voucher specimen.
b   Collected near Anasazi ruins.

branes usually long, teeth narrow, tapering, one or two sometimes exceeding tube. Corolla as broad as long, tubular part (17) 25 to 50 mm long, trumpet-shaped, in 5-merous varieties 2 to 2.5 mm wide in lower part, gradually broadened to 6 or 7 mm at mouth, outer surface pale virescent or with violet blush, oily glossy, limb 12 to 20 (30) mm wide, cleft into broadly triangular-ovate subacute lobes. Stamen filaments 3 to 10 (16) mm long, unequally inserted in upper 2/5 of tubular part of corolla, lowest inserted not reaching mouth, others often slightly exserted. Capsule narrowly ovoid, in some varieties ± globose, 15 (25) mm long, included. Seeds rotund-reniform, *ca.* 0.9 mm long, dull brown, surface reticulate with fluted or fluted-plicate ridges. Embryo bent. Chromosome number, 24 pairs. (Goodspeed 1954:447)

This important species has a confusing taxonomic history, with some researchers calling it *N. quadrivalvis*, others calling it *N. bigelovii*, and still others referring to it as *N. multivalvis*. It was first classified in 1814 as a cultivated tobacco of the Mandan and Arikara Plains Indians and called *N. quadrivalvis* Pursh. A decade later the plant collected by David Douglas in eastern Oregon was considered a separate species and named *N. multivalvis* Lindl. Still later, in 1871, another specimen was named *N. bigelovii* (Torrey) Watson.

In his detailed study of all three taxa in 1954, Goodspeed chose to consider *multivalvis* and *quadrivalvis* varieties of *N. bigelovii* and not separate species. Three years later, however, Gordon DeWolf (1957) criticized Goodspeed

for retaining the *bigelovii* name, and more recent researchers have added to the confusion by using one or another of the names. Brien Meilleur (1979) and Julia Hammett (this volume), for example, have followed DeWolf, whereas others (for example, Haberman 1984; Sisson and Saunders 1982; Sisson and Severson 1990; U.S. Tobacco Germplasm Catalog 1993–1994) have followed Goodspeed. The literature on the subject is therefore confusing, and it is made even more so by the fact that three of the species' four varieties (as defined by Goodspeed) have the same names as the species designations (that is, varieties *quadrivalvis*, *multivalvis*, and *bigelovii*). I have chosen to follow DeWolf.

Whatever it is called, this species of tobacco is very important to Native Americans. Indians in California, the Great Basin, the Southwest, the Northwest Coast, and even the Missouri River valley and far northern Great Plains gathered and at times grew it (table 26). All four

Table 26: Examples of Native American *Nicotiana quadrivalvis* in the Native American Plant Cooperative (NAPC), Albuquerque, New Mexico

| Specimen No. | Group | Variety | Source |
|---|---|---|---|
| 70 | Cahuilla | *Wallacei* | Los Coyotes Cahuilla Reservation, Calif. |
| 200, 217, 217A | Miwok | *Bigelovii?* | Miwok in California, via Bailey Hortorium, Cornell University |
| 135 | Pomo | Cf. *bigelovii* | Big Valley Pomo Rancheria, Calif. |
| 201, 202 | Crow | *Multivalvis* | Montana, via Bailey Hortorium, Cornell University |
| 230, 230A | Mandan | *Quadrivalvis?* | North Dakota, via University of New Mexico Herbarium |
| 89, 213, 213A | Chinook | *Multivalvis* | Collected by David Douglas in early 1800s along upper Columbia River, Oreg., via Rancho Santa Ana Botanic Gardens, Botanical Museum of Stockholm, and Komarov Institute |
| 203 | "Indian" | *Quadrivalvis* | Bailey Hortorium, Cornell University |
| 221, 229 | ?[a] | *Quadrivalvis* | From museums in Uppsala and Berlin |
| 249 | ?[a] | *Quadrivalvis* | U.S. Tobacco Germplasm Collection |
| 248 | ?[a] | *Multivalvis* | U.S. Tobacco Germplasm Collection |
| 221, 229 | ?[a] | *Multivalvis* | From museums in Uppsala and Berlin |

a  Since the varieties *quadrivalvis* and *multivalvis* were known only in cultivation by Native Americans, it is almost certain that the various seeds in museums, herbaria, and other locations are ultimately derived from Native American sources.

of the varieties have been affected by Native American use, such that two (*N. quadrivalvis* vars. *quadrivalvis* and *multivalvis*) are no longer able to seed themselves and therefore are sometimes considered "domesticates" (Yarnell 1989). The two fully domesticated species of tobacco, *N. tabacum* and *N. rustica*, also have problems disseminating their seeds. It is likely that this condition—indehiscence—is the result of thousands of years of human seed collecting. Prehistoric Indians gathered the seed capsules by snapping them off the stems, thereby producing an easier-to-collect capsule with a brittle stem, but one that could no longer open itself.

The ranges and archaeological discoveries of the apparent seeds of the species and varieties are shown on map 8. Each variety is described below, as well as in chapter 6, where Hammett analyses the history and distribution of the species. On the basis of her study of herbarium specimens, Hall (1985) concluded that the species originated in prehistoric times in southern California and that historically it was cultivated by Indians from central California north to the Oregon border and beyond that to the Queen Charlotte Islands in Canada and east to the Dakotas, where it cannot grow wild. She also concluded that the climatic conditions limiting its growth in the wild are frost (temperatures below 9.9 degrees C), precipitation over 29.4 centimeters annually, and possibly temperatures over 29.6 degrees C, and that these limitations were overcome by cultivation and careful tending of the plant, such as the Crow did (and still do) in the northern plains. Finally, she reached the conclusion that the decline in its range in California in the past century coincided with the cessation of cultivation by many indigenous groups.

*Nicotiana quadrivalvis* var. *bigelovii* (Torrey) DeWolf.
Low, dense to tall, coarse, erect plant; flowers ± numerous, 3 outer whorls 5-merous, calyx 15 to 20 mm long, corolla (33) 35 to 50 mm long exclusive of limb;

capsules *ca.* 15 mm long, 2-celled, narrowly ovoid, dehiscent. (Goodspeed 1954:449)

Variety *bigelovii* has been used by Native Americans throughout California, with both the Hupa and Pomo growing it and gathering it wild. The Takelma and Shasta to the north also use it. The seed capsule, with two cells, as shown in figure 10, can still open itself. This wild variety grows from sea level to about 350 meters.

In 1932, Harrington proposed that a very tall variety (up to 2 meters high) grew from San Francisco Bay north to southern Oregon. Basing his judgment on unpublished data provided by Setchell, he called it *N. bigelovii* var. *exhalta* Setchell. Goodspeed (1954), however, observed

Figure 10. *Nicotiana quadrivalvis* var. *bigelovii* Torrey. Inflorescence and leaf, 1/2X; entire flower, tubular part, limb, and stamen insertion, 1X; capsules (entire, cross sections), 1 1/3X. From Goodspeed 1954:fig. 104.

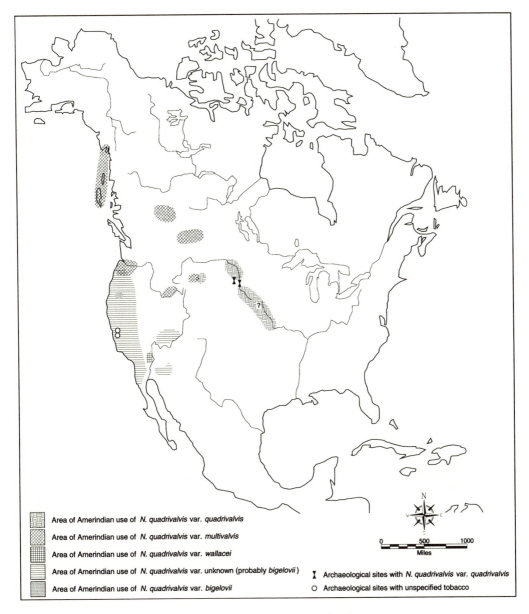

Area of Amerindian use of *N. quadrivalvis* var. *quadrivalvis*

Area of Amerindian use of *N. quadrivalvis* var. *multivalvis*

Area of Amerindian use of *N. quadrivalvis* var. *wallacei*

Area of Amerindian use of *N. quadrivalvis* var. unknown (probably *bigelovii*)

Area of Amerindian use of *N. quadrivalvis* var. *bigelovii*

**I** Archaeological sites with *N. quadrivalvis* var. *quadrivalvis*

O Archaeological sites with unspecified tobacco

0    500    1000
Miles

Map 8. Areas of native North American use of *Nicotiana quadrivalvis*.

that the variety bigelovii sometimes grew that high, so he rejected the *exhalta* classification.

*Nicotiana quadrivalvis* var. *wallacei*. Erect, rather delicate, loosely branched plant 6 to 12 dm high; flowers numerous, 3 outer whorls 5-merous, calyx 12 to 15 mm long, corolla 25 to 34 mm long exclusive of limb; capsule *ca.* 12 mm long, 2-celled, narrowly ovoid, dehiscent. (Goodspeed 1954:449)

Another wild California and Great Basin variety, this taxon grows in sand and along sandy river beds, from below sea level to 2,000 meters. Variety *wallacei* has dehiscent seed capsules with two cells. The Tubatulabal Indians in southeastern California "sucker" it and *N.*

attenuata (that is, they prune off the secondary stalks), and they eat the leaves mixed with lime. Photo 3 in chapter 1 illustrates a plant from one of the Cahuilla reservations.

*Nicotiana quadrivalvis* var. *quadrivalvis.* Compact plant 3 to 5 dm high; flowers few, solitary or nearly, 3 outer whorls 5-merous, calyx 9 to 15 mm long, corolla 17 to 20 mm long exclusive of limb; capsule *ca.* 12 mm long, truncately subglobose, (3-) 4-celled, dehiscent or indehiscent. (Goodspeed 1954:451)

This very special variety is known only in cultivation by the Mandan, Arikara, and Hidatsa of the upper Missouri River valley and by other Plains tribes along the lower Missouri. The Crow also use it. The type specimen was collected by Lewis and Clark in 1804, when they observed the Arikara growing it in South Dakota (Cutright 1989; Harrington 1932:41). This tobacco is sacred to the Crow and Hidatsa. Its seed capsules are both dehiscent and indehiscent, with three to four cells. Two archaeological sites in the Missouri River valley have produced its apparent seeds, though some authors have questioned their identification (Asch and Asch 1985a; Ford 1985; Haberman 1984). Haberman (1984) concluded that surface patterns on this variety, as well as on *N. quadrivalvis* var. *multivalvis,* *N. rustica,* and *N. attenuata,* are distinctive enough to allow the separate identification of the two varieties and three species. Copies of his micrographs are shown in photo 27. This is an extremely important variety, which Goodspeed considered an outlier of the California assemblage of *N. quadrivalvis.*

*N. quadrivalvis* var. *multivalvis* (Lindley) Mansfeld.
Rather broad, stocky plant 5 to 8 dm high; flowers few, solitary or in short false racemes, 6- to 8-merous, calyx 25 to 35 mm long, corolla 40 to 45 mm long exclusive of limb; capsule 19 to 25 mm long, depressed-globose, multilocular in 2 concentric series, indehiscent. (Goodspeed 1954:453)

This very significant variety (sometimes called *N. multivalvis*) is also known only in cultivation, with a complex distribution across northwestern North America (map 8). The Sarsi, Blackfoot, and Crow raise it. The Crow consider it so sacred that they do not even smoke it—just raising it is enough—and their tobacco society is organized around its growth. The Tlingit and Haida of extreme southern Alaska may have grown it, as did the Indians of the Snake River valley. David Douglas first recorded it in 1825 in the hands of an Indian at the great falls of the Columbia River in Oregon. The Indian planted it in ashes to make the plant large. Douglas learned that the species grew plentifully in the country of the Snake Indians, who may have obtained it from other Indians (the Crow?) at the headwaters of the upper Missouri (Harrington 1932).

Figure 11 illustrates how there are four or more irregular cells in the indehiscent seed capsule. Goodspeed considered this another outlier of the California *N. quadrivalvis* assemblage.

The exact history of evolution of the four varieties of *N. quadrivalvis* and the locations where they evolved through human and natural selection are unknown, primarily because the seeds and pollen of the different tobacco species and varieties are so difficult to differentiate. Nevertheless, it must have been a fascinating sequence. Hall (1984) concluded that prehistoric selection by native Californians influenced the emergence of the indehiscent form—*N. quadrivalvis* var. *multivalvis*—somewhere in northern California. The species itself probably originated in the deserts of southern California, where the *bigelovii* and *wallacei* varieties grow. Its seeds were then carried north, a few kilometers at a time, as prehistoric Indians encouraged its growth by broadcast sowing its seeds, pruning its dead leaves, suckering its secondary stalks, and burning the old plants in the autumn, until the partially indehiscent *quadrivalvis* and the almost totally indehiscent *multivalvis* varieties were developed. These varieties also have more compact plants and fewer flowers and are

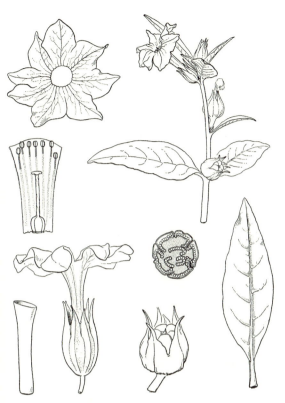

Figure 11. *Nicotiana quadrivalvis* var. *multivalvis* (Lindley) Mansfeld. Inflorescence and leaf, 1/2X; entire flower, tubular part, limb, and capsules (entire, cross sections), 1X. From Goodspeed 1954:fig. 102.

SUBGENUS *Petunioides* (Don) Goodspeed (1945: 339)

Section *Bigelovianae* Goodspeed (1945)

*Nicotiana clevelandii* Gray

Rapidly growing annual 2 to 6 dm high. Stem ± villose, moist to viscid, subsimple or loosely branched, later often several additional ascendant stems or well-developed basal branches. Leaves fleshy, both surfaces often moist asperulous from swollen, persistent bases of short, scattered, patent hairs, radical leaves rosulate, 6 to 19 cm long, blade rotund-elliptic and twice as long as the margined petiole to rhombic-ovate and 8 X as long as petiole, cauline leaves progressively smaller up stem, subsessile to sessile, ovate-acuminate. Lower flowers on leafy sympodial axes, by gradual reduction of leaves to bracts upper flowers falsely racemose, later entire flowering region often pinnately branched. Pedicels 2 to 5 mm long, later 4 to 7 mm. Flowers vespertine. Floral calyx cylindric-campanulate, narrow, 8 to 10 mm long, viscid-pubescent, membranes narrow, long, inconspicuous, segments subulate, 4 frequently as long as tube, fifth longer. Tubular part of corolla 14 to 20 mm long, nearly white, puberulent exteriorly, tube proper 3 or 4 mm long, *ca.* 1 mm wide, throat 2 to 4 mm wide, ± cylindric with apical dilation, mouth oblique, limb 3 to 5 mm wide, white within, cleft into broadly ovate, acute, unequal lobes. Stamens inserted on base of corolla throat, 4 erect, extending nearly to mouth, fifth curved, much shorter. Capsule oval, 4 to 6 mm long, included. Seeds rotund-reniform, 0.5 mm long, dark grey-brown, surface irregularly wavy- to fluted-reticulate. Embryo bent. Chromosome number, 24 pairs. (Goodspeed 1954:453–454)

*N. clevelandii* (fig. 12) is a diminutive form of *N. quadrivalvis* and may in fact be a hybrid of *N. quadrivalvis* and *N. attenuata*, with considerable

completely infertile when crossed with the wild varieties (Asch 1995:81; Goodspeed 1954: 10, 73). Over a period of several thousand years their seeds were then slowly taken east across the Cascade, Sierra Nevada, and Rocky Mountain ranges all the way to the upper Missouri River valley, then north into Canada, where the Sarsi and Blackfoot grow one of its varieties, as well as south to the lower Missouri, where the Pawnee and other groups grow it as well. Eventually the seeds may also have been taken west, back across the Canadian Rockies, to the Haida and Tlingit in extreme southern Alaska.

overlapping of characteristics (Goodspeed 1954: 454; Setchell 1921:412). Map 9 shows its range in Baja and southern California, as well as in the lower Colorado River valley and north-western Mexico, in dunes, washes, desert slopes, and sea cliffs, between sea level and 450 meters. Setchell (1921) and Goodspeed (1954:10) both suggested that *N. clevelandii* might have been the tobacco of the Luiseño, and Hall (1984, 1985) proposed that it was grown and traded in southern California. The Seri definitely use it, though they prefer *N. trigonophylla* when it is available. The one archaeological occurrence of unspecified tobacco seeds in the area of overlap of the three species is from a late prehistoric–early historic period Chumash site. *N. clevelandii* can sometimes be found growing on the old Chumash Indian shell middens along the coast and on the Channel Islands.

Based on her analysis of 42 herbaria speci-mens collected over a 100-year period, Hall (1984, 1985) concluded that this desert species was limited to extremely dry areas where the mean monthly temperature was 29.9 degrees C. By the time of historic contact it had invaded all favorable areas in southern California where it could grow (or be grown), but since then its range has shrunk, perhaps because humans have stopped using it. It was formerly noted on prehistoric middens along the Santa Barbara coast and can still be found on Santa Cruz and Santa Catalina islands, nearly always on middens. Much of its former habitat is now destroyed, so it is very rare (Jan Timbrook, review of a draft of this book, 1998).

## Nicotiana trigonophylla

SUBGENUS *Petunioides* (Don) Goodspeed (1945: 339)
Section *Trigonophylla* Goodspeed (1945:339)
*Nicotiana trigonophylla* Dun., *N. palmeri* Gray, *N. obtusifolia* Martens and Galeotti
   Pubescent annual or limited perennial 0.5 to 1 m high with few to many slender, brittle,

Figure 12. *Nicotiana clevelandii* Gray. Inflor-escence and leaf, 1/2X; entire flower, tubular part, limb, capsule, and stamen insertion, 2 1/2X. From Goodspeed 1954:fig. 103.

leafy stems. Leaves 5 to 20 cm long, seldom greatly reduced until close to inflorescence, lowest oblanceolate, spatulate or elliptic with short-winged petiole, remainder sessile, pan-duriform-elliptic, oblong-trigonate or trigon-ate, base somewhat clasping, apex obtuse, acute or acuminate. False racemes short, secund, sometimes 3 or 4 becoming strict branches of a narrow panicle. Pedicels 2 to 5 mm long, later 4 to 6 mm. Floral calyx 8 to 11 mm long, subcampanulate-cupshaped, asperulous, viscid-pubescent, 10 evident ribs, membranes short, teeth triangular to linear-triangular. Corolla virescent-cream, 12 to 23 mm long exclusive of limb, tube proper 3 to 6 mm long, 2 to 4 mm wide, tomentose

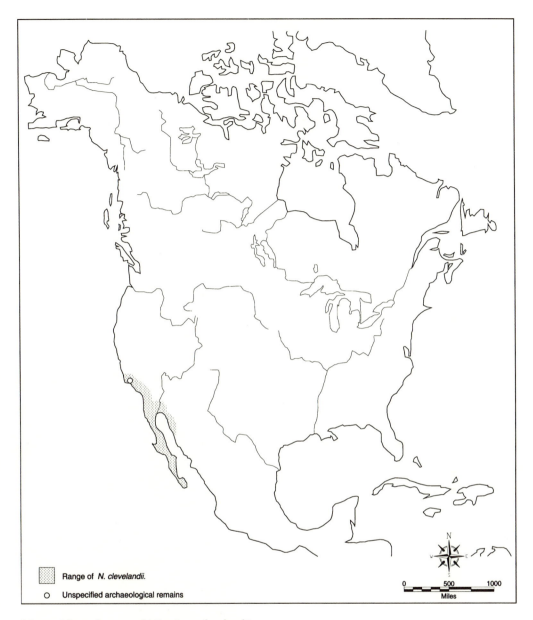

Map 9. Natural range of *Nicotiana clevelandii*.

within, throat 2 to 3 X as long, abruptly slightly wider than tube, limb 3 to 4 mm wide, pentagonal to circular-crenate. Stamens slightly hairy immediately above insertion on base of corolla throat, 4 longer sometimes kneed, fifth never kneed and usually curved away from corolla. Capsule broadly ovoid, acute, 8 to 11 mm long. Seeds oblong, sometimes subrotund, *ca.* 0.5 mm long, brown, surface reticulate, the ridges finely wavy. Embryo arcuate to bent. Chromosome number, 12 pairs. (Goodspeed 1954:100)

Another wild or semiwild tobacco used by Native Americans in the Southwest, California, and Mexico is *Nicotiana trigonophylla* Dunal (fig. 13), described by Goodspeed as a Mexican desert species. It is classified as *N.*

*obtusifolia* in *The Jepson Manual: Higher Plants of California* (Jepson 1993), but most authors still call it *N. trigonophylla*. It grows at elevations from sea level to 2,900 meters, from southern Mexico to east-central California and east through Arizona and New Mexico to the Austin, Texas, area (map 10). This highly variable species is fairly widespread in the deserts, and like *N. attenuata*, it grows in culturally and naturally disturbed habitats and is sometimes cultivated. Also like *N. attenuata*, it was most likely introduced into the Southwest and California in post-Pleistocene times, perhaps by human activity (Goodspeed 1954:46). It can tolerate very dry conditions with mean monthly temperatures up to 34.6 degrees C, and it may have entered California through west-central Arizona and/or southwest Nevada (Hall 1985:74). I have collected it from the Palm Canyon Agua Caliente Cahuilla Reservation and from an old Kumeyaay village site in California (photo 30), as well as from Petroglyph National Monument (a Sandia Pueblo site) and Tome Hill (an Isleta Pueblo site) in New Mexico (table 27). Several other collections have been made on the Havasupai Reservation in Arizona. *N. trigonophylla* prefers to grow in washes and on talus

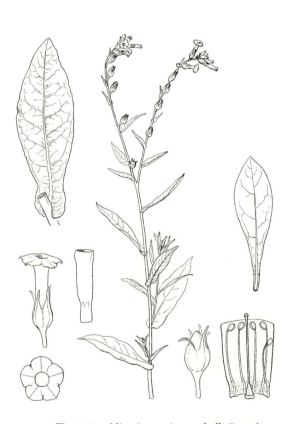

Figure 13. *Nicotiana trigonophylla* Dunal. Inflorescence and leaves (right, basal), 1/2X; entire flower, tubular part, limb, capsule, and stamen insertion, 2X. From Goodspeed 1954: fig. 78.

Photo 30. *Nicotiana trigonophylla* (Coyote's tobacco) grown in Albuquerque, New Mexico, from seed from old Kumeyaay village, California. Height 0.479 m. Photo by Joseph Winter. JCWSP74A.

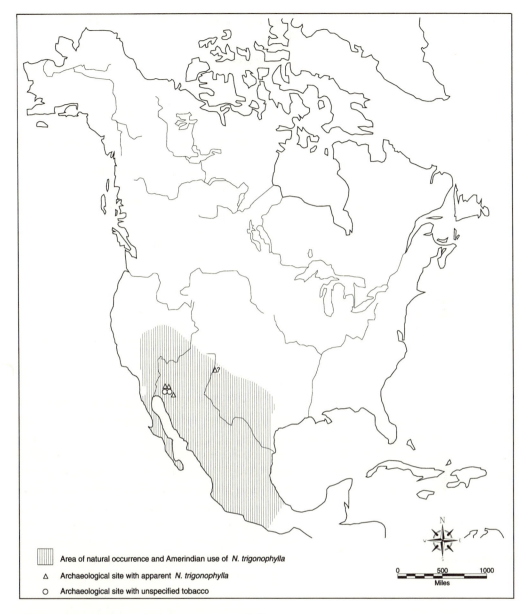

Map 10. Natural range of *Nicotiana trigonophylla*.

slopes in central and southern New Mexico and Arizona.

Apparent *N. trigonophylla* seeds have been recovered from several Hohokam (ancestral Akimel O'odham or Pima) sites in southern Arizona dating between A.D. 950 and 1200. Tijeras Pueblo in the Sandia Mountains of north-central New Mexico may also have yielded seeds of this species. It was probably used sporadically throughout the Mexican and southwestern deserts in prehistoric times, with its use sometimes extending into the mountains. As discussed in chapter 2, the Akimel O'odham gathered it, the Tohono O'odham gather and encourage it, the Yuma collected it, the Havasupai cultivate it, the Mohave grew and gathered it, and the Hopi

**Table 27: Examples of Native American *Nicotiana trigonophylla* in the Native American Plant Cooperative (NAPC), Albuquerque, New Mexico**

| Specimen No. | Group | Source[a] |
|---|---|---|
| SP76 | Cahuilla | Palm Canyon in Agua Caliente Cahuilla Reservation, Calif. |
| SP74A | Kumeyaay | Ancestral Kumeyaay village, Anza-Borrego State Park, Calif. |
| SP175 | Havasupai | Supai Village in Havasu Canyon, Ariz., via Harvard University Herbarium |
| SP170 | Havasupai | Havasu Canyon, Ariz., via Eastern Native Seed Conservancy |
| SP163 | Sandia Pueblo | Ancestral and current site, Petroglyph National Monument, N.M. |
| SP304 | Anasazi-Piro Pueblo?[b] | Turututu Butte, N.M. |
| SP281 | Anasazi-Piro Pueblo?[c] | Palo Duro Canyon, N.M. |
| SP287 | Anasazi-Isleta Pueblo?[d] | Tome Hill, N.M. |

a   Location where author collected the seeds, or other source.
b   From probable Piro Pueblo ancestral site with apparent shrines.
c   From canyon with Piro Pueblo pictographs.
d   From hill considered sacred by Isleta Pueblo.

also cultivate it. When the Indians have a choice, most prefer *N. attenuata* over *N. trigonophylla*, because the latter has less nicotine as well as a ranker smell and taste. Both the Kumeyaay and Havasupai believe that Coyote created it when he tried to make his own tobacco. The Seri prefer it over *N. clevelandii*.

The highly variable nature of *N. trigonophylla* is reflected in the confusion over the subspecies that is sometimes called *N. palmeri*, which is confined to western Arizona and southern Utah. Jones considered it a variety of *N. trigonophylla*, though Goodspeed (1954: 387) followed Gray by calling it a separate species with longer, whiter flowers. Phillip Wells (1959), in contrast, found a continuous intergradation of *N. palmeri* with *N. trigonophylla*, leading him to question the separate species designation, as did Verne Sisson and R. F. Severson (1990). Whatever it is called, there is only one ethnographic reference to it in the literature, by Washington Matthews (1902), who described its use in a Navajo Nightway ceremony.

## Other Tobacco Species Used by Native North Americans

No other species of tobacco was used by native North Americans until very recently, when a number of ornamentals were introduced from South America into the United States and Mexico and adopted by American Indians, who are opportunistic when it comes to using tobacco. When traditional types are unavailable, they often use commercial tobacco, tree tobacco, flowering garden tobacco, and whatever else they can find for ceremonial as well as social and recreational needs. All tobacco species contain nicotine, nornicotine, anabasine, and/or other powerful alkaloids, which make them ideal mood- and mind-altering psychotrophic substances.

During a recent collecting trip to Canada, I learned that at least one Huron was growing and using a white-flowered, fragrant ornamental tobacco that sounded suspiciously like *Nicotiana sylvestris*, which can be found in many flowerbeds throughout eastern Canada. One

Anishinabe (Ojibway) man in Ontario definitely grows and uses *N. sylvestris* for ceremonies and other ritual needs. Another ornamental species that has recently been adopted is *N. alata*, which is native to Brazil, Argentina, Paraguay, and perhaps other areas of South America. This beautiful flowering tobacco is a common ornamental used throughout North America, and I know one Native American who smokes it for religious purposes. In addition, it appears that the Huichol in western Mexico may have added it to their traditional tobacco complex. When I showed pressed specimens of six different tobacco taxa (two varieties of *N. alata*, two of *N. rustica*, and one each of *N. glauca* and *N. attenuata*) to a Huichol Indian shaman, the man identified a Pueblo Indian variety of *N. rustica* and a pink-flowered variety of *N. alata* as very similar to, if not the same as, tobaccos used by his tribe. He called both of them *makuchi*, a *muy fino* tobacco, which is discussed in more detail in chapter 13. *N. alata* is also used as traditional tobacco by at least one Native American group in South America, along the Río Putumayo in Columbia. Described as "very strong (*malo*) *tabaco*" on the voucher label, this specimen from a Putumayo Indian garden is in the herbarium at Harvard University (Harvard University Herbarium Voucher, specimen no. 7434, *Nicotiana alata*).

*Nicotiana langsdorffii* is another introduced species that may have been adopted by native North Americans. It is unknown whether it is used by Indians in South America, but there are two weak references to Huichol use of this pale, small-flowered species, both in ethnobotanical seed supply catalogs: "Potent leaves smoked as a sacred tobacco by the Huichols" (. . . Of the Jungle 1994:7), and "Incredibly potent leaves for smoking . . . ceremonially by the Huichol" (Seeds of Change n.d.:45). When I asked the two seed supply companies to clarify these references, neither was able to provide the original reference in the ethnographic literature, nor could they name the collector. This reflects a common problem among ethnobotanical seed supply companies: while providing valuable services by collecting and saving the seeds of rare plants used by Indians, their identifications are not always correct, and as a consequence, considerable confusion and incorrect information has been introduced into the literature. Readers should always grow their own specimens after obtaining seeds from these companies, then key them out using scientific manuals such as Goodspeed's definitive description of the *Nicotiana*s. The Huichol and other native North Americans may well be using *N. langsdorffii* and other recently introduced species, but until the seeds are carefully collected and grown out, and the resulting plants compared with voucher specimens, we will never know for sure.

## Notes

1. Charles Miksicek has identified tobacco in numerous reports from Arizona; see especially Miksicek 1983a, 1983b, 1983c, 1983d, 1984a, 1984b, 1984c. See also Adams 1990a; Adams and Toll, this volume; Haberman 1984; Stevenson 1985a.

2. See various works by Sissel Johannesson in the bibliography, especially 1985a, 1985b, 1987a, 1987b. See also Hammett 1993, and this volume.

3. See various works by Miksicek listed in the bibliography, including 1983a, 1983b, 1983c, 1983d, 1984b.

4. In her review of a draft of this book, Jan Timbrook wrote that "*N. glauca* was not regarded as traditional tobacco by Chumash earlier in this century. Any use of it today is a recent development. . . . Native people I know who use it now only do so because it is easier to find than the native species, and grows everywhere."

5. See various works by Matthews listed in the bibliography, including 1984, 1986a, 1986b. Also, Carol Brandt, personal communication.

# 6

# *Out of California*

## Cultural Geography of Western North American Tobacco

### Julia E. Hammett

Most current knowledge of tobacco is dominated by the history of European and Euro-American tobacco use. From archaeobotanical data, however, we now know that pipe, cigar, and cigarette smoking, as well as a number of other indigenous uses of tobacco, predate any contact with Europe. Paleoethnobotanists have partially traced the path of *N. rustica* from Mexico into the U.S. Southwest and the eastern woodlands, and we know a little about the distribution of *N. tabacum* in South America and the Caribbean. In addition, there are a number of lesser-known tobaccos having origins in the far west of North America, where two types were domesticated and eventually traded out of California (table 28).

Three source areas of native tobacco occur in western North America: (1) the Great Basin, where the species *N. attenuata* may have originated; (2) southern coastal California, where three taxa occur—*N. clevelandii*, *N. trigonophylla* var. *trigonophylla*, and *N. trigonophylla* var. *palmeri*; and (3) most of coastal, central valley, and northern California, where another complex, *N. quadrivalvis*, occurs.[1]

*N. quadrivalvis* includes four varieties: var. *bigelovii*, var. *wallacei*, var. *quadrivalvis*, and var. *multivalvis*. All but two of the tobaccos

### Table 28: *Nicotiana* Species Native to Western North America

| Species | Geographic Origin |
| --- | --- |
| *N. attenuata* Torrey ex. S. Wats | Great Basin |
| *N. trigonophylla* Dunal | |
| Var. *trigonophylla* | Southern California |
| Var. *palmeri* (Gray) M. E. Jones (syn. = *N. palmeri* Gray) | Southern California |
| *N. clevelandii* Gray | Southern coastal California |
| *N. quadrivalvis* Pursh | |
| Var. *bigelovii* (Torr.) Dewolf (syn. = *N. bigelovii* [Torr.] S. Wats.; syn. = *N. plumbaginifolia* var. *bigelovii* Torr.) | North-central California |
| Var. *wallacei* (Gray) Mansf. (syn. = *N. bigelovii* var. *wallacei* Gray) | Southern California |
| Var. *quadrivalvis* L. (syn. = *N. bigelovii* var. *quadrivalvis* [Pursh] Eastw.) | Northern California |
| Var. *multivalvis* (Lindl.) Mansf. (syn. = *N. bigelovii* var. *multivalvis* [Lindl.] Eastw.) | Oregon/Washington(?) |

Sources: Cronquist et al. 1984; Kartesz 1994.

native to western North America still occur in the wild. Two varieties of *N. quadrivalvis*, var. *quadrivalvis* and var. *multivalvis*, apparently were domesticated by prehistoric Native Americans. The two cultigens are distinguished from their wild relatives by having larger flowers and bigger seed capsules. The wild varieties of *N. quadrivalvis* have capsules with two or three locules (compartments), whereas var. *quadrivalvis* specimens typically have four locules, and var. *multivalvis* specimens have more than four, often six or more. Typically var. *multivalvis* and some of the var. *quadrivalvis* specimens have an indehiscent capsule—that is, one that does not naturally open to disperse its seeds.

In their *The Intermountain Flora*, Cronquist and colleagues (1984:72–73) state that *N. quadrivalvis* vars. *quadrivalvis* and *multivalvis* "ap-

Photo 31. Type specimen of *Nicotiana quadrivalvis* var. *multivalvis* (*N. quadrivalvis*) collected in trade by Meriwether Lewis along the Missouri River on October 12, 1804. Curated at the Philadelphia Academy of Science. Lewis Specimen no. 45; PH type specimen.

parently were maintained solely by primitive agriculture, and are no longer in cultivation." Both varieties were "discovered" and named by early historic expeditions. The type specimen of *N. quadrivalvis* was collected by Lewis and Clark among the Arikara (Ricara) along the Missouri River in the Dakotas on Columbus Day, 1804. Meriwether Lewis's specimen was presented in trade at a gathering of chiefs meeting their expedition. The "Lewis" specimen was carried back to Philadelphia, and the seed was dispersed among some young colonial gentlemen gardeners, including Thomas Jefferson and William Hamilton (Betts 1985). The specimen is curated at the Philadelphia Academy of Natural Sciences and is shown in photo 31.

In 1825, David Douglas, representing the Royal Horticultural Society in London, collected *N. multivalvis*, now named *N. quadrivalvis* var. *multivalvis*, on the banks of the Multnomah, a tributary of the Columbia River near present-day Portland, Oregon (fig. 14). According to his journal, Douglas's source declined to trade, but later, upon discovering Douglas pillaging his plot, the cultivator begrudgingly traded for some of the commercial tobacco Douglas was carrying (Lavender 1972). Douglas's seeds were later distributed by the Botanical Garden of Copenhagen to various other horticultural gardens for propagation. In 1907, this seed produced new specimens for Goodspeed and Setchell at the University of California at Berkeley.[2] In 1918, Hitchcock at Arlington Farms in Virginia and Safford at the USDA Greenhouse in Washington, D.C., obtained Arikara seed of var. *quadrivalvis* from Nebraska ethnobotanist Melvin Gilmore. In 1936, Dore and Breitung of the Central Experimental Farm in Ottawa obtained seeds from the UC-Berkeley gardens and from the USDA, which they propagated and deposited at the Dominion Arboretum and Gardens in Ottawa, Canada. Now, 76 years after the initial grow-out project, the historical specimens and progeny of the grow-out experiments account for two-thirds of the specimens of these two allegedly "extinct"

Figure 14. Drawing of *Nicotiana multivalvis* (*N. quadrivalvis* var. *multivalvis*) "made in the garden of the Horticultural Society, in September 1826" (Lindley 1827).

Photo 32. *Nicotiana quadrivalvis* var. *multivalvis* (*N. multivalvis*). Seeds were collected by David Douglas near the Columbia River in 1825 and propagated by the University of California Gardens at Berkeley in 1907. Curated at the National Herbarium, Washington, D.C. Specimen no. 1366005.

varieties that I have been able to locate in North American herbaria (photo 32, table 29).

In addition to the gene pool just described, there are a few other historical specimens, notably two samples of *N. quadrivalvis* var. *multivalvis*. One was collected in 1841 by Commander Charles Wilkes along the Umqua River near the coast of Oregon, and another in 1871 by Elihu Hall near Salem, Oregon (photo 33). Finally, three specimens, apparently from the same population of *N. quadrivalvis* var. *quadrivalvis*, were collected in 1899 by Blasdale and Davy in the Hoopa Valley of northwestern California.

Another possible population in the far Northwest Coast was observed and collected by several explorers and naturalists on the Queen Charlotte Islands and the coast of Alaska in the late 1700s and 1800s (Turner and Taylor 1972). Two specimens, both housed in Great Britain, appear to substantiate the presence of the *Nicotiana quadrivalvis* complex (Eastwood 1938; Turner and Taylor 1972). However, a more

Table 29: Herbarium Specimens of *Nicotiana quadrivalvis* Cultigens Native to Western North America

| Accession No. | Place Cultivated | Collector | Date | Determination/Comments |
|---|---|---|---|---|
| **var. multivalvis** | | | | |
| S 13382 | Umpqua R., Oreg. | Wilke, no. 1159 | 1841 | |
| H | Oregon | Hall | 1871 | |
| S 720836 | Salem, Oreg. | Hall | 1871 | |
| DAO 187543 | Oregon | Hall | 1871 | Raven in 1959 |
| H 751220 | Oregon | Hall | ca. 1875 | |
| S 1366005[a] | UC-Berkeley gardens; Copenhagen | Douglas, 1825 | 1907 | Goodspeed |
| MBO 930884[a] | UC-Berkeley gardens; Copenhagen | Douglas, 1825 | 1907 | Goodspeed |
| UC 313716[a] | UC-Berkeley gardens; Copenhagen | Douglas, 1825 | 1907 | Goodspeed |
| POM 118247[a] | UC-Berkeley gardens; Copenhagen | Douglas, 1825 | 1907 | Goodspeed |
| NA 19394[b] | Bismarck, N.D. | Gilmore | Feb. 1918 | |
| US 1038088 | Bismarck, N.D. | Gilmore | Feb. 1918 | |
| NA 19393 | Bismarck, N.D. | Gilmore | Sum. 1918 | |
| NA 19395 photo[b] | Bismarck, N.D. | Gilmore | Feb. 1918 | |
| DAO 423421 | USDA, 1936 | Dore and Breitung | Sept. 13, 1948 | Goodspeed |
| DAO 423420 | UC-Berkeley gardens, 1936 | Dore and Breitung | Sept. 13, 1948 | Goodspeed in 1952 |
| **var. quadrivalvis** | | | | |
| H[b] | Missouri R. | Lewis | Oct. 12, 1804 | Pursh |
| UC 1902 | Hoopa Valley, Calif. | Blasdale and Davy, no. 5709 | June 20, 1899 | |
| UC 73584 | Hoopa Valley, Calif. | Blasdale and Davy, no. 5709 | June 20, 1899 | |
| UC 73585 | Hoopa Valley, Calif. | Blasdale and Davy, no. 5709 | June 20, 1899 | |
| DAO[c] | Spearfish, S.D. | Haberman | June 20, 1981 | |
| NA 85329 photo | Ft. Berthold Res. | Gilmore | 1911–1912 | |
| US 1038095 | Bismarck, N.D. | Gilmore | Feb. 1918 | |
| NA photo | USDA Greenhouse | Gilmore | Feb. 18, 1918 | |
| US 1221025 | Arlington Farms, Va. | Hitchcock | July 5, 1918 | |
| NA photo | Arlington Farms, Va. | Hitchcock | July 5, 1918 | White flowered |
| NA photo | Arlington Farms, Va. | Hitchcock | July 5, 1918 | Small flowered |
| NA photo[b] | Arlington Farms, Va. | Hitchcock | July 5, 1918 | |
| NA | Arlington Farms, Va. | Hitchcock and Safford | Aug. 13, 1918 | White flowered |
| NA 5987 | USDA Greenhouse | Safford | July 13, 1918 | |
| MBO E007 (16–48)[d] | UC-Berkeley gardens | Harrington (Gilmore) | 1940 | |
| NA 48896/37024 | DAO423422 | Dore and Breitung | Sept. 7, 1948 | Goodspeed in 1953 |
| DAO 423422 | UC-Berkeley gardens, 1938 | Dore and Breitung | Sept. 13, 1948 | Goodspeed in 1952 |

Key to abbreviations:

DAO Dominion Arboretum and Gardens, Ottawa, Canada
MBO Missouri Botanical Gardens, St. Louis
NA United States National Arboretum, Washington, D.C.
H Philadelphia Academy of Natural Sciences
POM Pomona College, Claremont, California
UC University of California, Berkeley
US United States National Herbarium, Washington, D.C.
a Collected on Columbia River.
b Collected from Arikara.
c Collected in Hoopa Valley, 1899.
d Collected from Hidatsa.

Photo 33. *Nicotiana quadrivalvis* var. *multivalvis* (*N. multivalvis*). Collected by Elihu Hall in Salem, Oregon, in 1871. Curated at the U.S. National Herbarium, Washington, D.C. Specimen no. 720836.

complete inventory of Northwest Coast species awaits the discovery of further specimens (Meilleur 1979; Turner and Taylor 1972).

Even with this extremely small sample and widely divergent geographical distribution, several questions can be raised about relationships and origins. Does this distribution even remotely reflect Native American patterns of use prior to contact with Euro-American explorers? Setchell (1921) and Goodspeed (1954) have each suggested that the close botanical relationship between members of the *N. quadrivalvis* complex indicates that the cultivated varieties were derived from wild California stock, presumably *N. quadrivalvis* vars. *bigelovii* and/or *wallacei* (map 11). Where and when did the cultigens originate? What part did Cali-

fornia Native Americans play in the domestication process? And how did these tobaccos spread out of California?

Native California tobacco taxa not in the *N. quadrivalvis* complex include *N. attenuata*, which occurs throughout much of the western United States (map 12), and the southern desert complex, which includes *N. clevelandii*, *N. trigonophylla* var. *trigonophylla*, and *N. trigonophylla* var. *palmeri*. The latter is considered by most authorities to be a variety of *N. trigonophylla*. From an anthropocentric point of view, *N. clevelandii*'s geographic distribution (map 13) is intriguing, because the plant is often associated with ancient shell middens along the coast of southern California, which notably contained soapstone smoking tubes (Wheeler 1871).

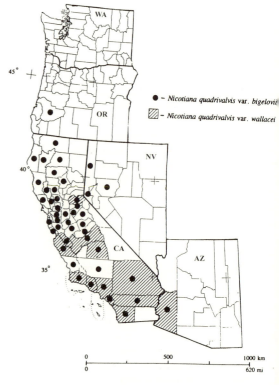

Map 11. Geographic distribution of *Nicotiana quadrivalvis* vars. *bigelovii* and *wallacei*.

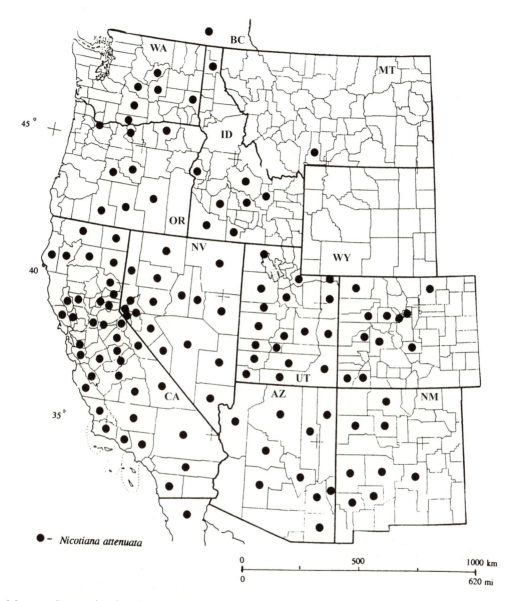

Map 12. Geographic distribution of *Nicotiana attenuata*.

Two other tobaccos found in California today are *N. glauca* and *N. acuminata* var. *multiflora*. Both are considered native to South America, not California. Their distributions indicate different habitat preferences (map 14). It is difficult to determine when either of these species arrived in California; both were documented by the 1880s. Further confounding the problem, herbaria sheets throughout the country document a practice in the 1890s of including *N. glauca* in the ballast of ships sailing to ports as far-flung as California, Florida, and New Jersey. For now, I accept the idea that these two species are entirely exotic to California and inconsequential to research related to the anthropogenic complex of *N. quadrivalvis*. Winter investigates

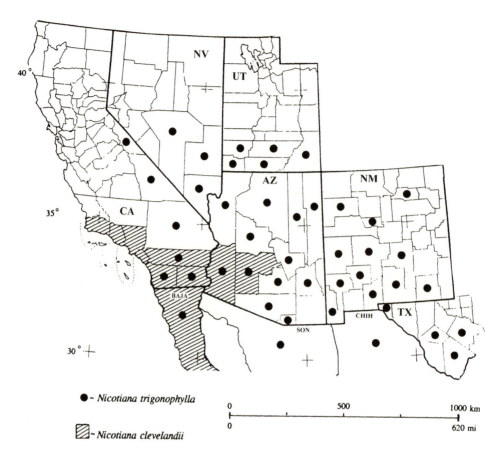

Map 13. Geographic distribution of *Nicotiana clevelandii* and *Nicotiana trigonophylla*.

the problem in more detail in chapters 2 and 5, since a number of Native American groups now consider *N. glauca* a traditional tobacco.

The cultigen members of the *N. quadrivalvis* complex are located at the margins of or outside the boundary of the wild stock. This is not surprising, given the requisite of isolation for the domestication process (Rindos 1984). But under what conditions did this process take place? Apparently *N. attenuata* was cultivated by the Thompson (Nlaka'pamux) and other interior groups in southern British Columbia with no evident genetic change (Setchell 1912, 1921; Turner et al. 1990).

Why did *N. quadrivalvis* change and not *N. attenuata*? Perhaps isolating *N. quadrivalvis* was easier than isolating *N. attenuata* because of their natural geographic distributions—*N. attenuata* has a broader range. Perhaps some qualitative characteristic of *N. quadrivalvis* was more desirable, and so domestication was a direct result of cultural selection. But if *N. attenuata* was also carried out of its natural range and planted by Native Americans, what allowed one species to be domesticated while the other remained wild? The answer may be a combination of cultural and natural processes. Perhaps *N. quadrivalvis* is genetically more plastic in the traits that allowed it to be domesticated, whereas *N. attenuata* is more resistent to human manipulation.[3] Recall that *N. quadrivalvis* var. *bigelovii* generally yields capsules having two or three

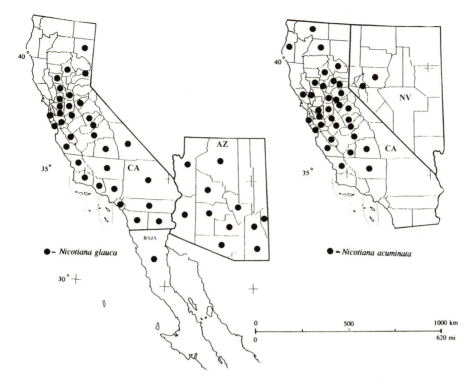

Map 14. Geographic distribution of *Nicotiana glauca* (left) and *N. acuminata* (right).

locules, whereas var. *quadrivalvis* capsules always have four locules and var. *multivalvis* capsules have more than four (six to eight are common). Through experimentation, Setchell (1921:407) was able to develop forms very close to var. *quadrivalvis* by crossing var. *multivalvis* with var. *bigelovii*. Apparently another cross resulted spontaneously in the botanical gardens at Berkeley. Setchell provided no information regarding the viability of these hybrids.

Even if such a cross was the source of the domesticated varieties, there is still no explanation for how and when these varieties were carried out of California, northward to the Columbia River, possibly as far north as the Queen Charlotte Islands, and eastward over the Rocky Mountains to the Missouri River. Presumably the cross would have taken place where both parent varieties occurred, such as in northern California or adjacent Oregon. In his treatment of the genus, Goodspeed (1954:285)

noted that "the high degree of compatibility of modern species of *Nicotiana*, even some which are widely separated taxonomically, suggests that natural hybridization may have been a factor in more instances of speciation than those in which its effect can today be recognized."

This conundrum is a compelling incentive to investigate the possibility of various crosses of *N. quadrivalvis* with *N. attenuata* and perhaps even with *N. rustica*. After all, *N. rustica* apparently was carried northward out of Mexico up the Missouri River, where it could have been bred with *N. multivalvis* (Setchell 1912). Or could var. *quadrivalvis* have been the result of a mutation in the Great Plains? If so, how do we account for the specimens of var. *quadrivalvis* collected the Hoopa Valley in 1899? Also, none of these scenarios accounts for the derivation of var. *multivalvis*. Setchell (1912) proposed that this variety might have originated from a simple mutation. Yet there have been no published reports of any laboratories reproducing such a mutation. On the basis of early ethnographies and ethnohistorical accounts, Brien Meilleur (1979) proposed a more circuitous route, relying upon evidence of trade ties. He suggested that tobacco was traded up the Columbia River, across the Rocky Mountains, northward to the Peace River, westward back across the Continental Divide, and then due west to the Queen Charlotte Islands, where var. *multivalvis* was observed. His proposal does not account for the genetic origin of var. *multivalvis*, but implicit in his model is its derivation from var. *quadrivalvis*. Meilleur's and Setchell's proposals, taken together, may yield a feasible explanation. However, an examination of locations where known specimens of var. *multivalvis* were collected indicates that a more direct route, essentially up the coast, is also a candidate. Given the current paucity of data, either or both routes are plausible.

Perhaps the human part of this anthropogenic equation is more informative. In the first part of the twentieth century, members of the Crow Indian tobacco society (which raised var. *multivalvis*) insisted that their tobacco was different from that of the Hidatsa (Lowie 1920). Setchell (1921) and other botanists agreed. David Douglas said that the Indian whose tobacco patch he raided told him that the Snake Indians also grew this kind of tobacco (var. *multivalvis*). Douglas suggested that these Indians may have traded it at the headwaters of the Missouri River, which they visited annually (Lavender 1972). Gilmore (1922:480) concluded, in contrast, from all the evidence he had, that the "Mandan and Hidatsa both obtained it from the Arikara, who had originally brought it with them in their northward migration from the southern Plains." Was the route out of California for both of these species northward? Or did they take separate tracks? Perhaps, considering how quickly a var. *quadrivalvis*–like specimen was developed in the Berkeley gardens (Setchell 1912), the specimen of var. *quadrivalvis* found at Hoopa, California, is not directly related to the plains variety at all but is of an entirely independent derivation.

## Out of the Ashes

No matter what the route, we cannot ignore Native American customs and traditions surrounding the traditional practice of cultivating tobacco throughout these regions. Indeed, the early ethnographies record a shared set of ideas and techniques regarding the mutualistic relationship between Native Americans and *N. quadrivalvis*. Recurring themes in these reports include isolation of the plants, preferences for uphill areas away from rivers and streams, burning plots prior to planting, prohibitions against visiting plots between planting and harvesting, guarding of the seed stock, and the idea that cultivated tobacco originally came from the mountains.

Our most extensive Native American word list for tobacco classification results from John P. Harrington's work in the 1930s on tobacco use among the Karok. The Karok are Hokan speakers who share the Klamath Mountains and Hoopa Valley of northwestern California with their Algonkian-speaking Yurok neighbors directly to the west, as well as with two Athapaskan groups, the Hupa to the south and Tolowa to the north.

The Karok term applied to wild, self-sown tobacco translates as "river tobacco." Cultivated tobacco was called on occasion "mountain tobacco" but more commonly "real tobacco" or "people's tobacco." Karok consultants gave Harrington (1932:75) this account of the origin of tobacco:

> The Ikxareyavs (ancient ones) said it. They
> left the plants, all the plants, our plants.
> They said the plants will all be medicine.
> Then they said: "Human will live on them."
> Then tobacco, one Ikxareyav threw the
> downslope tobacco down by the river bank.
> "But Human is not going to smoke it, that
> downslope tobacco." Then again, he threw

down another kind, real tobacco. "Human will smoke this, the good tobacco. Human will sow this, his own tobacco. Human will sow it back of his place, his own tobacco. Behold it will be strong. Human will sow his tobacco. Behold he will be feeding his tobacco to Mountains." They said, the Ikxareyavs. Behold, some of them became mountains, the Ikxareyavs did. So this is why they sow smoking tobacco, behold the Ikxareyavs threw it down, the smoking tobacco.

The acquisition of sacred tobacco from the mountains is also present in several origin legends recorded by Robert H. Lowie (1920: 177–178) among the Crow Indian tobacco society of the Great Plains. And in one Haida legend from the Northwest Coast, "the tobacco tree was said to grow on top of a high mountain, many days journey from the seashore, and was guarded by a powerful chief and his warriors. . . . A Haida man, hearing of the plant, managed to journey to the mountain, shoot off 'but two seeds' from the top of the tree, and escape with them back to the Queen Charlottes" (Turner and Taylor 1972:253).

Another reference to guarding seeds is provided by Gilmore (1919:114), whose Winnebago sources said that "the woodland tribes eagerly accepted presents of prepared tobacco of the species *N. quadrivalvis* from the tribes of the plains region and sought to obtain seed of the same, but that the plains tribes jealously guarded against allowing the seed to be exported to their woodland neighbors."

Both examples indicate that the control of seed stock was an element of the management of this resource. This would have been more feasible for varieties having indehiscent (non-opening) capsules. A clue to how this trait might have developed as a result of either deliberate or unintentional cultural selection is provided by one of Gilmore's Plains Indian consultants, who told him that "the crop was allowed to grow thick, and then the whole plant—leaves, unripe fruit capsules, and the tender, small parts of the

stems—was dried for smoking. The unripe seed capsules, dried separately, were specially prized for smoking on account of the flavor, pronounced by the Indians to be like the flavor now found in the imported Turkish tobacco" (Gilmore 1919:114).

Indehiscent fruit bodies are "thought to have developed from suppression of the naturally occurring opening mechanisms found in dehiscent structures" (Tootill and Blackmore 1984: 187). Indehiscent capsules replaced self-opening capsules partly because cultural selection pressures outweighed natural selection. No longer were self-seeders favored, but rather, through the process of domestication, the plants became dependent upon humans for their procreation and survival (Rindos 1984). Similarly, the larger and thicker pods enhanced the security of the seed harvest.

In northern California, specific methods of cultivating tobacco have been described for the Hupa, Yurok, and Karok. Central themes are fire and isolation. In 1903, Goddard (1903: 36–37) collected this account of tobacco cultivation among the Hupa: "Logs were burned and the seed sown in the ashes. The plant appears to be and probably is identical with the wild *Nicotiana bigelovii*, but the Hupa say the cultivated form is better. The wild form found along river, they say, is poison. . . . They believed an enemy's death may be caused by giving him tobacco from plants growing on a grave."

In 1925, A. L. Kroeber (1925:88–89) observed:

All tobacco smoked by the Yurok was planted by them. . . . Logs were burned on a hilltop, the seeds sown, and the plants nursed. Those who grew tobacco sold to those who did not. A woman's cap full or not full was the quantity given for a dentalium shell—a high price. Tobacco grows wild also, apparently of the same species as the planted, but is never used by the Yurok, who fear that it might be from a graveyard or from a trash midden or other unhealthy place. Otherwise it sprouts chiefly along sandy bars close to the river;

and this seems to have caused the choice of summits for the cultivated product.

Burning the ground to enhance conditions for tobacco plants was widely practiced by California natives as well as by Great Basin groups using *N. quadrivalvis* and *N. attenuata*, whether or not seeds were planted (Fowler 1986; Kroeber 1941). In the Great Plains, Gilmore's Pawnee consultant told him that in the old times "the ground was prepared by gathering a quantity of dried grass, which was burned where the patch was to be sown" (Gilmore 1919:114). Similar information was collected by Lowie (1920) among the Crow Indians at about this time. Lowie's consultants added that they currently did not burn the ground but plowed prior to planting.

From this information, we can conclude that western Native Americans developed a set of customs that selected for these large-capsuled, extremely pungent tobaccos. Strategies included isolation of gardens and plot preparation by clearing and burning. Availability of the seed pods was restricted in some instances, limiting access to the seed source. Perhaps as emphasis on guarding the seed stock increased, larger, indehiscent pods were encouraged through selection. Exactly how, when, and from what botanical origins these cultigens were derived remains untested. But the significance of this sacred herb to Native American society is irrefutable.

## Back From Extinction

Ethnobotanists working in the Great Plains in the early 1900s observed that because of pressures from Euro-Americans to discontinue traditional practices, and because of the availability of commercial tobacco, most Native American groups had ceased to cultivate tobacco. Some more traditional and more isolated groups in the northern plains were exceptions. Nevertheless, botanists declared these cultigens extinct.

Enter John Hellson and Morgan Gadd, ethnobotanists who reported collecting *Nicotiana multivalvis* (*N. quadrivalvis* var. *multivalvis*) from a northern Blackfoot tobacco society in 1971. Their text mentions taboos preventing visits to the plots between planting and harvesting because young plants were being tended by supernatural Small People (Hellson and Gadd 1974:14). Their ethnobotany indicates that they deposited a voucher specimen at the Museum of Man in Ottawa, now the Canadian Museum of Civilisation. Unfortunately, there is no tobacco specimen currently among the Hellson and Gadd vouchers at that institution.

Research continues as new herbarium specimens in Europe and Russia are investigated. Discovery of more historic specimens will expand our knowledge of the distributions. From the existing herbarium specimen gene pool, attempts are currently under way by Joseph Winter to propagate seeds.[4] Tests conducted in the early 1900s demonstrate the longevity of seed viability for the genus *Nicotiana* (Goodspeed 1913, 1915). But specimens and seeds of living populations of var. *multivalvis* and var. *quadrivalvis* are highly desired, if such populations exist.

Ultimately, one of the objectives of such research is to return these plants to Native American tribes for cultivation. From the standpoint of biodiversity, the rewards of such a program are obvious, but there are more humane motivations as well. Many tribes, particularly in California, were declared "extinct" by a previous generation of anthropologists, including Kroeber, and were therefore terminated by the federal government (Castillo 1978). These tribes are now striving for federal recognition, making their journey back from "extinction," at the same time that ethnobotanists are attempting to help revitalize the tobacco cultigens. Tobacco is arguably the single most sacred plant in all of North America. How fitting for their ancient sacred companion, tobacco, to accompany indigenous Californians as they reemerge from extinction.

## Conclusion

Examination of herbaria specimens, historical accounts, and plant distributions has generated new information about an anthropogenic complex of tobaccos native to western North America. *Nicotiana quadrivalvis* was the source of two domesticated varieties with enlarged seed capsules—*multivalvis* and *quadrivalvis*. These cultigens were traded through the Willamette, Columbia, and Missouri River valleys, possibly extending as far northward as the Queen Charlotte Islands. The management strategies used by Native Americans to sustain their tobacco cultigens included isolating their gardens, burning and clearing the plots, and controlling the seed stock. A set of traditions and rituals developed that served to perpetuate this anthropogenic system. Although now considered extinct by many botanists, research has indicated that these two cultigens may still be present among the native groups of western North America.

## Notes

Living expenses during this research project were underwritten by Constance H. and Ellis T. Hammett, the Nevada Employment Security Department, the Muwekma Tribe, the Ohlone Family Consulting Services, and the Stanford University Campus Archaeology Program. Travel grants were made available through the Estate of Christopher Raven, a University of North Carolina Research Grant, and the Stanford University Campus Archaeology Program. Logistical support for library research and communication between research teams was facilitated by the University of Nevada Computer Services.

A number of colleagues actively participated in data collection for this project; they include Joseph Winter, Ron Fritz, Jan Gish, Leonard Blake, Sheri Maktima, Annette G. Ericksen, Laura Jones, Mary Adair, Gayle Fritz, Kristen Gremillion and Andrea Hunter. Critical comments and additional information were provided by Karen Adams, M. Jean Black, Carole Crumley, Joel Gunn, Patricia Evans, Catherine Fowler, Gayle Fritz, Paul Gardner, Andrea Hunter, Chester King, Alan Leventhal, Paul Lewis, Alan May, Sandra Peacock, Belinda Rose, Ann Tippit, Nancy Turner, Susan Wallace, Joseph Winter, and Richard Yarnell.

Representatives of herbaria and libraries who assisted with my visits and inquiries include Sarah McNaull and Peter Masio of the National Arboretum, George Russell of the National Herbarium, Alfred Ernest Schuyler of the Philadelphia Academy of Natural Sciences, Jimmy Massey of the North Carolina University Herbarium in Chapel Hill, Steve Boyd of the Rancho Santa Ana Botanical Gardens, Belinda Rose of the University of Nevada Herbarium, Tim Noakes of the Stanford University Special Library Collections, Janet Jones of the California Academy of Sciences, Roy Goodman of the American Philosophical Society, Todd Burgess of the University of Nevada Life and Health Sciences Library, and Margaret Goodrich of the Douglas Library at the Denver Art Museum.

Herbarium collections used in this study include those at the University of Nevada, Reno; the Missouri Botanical Gardens, St. Louis; the Rancho Santa Ana Botanic Gardens, Claremont, California; Pomona College, Claremont, California; the California Academy of Sciences, San Francisco; the Dudley Herbarium of Stanford University; Ohio State University, Columbus; the University of California, Berkeley; the University of North Carolina; the United States National Herbarium, Washington, D.C.; the United States National Arboretum, Washington D.C.; the Dominion Arboretum and Gardens, Ottawa, Canada; the Philadelphia Academy of Natural Sciences; the Walter B. McDougall Herbarium, Northern Arizona University, Flagstaff; the Botanical Museum of Stockholm, Sweden; the Komarov Institute, St. Petersburg, Russia; the University of Copenhagen, Denmark; and Uppsala University, Sweden.

A preliminary version of this chapter was presented at the 1995 annual meeting of the Society for Ethnobiology in Tucson, Arizona.

1. Editor's note: *Nicotiana attenuata* and *N. trigonophylla* occur elsewhere as well, such as in Arizona and New Mexico, so these may not be the only places where they originated. *N. quadrivalvis* also grows elsewhere. See chapter 5.

2. Editor's note: Some of the 1907 UC-Berkeley seeds ended up in the Komorov Institute in Russia and the Botanical Museum of Stockholm, Sweden, where Jan Gish obtained them during her research for chapter 12 of this book. Gish gave them to me, and after repeated unsuccessful attempts at germinating them using standard techniques, I managed to germinate two of the seeds (one from each institute) with the aid of a German seed regeneration mixture—"Silpan, Das Naturliche Pflanzen Regenerativ Mit Germanium." The plants are now growing in my greenhouse.

3. Editor's note: Germination experiments carried out in my greenhouse have also demonstrated that *N. attenuata* is far more difficult to germinate and grow than *N. quadrivalvis*. Under natural conditions, fire may be a necessary ingredient.

4. Editor's note: After repeated unsuccessful attempts with standard germination approaches, I have been able, using Silpan (see note 2), to germinate old seeds from museum collections of the following specimens of *N. quadrivalvis*.

First, *N. quadrivalvis* var. *multivalvis* (*N. multivalvis*) Goodspeed no. 294: distributed by the UC-Berkeley Herbarium to the Botanical Museum of Sweden, Stockholm, from seeds cultivated at the UC-Berkeley Botanical Gardens from seed sent in 1907 from the botanical gardens at Copenhagen, Denmark, originally obtained by David Douglas in 1825 from Indians cultivating the plants along the Columbia River in Oregon. Jan Gish obtained the seeds in 1996 for her research for chapter 12 of this book and gave them to me (JCW no. 213).

Second, *N. quadrivalvis* var. *multivalvis* (*N. multivalvis*) Goodspeed no. 294: same as the preceding, except distributed by UC-Berkeley to the Komorov Institute in Russia, where Gish obtained them and gave them to me (JCW no. 213A).

Third, *N. quadrivalvis* var. *bigelovii* (*N. bigelovii*) Goodspeed no. 296: distributed by the UC-Berkeley Herbarium to the Botanical Museum at the University of Copenhagen, Denmark, from seeds cultivated at Berkeley from seeds obtained from Calaveras County, California, from plants used for smoking by the Miwok Indians and donated by Dr. S. A. Bartlett in 1907. Obtained by Gish in 1996 from the University of Copenhagen and given to me (JCW no. 217A).

Fourth, *N. quadrivalvis* var. *multivalvis* (*N. multivalvis*), "Crow Indian tobacco seeds, Montana": seeds collected by Melvin Gilmore in 1933. I obtained them in 1996 from a voucher specimen at the Bailey Hortorium at Cornell University (JCW no. 201).

# PART THREE

# The Archaeobotanical Study of Tobacco

# 7

## Tobacco Use, Ecology, and Manipulation in the Prehistoric and Historic Southwestern United States

### Karen R. Adams and Mollie S. Toll

This chapter provides an overview of Native American tobacco (*Nicotiana*) use in the four southwestern states of Arizona, New Mexico, Colorado, and Utah, on the basis of historic ethnographic observations and the rapidly accumulating archaeological record of tobacco remains. We discuss four wild species (*N. attenuata*, *N. trigonophylla*, *N. clevelandii*, and *N. palmeri*),[1] two domesticated taxa (*N. rustica*, *N. tabacum*), and one historic introduction (*N. glauca*). We also summarize data useful in identifying the archaeological remains of species or groups of species. Few archaeological reports from the northern Mexican states of Chihuahua and Sonora contain archaeobotanical analyses, and therefore little can be said at this time about ancient tobacco use in that region.

Several topics discussed in this chapter illustrate how tobacco and humans are well adapted to each other. They include the use of fire to increase supply; how range extensions and morphological changes could have resulted from aboriginal tobacco management; how range expansion could produce hybridization, heterosis, and polyploidy; and how these processes could be expressed in larger plants and seeds, indehiscent seed capsules, alterations in flowering seasons, larger capsules, and increased levels of variation. All of these processes could have resulted from increased interactions between humans and tobacco, thereby leading to managed, cultivated, and even domesticated plants.

## Southwestern Tobacco Species: Natural Habitat and Range

A worldwide view of tobacco ecology reveals that *Nicotiana* is composed largely of pioneer species that occupy coarse soils in disturbed sites (Wells 1959:642). Tobacco plants are highly adapted to move into recently opened habitats through their enormous production of minute seeds that are dispersed by wind, water, and animals.

### Native, Naturalized, and Domesticated Species

Annual *Nicotiana attenuata* Torr. is broadly distributed from northern Baja California east through the Great Basin to beyond the Rocky Mountains, and then north to southern Canada. It does especially well in naturally disturbed sites at 1,000–2,600 meters (Goodspeed 1954: 429; Wells 1959:642). The plants usually flower during the summer months (H. D. Harrington 1964:481; Kearney and Peebles 1960:761; Martin and Hutchins 1980:1750–1752; Wells 1959:640; Welsh et al. 1987:606).

The annual or limited perennial *N. trigonophylla* Dunal. does well in rocky or gravelly situations and along watercourses in arid or desert regions, from sea level to 2,900 meters in Mexico and the southwestern United States (Goodspeed 1954:385; H. D. Harrington 1964: 481; Kearney and Peebles 1960:761; Martin and Hutchins 1980; Wells 1959:642; Welsh et al. 1987:606). It flowers throughout the year, with a principal flowering season from March through October (Wells 1959:640).

The range of annual *N. clevelandii* Gray includes Mexico, the southern end of Baja California, southern California, and small portions of southern and western Arizona. The species prefers sandy ground or gravel, sea cliffs, dunes, washes, and desert slopes, from sea level to 450 meters (Goodspeed 1954:454; Kearney and Peebles 1960:761).

Spring flowering *N. palmeri* Gray (= *N. trigonophylla* Dun. var. *palmeri* [Gray] Jones) is an annual or limited perennial closely allied to *N. trigonophylla*. Plants are often found in sunny, rocky situations from western Arizona to southern Utah, between 250 and 1,300 meters (Goodspeed 1954:387; Kearney and Peebles 1960:761).

Tree tobacco, *Nicotiana glauca* Graham, is a shrub or small tree naturalized from South America in historic times (Goodspeed 1954:336; Kearney and Peebles 1960:761). It is included here because well-preserved, dry cave sites in southern and central Arizona might preserve tobacco evidence from a broad range of time periods, up to and including the historic.[2] This continuously flowering species prefers river banks, roadsides, and gullies, from sea level to 3,000 meters (Goodspeed 1954:336).

One cultivated tobacco, *Nicotiana rustica* L., is highly polymorphic in habit and generally unknown in the wild except for disturbed habitats in South America. *N. rustica* was the first tobacco grown and exported by American colonists; it was later replaced by the modern tobacco of commerce, *N. tabacum* L (Goodspeed 1954:353). Richard Ford (1985:344) suggested that the Spanish were responsible for first bringing *N. rustica* to the Southwest in the early years of their colonization. Reports of its presence in Southwestern archaeological contexts are, however, rare.

*Nicotiana tabacum*, which is not known to occur in the wild, exhibits a wide range of morphological variation and is found in both tropical and temperate regions (Goodspeed 1954:

373, 375). Although it is thought to have been imported to the North American continent from the West Indies by Virginia colonists, it is included in this chapter because of a reference to it in an ancient southwestern context and because some well-protected sites could easily include historically introduced materials. Contemporary southwestern tribes have also used it in historic times.

Examination of more than 400 specimens in the University of Arizona herbarium, collected primarily in Arizona and to a lesser extent in New Mexico, Utah, Nevada, California, Oregon, and Mexico, reveals that *Nicotiana attenuata*, *N. trigonophylla*, *N. clevelandii*, and *N. glauca* all do well in washes or near streams (38 percent of habitat citations), in sandy soil (18 percent), and along roadways or in other disturbed situations (18 percent). Indigenous groups could expect to find these tobaccos in well-drained, water-enriched, naturally and humanly disturbed locations. Phillip Wells (1959) came to a similar conclusion about habitat preferences of *N. attenuata* and *N. trigonophylla*. The data also document differences in species' elevational ranges: *N. attenuata* grows primarily above 1,525 meters, *N. clevelandii* prefers elevations below 300 meters, and *N. trigonophylla* and *N. glauca* both share the same 0–1,500 meters range.

## The Role of Fire in Encouraging Nicotiana

The response of *Nicotiana attenuata* to a lightning-caused fire that thoroughly burned a piñon-juniper woodland in southwestern Colorado has been documented by one of us (Adams 1991, 1993a). In the first summer following the July 1989 fire, a research team counted 86 healthy, robust tobacco plants, many over 1 meter in height and width and nearly all of them fully reproductive. In contrast, no tobacco plants were observed in the surrounding unburned area or in a nearby burned sagebrush-bitterbrush (*Artemisia-Purshia*) plot, although occasional tobacco plants have been documented in the area's natural flora (Welsh and Erdman 1964). In the second summer following the fire, the tobacco population included fewer plants, most of them measuring less than 15 centimeters in height. No tobacco plants were observed in the third year after the fire, suggesting that periodic burning would be needed to ensure continuing supplies.

Astute humans interested in harvesting tobacco could take advantage of natural fires or set some of their own in order to increase tobacco supplies. The role of fire in encouraging tobacco has been clearly recognized by historic southwestern groups. For example, the Havasupai in Arizona cut down mesquite trees and burned them, then threw tobacco seeds in the ashes (Spier 1928:105). Groups in California cultivated tobacco on newly burned ground (Setchell 1921:411), and a number of northern Paiute groups burned prior to planting (Stewart 1941:376).

Given the natural preference of southwestern tobacco plants for disturbed sites, and the response of a broadly distributed species like *N. attenuata* to fire, humans and tobacco seem well adapted to each other. Humans provide both the open habitats and the burned landscapes favored by tobacco. Tobacco, in turn, flourishes close to human habitats and is available for both the unconscious and conscious human selection pressures that might change its status from wild to managed, cultivated, or domesticated.

## Characteristics of Parts Most Commonly Recovered in the Southwestern Archaeological Record

The most common tobacco parts reported from southwestern archaeological sites are seeds, capsules, and stems. Other, rarely occurring parts are not discussed here. Thomas Goodspeed (1954) summarized the distinguishing features of most tobacco plant parts. As in other, similar attempts to identify archaeological materials, our ability to segregate tobacco parts rests upon (1) a detailed morphological and anatomical understanding of the part in question, based on direct comparison to specimens in herbarium collections; (2) descriptive morphometric data (means, standard deviations, ranges), based on populations whenever possible; (3) fully described modern comparative materials of all species known or expected in the region of study; and (4) knowledge of overlap between tobacco species and awareness of the possibilities for confusing tobacco with potential tobacco mimics. Well-supported identifications are based on more than one criterion.

## Seeds

Seeds are the parts most often recovered in archaeological sites, owing in part to the common use of flotation, an effective recovery technique for small organic items in archaeological sediments. Tobacco seeds "range from 0.4–1.3 mm in length, and are oval, elliptic, spherical, reniform or angularly several-sided" (Goodspeed 1954:89). They have an especially distinct "wavy-walled" appearance (Gunn and Gaffney 1974:8). However, badly degraded archaeological specimens may be difficult to identify, and researchers need to be familiar with other native genera within the Solanaceae that also have reticulate seed coat patterning, such as *Physalis*, *Solanum*, and *Lycium*. Seeds of southwestern tobacco species display variability in size, shape, and seed coat reticulation patterns, as is illustrated in photos 34–36 and summarized in table 30.

Two archaeobotanists (Adams 1990b; Hammett 1993) have gathered morphometric data on the seeds of five regional tobacco species, including some specimens that have been experimentally charred. For the five taxa examined, seeds smaller than 0.70 millimeter in length or 0.50 millimeter in width are likely to belong to *N. glauca*, *N. tabacum*, or *N. trigonophylla*, whereas those larger than 1.0 millimeter in length or 0.80 millimeter in width are *N. rustica*. Seeds between 0.70 and 1.00 millimeter in length and 0.50 and 0.80 millimeter in width likely represent *N. attenuata* or *N. rustica* (though a few

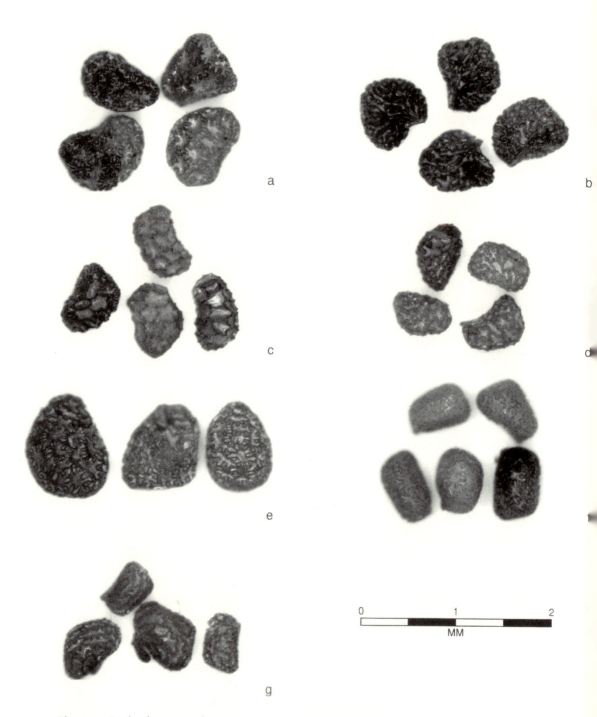

Photo 34. Seeds of seven southwestern U.S. *Nicotiana* species, photographed at 32X magnification. *a, N. attenuata* (Long Mesa fire of 1989, Adams 1991); *b, N. clevelandii* (specimen no. 129, J. Winter, seeds slightly immature); *c, N. palmeri* (specimen 106, J. Winter); *d, N. trigonophylla* (Tucson, Arizona); *e, N. rustica* (N1, Spanish settlers, Native Seeds/SEARCH; same as specimen 1, J. Winter); *f, N. tabacum* (specimen 24, J. Winter); *g, N. glauca* (specimen 72, J. Winter).

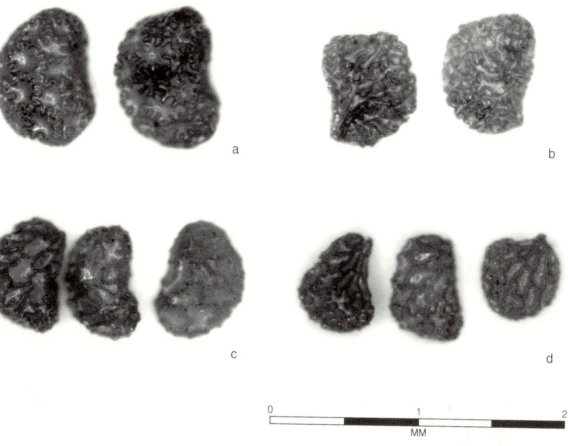

Photo 35. Seeds of four native southwestern U.S. *Nicotiana* species, photographed at 50X magnification. *a, N. attenuata* (Long Mesa fire of 1989, Adams 1991); *b, N. clevelandii* (specimen 129, J. Winter, seeds slightly immature); *c, N. palmeri* (specimen 206, J. Winter); *d, N. trigonophylla* (Tucson, Arizona). All three seeds of varied shape from same capsule.

larger seeds of *N. glauca* would also fall within this range). Seed measurements of *N. clevelandii* and *N. palmeri*, both relatively limited in the southwestern United States, remain to be documented. Whenever taxa exhibit overlapping population characteristics, identifications of ancient specimens should be based on data from multiple individuals insofar as possible.

Charring also has some effect on seed size. Length and width measurements may increase to a small degree, perhaps because of swelling from residual moisture trapped inside. Overall mean measurements of charred seeds are fairly close to the means of uncharred specimens, except in the case of *N. rustica*, for which mean seed length increased as much as 0.09 millimeter when the seeds were charred (table 31).

An increase in seed size can also be the response of a ruderal species undergoing domestication (Smith 1992). This could occur when selection pressures such as those arising from the harvesting and replanting of seeds are applied to tobacco plants, complicating direct comparisons of seed size between modern wild populations and archaeological specimens.

a

b

0                     1

MM

c

Photo 36. Seeds of *Nicotiana* species, two (a–b) domesticated and one (c) likely introduced into the southwestern United States in historic times. Photographed at 50X magnification. *a, N. rustica* (N1, Spanish settlers, Native Seeds/SEARCH; same as NAPC specimen 1, J. Winter); *b, N. tabacum* (specimen 24, J. Winter); *c, N. glauca* (specimen 72, J. Winter).

Table 30: Some General Features of Southwestern Nicotiana Seeds

| Species | Shape | Mean Length (mm) | Surface Pattern/ Reference |
|---|---|---|---|
| *N. attenuata* | Reniform, angular-reniform | 0.7 | Fluted reticulate (Goodspeed 1954:429) |
| *N. clevelandii* | Rotund-reniform | 0.5 | Irregularly wavy to fluted reticulate (Goodspeed 1954:454) |
| *N. palmeri* | Oblong to angular subreniform | 0.7 | Honeycombed-reticulate, with finely wavy ridges (Goodspeed 1954:387) |
| *N. trigonophylla* | Oblong or subrotund | 0.5 | Reticulate with finely wavy ridges (Goodspeed 1954:385) |
| *N. glauca* | Longer than broad | 0.5 | Honeycombed-reticulate (Goodspeed 1954:336) |
| *N. rustica* | Angular to elliptical | 0.7–1.1 | (Goodspeed 1954:355–356) |
| *N. tabacum* | Spherical or broadly elliptical | 0.5 | With fluted ridges (Goodspeed 1954:373) |

Table 31: Length and Width of Charred and Uncharred Seeds of Southwestern Tobacco Species

| Species | n | Condition | Length (mm) | | | Width (mm) | | |
|---|---|---|---|---|---|---|---|---|
| | | | Mean | S.D. | Range | Mean | S.D. | Range |
| N. attenuata | 60 | Uncharred | 0.83 | 0.05 | 0.72–0.93 | 0.65 | 0.07 | 0.49–0.78 |
| | 30 | Charred[a] | 0.82 | 0.06 | 0.74–0.98 | 0.59 | 0.04 | 0.49–0.66 |
| N. glauca | 30 | Uncharred | 0.62 | 0.06 | 0.53–0.73 | 0.47 | 0.06 | 0.35–0.63 |
| N. rustica[b] | 60 | Uncharred | 1.08 | 0.10 | 0.78–1.27 | 0.75 | 0.07 | 0.59–0.88 |
| | 30 | Charred | 1.13 | 0.09 | 0.88–1.27 | 0.74 | 0.06 | 0.62–0.88 |
| N. rustica[c] | 60 | Uncharred | 1.04 | 0.15 | 0.68–1.37 | 0.79 | 0.11 | 0.49–10.07 |
| | 30 | Charred | 1.13 | 0.12 | 0.78–1.36 | 0.79 | 0.10 | 0.49–0.98 |
| N. tabacum | 30 | Uncharred | 0.64 | 0.04 | 0.53–0.70 | 0.47 | 0.05 | 0.40–0.63 |
| N. trigonophylla | 60 | Uncharred | 0.58 | 0.04 | 0.49–0.68 | 0.41 | 0.04 | 0.29–0.49 |
| | 30 | Charred | 0.57 | 0.03 | 0.49–0.62 | 0.37 | 0.05 | 0.33–0.53 |

Source:   Adams 1990b; Hammett 1993. Raw data provided by Hammett permitted calculation of mean and standard
deviation for N. glauca and N. tabacum.

a   Seeds were charred in a frying pan for three minutes over a gas flame. All seeds were between 1 and 2 years old.
Charring freshly picked seeds might produce different results if their moisture content is higher.
b   Population from Talavaya along the northern Rio Grande.
c   Population from Santo Domingo Pueblo, middle Rio Grande.

Tight packing of hundreds of seeds inside a single rigid capsule may be responsible for variations in seed shape even within a single capsule (see photo 35d). Shape, therefore, cannot be considered useful in telling species apart, especially if only a few ancient specimens are available for scrutiny.

Seed coat reticulation patterns have also been reported as diagnostic (Haberman 1984), but as in the case of shape, the extent of intrataxon variation and interspecies overlap remains unknown (Asch and Asch 1985a). In a survey of 42 economically important species of North American Solanaceae, reticulation patterns were effective for distinguishing Nicotiana seeds from those of Petunia, a historically introduced taxon (Gunn and Gaffney 1974). Although we know of no other southwestern U.S. seed type with Nicotiana's wavy-walled reticulations, we caution that seeds of other Solanaceae may mimic those of tobacco when degraded. N. trigonophylla and N. clevelandii were included in a study of seed coat microsculpturing in which thickness of reticulation ridges, presence or absence of tubercles (raised areas), and the nature of the ridge junctions were all used to tell species apart (Farooqui and Bahadur 1985). This labor-intensive approach holds some hope for making species-level identifications of southwestern archeological tobaccos.

## Capsules

Nicotiana fruits are capsules with usually two (but sometimes four or more) carpels that each contain from 100 to 5,000 seeds. Distinguishing characteristics include size, shape, and whether or not the capsule is included within or extends beyond the surrounding calyx (Goodspeed 1954: 87). Capsules partially or fully indehiscent—that is, incapable of opening naturally to release seeds—are associated only with domesticated species.

Capsules of southwestern tobacco species display enough variability for well-preserved specimens to be identified (Goodspeed 1954; Kearney and Peebles 1960). For example, N. attenuata capsules are oval in shape, 8–12 millimeters long by 4 millimeters wide, and have four outward-curving teeth; the shortened calyx has four short teeth (Adams 1993b:25). Similar-sized capsules of N. palmeri and N. trigonophylla have an enclosing calyx with long, pointed teeth that extend to or beyond the top of the capsule. In contrast, the capsules of *N. tabacum*, *N. rustica*, and *N. glauca* are larger. *Nicotiana clevelandii* has the smallest capsules of all the southwestern tobacco species.

## Stems

Tobacco stems have long been reported from southwestern archaeological contexts (Cosgrove 1947:121; Grange 1952:418; Jones 1935; Martin et al. 1952:420). Anatomical and morphological criteria for identifying *Nicotiana* stems were described for materials inside "reed grass" (*Phragmites*) cigarettes at a Mogollon-Pueblo site in south-central Arizona (Adams 1990a: 130–135). In transverse view, the relative proportion of pith to stem wall, the spacing and abundance of rays, and the general arrangement of xylem cells of *Nicotiana* stems can be recognized. Among the southwestern tobacco species, alternate branching is common, though the leaves can be distinctly petiolate (e.g., *Nicotiana attenuata*), clasping (e.g., *N. trigonophylla*), or sessile. At high magnification, the nature of trichomes (hairs) can be used to distinguish species on the basis of diversity of types, nature of branching, presence or absence of glands, and general spacing and density (Adams 1990a:134–135; Goodspeed 1954).

## Other Forms of Tobacco Evidence: Nicotine, Quids, Artwork, Pollen

Traces of nicotine and nicotinic acid have been identified from dottle (the burned residue that remains inside a pipe) in pipes from the Prayer Rock district in northeastern Arizona (Johnson, Gager, and Holmes 1959 [cited in Switzer 1969: 13]). Other attempts at chemical analyses have not clearly established the presence of tobacco (Dixon and Stetson 1922; Jones and Morris 1960), perhaps because some of the alkaloid compounds in *Nicotiana* do not remain intact over time. Evidence in the form of tooth-marked yucca quids containing calcium carbonate and the seeds and stems of *N. attenuata* reveal tobacco ingestion via sucking (Jones and Morris

1960:116). An Aztec statue of the god Xochipilli, apparently in ecstatic repose, was adorned with carvings of hallucinogenic plants including the flowers of *Nicotiana* (Wasson 1973). Although not drawn from the southwestern United States, this example illustrates the possibility of recovering indirect evidence of *Nicotiana* in sculpture or other art forms. Examples of pollen recovery can be found in chapters 10–12 of this book.

## The Southwestern Ethnographic Record of Tobacco Use

References to use of wild tobaccos (*N. attenuata* and *N. trigonophylla*) are abundant in the historic record of southwestern groups (Adams 1990a:133–134). Wild species were both smoked and traded. Volunteer tobacco plants in a garden were sometimes left to be harvested later. More formal management or cultivation included scattering the seeds in a favored garden spot, burning over a plot and then planting seeds in the ashes, pruning and pinching to increase leaf size, and suckering plants (Adams 1990a: 133–134).

Domesticated species of tobacco (*N. rustica* and *N. tabacum*) have also received care by historic groups. *N. rustica* was grown in a number of eastern Pueblos (Jemez, Picuris, Cochiti, Santo Domingo, Taos, Acoma, Isleta, and Santa Ana) in the early part of the twentieth century, although the seed may have been provided by a modern tobacco company executive stationed in New Mexico (Beinhart 1941; Castetter 1943; White 1942:59). A search of the field notes and specimens of Dr. Edward Palmer, who made extensive botanical collections in the Southwest prior to 1890, failed to turn up evidence that *N. rustica* was under cultivation among the Pueblos (White 1942: 60). Nevertheless, Edward Castetter's native consultants stated that *N. rustica* had been cultivated in the Southwest for quite some time (Castetter 1943:323). As discussed in chapters 2 and 5, various eastern Pueblos still grow *N. rustica*.

For historic southwestern groups, tobacco has primarily served religious and ceremonial needs (Elmore 1944:75; Stevenson 1915:95; Whiting 1939:90). By smoking reed-grass (*Phragmites*) "cigarettes," one provides smoke to make a path for prayer to the gods for the general good of the group (Bohrer 1962:87). Modern Puebloans often touch cane cigarettes with a live coal before depositing them in shrines to be smoked by supernaturals (Switzer 1969: 40). The antiquity of this practice is revealed by archaeological contexts in which cigarettes are associated with other sacred paraphernalia but none (Haury 1945:194) or only a few (J. Gifford 1980:11, 78) show any evidence of actually having been smoked.

The reproductive parts of tobacco (flowers, capsules, and seeds) have been especially desirable as smoking materials among modern North American groups (Gilmore 1919:62; Goodspeed 1954:452; Harshberger 1906:34; Weitzner 1979: 191–192). In one example, the calyx of certain California species was preferred over the corolla (Goodspeed 1954:453). In contrast, it is the leaf of the commercial tobacco plant (*N. tabacum*) that is currently smoked for pleasure in the United States and elsewhere.

Although contemporary tobacco-smoking habits lead us to think of wild tobacco as a logical ancient antecedent, a wide variety of other smoked substances (not all of them botanical) have been reported in the archaeological and ethnographic literature (Adams 1990a). The archaeological record lists aromatic herbs such as "artemisia," possibly the scaly bark of "ocotillo," "red willow," *Larrea* (creosote bush) and "cedar" (Bandelier 1890:49–50; Haury 1945:194; Jones 1935:289), while the ethnographic literature includes such materials as *Abies* (fir) and *Pinus* (pine) needles; *Rhus* (sumac), *Arctostaphylos* (manzanita), and *Portulaca* (purslane) leaves; Mentha (mint), *Verbascum* (mullein), and *Onosmodium* (borage) plants; and minute yellow feathers (Adams 1990a:table 2). Because of this diversity, when the only items recovered archaeologically are

paraphernalia such as reed-grass (*Phragmites*) cigarettes or stone, clay, or bone pipes, we cannot automatically assume that it was *Nicotiana* that was smoked.

## Possible Changes to *Nicotiana* under Aboriginal Management

The idea that tobacco plants were being moved over the North American landscape in ancient times was advanced by Ralph Linton more than 70 years ago (Linton 1924:3). Goodspeed (1954: 43) wondered whether the widespread use of *N. attenuata* by historic groups in the western United States was in part a result of past movement of the plants between ancient groups. William Setchell (1921:410) believed it to have been cultivated north of the range of *N. bigelovii*.[3] Wells (1959:626), too, noted that *N. attenuata* may owe part of its present range to Native Americans, and certainly its modern range is being extended along the ever-increasing number of modern roads that cross the landscape. An analysis of DNA from *N. attenuata* plants across its range might shed light on the timing of isolation of some of its populations.

Increasing the range of a species can bring it rapidly into contact with other tobacco populations and species and new environmental settings. Hybridization, heterosis (hybrid vigor), and polyploidy (for example, a doubling or quadrupling of the number of chromosomes) might be expressed as larger plants and/or plants with unusual traits. Humans might opportunistically select appealing new characteristics such as larger, more robust plants or seeds, change(s) in nicotine content, or a shift in the timing of flowering. Both polyploidy and hybridization may have played major roles in the evolution of *Nicotiana* (Goodspeed 1954: 102). Again, a DNA analysis might provide a helpful perspective on such matters.

Characteristics of the seeds, capsules, and stems should be monitored closely for indications of human management. Larger seeds (above

1.0 millimeter) reported from southwestern archaeological sites are currently considered likely to represent the domesticated *N. rustica*, but ancient manipulation of other species such as *N. attenuata* might also have resulted in increased seed size. In the eastern United States, morphological changes to seeds undergoing domestication have included increased seed size, as in the cases of sumpweed (*Iva annua*) and sunflower (*Helianthus annuus*), or a reduction in seed coat thickness, as in the case of goosefoot (*Chenopodium berlandieri*) (Smith 1992). When seeds are deliberately planted, selection pressures favor either quick sprouting or seedlings that grow rapidly from seeds with greater available food reserves (Harlan, de Wet, and Price 1973; Heiser 1988). Capsules should be examined for tendency toward indehiscence, a recognized feature of domesticated tobaccos. An increased level of species variation coincides with domestication for both *N. tabacum* and *N. rustica* (Goodspeed 1954:353). A valuable approach might be to develop measures of variation to apply to both archaeological and extant wild tobacco populations. Any ancient tobacco populations with both larger seed size and higher levels of overall variability might represent species undergoing domestication.

## The Southwestern Archaeological Record of Tobacco Recovery

Recognition of ancient tobacco use in the southwestern United States came early in the twentieth century when Jesse Walter Fewkes (1912) reported that "a small dish containing native tobacco (*Nicotiana attenuata*) was found in one of the rooms" at Casa Grande Pueblo in Arizona. Later, Volney Jones (1944) questioned the identification of these specimens, and recent efforts to relocate them have failed. Two other early researchers attempted unsuccessfully to chemically identify the dottles clinging to the insides of Basketmaker pipe stems (Dixon and Stetson 1922). Over the next four decades,

tobacco was occasionally reported present in well-preserved archaeological contexts in Arizona and New Mexico (Cosgrove 1947; Grange 1952; Haury 1945; Jones 1935; Jones and Morris 1960; Yarnell 1977).

The two decades after 1975 produced a long list of citations for tobacco remains from ancient southwestern sites. This profusion of finds can be tied to the enhanced recovery of small organic materials provided by water flotation of archaeological sediments and to the proliferation of "contract" archaeology, which encourages the analysis of significant numbers of samples from archaeological contexts likely to be destroyed or damaged by modern land use. The sporadic earlier recoveries of tobacco remains were largely dependent on researchers' encountering assemblages in situations of exceptional preservation, whereas flotation has allowed the recovery of the tiny seeds even when they occur in very low frequencies and/or situations of poor preservation.

The analysis of macrobotanical specimens recovered through flotation has itself required some modifications in order to become a dependable method for identifying tobacco. At magnification levels widely used (often between 10X and 20X), the distinctive sculpturing of tiny tobacco seeds may not be evident; without the proper search image, the seeds look like yellow sand grains or bits of amorphous organic material. Analysts now recognize the importance of examining these yellow rectangular bits and of working at higher magnifications in the smaller screen sizes. Nevertheless, it is altogether possible that many *Nicotiana* seeds have gone unrecognized in the past.

The best evidence for early southwestern tobacco use comes from the Tucson area in southern Arizona, where 108 carbonized seeds have been recovered from an early agricultural village site dating to 398–169 B.C. (map 15, table 32) (Huckell 1995). The abundant carbonized seeds in appropriate cultural contexts (on pit-structure floors and in interior pits, associated in one case with an elegant and intact steatite pipe) leave little doubt about their cultural role at this site. Both material and design attributes suggest a California origin for the pipe, which raises questions about whether smoking was a local or an introduced practice.

Of the 31 sites known to us from the Archaic and Basketmaker eras, all but Tularosa Cave and the Stone Pipe site are Ancestral Puebloan (Anasazi), and 87 percent of them are located on the Colorado Plateau, including adjacent areas of southwestern Colorado, northwestern New Mexico, and northeastern Arizona. Carbonized tobacco seeds were recovered from 71 percent of the sites, and uncharred seeds or other tobacco remains occurred at 58 percent. These early assemblages include some of the largest and most informative collections of southwestern tobacco, such as the Prayer Rock quids and plant

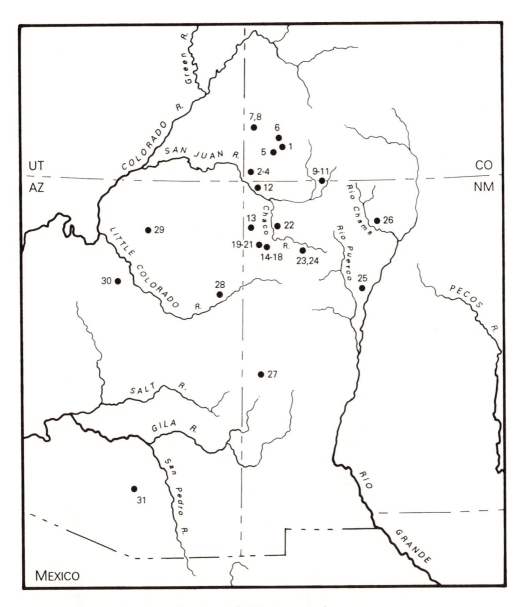

Map 15. Archaic and Basketmaker sites with *Nicotiana* remains.

Table 32: Archeological Recoveries of *Nicotiana* in Archaic to Late Basketmaker Sites (prior to A.D. 750 in Most Areas)

| Project or Site Name | Site No. | Reference | No. on Map 15 | Occurrence | | | | Context | | | |
|---|---|---|---|---|---|---|---|---|---|---|---|
| | | | | No. Locations | Charred Seeds | Uncharred Seeds | Other | Primary Deposits | | Secondary Deposits | Other/ Unknown |
| | | | | | | | | Feature | Strat | | |
| **Southwestern Colorado** | | | | | | | | | | | |
| Prairie Dog Hamlet | 5MT4614 | Benz and Matthews 1982 | 1 | 1 | 1–10 | 1–10 | | + | | | |
| Towaoc Canal | 5MT8937 | Brandt 1991a | 2 | 5 | >25 | >25 | | + | | + | |
| | 5MT8938 | | 3 | 7 | 1–10 | >25 | | + | + | | |
| | 5MT9072 | | 4 | 5 | >25 | >25 | | + | | | + |
| Poco Tiempo Hamlet | 5MT2378 | Brisbin 1984 | 5 | 5 | 1–10 | >25 | | + | + | + | |
| Le Moc Shelter | 5MT2151 | Matthews 1983b | 6 | 2 | — | 11–25 | | + | + | | |
| South Canal | 5MT8822 | Matthews 1988b | 7 | 1 | — | 1–10 | | + | | | |
| | 5MT8837 | Matthews 1988b | 8 | 3 | >25 | >25 | | + | | | |
| Bodo Canyon | 5LP478B | Matthews 1988a | 9 | 1 | 1–10 | — | | + | | | |
| | 5LP483 | 1988a | 10 | 2 | 1–10 | 1–10 | | + | | | |
| | 5LP1100 | | 11 | 1 | — | >25 | | | | + | |
| La Plata Valley | LA 60751 | Toll 1995a | 12 | 21 | 1–10 | >25 | | + | + | + | + |
| **Northwestern New Mexico** | | | | | | | | | | | |
| Prayer Rock Caves | Broken Flute | Morris 1980:77, 103; Jones and Morris 1960: 115–116 | 13 | ? | — | + | See note a | + | + | + | + |
| El Paso North | 2501 | McVickar 1995 | 14 | 5 | + | — | | | | | + |
| | 2506 | | 15 | 14 | + | — | | | | | + |
| | 2507 | | 16 | 3 | + | — | | | | | |
| | 80422 | | 17 | 2 | + | — | | | | | |
| | 80434 | | 18 | 2 | + | — | | | | | + |

Table 32: Archeological Recoveries of *Nicotiana* in Archaic to Late Basketmaker Sites (prior to A.D. 750 in Most Areas) (continued)

| Project or Site Name | Site No. | Reference | No. on Map 15 | No. Locations | Occurrence | | | Context | | | |
| | | | | | Charred Seeds | Uncharred Seeds | Other | Primary Deposits | | Secondary Deposits | Other/ Unknown |
| | | | | | | | | Feature | Strat | | |
| Mexican Springs | 61955 | Brandt 1992b | 19 | 4 | 11–25 | — | | + | + | + | |
| | 61956 | | 20 | 1 | 11–25 | — | | | + | | |
| | 61958 | | 21 | 1 | 11–25 | — | | + | | | |
| ENRON— Ram Mesa | 423–131 | Hammett 1993 | 22 | 10 | >25 | 11–25 | | | | | + |
| Chaco Canyon | 29SJ721 | Toll 1993a | 23 | 1 | — | 1–10 | | | + | | |
| | 29SJ724 | | 24 | 7 | — | >25 | | + | + | | |
| **Northern Rio Grande Valley** | | | | | | | | | | | |
| River's Edge | LA 59617 | Brandt 1991b | 25 | 1 | 1–10 | — | | | | | + |
| Chama Alcove | LA 24807 | McBride 1994 | 26 | 1 | — | 1–10 | | | | + | |
| **West-central and southwestern New Mexico** | | | | | | | | | | | |
| Tularosa Cave | LA 4427 | Grange 1952 | 27 | ? | — | — | See note b | | | +? | |
| **Northeastern Arizona** | | | | | | | | | | | |
| N-2015 | P:60:31 | Brandt 1991c | 28 | 1 | 1–10 | — | | | | + | |
| Turquoise Trail | PAO-83-33 | Toll 1985b | 29 | 1 | 1–10 | — | | | | | |
| ENRON— Sinagua | 442-96 | Hammett 1993 | 30 | 1 | — | 1–10 | | | | | + |
| **Southern Arizona** | | | | | | | | | | | |
| Miracle Mile Project; Stone Pipe Site | BB:13:425 1995 | Huckel 1995 | 31 | 5 | >25 | — | | + | + | | |

Note: Numbers of seeds are given simply as one of three categories: 1–10, 11–25, and greater than 25. A plus sign (+) indicates that one or more specimens were present (quantity unspecified).

a  *Nicotiana* stems, leaves, corollas, capsules, and seeds in a vessel; 27 yucca quids with *Nicotiana* seeds and capsules; pipes with nicotine residue.

b  A few reed cigarettes filled with tobacco stems and leaves.

parts in a jar, the Tularosa Cave cane cigarettes filled with tobacco stems, and the flotation samples with high densities of tobacco seeds from the Towaoc Canal project in southwestern Colorado (Brandt 1991a; Grange 1952).

For the period A.D. 750–950, corresponding roughly to the Ancestral Pueblo I period, 28 sites with tobacco remains have been identified solely on the basis of flotation. Seeds have been

found at numerous sites in southwestern Colorado (43 percent), as well as in the Totah region of northwestern New Mexico (29 percent) (map 16, table 33). Other occurrences in this period are rare and scattered far and wide across the southwestern landscape (for example, in the central Rio Grande Valley, west-central New Mexico, and southern Arizona). Areas where early Pueblo tobacco recoveries are few (as in

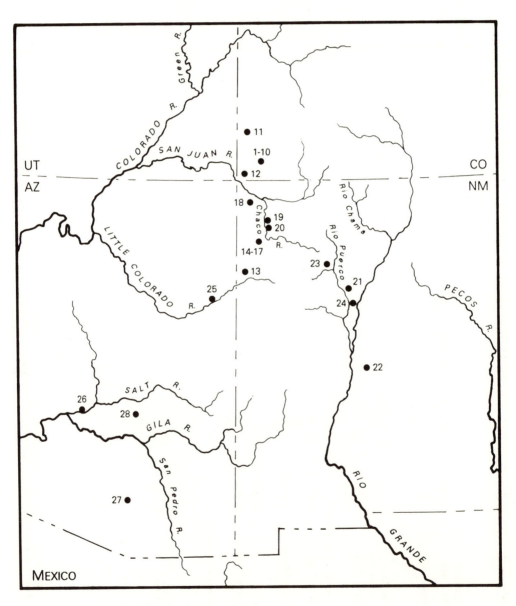

Map 16. Pueblo I sites with *Nicotiana* remains.

Table 33: Archaeological Recoveries of *Nicotiana* in Early Pueblo Sites (A.D. 750 to 950 in Most Areas)

| Project or Site Name | Site No. | Reference | No. on Map 16 | No. Locations | Charred Seeds | Uncharred Seeds | Other | Feature | Strat | Secondary Deposits | Other/ Unknown |
|---|---|---|---|---|---|---|---|---|---|---|---|
| **Southwestern Colorado** | | | | | | | | | | | |
| Grass Mesa | 5MT23 | Matthews 1983c | 1 | 21 | 11–25 | >25 | | + | | | |
| Aldea Sierritas | 5MT2854 | Matthews 1983e | 2 | 3 | 1–10 | 1–10 | | + | | + | |
| Windy Wheat | 5MT4644 | Matthews 1986c; Scott 1983, 1986 | 3 | 49 | >25 | >25 | See note a | + | + | + | |
| Kin Tl'iish | 5MT2336 | Dohm and Gould 1985 | 4 | 6 | — | >25 | | + | + | | + |
| Rio Vista Shelter | 5MT2182 | Wilshusen 1985 | 5 | 19 | 11–25 | >25 | | + | + | | |
| Periman Hamlet | 5MT4671 | Matthews 1983d | 6 | 3 | — | 11–25 | | + | + | | |
| Prince Hamlet | 5MT2161 | Matthews 1983a | 7 | 1 | 1–10 | — | | + | | | |
| Dovetail Hamlet | 5MT2226 | Nelson 1985 | 8 | ? | + | + | | + | | | + |
| House Creek Village | 5MT2320 | Robinson and Brisbin 1984 | 9 | 1 | — | 1–10 | | + | | | |
| Singing Shelter | 5MT4688 | Matthews 1985 | 10 | 16 | 1–10 | >25 | | + | + | + | + |
| South Canal | 5MT8838 | Matthews 1988b | 11 | 7 | >25 | 11–25 | | + | + | | |
| Towaoc Canal | 5MT8937 | Brandt 1991a | 12 | 4 | >25 | >25 | | + | | + | |
| **Northwestern New Mexico** | | | | | | | | | | | |
| Pittsburgh-Midway Coal | PM 240 | Toll and Donaldson 1982:762 | 13 | 1 | — | >25 | | | + | | |
| El Paso North | 2508A | McVickar 1995 | 14 | 1 | + | — | | + | | | |
| | 80407 | | 15 | 2 | + | + | | | | | + |

Table 33: Archaeological Recoveries of *Nicotiana* in Early Pueblo Sites (A.D. 750 to 950 in Most Areas) (continued)

| Project or Site Name | Site No. | Reference | No. on Map 16 | Occurrence | | | | Context | | | |
| --- | --- | --- | --- | --- | --- | --- | --- | --- | --- | --- | --- |
| | | | | No. Locations | Charred Seeds | Uncharred Seeds | Other | Primary Deposits | | Secondary Deposits | Other/ Unknown |
| | | | | | | | | Feature | Strat | | |
| El Paso North | 80410 | McVickar 1995 | 16 | 4 | + | + | | + | + | + | |
| | 80934 | | 17 | 2 | + | + | | | + | + | + |
| Fruitland | LA 79489 | Brandt 1993b | 18 | 2 | 1–10 | — | | +? | | + | + |
| ENRON— Escalante | 423-101 | Hammett 1993 | 19 | 3 | — | 1–10 | | | | | + |
| ENRON— Ram Mesa | 423-1241 | Hammett 1993 | 20 | 4 | >25 | >25 | | | | | + |
| **Northern and central Rio Grande Valley** | | | | | | | | | | | |
| Arroyo de las Montoyas | LA 45996 | Brandt 1990a | 21 | 1 | 1–10 | — | | + | | | |
| Bingham | LA 71726 | Toll 1997c | 22 | 3 | — | 11–25 | | | | + | |
| I-40 | LA 3558 | Toll 1994a | 23 | 3 | — | 1–10 | | + | | | |
| River's Edge | LA 59617 | Brandt 1991b | 24 | 1 | 1–10 | — | | | | | + |
| **Northeastern Arizona** | | | | | | | | | | | |
| Sanders High School | P:54:11 | McBride 1997 | 25 | 1 | 1–10 | — | | | | + | |
| **Southern Arizona** | | | | | | | | | | | |
| Dutch Canal | T:12:62 | Kwiatkowski 1994 | 26 | 1 | 1–10 | — | | + | | | |
| Fastimes | AA:12:384 | Kwiatkowski and Gasser 1988 | 27 | 2 | 1–10 | — | See note b | | + | | |
| Farmstead | U:15:84 | Miksicek 1983d | 28 | 1 | 1–10 | — | — | + | | | |

Note: Numbers of seeds are given simply as one of three categories: 1–10, 11–25, and greater than 25. A plus sign (+) indicates that one or more specimens were present (quantity unspecified).

a  Pollen.

b  Leaves.

central New Mexico) often suffer from a combination of poor preservation conditions for perishable materials and poor flotation coverage. The recovery of ceramic and stone pipes at excavations antedating routine flotation sampling suggests that smoking may have been more widespread during this era than botanical remains indicate, but direct evidence of the smoking materials is for the most part lacking.

Tobacco-related activity picked up in the years between A.D. 950 and 1250, corresponding to the Ancestral Pueblo II–III period. This period comprises the majority of sites with tobacco (62 sites, or 74 percent of all known sites with tobacco), but the emphasis shifts away from southwestern Colorado (now with 29 percent of the sites) to northwestern New Mexico (with 32 percent), mainly in the Chaco Canyon area (map 17, table

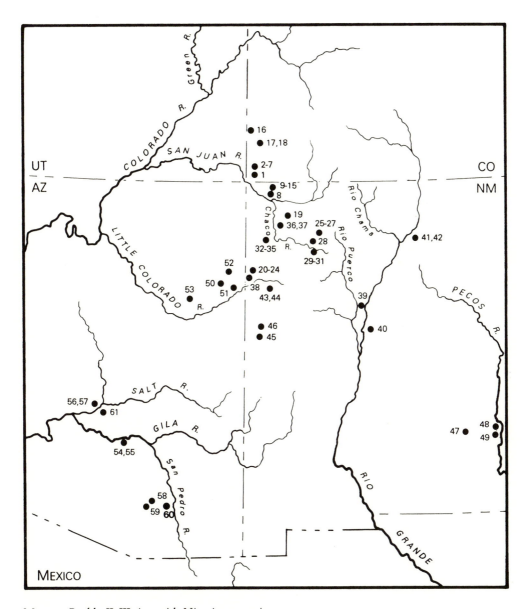

Map 17. Pueblo II–III sites with *Nicotiana* remains.

Table 34: Archaeological Recoveries of *Nicotiana* in Pueblo II to III Sites (A.D. 950 to 1250 in Most Areas)

| Project or Site Name | Site No. | Reference | No. on Map 17 | No. Locations | Occurrence | | | Context | | | |
|---|---|---|---|---|---|---|---|---|---|---|---|
| | | | | | Charred Seeds | Uncharred Seeds | Other | Primary Deposits | | Secondary Deposits | Other/ Unknown |
| | | | | | | | | Feature | Strat | | |
| **Southwestern Colorado** | | | | | | | | | | | |
| Towaoc Canal | 5MT8943 | Brandt 1991a | 1 | 1 | 1–10 | 1–10 | | | | + | |
| Ute Mountain Ute | 5MT8653 | Miller 1995 | 2 | 1 | — | + | | + | | | |
| | 5MT9847 | | 3 | 9 | — | + | | + | + | | |
| | 5MT9863 | | 4 | 1 | — | + | | | + | | |
| | 5MT9869 | | 5 | 5 | — | + | | + | + | | |
| | 5MT9873 | | 6 | 12 | — | + | | + | + | | |
| | 5MT9949 | | 7 | 6 | — | + | | + | + | | |
| La Plata Valley | LA 50337 | Toll 1993c | 8 | 1 | — | 1–10 | | + | | + | |
| | LA 37592 | Toll 1995a | 9 | 9 | — | >25 | | + | + | | |
| | LA 37593 | | 10 | 2 | — | 1–10 | | + | + | | |
| | LA 37595 | | 11 | 7 | — | 1–10 | | + | + | | |
| | LA 37599 | | 12 | 5 | — | 1–10 | | + | + | | |
| | LA 37601 | | 13 | 3 | — | 1–10 | | + | | + | |
| | LA 37606 | | 14 | 3 | — | >25 | | + | | + | |
| | LA 65030 | | 15 | 4 | — | 1–10 | | + | + | | |
| Hovenweep | | Woosley 1977 | 16 | ? | — | — | See note a | | | | + |
| South Canal | 5MT8836 | Matthews 1998b | 17 | 1 | — | 1–10 | | + | | | |
| | 5MT8839 | | 18 | 4 | 1–10 | 1–10 | | + | | | |
| **Northwestern New Mexico** | | | | | | | | | | | |
| Navajo Indian Irrigation | H28-19 | Struever and Knight 1979:1714 | 19 | 1 | — | 1–10 | | | | + | |
| Pittsburgh and Midway Coal Lease | PM 224 | Toll and Donaldson 1982:756,760 | 20 | 1 | 11–25 | — | | + | | | |
| | PM 218 | | 21 | 1 | — | 1–10 | | | + | | |

Table 34: Archaeological Recoveries of *Nicotiana* in Pueblo II to III Sites (A.D. 950 to 1250 in Most Areas) (continued)

| Project or Site Name | Site No. | Reference | No. on Map 17 | No. Locations | Occurrence Charred Seeds | Occurrence Uncharred Seeds | Occurrence Other | Context Primary Deposits Feature | Context Primary Deposits Strat | Context Secondary Deposits | Context Other/Unknown |
|---|---|---|---|---|---|---|---|---|---|---|---|
| | PMMC 265 | Powell n.d. | 22 | 1 | 1–10 | — | | + | | | |
| | PMMC 1004 | | 23 | 2 | 1–10 | — | | + | | | |
| | SW 180 | | 24 | 1 | 1–10 | — | | + | | | |
| Bis sa'ani Pueblo | NMG-63-1&2 | Donaldson and Toll 1982 | 25 | 1 | — | 1–10 | | | | + | |
| Bis sa'ani Community | NMG-63-23 | | 26 | 1 | — | 1–10 | | | + | | |
| | NMG-63-26 | | 27 | 1 | — | 1–10 | | | | + | |
| Pueblo Alto | 29SJ389 | Toll 1985a | 28 | 4 | — | 1–10 | | + | + | | |
| Chaco small sites | 29SJ626 | Toll 1985a | 29 | 2 | — | 11–25 | | + | | + | |
| | 29SJ627 | Toll 1985a | 30 | 7 | — | >25 | | + | + | + | + |
| | 29SJ629 | Toll 1993b | 31 | 11 | — | 11–25 | | + | + | | |
| El Paso North | 2505 | McVickar 1995 | 32 | 1 | + | + | | + | | | |
| | 2508C | | 33 | 1 | + | — | | | | | + |
| | 80425 | | 34 | 1 | — | — | | + | | | |
| | 80428 | | 35 | 1 | — | + | | + | | | |
| ENRON— | 423-123 | Hammett 1993 | 36 | 1 | — | 1–10 | | | | | + |
| Ram Mesa | 423-130 | | 37 | 2 | — | 1–10 | | | | | + |
| ENRON | 442-1 | | 38 | 1 | >25 | 11–25 | | | | | + |
| **Northern and central Rio Grande Valley** | | | | | | | | | | | |
| Belen Bridge | LA 53662 | Toll 1995c | 39 | 1 | — | >25 | | + | | | |
| Sevilleta Shelter | LA 20896 | Struever 1980 | 40 | 1 | — | 1–10 | | | + | | |
| Pot Creek | LA 2742 | Toll 1994b | 41 | 6 | — | 1–10 | | + | + | | + |
| | LA 70577 | | 42 | 7 | — | 11–25 | | + | | | |
| **West-central and southwestern New Mexico** | | | | | | | | | | | |
| Michael's Land Exchange | AR 03-03-02-520 | Bohrer 1984:4–10 | 43 | 1 | 1–10 | — | | + | | | |

Table 34: Archaeological Recoveries of *Nicotiana* in Pueblo II to III Sites (A.D. 950 to 1250 in Most Areas) (continued)

| Project or Site Name | Site No. | Reference | No. on Map 17 | Occurrence | | | | Context | | | |
|---|---|---|---|---|---|---|---|---|---|---|---|
| | | | | No. Locations | Charred Seeds | Uncharred Seeds | Other | Primary Deposits | | Secondary Deposits | Other/ Unknown |
| | | | | | | | | Feature | Strat | | |
| Vogt Ranch | LA 56716 | Brandt 1990c | 44 | 3 | 1–10 | 1–10 | | + | | | + |
| Spurgeon Draw | LA 39968 | Toll and McBride 1996 | 45 | 2 | — | 1–10 | | + | | + | |
| Gallo Mountain | LA 6075 | Toll and McBride 1998a | 46 | 1 | — | 1–10 | | | | | + |
| **Southeastern New Mexico** | | | | | | | | | | | |
| Picacho | LA 71167 | Toll 1996 | 47 | 6 | — | 11–25 | | | + | | |
| Henderson Pueblo | LA 1549 | Huckell and Toll 1995 | 48 | 1 | 1–10 | — | | | + | | |
| Fox Place | LA 68188 | Toll 1993d | 49 | 1 | — | 1–10 | | | | | + |
| **Northeastern Arizona** | | | | | | | | | | | |
| Navajo, Ariz. | K:14:26 | Brandt 1990b | 50 | 1 | 1–10 | — | | +? | | | |
| Sanders High School | P:54:9 | McBride 1996a | 51 | 2 | 1–10 | 1–10 | | | | + | |
| ENRON— Wide Ruin | 442-15 | Hammett 1993 | 52 | 2 | — | 1–10 | | | | | + |
| ENRON— Hopi Buttes | 442-30 | | 53 | 1 | — | 1–10 | | | | | + |
| **Southern Arizona** | | | | | | | | | | | |
| Frogtown | U:15:61 | Miksicek 1984b:571 | 54 | 1 | 1–10 | — | | + | | | |
| Smiley's Well | U:14:73 | | 55 | 1 | 1–10 | — | | | | | |

Table 34: Archaeological Recoveries of *Nicotiana* in Pueblo II to III Sites (A.D. 950 to 1250 in Most Areas) (continued)

| Project or Site Name | Site No. | Reference | No. on Map 17 | Occurrence | | | | Context | | | |
|---|---|---|---|---|---|---|---|---|---|---|---|
| | | | | No. Locations | Charred Seeds | Uncharred Seeds | Other | Primary Deposits | | Secondary Deposits | Other/ Unknown |
| | | | | | | | | Feature | Strat | | |
| Las Colinas | T:12:10 | Miksicek and Gasser 1989:97, 108 | 56 | 3 | 1–10 | — | | | | + | |
| Double Butte Cave | U:9:59 | Haury 1954:194 | 57 | ? | — | — | See note b | + | | + | |
| Los Morteros | AA:12:57 | Wallace and Miksicek 1995 | 58 | 1 | 1–10 | — | | | | | |
| West Branch | AA:16:3 | Miksicek 1986:301 | 59 | — | — | — | | | | | |
| Red Cave | EE:3:18 | Adams 1993b | 60 | 1 | — | — | See note c | + | | | |
| Siphon Draw | U:10:6 | Miksicek 1984c | 61 | 1 | 1–10 | — | | | | + | |
| Pueblo Grande | U:9:2 | Miller 1994 | 62 | 1 | >25 | — | | + | | | |

Note: Numbers of seeds are given simply as one of three categories: 1–10, 11–25, and greater than 25. A plus sign (+) indicates that one or more specimens were present (quantity unspecified).

a   Pollen.
b   Leaves in reed-grass cigarette.
c   Capsule in reed-grass cigarette.

34). Tobacco recoveries increase significantly in the Hohokam region of southern Arizona in this period, accounting for 15 percent of the sites (these remains are often identified as *Nicotiana trigonophylla*). The only known tobacco from southeastern New Mexico dates to this period.

Identifications of tobacco remains fall off sharply for the period from A.D. 1250 to the sixteenth-century Spanish contact, with only 11 sites noted (map 18, table 35). Late Classic Hohokam sites make up 27 percent of this small sample, and southwestern Colorado and northwestern New Mexico are not represented at all. Reed-grass cigarettes with *Nicotiana attenuata* stems at Red Bow Cliff Dwelling in northeastern Arizona belong to the earlier part of this time period (Adams 1990a). There is clear evidence of tobacco use in several large,

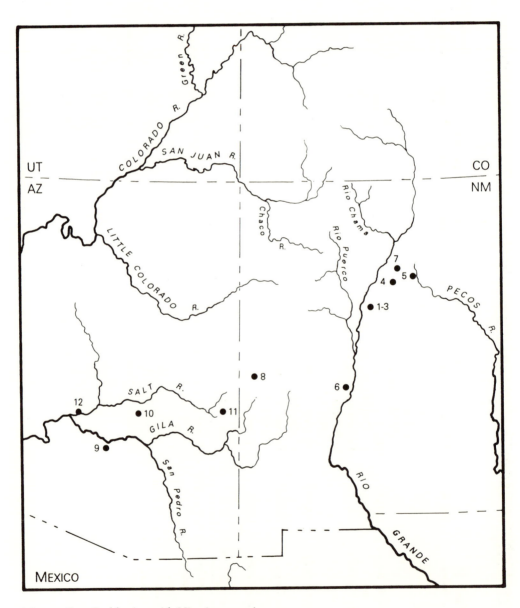

Map 18. Late Pueblo sites with *Nicotiana* remains.

Table 35: Archaeological Recoveries of *Nicotiana* in Late Pueblo and Late Classic Hohokam Sites (A.D. 1250–1300 to European Contact in Most Areas)

| Project or Site Name | Site No. | No. on Map 18 | Reference | Occurrence | | | | Context | | | |
| | | | | No. Locations | Charred Seeds | Uncharred Seeds | Other | Primary Deposits | | Secondary Deposits | Other/ Unknown |
| | | | | | | | | Feature | Strat | | |
| **Northern Rio Grande Valley** | | | | | | | | | | | |
| Cedro Canyon[a] | LA 581 | 1 | Yarnell 1977:871 | 1 | — | >25 | See note b | + | | | |
| Tijeras Pueblo | LA 581 | 2 | Garber 1980: 72, 75–78 | ? | — | >25 | | +? | | + | + |
| San Antonio Pueblo | LA 24 | 3 | Toll 1997a | 5 | — | 11–25 | | + | | + | |
| Galisteo Pueblo | LA 3333 | 4 | Toll 1995d | 17 | — | >25 | | + | | + | |
| Rowe Pueblo | LA 108 | 5 | Toll 1997b | 8 | — | >25 | | + | | + | |
| Tri-Sect | LA 98670 | 6 | McBride 1996b | 1 | — | 1–10 | | + | | | |
| San Lazaro Pueblo | [none] | 7 | Toll 1995b | 1 | — | 1–10 | | + | | | |
| **West-central and southwestern New Mexico** | | | | | | | | | | | |
| Upper Gila Caves | — | 8 | Cosgrove 1947:121 | ? | — | — | See note c | + | | | |
| **Southern Arizona** | | | | | | | | | | | |
| Casa Grande | AA:2:1 | 9 | Fewkes 1912 | 1? | — | >25 | See note d | + | | | |
| Las Fosas | U:15:19 | 10 | Miksicek 1983c | 2 | 1–10 | — | | + | | + | |
| Red Bow Cliff Dwelling | W:9:72 | 11 | Adams 1990b | — | — | + | C | + | | | |

Note: Numbers of seeds are given simply as one of three categories: 1–10, 11–25, and greater than 25. A plus sign (+) indicates that one or more specimens were present (quantity unspecified).

a   Material from unpublished 1948 excavations of Tijeras Pueblo (then referred to as the Cedro Canyon site) by Fred Wendorf and Stanley Stubbs.

b   Seeds in a dish.

c   Stems in reed-grass cigarette.

d   Unspecified plant parts in reed-grass cigarettes.

late settlements east of the Rio Grande Valley, centered in the Galisteo basin and Tijeras Canyon areas (64 percent of sites from this era).

Most occurrences of tobacco seeds in historic-period sites consist solely of small numbers of uncharred seeds, with an unfortunate risk of contamination by noncultural, intrusive seeds. Sites from this period include Navajo dwellings from the Four Corners area and sites of His-panic and Puebloan ethnicities in the central and northern Rio Grande Valley (map 19, table 36).

## Summaries of Ancient Uses

Tobacco stems, leaves, corollas, capsules, pollen, seeds, and dottles have been identified from archaeological sites. By far the largest

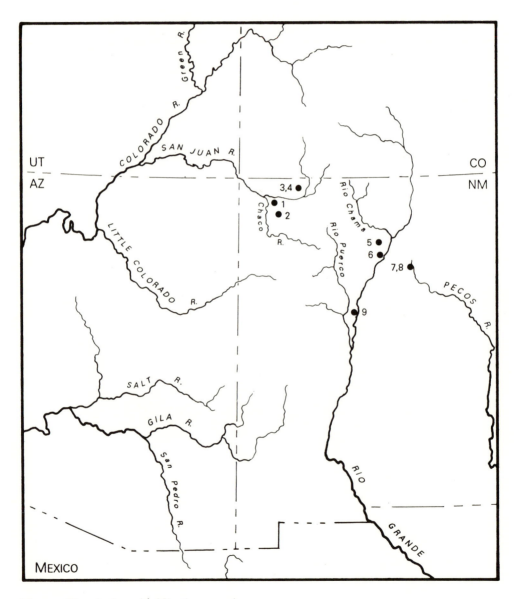

Map 19. Historic sites with *Nicotiana* remains.

Table 36: Archaeological Recoveries of *Nicotiana* in Historic Sites (Post-European Contact)

| Project or Site Name | Site No. | Reference | No. on Map 19 | Occurrence | | | | Context | | | |
|---|---|---|---|---|---|---|---|---|---|---|---|
| | | | | No. Locations | Charred Seeds | Uncharred Seeds | Other | Primary Deposits | | Secondary Deposits | Other/ Unknown |
| | | | | | | | | Feature | Strat | | |
| **Northwestern New Mexico** | | | | | | | | | | | |
| El Paso North | LA 80986 | McVickar 1995 | 1 | 1 | + | — | | + | | | |
| El Campo Navahu | LA 38946 | Toll 1985c: 225 | 2 | 1 | — | 1–10 | | | | + | |
| Arkansas Loop | LA 80910 | Brandt 1993b | 3 | 1 | 11–25 | 1–10 | | +? | | | |
| | LA 81175 | | 4 | 1 | 1–10 | 1–10 | | +? | | | |
| **Northern and central Rio Grande Valley** | | | | | | | | | | | |
| La Puente | LA 54313 | Toll 1989 | 5 | 2 | — | 1–10 | | | | + | |
| Bandelier Cliff Dwellings | LA 50972 | Hendron 1946; H.W. Toll 1995:9–11 | 6 | 1 | — | — | See note *a* | | | | + |
| Pecos Mission | LA 625 | Toll 1995c | 7 | 2 | — | 1–10 | | + | | | |
| Pecos | LA 76138 | Toll and McBride 1998b | 8 | 1 | — | 1–10 | | | + | | |
| Alameda Road | LA 87058 | McBride and Brown 1997 | 9 | 3 | 1–10 | 1–10 | | | | | |

Note: Numbers of seeds are given simply as one of three categories: 1–10, 11–25, and greater than 25. A plus sign (+) indicates that one or more specimens were present (quantity unspecified).

a   Leaves and seeds in a bowl.

proportion of tobacco remains known to us consists of seeds recovered by flotation. In lieu of more abundant and obvious indicators of where and how tobacco was used, we consider these scattered instances of usually small numbers of seeds to be incidental signs of the use of tobacco. Many of these seeds are unburned, and uncharred seeds in open, unprotected sites are often conservatively considered noncultural (Minnis 1981). However, two factors suggest that uncharred tobacco seeds in archaeological sites may represent residues of ancient human activities. First, their contexts and associated remains strongly suggest use by humans (Hammett 1993:510; Matthews 1996c; Toll 1985a), and second, their high alkaloid content may inhibit the normal trajectory of degradation of parts. Examination of samples from post-occupational fill would help archaeobotanists assess whether tobacco seeds are regularly contributed to the natural "seed rain" at archaeological sites.

Unusually good preservation conditions provide us with some of our best contextual clues to tobacco use. *Nicotiana* stems and/or leaves in reed-grass cigarettes at Tularosa Cave, Red Bow Cliff Dwelling, Double Butte Cave, and upper Gila River Cave suggest that the vegetative parts were smoked (Adams 1990a; Cosgrove 1947; Grange 1952; Haury 1945). At Red Cave, cigarette contents included a capsule as well (Adams 1993b). Spectacular preservation of Basketmaker remains in the Prayer Rock Caves in the extreme northeastern corner of Arizona provided both a firm taxonomic identification at the species level (*Nicotiana attenuata*) and important contextual information about attributes of storage and use (Jones and Morris 1960). Vegetative and reproductive parts (stems, leaves, corollas, capsules, and seeds) were stored together in a ceramic vessel, and about two dozen yucca quids containing tobacco seeds, capsule fragments, and lime indicate that nicotine was ingested by sucking. Tobacco remains in a bowl at Bandelier National Monument included seeds and leaves (Hendron 1946). Other instances of tobacco storage in

vessels are limited to seeds (Fewkes 1912; Yarnell 1977).

Tobacco seeds recovered by flotation in sites with poorer preservation of perishables have been found frequently on floors, especially around central hearths and other features where activities were likely concentrated. Carbonized seeds have often turned up in the burned features that produced them, or where trash from thermal features was redeposited (on floors, in middens, in the trash fill of pits and residential structures).

## Discussion

The recovery of wild tobacco species in southwestern archaeological contexts generally coincides with current distributions of tobacco species. *Nicotiana attenuata* is the type most often cited in higher-elevation Colorado Plateau and upland archaeological sites, and *Nicotiana trigonophylla* is regularly identified from ancient lower desert settings. Archaeological recoveries follow a pattern, increasing in intensity in the Four Corners Ancestral Puebloan area, peaking in southwestern Colorado, then expanding out to include areas of New Mexico and the southern Hohokam region. Whether this pattern is real or in part a reflection of heavy emphasis on flotation in conjunction with major archaeological contract projects in the 1980s and early 1990s remains to be seen. Clearly, more archaeobotanical analyses are needed in areas to the north and east in Colorado, in Utah, and from within those parts of the Southwest that have witnessed little excavation in recent decades. Central and southern Arizona and southeastern Utah also require thorough searches for tobacco remains, especially considering the poor preservation in the often spectacular sites. The recent recovery of tobacco from buried deposits at the Stone Pipe site in Tucson suggests that this region holds especially good potential for increasing our knowledge about this important plant.

The presence of a domesticated tobacco in ancient southwestern sites is a tantalizing possibility. In 1981, Ford (1981:21–22) concluded that there was no direct evidence for long-term *Nicotiana* cultivation north of Mexico. During the mid-1980s, however, *Nicotiana rustica* seeds were identified at a number of Hohokam sites in central and southern Arizona (Hammett 1993), though the case is less than secure because size, the prime criterion of identification, was described qualitatively rather than measured. More recently, measured populations of tobacco seeds from Ancestral Puebloan and Sinagua contexts have demonstrated the presence of seeds in the size range of *N. rustica*. At this point we also entertain the possibility that regular interactions between ancient humans and one or more of the wild tobacco species might have fostered changes that included increased seed size. We need to continue to accumulate measurements and descriptions of preserved ancient populations of tobacco seeds, as well as seeds of modern, native populations growing in diverse environments, in order to both document and compare variability in shape, size, seed coat sculpturing, and other characters.

## Summary

Tobacco was used extensively throughout what is now the southwestern United States from at least late Basketmaker times. Regions of high usage include the Four Corners area, especially southwestern Colorado during the Basketmaker to early Pueblo periods, and north-central New Mexico and central and southern Arizona in the later Puebloan era. Recoveries from archaeological sites consist most often of charred and uncharred seeds from flotation. Prime locations for these seeds are burned features and storage pits inside pit structures and rooms. Interior floors and fill, and to a lesser extent extramural storage features, also preserved tobacco seeds with some regularity. Vegetative parts are far less likely to survive over the centuries, but it is the rare cases of their recovery, often in their original context of storage or use, that give special insight into tobacco's ancient usage. Seeds and other parts were stored in ceramic vessels. Important clues to ingestion techniques are revealed by nicotine identified in pipe dottles, by stems and capsule fragments found in reed-grass cigarettes, and by seeds and capsules found in tooth-marked yucca quids.

## Notes

We thank Joe Winter for encouraging us to summarize the southwestern tobacco record and to include the important anatomical and morphological criteria that permit sound identifications of ancient tobacco parts. He also kindly loaned seed specimens for photos 34–36. We also appreciate the courtesy of all our southwestern archaeobotanical colleagues, especially Carol B. Brandt, Pamela McBride, Lisa Huckell, Janet McVickar, Jo Anne Miller, Julia Hammett, Meredith Matthews, Scott Kwiatkowski, and Gina Powell, who have shared with us their accumulating manuscripts and reports on *Nicotiana* recoveries. To access reports in the hard-to-find literature of contract archaeology, as well as in the drafts of reports that were "in preparation" when this summary was written, readers should directly contact the companies listed in the bibliographic citations. Crow Canyon Archaeological Center provided funds toward technical and editorial support. Adams thanks Wendy Youmans for patiently accumulating tobacco ecology data from more than 400 University of Arizona herbarium specimens. She also acknowledges Agnese Lindley Haury and the late Dr. Emil Haury for their interest in and funding of a study of reed-grass cigarettes with *Nicotiana* contents at Red Bow Cliff Dwelling; it was this study that firmly directed her onto the southwestern tobacco road.

This summary of the archaeological occurrences of tobacco remains in the Southwest is current as of 1995, when the manuscript was originally prepared for publication.

1. Editor's note: Elsewhere in this book *Nicotiana palmeri* is considered a variety of *N. trigonophylla*.

2. Editor's note: As discussed in chapters 2 and 5, I have found that several native groups in southern California and Arizona consider *N. glauca* to be a traditional form of tobacco, despite its introduction from South America during the historic period.

3. In this book, *N. bigelovii* is called *N. quadrivalvis*.

# 8

# Tobacco on the Plains

## Historical Use, Ethnographic Accounts, and Archaeological Evidence

### Mary J. Adair

The Great Plains region, a vast grassland in central North America, was inhabited in prehistoric times by diverse cultures, some of whom came to rely on agricultural crops for a major portion of their diet. Others remained hunters and foragers, although they traded with the agriculturalists for portions of their diet. Remains of cultivated maize (*Zea mays*), squashes and pumpkins (*Cucurbita pepo*), beans (*Phaseolus vulgaris*), sunflowers (*Helianthus annuus*), marshelder (*Iva annua*), goosefoot (*Chenopodium berlandieri*), and little barley (*Hordeum pusillum*) have been recovered from prehistoric sites ranging from the southern plains to the Canadian provinces. Tobacco (*Nicotiana* spp.) was added to the agricultural complex well before Euro-American contact. Early historical accounts indicate that almost all plains groups either grew or traded for native tobacco, and no other plant figured so prominently in religious and secular ceremonies, rites of passage, economic and political alliances, or social events and relaxation (see Fletcher 1904; Gilmore 1913, 1919; Turnbaugh 1975; Weltfish 1965; West 1934; Wilson 1977 [1917]; Winter, chapter 2, this volume). Moreover, some researchers have argued that the calumet ceremony, an elaborate ritual that involved a distinctive pipe stem, an associated dance, the establishment of fictive kinship relationships, and the smoking of tobacco in a distinctively styled pipe, originated on the prehistoric plains as a response to intertribal trade networks (Blakeslee 1975, 1981).

The aboriginal distribution and use of native tobacco on the Great Plains can be determined by combining data from historic and ethnographic records and archaeological investigations. Each source, however, involves limitations. As discussed elsewhere in this volume, archaeological evidence for tobacco comes primarily in the form of charred seeds, which, owing to their size and context, are often not recovered. Although flotation can offer a viable technique for recovering these small particles, issues such as the fine mesh size used during flotation and the laborintensive sorting of the recovered light fraction are real concerns that go beyond field methods. Tobacco seeds, among the smallest botanical remains that can be recovered with flotation, measure 0.4–1.1 millimeter in length (taking into account the ranges of several species; see Adams and Toll, this volume; Wagner, this volume). In addition, the manner of aboriginal use of tobacco suggests that seeds likely were not preserved in the same context as food remains.

For the historic and ethnographic records, the major limitation centers on the descriptions of the various plants cultivated and gathered. Although extant historical records often mention the presence of tobacco, the cultivated variety is not always noted. Occasionally, some description of the plant is offered, making it possible to speculate on the taxa cultivated. For the most part, however, the agricultural practices of aboriginal plains tribes were poorly recorded, because more attention was given to the bison, its various uses, and the hunting of it. Most ethnographic observations were made in the eighteenth and nineteenth centuries, well after the

EuroAmerican presence had been established. The extent to which the use of native tobacco changed between the prehistoric period and the time when these accounts were written may be difficult to reconstruct.

## Taxonomy and Distribution

Of the nine or more taxa of *Nicotiana* that occur in North America, four are found in the Great Plains and are considered in this chapter. As was suggested by William Setchell (1921: 414, pl. 3), the general distributions of the four taxa converge on the plains (map 20). The four differ in growing conditions and in the characteristics of the plant and flower. *Nicotiana rustica* L., originally native to South America, was the tobacco cultivated prehistorically in the eastern woodlands, eastern and northern Canada, and parts of northern Mexico (Goodspeed 1954). *Nicotiana attenuata* Torr. also exhibited (and continues to exhibit) a relatively wide range throughout the southwestern United States and Great Basin, parts of the Great Plains, and the southern sections of the western Canadian provinces. The remaining two taxa, *N. quadrivalvis* Pursh var. *quadrivalvis* and *N. quadrivalvis* Pursh var. *multivalvis* (Lindley) Gray,[1] are varieties of the closely related *quadrivalvis* group that exhibited a natural and cultural distribution along the west coast of California and Oregon, inland along tributaries of the Columbia River, and across the continental divide into Montana and North Dakota (Setchell 1921: 404).

Setchell constructed his distribution map using species characteristics as described in the literature; known use of a species by existing Indian groups; herbarium samples collected during the eighteenth and nineteenth centuries; and a certain amount of guesswork in areas where sufficient data were lacking. For the Great Plains in particular, he was admittedly arbitrary in drawing the eastern boundary of the distribution of *Nicotiana rustica*, stating that "it was prob-

ably along the line of the eastern boundary of the 'Plains Area', as outlined by Wissler" (Setchell 1921:402). Without an appreciation of the diversity of Plains Indian cultures or a knowledge that prehistoric populations throughout the plains had adopted a sedentary farming lifestyle, Setchell viewed all of the Great Plains as one culture area of "nomads" and felt that their use of tobacco must have differed from that of the more sedentary villagers of the eastern woodlands. In addition, he was influenced by Thomas Nuttall (1818), who stated that *Nicotiana quadrivalvis* was cultivated by all of the tribes along the Missouri River (Gilmore 1919:62).

It is interesting that Setchell chose to include all of South Dakota and the central plains (including Nebraska and Kansas) within the distribution of *Nicotiana attenuata*. Again, however, he admitted that the reasons for doing this were "not as yet clear to me" (Setchell 1921:410), and he acknowledged that his distribution for this taxon might not reflect the aboriginal distribution. As Joseph Winter (1990a) points out, *Nicotiana attenuata* is essentially a montane, high desert taxon, and the lower grasslands of the plains would have moisture balances unfavorable to it (also see chapter 5, this volume). On this basis, it seems unlikely that *N. attenuata* was cultivated on the Great Plains.

Although Setchell's map continues to be used in determining the aboriginal distributions of tobacco taxa, such use should be approached with a certain amount of caution. A review of the historic and ethnographic literature, combined with direct archaeological evidence of tobacco on the plains, may offer a better approach to understanding the specific use of this plant.

## Historic and Ethnographic Data

In summarizing ethnohistoric accounts of the presence or use of tobacco on the Great Plains, I emphasize the aboriginal distribution of the plant and so omit information about immigrant tribes (that is, the Cheyenne, Comanche, Dela-

1. *Nicotiana rustica*
2. *Nicotiana attenuata*
3. *Nicotiana quadrivalis* var. *quadrivalis*
4. *Nicotiana quadrivalis* var. *multivalis*

0        400
Scale in Miles

Map 20. Distribution of aboriginal tobacco on the Great Plains, according to Setchell (1921).

ware, Lakota, and Potawatomi). Native tribes, historically identified as the Wichita, Pawnee, Mandan, Hidatsa, Arikara, Plains Apache, Crow, Cree, Blackfoot, and Kansa, are included.

### The Wichita

The Great Bend aspect, or protohistoric Wichita, is identified in archaeological sites located in central and southcentral Kansas that date from A.D. 1400 to 1700. Sites along the Arkansas River in central Kansas are believed to have been visited by the first Spanish *entrada* led by

Francisco Vázquez de Coronado into the interior in 1541 (Udden 1900; W. Wedel 1959). A subsequent Spanish expedition led by Juan de Oñate in 1601 is thought to have visited sites along the lower Walnut River in southcentral Kansas (Vehik 1992; M. Wedel 1982). Because these Spanish expeditions were conducted primarily to seek gold and silver and to introduce the natives to Christianity, information about subsistence, customs, and rituals is extremely limited in the written accounts they left. The Spaniards found no precious metals, and the impact of these early encounters, if judged by the number and distribution of trade goods, may have been insubstantial (Lees 1990).

In a settlement visited by Oñate in 1601, Fray Alonso Martínez (Hammond and Rey 1953: 846) described fields of maize and noted that smaller gardens were planted in beans and "calabashes" (a term that may collectively refer to a mixture of squash and pumpkin). Although there is no mention of tobacco, smoking, or even the presence of the calumet ceremony in the early Spanish accounts, this should not be interpreted to mean that the Wichita did not possess or cultivate tobacco. To the Spaniards, the calumet ritual would have been a pagan ceremony and not likely recorded (Blakeslee 1981).[2] Stylized catlinite or red pipestone elbow pipes, which are viewed as archaeological evidence of this ceremony, have been recovered from several Great Bend sites (Lees et al. 1989: 57; W. Wedel 1959:286). Tobacco fields, if separated from those of other crops as described for the Hidatsa (Wilson 1977 [1917]), may have gone unnoticed by the Spaniards. That the Spaniards did not record the cultivation of the easily recognized sunflower suggests that they noted the horticultural practices of the Wichita very casually. Further, as I discuss later in this chapter, tobacco seeds have been recovered from flotation samples collected systematically during the excavation of the Great Bend Mems site (14MN328) (Adair 1989), as well as at several Great Bend sites excavated in the Lower Walnut River valley (Adair, unpublished notes, 1995).

The Wichita experienced limited additional European contact until the beginning of the eighteenth century and the advance of the French traders. In 1719, J. B. Bénard, Sieur de la Harpe, visited a Tawakoni village along the Arkansas River below present-day Tulsa, Oklahoma, where a large group of Wichita had gathered (John 1975:200; M. Wedel 1988 [1971]:140). There he documented the Wichita cultivation of a "prodiguous quantity of tobacco" (Margry 1875–1878, 6:294). The ripe tobacco plants were pounded between two stones and made into flat loaves for future use. La Harpe received several of these tobacco cakes along with numerous other gifts. He was further honored with the calumet ceremony (M. Wedel 1988 [1971]).

In 1778, while visiting two villages of the Taovaya (Wichita speakers) along the Vermejo (Red?) River, Athanase de Mézèires commented that "there is no house in which at present there may not be seen four or five vessels full of maize, each one estimated at 4 1/2 faneges, besides a great quantity of beans and calabashes. They preserve the latter from year to year, weaving them curiously like mats. In addition, they raise watermelons and tobacco in great quantity" (Bolton 1914, 2:202).

A half century later, in 1832, John Sibley (1832:723) noted that "their tobacco they manufacture and cut as fine as tea, which is put into leather bags . . . and is . . . an article of trade."

Accounts from the eighteenth and early nineteenth centuries are unclear, however, about whether the tobacco the Wichita grew for trade or export was a native species or the introduced N. tabacum. Even determining the native species is no easy task, because the historical records provide confusing information and the archaeological remains cannot be identified beyond the genus level. Melvin Gilmore (1922:481) stated that "Nicotiana quadrivalvis was the species cultivated by all the tribes of the Plains from Texas to and including the country of the Mandans." As David Asch and William Green (1992: 81) argue, however, the claim that N. quadrivalvis was the original tobacco of the entire plains region is supported by no other documentation or current research. Nor was it verified by Gilmore, but rather gathered from several secondhand sources and oral traditions.

In addition, by the 1700s and 1800s the Wichita's use of tobacco may have been heavily influenced by their association with the French. As Wagner notes in chapter 9, N. tabacum had been introduced in the English colonies and was an established commercial crop by the mid-seventeenth century, roughly 100 years before de Mézières visited the southern plains. One suggestion that *N. tabacum* might have been the tobacco cultivated by the Wichita comes from Father Abad's account in 1772 that the Tawakoni were well supplied with French guns and French tobacco (Bolton 1914, 1:101). W. W. Newcomb and W. T. Field (1967:310) add that although the Wichita received tobacco from Europeans as early as the mid-eighteenth century, the native-grown product was not entirely displaced, perhaps suggesting that the two species were cultivated at the same time. Or perhaps only the native species was grown while *N. tabacum* was added through trade.

## The Pawnee

The Pawnee historically occupied an area around the Loup and Platte rivers in present-day central Nebraska and southward along the Republican River into north-central Kansas. The Lower Loup (Itskari) phase (A.D. 1650–1700) was probably ancestral Pawnee. Although the Pawnee may have had some earlier contact with Spaniards (either directly or through trade) (M. Wedel 1982), their actual location and identity were not well known until the early 1700s, when the French trade with the Missouri River tribes became established (W. Wedel 1986:173). The archaeological record of early Pawnee sites indicates the presence of more French trade items than Spanish. The location of the French at Kaskaskia and at Fort de Cavagnial in 1743 gave their traders easier access to the Pawnee via major waterways than was available to the Spanish, who traveled overland from the Southwest. In 1724, Étienne de Bourgmont mentioned the presence of nine villages of the Panimaha (Pawnee). Although known to French fur traders, these villages also maintained trade relations with Spaniards (Giraud 1958:16).

Perhaps the first recorded information on Pawnee tobacco comes from the early 1800s. Zebulon Pike in 1806, John Dunbar in 1833, and Charles Murray in 1834–1836 all provided information on the Pawnee, and all noted the presence of tobacco. At his famous council with the Pawnee in 1806 (now recognized as having taken place at the Hill site [25WT1] in south-central Nebraska), Pike and his men, as well as several Osage who accompanied them, were offered a pipe (Quaife 1925:47). Pike also noted that the Kansa and Osage had already smoked the pipe of peace together (Quaife 1925:49), thereby acknowledging the importance of the pipe (and presumably the calumet ceremony) in forming alliances. Dunbar and Murray were less formal in their recognition of tobacco; Murray (1839:321) commented only that Pawnee men were lazy and "passed the time in smoking, feasting, mending and sharpening their knives and arrows." Although Murray mentioned a first offering of smoke to the Great Spirit, neither account recognized the importance of Pawnee beliefs and rituals. One important ceremony was the Hako, in which smoking and pinching tobacco were critical elements (Fletcher 1904).

Like the Wichita, the Pawnee practiced a mixed economy of hunting and farming. At the time of contact, they raised crops of maize, several varieties of squash, sunflowers, beans, and tobacco (W. Wedel 1986). Gilmore (1919:61) stated that all the tribes of Nebraska cultivated *Nicotiana quadrivalvis*, a variety they eagerly traded as prepared tobacco leaves, although they jealously guarded against export of the seeds. Pawnee men were traditionally responsible for the tobacco patches, which they planted and tended from late spring until frost. According to Gilmore: "The crop was allowed to grow thick, and then the whole plant—leaves, unripe fruit capsules, and the tender small parts of the stems—was dried for smoking. The unripe seed capsules, dried separately, were specially prized for smoking on account of the flavor, pronounced by the Indians to be like the flavor now found in the imported Turkish tobacco" (Gilmore 1919:62).

Gene Weltfish (1965:159) added that tobacco was always mixed with the inner bark of the red dogwood (*Cornus amomum*) and that smoking was a critical part of structured secular visits, chiefs' meetings, ritual cleansing, harvest ceremonies, rites of passage, and political alliances. To date, no remains of tobacco have been identified from a precontact or historic Pawnee site.

## The Mandan, Hidatsa, and Arikara

The middle Missouri area is an 800-mile segment along the Missouri River trench north of the Niobrara River in northern Nebraska, reaching to the mouth of the Yellowstone River in northern North Dakota. During the late prehistoric and early historic periods, this area was occupied by sedentary, village dwelling Arikara, Mandan, and Hidatsa Indians. The Arikara were in the vicinity of the Grand River in what is now South Dakota, while the Mandan and Hidatsa were located upstream at the confluence of the Knife and Missouri rivers in present-day North Dakota. After the early 1800s, the three groups lived together in the vicinity of the mouth of the Knife River, and it was in this area that most of the historical accounts were written. The three groups shared a similar hunting and farming adaptation (Wood 1967).

In 1738, Sieur de la Vérendrye made the first recorded visit by a European to the Mandan and Hidatsa villages along the Missouri (Lehmer 1971; Ronda 1984). By this time, trade goods were already well known to these groups, and la Vérendrye referred to the well-established trade pattern that the Mandan and Hidatsa maintained with the Assiniboin and Cree in the north and east and the Crow and Cheyenne in the west. Operating as middlemen, the Mandan and Hidatsa, and later the Arikara, were responsible for the transport of a considerable quantity of goods across the northern plains from as far away as the Pacific coastal region (Ewers 1968). In return for English and French goods possessed by the Cree and Assiniboin, the Mandan and Hidatsa exchanged agricultural produce and tobacco. La Vérendrye commented that the villagers "knew well how to profit by it in selling their grains, tobaccos, skins, and colored plumes which they knew the Assiniboin prize highly" (Burpee 1927:76). To the west, the Cheyenne,

who had abandoned farming and moved onto the plains, depended heavily on the Arikara for foodstuff and tobacco (Ronda 1984:50). Buffalo Bird Woman recounted to Gilbert L. Wilson (1977 [1917]:126) that the village tribes also traded with the Sioux. Archaeological data from several northern plains sites suggest that the trade network between the northern plains and the Pacific coast was established before Euro-American contact (Lehmer 1971; Wood 1980).

Ethnographic and historic accounts of the Mandan, Hidatsa, and Arikara provide good information on the varieties of tobacco cultivated. In 1804, Lewis and Clark identified the Arikara tobacco as *N. quadrivalvis* and noted that it was quite different from the Chesapeake varieties. Lewis described the tobacco plant as growing about 3 feet high; it was planted in hills and harvested in late summer. Photo 31 (see chapter 6) illustrates the actual type specimen of *N. quadrivalvis* collected by Lewis. During his visit to the middle Missouri area in 1833, Prince Maximilian of Weid also commented on the cultivation of *N. quadrivalvis* (Thwaites 1905b:108).

In 1811, John Bradbury and Thomas Nuttall traveled up the Missouri River, collecting and recording the distribution of the native flora. Bradbury wrote that the Arikara grew the "small tobacco, *Nicotiana rustica*," which he identified as the same variety grown by the Maha (Omaha) to the east (Thwaites 1904:175). It has been suggested that Bradbury made an incorrect taxonomic identification, because he described the plant as having *white* flowers—a distinctive characteristic of *N. quadrivalvis* (Will and Hyde 1917:62). Gilmore (1913) later identified *N. quadrivalvis* as the variety cultivated historically by the Omaha. Bradbury, however, was a botanist and is noted for his careful records on native plants. Gilmore based his identification on Omaha oral tradition rather than on herbarium specimens, because the Omaha no longer possessed their native variety in the early 1900s. Gilmore (1919:61–62) also stated that the oldest living Omaha in 1914 had never seen *N. quad-*

*rivalvis* growing but used European tobacco instead. He obtained *N. quadrivalvis* seed from a 73-year-old Hidatsa man from North Dakota. In addition, Cutler and Blake (1973) identified *Nicotiana rustica* seeds from a protohistoric Hidatsa medicine bundle recovered from the Mahhaha site in North Dakota. These identifications do not dispute the cultivation of either taxa but rather suggest that both *N. rustica* and *N. quadrivalvis* might have been cultivated in the middle Missouri area during the late prehistoric and early historic periods.

As in the case of the Pawnee, tobacco growing among the Arikara, Mandan, and Hidatsa was the responsibility of the men. Individual tobacco gardens were planted apart from the cornfields because it was thought that tobacco was harmful to the corn if planted too close. Tobacco seed, planted at the same time as sunflower seed, was sown in rows made with a digging stick, and the young plants were tended with a bison-rib cultivation tool. Tobacco was gathered in two harvests, starting with the collecting of the white blossoms (which suggests that the variety grown was of the *N. quadrivalvis* group). Gathered every fourth day, the delicate blossoms were spread out to dry on a hide in the lodge. Once dried, they were gently mixed with buffalo fat and stored in tobacco bags. The stems and leaves of the tobacco plant were harvested before the frost and were also dried inside the lodge and stored in tobacco bags or underground cache pits (Wilson 1977 [1917]:123–125).

## The Crow, Blackfoot, and Cree

North and west of the middle Missouri area are the high plains and the prairies of the Canadian provinces. Within these areas are found the historic tribes of the Crow, the Blackfoot, and the Cree. Although data are not abundant on the subsistence practices of these groups, they are usually described as hunters and foragers (Driver 1970). Tobacco was the only domesticated plant cultivated among the Crow, and it was ceremonially important in their tobacco society (Lowie 1920, 1935). The species cultivated by

the Crow was probably *Nicotiana quadrivalvis* var. *multivalvis*, which is part of the *N. quadrivalvis* group but botanically different from the *N. quadrivalvis* var. *quadrivalvis* grown by the middle Missouri groups. The Blackfoot are reported to have acquired tobacco from the Crow (Castetter 1944), although the variety may not have been *N. multivalvis*. Setchell (1921:411) commented that Blackfoot tobacco was *Nicotiana attenuata*. The Crow's use of tobacco is described in detail in chapter 13.

## The Plains Apache

The Apache occupied portions of the high plains of present-day Nebraska, Kansas, Colorado, and New Mexico and the southern plains in Oklahoma and Texas during the late prehistoric and historic periods. Here I devote attention to Apache groups referred to in early historical accounts as Paloma, Paduca, and Cuartelejo (Gunnerson and Gunnerson 1971; Thomas 1935; W. Wedel 1986). Although it is unclear whether some of these groups adopted agriculture and irrigation prior to late-sixteenth- and early-seventeenth-century contact with Puebloan groups in the Southwest, early accounts describe the economy of the Cuartelejo as a mixture of hunting and agriculture. Cultivated plant remains from the seventeenth-century El Quartelejo site (14SC1) in western Kansas include corn, melons, and watermelons (Adair 1992). The Apache reportedly traded with both the Wichita to the east and Puebloan groups in New Mexico (Gunnerson and Gunnerson 1971). John Upton Terrell referred to the plains Apache as enterprising traders and described seasonal visits to Taos and Pecos for purposes of trade (Terrell 1975). Although early accounts do not mention tobacco cultivation by the Apache, one can assume that their geographic location gave them access to the plant. Indeed, the earliest reference to the calumet ceremony is found in a description of a performance by the plains Apache in 1634 (Blakeslee 1981). The Apache probably did not originate the ceremony but received it from plains Caddoan-speaking tribes to the east (Blakeslee 1981). The tobacco used by the Apache could be one of several varieties or species.

## The Kansa

The final historic, indigenous tribe on the plains for whom there is an ethnographic record of the use of tobacco is the Kansa. Historically, this tribe occupied an area along the Missouri River north of the mouth of the Kansas River and west along the Kansas to the Blue River in the vicinity of present-day Manhattan, Kansas (Unrau 1965). Although the 1724 visit by Étienne de Bourgmont was the first well-documented contact between the Kansa and Europeans, de Bourgmont's account fails to describe much of their way of life. Almost 100 years later, Thomas Say, who accompanied the Long expedition to the central plains in 1819, spent four days at the principal Kansa village, then located near the confluence of the Bleu Earth (Blue River) and Kansas rivers, where he was offered a pipe, beef jerky, and boiled corn (Thwaites 1905a: 187). Although this is not strong evidence of precontact possession of tobacco, the Kansa are believed to be descendants of the prehistoric Oneota (Henning 1970; W. Wedel 1959). Clay and pipestone pipes have been recovered from both the Doniphan (14DP2) and Fanning (14DP1) sites in northeastern Kansas, which are believed to have been in part ancestral Kansa (W. Wedel 1959). Tobacco seeds have been identified from several prehistoric Oneota sites.

## Archaeological Tobacco

Despite the numerous ethnographic records of the use of tobacco on the plains, there is relatively little direct evidence to corroborate its importance prehistorically. To date, archaeological tobacco has been identified from only 18 sites on the Great Plains (map 21, table 37). Direct evidence comes from the recovery and identification of distinctive seeds and the analysis of pipe dottle. Although attempts have been made to identify a distinctive tobacco phytolith from experimental gardens, they have not produced taxonomically useful results (Steve Bozarth, personal communication, 1991). In what follows, I describe the context of each of the 18 discoveries of archaeological tobacco, in order to contribute to a broad understanding of the plant's prehistoric distribution and the possible taxa utilized.

## Woodland Period

The earliest evidence of tobacco on the plains comes from several early Late Woodland, Boyer phase occupations in eastern Iowa. The Boyer phase is dated between A.D. 450 and 660 (Tiffany

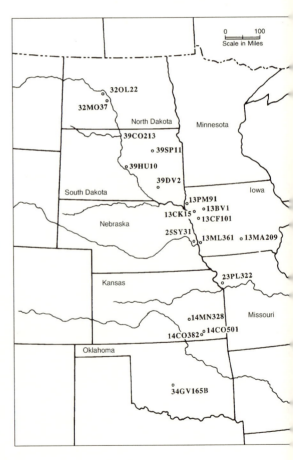

Map 21. Sites at which archaeological tobacco has been identified on the Great Plains.

Table 37: Archaeological Tobacco on the Great Plains

| Site | Component | Date A.D. | No. Seeds | No. Proveniences | Reference |
|------|-----------|-----------|-----------|------------------|-----------|
| Rainbow 13PM91 | Late Woodland Boyer phase | 450-660 | 14 | 3 | Benn 1990 |
| M.A.D. 13CF101, 13CF102 | Late Woodland Boyer phase | 450-660 | 1 | 1 | Benn 1981a |
| Brewster 13CK15 | Mill Creek | 1005 (15 C14 dates) | 1 | 1 | Stains 1972 |
| Chan-Ya-Ta 13BV1 | Mill Creek | 1077 (7 C14 dates) | 4 | 1 | Wegner 1979 |
| Millipede 13ML361 | Nebraska phase | 1260 ± 60 | 96 | 4 | Green and Billeck 1993 |
| Mitchell 39DV2 | Initial Middle Missouri | 985-1125 | 8 | 2 | Benn 1974 |
| Humphrey 23PL322 | Steed-Kisker | 950-1200 | | | Johnson 1994 |
| Patterson 25SY31, House 3 | Nebraska phase | ca. 1300 | 1 | 1 | Adair, unpublished notes |
| 34GV165B | Paoli phase | 1100-1250 | 1 | 1 | Drass 1995 |
| Wildcat 13MA209 | Oneota | 1200-1400 | 1 | 1 | Parker 1990 |
| Dirt Lodge 39SP11 | Late Woodland Randall phase | 1030-1250 | 1 | 1 | Haberman 1984 |
| Travis 1 39CO213 | Extended Middle Missouri | 1100-1550 | 10 | 1 | Haberman 1982 |
| Indian School 39HU10 | Postcontact Coalescent | 1675-1780 | 1 | 1 | Haberman, pers. comm., 1991 |
| Boley 32MO37 | Postcontact Coalescent | 1675-1780 | | | Adair, unpublished notes |
| Mahhaha 32OL22 | Protohistoric Hidatsa | 1780-1804 | | | Cutler and Blake 1973 |
| Mems 14MN328 | Great Bend | 1400-1700 | 4 | 2 | Adair 1989 |
| 14CO501 | Great Bend | 1550-1700 | | | Adair, unpublished notes |
| 14CO382 | Great Bend | 1550-1700 | | | Adair, unpublished notes |

1981). David Benn (1981b:196, 200) described 13 carbonized seeds from features and one seed from a level of the Boyer component at the Rainbow site (13PM91). He identified the species tentatively as *N. rustica*. At the M.A.D. sites (13CF101 and 13CF102), one carbonized seed was recovered and also identified as *N. rustica* (Benn 1981a).

## Village Period

Additional evidence of *Nicotiana* has been found at Village period sites along the eastern border of the plains and in the northern, central, and southern plains. Two Mill Creek sites in northwestern Iowa yielded charred tobacco seeds. At the Brewster site (13CK15), Donna Jean Stains (1972) identified one carbonized seed. Fifteen radiocarbon dates from the site averaged A.D. 1005 (Tiffany 1981). At the nearby site of Chan-Ya-Ta (13BV1), Steven Wegner (1979) reported the recovery of four charred seeds. Joseph Tiffany (1981) averaged the seven radiocarbon dates from the site at A.D. 1077. An analysis of archaeobotanical remains from the Millipede site (13ML361), a central plains earthlodge in southwestern Iowa, identified 96 *N. rustica* seeds from storage features and house midden (Green and Billeck 1993). Of particular interest at this site is the association of a relatively large number of the tobacco seeds with nightshade (*Solanum americanum*) seeds. The seeds of this plant, which is also a member of the Solanaceae family, are known to have been used for medicinal purposes (Bocek 1984; Reagan 1928, 1929), and they are frequently associated with tobacco in archaeological contexts (see Wagner, this volume). At the Wildcat Creek site (13MA209) in south-central Iowa, excavation of an Oneota occupation yielded one carbonized tobacco seed. Kathryn Parker (1990: 359) identified it as *N. rustica* on the basis of the known distribution of this variety, stating that "most tobacco from sites in the Northern Plains eastward has been identified as *rustica*."

Tobacco roughly contemporaneous with that found at Mill Creek has also been identified at several sites in the northern plains. In the Initial Middle Missouri occupation at the Mitchell site (39DV2) in southeastern South Dakota, eight carbonized seeds from two contexts were identified as *Nicotiana rustica* (Benn 1974). Tobacco is also associated with the Extended Middle Missouri complex, dated from A.D. 1100 to 1550. Thomas Haberman (1982, 1984:282) identified 10 carbonized seeds at the Travis I site (39CO213) as western tobacco of the *quadrivalvis* group, probably *N. quadrivalvis* var. *quadrivalvis*.

Tobacco has also been recovered from two central plains sites. A sandstone pipe from the Humphrey site (23PL322), a Steed-Kisker Mississippian occupation in northwestern Missouri, yielded dottle fragments identified on the basis of leaf stomata as *Nicotiana* sp. (A. E. Johnson 1994) (photo 37). This complex is radiocarbon dated at A.D. 950 to 1200. One tobacco seed has additionally been identified from an interior storage feature in House 3 at the Patterson site (25SY31) in east-central Nebraska (Adair, unpublished notes, 1995). Radiocarbon dates from the structure at this Nebraska phase site indicate an occupation during the late thirteenth to early fourteenth century (Rob Bozell, personal communication, 1995).

Excavations at site 34GV165B, on the Washita River in south-central Oklahoma, also produced one charred tobacco seed associated with several other native and tropical domesticates, including *Iva annua, Zea mays, Phaseolus vulgaris,* and *Hordeum pusillum.* Radiocarbon dates place the occupation at around A.D. 1100 to 1250 (Drass 1995).

## Late Prehistoric

For the protohistoric and postcontact time periods, tobacco has been identified at four sites on the Great Plains. As noted previously, *Nicotiana rustica* was identified in a medicine bundle at

Photo 37. Dottle residue from a sandstone pipe (23PL322), showing *Nicotiana* sp. leaf stomata. Photo by Mary J. Adair.

the protohistoric Hidatsa site of Mahhaha (Cutler and Blake 1973). Tobacco has also been recovered from the postcontact Coalescent Indian School site (39HU10) in central South Dakota, but a species identification is unconfirmed (Haberman, personal communication, 1991). Ongoing analysis of archaeobotanical remains from storage pits at the Boley site (32MO37), a postcontact Coalescent site in North Dakota, has identified many *Nicotiana* sp. seeds clumped together in a mass (Adair, unpublished notes, 1995). In south-central Kansas, four carbonized tobacco seeds were recovered from two storage pit features at the protohistoric Wichita Mems site (14MN328). The seed surface compares to that of *N. rustica* (Adair 1989). Additional evidence of the protohistoric Wichita use of tobacco comes from ongoing excavations and analyses of flotation samples recovered from several sites attributed to the Lower Walnut focus of the Great Bend aspect. To date, tobacco seeds have been tentatively identified from 14CO501 and 14CO382.

## Indirect Evidence

There are several lines of indirect archaeological evidence for the use of tobacco on the Great Plains. As outlined by Haberman, these include the occurrence of stone and ceramic pipes and related accessories such as tobacco-cutting tablets, the recognition of other plant materials that are known additives in tobacco mixtures, and the identification of archaeological features related to tobacco cultivation (Haberman 1984: 270–271). Of primary concern for this chapter is the occurrence and distribution of pipes. Although several authors have referred to aboriginal smoking mixtures other than tobacco (see Adams and Toll, this volume; Harshberger 1906; Jones 1944; Linton 1924; McGuire 1897, 1910; Winter, chapters 2 and 13, this volume; Yarnell 1964) and/or have urged caution in equating the archaeological occurrence of pipes with the use of tobacco (Ford 1981; Yarnell 1964), still others have accepted the close association of pipes with native tobacco (Castetter

1943; Safford 1916b). Indeed, one author argued "that all smoking pipes in the eastern United States are associated with the use of cultivated *N. rustica*" (Lathrap 1987:350). Part of the hesitation over using pipes as indirect evidence for the presence of tobacco results from the relatively recent recognition of the widespread prehistoric distribution of tobacco in eastern North America (see Wagner, this volume) in conjunction with the difficulty of recovering tobacco remains. Given our current knowledge of the prehistoric use and distribution of tobacco, however, the suggestion that pipes recovered from archaeological deposits probably indicate the use of tobacco seems reasonable.

On the basis of data available from the central plains, the initial appearance of pipes is associated with the Middle Woodland Hopewell complex, dated at A.D. 1 to 500. Although tobacco has not been identified from a Kansas City Hopewell site, it does appear in northwestern Iowa in roughly contemporaneous contexts (Benn 1981b). Platform pipes and undecorated clay pipes are associated with numerous Hopewell and later Plains Woodland period sites (ca. A.D. 500 to 1000) (Bozell and Winfrey 1994; A. E. Johnson 1979, n.d.; Kivett 1952), where they are frequently recovered from midden deposits or cache pits. Stone and ceramic pipes have also been recovered from several later Village period occupations of around A.D. 1000 to 1500 (K. Brown 1984; Calabrese 1969; A. E. Johnson 1994; Logan 1990; Ludwickson 1978; Shippee 1972; W. Wedel 1943).

It was during this time period that red argillite stone pipes, stylized in elbow, disk, or effigy forms, made their first appearance. Although some of these pipes may indeed have been manufactured from Minnesota catlinite, the mineralogy of others indicates that the stone was quarried from local Kansas and Nebraska glacial tills (Gunderson 1993). Donald Blakeslee (1981: 763) argued that pipes stylized like these were made for use with a wooden stem and are similar to the pipe bowls used in the sacred calumet ceremony. Large effigy sandstone pipes, thought to have had a special function, have also been recovered from SteedKisker Mississippian sites in northwestern Missouri (A. E. Johnson 1994). As noted earlier, residue of *Nicotiana* sp. was identified in the effigy pipe from 23PL322, indicating that tobacco might have been used as part of a ritual performance (A. E. Johnson 1994:191).

An analysis of smoking remains from pipe bowls and a greater emphasis on the recovery of small-scale botanical remains through systematic flotation techniques will certainly increase our knowledge of prehistoric tobacco on the Great Plains. Given the eastern orientation of several plains cultural complexes, it would not be surprising to recover tobacco from plains Early or Middle Woodland sites. *Nicotiana rustica* would likely be the species identified, since it is the only species so far identified from early sites in Illinois and Iowa. The likelihood of such a recovery is strengthened by the fact that the earliest agricultural complex of squash, corn, and marshelder, identified from sites on the eastern margins of the plains, is very similar in context to that identified from temporally equivalent sites in the eastern woodlands (Adair 1988).

## Discussion and Conclusion

Although increased knowledge of the distribution of prehistoric tobacco on the Great Plains is desirable, of perhaps equal interest is the identification of the different species and varieties that were cultivated. Tobacco seeds as a genus are distinctive, but identifying species from archaeological remains is problematical in that differences in seed morphology between taxa are neither easily recognized nor agreed upon by researchers (Asch and Green 1992; Haberman 1984; Wagner, this volume). For example, only one researcher has identified archaeologically derived *N. quadrivalvis* seeds east of the Rockies (Haberman 1984), and doubts have been expressed about that identification (Asch and Asch 1985a). The historic range of this variety is equally unresolved, as is the terminological disagreement concerning its name (see chapter 5).

If seeds of *N. quadrivalvis* cannot be distinguished from those of *N. rustica*, then identifications of tobacco seeds as *N. rustica* are potentially invalid as well, and all tobacco recovered from plains sites should be identified only to genus. In the eastern woodlands, this dilemma is often resolved by identifying archaeological tobacco as *N. rustica* solely on the basis of the known historic distribution of this species, rather than on the characteristics of the seeds alone. There seems to be little disagreement that this was the only taxon of native tobacco grown east of the Mississippi River at the time of contact. A similar argument cannot be made for the Great Plains.

In light of ethnographic and archaeological data, we must consider the distribution and use of four taxa of tobacco. The Mandan, Hidatsa, and Arikara and possibly the Pawnee are recorded as having cultivated *N. quadrivalvis* var. *quadrivalvis*, a variety also identified from prehistoric sites in the northern plains. The Crow cultivated *N. quadrivalvis* var. *multivalvis* and *N. quadrivalvis* var. *quadrivalvis*, whereas the Blackfoot may have used *N. attenuata*. *N. rustica*, which was also associated with the protohistoric Hidatsa, Arikara, and Wichita, had a relatively wider prehistoric distribution. This taxon has been identified from several early Late Woodland to Village period sites in the northern and central plains and is considered the likely taxon at other sites where identifications have not been confirmed. The question that needs to be addressed is, what is the significance of the presence of different tobacco taxa? Data relevant to early trade networks and to the ritual or shamanistic use of tobacco may be of value in addressing this question.

Historic and archaeological data from the middle Missouri region indicate that *N. quadrivalvis* was the species of tobacco cultivated at the time of contact. Its initial use in the northern plains may have occurred around A.D. 900 to

1000 as a result of trade networks established with western and Pacific coastal groups (Haberman 1984). Prior to that, the taxon most likely to have been cultivated was *Nicotiana rustica*, judging from its identification in archaeological contexts to the south and east. Haberman may be correct in suggesting that the use of *N. quadrivalvis* was widespread in the plains, but the implication that central plains groups were involved in the elaborate Northwest Coast trade network has not been confirmed in the ethnographic or archaeological record. The Mandan and Hidatsa traded agricultural crops to the Rocky Mountain Indians (identified as Crow and Shoshoni) in return for meat and animal pelts (Will and Hyde 1917:172, 183). The Rocky Mountain tribes knew that the Mandan and Hidatsa villages were the only places where crops could be procured, because the Pawnee and other central plains tribes were not involved in the trade network. Dunbar (1910) also noted that the Pawnee never traded or sold their corn. Exotic items have been recovered from several prehistoric central plains sites, but the small quantity of these artifacts appears not to reflect an elaborate trade network or long-term relationship with Indians in other geographical areas.

If the cultivation of *Nicotiana quadrivalvis* in the northern plains was directly associated with an extensive trade network, then one must account for the continued presence of *N. rustica* in archaeological and historical contexts. Although the two taxa have slightly different morphological characteristics, one of their more pronounced differences is the mean percentage of nicotine in their dried leaves. Research indicates that the *N. quadrivalvis* group exhibits a fairly low nicotine content—roughly 0.16 percent—whereas the nicotine content of *N. rustica* measures significantly higher—2.77 percent to at least 8.26 percent (Siegel, Collings, and Diaz 1977; Smith and Bacon 1941; Smith and Smith 1942; Winter, chapter 14, this volume). Richard Schultes (1979:152) also describes several ß-carboline compounds in tobacco that are related

to known hallucinogenic compounds. During burning, the concentration of these compounds may be increased to 40 to 100 times the concentration found in fresh leaves. In combination with other constituents in tobacco, such as nicotine, the ß-carbolines could act psychoactively as hallucinogens (Schultes 1979:152), especially when used in a proper cultural context, such as during shamanistic and medicinal rituals, trance states, and vision quests. All of these involved the ingestion and at times inhalation of a significant amount of tobacco smoke or tobacco plants, often accompanied by fasting (Fletcher 1904; Weltfish 1965). The intake of tobacco to produce hallucinogenic or mind-altered effects was practiced among several Native American tribes on the Northwest Coast, in the Southeast, and in the Great Lakes region (Moerman 1986: 303–307). The presence of more than one taxon of tobacco on the Great Plains might indicate that the more potent variety was used in ritual contexts while the milder variety functioned in the establishment of alliance and fictive kinship relationships. Combined archaeological, ethnographic, and linguistic data might be used to investigate the possible uses of the different varieties. A medicine bundle containing *N. rustica* and midden deposits in which *N. quadrivalvis* has been identified at northern plains sites exemplify the kinds of archaeological contexts that are necessary if we are to interpret why one taxon was chosen over another.

In summary, it may be that more than one taxon of tobacco was cultivated or traded prehistorically on the Great Plains. *Nicotiana rustica*, probably the earliest species on the plains, may have been supplemented in the northern plains by *N. quadrivalvis*. Exactly where one draws the lines of distribution for these taxa is speculative and may remain so for some time. Direct archaeological evidence has not yet solved the distributional problem, and the co-occurrence of these taxa for potentially different uses might render distribution maps meaningless. Certainly, greater attention to the recovery and identification of archaeobotanical collections is needed, as are improved techniques for identifying the different tobacco taxa.

## Notes

I would like to recognize the following people for their assistance in compiling information on the presence of tobacco in archaeological contexts: David Benn, Richard Drass, William Green, the late Thomas W. Haberman, and C. Thomas Shay. In particular, I thank Gail Wagner for including Great Plains sites in her distribution maps of archaeological tobacco, a measure that offers readers a greater appreciation of the widespread use of this domesticate. I also thank Alfred E. Johnson for reading and commenting on earlier drafts of this chapter; Meredith Lane for identifying tobacco from pipe dottle recovered from the Humphrey site; Karen Adams and Joseph Winter for chairing and organizing the 1991 SAA symposium from which this volume grew; and Joseph Winter for his hard work and persistence in bringing the book to a successful completion.

1. See chapter 5 for a discussion of the terminological confusion over these names.

2. Editor's note: In other places, such as California and the Southwest, the Spanish did report on "pagan" ceremonies.

# 9

# Tobacco in Prehistoric Eastern North America

## Gail E. Wagner

The earliest tobacco in eastern North America dates to Middle Woodland contexts—as early as the first century B.C. to the second century A.D.— at sites in west-central Illinois at the confluence of the Mississippi, Illinois, and Missouri rivers. To date, these are the second earliest finds of tobacco in archaeological contexts in all of North America. Its more widespread occurrence in eastern North America postdates A.D. 300. This survey of published and unpublished reports tracks tobacco's distribution through space and time, as well as the contexts of its disposal.

Although tobacco can be identified by different sorts of evidence such as leaves, stems, capsules, trichomes, pollen, and residues,[1] the most commonly recovered form of evidence in eastern North America is charred seeds. Without the use of flotation to recover small botanical remains, an archaeologist is unlikely to recover tobacco seeds. Tobacco has rarely been recovered by water screening. Our knowledge of the distribution of tobacco in eastern North America is therefore limited to those areas and periods for which archaeologists have employed flotation.

Researchers agree that *Nicotiana rustica* likely spread to eastern North America from Mexico rather than from the Southwest (Asch and Asch 1985a; Ford 1985; Fritz 1990; Riley, Edging, and Rossen 1990; Setchell 1921). Unfortunately, tobacco so far has not been recovered from early contexts in Texas, the Caribbean, or along the Gulf coast, and thus no evidence exists to trace a northward route through the Caribbean or a northeastward

route through Mexico and Texas (Fritz 1990; Riley, Edging, and Rossen 1990; Setchell, 1921). Until more flotation and paleoethnobotanical analyses are carried out in these areas, the route and timing of transmission from south to north will remain unknown.

## Identification of Tobacco Species

Archaeological tobacco in North America east of the Great Plains is presumed to be *Nicotiana rustica*, on the basis of the early historic distribution of this species rather than on strict morphological comparison of the remains with modern or ethnographic material (Asch and Asch 1985a; Ford 1985; Goodspeed 1954; Setchell 1921). William Strachey's 1612 description of *N. rustica* grown by the Indians in Virginia clearly differentiates it from the *N. tabacum* grown in Trinidad and elsewhere:

> There is here great store of Tobacco which the Saluages call *Apooke*, howbeyt yt is not of the best kynd, yt is but poore and weake, and of a byting tast, yt growes not fully a yard aboue ground, bearing a little yellow flower like to henn-bane, the leaves are short and thick, somewhat round at the vpper end: whereas the best Tobacco of Trinidado and the Oronoque, is large sharpe and growing 2. or 3. yardes from the ground, bearing a flower of the breadth of our Bel-flowers in England. (Wright and Freund 1953:122–123)

Other early historic accounts from eastern North America are not nearly so clear in identifying the species of tobacco grown by the Indians. For example, James Rosier wrote the following about his 1605 voyage to Cape Cod with Captain George Waymouth: "They gave us the best welcome they could, spreading deer-skins for us to sit on the ground by their fire, and gave us of their tobacco in our pipes, which was most excellent, and so generally commended of us all to be as good as any we ever took, being the simple leaf without any composition, very strong and of a pleasant sweet taste" (Viereck 1967:68–69).

A closer look at the historical records might be fruitful, especially because the Spanish and English quickly adopted the use of tobacco and soon began commercial cropping of N. tabacum. During the seventeenth century the eastern seaboard Indians themselves came to favor Brazilian N. tabacum over N. rustica (Goodman 1993: 164–165). Spaniards were cultivating tobacco commercially in the West Indies by A.D. 1531, in Cuba and Venezuela by 1580, and in Brazil by around 1600 (Doub and Crabtree 1973). The earliest European description of tobacco was that of N. rustica by Rembrandt Dodoens in 1554, and tobacco appeared in European herbals in 1563 and 1565 (Spinden 1950). In 1557 N. tabacum was taken from Brazil to France by Jean André Thevet, and in 1560 N. rustica was taken from Florida to Portugal (Spinden 1950). Tobacco was grown as an ornamental and medicinal plant in Europe by 1560, and by 1600 it had been introduced into many other parts of the world, including China, Japan, and southern Africa (Doub and Crabtree 1973). Thus, in 1590 Thomas Hariot was already comparing the Virginia herb to the West Indies and Spanish tobacco (de Bry 1966 [1590]: 16). The first commercial crop of N. tabacum in the English colonies was grown by John Rolfe at Jamestown in 1612, and the resulting shipment was sent to England in 1613 (Doub and Crabtree 1973). In 1628 Virginia exported 370,000 pounds of tobacco to England (Goodman 1993:135). By the 1630s, tobacco was a commercial crop in Maryland (Doub and Crabtree 1973), and by the early 1640s it was being grown by the Swedish in Delaware (Goodman 1993:135).

## Seed Size and Shape

Tobacco seeds are small: in layman's terms, just a little larger than the period at the end of this sentence. The sizes and shapes of tobacco seeds within any one species are also quite variable (Akehurst 1981:48; Asch 1991; Goodspeed 1954). Whereas N. rustica seeds are larger than those of N. tabacum, the sizes of N. rustica seeds may overlap with those of N. attenuata and N. quadrivalvis (table 38). The uncharred seeds of N. tabacum are 0.4–0.6 millimeter in length and spherical or broadly elliptical in shape; N. attenuata seeds are approximately 0.7 millimeter in length and reniform to angular reniform in shape; N. quadrivalvis seeds are approximately 0.9 millimeter in length; and N. rustica seeds are 0.7–1.1 millimeter in length and elliptical, oval, or angular in shape (Goodspeed 1954:353, 373, 429, 447). B. C. Akehurst (1981:48) notes that the length-to-width ratio (presumably of N. tabacum seeds) is approximately 1.5 to 1.

The size range of the archaeological tobacco seeds from eastern North America that have been measured so far better fits N. rustica than it does N. tabacum, another domesticated species. However, considering that the seeds of N. attenuata and N. quadrivalvis fall within the same size range (Adams and Toll, this volume; Goodspeed 1954:353, 373, 429, 447) and that the earliest tobacco in eastern North America is found along river routes leading east from the Great Plains, we should not automatically assume that the eastern seeds are N. rustica. Table 39 lists the measurements that so far have been published for prehistoric tobacco from eastern North America. The charred seeds range from 0.80 to 1.19 millimeter in length and 0.60 to 0.90 millimeter in width.

| ɔecies | Length (mm) | Width (mm) | Thickness (mm) | Shape | Reticulations | No. Seeds per Capsule or Berry | Reference |
|---|---|---|---|---|---|---|---|
| rustica | 0.7–1.1 | — | — | Elliptical, oval, or angular | Fluted–reticulate | — | Goodspeed 1954:353 |
| | 1.0–1.3 | 0.5–0.9 | — | Oblong | With wavy, thin walls | 450–710 | Gunn and Gaffney 1974:8, 17 |
| | — | — | — | — | — | 500–600 | Voges 1984: 281–282 |
| | — | — | — | — | Straighter lines adjacent to hilum | — | Haberman 1984:281 |
| . quadrivalvis | 0.7–0.9 | — | — | Rotund-reniform | Medium to large numerous regular, closely spaced meshes; with fluted or fluted-plicate ridges | — | Goodspeed 1954:87, 92, 447 |
| | — | — | — | Reniform | No straight lines near hilum; oblong patterns between wavy lines | — | Haberman 1984:281 |
| . attenuata | 0.7–0.9 | — | — | Reniform, reniform-angular | Fluted-reticulate | — | Goodspeed 1954:92, 429 |
| | — | — | — | Reniform | Nearly circular patterns between wavy lines | — | Haberman 1984 |
| . tabacum | 0.3 | — | — | Spherical or broadly elliptical | Ridges fluted | — | Goodspeed 1954:373 |
| | 0.6–0.8 | 0.3–0.4 | — | Ovate to oblong | Straight-sided around hilum, radiating like spokes of a wheel | 3500 | Gunn and Gaffney 1974:8, 17 |
| | — | — | — | — | — | 1500–3500 | Voges 1984:455 |
| | 0.5 | — | — | Oval to spherical | — | 2000–3000 | Purseglove 1968 |
| americanum | 1.5–1.7 | 1.0–1.2 | 0.5 | Obovate | Wavy, thin to moderately thickened walls | 70–150 | Gunn and Gaffney 1974:25 |
| | 1.4–1.6 | — | — | — | — | 50–110 | Rogers and Ogg 1981 |
| nigrum | 1.0–1.6 | 0.9 | 1.3 | Obovate; slightly extended, narrow base often oblique and truncate | Network in a definite pattern | — | Delorit 1970: 94 |
| | 1.2 | 0.9–1.7 | 0.4–0.6 | Obovate to C-shaped | Straight, thin walls | 70–100 | Gunn and Gaffney 1974:27 |

Table 39: Sizes of Charred Prehistoric Eastern Tobacco Seeds

| Site | Length (mm) | Width (mm) | Thickness (mm) | Feature or Sample No. | Reference |
|------|------------|-----------|----------------|----------------------|-----------|
| Bonham, Va. | 1.00 | 0.70 | 0.70 | n = 3 | Gardner 1992a |
| Cahokia, Ill. | — | 0.60 | — | F12 | Measured by Wagner from photocopy supplied by Neal Lopinot, pers. comm. 1991 |
| Hill Creek, Ill. | 0.80 | 0.60 | 0.50 | F3 | Asch 1991 |
| Hine Village, Ohio | ca. 0.83+ | 0.70 | — | F6 | Measured by Wagner from figure in Macaulay 1990:189 |
| Incinerator, Ohio | 0.84 | 0.80 | 0.48 | 155 | Wagner, this volume |
| | 0.91 | 0.77 | 0.67 | 587 | |
| | 0.93 | 0.75 | 0.60 | 198 | |
| | 0.95 | — | 0.70 | 235 | |
| | 1.19 | 0.90 | 0.56 | 1025 | |
| Leonard Haag, Ind. | ca. 1.20 | — | — | — | Crawford 1981 |
| Chambers, Ky. | 1.00 | 0.60 | — | Unit 4 | Rossen 1987 |
| Mortland Island, Ill. | 1.00 | 0.80 | 0.60 | F126 | Asch 1991 |
| Pere Marquette, Ill. | 0.90+ | 0.70 | 0.70 | F63 | Asch 1991 |
| | 0.90+ | 0.80 | 0.60 | F17 | |
| | 1.10 | 0.80 | 0.70 | F17 | |
| Petitt, Ill. | ca. 0.83 | 0.60 | — | F13 | Measured by Wagner from photocopy supplied by Neal Lopinot, pers. comm., 1991 |
| Smiling Dan, Ill. | ca. 0.90 | 0.60 | — | Sq 960 | Asch 1991 |
| | 0.90 | 0.70 | — | F231 | |
| | ca. 1.00 | 0.70+ | 0.50+ | Sq 39 | |
| | 1.10 | 0.90 | 0.80 | F2 | |

## Seed Coat Sculpturing

Like other members of the family Solanaceae, tobacco seeds are distinguished by reticulations or sculpturing on the seed coat caused by the sinking or bending in at maturity of portions of the epidermis (Akehurst 1981:48). Studies that have used seed coat sculpturing to differentiate among tobacco species suggest that key characters may include the thickness, height, and pattern of the reticulations (Bahadur and Farooqui 1986; Farooqui and Bahadur 1985). Other useful characters include seed shape, seed size, and hilum shape (Bahadur and Farooqui 1986; Gunn and Gaffney 1974). So far few paleoethnobotanists have reported any details about seed coat sculpturing on seeds recovered (Asch 1991; Haberman 1984), and no descriptions closely follow the terminology for reticulations established in botanical studies by Charles Gunn and Frederick Gaffney (1974) and by Bir Bahadur and S. M. Farooqui (1986).

*Solanum* sp. (nightshade) has somewhat similar seed coat reticulations, and charred seeds of this species may be confused with those of tobacco. The charred *Solanum* sp. seeds (n = 23) from the Incinerator site in southwestern Ohio measure 1.06–1.37 millimeter in length and 0.77–1.18 millimeter in width. Modern, uncharred *S. americanum* seeds measure 1.4–1.7 millimeter in length (Gunn and Gaffney 1974:25; Rogers and Ogg 1981).

## Discussion

On the basis of seed size, shape, and pattern of seed coat sculpturing, Thomas Haberman (1984) argued that the similarly sized seeds of *N. rustica*, *N. attenuata*, and the *N. quadrivalvis* group were morphologically distinct from each other. Although other paleoethnobotanists do not disagree that species may be differentiated by their seeds, they would like to see morphological comparisons based upon large modern and ethnographic populations that also take into account any effects of carbonization (Asch 1991; Asch and Asch 1985a; Jones and Dunavan n.d.). So far, such studies have not been undertaken for the species under discussion. Although Gunn and Gaffney (1974) based their averages of seed size and shape on at least 50 seeds from 4 to 20 samples for each species, their study did not include a detailed analysis of seed coat sculpturing. In addition, their study is of limited usefulness to paleoethnobotanists because in emphasizing the means, they did not detail the extremes.

Even though the identification of *N. rustica* is likely for archaeological tobacco seeds recovered east of the Great Plains, it might be wise to consider species identification of seeds unverified until further morphological and population studies have been completed. Therefore, in the rest of this chapter, species identification is not attempted.

## The Distribution and Spread of Tobacco

Tobacco has been recovered from more than 100 archaeological sites in eastern North America—from the lower to the upper reaches of the Mississippi River and from the Great Plains to

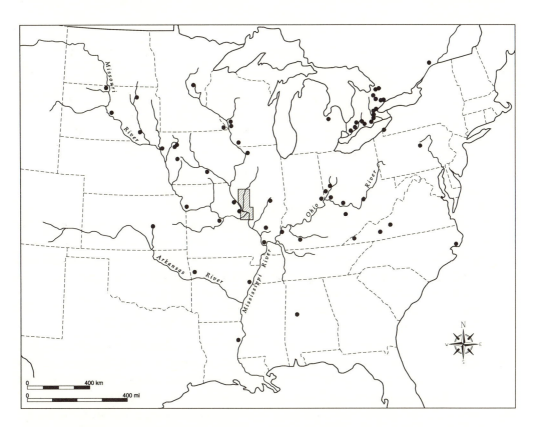

Map 22. Distribution of archaeological tobacco across eastern North America. See map 23 for enlargement of shaded area.

the Appalachians and southern Ontario (maps 22–23, table 40). These finds represent approximately 91 components at 75 sites in 20 states, as well as 30 components at 29 sites in Ontario, Canada. So far tobacco has rarely been recovered from sites east of the Appalachians or from the South.

Although no archaeological tobacco has yet been directly dated, tobacco has been recovered from at least 15 features with radiocarbon dates. In addition, several midden samples have been dated. Other tobacco remains can be placed in cultural periods based on their association with diagnostic artifacts.

In the following sections, I summarize the occurrences of charred seeds by cultural-temporal period. The number of seeds recovered and the types and numbers of contexts of recovery provide some indication of the ubiquity of tobacco in various contexts. Next follows a short summary of tobacco from undated or questionable contexts and tobacco identified from material other than charred seeds. Finally, I discuss the distribution of tobacco across eastern North America.

## Middle Woodland Tobacco

The earliest tobacco dates to Middle Woodland period domestic contexts at four sites near the confluence of the Mississippi and Illinois rivers. One possible, fragmentary seed was recovered in midden dated from 100 B.C. to A.D. 250 at the Naples-Abbot site on the Illinois River (Asch 1991; Asch and Asch 1987). Two of the Smiling Dan seeds (70 B.C.–A.D. 320) were recovered from exterior pits, and two positive and one possible seed have been identified from the lower levels of a Middle Woodland midden that filled a gully at this site (Asch 1991; Asch and Asch 1985a). At least three seeds have been identified from three late Holding to early Hill Lake phase (A.D. 100–200) pits at the Meridian Hills site in the uplands above the American Bottom (Kathryn Parker, personal communication, 1991, 1994). Two tobacco seeds were recovered in one Middle Woodland exterior pit at the

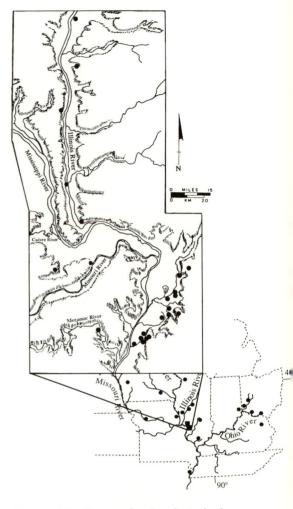

Map 23. Distribution of archaeological tobacco in the confluence area.

Burkemper 2 site near the junction of the Cuivre and Mississippi rivers in eastern Missouri. An additional 16 seeds were recovered in four mixed Middle Woodland–Late Woodland exterior pits at this site (Pulliam 1989).

## Late Woodland Tobacco

Tobacco has been identified from six early Late Woodland period sites in components that date between A.D. 300 and 600. Two sites, Rainbow and M.A.D., are in the plains (Benn 1981a, 1981b). The remaining four are in the confluence area near the previous Middle Woodland occurrences. These include the Rosewood phase

# Table 40: Archaeological Tobacco in Eastern North America

| Site | Component | Date | Reference |
|------|-----------|------|-----------|
| **Alabama** | | | |
| Moundville, 1TU500 | Moundville III | 1400–1550 | Margaret Scarry, pers. comm., 1994 |
| **Arkansas** | | | |
| Belle Meade, 3CT30 | Mississippian | 1250–1550 | Wagner, this volume |
| Craddock Shelter, 3CW2 | Mississippian? | 1290–? | Fritz 1986b |
| **Illinois** | | | |
| Naples-Abbott, 11ST121 | Middle Woodland | 100 B.C.–A.D. 250 | Asch 1991; Asch and Asch 1987 |
| Smiling Dan, 11ST123 | Middle Woodland | 70 B.C.–A.D. 320 | Asch and Asch 1985a |
| Meridian Hills, 11MS1258 | MW/late Holding to early Hill Lake | 100–200 | Kathryn Parker, pers. comm., 1991, 1994 |
| Leingang, 11MO722 | LW/Rosewood | 300–450 | Johannessen and Whalley 1988 |
| Mortland Island | LW/Whitehall | 370 | Asch 1991; Panet 1987 |
| Cunningham, 11MS1353 | LW/Rosewood to Mund | 300–600 | Kathryn Parker, pers. comm., 1994 |
| George Reeves, 11S650 | LW/Rosewood | 300–450 | Johannessen 1987a |
| | EM/Dohack | 800–850 | Johannessen 1987a |
| | EM/George Reeves | 900–950 | Johannessen 1987a |
| | EM/Lindemann | 950–1000 | Johannessen 1987a |
| Mund, 11S435 | LW/Mund | 450–600 | Johannessen 1983 |
| Holdener, 11S685 | LW/Patrick | 600–750 | Simon 1994 |
| Fish Lake, 11MO608 | LW/Patrick | 600–800 | Johannessen 1984b |
| Hays, 11FK32 | Late Woodland | 580–840 | Lopinot 1990a |
| Range, 11S47 | LW/Patrick | 600–800 | Johannessen 1987b |
| | EM/Dohack | 800–850 | Whalley 1990a |
| | EM/Range | 850–900 | Whalley 1990b |
| | EM/George Reeves | 900–950 | Kathryn Parker, pers. comm., 1991 |
| | EM/Lindemann | 950–1000 | Kathryn Parker, pers. comm., 1991 |
| Sponemann, 11MS517 | EM/Sponemann | 700–800 | Parker 1988, 1991 |
| | M/Stirling | 1050–1150 | Parker 1988, 1992a |
| Dohack, 11S642 | EM/Dohack | 800–850 | Johannessen 1985a |
| Petitt, 11AX253 | EM/Dillinger | 850–950 | Lopinot 1992 |
| Goshen, 11MS1273 | EM | 800–1000 | Lopinot 1989 |
| Radic, 11MS584 | EM/Merrell | 900–950 | Parker 1987 |
| | Mississippian | 1150–1400 | Parker 1987 |
| Pere Marquette, 11JY8 | EM/Jersey Bluff | 940 | Asch 1991 |
| BBB Motor, 11MS595 | EM/Edelhardt | 950–1000 | Johannessen 1984c |
| Olszewski, 11S465 | M/Lohmann | 1000–1050 | Dunavan 1990 |
| Cahokia ICT–II, 11S34 | M/Lohmann | 1000–1050 | Lopinot 1991 |
| | M/early Stirling | 1050–1100 | Lopinot 1991 |
| | M/late Stirling | 1100–1150 | Lopinot 1991 |
| | M/Moorehead | 1150–1250 | Lopinot 1991 |
| Walmart, 11MS1369 | M/Lohman–Stirling | 1000–1150 | Parker 1992b |
| Cahokia, 11S34 | M/Stirling | 1050–1150 | Lopinot et al. 1989 |
| Lundy, 11JO140 | M/Bennett | 1070 | Asch 1991; Schroeder 1989 |
| Robert Schneider, MS1177 | M/Stirling | 1050–1150 | Johannessen 1985a |
| Turner, 11S50 | M/Stirling | 1050–1150 | Whalley 1983 |
| Hill Creek, 11PK125 | M/Pearl | 1150–1300 | N. Asch and D. Asch 1985 |
| Doctor's Island, 11MT53 | Shelbyville II | 1200–1250 | Wagner 1985b, this volume |
| 78th Street, 11S821 | Oneota | ca 1400 | Neal Lopinot, pers. comm., 1991 |

| Site | Component | Date | Reference |
|------|-----------|------|-----------|
| **Indiana** | | | |
| Leonard Haag, 12D19 | LW/Ft. Ancient | 900?–1300 | Crawford 1981 |
| **Iowa** | | | |
| Rainbow, 13PM91 | LW/Boyer | 550–620 | Benn 1981b, 1990 |
| M.A.D., 13CF102 | LW/Boyer | 450–650 | Benn 1981a |
| Brewster, 13CK15 | Mill Creek | 925–1200 | Stains 1972 |
| Chan–Ya–Ta, 13BV1 | Mill Creek | 995–1215 | Wegner 1979 |
| Millipede, 13ML361 | Nebraska | 1260 | Green and Billeck 1993 |
| Wildcat Creek, 13MA209 | Oneota/Moingona | 1200–1400 | Parker 1990 |
| **Kansas** | | | |
| Mems, 14MN328 | PH/Wichita | 1400–1800 | Adair, this volume |
| **Kentucky** | | | |
| Carlston Annis, 15BT5 | Woodland? | — | Wagner 1995 |
| Newt Kash Hollow | Unknown | — | Jones 1936 |
| Slack Farm, 15UN28 | Caborn–Welborn | 1400–1650 | Jack Rossen, pers. comm., 1994 |
| **Louisiana** | | | |
| Osceola, 16TE2 | Coles Creek | 1000–1200 | Fritz and Kidder 1993; Kidder and Fritz 1993 |
| **Michigan** | | | |
| 20SA1034 | Late Woodland | 1100 | Parker n.d. |
| **Minnesota** | | | |
| Farley Village, 21HU2 | Oneota/Orr | Ca. 1650–1720 | Arzigian 1990 |
| Wilford, 21ML12 | Eastern Dakota | Early historic | Schaaf 1981 |
| **Missouri** | | | |
| Burkemper 2, 23LN104 | Middle Woodland | — | Pulliam 1987, 1989 |
| | Mixed MW/LW | — | Pulliam 1989 |
| | Late Woodland | — | Pulliam 1987, 1989 |
| Little Hills, 23SC572 | LW/Patrick | 600–800 | Lopinot 1990b |
| Boschert, 23SC609 | LW/Patrick | 600–800 | Pulliam 1988 |
| Algoa, 23CO156 | Late Woodland | 720 | Baker 1984 |
| Riverside, 23SL481 | EM | 930 | P. Wright 1990 |
| Bundy, 23PI177 | Late Woodland | 750–1000 | Fritz 1986a |
| Humphrey Bridge, 23PL322 | Steed–Kisker | 950–1200 | Adair, this volume |
| **New York** | | | |
| Ripley, NYSM2490 | Mississippian | 1300–1650 | Bodner 1989; Sullivan et al. 1995 |
| **North Carolina** | | | |
| Whalen, 31BF26 | Early MW | Ca. 800 | Oliver 1986 |
| **North Dakota** | | | |
| Mahhaha, 32O122 | PH/Hidatsa | 1780–1804 | Cutler and Blake 1976 |
| **Ohio** | | | |
| Incinerator, 33MY57 | FA/Anderson | 1250 | Wagner 1987, this volume |
| Hine Village, 33BU33 | FA/Schomaker | 1270 ± 80 | Macaulay 1990 |
| Island Creek, 33AD25 | Fort Ancient | 1326 | Wagner 1985a |
| Madisonville, 33HA36 | FA/mixed | 1200–1650 | Dunavan n.d. |
| | FA/Mariemont | 1400–1650 | Dunavan n.d. |
| **Pennsylvania** | | | |
| Memorial Park, 36CN164 | MW–LW/Clemson's Island | 800–1000 | Nancy Asch Sidell, pers. comm., 1992 |

Table 40: Archaeological Tobacco in Eastern North America (continued)

| Site | Component | Date | Reference |
|------|-----------|------|-----------|
| **South Dakota** | | | |
| Mitchell, 39DV2 | Init. Middle Missouri | 985–1250 | Benn 1974 |
| Dirt Lodge SP11 | Lower James | 1030–1250 | Haberman 1984 |
| Travis I, 39CO213 | Extended Middle Missouri | 1100–1550 | Haberman 1982 |
| Indian School, 39HV10 | PH/Arikara | 1675–1780 | Adair, this volume |
| **Virginia** | | | |
| Bonham, 44SM7 | Late Woodland | 1480 | Boyd et al. 1992; Gardner 1992a |
| Daugherty's Cave, 44RU14 | Mixed, poss. historic | Post–1470 | Gardner 1992b |
| Graham-White | Protohistoric | 1650–1700 | Gremillion 1995 |
| **West Virginia** | | | |
| Childers, 46MS121 | Late Woodland | 600 | Wymer 1990 |
| **Wisconsin** | | | |
| Fred Edwards, 47GT377 | LW/Middle M | 1050–1150 | Arzigian 1987 |
| Gunderson, 47LC394 | Oneota | 1300–1400 | Arzigian 1994 |
| Pammel Creek, 47LC61 | Oneota | 1380–1550 | Constance Arzigian 1989, pers. comm., 1991 |
| Sand Lake, 47LC44 | Transitional Oneota | 1400–1500 | Stevenson 1985a |
| | Oneota | 1450–1550 | Stevenson 1985a |
| Valley View, 47LC34 | Protohistoric/Oneota | 1550–1600 | Stevenson 1985b |
| **Ontario** | | | |
| Stratford Flats | Princess Point | 700–800 | Fecteau 1983a |
| Boisclair | — | 1000 | Ounjian 1986 |
| Elliott Village I | Glen Meyer | 1000–1100 | Fecteau 1983a |
| Elliott Village II | Glen Meyer | 1150–1200 | Fecteau 1983a |
| Dymock I | Younge | 1000–1100 | Cooper 1982 |
| Kelly | Glen Meyer | 1100–1125 | Ounjian 1986; Fecteau 1979 |
| Yaworsky | Glen Meyer | 1100–1200 | Rudolph Fecteau, pers. comm., 1991 |
| Wilcocks | Glen Meyer | 1250–1300 | Fecteau, pers. comm., 1991 |
| Force | Glen Meyer | 1250–1300 | Fecteau, pers. comm., 1991 |
| Gunby | Pickering | 1250–1300 | Rozel 1979 |
| Unick | Middleport | 1300–1400 | Ounjian 1986 |
| Dunsmore | Iroquois | 1300–1400 | Monckton 1990c |
| Finch | Iroquois | 1300–1400 | Monckton 1990d |
| Myer's Road | Iroquois | 1300–1400 | Monckton 1989 |
| Wiacek | Late Middleport | 1350–1400 | Lennox et al. 1986; Macaulay 1990:98 |
| Rife | Middleport | 1350–1400 | Fecteau, pers. comm., 1991 |
| Pipeline | Pre–Neutral | 1400–1450 | Busby 1979 |
| Keffer | Huron | 1400–1500 | Finlayson et al. 1985, 1987 |
| Parson | Iroquois | 1400–1500 | Monckton 1990b |
| Harrietsville | Neutral | 1400–1500 | Fecteau 1983b |
| Coleman | Prehistoric Neutral | 1450–1500 | MacDonald 1986; Ounjian 1986 |
| Steward | St. Lawrence | 1450–1500 | Fecteau 1981a |
| Wallace | Proto–Huron | ca. 1500 | Letts 1990 |
| Draper | Huron | 1500–1550 | Fecteau 1978, pers. comm., 1991; Finlayson 1975; King and Crawford 1974 |
| Robin Hood | Huron | 1500–1550 | Fecteau 1980; Williamson 1983 |

Table 40: Archaeological Tobacco in Eastern North America (continued)

| Site | Component | Date | Reference |
|---|---|---|---|
| Seed–Barker | Late Iroquois | 1550–1600 | Gary Crawford, pers. comm., 1991 |
| Wolfe Creek | Neutral | 1550–1600 | Fecteau 1981b; Foster 1990 |
| Bidmead | Huron | 1600–1610 | Monckton 1990a |
| Auger | Huron | 1620 | Monckton 1990a |
| Norton | Iroquois | 1600–1700 | Monckton 1988 |
| Report of tobacco now discounted: | | | |
| Chambers, Ky. 15ML109 | Mississippian | 1250–1350 | Jack Rossen 1987, pers. comm., 1991 |

Note: All remains are carbonized seeds unless otherwise noted. All dates are A.D. unless otherwise noted.

Key:
| | | |
|---|---|---|
| ? | Identification uncertain |
| MW | Middle Woodland |
| LW | Late Woodland |
| EM | Emergent Mississippian |
| FA | Fort Ancient |
| M | Mississippian |
| PH | Protohistoric |

components at the Leingang and George Reeves sites (Johannessen 1987a); the Rosewood-Mund phase component at the Cunningham site (Kathryn Parker, personal communication, 1994); the Mund phase component at the Mund site (Johannessen 1983); and a Whitehall component at the Mortland Island site (Asch 1991; Panet 1987). Altogether nine positive seeds and one possible tobacco seed were recovered from eight different domestic proveniences (such as exterior and interior pits and hearths) at these Mississippi-Illinois valley sites.

Tobacco has also been recovered from nine late Late Woodland to early Emergent Mississippian components dating between A.D. 600 and 800. These include the Patrick phase components at the Fish Lake and Range sites and the Emergent Mississippian Sponemann phase component at the Sponemann site in the American Bottom (Johannessen 1984b, 1987b; K. Parker 1988, 1990); the Late Woodland components at the Algoa site in Missouri and the Hays site in Illinois (Baker 1984; Lopinot 1990a); and the Patrick phase components at the Boschert and Little Hills sites in Missouri (Pulliam 1988; Lopinot 1990b). One seed was found at the ter-minal Late Woodland Childers site along the Ohio River in West Virginia (Wymer 1990). More than 290 seeds were recovered from at least 30 different domestic contexts, including pits and structures. The first tobacco in southern Ontario made its appearance in a Princess Point component (A.D. 700–800) at the Stratford Flats site in the Grand River valley. Two seeds were recovered, one from a hearth and one from midden (Fecteau 1978).

Post–A.D. 800 Tobacco

Tobacco has also been identified from 18 late Late Woodland to Emergent Mississippian components dating between A.D. 800 and 1000. This amounts to at least 169 positively and 10 tentatively identified seeds from at least 43 different, mostly domestic contexts, including exterior pits, midden, structures, and an interior pit. Only 5 of the exterior pits containing tobacco were identified as special rather than domestic in context. At least 186 positively and 2 tentatively identified seeds were recovered from 40 Mississippian components dating between A.D. 1000 and 1500 in the United States. The seeds were recovered from at least 75 different proveniences, including pits, structures, and midden in both domestic and special contexts. At least 2,816 additional seeds have been identified from 21 components in southern Ontario. Proto-historic and historic sites postdating A.D. 1500 in Ontario have so far returned 547 tobacco seeds from 7 components. At post–A.D. 1500 sites in the United States, at least 56 seeds have been recovered from 6 components, plus several hundred from one additional component.

## Undated Tobacco

A number of the tobacco finds are of uncertain age, including the three desiccated capsules from the Newt Kash Hollow Rockshelter in eastern Kentucky, which have been variously interpreted as recent or undated (Jones 1936). One charred seed from near the top of the Late Archaic midden at the Carlston Annis shell mound in west-central Kentucky is thought to belong to the overlying undated Woodland midden (Wagner 1995). One other occurrence with less than secure contexts is a seed from the upper, historically disturbed, post–A.D. 1470 midden in Daugherty's Cave, western Virginia (Gardner 1992b). Finally, tobacco has been recovered from mixed components at a number of sites, and the charred tobacco seed reported from the Chambers site in Kentucky is now thought to be *Solanum* sp. (nightshade) rather than tobacco (Jack Rossen, personal communication, 1991).

## Other Types of Tobacco Remains

In addition to desiccated capsules, several iden-tifications have been made on material other than charred seeds. The seed identified from the late prehistoric component at Craddock Shelter in northwestern Arkansas is desiccated rather than charred (Fritz 1986b). Nicotine residue and trichomes have been identified by R. J. Rey-nolds scientists from a pipe recovered in a shovel test at the Whalen site, eastern North Carolina. The style of the pipe and associated ceramics indicate a late Middle Woodland to early Late Woodland age, or about A.D. 900–

1000 (Oliver 1986). Tobacco pollen (possibly *Nicotiana tabacum*) has been identified in a sediment core at the A.D. 1050 Sanate Abajo site in eastern Dominican Republic (Fortuna 1978),[2] but Lee Newsom (1993:25–26) notes that there is no direct association between the radiocarbon date and the pollen sample. Other unusual finds were made on the Great Plains (Adair, this volume).

## Discussion

So far, the distribution of archaeological tobacco specimens in the eastern United States is strik-ingly concentrated in the Mississippi, Missouri, Illinois, and Ohio river drainages. Undoubtedly, the major rivers in the midwestern United States were conduits for the transmission of many goods, including material ones such as tobacco and, through the people moving along these conduits, less tangible ones such as the concepts or beliefs associated with tobacco. The distri-bution of seeds through space and time in the archaeological record, however, does not neces-sarily reflect the actual prehistoric spread and distribution of tobacco. It is more likely that our record favors those areas where flotation has regularly been performed as a recovery technique, particularly in view of the early historic accounts that describe the widespread use of tobacco across eastern North America (Winter, chapter 2, this volume; von Gernet, this volume). Certainly, tobacco was well recorded in historic contexts in the South and along the eastern seaboard, where little or no tobacco has been recovered from sites of any time period. What we presently know about the distribution of tobacco across eastern North America may be based more on the methods of archaeologists than on the habits and customs of the sites' inhabitants.

## Contexts for the Recovery of Tobacco

I initiated this survey with the thought that tobacco might be found in special contexts or in association with other unusual or special plants. To test this, I researched details about the context and associations of each tobacco find. For example, was the tobacco recovered from a pit or from midden, and was the location inside or outside a structure? Did the archaeologist consider it a special or a domestic context? What other plant remains were found in the same sample, level, or feature? In particular, was the tobacco associated with eastern red cedar (*Juniperus virginiana*)? This wood has been shown to occur most often in public or special structures or fires rather than in domestic or common structures or fires, from about A.D. 800 throughout the late prehistoric period in eastern North America (Wagner 1987). I also researched tobacco's association with nightshade (*Solanum* sp.). Although no unusual purpose has been ascribed to nightshade, it is unclear why it is found in prehistoric contexts (for example, K. Parker n.d.). Andrew Fortier noted that nightshade occurred only in features located in the apparent ceremonial precinct in the Stirling phase component at the Sponemann site in the American Bottom (Fortier 1992a).

In the following sections, I examine domestic and special contexts and then several masses of tobacco seeds that have been excavated. The implications of the contexts of tobacco recovery are discussed in terms of archaeological sampling strategies and how tobacco fit into the daily lives of the Indians.

## Domestic Contexts

Tobacco is overwhelmingly recovered from domestic rather than special contexts. In fact, most tobacco has been found in secondary fill in exterior pits. Some seeds have also been found in secondary fill in structures or in pits or hearths inside structures. In nearly every case, tobacco occurs in direct association (in the same flotation sample) with the most common cultivated food plant remains found at the site. In Illinois and Missouri, these are the starchy seed complex of maygrass (*Phalaris caroliniana*), chenopod (*Chenopodium berlandieri* ssp. *jonesi-*

*anum*), erect knotweed (*Polygonum erectum*), little barley (*Hordeum pusillum*), and sometimes maize (*Zea mays*). In Ohio the crop is corn, in Wisconsin the crops are maize and chenopod, and in Ontario they are corn, fleshy fruits, and sometimes chenopod and common bean (*Phaseolus vulgaris*).

Tobacco is generally not directly associated with red cedar, but when it is, that context is often considered special rather than domestic. Tobacco and nightshade occur together on 2 out of 10 domestic structure floors, in 6 of 14 interior pits, in 27 of 107 exterior pits, and in 1 of of the 9 domestic midden samples that have tobacco remains (table 41). Nightshade occurs most often, however, without any associated tobacco. Jimsonweed (*Datura stramonium*), which contains hallucinogenic alkaloids such as atropine (Foster and Duke 1990:182), has rarely been identified from eastern archaeological sites. At the BBB Motor site in the American Bottom of west-central Illinois, two jimsonweed seeds were recovered from a special-context Stirling phase pit associated with eastern red cedar wood (Whalley 1984). The association between tobacco and jimsonweed in one interior and one exterior pit in the Moorehead phase component at the nearby Cahokia ICT-II site has been interpreted as occurring in a domestic rather than a special context (Collins 1990; Lopinot 1991).

## Special Contexts

Tobacco has been recovered from only a handful of recognizably special contexts, including a few structures. At the Cahokia ICT-II tract, one tobacco seed was found in a T-shaped Lohmann phase (A.D. 1000–1050) structure thought to be a council house or chief's cabin (Collins 1990:76–81; Lopinot 1991). The structure, which has been radiocarbon dated, also contained five nightshade seeds and unusual quantities of exotic material. In addition, one tobacco and one nightshade seed were recovered from an interior pit in an isolated, possibly unusual early Stirling phase (A.D. 1050–1100) structure

**41: Frequency of Occurrence of Tobacco Seeds in Domestic and Special Contexts and in Association with
[Night]shade and Cedar in Archaeological Sites in the Eastern United States**

| [Cont]ext | Domestic Contexts | | | Special Contexts | | |
|---|---|---|---|---|---|---|
| | No. of Occurrences | No. with Nightshade | No. with Cedar | No. of Occurrences | No. with Nightshade | No. with Cedar |
| [...]en | 9 | 1 | — | 1 | — | — |
| Concentration | 1 | — | — | — | — | — |
| [Inter]ior Pit | 107 | 27 | 2 | 4 | 2 | 2 |
| [...]n mound | — | — | — | 1 | — | — |
| [...]plaza | — | — | — | 4 | — | — |
| [c]harnel | — | — | — | 1 | — | — |
| [struc]ture | 10 | 2 | — | 3 | 1 | 1 |
| [ex]terior pit | 14 | 6 | 1 | 2 | 2 | 1 |
| [ex]terior hearth | 3 | — | — | 1 | 1 | 1 |
| [r]e-use as earth oven | 1 | — | — | — | — | — |

Counts exclude those with uncertain dates. Nightshade is *Solanum* sp.; cedar is eastern red cedar (*Juniperus virginiana*).

at Cahokia ICT-II (Collins 1990; Lopinot 1991). Tobacco and sometimes eastern red cedar wood, nightshade seeds, and exotic or unique goods were also found in five features in the ceremonial precinct in the Stirling phase (A.D. 1050–1150) occupation at the Sponemann site in Illinois (Fortier 1992a; K. Parker 1988, 1992a). One of these features is a structure possibly representing a household temple. In addition to one tobacco seed, this structure contained one nightshade seed, cached hoes, many grinding stones, and the majority of the bauxite figurine fragments from the ceremonial precinct. It should be noted that the only tobacco found outside the ceremonial precinct of this component was recovered from a pit in structure F830, which was also the only structure containing eastern red cedar wood located outside the ceremonial precinct.

Tobacco has been recovered from a variety of exterior pits with possible special functions. Specimens include 1 seed each from two external pits and 10 seeds from one external pit in the ceremonial precinct in the Stirling phase (A.D. 1050–1150) occupation at the Sponemann site, Illinois (K. Parker 1992a). One of these pits, identified as a "busk pit" associated with corn harvest ceremonies, also contained eastern red cedar wood and 14 nightshade seeds. Wood from this pit, feature 183, was radiocarbon dated. One of the other external pits also contained 8 nightshade seeds.

Two tobacco seeds were found in a Lohmann phase (A.D. 1000–1050) pit at the Olszewski site, Illinois, which also contained eastern red cedar wood and 35 sprouted morning glory (*Ipomoea* sp.) seeds (Dunavan 1990). In the site report, this pit was designated domestic, yet its contents point to possible ritual use. A Morehead–Sand Prairie phase (A.D. 1150–1400) pit with cremated human bones, associated with a charnel structure containing the only eastern red cedar found at the Radic site, Illinois, returned one tobacco seed (K. Parker 1987). A few tobacco seeds were recovered from the central pits in two large plazas in the Emergent Mississippian George Reeves phase (A.D. 900–950) occupation at the Range site, Illinois, as well as from the two central pits in the northern courtyard in the Emergent Mississippian Lindemann phase (A.D. 950–1000) occupation at the Range site (K. Parker 1990). Finally, 11 tobacco seeds associated with corn were recovered from a small, likely special pit dug into the cap of Mound B, attributed to the A.D. 1000–1200 Balmoral or Preston phase of the Coles

Creek component at the Osceola site, Louisiana (Fritz and Kidder 1993; Kidder and Fritz 1993).

Tobacco, nightshade, and eastern red cedar wood are highly correlated in this small sample of special contexts. Altogether one-third of the structures with tobacco contained all three, as did one-half of the interior and exterior pits that contained tobacco. In fact, in the Stirling phase component at the Sponemann site in the American Bottom, nightshade seeds co-occurred with tobacco seeds only in features located in the ceremonial precinct (Fortier 1992a; K. Parker 1992a).

Although it is true, as Kathryn Parker (1990) has pointed out, that tobacco in the American Bottom rarely occurs in contexts that suggest ritual use, it is striking that so far nearly all contexts with tobacco that do suggest ritual use occur in the American Bottom. All special contexts for tobacco that have been identified date between A.D. 900 and 1200. During this period, tobacco in ritual contexts appears to have been associated with chiefdom-level societies.

### Seed Masses

A few masses of tobacco seed have also been recovered, such as that from a single pit at the Bundy site in eastern Missouri, where Gayle Fritz (1986a) identified 91 tobacco seeds. Clumps of the burnt seeds were adhering to each other, as they were among the 32 seeds recovered in one of the pits at the 20SA1034 site in Michigan (K. Parker n.d.). Clumps of nightshade seeds were recovered from the same pit at 20SA1034. Some of the seeds recovered from a pit at the Travis I site in South Dakota were also fused together (Haberman 1982).

A clumped or fused mass of tobacco seed likely represents a container of seed saved for planting or trade, whereas a mass of unfused seed could result from concentration of seed by sweeping. Sissel Johannessen (1984b) has identified 170 tobacco seeds from an ash lens in a pit at the Late Woodland Fish Lake site. Stephen Monckton (1990a) identified 161 tobacco seeds from midden in a sample at the Auger site in southern Ontario. He also found 1,310 tobacco and 2 nightshade seeds in one feature at the Myer's Road site, and another feature with 150 nightshade and 2 tobacco seeds (Monckton 1989, personal communication 1991). Other seed masses were found at the Gunby, Wiacek, Pipeline, Steward, and Wolfe Creek sites in southern Ontario (Busby 1979; Fecteau 1981a, 1981b; Macauley 1990:98; Rozel 1979).

Like other crop seeds, tobacco seed doubtless was saved by all groups who cultivated it. The Pilgrims included tobacco seed in a list of household contents they observed in Indian houses at Cape Cod in 1620: "In the houses we found wooden bowls, trays, and dishes, earthen pots. . . . There were also two or three baskets full of parched acorns, pieces of fish, and a piece of broiled herring. We found also a little silk grass, and a little tobacco seed, with some other seeds which we knew not" (Viereck 1967:19).

### Discussion

In general, tobacco seeds are scarce in sites in the eastern United States. They usually constitute less than 1 percent and often around 0.5 percent of the total identifiable seeds from any particular site. They have been found in as few as 1 out of 83 proveniences sampled; the high is 1 out of 3.5 proveniences. Tobacco may not be found when only a few features are sampled at any one site; the chances for finding it improve when more and varied contexts are studied. That one of the many capsules on an *N. rustica* plant contains 450–710 seeds (Gunn and Gaffney 1974:17) underscores how few seeds we are recovering. By comparison, *Solanum americanum* berries contain 50–150 seeds per fruit (Gunn and Gaffney 1974:25; Rogers and Ogg 1981), yet these similarly sized seeds are often comparable to tobacco seeds in frequency and ubiquity at archaeological sites. Perhaps the juicy nightshade berries afford protection during carbonization, thus enhancing seed preservation, whereas tobacco seeds are afforded no protection by the dry, papery capsule that encloses them.

Why are we finding tobacco seeds where we find them—that is, most often in secondary, domestic contexts and rarely in special or ritual contexts? One reason is that it is notoriously difficult to define a ritual context. Keep in mind also that when tobacco is burned or used, it is blossoms, leaves, or stems (and not the seeds) that are most likely smoked. When blossoms are ready for collection, there are few or no ripe seeds. However, if at least some blossoms are left unharvested and the seed heads are left on the plant, then when an entire plant is uprooted and hung to dry, the drying capsules split open and release seeds whenever the drying plant is disturbed (although some races of *N. rustica*, *N. quadrivalvis*, and *N. tabacum* are indehiscent; Goodspeed 1954:87). These seeds fall to the ground or are caught in the sticky, hairy leaves and stems of the drying plant.

Seeds that are caught in the leaves or stems of the plant may subsequently be charred through smoking. If this is the source of most of the charred seeds recovered, then smoking frequently occurred in domestic contexts. Uncarbonized seeds that fell to the ground from drying plants may have been incorporated into sweepings and middens, then subsequently burned during trash maintenance. Thus, one likely explanation for finding tobacco seeds in refuse pits, middens, and house floors is that this distribution reflects the storage and/or drying of tobacco rather than the direct use of tobacco in ritual situations. Parker (n.d.) proposed that the association she found between tobacco seeds and small stems and ash sticks at the 20SA1034 site in Michigan might represent the remains of a tobacco drying rack.

It may be significant that storing or drying tobacco was not segregated from other household activities. A number of historic accounts indicate that tobacco plots were kept separate from those of other cultivated crops. Sometimes care of the agricultural fields fell largely within the domain of women, whereas tobacco plots

were attended by men.[3] Judging from our present archaeological record, regardless of who tended the tobacco in the fields, or how or where the tobacco was grown, most of the harvested tobacco seed that became charred ended up in trash deposits that also included other common domesticated crops. This observation does not help define the function or meaning of tobacco within any of these societies, other than that tobacco seems to have been a part of daily life.

Although the archaeological evidence for ritual use of tobacco is limited, a few patterns are present. Within nondomestic, special contexts, tobacco is highly correlated with nightshade seeds and eastern red cedar wood. At the Osceola site, the pit in the top of Mound B is unusual in that besides tobacco, it contained quantities of maize, which was not yet substantially part of the local diet (Fritz and Kidder 1993). At the Olszewski site, both eastern red cedar wood and sprouted morning glory seeds were found in the same pit with tobacco (Dunavan 1990). It should be noted, however, that in nearly all contexts, tobacco also co-occurs with the prevalent common plant food remains.

## Conclusion

All prehistoric tobacco in North America east of the Great Plains has been assumed to be *Nicotiana rustica*, judging only from the presumed early historic distribution of this species. This kind of identification is very tenuous and requires confirmation by morphological comparisons with modern and ethnographic collections of material, whether seeds, pollen, trichomes, or residue.

The earliest eastern tobacco dates to Middle Woodland contexts from the confluence of the Illinois, Missouri, and Mississippi rivers. Finds of tobacco are most common at Late Woodland and later sites from the lower to the upper reaches of the Mississippi River and from the plains to the Atlantic Ocean. Tobacco is common and often abundant at late prehistoric sites in southern Ontario. Although the tobacco in eastern North America is thought to have been derived from South America via Mexico, the route, timing, and mechanisms of transmission are unknown. So far no early tobacco has been recovered from the region between the confluence area and South America. Instead, present evidence suggests a link between the plains and eastern North America.[4]

Tobacco seeds, the most common type of tobacco remains recovered, may have entered the depositional record in a number of ways. For the most part, only seeds that were charred have been preserved. Seed that was saved for planting or trade may be recovered as a charred clump or mass. Seeds could also have been amassed by sweeping and subsequent dumping of dirt and debris. The drying of entire tobacco plants may have resulted in loose seed falling to the ground or becoming caught in the sticky leaves and stems of the drying plant. The seeds that fell to the ground may then have been caught or concentrated in sweepings. Seeds that caught in the leaves or stems could have become charred through the smoking of these other tobacco products, whether in a pipe or as an offering on a fire. For all we know, tobacco seed itself may have been smoked or used in ceremonies.

If eary historic accounts are any indication of past customs, then tobacco as a crop may have been handled differently from the other cultivated plants. Furthermore, it seems likely that tobacco products were important in many rituals. Nevertheless, charred tobacco seeds are recovered mostly in secondary, domestic contexts in direct association with important cultivated plant food remains. So far few finds of tobacco have been from recognizably ritual or special contexts.

This pattern does not preclude the possibility that tobacco was targeted for ritual uses. If the charred seeds resulted from the smoking of other tobacco parts that had seeds adhering to them, then the smoking of tobacco appears to have permeated daily life in these Native American societies. If the charred seeds are interpreted as resulting from the incorporation of dropped seeds into daily midden sweepings, then the drying and/or storage of tobacco was a part of regular household activities rather than segregated in special areas or structures. It is likely, however, that seeds were incorporated into the depositional record in all of the ways just outlined. It also is not unreasonable to propose that tobacco did not hold the same meaning for all societies. The regulations or customs regarding its planting, tending, harvesting, processing, storing, smoking, and disposal may have differed from place to place.

Flotation is the most likely means for recovering tobacco seeds. Judging from the examples at hand, many rather than few contexts should be sampled before tobacco is likely to be noted at a site, and those samples will probably be from domestic rather than special contexts. Distinctive phytoliths are rare (Adair, this volume; Piperno 1988), but pipe contents can be identified by chemical content and the presence of distinctive trichomes. With widespread flotation and intensive analysis, the timing and route of transmission of this important plant into eastern North America may eventually be understood.

## Notes

This summary would not have been possible without the cooperation of David L. Asch, Leonard W. Blake, C. Wesley Cowan, Gary Crawford, Gary D. Crites, David H. Dye, John Hart, Lawrence Kaplan, John and Cricket Kelly, Frances B. King, Deborah Pearsall, Christopher B. Pulliam, C. Margaret Scarry, Nancy Asch Sidell, University of South Carolina Interlibrary Loan, Marie Standifer, Joseph Winter, and Patti Wright. In particular, I would like to thank Mary J. Adair, Karen R. Adams, Constance M. Arzigian, David W. Benn, Connie Cox Bodner, Gary W. Crawford, Sandra Dunavan, Rudolph D. Fecteau, Gayle J. Fritz, Paul S. Gardner, Kristen J. Gremillion, John Letts, Neal H. Lopinot, Stephen Monckton, Lee Newsom, Billy

L. Oliver, Kathryn E. Parker, Jack Rossen, Jane Macaulay Sutton, and Richard Yarnell, all of whom contributed substantially to this chapter. The maps were drafted by Marcus Fellbaum and Ginger McGuinness.

1. See Adams 1990a; Adams and Toll, this volume; Cummings, this volume; Gager, Johnson, and Holmes 1960; Gish, this volume; Goodspeed 1954; Holloway and Dean, this volume.

2. As discussed in chapters 5, 10, 11, and 12, tobacco pollen can probably be identified at the genus level (*Nicotiana*) but not at the species level (e.g., *tabacum*).

3. Compare Goodman 1993, Paper 1988, and Springer 1981.

4. In his review of a draft of this chapter and volume, Richard Yarnell wrote: "It seems odd to me that no one else sees the association between early tobacco in the East and its concentration in the region of the Mississippi River/Missouri River confluence as significant. Only two claimed occurrences of tobacco occur eastward before ca. A.D. 900. This could mean that *N. quadrivalvis* was earlier and that *N. rustica* did not arrive in the East until ca. A.D. 900. It should be emphasized that archaeological tobacco could be acquired by trade and was not necessarily grown where it was found."

# PART FOUR

# The Identification of Tobacco Pollen

# Prehistoric Tobacco Pollen in Southwestern Colorado

## Distribution and Possible Contamination

### Linda Scott Cummings

Tobacco pollen is rarely found in archaeological sites, so when it is noted it becomes extremely important. In this chapter I examine the distribution of tobacco pollen on the floor of a prehistoric structure and raise the question of contamination by modern tobacco use. Current interpretations of tobacco pollen from archaeological settings rely upon the absence of modern contamination.

## Archaeological Tobacco Pollen

The largest archaeological sample of *Nicotiana* (tobacco) pollen in North America was recovered in 1979 by the Dolores Archaeological Project, funded by the U.S. Bureau of Reclamation in Montezuma County, southwestern Colorado. Eighty-nine pollen samples were analyzed from the floor of a single pit structure (site 5MT4644, pit structure 1). This floor was divided into quarter-meter squares, each of which was sampled for pollen. Pollen recovery was sporadic across the floor because the structure had been abandoned after a catastrophic fire. Some areas of the floor appeared to have been more severely burned than others. In some areas pollen recovery was minimal to nonexistent, whereas in other areas of the floor the burning appeared to have been less intense, and pollen protected in the floor matrix survived. When structures collapse and burn unexpectedly during occupation, they trap paleoethnobotanic evidence in situ, thus preserving evidence of activity for later interpretation.

Identification of *Nicotiana* pollen was made under oil immersion. *N. attenuata* is the native tobacco that grows in the study area today, and *N. attenuata* seeds were identified from this structure (Matthews 1986a), suggesting that the pollen, too, represented this species. Although *Nicotiana* pollen was identified at the genus level, no attempt was made to identify the pollen as *N. attenuata* as opposed to other tobacco species. Pollen grains were compared with those of the closely related genus *Lycium*. Under oil immersion, the archaeological pollen grains more closely resembled *Nicotiana* than *Lycium*.

The 89 samples from the floor were intensively analysized for both pollen and macrofloral remains. The majority of pollen representing food plants was concentrated around the hearth, along the wing walls, behind the wing walls, and to some extent near pot rests, as is shown in the accompanying floor plans. (See Scott 1983 for pollen diagrams and Scott 1986 for the raw pollen data.) In historic ethnobotanic studies, these locations are described as traditional food processing areas. The distribution of *Zea mays* (maize) pollen, the most common pollen representing a cultigen at this site, fits this pattern very well in pit structure 1 (fig. 15). The distribution of *Cleome* (Rocky Mountain beeweed) pollen, the most common pollen representing an exploited native plant, fits the pattern even more closely (fig. 16). The distribution of *Nicotiana* (tobacco) pollen, however, only partially fits the pattern (fig. 17).

*Nicotiana* pollen occurred primarily in association with the hearth and the pot rest in the

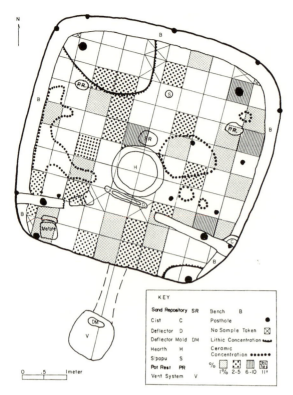

Figure 15. Distribution of *Zea mays* pollen percentages on the floor of pit structure 1, 5MT4644.

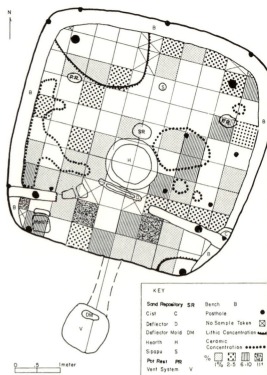

Figure 16. Distribution of *Cleome* pollen percentages on the floor of pit structure 1, 5MT4644.

northeastern portion of the pit structure. The highest frequencies of *Nicotiana* pollen were observed on the northwestern edge of the hearth and in the southwest corner of the main chamber near the west wing wall. This corner also contained a large variety of other economic pollen types (*Zea mays, Cleome, Sphaeralcea*), as well as members of the Apiaceae (Umbelliferae) family and the cheno-am group (Scott 1982, 1986). The southwest corner may have been used either as a common or collective storage location or for the processing of plant materials.

The historic Pueblo Indians used *Nicotiana* for both ceremonial and medicinal purposes (Whiting 1939). W. W. Robbins, John P. Harrington, and Barbara Freire-Marreco (1916) provided an excellent description of the method of rolling and smoking native tobacco cigarettes.

The dried leaves and stems of tobacco also were smoked in pipes. The Tewa smoked native tobacco at all formal occasions, at religious ceremonies, at council and society meetings, and at receptions for visitors from distant pueblos—in preference to commercial tobacco, which was also available. Robbins, Harrington, and Freire-Marreco described in detail the ritual for smoking at Santa Clara. Individual bundles or bags of clean corn husks and tobacco were laid on the floor. As each person was ready to smoke, he

removes a husk from the bundle, creases it with his fingers and teeth, and cuts it to a convenient size with his thumb-nail, unless the host has already trimmed a number of husks with scissors to save trouble. . . . [Then each person takes a pinch and a few

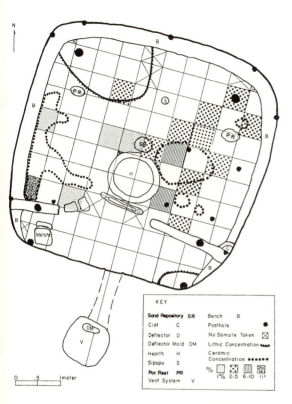

KEY

| | | | |
|---|---|---|---|
| Sand Repository | SR | Bench | B |
| Cist | C | Posthole | ● |
| Deflector | D | No Sample Taken | ⊠ |
| Deflector Mold | DM | Lithic Concentration | |
| Hearth | H | Ceramic Concentration | ●●●●● |
| Sipapu | S | | |
| Pot Rest | PR | % | |
| Vent System | V | 1% 2-5 6-10 11+ | |

Figure 17. Distribution of *Nicotiana* pollen percentages on the floor of pit structure 1, 5MT4644.

leaves of tobacco from the bag and] rolls and bruises them with his right thumb and finger in the palm of his left hand. He dampens the slip of cornhusk in his mouth and draws it between his teeth to make it flexible, lays a pinch of mixed tobacco in the middle of the slip, rolls it into a cigarette about 2 1/2 inches long, licks the outer edge and pinches the cigarette together, folds up and pinches the ends, and looks around for a light. At this point, one of the younger men of the household . . . ought to present the glowing end of a fire-stick, a slender rod about 3 feet long, which has been allowed to smolder in the fireplace; but it is now quite usual to provide ceremonial matches. The smoker lights the cigarette and smokes it, coughing and spitting freely; the small quantity of tobacco is soon consumed and

the rest of the cigarette is thrown on the floor. (Robbins, Harrington, and Freire-Marreco 1916:104)

Native tobacco appears to be more irritating to the throat and eyes than commercial tobacco; few men at Santa Clara smoked it for pleasure. Three or four cigarettes were enough to elicit complaints from the smoker the next day.

These activities, including grinding the tobacco in the palm of the hand, filling and rolling the cigarettes, and throwing the unsmoked portion of the cigarettes on the floor, would all tend to deposit tobacco pollen on the floor of a structure—including the pit structure under discussion here. Some of the activities, such as getting the corn husk, moistening it, filling and rolling the cigarette, and throwing the unsmoked portion of the cigarette onto the floor, would also introduce *Zea mays* pollen onto the floor. *Nicotiana* leaves are sticky and glandular, and they usually collect and hold any pollen that falls on them. The use of tobacco might therefore be responsible for the presence of pollen types other than *Nicotiana* in a structure. The spitting that accompanies native tobacco smoking might also help distribute a variety of pollen on the floor.

## Modern Contamination

Modern contamination is presumed to come primarily from activities associated with smoking cigarettes, cigars, or pipes and using chewing tobacco or snuff. Past and present archaeological policies regarding on-site smoking by workers include requiring all smokers to go at least as far away as the back-dirt pile to smoke, thereby removing them from the immediate excavation area. Although these precautions are a step in the right direction, they do not fully address problems associated with modern tobacco use.

In 1980 I conducted an experiment to determine the origin of contamination from tobacco products. Samples of a fresh cigarette, cigarette ash, and chewing tobacco (snuff) were processed in the laboratory in order to observe the pollen types present and to determine whether these items had contaminated the samples from the pit structure. The cigarette sample contained some *Nicotiana* pollen along with abundant quantities of Asteraceae pollen, primarily low-spine Asteraceae (fig. 18). The snuff sample was similar, although the frequencies of the various pollen types varied somewhat from those of the cigarette. This was thought to reflect the area in which the tobacco was grown, and the frequency probably varies between brands of cigarettes and snuff. The ash sample, however, contained no pollen. Although it is reassuring to know that the pollen is destroyed when the cigarette is smoked, there is always the possibility of contamination before the cigarette is lit

and when the butt is discarded. Snuff poses a greater problem, as would chewing tobacco, because the pollen present in these forms of tobacco is never burned but is mixed with saliva, which may then contaminate the site if one spits (or even spills) the tobacco. Several pollen types that are exotic to the Southwest and that remained unidentified at the time of the original study were noted in small quantities in the cigarette and snuff samples.

Contamination from tobacco products may occur simply from having the tobacco on-site. Any open pack of cigarettes or can of chewing tobacco or snuff is a potential problem. An open pack of cigarettes contains particles, dust, and loose fragments of tobacco leaves, any or all of which might spill out as an excavator bends over—and will certainly spill if the pack falls

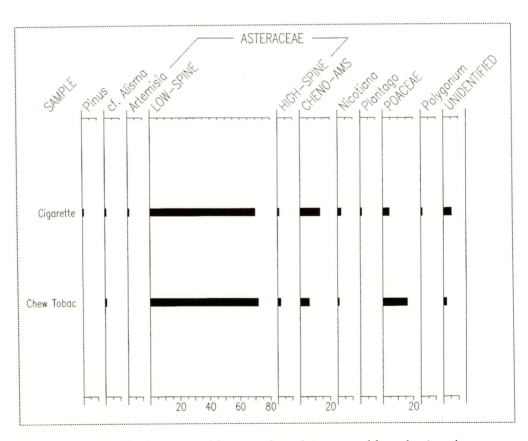

Figure 18. Diagram of pollen recovered from an unburned cigarette and from chewing tobacco.

from his or her pocket. Also, when the excavator takes the package out of a pocket, backpack, or car and handles the cigarettes, tobacco and other pollen are transferred from the tobacco product to the hands.

I should stress that the potential source of contamination is not the cigarette ash. Pollen, like tobacco, is burned when the cigarette is smoked. It is the cigarette before it is smoked, the package of cigarettes, and the butt, as well as the person's hands, that are the source of contamination.

Using chewing tobacco or snuff is more likely to contaminate a site than is smoking cigarettes, because the person chewing tobacco dips his or her fingers into the tobacco before placing it in the mouth. The practice of spitting by anyone chewing tobacco is guaranteed to contaminate.

Pipe smokers also use their hands to fill the bowls of their pipes with tobacco. Again, it is handling the tobacco that is the source of contamination, not the fact that someone has a pipe in his or her mouth.

And then there are cigars, which are wrapped in tobacco leaves, making them a source of almost certain contamination from agricultural weed pollen as well as from tobacco pollen. Having a cigar at a site is a likely source of tobacco and other pollen contamination.

Tobacco representatives maintain that tobacco is harvested before it pollinates. This certainly has not always been the case in the past and may not be at present. The analyzed cigarette contained nearly 5 percent *Nicotiana* (tobacco) pollen, which was easily recognized, in addition to pollen from agricultural weeds and other elements of the local vegetation communities.

To prevent contamination, a hand-washing station, which must be used by all smokers, tobacco chewers, and snuff users after each smoking break or every time they handle tobacco products, would help alleviate problems of contamination. Washing should be under running (not standing) water, such as water from an Igloo cooler maintained specifically for washing hands, rather than using drinking water in a canteen, which may already have been contaminated by the smoker. It would also be immensely helpful if all smokers and chewers routinely kept their tobacco products off-site at all times, used them only in a designated tobacco use area, and washed their hands afterward. Visitors to the site also pose a threat of contamination, particularly if they have been smoking in their vehicles prior to arriving at the site.

Analytical procedures have become sophisticated enough that we need to consider employing additional measures of protection to avoid tobacco pollen contamination. When sampling especially sensitive areas, it makes sense to consider wearing unpowdered surgical gloves, as uncomfortable as this would be in most field situations. Unpowdered surgical gloves are recommended over the standard, powdered gloves, which have the potential for introducing cornstarch or talc into the excavation.

Some sensitive areas in which one might take extra care to prevent tobacco pollen contamination include fields where tobacco might have been grown, field houses where tobacco might have been stored after harvest, kivas or pit structures where tobacco might have been used, and rock shelters displaying ceremonial rock art, where one would expect that tobacco might have been used or available in the local flora. Any pit structure floor that was abandoned because of catastrophe and therefore could represent activities in progress at the time of the "accident," whether or not there appear to be indications of ceremonial activities, should be considered an especially sensitive area.

These recommendations for avoidance of contamination have not been field tested. Nevertheless, they should help prevent contamination in the form of introduction of both tobacco pollen and the suite of pollen representing weedy plants that grow in or around commercial tobacco fields.

## Summary and Conclusion

Recovery of *Nicotiana* pollen, observed primarily in the eastern and northeastern portion of a prehistoric Colorado pit structure and mostly to the north of the wing wall, raised many issues, including the possibility that modern tobacco pollen was unintentionally introduced into the structure. Studies of modern tobacco contamination and the macrobotanical identification of *Nicotiana attenuata* seeds led to the conclusion that the *Nicotiana* pollen represented the presence of native tobacco within the structure. *N. attenuata* seeds were recovered from the pit structure, with the greatest number of seeds immediately to the north and east of the hearth, as well as against the eastern portion of the north wall of the structure, where large quantities of *Nicotiana* pollen were also present. Smaller quantities of seeds were noted behind the east wing wall, scattered along the front edge of both wing walls, along the back side of the hearth, and along the entire northern edge of the structure, into the lithic concentration. The recovery of charred *N. attenuata* seeds along with *Nicotiana* pollen was very important in helping to establish that the pollen represented prehistoric use rather than modern contamination, since at least one crew member smoked on-site. In addition, the frequency of *Nicotiana* pollen recovered from the southwest corner of the main chamber was higher than the frequency of *Nicotiana* pollen in a modern cigarette, and none of the exotic pollen types in the cigarette were present in the pit structure. Therefore it is unlikely that *Nicotiana* pollen was present as the result of modern contamination.

The pattern of recovery of tobacco pollen in the northeast quadrant of this structure suggests that the prehistoric inhabitants used this area for smoking. In contrast, the concentration of tobacco pollen in the southwest corner of the main chamber, next to the wing wall, is interpreted as representing a storage area that contained tobacco.

# 11

# Morphological Studies of
# New Mexico Solanaceae Pollen

Richard G. Holloway and Glenna Dean

Although palynologists have routinely identi-fied pollen of the Solanaceae at the family level, questions of archaeological importance make the identification of Solanaceae pollen at the generic level highly desirable. In some cases palynologists have identified solanaceous pollen at the genus level, but the criteria used were unspecified (Bohrer 1986; Scott 1986). As part of an investigation into the Solanaceae, we were asked by the editor of this book to examine a number of genera of this family that occur naturally in the U.S. Southwest. This is a pre-liminary investigation to test the feasibility of identifying members of this family, especially *Nicotiana*, at the generic level.

We had expected to rely on L. E. Murry and W. H. Eshbaugh's work (1971) as the primary source material for the pollen morphology of many of the genera we investigated. We noted, however, that they apparently calculated the polar area index (PAI) incorrectly, because throughout their paper they consistently achieved polar area indices greater than unity. K. Faegri and J. Iversen (1975:44) define the polar area as "the greatest distance between the ends of two furrows, and the 'polar area index' as the ratio between this measure and the greatest breadth of the pollen grain." According to this definition, PAIs greater than one require that the distance between two adjacent furrows be greater than the greatest diameter of the grain, which is impossible. This published error may be responsible for secondary errors committed by some archaeological palynologists, as will be discussed shortly.

## Methods and Materials

Ten genera were found to occur naturally in New Mexico (Martin and Hutchins 1980). Pollen from one species of each genus was taken from herbarium specimens at the University of New Mexico and New Mexico State University, as well as from fresh collections we made from local populations. The taxa examined were *Capsicum annuum* L., *Chamaesaracha conioides* (Moric.) Britt., *Datura meteloides* DC, *Hyocyamus niger* L., *Lycium pallidum* Miers, *Margaranthus pur-purascens* Rydb., *Nicotiana glauca* Graham, *Petunia parviflora* Juss., *Physalis heterophylla* Nees, and *Solanum eleagnifolium* Cav. (photo 38). (Although the species *glauca* is introduced, the genus *Nicotiana* is native to the Southwest.) Whole flowers, anthers, and/or buds were re-moved from the herbarium specimens and aceto-lyzed using G. Erdtman's methodology (1960). The residue was passed through a 200-micron screen and then was stained with safranin O and dehydrated using methanol. The pollen residue was transferred to 1,000 cks silicon oil using Butanol. The stained polliniferous residue was mounted on microscope slides and examined at 1,000X magnification.

Each analyst independently measured 25 different grains of each genus, according to attributes that were thought to be significant. These measurements included polar axis (P), equatorial diameter (E) in equatorial view, the distance between the ends of two furrows at the pole, the colpus length in equatorial view, the colpus width at the equator, the thickness

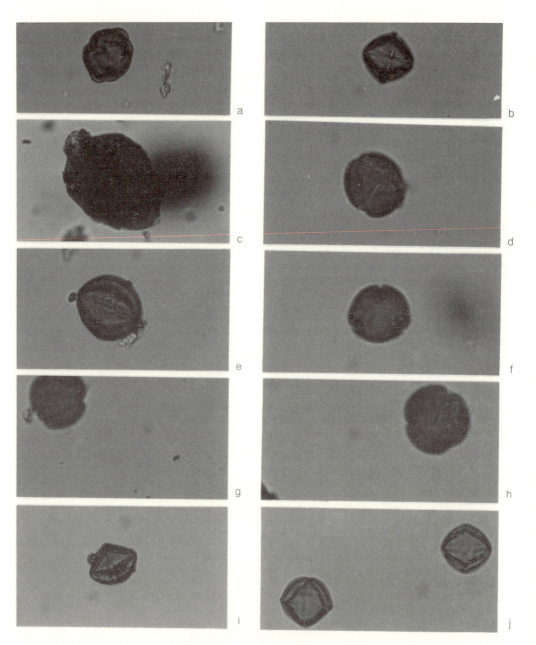

Photo 38. Examples of New Mexico Solanaceae pollen grains (magnification at 400X). *a, Capsicum annum* L.; *b, Chamaesaracha conioides* (Moric.) Britt.; *c, Datura meteloides* DC; *d, Hyocyamus niger* L.; *e, Lycium pallidum* Miers; *f, Margaranthus purpurascens* Rydb.; *g, Nicotiana glauca* Graham; *h, Petunia parviflora* Juss.; *i, Physalis heterophylla* Nees; *j, Solanum eleagnifolium* Cav.

of any colpus margo, and the thickness of the exine. From several of these measurements, the polar-equatorial index (P/E) and the polar area index (PAI) were calculated following the method of Faegri and Iversen (1975). Numer- ical analyses including simple statistics and cluster and discriminant analyses were run on the IBM mainframe at the University of New Mexico using the Statistical Analysis System (SAS). The resulting measurements and morphological observations are summarized in the next section.

## Results

Simple statistics calculated individually by both analysts and for the combined data set are available from the authors. The means and ranges of one standard deviation are graphed in figures 19–23 for the primary numerical variables. The findings are summarized in the following list.

1. *Capsicum.* Shape: prolate spheroidal. Size: 24.54 ± 1.417 μ (P) by 22.14 ± 1.37 μ (E); .156 ± .038 (PAI). Furrows entirely bordered by margos, lalongate os present. Pronounced vestibulum present. Tectate, verrucate/scabrate surface ornamentation.
2. *Chamaesaracha.* Shape: prolate spheroidal. Size: 22.54 ± 1.249 μ (P) by 20.14 ± 1.325 μ (E); .101 ± .051 (PAI). Vestibulum present but small, furrows completely bordered by margo. Attenuate lalongate os present. Tectate, verrucate surface sculpturing.
3. *Hyocyamus.* Shape: prolate spheroidal. Size: 22.55 ± 1.679 μ (P) by 22.56 ± 1.473 μ (E); .143 ± .038 PAI. Colpus lacking margo. Os lalongate, attenuate with small vestibulum present. Tectate, verrucate surface sculpturing.
4. *Lycium.* Shape: subprolate. Size: 29.46 ± 2.636 μ (P) by 24.1 ± 3.151 μ (E); .135 ± .05 PAI. Vestibulum present, furrows bordered by margo. Os lalongate, attenuate. Tectate, verrucate surface sculpturing.
5. *Margaranthus.* Shape: prolate spheroidal. Size: 22.88 ± 1.043 μ (P) by 21.17 ± 1.497 μ (E); .38 ± .051 PAI. Small vestibulum present. Colpus completely bordered by margo. Os lalongate. Tectate, verrucate.
6. *Nicotiana.* Shape: prolate spheroidal. Size 24.88 ± 1.698 μ (P) by 22.36 ± 1.481 μ (E); .131 ± .039 PAI. Vestibulum lacking, colpus completely bordered by margo. Os circular. Tectate, verrucate/scabrate surface sculpturing.
7. *Petunia.* Shape: subprolate. Size 28.522 ± 2.145 μ (P) by 24.402 ± 1.671 μ (E); .091

± .042 PAI. Colpus wide, bordered by margo, vestibulum lacking. Tectate, coarse verrucate surface sculpturing.
8. *Physalis.* Shape: subprolate. Size 20.0 ± 1.591 μ (P) by 16.46 ± 1.729 μ (E); .127 ± .029 PAI. Furrows bordered by distinct margo. Slight vestibulum present. Os lalongate. Tectate, psilate/verrucate surface sculpturing.
9. *Solanum.* Shape: oblate spheroidal. Size: 18.758 ± 1.154 μ (P) by 19.562 ± 1.796 μ (E); .08 ± .028 PAI. Furrows bordered by distinct margos. Small vestibulum appears to be present. Os lalongate. Tectate, verrucate surface sculpturing.
10. *Datura.* Large grain. Gemmate surface sculpturing. Numerical measurements not taken because unique surface sculpturing obscures colpus features.

## Discussion

Exine sculpturing and the construction of the apertures were two primary types of qualitative observations that could be made. Combined with traditional measurements of grain shape and size, these observations permitted a separation of the 10 genera into 8 groups. Both the presence or absence of a transverse furrow and the degree of development of a vestibulum of the transverse furrow appeared to be very important in distinguishing the genera. Yet even these features could not separate all 10 genera from one another. We then explored some of the quantitative measurements by means of statistical analysis. Datura, however, was excluded from statistical analyses because we found its characters to be unique among the 10 genera.

Because none of the measurements alone was sufficient to separate the individual genera, we decided to attempt a numerical analysis that considered all variables together. We used linear discriminant analysis for this approach. According to J. F. Hair, R. E. Anderson, and R. L. Tatham (1987), discriminant analysis involves solving the equation:

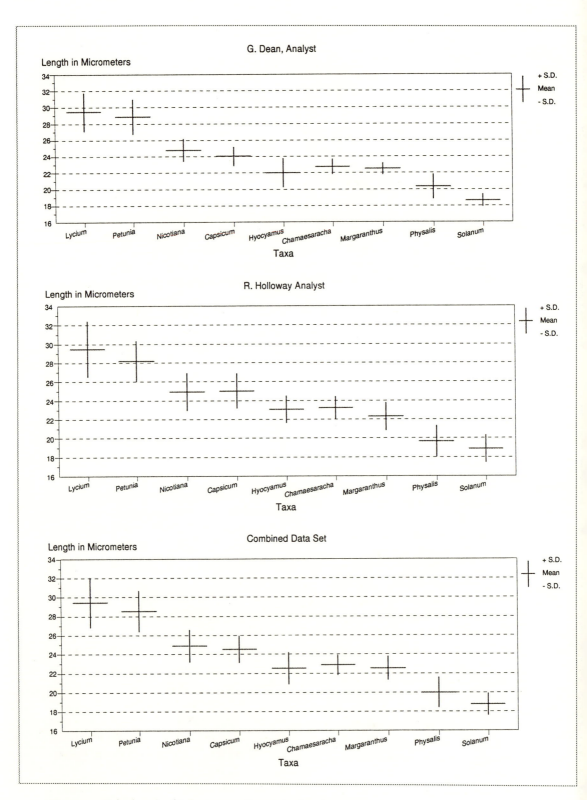

Figure 19. Polar length of Solanaceae pollen grains in micrometers.

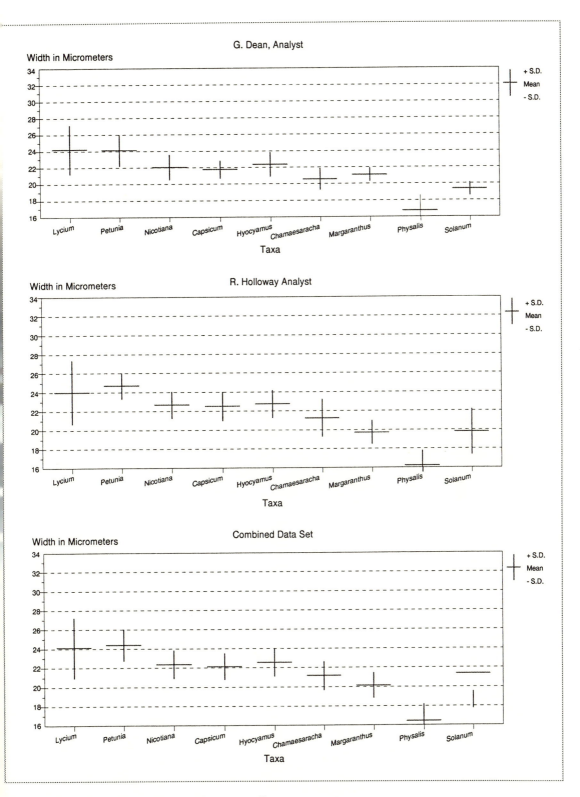

Figure 20. Equatorial width of Solanaceae pollen grains in micrometers.

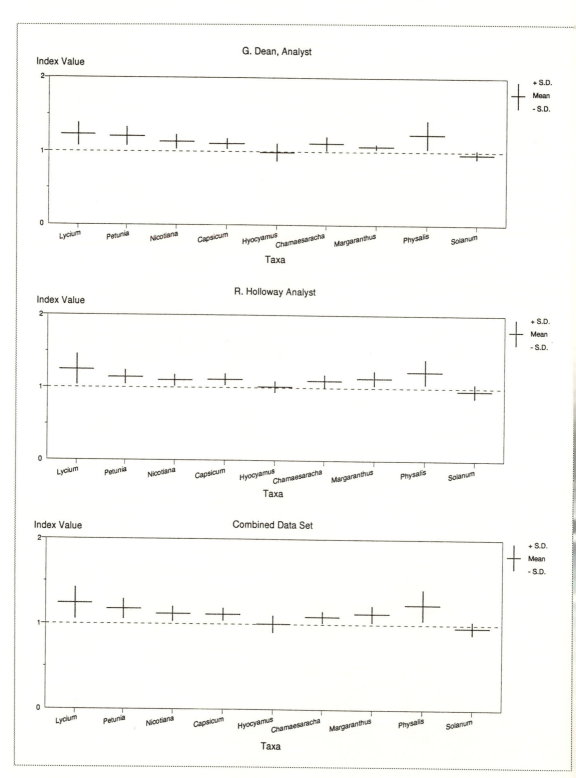

Figure 21. P/E index for Solanaceae pollen grains.

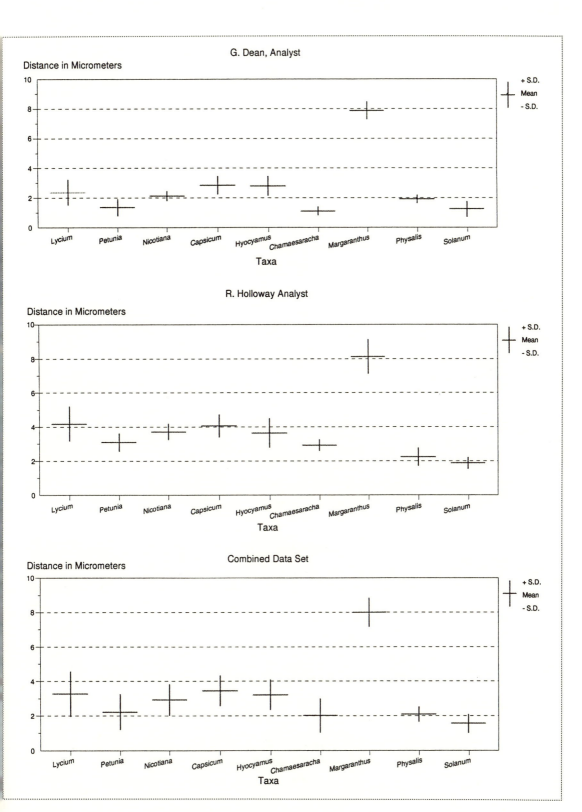

Figure 22. Polar area measurements for Solanaceae pollen grains.

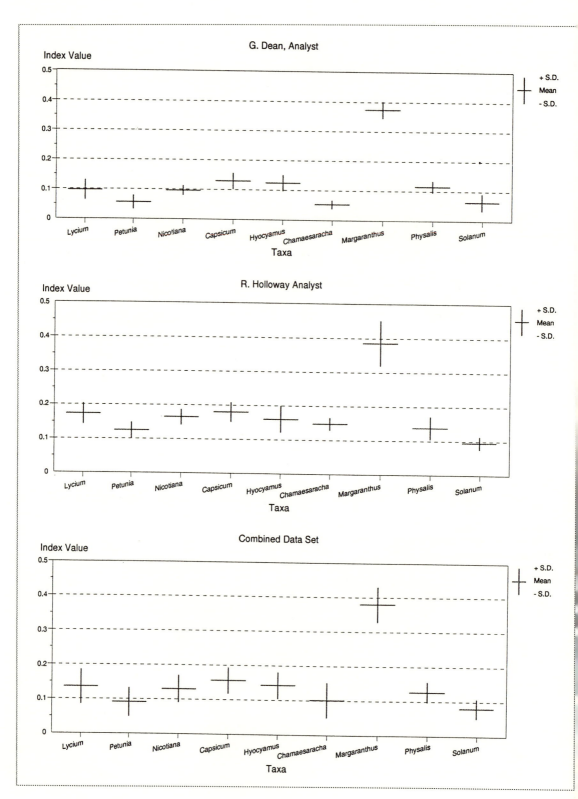

Figure 23. Polar area index for Solanaceae pollen grains.

$$d_f = (\lambda_1 x_1) + (\lambda_2 x_2) + \ldots + (\lambda_n x_n)$$

Where $d_f$ = discriminant function

$\lambda_1$ = discriminant coefficient for variable 1

$x_1$ = variable $x_1$ measurement

The mid-point between two adjacent groups therefore becomes the discriminant index for the separation of these groups. Table 42 provides these calculated measurements for discriminant indices based on six and seven variables. The discriminant index or cutting score was calculated on the basis of the following equation:

$$CS = (d_{f1} + d_{f2})/2$$

Where CS = discriminant index or cutting score

$d_{f1}$ = mean discriminant coefficient for group 1

$d_{f2}$ = mean discriminant coefficient for group 2

Utilizing six numerical variables does not effectively discriminate between the nine genera. Using seven variables, however, does serve to break up the grouping somewhat more effectively. A discriminant coefficient of less than −100 can be utilized to identify the *Nicotiana-Petunia* group. Two qualitative variables—the presence or absence of a margo and the width of the colpus (narrow versus wide)—can break these apart further. A discriminant coefficient of greater than 100 effectively identifies the *Lycium-Margaranthus* group. The remaining five genera show a gradual trend toward increasing discriminant coefficients, but the overlap is so great that numerically it would be impossible to separate these genera.

As an additional check on these data, separate cluster analyses were conducted on both the individual and the combined data sets (fig. 24). Although the order of the taxa is slightly different in each case, the taxa joined together are in identical sequences. Thus, we feel confident

Table 42: Discriminant Index Scores by Six and Seven Variables

| Taxon | Minimum Z-Score | Centroid | Maximum Z-Score | Cutting Score |
|---|---|---|---|---|
| **Six Variables** | | | | |
| Solanum | −112.8104 | −70.8676 | −25.2092 | — |
| Physalis | −111.4671 | −51.4746 | −15.7366 | −61.1711 |
| Chamasaracha | −119.1624 | −51.1331 | 23.1962 | −51.3039 |
| Hyocyamus | −90.9344 | −4.3069 | 76.0904 | −27.7200 |
| Nicotiana | −132.7511 | −0.2052 | 96.2819 | −2.2560 |
| Capsicum | −73.9109 | 6.8697 | 93.3574 | 3.3323 |
| Petunia | −89.1761 | 17.2425 | 140.1515 | 12.0561 |
| Lycium | −65.8542 | 74.3599 | 219.0016 | 45.8012 |
| Margaranthus | 69.5962 | 140.4866 | 221.4368 | 107.4233 |
| **Seven Variables** | | | | |
| Nicotiana | −297.9301 | −151.9535 | −126.8624 | — |
| Petunia | −232.4356 | −160.0898 | −90.5193 | −156.0216 |
| Solanum | −88.6205 | −23.9107 | 60.2819 | −92.0002 |
| Physalis | −94.4342 | −22.1204 | 70.4386 | −23.0155 |
| Chamaesaracha | −59.5080 | 15.9742 | 63.0613 | −3.0731 |
| Hyocyamus | −18.2774 | 44.3783 | 86.3371 | 30.1762 |
| Capsicum | 0.7210 | 49.4257 | 103.6350 | 46.9020 |
| Lycium | 23.4190 | 114.4178 | 191.3471 | 81.9218 |
| Margaranthus | 66.8334 | 107.0990 | 356.0713 | 110.7584 |

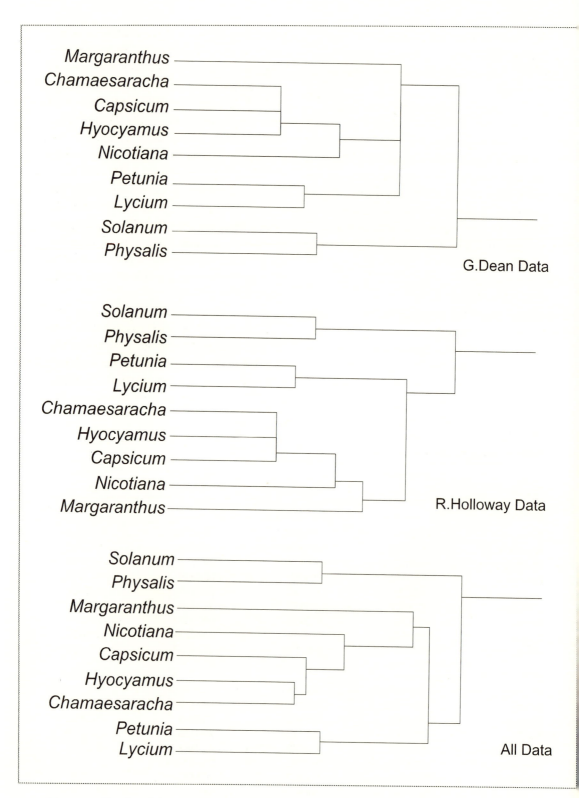

Figure 24. Results of cluster analysis for the New Mexico Solanaceae.

that these represent "real" similarities between specific pollen taxa.

Table 43 provides a key to the 10 genera of the Solanaceae based on both numerical and qualitative characters. As others have observed (Anderson and Gensel 1976; Erdtman 1952; Murry and Eshbaugh 1971), pollen morphology within the Solanaceae is fairly consistent. Our analyses indicate, however, that the presence or absence of features such as the transverse furrow and the vestibulum is important in separating these taxa. Many of the genera included in this study occur only rarely, and only a few (*Capsicum*, *Nicotiana*, *Solanum*, *Physalis*, and *Datura*) are archaeologically important.

Murry and Eshbaugh (1971) reported that they were able to separate *Physalis* and *Solanum*. We were not able to duplicate their results. As mentioned earlier, at least part of the problem appears to lie in the calculation of the polar area index, which they used to segregate members of the two genera. Our results indicate that the ranges of the PAI overlap too much to enable

the use of this character to differentiate the two genera. We have opted instead to combine these genera into a group.

*Capsicum* pollen was easily distinguished on the basis of the large vestibulum that characterizes the genus. This character was also emphasized in Murry and Eshbaugh's investigation (1971). *Nicotiana* pollen, although similar to several of the other genera, was distinct enough to be recognizable by several measurements. The primary determining character in our investigation was a circular pore with a distinctly marginate colpus. The presence of the marginate colpus permitted separation of *Nicotiana* from *Petunia*, the only other genus with a circular pore.

The characters used to separate the genera are easily recognized using transmitted light microscopy at 400X total magnification. Thus these characters should enable the microscopist to assign a particular grain to one of the groups with a minimum of measurement. Most of our characters are based on ratios between measurements, and these should remain intact even when

## Table 43: Morphological Key to Genera of Solanaceae

| Morphology | | | | | Genus |
|---|---|---|---|---|---|
| I | Grain large, surface sculpturing gemmate | | | | *Datura* |
| I | Grain size smaller, surface sculpturing otherwise | | | | 2 |
| | 2 | Circular pore, no vestibulum present | | | 3 |
| | | 3 | Colpus wide, coarse verrucate sculpturing, margo absent | | *Petunia* |
| | | 3 | Colpus narrow, verrucate/scabrate sculpturing, margo present | | *Nicotiana* |
| | 2 | Transverse furrow present | | | 4 |
| | | 4 | Polar Area Index > .27 | | *Margaranthus* |
| | | 4 | Polar Area Index < .27 | | 5 |
| | | | 5 | Os attenuate | 6 |
| | | | | 6 Margo not present | *Hyocyamus* |
| | | | | 6 Margo present | *Chamaesaracha/Lycium* group |
| | | | 5 | Os not as above | 7 |
| | | | | 7 Grain < 22μ polar diameter, small vestibulum | *Solanum/Physalis* group |
| | | | | 7 Grain > 23μ, large vestibulum | *Capsicum* |

Note: The numbers in the "Genus" column are a descending key of identification. If the "answer" to number I is number 2, then the reader proceeds to number 2, and so forth.

the grains have been weathered, as normally occurs in archaeological sediments. The results of the numerical analysis did not permit the calculation of a discriminant index like that computed by H. J. B. Birks and S. M. Peglar (1980), which would effectively separate genera. The degree of overlap was too great within the genera investigated for this procedure to be effective. This supports the contention of other investigators that pollen of this family is homogeneous.

Previous archaeological investigations have reported generic identification of members of the Solanaceae. *Datura* pollen has been reported from Arroyo Hondo, New Mexico (Bohrer 1986), and Hovenweep, Utah (Woosley 1977). Our results confirm that *Datura* pollen is distinct enough to be distinguishable from the other nine genera likely to occur in New Mexico archaeological sediments. Anne Woosley's other Hovenweep data are difficult to test, however, because she reports the presence of *Datura*, *Lycium*-type, *Nicotiana*-type, *Physalis*-type, and *Solanum*-type in her discussion, whereas only *Lycium*-type and *Datura* are identified in her table of raw data (Woosley 1977). Additionally, our data fail to support her segregation of *Solanum*-type and *Physalis*-type pollen. Since she failed to report the criteria utilized for her identifications, her interpretations are ambiguous at best.

*Nicotiana* pollen was identified from Windy Wheat Hamlet, Colorado (site 5MT4644), excavated as part of the Dolores Archaeological Project (Scott 1986). To our knowledge, the statistical analyses necessary for a more precise species identification have not yet been performed, so Linda Scott Cummings's assignment of those pollen grains to a specific taxon (*N. attenuata*) may have been premature (see Cummings, this volume). Luis Fortuna (1978) reported the occurrence of *Nicotiana tabacum* in the Dominican Republic. Again, no basis

was provided for his identification of a species for these pollen grains, and thus his data cannot be verified.

## Conclusion

Numerical analysis of the 10 genera of the Solanaceae family that occur naturally in New Mexico reveals the high degree of similarity between taxa. Based on the numerical criteria we examined, *Datura*, *Petunia*, *Nicotiana*, *Margaranthus*, *Hyocyamus*, and *Capsicum* can be identified at the generic level. Two additional groups comprising, respectively, the genera *Chamaesaracha* and *Lycium* and the genera *Solanum* and *Physalis* can also be identified. Using these characters in conjunction with the qualitative characters listed in table 43, a more precise separation of genera appears possible. The next step in the analysis is to apply these techniques to a larger suite of species of these genera. This will test the degree of overlap of the genera, and it might also permit the identification of individual species. In the present study, *Nicotiana glauca* was used as the representative of the genus *Nicotiana*, but we do not know whether the pollen of the other tobacco species is identical. The next chapter addresses all of these issues.

## Notes

A version of this chapter was presented at the 1991 Society for American Archaeology Annual Meeting, in New Orleans. An earlier version appeared as report no. 290 in the Castetter Laboratory for Ethnobotanical Studies Technical Series. The research was carried out with a grant from the Office of Contract Archeology at the University of New Mexico.

# 12

# Morphologic Distinctiveness of Nicotiana Pollen and the Potential for Identifying Prehistoric Southwestern Tobacco Use through Pollen Analysis

Jannifer W. Gish

Nicotiana (tobacco) has been identified in prehistoric archaeological contexts in California by Pat Hall (1984) and in Colorado by Linda Scott Cummings (1986) through pollen analysis, and in Arizona, California, Colorado, and New Mexico through archaeobotanical identification of seeds and other remains (Winter 1990b, 1991). From the perspective of palynology, a recent study of southwestern members of the Solanaceae plant family suggested that *Nicotiana* was sufficiently distinct to be identified consistently (Holloway and Dean 1990, and this volume). On the basis of this recent research, it appears possible to identify tobacco at archaeological sites through pollen analysis. The objectives of the current study were to test this view of morphological distinctiveness by examining additional species of common southwestern Solanaceae genera, particularly those that have ethnobotanical significance, and also to test the hypothesis that *Nicotiana* species are distinct from each other in pollen morphology.

## Research Design

The current research focused on four topics: (1) the geographic distribution of Solanaceae species in the greater Southwest (table 44); (2) the detailed pollen morphology of selected Solanaceae species; (3) the overlap in pollen morphology among tobacco species and other members of the Solanaceae family relative to the natural overlap in their geographic ranges; and (4) the archaeological implications of the results. If the

pollen of tobacco and its species is distinct from that of other Solanaceae, then their identification at archaeological sites could contribute enormously to our understanding of the diffusion of tobacco throughout the Americas. Although tobacco has been one of the most intensely studied of New World plants, its prehistoric development is poorly understood, especially in South America, where the two domesticated species originated. For this reason alone, the science of palynology holds great potential for the study of tobacco.

Since it was first documented by Europeans more than 500 years ago, tobacco has undergone many changes, especially through commercial crop breeding. To control for this as much as possible, early historic specimens were sought for this comparative study. Hence, many specimens dating to the early 1800s were collected from Old World herbaria, although the study also included many younger specimens.

## Methods and Materials

Evaluation of the geographic distribution of Solanaceae species in the greater Southwest depended on a thorough literature search and a check of available herbarium specimens at the University of New Mexico. Some genera of southwestern Solanaceae are undergoing revision, making it a complicated task to track certain species. In this chapter I use the botanical nomenclature of John Kartesz and Rosemarie Kartesz (1980), which takes precedence over

Table 44: Distribution of Solanaceae Species in the Greater Southwest

| Species | Ariz. | Calif. | Colo. | N.M. | Nev. | Texas | Utah | Mexic |
|---|---|---|---|---|---|---|---|---|
| Capsicum annuum L. = | | | | | | | | |
|   C. baccatum L. | x | | | x | | x | x | x |
| C. frutescens L.* | | | | | | | | x |
| Cestrum flavescens L.* | | | | | | | | x |
| Chamaesaracha conioides | | | | | | | | |
|   (Moric. ex Dunal) Britt. | x | | x | | | x | | x |
| C. coronopus (Dunal) Gray | x | x | x | x | x | x | x | x |
| Datura discolor Bernh. | x | x | | | | | | B, S |
| D. metel L. = D. fastuosa L. | | | | | | | x | |
| D. ferox L. | | x | | | | | | |
| D. innoxia P. Mill. = | | | | | | | | |
|   D. meteloides DC. = | | | | | | | | |
|   D. wrightii Regel | x | x | x | x | x | x | x | x |
| D. quercifolia H. B. K. | x | x | | x | | x | | x |
| D. stramonium L. | x | x | x | x | x | x | x | |
| Hyoscyamus niger L.* | | | x | x | | | x | |
| Leucophysalis nana (Gray) | | | | | | | | |
|   Averett = Chamaesaracha | | | | | | | | |
|   nana (Gray) Gray | | x | | | x | | | |
| Lycium andersonii Gray | x | x | | x | x | | x | B, S |
|   Var. deserticola (C. L. | | | | | | | | |
|     Hitchc. ex Munz) Jepson | x | | | | | | | B, S |
|   Var. wrightii Gray | x | | | | | | | S |
| L barbarum L.* = | | | | | | | | |
|   L halimifolium P. Mill | | | x | x | x | | x | |
| L berlandieri Dunal | | | | | | | | |
|   Var. longistylum C. L. Hitchc. | x | | | | | | | |
|   Var. parviflorum | | | | | | | | |
|     (Gray) Terracc. | x | | | | | | | S |
|   Var. peninsulare (Brandegee) | | | | | | | | |
|     C. L. Hitchc. | x | | | | | | | B, S |
| L californicum Nutt. | x | x | | | | | | B, S |
| L carinatum S.Wats. | | | | | | | | S |
| L chinense P. Mill. | | x | | | | | | |
| L cooperi Gray | x | x | | | x | | x | |
| L densifolium Wiggins | | | | | | | | B |
| L dispermum Wiggins | | | | | | | | S |
| L exsertum Gray | x | | | | | | | B, S |
| L fremontii Gray | x | x | | | | | | B, S |
|   Var. congestum C.L. Hitchc. | | | | | | | | B, S |
|   Subsp. viscidum Wiggins | | | | | | | | B |
| L macrodon Gray | x | | | | | | | S |
| L megacarpum Wiggins | | | | | | | | B |
| L pallidum Miers | x | x | x | x | x | x | x | S |
| L parishii Gray | x | x | | | | | | S |
| L richii Gray = | | | | | | | | |
|   L brevipes Benth. | | x | | | | | | B |
| L torreyi Gray | x | x | | x | x | x | x | C, S |
| L verrucosum Eastw. | | x | | | | | | |
| Lycopersicon esculentum P. Mill.* | | x | | | | | x | |
| Margaranthus solanaceus | | | | | | | | |
|   Schlecht. = | | | | | | | | |
|   M. lemmonii Gray | x | | | x | | x | | x |

Table 44: Distribution of Solanaceae Species in the Greater Southwest (continued)

| Species | Ariz. | Calif. | Colo. | N.M. | Nev. | Texas | Utah | Mexico |
|---|---|---|---|---|---|---|---|---|
| *Nicandra physalodes* (L.) Gaertn.* | | | x | | | | | |
| *Nicotiana acuminata* (Graham) Hook.* | | | x | | | | | |
| *N. attenuata* Torr. ex S.Wats. | x | x | x | x | x | x | x | B, S |
| *N. bigelovii* (Torr.) S.Wats. = *N. quadrivalvis* Pursh = *N. multivalvis* Lindl. | | | x | | | | x | |
| *N. clevelandii* Gray | x | x | | | | | | B |
| *N. glauca* Graham* | x | x | | x | | | | x |
| *N. greeneana* Rose | | | | | | | | B |
| *N. mexicana* Schlecht. | | | | | | | | S |
| *N. palmeri* Gray | x | | | | x | | | B, S |
| *N. plumbaginifolia* Viviani | | | | | | | | S |
| *N. rustica* L. | | | | | | | | B, S |
| *N. sylvestris* Speg. & Comes* | | | | | | | x | |
| *N. tabacum* L.* | | | | | | x | x | |
| *N. trigonophylla* Dunal | x | x | | x | x | x | x | B |
| *Oryctes nevadensis* S.Wats. | | x | | | x | | | |
| *Petunia parviflora* Juss. | x | x | | x | | x | | x |
| *Petunia violacea* Lindl.* = *P. hybrida* Vilm. | | | | | | | | x |
| *Physalis acutifolia* (Miers) Sandw. = *P. wrightii* Gray | x | x | | | | x | | S |
| *P. angulata* L. var. *lanceifolia* | x | x | | | | | | |
| *P. caudella* Standl. | x | | | | | | | |
| *P. crassifolia* Benth. = *P. crassifolia* Var. *cardiophylla* (Torr.) Gray | x | x | | | x | x | x | B, S |
| Var. *infundibularis* I. M. Johnston | | | | | | | | B |
| Var. *versicolor* (Rydb.) Waterfall | x | | | | | | | |
| *P. filipendula* Brandegee | | | | | | | | B |
| *P. flava* Wiggins | | | | | | | | B |
| *P. glabra* Benth. | | | | | | | | B |
| *P. greenei* Vasey & Rose | | x | | | | | | B |
| *P. hederaefolia* Gray (also spelled *P. hederifolia*) | x | x | | | | x | x | x |
| Var. *cordifolia* (Gray) Waterfall | x | x | x | x | | | x | |
| *P. heterophylla* Nees | | | | | | | x | |
| *P. ixocarpa* Brot. ex Hornem. | | x | | | | | | x |
| *P. leptophylla* Waterfall | | | | | | | | S |
| *P. muriculata* Greene | | | | | | | | B |
| *P. nicandroides* Schlecht. | | | | | | | | B, S |
| *P. pubescens* L. | x | x | | | | | x | B, S |
| *P. purpurea* Wiggins | | | | | | | | S |
| *P. subulata* Rydb. var. *neomexicana* (Rydb.) Waterfall | x | x | x | x | | | | |
| *P. versicolor* Rydb. | x | | | x | | | | |
| *P. virginiana* P. Mill var. *sonorae* (Torr.) Waterfall = *P. longifolia* (Nutt.) Trel | x | | | | x | x | x | |

Table 44: Distribution of Solanaceae Species in the Greater Southwest (continued)

| Species | Ariz. | Calif. | Colo. | N.M. | Nev. | Texas | Utah | Mexic |
|---|---|---|---|---|---|---|---|---|
| *P. viscosa* L. | | x | | | | | | |
| *Quincula lobata* (Torr.) Raf. | | | | | | | | |
|   = *Physalis lobata* Torr. | x | | x | | | x | x | x |
| *Salpichroa origanifolia* (Lam.) Baill. | x | x | | | | x | | |
| *Saracha procumbens* (Cav.) R. & P. | x | | | | | | | |
| *Solanum amazonium* Ker. | | | | | | | | C, S |
| *S. americanum* P. Mill. | x | | | | | | | |
| *S. aviculare* Forst. f. | | | | | | | | |
|   *bahamense* L. | | x | | | | | | |
| *S. carolinense* L.* | x | x | | x | | x | x | |
| *S. deflexum* Greenm. | x | | | | | | | x |
| *S. dimidiatum* Raf. = | | | | | | | | |
|   *S. torreyi* Gray | | x | | | | | | |
| *S. douglasii* Dunal = *S. nigrum* L. | x | x | | | | | x | B |
| *S. dulcamara* L.* | | x | | | | | x | |
| *S. elaeagnifolium* Cav. (Calif.*) | x | x | | | | x | x | x |
| *S. fendleri* Gray | x | | | | | | | |
| *S. furcatum* Dunal* | | | x | | | | | B |
| *S. heterodoxum* Dunal var. | | | | | | | | |
|   *novomexicanum* Bartlett | x | | | | | | | |
| *S. jamesii* Torr. | x | | | | | | x | |
| *S. lanceolatum* Cav. | | x | | | | | | |
| *S. lumholtzianum* Bartlett | x | | | | | | | |
| *S. madrense* Fernald | | | | | | | | C, S |
| *S. marginatum* L. | | x | | | | | | |
| *S. nodiflorum* Jacq. | x | x | | | | | | x |
| *S. parishii* Heller | | x | | | | | | |
| *S. rostratum* Dunal (Calif.*) | | x | x | | | x | x | x |
| *S. sarachoides* Sendtner* | x | x | | | | | x | |
| *S. seaforthianum* Andr. | | | | | | | | B |
| *S. sisymbriifolium* Lam.* | x | x | | | | | | |
| *S. tenuilobatum* Parish | | x | | | | | | |
| *S. triflorum* Nutt. | x | x | | | x | x | x | |
| *S. tuberosum* L.* | | | | | | | x | |
| *S. umbelliferum* Eschsch. | | x | | | | | | |
| *S. wallacei* (Gray) Parish | | x | | | | | | |
| *S. xantii* Gray | x | x | | | | | | B |
|   Var. *glabrescens* Parish | | x | | | | | | B |
|   Var. *hoffmannii* Munz | | x | | | | | | |

Sources: Arizona, Kearney and Peebles 1960; McDougall 1973; Shreve and Wiggins 1964; California, Munz and Keck 1968; Colorado, Great Plains Flora Association 1986; H. D. Harrington 1964; Mexico, Shreve and Wiggins 1964; Wiggins 1980; Nevada, Cronquist et al. 1984; New Mexico, Martin and Hutchins 1980; Texas, Correll and Johnston 1970; Utah, Albee, Shultz, and Goodrich 1988; Welsh et al. 1987.

Editor's note: In contrast to the rest of this book, where the *Nicotiana quadrivalvis* nomenclature has been used, in this chapter I chose to retain Jan Gish's use of the *Nicotiana bigelovii* name, to avoid any possibility of misinterpreting or misrepresenting her data.

Key: * Non-native to the southwestern United States
    B Baja California
    C Chihuahua
    S Sonora

other approaches.[1] Distributions were recorded for Arizona, California, Colorado, New Mexico, Nevada, Texas, and Utah in the United States and for Baja California, Chihuahua, and Sonora in Mexico. The herbarium check provided data primarily for New Mexico, but specimens from adjacent states also served as cross-checks for distributions noted in floras for those states. The Four Corners states were of particular interest in this study because of the substantial archaeobotanical evidence for tobacco in Anasazi (ancestral Pueblo), Hohokam (ancestral Pima), and Mogollon archaeological sites.

Most of the pollen specimens were chemically processed at the Palynology Laboratory of the Swedish Museum of Natural History, although some chemical work also took place at the Palynology Laboratory of Northern Arizona University. All specimens were acetolated following G. Erdtman's procedure (1943). Specimens were left in alcohol and transferred by pipette to aluminum stubs that had been coated with tar. Then they were spatter-coated with gold for scanning electron microscope (SEM) photography. Additionally, *Datura* specimens were treated with hexamethyldisilazane (HMDS) (Chissoe, Vezey, and Skvarla 1994), since they tended to collapse during standard SEM specimen preparation. Tar cannot be used with HMDS, so these specimens were transferred onto pieces of exposed negative film that had been glued to the stubs and then spatter-coated. A Jeol 6300 microscope was used in the SEM photography. Most grains were photographed at 2,500X and 10,000X magnification. After the SEM work was completed, the specimens were treated with tertbutyl alcohol, and then silicon oil was added as a preservative. A Bausch and Lomb research microscope was used for the light microscope (LM) photography. Grains were photographed at 400X magnification and also examined under oil (1,000X magnification).

In this microscopic evaluation of morphology, pollen nomenclature follows the systems of Ronald Kapp (1969), L. E. Murry and W. H. Eshbaugh (1971), and W. Punt and colleagues (1994). Although it did not deal specifically with *Nicotiana*, Murry and Eshbaugh's study of pollen of the Solanaceae family (1971) was fairly comprehensive. The morphological information in this earlier work provided the basic guidelines for comparative detail that I applied in the current study. The variables studied are also comparable to those addressed by Richard Holloway and Glenna Dean in chapter 11 (and see Holloway and Dean 1990). These variables include aperture class (kinds of furrows and pores), grain size (polar axis, measured from pole to pole, and equatorial diameter, with measurements in microns), shape class, exine (pollen wall) surface sculpturing and structure, and aperture details (such as details about the pore, which can be a distinct break in the furrow or simply an equatorial constriction). A vestibulum (a cavity of the exine around the pore) might also be present, as might a transverse furrow (an elongated pore running at right angles to the longitudinal furrows). Certain of these variables can be used together to generate other morphological indices. For example, the polar axis (P) divided by the equatorial diameter (E) provides the P/E index, which determines the shape class. Shape classes include perprolate (P/E index greater than 2.0), prolate (P/E index 1.33–2.00), subspheroidal (P/E index 0.75–1.33), oblate (P/E index 0.50–0.75), and peroblate (P/E index less than 0.5) (Kapp 1969).

I describe 56 specimens representing 34 species. Included are a few non-native species that are adventive in the Southwest and could occur in archaeological sites as contaminants. Both SEM and LM photographs are provided; the SEM photography permits insight into details that are visible or invisible at the LM level of magnification. The SEM work was especially valuable in determining intraspecies variation in pollen morphology as well as interspecies variation.

I also used the morphological details observed in this study to generate a pollen key for southwestern Solanaceae. This key is designed for LM microscopy, since that is the level used in most archaeological studies. The key is nonetheless guided by the SEM results for clarification of morphological overlap. I then compared the results with the geographic distribution of species in order to assess the potential for confusing tobacco pollen with pollen of the other Solanaceae species. Even if overlap in pollen morphology is evident, the species might be sufficiently separate in geographic range to eliminate the likelihood of confusing tobacco pollen in archaeological sites with pollen of other Solanaceae species. Alternatively, occurrences of species with similar morphology in the same area indicates that they should be grouped together as a single pollen class. Even where no geographic overlap occurs, the species might still not be distinct, owing to other complicating factors. The potential exists, for example, for overlap in morphology with species of other families. Extinction of taxa that might have overlapped in morphology in the past is another complicating factor. I do not address these matters in this study.

For the archaeological sites, known occurrences of *Nicotiana attenuata*, *N. rustica*, and *N. trigonophylla* were plotted for the Four Corners states (see maps 24–27). These distributions were then assessed in terms of potential overlap in pollen morphology with other Solanaceae species. It should be noted that many members of the Solanaceae besides tobacco have been documented ethnographically as utilized plants. The focus of this research, however, is the possibility of identifying prehistoric southwestern tobacco species and use through pollen analysis.

## The Pollen Taxa

As shown in table 44 and photos 39–63, 14 genera were studied: *Capsicum*, *Cestrum*, *Chamaesaracha*, *Datura*, *Hyoscyamus*, *Lycium*, *Margaranthus*, *Nicandra*, *Nicotiana*, *Petunia*, *Physalis*, *Salpichroa*, *Saracha*, and *Solanum*. At least one species of each genus was analyzed; alto-

gether, descriptions of the pollen of 56 specimens are presented in the next section. Brief notations on the location and date of each specimen are given along with the morphological details. For some of the oldest tobacco specimens, locational details were unavailable. All identifications on herbaria sheets were accepted as accurate. On the basis of an earlier study (Gish 1993), I expected that morphological overlap would be evident between *Lycium* and *Nicotiana*. I also expected that substantial intraspecies variation would be evident in those taxa and others. To better define the nature of the variation and potential degree of overlap, I considered replication and redundancy to be important aspects of the methods. Therefore I included multiple specimens of most *Lycium* and *Nicotiana* species. The number of specimens presented here actually reflects only a portion of the material studied. For *Nicotiana rustica*, for example, 17 specimens were studied and six are described. Those six, however, are representative of the morphological findings for *N. rustica*. Additional publications on these pollen results are planned for a later date.

## The Pollen Morphology

1. *Datura quercifolia* H. B. K.
   New Mexico, 1974
   LM: photo 39, no. 2
   Shape: subspheroidal; meridional bulge
   Dimensions: E = 30.8
   Apertures: 3-colporate (appearing 3-colpate), colpi short
   Exine: striate to striate-reticulate
   SEM: photo 39, nos. 1, 3, and 4
   Apertures: colpi with granules
   Exine: more reticulate in polar view and striate-reticulate in equatorial view; striae are also present on the muri of the reticulum
2. *Datura innoxia* P. Mill.
   New Mexico, 1938
   LM: photo 39, nos. 7 and 8
   Shape: subspheroidal; meridional bulge
   Dimensions: P = 41.8, E = 37.4

Photo 39. Scanning electron microscope (SEM) and light microscope (LM) photographs of selected southwestern Solanaceae species. Numbers preceding species names correspond to list in text. 1. *Datura quercifolia*:

1, 1500X;

2, 400x;

3 and 4, 10000X.

2. *D. innoxia*:

5 and 6, 1500X;

7 and 8, 400X;

9, 10000X.

3. *D. meteloides*:

10, 1500X;

11, 400X;

12, 10000X.

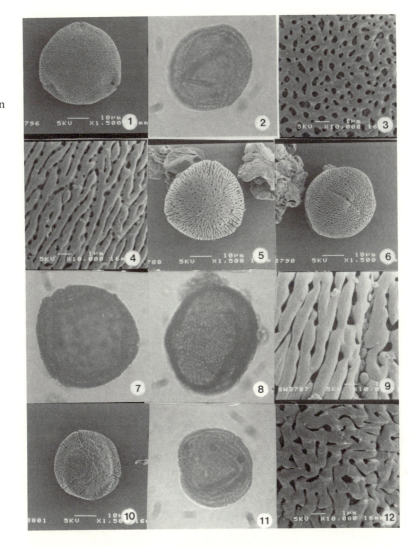

Apertures: 3-colporate (appearing 3-colpate), colpi short
Exine: striate-reticulate
SEM: photo 39, nos. 5, 6, and 9
Apertures: colpi with granules
Exine: striae are also present on the muri of the reticulum

3. *Datura meteloides* DC.
New Mexico, 1994
LM: photo 39, no. 11
Shape: subspheroidal; meridional bulge
Dimensions: P = 33.0, E = 35.2
Apertures: 3-colporate (appearing 3-colpate), colpi short
Exine: coarsely reticulate to striate-reticulate

SEM: photo 39, nos. 10 and 12
Apertures: colpi with granules
Exine: more rugulate in polar view and striate-reticulate in equatorial view; striae are also present on the muri of the reticulum

4. *Nicandra physalodes* (L.) Gaertn.
Malawi, 1985
LM: photo 40, nos. 3, 4, and 5
Shape: subspheroidal
Dimensions: P = 28.6, E = 24.2
Apertures: 3-colporate, colpi short, pores vestibulate, pores round and usually not exceeding furrow margins but occasionally transverse furrows appear present
Exine: granulate
SEM: photo 40, nos. 1, 2, and 6

Apertures: occasional transverse furrows are actually thickenings or wrinkles of the exine and not true furrows
Exine: micro-echinate, perforate, and faintly rugulate

5. *Hyoscyamus niger* L.
Bergianska Botanical Garden, 1969
LM: photo 40, nos. 9 and 10
Shape: subspheroidal
Dimensions: P = 37.4, E = 28.6
Apertures: 3-colporate, colpi long, pores distinct or constrictions
Exine: reticulate
SEM: photo 40, nos. 7, 8, 11, and 12

Apertures: colpi with granules
Exine: more reticulate in polar view and striate-reticulate in equatorial view; micro-echinae are also present on the muri of the reticulum

6. *Saracha procumbens* (Cav.) R. & P.
Komorov Botanical Institute, n.d.
LM: photo 41, nos. 3, 4, and 5
Shape: subspheroidal
Dimensions: P = 19.8, E = 22.0
Apertures: 3-colporate, colpi long, pores distinct or constrictions
Exine: rugulate-verrucoid
SEM: photo 41, nos. 1, 2, and 6

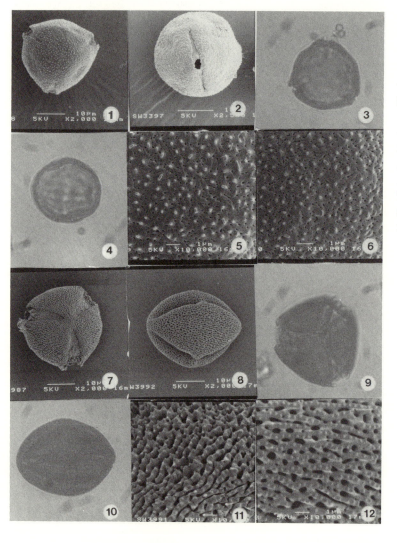

Photo 40. SEM and LM photographs of southwestern Solanaceae species.
4. *Nicandra physalodes*:
1, 2000X;
2, 2500X;
3 and 4, 400X;
5 and 6, 10000X.
5. *Hyoscyamus niger*:
7 and 8, 2000X;
9 and 10, 400X;
11 and 12, 10000X.

Photo 41. SEM and LM photographs of southwestern Solanaceae species.
6. *Saracha procumbens*: 1 and 2, 2500X; 3 and 4, 400X; 5 and 6, 10000X.
7. *Capsicum annuum* var. *aviculare*: 7, 8, and 9, 2500X; 10, 400X; 11, 1500X; 12, 10000X.

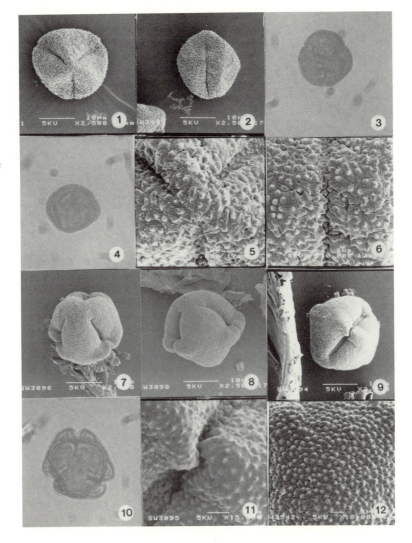

Apertures: colpi with granules
Exine: striae and micro-echinae are also present on the raised elements of the rugulate(?) pattern

7. *Capsicum annuum* var. *aviculare*
Arizona, 1989
LM: photo 41, no. 10
Shape: subspheroidal
Dimensions: P = 24.2, E = 19.8
Apertures: 3-colporate, colpi long, pore vestibulate, transverse furrows present
Exine: psilate, micro-echinate (oil)
SEM: photo 41, nos. 7, 8, 9, 11, and 12
Apertures: colpi with granules; transverse furrows are actually thickenings of the exine and not true furrows

Exine: micro-echinate, perforate

8. *Capsicum baccatum* L.
Paraguay, 1897
LM: photo 42, nos. 4 and 5
Shape: subspheroidal
Dimensions: P = 22.0, E = 22.0
Apertures: 3-colporate, colpi long, pores vestibulate, transverse furrows present
Exine: psilate, micro-echinate (oil)
SEM: photo 42, nos. 1, 2, 3, and 6
Apertures: colpi with granules; transverse furrows are actually thickenings of the exine and not true furrows
Exine: micro-echinate, perforate

9. *Physalis acutifolia* (Miers) Sandw.
New Mexico, 1950

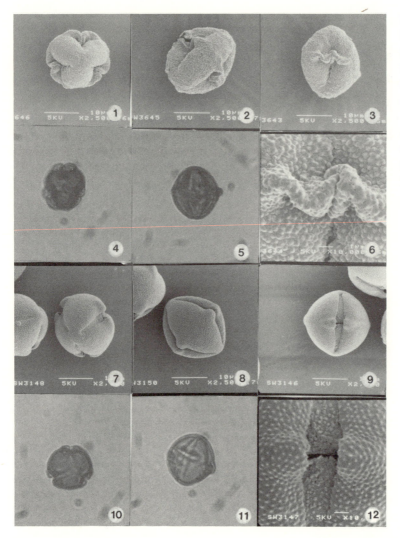

Photo 42. SEM and LM photographs of southwestern Solanaceae species. 8. *Capsicum baccatum*: 1, 2, and 3, 2500X; 4 and 5, 400X; 6, 10000X. 9. *Physalis acutifolia*: 7, 8, and 9, 2500X; 10 and 11, 400X; 12, 10000X.

LM: photo 42, nos. 10 and 11
Shape: subspheroidal
Dimensions: P = 19.8, E = 19.8
Apertures: 3-colporate, colpi long, pores vestibulate, transverse furrows present
Exine: psilate, faintly micro-echinate (oil)
SEM: photo 42, nos. 7, 8, 9, and 12
Apertures: colpi with granules; transverse furrows are actually thickenings of the exine and not true furrows
Exine: micro-echinate

10. *Physalis hederaefolia* Gray
New Mexico, 1971
LM: photo 43, no. 3

Shape: subspheroidal
Dimensions: P = 19.8, E = 15.4
Apertures: 3-colporate, colpi long, pores vestibulate, transverse furrows present
Exine: psilate, faintly micro-echinate (oil)
SEM: photo 43, nos. 1, 2, and 4
Apertures: colpi with granules; transverse furrows are actually thickenings of the exine and not true furrows
Exine: micro-echinate

11. *Solanum douglasii* Dunal
New Mexico, 1948
LM: photo 43, no. 8
Shape: subspheroidal

Photo 43. SEM and LM photographs of southwestern Solanaceae species. 10. *Physalis hederaefolia*: 1 and 2, 3000X; 3, 400X; 4, 10000X. 11. *Solanum douglasii*: 5, 6, and 7, 2500X; 8, 400X. 12. *S. jamesii*: 9 and 10, 2500X; 11, 400X; 12, 10000X.

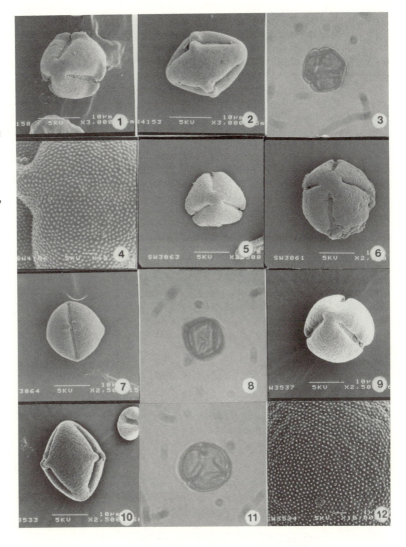

Dimensions: P = 17.6, E = 17.6
Apertures: 3-colporate, 4-colporate (rare), colpi long, pores vestibulate, transverse furrows present
Exine: psilate
SEM: photo 43, nos. 5, 6, and 7
Apertures: colpi with granules; transverse furrows are actually thickenings of the exine and not true furrows
Exine: micro-echinate

12. *Solanum jamesii* Torr.
New Mexico, 1950
LM: photo 43, no. 11
Shape: subspheroidal

Dimensions: P = 19.8, E = 19.8
Apertures: 3-colporate, 4-colporate (rare), colpi long, pores vestibulate, transverse furrows present
Exine: psilate
SEM: photo 43, nos. 9, 10, and 12
Apertures: colpi with granules; transverse furrows are actually thickenings of the exine and not true furrows
Exine: micro-echinate

13. *Solanum fendleri* Gray
New Mexico, 1970
LM: photo 44, nos. 6 and 7
Shape: subspheroidal

Dimensions: P = 19.8, E = 19.8
Apertures: 3-colporate, 4-colporate plus 2-colpi (rare), colpi long, pores vestibulate, transverse furrows present
Exine: psilate
SEM: photo 44, nos. 1, 2, and 3
Apertures: colpi with granules; transverse furrows are actually thickenings of the exine and not true furrows
Exine: micro-echinate

14. *Chamaesaracha conioides* (Moric. ex Dunal) Britt.
New Mexico, 1979
LM: photo 44, nos. 11 and 12
Shape: subspheroidal
Dimensions: P = 22.0, E = 22.0

Apertures: 3-colporate, colpi long, pores vestibulate, transverse furrows present
Exine: psilate
SEM: photo 44, nos. 9 and 10
Apertures: colpi with granules; transverse furrows are actually thickenings of the exine and not true furrows
Exine: micro-echinate

15. *Chamaesaracha coronopus* (Dunal) Gray
New Mexico, 1941
LM: photo 45, nos. 1 and 2
Shape: subspheroidal
Dimensions: P = 22.0, E = 22.0
Apertures: 3-colporate, colpi long, pores vestibulate, transverse furrows present
Exine: psilate

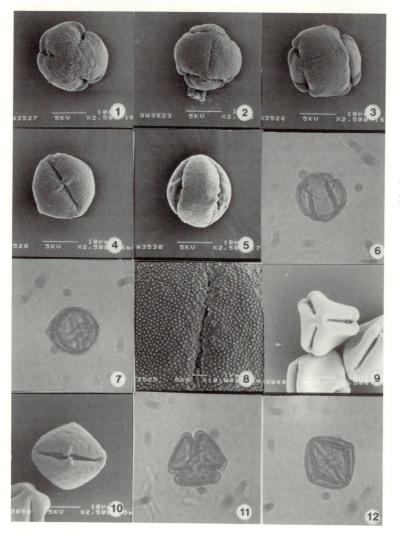

Photo 44. SEM and LM photographs of southwestern Solanaceae species.
13. *Solanum fendleri*: 1, 2, 3, 4, and 5, 2500X;
6 and 7, 400X;
8, 10000X.
14. *Chamaesaracha conioides*:
9 and 10, 2500X;
11 and 12, 400X.

Photo 45. SEM and LM photographs of southwestern Solanaceae species.

15. *Chamaesaracha coronopus:*
1 and 2, 400X;
3, 10000X.

16. *Margaranthus solanaceus:*
4 and 5, 2500X;
6 and 7, 400X;
8, 10000X.

17. *Salpichroa organifolia:*
9 and 10, 2500X;
11, 400X;
12, 10000X.

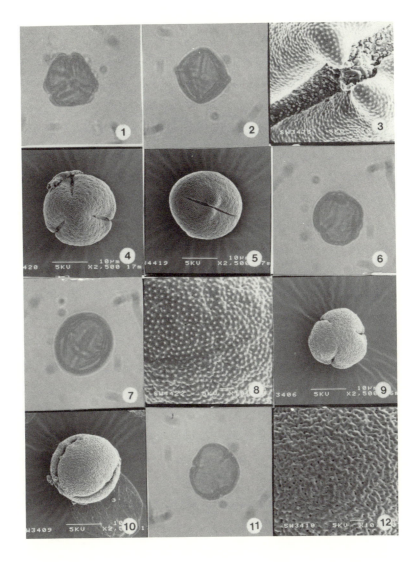

SEM: photo 45, nos. 4 and 5
Apertures: colpi with granules; transverse furrows are actually thickenings of the exine and not true furrows
Exine: micro-echinate

16. *Margaranthus solanaceus* Schlecht.
Mexico, 1898
LM: photo 45, nos. 6 and 7
Shape: subspheroidal
Dimensions: P = 26.4, E = 22.0
Apertures: 3-colporate, colpi long, pores vestibulate, transverse furrows present
Exine: psilate
SEM: photo 45, nos. 4, 5, and 8

Apertures: colpi with granules; transverse furrows are actually thickenings of the exine and not true furrows
Exine: micro-echinate, irregularly perforate

17. *Salpichroa origanifolia* (Lam.) Baill
France, 1934
LM: photo 45, no. 11
Shape: subspheroidal
Dimensions: P = 19.8, E = 17.6
Apertures: 3-colporate, colpi moderately long, pores vestibulate, transverse furrows present
Exine: psilate
SEM: photo 45, no. 9, 10, and 12

Apertures: transverse furrows are actually thickenings of the exine and not true furrows
Exine: finely rugulate

18. *Cestrum flavescens* Greenm.
Mexico, 1962
LM: photo 46, no. 3
Shape: subspheroidal to prolate
Dimensions: P = 33.0, E = 30.8; P = 44.0, E = 28.6
Apertures: 3-colporate, colpi long, pores vestibulate, transverse furrows present or absent (weakly pronounced)
Exine: psilate
SEM: photo 46, nos. 1, 2, and 4
Apertures: transverse furrows are actually thickenings of the exine and not true furrows

Exine: faintly rugulate, smoother on poles

19. *Cestrum flavescens* Greenm.
Mexico, 1962
LM: none
Shape: prolate
Dimensions: P = 39.6, E = 28.6
Apertures: 3-colporate, colpi long, pores vestibulate, transverse furrows present or absent (weakly pronounced)
Exine: psilate
SEM: photo 46, no. 6
Apertures: transverse furrows are actually thickenings of the exine and not true furrows
Exine: faintly rugulate, smoother on poles, irregularly perforate

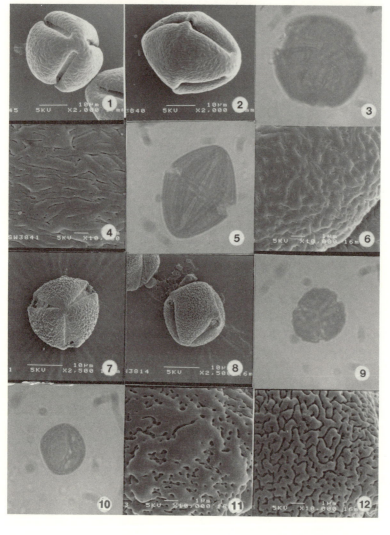

Photo 46. SEM and LM photographs of southwestern Solanaceae species.
18. *Cestrum flavescens*:
1 and 2, 2000X; 3, 400X; 4, 10000X.
19. *C. flavescens*:
5, 400X; 6, 10000X.
20. *Petunia parviflora*:
7 and 8, 2500X; 9 and 10, 400X; 11 and 12, 10000X.

Photo 47. SEM and LM photographs of southwestern Solanaceae species.
21. *Lycium andersonii*: 1, 2500X; 2, 400X; 3 and 4, 10000X.
22. *L. pallidum*: 5 and 6, 2500X; 7, 400X; 8, 10000X.
23. *L. torreyi*: 9, 2500X; 10, 400X; 11 and 12, 10000X.

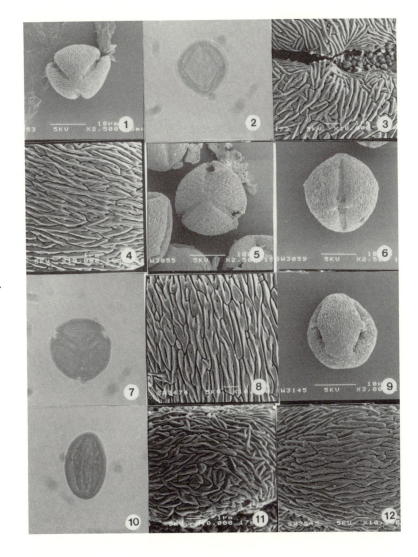

20. *Petunia parviflora* Juss.
Texas, 1966
LM: photo 46, nos. 9 and 10
Shape: subspheroidal
Dimensions: P = 19.8, E = 19.8
Apertures: 3-colporate, 4-colporate (rare), colpi long
Exine: rugulate to rugulate-verrucoid
SEM: photo 46, nos. 7, 8, 11, and 12
Apertures: colpi granulate
Exine: rugulate to rugulate-verrucoid, smoother on poles

21. *Lycium andersonii* Gray
Arizona, 1978
LM: photo 47, no. 2
Shape: subspheroidal to prolate
Dimensions: P = 19.8, E = 19.8; P = 28.6, E = 19.8
Apertures: 3-colporate, colpi long, pores distinct or constrictions
Exine: faintly reticulate to striate-reticulate
SEM: photo 47, nos. 1, 3, and 4
Apertures: colpi granulate
Exine: striate to striate-rugulate; striae are also present on the raised elements of the striate-rugulate pattern

22. *Lycium pallidum* Miers
New Mexico, n.d.
LM: photo 47, no. 7
Shape: subspheroidal

Dimensions: P = 24.2, E = 22.0
Apertures: 3-colporate, colpi long, pores distinct or constrictions, transverse furrows appear evident in some specimens
Exine: faintly striate-reticulate
SEM: photo 47, nos. 5, 6, and 8
Apertures: colpi granulate; transverse furrows are actually slight thickenings of the exine and not true furrows
Exine: striate to striate-rugulate; striae are also present on the raised elements of the striate-rugulate pattern

23. *Lycium torreyi* Gray
Jemez Pueblo, New Mexico, 1931
LM: photo 47, no. 10

Shape: prolate
Dimensions: P = 24.2, E = 15.4
Apertures: 3-colporate, colpi long, pores distinct or constrictions
Exine: faintly striate-reticulate
SEM: photo 47, nos. 9, 11, and 12
Apertures: colpi granulate
Exine: striate to striate-rugulate; striae are also present on the raised elements of the striate-rugulate pattern

24. *Lycium pallidum* Miers
New Mexico, 1939
LM: photo 48, nos. 4 and 5
Shape: subspheroidal
Dimensions: P = 22.0, E = 22.0

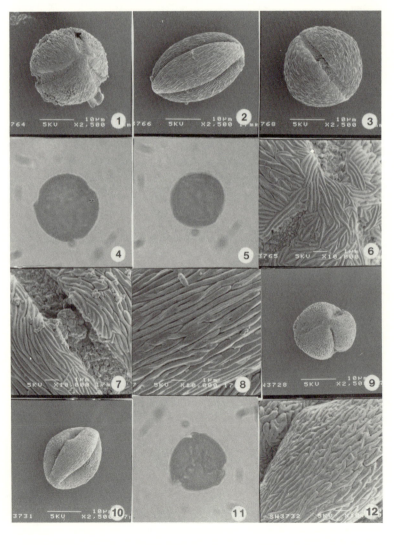

Photo 48. SEM and LM photographs of southwestern Solanaceae species.
24. *Lycium pallidum*: 1, 2, and 3, 2500X; 4 and 5, 400X; 6, 7, and 8, 10000X.
25. *L. torreyi*: 9 and 10, 2500X; 11, 400X; 12, 10000X.

Apertures: 3-colporate, colpi long, pores distinct or constrictions

Exine: striate to striate-rugulate

SEM: photo 48, nos. 1, 2, 3, 6, 7, and 8

Apertures: colpi granulate

Exine: striate to striate-rugulate to striate-rugulate-verrucoid; striae are also present on the raised elements of the striate-rugulate pattern

25. *Lycium torreyi* Gray
New Mexico, 1957
LM: photo 48, no. 11
Shape: subspheroidal
Dimensions: P = 22.0, E = 19.8
Apertures: 3-colporate, colpi long, pores distinct or constrictions

Exine: faintly striate-rugulate

SEM: photo 48, nos. 9, 10, and 12

Apertures: colpi granulate

Exine: striate to striate-rugulate; striae are also present on the raised elements of the striate-rugulate pattern

26. *Nicotiana attenuata* Torr. ex S. Wats.
California, n.d.
LM: photo 49, nos. 3, 4, and 5
Shape: subspheroidal
Dimensions: P = 24.2, E = 24.2
Apertures: 3-colporate, colpi long, pores distinct or constrictions
Exine: psilate to faintly striate-rugulate (oil)
SEM: photo 49, nos. 1, 2, and 6

Photo 49. SEM and LM photographs of southwestern Solanaceae species.
26. *Nicotiana attenuata*:
1 and 2, 2500X;
3, 4, and 5, 400X;
6, 10000X.
27. *N. attenuata*:
7 and 8, 2500X;
9, 2000X,
10 and 11, 400X;
12, 10000X.

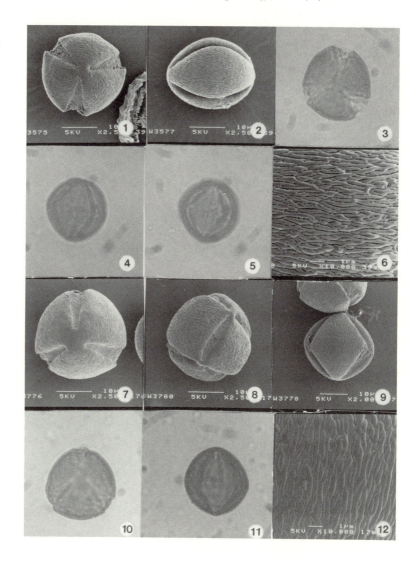

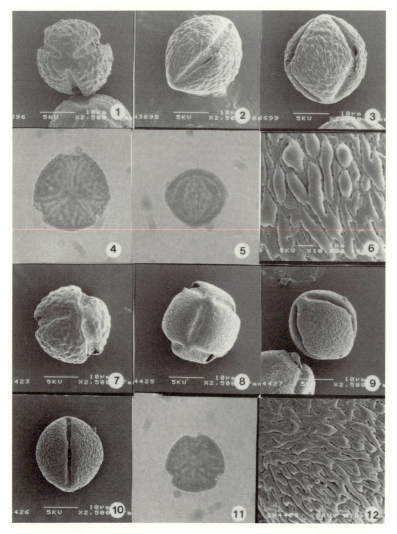

Photo 50. SEM and LM photographs of southwestern Solanaceae species. 28. *Nicotiana trigonophylla*: 1, 2, and 3, 2500X; 4 and 5, 400X; 6, 10000X. 29. *N. trigonophylla*: 7, 8, 9, and 10, 2500X; 11, 400X; 12, 10000X.

Apertures: colpi granulate
Exine: striate to striate-rugulate, smoother on poles

27. *Nicotiana attenuata* Torr. ex S. Wats.
New Mexico, 1995
LM: photo 49, nos. 10 and 11
Shape: subspheroidal
Dimensions: P = 22.0, E = 24.2
Apertures: 3-colporate, 4-colporate plus 2-colpi or 6-colporate (both rare), colpi long, pores distinct or constrictions
Exine: psilate to faintly striate-rugulate (oil)
SEM: photo 49, nos. 7, 8, 9, and 12
Apertures: colpi granulate
Exine: striate to striate-rugulate, smoother on poles

28. *Nicotiana trigonophylla* Dunal
California, 1952
LM: photo 50, nos. 4 and 5
Shape: subspheroidal
Dimensions: P = 22.0, E = 24.2
Apertures: 3-colporate, colpi long, pores distinct or constrictions
Exine: striate-rugulate to striate-rugulate-verrucoid
SEM: photo 50, nos. 1, 2, 3, and 6
Apertures: colpi granulate
Exine: rugulate to striate-rugulate to striate-rugulate-verrucoid, smoother on poles, perforate

29. *Nicotiana trigonophylla* Dunal
Tehuacan, Mexico, 1841

LM: photo 50, no. 11
Shape: subspheroidal
Dimensions: P = 22.0, E = 22.0
Apertures: 3-colporate, 4-colporate plus 2-colpi (rare), colpi long, pores distinct or constrictions
Exine: striate-rugulate to striate-rugulate-verrucoid
SEM: photo 50, nos. 7, 8, 9, 10, and 12
Apertures: colpi granulate
Exine: rugulate to striate-rugulate to striate-rugulate-verrucoid, smoother on poles, perforate

30. *Nicotiana trigonophylla* Dunal
Mexico, 1897

LM: photo 51, no. 3
Shape: subspheroidal
Dimensions: P = 26.4, E = 22.0
Apertures: 3-colporate, colpi long, pores distinct or constrictions
Exine: faintly rugulate
SEM: photo 51, nos. 1, 2, and 4
Apertures: colpi granulate
Exine: rugulate to striate-rugulate, smoother on poles, perforate

31. *Nicotiana rustica* L.
Sweden, 1842
LM: photo 51, nos. 10 and 11
Shape: subspheroidal
Dimensions: P = 26.4, E = 22.0

Photo 51. SEM and LM photographs of southwestern Solanaceae species.
30. *Nicotiana trigonophylla*:
1 and 2, 2500X;
3, 400X;
4, 10000X.
31. *N. rustica*:
5, 6, 7, 8, and 9, 1500X;
10 and 11, 400X;
12, 10000X.

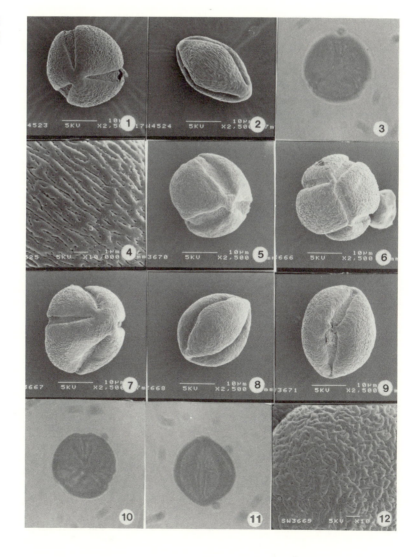

Apertures: 3-colporate, 4-colporate, 4-colporate plus 2 colpate, colpi long, pores distinct or constrictions
Exine: faintly striate-rugulate
SEM: photo 51, nos. 5, 6, 7, 8, 9, and 12
Apertures: colpi granulate
Exine: rugulate to striate-rugulate, smoother on poles

32. *Nicotiana rustica* L.
New Mexico (Santa Domingo Pueblo), 1995
LM: photo 52, nos. 4, 5, 6, 7, and 8
Shape: prolate
Dimensions: P = 33.0, E = 22.0
Apertures: 3-colporate, 4-colporate plus 2 colpate, colpi long, pores distinct or constrictions

Exine: psilate to faintly striate-reticulate
SEM: photo 52, nos. 1, 2, 3, 9, and 10
Apertures: colpi granulate
Exine: striate to striate-rugulate, smoother on poles, perforate

33. *Nicotiana rustica* L.
Komarov Botanical Institute, 1826
LM: none
Shape: subspheroidal
Dimensions: P = 28.6, E = 22.0
Apertures: 3-colporate, colpi long, pores distinct or constrictions
Exine: psilate
SEM: photo 52, nos. 11 and 12
Apertures: colpi granulate
Exine: striate-rugulate, smoother on poles

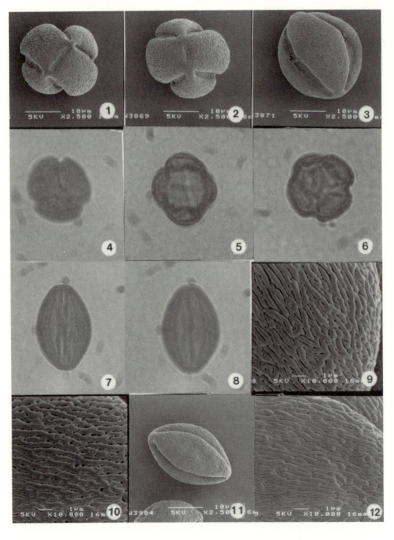

Photo 52. SEM and LM photographs of southwestern Solanaceae species.
32. *Nicotiana rustica*: 1, 2, and 3, 2500X; 4, 5, 6, 7, and 8, 400X; 9 and 10, 10000X.
33. *N. rustica*: 11, 2500X; 12, 10000X.

34. *Nicotiana rustica* L.
New Mexico (Isleta Pueblo), 1995
LM: none
Shape: subspheroidal
Dimensions: P = 28.6, E = 24.2
Apertures: 3-colporate, 4-colporate plus 2-colpi, colpi long, pores distinct or constrictions
Exine: psilate to faintly striate-rugulate (oil)
SEM: photo 53, nos. 1, 2, 3, 4, and 5
Apertures: colpi granulate
Exine: rugulate to striate-rugulate, smoother on poles, perforate

35. *Nicotiana rustica* L.
New Mexico (San Juan Pueblo), 1995

LM: none
Shape: subspheroidal to prolate
Dimensions: P = 30.8, E = 26.4; P = 30.8, E = 22
Apertures: 3-colporate (can appear 3-colpate), 4-colporate plus 2-colpi, colpi long, pores distinct or constrictions
Exine: psilate to faintly striate-rugulate (oil)
SEM: photo 53, nos. 6, 7, 8, 9, 10, 11, 12
Apertures: colpi granulate
Exine: rugulate to striate-rugulate, smoother on poles

36. *Nicotiana rustica* L.
New Mexico (seed originally from Mohawk Indian Reservation, New York), 1995

Photo 53. SEM and LM photographs of southwestern Solanaceae species.
34. *Nicotiana rustica*: 1, 2, and 3, 2500X; 4, 2000X; 5, 10000X.
35. *N. rustica*: 6 and 7, 2500X; 8 and 9, 2000X; 10, 11, and 12, 10000X.

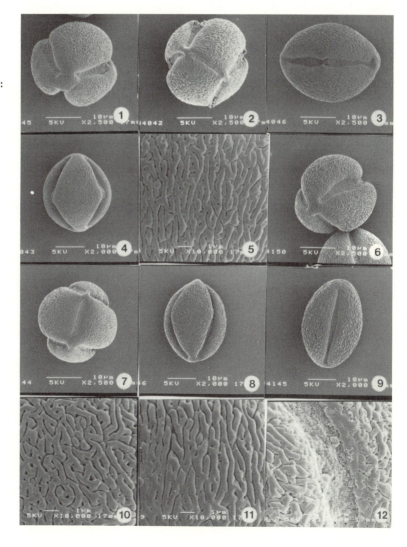

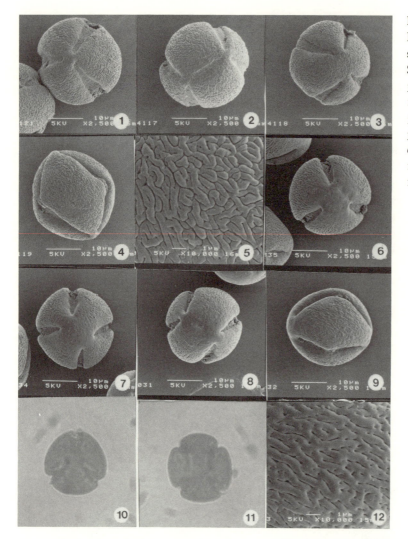

Photo 54. SEM and LM photographs of southwestern Solanaceae species.
36. *Nicotiana rustica*: 1, 2, 3, and 4, 2500X; 5, 10000X.
37. *N. tabacum*: 6, 7, 8, and 9, 2500X; 10 and 11, 400X; 12, 10000X.

LM: none
Shape: subspheroidal to prolate
Dimensions: P = 28.6, E = 24.2; P = 33.0, E = 24.2
Apertures: 3-colporate, 4-colporate, 4-colporate plus 2-colpi, colpi long, pores distinct or constrictions
Exine: psilate to faintly rugulate (oil)
SEM: photo 54, nos. 1, 2, 3, 4, and 5
Apertures: colpi granulate
Exine: rugulate, smoother on poles

37. *Nicotiana tabacum* L.
New Mexico, 1995
LM: photo 54, nos. 10 and 11
Shape: subspheroidal
Dimensions: P = 24.2, E = 22.0
Apertures: 3-colporate, 4-colporate, 4-colporate plus 2-colpi, colpi long, pores distinct or constrictions
Exine: faintly striate
SEM: photo 54, nos. 6, 7, 8, 9, and 12
Apertures: colpi granulate
Exine: striate-rugulate, smoother on poles

38. *Nicotiana tabacum* L.
Mexico, 1897
LM: photo 55, no. 3
Shape: subspheroidal
Dimensions: P = 24.2, E = 19.8
Apertures: 3-colporate, 4-colporate, colpi long, pores distinct or constrictions
Exine: rugulate to rugulate-verrucoid
SEM: photo 55, nos. 1, 2, and 4

Photo 55. SEM and LM photographs of southwestern Solanaceae species.

38. *Nicotiana tabacum*:

1 and 2, 2500X;

3, 400X;

4, 10000X.

39. *N. tabacum*:

5, 6, and 7, 2500X;

8, 2000X;

9, 10, and 11, 400X;

12, 10000X.

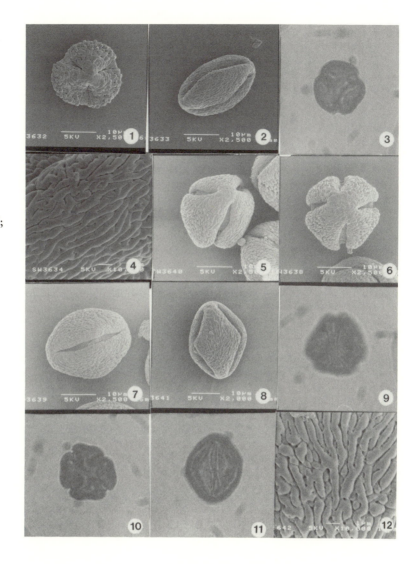

Apertures: colpi granulate

Exine: striate-rugulate to rugulate to rugulate-verrucoid, smoother on poles

39. *Nicotiana tabacum* L.

Bolivia, 1817

LM: photo 55, nos. 9, 10, and 11

Shape: subspheroidal

Dimensions: P = 26.4, E = 22.0

Apertures: 3-colporate, 4-colporate, colpi long, pores distinct or constrictions

Exine: striate-rugulate

SEM: photo 55, nos. 5, 6, 7, 8, and 12

Apertures: colpi granulate

Exine: striate-rugulate to rugulate to rugulate-verrucoid, smoother on poles

40. *Nicotiana tabacum* L.

New Mexico, 1995

LM: photo 56, nos. 3 and 4

Shape: subspheroidal

Dimensions: P = 22.0, E = 22.0

Apertures: 3-colporate, colpi long, pores distinct or constrictions

Exine: striate to striate-reticulate

SEM: photo 56, nos. 1, 2, 5, and 6

Apertures: colpi granulate

Exine: striate-rugulate to rugulate to rugulate-verrucoid, smoother on poles, perforate

41. *Nicotiana tabacum* L.

Hispaniola, 1932

LM: photo 56, nos. 9, 10, and 11

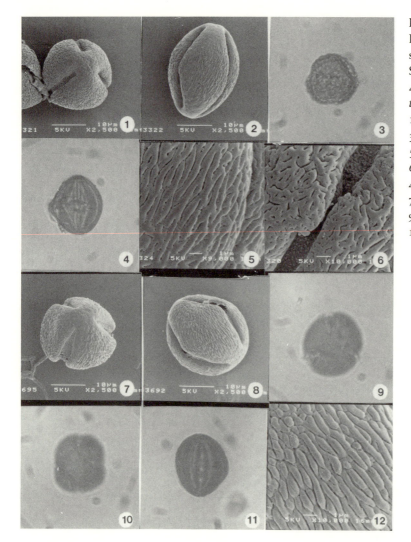

Photo 56. SEM and LM photographs of southwestern Solanaceae species. 40. *Nicotiana tabacum*: 1 and 2, 2500X; 3 and 4, 400X; 5, 9000X; 6, 10000X. 41. *N. tabacum*: 7 and 8, 2500X; 9, 10, and 11, 400X; 12, 10000X.

Shape: subspheroidal
Dimensions: P = 24.2, E = 22.0
Apertures: 3-colporate, 4-colporate, colpi long, pores distinct or constrictions
Exine: striate-rugulate to rugulate-verrucoid
SEM: photo 56, nos. 7, 8, and 12
Apertures: colpi granulate
Exine: striate-rugulate to striate-rugulate-verrucoid, smoother on poles, perforate

42. *Nicotiana bigelovii* (Torr.) S. Wats. (see note 1)
New Mexico, 1995
LM: photo 57, nos. 3 and 4
Shape: subspheroidal
Dimensions: P = 26.4, E = 26.4

Apertures: 3-colporate, colpi long, pores distinct or constrictions
Exine: striate-rugulate to rugulate-verrucoid
SEM: photo 57, nos. 1, 2, 5, and 6
Apertures: colpi granulate
Exine: rugulate to striate-rugulate to striate-rugulate-verrucoid, smoother on poles, perforate

43. *Nicotiana bigelovii* (Torr.) S. Wats. var. *wallacei*
New Mexico (seeds originally from Los Coyotes Cahuilla Reservation, California), 1995
LM: photo 57, no. 11
Shape: subspheroidal

Photo 57. SEM and LM photographs of southwestern Solanaceae species.

42. *Nicotiana bigelovii*:
1, 2500X;
2, 2000X;
3 and 4, 400X;
5 and 6, 10000X.

43. *N. bigelovii* var. *wallacei*:
7, 8, 9, and 10, 2000X;
11, 400X;
12, 10000X.

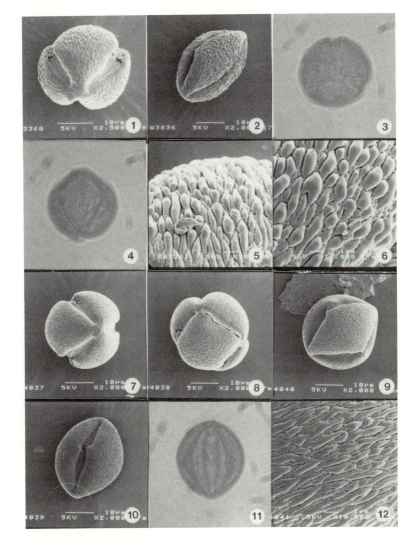

Dimensions: P = 28.6, E = 26.4
Apertures: 3-colporate, 4-colporate plus 2-colpi, colpi long, pores distinct or constrictions
Exine: faintly rugulate to striate-rugulate
SEM: photo 57, nos. 7, 8, 9, 10, and 12
Apertures: colpi granulate
Exine: striate-rugulate, smoother on poles, perforate

44. *Nicotiana bigelovii* (Torr.) S. Wats.
Oregon, 1881
LM: photo 58, no. 3
Shape: subspheroidal
Dimensions: P = 28.6, E = 26.4

Apertures: 3-colporate, colpi long, pores distinct or constrictions
Exine: faintly striate-rugulate
SEM: photo 58, nos. 1, 2, 4, 5, and 6
Apertures: colpi granulate
Exine: rugulate to striate-rugulate, smoother on poles

45. *Nicotiana multivalvis* Lindl.
Komarov Botanical Institute, 1832
LM: photo 58, nos. 10 and 11
Shape: subspheroidal
Dimensions: P = 30.8, E = 24.2
Apertures: 3-colporate, colpi long, pores distinct or constrictions

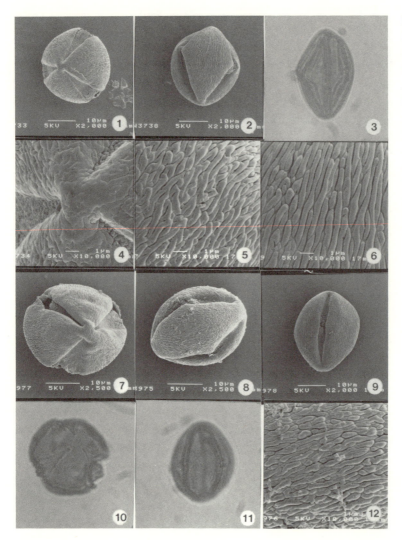

Photo 58. SEM and LM photographs of southwestern Solanaceae species. 44. *Nicotiana bigelovii*: 1 and 2, 2000X; 3, 400X; 4, 5, and 6, 10000X. 45. *N. multivalvis*: 7 and 8, 2500X; 9, 2000X; 10 and 11, 400X; 12, 10000X.

Exine: psilate to faintly striate
SEM: photo 58, nos. 7, 8, 9, and 12
Apertures: colpi granulate
Exine: striate-rugulate, smoother on poles

46. *Nicotiana multivalvis* Lindl.
Komarov Botanical Institute (from Berlin Garden), n.d.
LM: photo 59, nos. 3 and 4
Shape: subspheroidal
Dimensions: P = 30.8, E = 24.2
Apertures: 3-colporate, colpi long, pores distinct or constrictions
Exine: psilate to faintly striate

SEM: photo 59, nos. 1, 2, and 5
Apertures: colpi granulate
Exine: rugulate to striate-rugulate, smoother on poles

47. *Nicotiana quadrivalvis* Pursh
Komarov Botanical Institute, 1827
LM: photo 59, nos. 9, 10, and 11
Shape: subspheroidal
Dimensions: P = 28.6, E = 22.0
Apertures: 3-colporate (can appear 3-colpate), colpi long, pores distinct or constrictions
Exine: faintly rugulate

Photo 59. SEM and LM photographs of southwestern Solanaceae species.
46. *Nicotiana multivalvis:*
1 and 2, 2000X;
3 and 4, 400X;
5, 10000X.
47. *N. quadrivalvis:*
6, 7, and 8, 2500X;
9, 10, and 11, 400X;
12, 10000X.

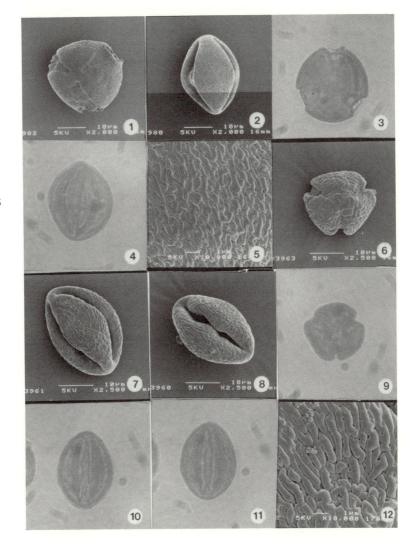

SEM: photo 59, nos. 6, 7, 8, and 12
Apertures: colpi granulate
Exine: rugulate to striate-rugulate, smoother on poles

48. *Nicotiana quadrivalvis* Pursh
Komarov Botanical Institute, 1826
LM: photo 60, nos. 5 and 6
Shape: subspheroidal
Dimensions: P = 24.2, E = 22.0
Apertures: 3-colporate (can appear 3-colpate), 4-colporate plus 2-colpi, colpi long, pores distinct or constrictions
Exine: faintly rugulate to striate-rugulate

SEM: photo 60, nos. 1, 2, 3, 4, and 7
Apertures: colpi granulate
Exine: rugulate to striate-rugulate, smoother on poles, perforate

49. *Nicotiana quadrivalvis* Pursh
Komarov Botanical Institute, 1836
LM: photo 60, nos. 10 and 11
Shape: subspheroidal
Dimensions: P = 28.6, E = 26.4
Apertures: 3-colporate (can appear 3-colpate), colpi long, pores distinct or constrictions
Exine: faintly rugulate to striate-rugulate

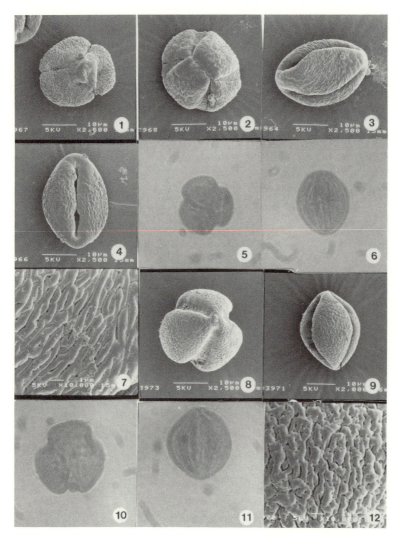

Photo 60. SEM and
LM photographs of
southwestern
Solanaceae species.
48. *Nicotiana
quadrivalvis*:
1, 2, 3, and 4, 2500X;
5 and 6, 400X;
7, 10000X.
49. *N. quadrivalvis*:
8, 2500X;
9, 2000X;
10 and 11, 400X;
12, 10000X.

SEM: photo 60, nos. 8, 9, and 12
Apertures: colpi granulate
Exine: rugulate to striate-rugulate, smoother
on poles, perforate
50. *Nicotiana glauca* Graham
Texas, 1929
LM: photo 61, nos. 3 and 4
Shape: prolate
Dimensions: P = 24.2, E = 17.6
Apertures: 3-colporate, colpi long, pores
distinct or constrictions
Exine: psilate to faintly striate-reticulate
(polar view) or striate-rugulate

SEM: photo 61, nos. 1, 2, and 5
Apertures: colpi granulate
Exine: striate-rugulate, smoother on poles
51. *Nicotiana glauca* Graham
New Mexico, 1995
LM: photo 61, nos. 8 and 9
Shape: subspheroidal to prolate
Dimensions: P = 26.4, E = 19.8; P = 26.4,
E = 15.4
Apertures: 3-colporate, colpi long, pores
distinct or constrictions
Exine: psilate to faintly striate
SEM: photo 61, nos. 6, 7, and 10

Apertures: colpi granulate
Exine: striate-rugulate, smoother on poles,
perforate

52. *Nicotiana glauca* Graham
California (Morongo Cahuilla Reservation),
1994
LM: none
Shape: subspheroidal
Dimensions: P = 22.0, E = 19.8
Apertures: 3-colporate, 4-colporate (rare),
colpi long, pores distinct or constrictions
Exine: psilate to faintly striate
SEM: photo 61, nos. 11 and 12

Apertures: colpi granulate
Exine: striate-rugulate, smoother on poles,
perforate

53. *Nicotiana acuminata* (Graham) Hook.
California, 1955
LM: photo 62, nos. 3 and 4
Shape: subspheroidal
Dimensions: P = 28.6, E = 26.4
Apertures: 3-colporate, colpi long, pores
distinct or constrictions
Exine: faintly striate to striate-reticulate
(polar) or striate-rugulate
SEM: photo 62, nos. 1, 2, 5, and 6

Photo 61. SEM and
LM photographs of
southwestern
Solanaceae species.
50. *Nicotiana glauca*:
1 and 2, 2500X;
3 and 4, 400X;
5, 10000X.
51. *N. glauca*:
6 and 7, 2500X;
8 and 9, 400X;
10, 10000X.
52. *N. glauca*:
11, 2500X;
12, 10000X.

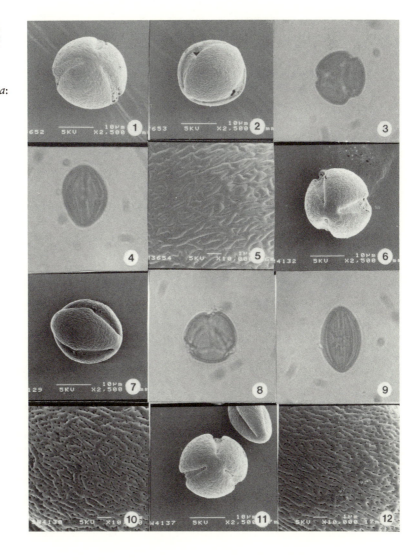

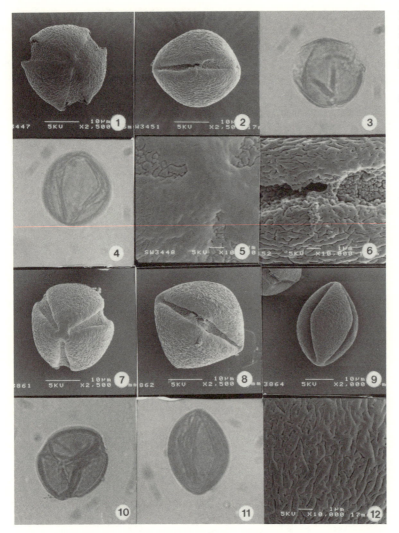

Photo 62. SEM and LM photographs of southwestern Solanaceae species.
53. *Nicotiana acuminata*:
1 and 2, 2500X;
3 and 4, 400X;
5 and 6, 10000X.
54. *N. clevelandii*:
7 and 8, 2500X;
9, 2000X;
10 and 11, 400X;
12, 10000X.

Apertures: colpi granulate
Exine: rugulate to striate-rugulate, smoother on poles, perforate

54. *Nicotiana clevelandii* Gray
Mexico, 1925
LM: photo 62, nos. 10 and 11
Shape: prolate
Dimensions: P = 33.0, E = 24.2
Apertures: 3-colporate, colpi long, pores distinct or constrictions
Exine: psilate to faintly rugulate
SEM: photo 62, nos. 7, 8, 9, and 12
Apertures: colpi granulate
Exine: rugulate to striate-rugulate, smoother on poles

55. *Nicotiana palmeri* Gray
Nevada, 1919
LM: photo 63, nos. 4 and 5
Shape: subspheroidal to prolate
Dimensions: P = 26.4, E = 26.4; P = 33.0, E = 22.0
Apertures: 3-colporate, colpi long, pores distinct or constrictions
Exine: faintly rugulate to striate-rugulate
SEM: photo 63, nos. 1, 2, 3, and 6
Apertures: colpi granulate
Exine: rugulate to striate-rugulate, smoother on poles, perforate

56. *Nicotiana sylvestris* Speg. & Comes
New Mexico, 1995

Photo 63. SEM and LM photographs of southwestern Solanaceae species. 55. *Nicotiana palmeri*: 1, 2, and 3, 2500X; 4 and 5, 400X; 6, 10000X. 56. *N. sylvestris*: 7 and 8, 2500X; 9 and 10, 400X; 11 and 12, 10000X.

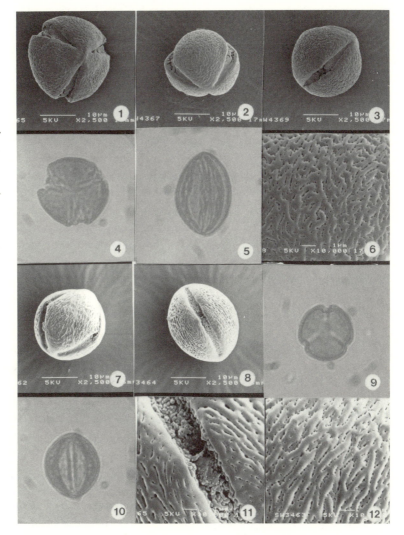

LM: photo 63, nos. 9 and 10
Shape: subspheroidal
Dimensions: P = 24.2, E = 22.0
Apertures: 3-colporate, colpi long, pores distinct or constrictions
Exine: faintly striate-rugulate
SEM: photo 63, nos. 7, 8, 11, and 12
Apertures: colpi granulate
Exine: striate-rugulate, smoother on poles, perforate

As the photographs illustrate, the pollen grains of all of the studied genera have certain characteristics in common, as well as many differences. All of them are radiosymmetric, isopolar monads, which means that the pollen occurs as single grains with identical halves. All grains are distinctly (or indistinctly) tectate, in that they have a continuous outer layer over the structural elements of the grain wall. For the Solanaceae, the sculptural elements and patterns on this outer layer of the exine are the main distinguishing traits.

Among sculptural elements, micro-echinae (small spines) occur in several genera. Granules (small, rounded projections) are often apparent on the furrows under SEM. Some grains appear to have verrucae, which are rounded projections that are wider at the base than they are high. In the case of the Solanaceae, these projections are actually part of the dense sculpturing that characterizes some grains. They occur in the rugulate pattern, where elements are elongated and irregularly arranged on the grain surface. These elements can be so coarse that portions project out from the grain surface. This pattern is referred to here as "rugulate-verrucoid." The projections are, therefore, not true verrucae. Other grains exhibit patterns that are psilate (smooth), reticulate (netlike), or striate (with parallel elongated elements). The ridges (raised elements) in the rugulate, reticulate, and striate patterns are referred to as muri (walls). In the Solanaceae, these muri can exhibit additional patterning under SEM. They are sometimes striate, sometimes micro-echinate, and sometimes both.

Many of the Solanaceae do not fall neatly into the standard descriptive terms used for surface patterns. Consequently, some grains are described as "striate-reticulate," "striate-rugulate," "striate-rugulate-verrucoid," and so on. Different patterns can occur on different parts of the same grain or are evident in different views of the same grain. Under LM, polar views might show a more reticulate pattern and equatorial views a more striate pattern for the same grain. This might be an actual condition of the grain (as in some *Datura* pollen, in which the equatorial region can be striate and the polar region reticulate). In LM, it is also a factor of the compressed view one has of a grain. Consequently, in the descriptions of many of the pollen grains in this study, the LM and SEM terminologies do not match. Also, morphological variation among grains from the same specimen is reflected in the exine descriptions. Hence, from the same specimen, grains might be "rugulate to striate-rugulate to striate-rugulate-verrucoid," and variations in patterning can also occur on the same individual grains. The photographs illustrate these complicated characteristics.

Most Solanaceae grains are 3-colporate, which means that they have three furrows, each of which has a pore. Some grains here are 4-col-

porate or are described as 4-colporate plus 2-colpi. Such grains have, respectively, four furrows with pores or four furrows with pores and an additional two furrows that lack pores. The two additional furrows can be distinctly formed or only partly formed. In a few instances they do have pores, and such grains are termed 6-colporate. The specimens that include grains with more than three colpori are still dominated by 3-colporate grains. The pollen of such specimens is termed dimorphic.

The grains with more than three colpori could have at least two different explanations—they could be abnormal single grains, or they could be microspore mother cells that never completely divided during meiosis and hence failed to fully form microspore tetrads (which then separate into the individual pollen grains). In either case, the pollen is probably not viable.

Interestingly, the highest proportions of such anomalous grains occur in some *Nicotiana rustica* and *N. tabacum* specimens—the two domesticated tobacco taxa. It is therefore possible that the pollen dimorphism is an effect of domestication. If the anomalous pollen is not viable, this could help explain why these plants do not readily grow outside of cultivation. Growing the plants close together would aid in the transfer of pollen by insects and result in transportation of more pollen than would probably occur if the plants were dispersed in the wild. Hence, cultivation would help counter the effects of nonviable pollen and enable the plants to survive. This idea requires further testing, since there are other tobacco species, besides these two key domesticates, that exhibit substantial dimorphism. *Nicotiana alata* is an example, though it is not included in this chapter. Also, not all specimens of *N. rustica* and *N. tabacum* exhibit substantial dimorphism. In specimen 40, for example, only 3-colporate grains were recorded, while in specimen 31, 32 percent of the grains were 4-colporate or 4-colporate plus 2-colpi (based on observations of 100 grains).

Still another explanation of the dimorphism could simply involve the phylogenetic position of the tobaccos in the Solanaceae family. J. G. Hawkes, R. N. Lester, and A. D. Skelding (1979:14) list the *Nicotiana* genus in the Cestroideae subfamily of the Solanaceae, whereas most of the other genera examined in this study fall in the Solanoideae subfamily. The Cestroideae subfamily is more advanced, which may be a factor in the morphologic development of *N. rustica* and *N. tabacum* pollen. It should be noted that these findings of dimorphic tobacco pollen contradict the preliminary descriptions of Thomas Goodspeed (1954), who considered the pollen of the different tobacco species all very similar.

## Pollen Results

Morphological contrasts among the studied species are generally sufficient to separate most of the genera in this study (table 45). The *Datura* species, for example, are distinguished by an equatorial bulge and meridional striations. *Nicandra* has short furrows, vestibulate pores, and is granulate (micro-echinate under SEM). *Hyoscyamus* has long furrows and is reticulate. *Saracha* has long furrows and is rugulate-verrucoid (with echinae and striae on the muri under SEM).

*Capsicum, Physalis, Solanum, Chamaesaracha,* and *Margaranthus* are similar to one another. They all have long furrows, vestibulate pores, and transverse furrows and are psilate under LM, or faintly micro-echinate. All are clearly micro-echinate under SEM. Also under SEM, the transverse furrows actually are transverse thickenings of the exine, and not true furrows. These five genera could be lumped in a single group, but there are some subtle traits that further differentiate them. *Physalis* and *Solanum,* for example, are the two smallest and can be placed in their own group. *Capsicum* has bigger vestibulae; *Chamaesaracha* and *Margaranthus* have far less pronounced vestibulae and could be another group, since they are larger than *Physalis* and *Solanum.* Hence, these five genera can be keyed to three groups.

*Salpichroa* is another separate taxon, its pollen differentiated by only moderately long furrows that also have vestibulate pores and transverse furrows (thickenings under SEM). The grains appears psilate under LM, with no hint of echinae. They are finely rugulate under SEM. *Cestrum* has long furrows, with vestibulae and transverse furrows weakly evident. The grains are psilate (faintly rugulate under SEM). *Cestrum* could be confused under LM with some specimens of tobacco, particularly those with only faint rugulate sculpturing (such as specimen 54, *Nicotiana clevelandii*), especially when the vestibulae and transverse furrows in the *Cestrum* grains are not well pronounced. Because *Cestrum* is non-native to the Southwest, this would not be a concern unless contamination of an archaeological site's deposits was a possibility. *Petunia* has long furrows but is coarsely rugulate to rugulate-verrucoid. It is quite different from *Cestrum* but is similar to some specimens of tobacco (such as specimen 28, *Nicotiana trigonophylla*) and could also be confused with tobacco. Both *Cestrum* and *Petunia* are closely related to the *Nicotiana* genus, and this appears evident in the different pollen forms.

The remaining two genera, *Lycium* and *Nicotiana,* are more problematical. Although they are dissimilar from most of the genera previously described, they are very similar to each other. They also overlap in much of their geographic ranges (maps 24–27). Most *Lycium* grains overlap in size with members of the tobacco genus, particularly the wild tobaccos. Most *Lycium* grains are 3-colporate, although there are 4-colporate exceptions (not illustrated in this chapter). The surface sculpturing of *Lycium* grains often appears only faintly striate or striate-reticulate (polar view) and sometimes only psilate under LM. The surface sculpturing of many *Nicotiana* grains also appears striate or striate-rugulate. The SEM photography clearly shows that the surface sculpturing of *Lycium* is striate. Sometimes the striae are so pronounced that they appear verrucoid. Usually faint striae also appear

## Table 45: Pollen Key

| Description | Taxon |
|---|---|
| Grains with short furrows and a meridional bulge | *Datura* |
| Grains granulate with short furrows and vestibulate pores | *Nicandra* |
| Grains reticulate with long furrows | *Hyoscyamus* |
| Grains rugulate-verrucoid (and micro-echinate) | *Saracha* |
| Grains psilate to micro-echinate, strongly vestibulate, with transverse furrows (thickenings) | *Capsicum* |
| Grains small, psilate to micro-echinate, vestibulate, with transverse furrows (thickenings) | *Physalis/Solanum* |
| Grains psilate to micro-echinate, weakly vestibulate, with weakly developed transverse furrows (thickenings) | *Chamaesaracha/Margaranthus* |
| Grains psilate (finely rugulate) with moderately long colpi | *Salpichroa* |
| Grains psilate, weakly vestibulate (or not), with weakly developed transverse furrows (thickenings) (or not) | *Cestrum* (*Cestrum/Nicotiana*) |
| Grains coarsely rugulate-verrucoid | *Petunia* (*Petunia/Nicotiana*) |
| Grains striate-rugulate | *Lycium/Nicotiana* |
| Grains rugulate | *Nicotiana* |
| Grains rugulate to striate-rugulate to striate-rugulate-verrucoid, 4-colporate, 4-colporate plus 2-colpi | *Nicotiana* |

on the muri that constitute the ridges of the pattern. There is often a "cross-hatching" effect in Lycium grains, particularly across the poles, that would be described as rugulate, but it is not the same type of rugulate pattern as that which characterizes many *Nicotiana* specimens (under SEM). This polar sculpturing is a clear point of contrast with many tobacco species, since the polar areas in *Nicotiana* grains are often psilate, or at least much smoother than the rest of the grain surface. Unfortunately, despite the presence of these details under SEM, the polar traits are not strongly evident under LM. The polar areas in *Lycium* and *Nicotiana* are usually very small, which contributes to the weak visibility of the polar distinctions at the LM levels of magnification.

It should be noted that the descriptions of *Lycium*, as well as other taxa, presented here are in only partial agreement with other studies. Using LM, Holloway and Dean (1990) keyed *Lycium pallidum* as having a transverse furrow. This agrees, in part, with the findings of other researchers using LM (Heusser 1971:57; Murry and Eshbaugh 1971:69). Murry and Eshbaugh (1971:69), however, also keyed *Lycium* as vesti-

bulate, whereas this was not observed by Holloway and Dean (1990). In the current study, thickening of the poroid area is evident in specimen 22 but is not regularly found, and the *Lycium* grains here are perceived as having neither transverse furrows nor vestibulae. This view is supported by SEM examinations of grain morphology, which were unavailable to the other researchers. In general, these differences in descriptions reflect the large degree of intraspecies variation and morphological complexity that characterizes the Solanaceae.

Overall, then, pollen morphological overlap is apparent in the current study between *Lycium* and *Nicotiana* grains, and a group taxon of *Lycium-Nicotiana* seems warranted. The overlap is particularly evident in the surface sculpturing patterns. Both grains can exhibit striate to striate-regulate patterns that appear very similar under LM. All of the *Lycium* grains that were observed, however, did exhibit some kind of striations. Some *Nicotiana* specimens can also be only rugulate or rugulate-verrucoid. In the latter case, some overlap with *Petunia* could occur. Overall then, most expressions of *Lycium* pollen overlap with *Nicotiana*, but some forms of *Nicotiana* are distinct (rugulate grains). The most distinct characteristic is the abundant occurrence of 4-colporate or 4-colporate plus 2-colpi pollen among some tobaccos. The oldest specimens with this trait included here date to 1817 (specimen 39) and 1842 (specimen 31). While it is not certain that this dimorphic trait has a time depth that extends back into prehistory, it is possible. Dimorphism, specifically the occurrence of 4-colporate kinds of pollen, could most clearly identify past tobacco pollen.

## Geographic Ranges, Pollen Morphology, and Archaeological Sites

Representatives of most of the studied genera are plotted by county on maps 24–27. A few are excluded if they are solely adventive (e.g., *Cestrum*) or are very limited in distribution (e.g., *Margaranthus*). While much of the distributional information is drawn from published sources, the information for Colorado is based primarily on a study of herbarium specimens at

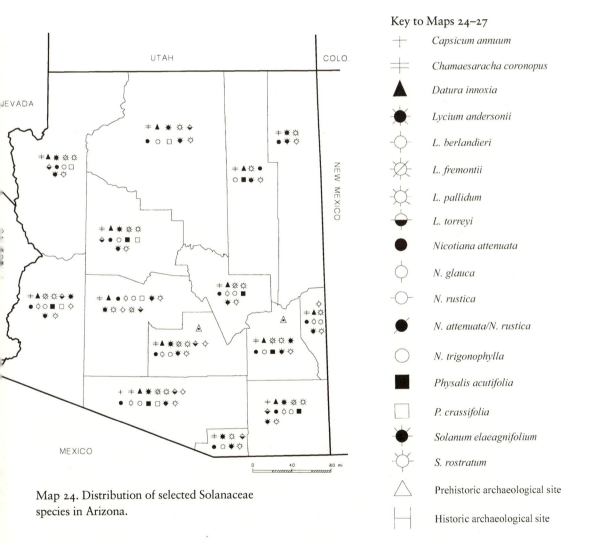

Map 24. Distribution of selected Solanaceae species in Arizona.

Key to Maps 24–27

| | |
|---|---|
| + | *Capsicum annuum* |
| ‡ | *Chamaesaracha coronopus* |
| ▲ | *Datura innoxia* |
| ◑ | *Lycium andersonii* |
| ○ | *L. berlandieri* |
| ⊘ | *L. fremontii* |
| ☼ | *L. pallidum* |
| ◒ | *L. torreyi* |
| ● | *Nicotiana attenuata* |
| ○ | *N. glauca* |
| ⊖ | *N. rustica* |
| ◕ | *N. attenuata/N. rustica* |
| ○ | *N. trigonophylla* |
| ■ | *Physalis acutifolia* |
| □ | *P. crassifolia* |
| ◉ | *Solanum elaeagnifolium* |
| ✺ | *S. rostratum* |
| △ | Prehistoric archaeological site |
| ⊢ | Historic archaeological site |

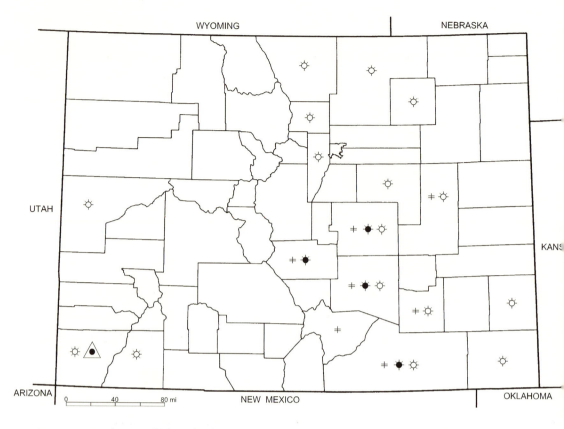

Map 25. Distribution of selected Solanaceae species in Colorado. Key accompanies map 24.

the University of Colorado, Boulder. There are many contradictions in the published discussions of distributions of the floras for this state (compare H. D. Harrington 1964 and Great Plains Flora Association 1986).

With regard to the *Lycium* species and wild tobaccos, the potential for overlap in occurrence and confusion in pollen identification appears high for certain geographic areas. *Lycium andersonii*, for example, overlaps in distribution with *Nicotiana attenuata* and *N. trigonophylla* throughout much of Arizona, southern Utah, and parts of New Mexico. It occurs in several counties in Arizona (Graham and Pinal) and New Mexico (Bernalillo and Cibola) where *Nicotiana attenuata* or *N. attenuata/rustica* has been identified in archaeological sites. The geo-

graphic range of *Lycium berlandieri* also overlaps with that of tobacco and its occurrences in archaeological sites in Arizona. Likewise, *Lycium pallidum* overlaps with a recorded occurrence of *N. attenuata* at an archaeological site in Montezuma County, southwestern Colorado. H. D. Harrington (1964) described *N. attenuata* as growing in the western part of Colorado and *N. trigonophylla* in the southern part. The actual distributions in Colorado require additional research for clarification.

In much of the Four Corners states, it appears that our ability to differentiate tobacco through pollen analysis is limited, unless morphologically anomalous grains are found. Fortunately for archaeologists, few of the *Lycium* species range very far north. *Lycium berlandieri*, for

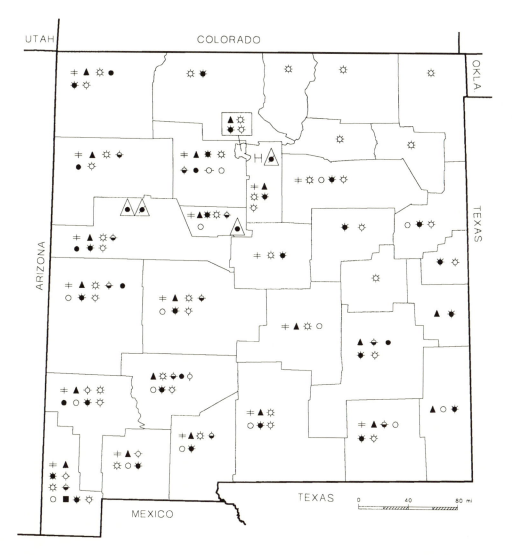

Map 26. Distribution of selected Solanaceae species in New Mexico. Key accompanies map 24.

example, is recorded only for Arizona and extreme southwestern New Mexico, although several other, as yet unstudied *Lycium* species are present in these states and Utah. Still, the likelihood for confusing tobacco pollen with wolfberry pollen obviously decreases where the natural occurrence of wolfberry is less likely. Thus the potential for confusing tobacco with *Lycium* is especially low for Colorado. Only *Lycium barbarum* (= *L. halimifolium*, non-native) and *L. pallidum* are recorded for this state (H. D. Harrington 1964:481). This is noteworthy, considering that most evidence for prehistoric tobacco comes from Anasazi sites in Montezuma County in the extreme southwestern corner of the state (Winter 1990b, 1991, chapter 7 this volume). The pollen evidence for tobacco reported by Scott (1986, and Cummings, this volume) also comes from a site in this county.

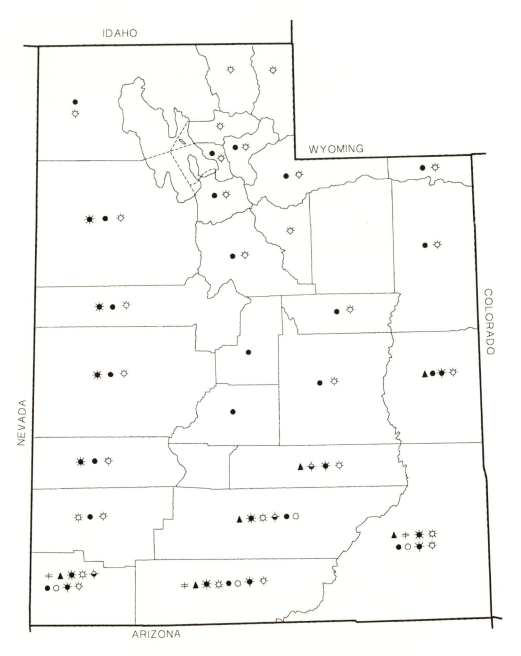

Map 27. Distribution of selected Solanaceae species in Utah. Key accompanies map 24.

### Conclusion

It appears that tobacco pollen can be differentiated from pollen of other members of the Solanaceae, but only when it occurs as rugulate grains or anomalous 4-colporate or 4-colporate plus 2-colpi grains. It might also be identified in areas beyond the natural range of *Lycium*, with its potentially overlapping pollen, assuming that *Lycium* did not grow there in the past. These findings suggest that southwestern archaeological sites warrant intensive investigation for tobacco pollen. This does not mean that tobacco will be easily identified. It is still possible that its pollen might be confused with that of other plant families, a matter not considered in this chapter.

The results of this study indicate that tobacco pollen is potentially distinct from the pollen of other Solanaceae, albeit with certain serious limitations, especially with regard to *Lycium*. Pollen studies can therefore provide key information on the diffusion of tobacco and the processes of plant domestication in the New World. All of the tobacco species described in this chapter have the potential to provide such information. The two domesticated species (*Nicotiana rustica* and *N. tabacum*) produced a high proportion of dimorphic, probably nonviable pollen grains, a condition that could well be a product of the domestication process. Replication of the current findings is needed, however, to substantiate the strikingly different results obtained for cultivated as opposed to wild tobacco.

## Notes

This research would not have been possible without the cooperation and contributions of many institutions and individuals. Grateful appreciation is extended to the institutions that provided specimens and/or permitted photography of specimens: Bergianska Botanical Garden, Stockholm; Komorov Botanical Institute, St. Petersburg; Native Seeds/SEARCH, Tucson; Deaver Herbarium and Palynology Laboratory of Northern Arizona University, Flagstaff; Rancho Santa Ana Botanical Garden and Herbarium, Claremont; Royal Botanic Gardens, Kew; Herbarium of the Swedish Museum of Natural History, Stockholm; Palynology Laboratory of Texas A&M University, College Station; United States National Arboretum and United States National Herbarium, Washington, D.C.; Herbarium of the University of Colorado, Boulder; Botanical Garden and Herbarium of the University of Copenhagen, Copenhagen; Herbarium of the University of New Mexico, Albuquerque; Herbarium of the University of North Carolina, Chapel Hill; and the Botanical Garden and Herbarium of Uppsala University, Uppsala.

It is, regretfully, not possible to name all of the individuals who contributed to this study, but I greatly appreciate the time, effort, and interest my colleagues have invested in it. I particularly wish to thank Siwert Nilsson, who provided access to the Palynology Laboratory of the Swedish Museum of Natural History and made many helpful comments on the results of the study, and to Elisabeth Grafstrom, who guided the SEM photography that I conducted there. I also extend thanks to R. Scott Anderson, who provided access to the Palynology Laboratory of Northern Arizona University for portions of the chemical processing, and to Susan Smith, who helped with the chemical work. I additionally want to thank Julia Hammett and Joseph Winter for collecting many of the specimens used here. This research was supported in part by grants from the University of New Mexico's Office of Contract Archeology, Office of Graduate Studies, and Student Research Allocations Committee.

A preliminary version of this paper can be found in Gish et al. 1993.

1. Editor's note: Elsewhere in this book the *Nicotiana quadrivalvis* nomenclature has been used, rather than *N. bigelovii*. However, because of Gish's very detailed data, especially in the captions to photos 39–63, I have retained her use of *N. bigelovii* in order to avoid misinterpretation or misunderstanding of her data.

# PART FIVE

# Evolution of the Use of Tobacco
# by Native Americans

# From Earth Mother to Snake Woman

## The Role of Tobacco in the Evolution of
## Native American Religious Organization

### Joseph C. Winter

From the Inuit in Alaska to the Cuna in Panama, the tobacco-using natives of North America encompass an incredible array of shamans, medicine men, singers, spirit impersonators, secret societies, World Renewal formulists, organized priesthoods, and other types of religious actors and organizations. Chapter 2 summarized tobacco use by 327 different groups, revealing its religious importance at three basic levels: individual use of tobacco by shamans, medicine men, other religious practitioners, and the ordinary members of their tribes; group use by voluntary, sometimes secret societies; and formal, institutionalized use by priests and other elites.

The boundaries between these three general levels are often subtle and difficult to determine, and the levels are not necessarily mutually exclusive. For example, the Haudenosaunee (Iroquois) have both shamans and societies. The Aztec may have had all three and definitely had some priests who were shamans. Moreover, there are other ways of categorizing the different types of religious organization in North America; the situation is far more complex than this simple generalization implies. Nevertheless, it appears safe to conclude that there are three basic types of tobacco use for religious purposes, and they seem to correlate with three general levels of religious organization.[1] The presence or absence of tobacco use in one of the levels and variations in the intensity of use in all three permit the identification of seven recognizable categories of tobacco-related religious organization in North America: shamans who use neither tobacco nor any other psychoactive plant to obtain visions; shamans and other individual practitioners who use moderate amounts of tobacco; shamans who use so much tobacco that they are called tobacco shamans; medicine societies whose members use moderate to large amounts of tobacco; tobacco societies that are dedicated to the care and veneration of tobacco; priests who regularly use tobacco; and tobacco priesthoods. Each category is discussed in the next section.

The central point of this chapter is that the use and domestication of tobacco in North and South America evolved in association with the development of complex forms of religious organization. At first, the most basic and fundamental level of religious organization—shamanism or a similar type of individual practice—appeared in North America *without* tobacco as the earliest paleo-Indians crossed the Bering land bridge and slowly migrated south through North America and into South America. At some point (perhaps in the Great Basin, northern California, and/or the Southwest) wild tobacco was encountered, experimented with, and added to this shamanistic base. Over time its use and manipulation increased to the point that wild tobacco may have been semi-domesticated by shamans and other medicine men who came to depend upon it for visions and communication with the supernatural. Eventually, several species were fully domesticated in South America and one was almost domesticated in North America. The use of tobacco was then maintained, expanded, and elaborated as more complex forms of religious organization evolved, including individual practitioners with apprentices, formal curing societies with initiation rites, and organized priesthoods.

After its initial adoption, tobacco became a constant, elemental force. The basic shamanistic or other individualistic substrate was often retained; tobacco formed an essential part of the substrate; and as more complex forms of individual use, curing societies, and supernatural contact developed—up to and including state theocracies with institutionalized, hereditary priesthoods—tobacco use remained at the heart of the religious experience for most members of the tribe and, in most groups, for all members of the group. Other psychoactive plants and drugs derived from plants were added, such as *toloache* (datura), peyote, mescal, *tesquino* (corn beer), and *ololiuhqui* (morning-glory seeds), but tobacco remained the core religious drug of choice—the primary way in which supernatural beings were contacted and placated, a food of the gods, at times a god itself.

## Basic Forms of Tobacco-Related Religious Organization in North America

### Shamanism without Tobacco

In precontact times, before the introduction of the commercial tobacco trade by the Russians, Danes, English, and other Euro-Americans, the only North American groups who lacked tobacco in their religious systems appear to have been the Inuit, Aleut, and certain subarctic Indians at the far northern edge of the continent. As soon as commercial tobacco became available, either directly from traders or indirectly through Siberian and Indian intermediaries, it was added and in some cases marginally incorporated into their religions, as is shown by the St. Lawrence Island Inuit, who sacrificed tobacco in whaling rites. For the most part, however, tobacco was and is almost completely absent from the ideology, rituals, and other aspects of these northern peoples' shamanistic religions,

for the simple reason that they did not know about it until only a few hundred years ago. Now they use it for recreational and other purposes, but it does not grow locally, it cannot be raised or gathered, and it remains essentially on the surface of their cultures, at the interface with the Euro-American societies that provide it. Readers who are interested in how Inuit shamans enter trance states without the use of tobacco or other psychoactive plants should read Dan Merkur's detailed study (1992).

### Shamans and Other Individual Practitioners Who Use Moderate Amounts of Tobacco

The majority of native groups in North America have shamans or other individual practitioners such as medicine men, curers, and singers who have access to supernatural power or who have the power to call upon the spirits. Medicine people and other individual medico-religious practitioners use their power to diagnose and cure disease, control the weather, and otherwise help (and sometimes harm) the members of their social group. Shamans often have a personal relationship with one or more supernatural beings, and the other types of individual practitioners know secret spells or rituals and medicinal herbs that enable them to contact these beings. First and foremost among the herbs and drugs used by shamans, medicine men, and other healers is tobacco. Almost every native group in North America—with the exception of the far northern tribes already mentioned—uses or used tobacco as a tool to divine and treat illness. Blowing tobacco smoke on the patient, throwing tobacco on the ground, offering it in the air, in fire, and in water, and many other usages are known among hunters, gatherers, fishermen, herders, and other native groups with individual religious practitioners.

Most medicine men and women and other healers in North America do not, however, ingest such large amounts of nicotine that it produces hallucinations, visions, trances, and other states of altered consciousness. They may have done so in the past, before curing societies and elaborate priesthoods developed, but in general the average Native American medico-religious practitioner does not use tobacco to enter a trance state, although he or she does use it for many other purposes. Later in this chapter the Navajo of the southwestern United States are discussed as an example of a basic tobacco-using religion organized around the activities of individual singers and other practitioners.

## Tobacco Shamanism

Following Johannes Wilbert (1987:150), I define a tobacco shaman as "the religious practitioner who uses tobacco, whether exclusively or not, to be ordained, to officiate, and to achieve altered states of consciousness." Contemporary, full-blown tobacco shamans in North America are restricted almost exclusively to the southernmost tribes of Mesoamerica, such as the Cuna, Talamanca, Miskito, and Sumu of Panama, Costa Rica, and Nicaragua, who form a cultural continuum with a number of cultures in South America that have tobacco shamans. Several hundred miles to the north, in Mexico, the Huichol also have tobacco shamans, as I discuss later in this chapter. Prehistoric groups located between the Huichol and Sumu, such as the ancestors of the Aztec and Toltec, probably had tobacco shamans, who later developed into tobacco societies and priesthoods. There may also have been many groups to the north who had tobacco shamans far back in the past, as von Gernet discusses in chapter 3. He concludes that many historic tobacco practices are vestiges of this ancient and elemental form of religious expression.

## Medicine Societies Using Tobacco

Native American curing societies such as the Haudenosaunee Company of False Faces are communal organizations that often perform public rituals of benefit to the whole tribe. These societies are rarely divorced from individual practitioners, and some societies on the Great Plains were basically groups of individuals endowed with shamanistic power. Other Plains

Indian societies are based on voluntary affiliation, with membership achieved by dreams, purchase, age, war record, and other means. In the Southwest, there are a number of different kinds of societies, such as the Pueblo kachina cult and various Pueblo medicine societies, that appear to have replaced individual practice as the basis of curing and dealing with the supernatural. Kachina spirit-impersonator societies also cure, but their main function is to bring rain and encourage fertility.

In California, there are several major societies, such as the Kuksu of the Pomo, Miwok, and other north-central tribes, that are organized around spirit impersonators, spectacular dances, and initiation rites. The Midewiwin of the Midwest is another Native American society, as are various societies on the Northwest Coast.

All of these North American religious societies share the use of tobacco, as well as communal ceremonials that are performed for the public, and initiation rites. A. L. Kroeber (1973 [1932]: 487) suggested that they evolved out of a very ancient substrate of tribal-wide initiation ceremonies. However they evolved, tobacco use is prevalent; I illustrate it later in the chapter with the Haudenosaunee Company of False Faces.

## Tobacco Societies

Along the headwaters of the Missouri River and on the far northern plains in Canada, organized tobacco use became so intense that a number of tribes developed formal tobacco societies whose sole purpose was to grow and revere tobacco, which was considered a deity, essential for the survival of the tribe. The Siksika (Blackfoot), Sarsi, and Crow still have tobacco societies; I discuss the Crow in detail elsewhere in this chapter. The Hidatsa used to have a tobacco society, before the group that became the Crow split off, and the Mandan and Arikara may have had them. Tobacco ceremonies, dances, songs, prayers, dreams, medicine bundles, pipes, and other equipment and activities are important aspects of the Crow tobacco society. Its members' lives are almost totally devoted to the care of tobacco during the day, as their dreams are at night.

## Priests Who Regularly Use Tobacco

Priests are religious specialists who mediate between the members of their congregations and the supernatural beings who control life and death. Priests usually do not cure, but they do lead their tribes, temple groups, parishes, and other congregations in regular, scheduled rites, and they help their followers petition the supernatural for health, help, and good fortune. Priests seldom possess supernatural powers in and of themselves, although some also function as shamans or medicine people. Others have been ordained and given the power to transform the ordinary into the supernatural, such as the Catholic priest who changes bread and wine into the body and blood of Christ. Priests know the esoteric formulas and rites that propitiate the gods or spirits, and some Native American priests, especially among the Aztec, were organized in schools of trained priesthoods that served specific gods and supported state religions—the Aztec empire was essentially a highly organized, complex theocracy.

Most priesthoods in native North America developed in the southern part of the continent, among the prehistoric Maya and Toltec and the historic Aztec, Tarascan, Zapotec, and other state-level civilizations. To the north, true priesthoods were few and far between, and not fully developed. There appear to have been no hereditary priests to the north of Mexico, and there was hardly a recognized class of priests. The old man who knew the formulas for a particular ceremony was most likely to pass his knowledge down to his son or his sister's son, but it was not a formal, hereditary, institutionalized priesthood. The Pueblos are one of the only groups north of Mexico with a fairly developed series of what are often called priesthoods, such as the Zuni Bow Priests, yet they are not full-time, institutionalized functionaries. The Aztec, in contrast, had hundreds (if not thousands) of full-time priests who were raised and trained in special schools.

The World Renewal priests (or *fatewenan*) of the Karok, Hupa, and Yurok along the Klamath and Trinity rivers in far northwestern California are quasi-priests who know the ancient formulas established by the Immortals that must be recited every year at a set time, in a specific sequence, to reestablish the world. Tobacco use was and is an important element of the World Renewal ceremony and its priests, as I discuss later.

## Tobacco Priesthoods

The use of tobacco was absolutely essential for the priests and organized priesthoods of the various Aztec deities, as well as for the royalty, warriors, other elites, merchants, and most other inhabitants of the empire. All Aztec priests appear to have ingested tobacco in order to enter into contact with the deities, but one priesthood—that of Cihuacoatl, the earth goddess—stood above all others as a true tobacco priesthood. Cihuacoatl, in fact, was manifested on earth as the tobacco plant. In various of her other aspects she was the mother of the rest of the Aztec gods, the protector of plants and animals, and the patron of midwives and women in labor. Her cult was one of the oldest Aztec priesthoods, most likely having evolved from an earlier tobacco society, and before that from tobacco shamanism.

The rest of this chapter describes six examples of tobacco-based religious organizations in North America. No additional information is presented concerning shamans who do not use tobacco.

## Individual Religious Practitioners and Tobacco: The Navajo Ceremonial System

The Athabaskan-speaking Navajo are relative newcomers to the deserts of the southwestern United States, most of their ancestors having arrived in the San Juan Valley of northwestern New Mexico by about A.D. 1450, if not earlier (Hogan 1989). Prior to that, prehistoric Athabaskans may have lived in northeastern New

Mexico along the Dry Cimarron River and on the nearby Park Plateau (Winter 1986). Even earlier, they migrated south from Canada and Alaska, where many Athabaskan-speaking tribes, such as the Gwitch'in, still live. Because of their relatively recent arrival in a region already inhabited by the Hopi, Zuni, Jemez, and other Pueblo Indians, and because of their intermarriage with these people after the Pueblo Revolt of 1680, their ceremonial system and ideology reflect a combination of ancient, northern, hunting-and-gathering elements, such as an emphasis on individualistic curing, and their Pueblo neighbors' belief in deities and an emergence from a previous underworld.

The Navajo ceremonial system, which is transmitted from singer (curer) to apprentice, is explained and sanctioned by a large body of myths, consisting of a general origin story organized around the events of emergence from the underworld and the origin legends of the various chantway ceremonials that are used to invoke blessings, to cure, and to restore harmony. Tobacco is woven throughout the mythology and the ceremonials. Its critical importance is reflected by the fact that creation itself was brought about when Sky Father and Earth Mother smoked this sacred plant (fig. 25) (Reichard 1950:432). Sky Father needed the smoke to think about the awesome task that lay ahead:

> First Man had already guessed this. "All right, I see, so it is indeed," he said, "there should be tobacco for you!" That is called the wide leaf, the slender leaf, the dark-tipped and the white-tipped. "This will be your tobacco," he told him. "By this token it will become mutually known to us," he told him. "You see, in . . . occasion for sorrow (worry) at any time in your mind, you can smoke it!" (Wyman 1987:349)

Because of its critical role in the creation of the world, tobacco figures prominently in numerous Navajo myths, songs, stories, ceremonies, and activities. All ceremonies require it, most

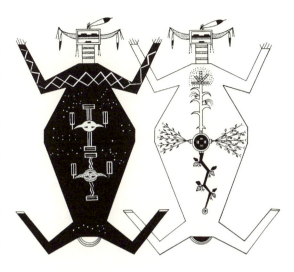

Figure 25. Sky Father and Earth Mother as depicted in Navajo sandpaintings and rugs. The four sacred plants growing on Earth Mother are (clockwise) corn, beans, squash, and tobacco.

prayer sticks contain it, and it is one of the four sacred plants, along with corn, beans, and squash. Tobacco is also a supernatural food—when the *ye'ii* and other deities smoke it, it is a test of their supernatural power. Reed prayer sticks containing tobacco are offered to the deities and then are ritualistically lighted by holding a crystal to the sun. Commonly called "cigarettes," these prayer sticks are filled with mountain tobacco (*N. attenuata*), along with blue, white, yellow, black, and brown mineral paints, bluebird and yellow bird feathers, eagle plumes, and special pollen. *N. palmeri* (*N. trigonophylla*) is also used in the cigarettes (Elmore 1944:102; Kluckhohn and Wyman 1940:29).[2]

Navajo creation mythology and the innumerable stories associated with it are filled with tobacco. Beaver goes to Rainbow for tobacco. Owl trades his aromatic sumac medicine to Monster Slayer for four kinds of tobacco. One of Sun's cherished possessions is his tobacco pouch. His twin sons—Monster Slayer and Born For Water—survive a tobacco smoking test, after which Sun spit upon the ashes in his pipe "and rubbed them on the boys' feet, as he molded their bodies" (Reichard 1950:516).

To help the twins survive their smoking test, Hornworm (sphinx moth caterpillar, also known as tobacco hornworm caterpillar) gives them his special gift:

> "Your father is not an easy one, he kills with his tobacco," he told them. Directly he vomited, which he gave to the one who was first mentioned (Monster Slayer). Again he vomited, which he gave to the second one mentioned (Born for Water). "When he has prepared a smoke for you, you must put this into your mouths, then he cannot kill you with it," he told them. (Wyman 1987:538)

Tobacco was also used by their mother, Changing Woman, to help the twins when they were tested by their father.

> Then their mother, at their home (on Huerfano Mountain), had some tobacco, some kind of tobacco. It was hanging up and it would light up. When it would light it was telling her that her children were in danger. The breeze was what was telling her. And when the tobacco would light up she would put it out, and the Twins would be all right again. (Kelley and Francis 1994:66)

Black God and the other gods and all of the beings in the world also valued tobacco. Black God hummed a tune and tapped his toe when the people gave him a tobacco pouch. "He looked at it, smelled it, reached into the pouch, took out the prayer stick and inspected it more carefully, took out the turquoise pipe and the tobacco, and, by smoking, accepted" (Reichard 1950:507). After a fight with the Ute, both the Navajo and their enemies smoked a peace pipe, embraced, and exchanged gifts. At a Navajo-Hopi peace conference, the delegates made cigarettes their own way, with each Navajo filling a corn husk with mountain tobacco. A tobacco pouch is Black God's and Gila Monster's offering.

Deer Owner has a tobacco pouch with sun and moon figures on it; his pipe has drawings of rare game. Self Teacher smokes as the gods examine his offerings. When Rainboy was a frog he couldn't smoke, lest he fail to resume his proper form.[3]

Tobacco is used in varying amounts in all of the Navajo ceremonials, or chantways. There are several dozen chantways, the most common being Blessingway (to invoke blessings), Enemyway (to exorcise the ghosts and other harmful effects of contact with non-Navajo), Nightway, or *ye'ii bicheii* (to cure head ailments and other sicknesses brought on by contact with the *ye'ii*, or deities), Shootingway (to alleviate troubles caused by thunder, lightning, snakes, and arrows), Mountainway (which deals with bear disease and the effects of other animals living in the mountains), Beautyway (also concerned with snakes as etiological factors), and Windway (for diseases associated with whirlwinds and other winds).

All of the chantways except Blessingway are aimed at appeasing or exorcising the factors that caused a disease or illness, rather than treating the symptoms of the disease itself. Blessingway, in contrast, is used for good luck, to avert misfortune, and to invoke positive blessings, such as for a new house, a job change, the protection of livestock, and aid to a woman in childbirth. Even the *kinaalda*, or girl's adolescence rite, is a special form of the ceremony, and there are many other occasions when a Blessingway is given.

In contrast to full-blown tobacco shamanism, in which a medicine man uses tobacco to enter a trance state so that he can communicate directly with supernatural beings, the Navajo singer and other chantway participants use tobacco and other sacred materials as invocatory offerings to attract the Holy People. If the prayer sticks, smoke medicine, other offerings, songs, sand paintings, and other parts of the ceremonials are correct, the Holy People come to the ceremonial and are obliged to render aid. Throughout the ceremony both the singer and patient are extremely powerful—almost as powerful, in fact, as the Holy People that the singer attracts with offerings and with sand paintings that depict specific deities (Kluckhohn and Wyman 1940:15, 19, 89, 99–100).

Different herbal medicines and types of "tobacco" (both true *Nicotiana* and other plants that are considered to be tobacco) are appropriate for different chants. Many of these medicines have large numbers of plants mixed together—for example, emetics that contain up to 40 different species (Kluckhohn and Wyman 1940:48–49). In the Nightway, Mountain tobacco (*N. attenuata*) is fed to the sacred *ye'ii bicheii* masks, which smoke it: "The masks smoke (*jish badilhilya*), that is, the singer prepares a smoke for them from mountain tobacco (*nat'o wa'i* and *dzil nat'o*), which he blows up and downward four times, following this by blowing the smoke towards each mask" (Franciscan Fathers 1910:389).

Tobacco is common in other Nightway medicines and rituals. Three different types of tobacco were given to Beaver in the story of the Hailway, and smoking transformed Snake and Bear—the ugly old men of the Beautyway—into handsome young men (Reichard 1950:606–607). Snake and Bear were also able to seduce two girls with tobacco in the Enemyway story (Wyman 1987: 61). Throughout the Hailway, tobacco is closely associated with Frog. Smoking a ceremonial pipe occurs in the Rain ceremony, and although few Navajo eat tobacco, unlike the Mesoamerican and California Indians, smoke is still considered a refreshing food. Also, the contents of the Rain ceremony medicine bundle include a tubular pipe with tobacco "from everywhere" (Reichard 1950:606–607, 631–632).

Tobacco smoke is blown as a fumigant in most if not all ceremonials, and in the Plumeway it is used as a special medicine (Wyman and Harris 1941:61). Prayer sticks are "dressed" for animals by "feeding" them with tobacco. Mountain tobacco is also used in the Beadway (Franciscan Fathers 1910:171, 395). *Phragmites* reeds are rubbed with finely ground tobacco

and made into prayer sticks for the Mountainway. *N. palmeri* is sometimes used in filling the ceremonial prayer sticks for the Nightway, whereas commercial tobacco (*N. tabacum*) is occasionally used with *N. attenuata* in the Mountainway (Elmore 1944:28, 74–75, 99). *N. attenuata* is also smoked in the Evilway and is used as a fumigant, with bird feathers, for nosebleeds (Wyman and Harris 1941:73–74, 1951:41). *Nicotiana* is applied externally to cure sores on the hands (Elmore 1944:97).

As one of the four sacred plants, tobacco is a common feature in Blessingway and other chantway sand paintings, such as the one depicted in figure 25. A large tobacco pouch "for pleasant company" is also shown in many of the sand paintings, and Blessingway stories and songs often mention tobacco. In the Blessingway Songs of Earth's Inner Form,

the Earth People sang, and the Mountain Woman People and Water Woman People. And they continued singing all night long without interruption. . . . That done they returned inside where they sat down. At once a smoke was prepared for them.

"Prepare a smoke for them . . . now long ago he had placed it, prepare a smoke for them!
Now earth he has placed, prepare a smoke for them!
Now long life, now happiness he has placed, prepare a smoke for them!" . . .

That done they blew the tobacco in all four directions where it appeared as a fog in which they moved away. Those were the sun's inner form, the moon's inner form, and the inner forms of the mountains that had been made. For these the (smoke) ceremony had been performed (to show respect for the inner forms to be). For these, what was to be dark cloud and dark mist, male rain and female rain, sunray, pollens of dawn and evening twilight, rainbow, all of these were laid down before them, in these they clothed themselves. (Wyman 1987:124–127)

For the Navajo, tobacco symbolism is the very essence of poetry. In the Blessingway story of the mating of corn, where Rock Crystal Talking God gives the procedure for making sacrificial offerings, he asks for choice jewels, hematite, blue and ordinary pollen, tobacco, and a turquoise tobacco pipe. Ever since then, the jewels, hematite, pollen, and tobacco must be present when a Navajo visits the four primary mountains to make his mountain soil bundle. Also, the Blessingway story that explains how Talking God was "placed" (that is, created) states that he was placed with a white buckskin tobacco sack and a crystal doeskin tobacco sack (Wyman 1987:227, 364–365).

The central role of tobacco in the Navajo ceremonial system and in the overall culture was brought home to me in the summer of 1994 when I asked a resident of the Nageezi, New Mexico, area if he knew where any wild tobacco was growing. The man (LN) took me to the site of his grandfather's old homestead along Escavada Wash, where he showed me a large patch of mountain tobacco (*N. attenuata*). The tobacco was growing on his grandfather's former garden at an elevation of 2,070 meters. The grandfather had brought the seeds from the mountains 40 to 50 years earlier and scattered them on the surface of the garden. Now there were hundreds of tobacco plants growing in and around the old garden plot, and despite the very hot, dry summer (102 degrees F at the time of the visit), the plants were thriving, with many of them over 1 meter tall (see photo 4 in chapter 1). LN said that he did not have to water, weed, or prune them, nor did he burn the old plants in the fall. All he did was "take care of them" by visiting them often to make sure that they were all right and no one else had come by to pick their leaves or pull them up. They were very rare in this region, he said, and he was afraid that if given the chance, some people would take them, for the plants were Holy People themselves—they were *diyin*, which are smoked only during ceremonials such as the Blessingway, when the smoke goes back to the spirits and the

spirits give their blessings. His mountain tobacco (*dzil nat'oh*) was also smoked in the curing ceremonials, such as the Nightway and the Beautyway, when the singer blows smoke on the patient and special cigarettes are smoked clockwise around the ceremonial hogan. LN's grandfather was a medicine man, so he used the tobacco in his ceremonials. LN brings his tobacco to ceremonials if asked, but he does not do so every time, because the patient and singer bring their own, if they have any.

LN's brother has his own patch of *N. attenuata* growing from seeds from the grandfather's garden. LN showed me the brother's patch, about a mile from his, where hundreds of small tobacco plants are growing around two structures and in the area between them (photo 64). He could not give me any of the plants, because they belonged to his brother, but LN generously gave me some of his. Both men pick only as many leaves as they need for a year, in August when the plants are mature.

Later LN introduced me to JL, a Navajo herbalist who knows the uses and names of many species of plants, collects them for singers and other traditionalists, and teaches Navajo plant lore to students. JL also has a private patch of mountain tobacco that he had started about six

Photo 64. Patch of young mountain tobacco growing in front of a Navajo hogan. Photo by Joseph Winter. JCWSP5.

years earlier with seeds brought down from the La Plata Mountains to the north, in Colorado. He took us to the patch, where he collected a large bunch of whole plants (see photo 18 in chapter 2), which would last for about a year's worth of ceremonials. He smokes the leaves and flowers, but only for ceremonial purposes, not for recreation or relaxation. He also carries tobacco in his personal medicine pouch, mixed with pollen. He deposited a tiny pinch of the mixture and sang a prayer as we collected other types of plants.

JL's tobacco patch was in an old, filled-in earthen stock tank, so no irrigation or encouragement was necessary, other than the initial broadcast sowing. The patch was in the hills north of Betonnie Tsosie Wash, at an elevation of 2,100 meters, several kilometers from LN's patch. It was very similar to LN's, but neither man knew of the existence of the other's. LN said that you did not have to be a medicine man to bring tobacco to a ceremonial or to use it there. Even commercial tobacco could be used at a ceremonial, since it was from the sacred tobacco plant. He believed the reason people died from cancer and other diseases due to tobacco was that they smoked it for purposes other than those intended by the supernatural beings. Sickness and death resulted from using this powerful and sacred plant for everyday, recreational smoking.

Not everything that the Navajo call tobacco is actually *Nicotiana*. Bighorn tobacco, for example, is *Oxytropis*, which is offered to the Bighorn *ye'ii* in the Nightway. Bear tobacco is *Tribulus maximus*, snake tobacco is *Psoralea tenuiflora*, and eagle tobacco is *Gilia longifolia* (Franciscan Fathers 1910:394–395). LN's aunt showed me a patch of "thin tobacco," which turned out to be brickellbush (*Brickellia oblongifolia*). Sometimes it is called bat's tobacco. Thin tobacco might also be the "narrow-leaved" tobacco in the Hailway story, or perhaps it is the "slender leaf" in the Creation story (Franciscan Fathers 1910:606). Thin tobacco is dried and ground up, then smoked in corn-husk cigarettes, like mountain tobacco. It is also mixed with water and rubbed on a sick person's body. LN's uncle used it in the Beautyway, Windway, and Shootingway. It is also smoked in the Blessingway, Nightway, and Enemyway.

At least 53 non-*Nicotiana* species are called tobacco and/or are explicitly used as tobacco by the Navajo (table 46). Many of these plants are used as tobacco by a certain animal or other being that has religious importance. There is considerable variation among the Navajo names used for these plants; one Navajo might call a particular plant "sheep tobacco" while another calls it "big tobacco" or something else. Conversely, the same name (sheep tobacco) can be applied to several different species, including *Nicotiana attenuata*.

Several versions of a Navajo myth help explain why the animals need tobacco. In one version, Reared-in-the-Mountain knocked out the bears by providing them with Ute tobacco; then he brought them back to consciousness by rubbing them with tobacco ash (Reichard 1950:594). In another version, BearBoy (who appears to be the same as Reared-in-the-Mountain) is given tobacco by one of the People (the Navajo), and he enjoys it. Later, his stepmother, BearMother, sees him smoking and asks:

"What are you doing?" BearMother asked in alarm.

"I am smoking tobacco. It is a sacred herb of The People. They are the only ones who smoke it," he replied.

"Well, you are a bear! Bears must be able to smoke tobacco too," she said.

"Would you like to try some?" BearBoy asked his BearMother.

"Yes," she said, and she took a cautious puff and fell into a faint.

Concerned, BearBoy gathered his few things together, and then stooped down beside his BearMother. He kissed her, and rubbed some tobacco onto her large paws. She woke up quietly. (Santa Fe Natural Tobacco Company 1993)

Table 46: Non-*Nicotiana* Species Called Tobacco and/or Explicitly Used as Tobacco by the Navajo

| Scientific Name | Common Name[a] | Navajo Name |
| --- | --- | --- |
| *Amaranthus graecizans* (*A. albus*) | Pigweed | The ones that lie spreading (*A. blitoides*); heaped grass (*A. retroflexus*) |
| *Antennaria aprica* | Pussytoes | Coyote bed |
| *Apocynum suksdorfii* var. *angustifolium* | Dogbane; Indian hemp | Green frog food or green frog tobacco |
| *Arctostaphylos patula* | Bearberry; manzanita; kinnikinick | Big *dinas*; it rolls up |
| *Artemisia carruthi* | Sagebrush | Corn tobacco |
| *A. tridentata* | Sagebrush | Black coyote tobacco |
| *Aster oblongifolius* | Aster | Sheep tobacco |
| *Astragalus lonchocarpus* | Milkvetch; vetch | Brown crane's tobacco |
| *A. scaposus* (*A. calycosus*) | Milkvetch; vetch | Furry plant |
| *Atriplex* sp.? | Saltbrush | ? (tobacco ingredient) |
| *Baccharis glutinosa* | Groundsel tree | Waterway lotion (Excessway tobacco) |
| *Brickellia oblongifolia* var. *linifolia* | Brickellbush | Bat's tobacco, thin tobacco |
| *Castilleja minor* (*C. affinis*) | Indian paint brush | Smelly tobacco |
| *Chrysothamnus* sp. | Rabbit brush | Yellow on top (a tobacco in Evilway prayer sticks) |
| *Cleome lutea* | Bee-plant | Yellow bee weed |
| *Comandra pallida* | Bastard toadflax | Slim beetle's tobacco |
| *Corydalis aurea* | Corydalis | Raven's tobacco |
| *Cryptantha jamesii* | Borage | Racer's tobacco |
| *Daucus carota* | Carrot | Big Pleiades tobacco |
| *Encelia frutescens* var. *resinosa* | ? | Red-headed red ant tobacco |
| *Epilobium angustifolium* | Willowweed; willow herb | Red blackbird's tobacco |
| *Eriogonum alatum* | Umbrella plant | Earth medicine; knotted medicine |
| *E. divaricatum* | Umbrella plant | Resembling big snake's horns |
| *E. jamesii* | Umbrella plant | Yellow flower; with tobacco |
| *E. umbellatum* | Umbrella plant | Mountain tobacco; horned worm's tobacco |
| *Eurotia* sp.? | Winterfat | Jackrabbit food |
| *Fendlera rupicola* | Fendlerbush | Talking God's tobacco |
| *Gilia longifolia* | Gilia | Eagle tobacco; Blessingway tobacco |
| *Helianthus annuus* | Sunflower | Sun's tobacco |
| *Heuchera parvifolia* | Alumroot | Canyon rat's tobacco; sparkling (spotted) wind's tobacco |
| *Hymenopappus lugens* | ? | Moon's tobacco |
| *Lygodesmia rostrata* | Skeleton plant | Antelope tobacco; Navajo tobacco; alarmed Navajo tobacco |
| *Mentzelia pumila* | Blazingstar | Slender or big tenacious |
| *Mirabilis oxybaphoides* | Four-o'clock | Snake tobacco (part of Beadway tobacco) |
| *Monarda pectinata* | Horsemint; beebalm | Jagged medicine |
| *Oenothera multijuga* | Evening primrose | Lizard's tobacco; waterstrider's tobacco |
| *O. scapoidea* | Evening primrose | Lizard's tobacco |
| *Oxytropis lambertii* | Locoweed | Odiferous crow's tobacco; sheep tobacco; sheep food or sheep tobacco; bighorn tobacco |
| *Parosela lanata* | Indigo bush | Centipede's tobacco |

Table 46: Non-*Nicotiana* Species Called Tobacco and/or Explicitly Used as Tobacco by the Navajo (continued)

| Scientific Name | Common Name[a] | Navajo Name |
|---|---|---|
| Penstemon neomexicanus | Beardtongue | Sheep tobacco |
| P. palmeri | Beardtongue | Talking God's tobacco |
| Portulaca retusa | Purslane | Fringed juniper or juniper basket |
| Psilostrophe sparsifolia | Paperflower | Stick medicine; owl's feet |
| Psoralea tenuiflora | Scurfpea | Tobacco beeweed |
| Rumex fueginus | Dock | Sky tobacco |
| Salix exigua | Willow | Big star's tobacco |
| Salvia lanceaefolia | Sage | Sheep tobacco |
| Senecio neomexicanus | Groundsel | Born for Water's tobacco |
| Silene douglasii | Catchfly, campion | (part of the Bead Chant tobacco); coyote tobacco |
| Solidago canadensis | Goldenrod | Blue lizard's tobacco |
| Sphaeralcea coccinea | Globemallow | Whirling coyote |
| Spirea caespitosa | ? | Pleiades tobacco |
| Stellaria jamesiana | Chickweed; starwort | Big Dipper's tobacco |
| Tribulus terrestris (maximus) | Puncture vine | Bear tobacco, part of Bead Chant tobacco |
| Verbascum thapsus[b] | Mullein | Big tobacco; sheep tobacco |
| Vicia americana | Vetch | Water tobacco; Navajo tobacco |

Sources: Franciscan Fathers 1910; Young and Morgan 1987; Wyman and Harris 1941, 1951; Elmore 1943; Winter 1994b; Roberts et al. 1995; and Matthews 1886.

a   From H. D. Harrington 1964.

b   *Verbascum* is also used by the Hopi as tobacco, as are *Salvia carnosa* and *Onosmodium thurberi*. The latter is even called "sacred tobacco" by the Hopi and is thought to be more effective than native tobacco in bringing rain (Whiting 1939:88, 91).

Bears and other animals want to smoke tobacco, but real tobacco is far too strong, so they smoke other plants instead, such as bear tobacco (*Tribulus*). The Navajo adopted these plants for use in their ceremonies, perhaps because animals figure prominently in the ceremonies. Thus bear tobacco, snake tobacco, eagle tobacco, catchfly, and four-o'clock are mixed together to form Bead Chant tobacco.

As is illustrated by all of this information, tobacco—especially real tobacco but also many wild plants that serve as tobacco for other beings—is used throughout the Navajo ceremonial system to attract the Holy People so that they will come to a ceremonial and offer their blessings. It is also smoked socially a great deal at the ceremonials, as well as on hunting trips for luck and to prevent injuries from bears,

snakes, lightning, "bad deer," and "deer sickness" (Switzer 1969:35; Tschopic 1941:57, 63). The Navajo ceremonial system cannot be classified as tobacco shamanism, because the singers do not ingest it in large enough quantities to enter trances and to have visions. Nevertheless, tobacco is a very important element in Navajo religion, as well as in other facets of Navajo life.

## Deer Person's Gift: Huichol Tobacco Shamanism

The Huichol Indians of west-central Mexico live at the southern end of the Sierra Madre Occidental mountain chain in the states of Zacatecas, Jalisco, and Nayarit. Approximately half of the Huichol (about 8,000 people) still live in their mountainous homeland while another 7,000 live in and around the urban centers of Guadalajara and Tepic (Weigand 1978:102). There are two systems of Huichol tobacco use: the traditional system of cultivating *Nicotiana rustica* and possibly *N. tabacum* in the highlands for religious use, and the seasonal movement of large numbers of Huichol to the lowlands to the west, where they work on commercial tobacco plantations for meager pay. Instead of finding work in the commercial fields, many Huichol "find themselves jobless, homeless, disoriented, exploited, and incapable of solving the problems they encounter" (Valadez 1989:20).

The Huichol raise corn and other crops and have (or had until recently) a heavy dependence on deer hunting. For the most part, they live in small *ranchos* (farmsteads) of 4 or 5 to 50 persons, each *rancho* located about 15 minutes' walk from the next one. The farmsteads are aggregated into larger *rancherías*, which in turn are clustered in five regional and political subdivisions (*comunidades*).

Because of their geographical isolation, the Huichol continue to practice slash-and-burn agriculture and to gather wild and semi-domesticated plants (Bauml 1994:2). Corn, beans, and squash are their main crops, supplemented by melons, chilies, tobacco, and other cultivated plants (Dutton 1962:5–6). Tobacco, chilies, and tomatoes—the usual dry-season produce—are grown in small, hand-irrigated plots rarely larger than a meter square (Weigand 1972:43). Larger tobacco gardens measure a half acre or more, surrounded by brush and rock corrals near the homestead (Bauml 1994:7). Wild tobacco is also gathered.

The Huichol can no longer support themselves entirely by slash-and-burn agriculture. They periodically need cash to buy religious paraphernalia for ceremonies and to pay for transportation to distant shrines, including several along the ocean to the west and others in the sacred desert far to the east, where they gather peyote. Many Huichol therefore leave their homeland temporarily or permanently to work

Photo 65. Huichol Indian child laborer drinking water from a pesticide container in a commercial tobacco field, Nayarit, Mexico. Courtesy of Patricia Díaz-Romo.

in the commercial tobacco fields in the lowlands of Nayarit (photo 65). The tobacco poisoning, pesticide contamination, and other illnesses that occur as a result are discussed in chapter 16.

*Nicotiana rustica* is grown by the Huichol, although it sometimes grows wild in the mountains. Calling it *ye* or *ya* (from the Aztec *yetl*, meaning tobacco), the Huichol plant the seeds in soil containing ash, then top and sucker the plants to produce larger leaves. All of the leaves and stems are smoked, since tobacco is in short supply. Normally they smoke it in corn-husk cigarettes, rarely in pipes (Siegel, Collings, and Diaz 1977:17). Commercial cigarettes are also purchased in town, to be smoked recreationally or to be sold or given to friends and neighbors (Sedlak 1975:15).

The Huichol also grow *Nicotiana tabacum*, at least in the community of San Andrés and in the pueblo of Nueva Colonia (James Bauml, personal communication, 1995; Winter, field notes). I also obtained a sample of *N. tabacum* from a mestizo farmer in Cofradía Acuitapilco, southwest of San Andrés, who reportedly collected it in the mixed Huichol-mestizo *ejido* of Cantilez.

Shamanism is at the heart of Huichol culture and religion, and the shaman is able to communicate with the deities through peyote-induced hallucinations. Shamans also use tobacco to induce visions by violently inhaling and swallowing large quantities of smoke, which results in stupor and intoxication. During ceremonial periods the smoking is carried out almost continuously for up to four days by the shamans and other men. Recreational smoking also occurs, but because of the priority of the need for ceremonial tobacco, its extent is governed by the availability of *N. rustica*.

Peyote is also used to produce visions, but the two plants are generally used together, with the smoking of *N. rustica* "integral to Huichol use of the potent little cactus and its effects on the central nervous system" (Schaefer 1996a:140). There are strong religious links between the two plants—tobacco was created by Deer Person, who turned into peyote—and *N. rustica* is smoked "to 'help one feel the peyote' . . . [and] to reach greater depths in . . . visionary experiences" (Schaefer 1996a:155).

After analyzing specimens of Huichol *N. rustica*, Ronald Siegel, P. R. Collings, and J. L. Diaz found that three samples contained 1.9 percent, 3.9 percent, and 4.0 percent nicotine, respectively, by dry leaf weight. *N. tabacum* cigarettes in the United States average about 2.0 percent nicotine, with a range of 0.43 percent to 3.85 percent, so the Huichol tobacco is considerably higher. In fact, two very special samples of Huichol *N. rustica* were found to contain 12.7 percent and 18.8 percent nicotine, respectively, which are concentrations high enough to produce hallucinations and catatonia (Siegel, Collings, and Diaz 1977:18, 22). I have used Huichol *makuchi* (*N. rustica*) on several occasions and have found that even small doses (one or two puffs) produce mood altering effects that are much stronger than those produced by commercial tobacco.

James Bauml (1994:250) gives the following description of *makuchi*, as told to him by a Huichol: "Es un tabaco, este [es] mas fino, mas fuerte, no es tabaco grande, es chiquito. Se planta donde quiera. Lo usan los caviteros. Lo usan también los chamanes."

The Huichol also smoke *tumutsali* or *yauhtli*, either alone or in a 50 percent mixture with tobacco, for ceremonial and recreational purposes. Identified by Siegel, Collings, and Diaz (1977:19) as *Tagetes lucida* Cav. (marigold), this may have been the *yauhtli* of the Aztec. The Huichol report that it reduces the harshness of tobacco, aids in deep inhalation, and enhances intoxication and visions. While smoking the mixture they frequently ingest peyote and drink tesquino (corn beer), sotol (cactus liquor), and other alcoholic beverages, which also produce intense visions. Even when the other drugs are not used, the Huichol smoke the tobacco-*yauhtli* mixture all night long, as the *mara'akame* (shaman) sings. The shaman also blows tobacco smoke to treat the patient. Sometimes Huichol shamans mix tobacco with bat blood and turtle meat to purify and protect against witchcraft (Siegel, Collings, and Diaz 1977:19–21; Grimes and Hinton 1969:809).

The *mara'akame* communicates with the spirits through tobacco, chants, and prayers and by shaking hawk feathers. The chants account for the origins and functions of the deities, who cause illness when neglected. Illness is also brought about by dead relatives wanting company, by sorcery and the neglect of customs, and by natural causes. The shamans diagnose the sickness by dreaming, chanting, or ingesting peyote; then they treat the patient by blowing tobacco smoke, brushing him with hawk plumes, and sucking small objects from the afflicted part of the body. Follow-up treatment includes a ceremonial pilgrimage, with offerings, to the place where the deities reside (Grimes and Hinton 1969:806–810).

The shaman's chants last for up to three nights, with the *mara'akame* singing to the gods to effect cures and to let rain fall. The shamans guard both the physical and spiritual well-being of the Huichol, nurture the magic in nature, and bring ceremonies and rituals from the world of the spirits to the world of humans. They also act as mediators between the gods and sick humans. They consult their dreams to determine the reasons for the sickness and then use their power objects—including feathered wands and tobacco gourds—to communicate with the spirit world (Valadez 1989:24–25).

The feathered wands, tobacco gourds, other power objects, and peyote are also used to ensure that rain will fall, the sun will shine, night will turn to day, and males and females of all species will live in harmony. The shamans communicate directly with plants and animals, and they use tobacco and other herbal remedies and rituals to protect the health of their families and communities. The shamans and their patients work together to contact the spirits responsible for causing illness, and then the rituals help to send healing white energy that effects the cure (Valadez and Valadez 1992, 1995). Tobacco is also essential for the survival of the deities: along with the blood of sacrificed animals, it feeds the deities and embodies the essential life force (Schaefer and Furst 1996:19). It is the special food of fire, so it belongs to Tatevari, the god of fire (Lemaistre 1996:315).

There are five principal Huichol deities, and tobacco use and symbolism are important to each one. These deities are Grandfather Fire (photo 66), Grandfather Deer-Tail, Grandmother Growth, Sun, and Elder Brother (also known as Deer Person). Other important deities are the God of Wind, the Rain Mothers, and the Mother of the Sea. There was no rain, crops,

or abundance until the first people learned about the peyote cactus living in the land where the sun is born. Peyote visions put the people into contact with Grandfather Deer-Tail and the other deer spirits, who are in contact with the Rain Mothers and the Mother of the Sea. The Huichol perform ceremonies that honor the Rain Mothers (the goddesses of cultivation and fertility) and the other gods and goddesses (Valadez and Valadez 1992, 1995).

The main Huichol deity is Tatevari—Grandfather Fire—who owns tobacco, which was once a hawk (Furst 1972:176). Tatevari is the god of fire and the patron of life and health. After many journeys he settled in Te-akata, where his main temple is located. The temple contains his image, with two tobacco gourds hanging from his left shoulder, thereby identifying him as a shaman or priest. He communicates the will of all of the gods to the shamans at ceremonies (Valadez 1989:19).

Photo 66. Grandfather Fire, in a yarn painting, or *tabla*, by Mariano Valadez. Deer Person, Toad, Kieri Plant, Tobacco, and other sacred beings are also shown in the *tabla*. Photo by Damian Andrus.

Little chairs are made for Grandfather Fire and the other gods to sit on at feasts, when the gods are brought into the presence of the people. The fire god's chair has two small tobacco gourds attached to it, one for luck in raising gourds and the other for luck in hunting deer (Lumholtz 1902, 2:31, 115, 169).

Most Huichol *rancherías* have their own *xiriki* (temples), where offerings are made to the deities for the souls of the dead. The temples contain gourds of sacred water collected on the annual peyote pilgrimage, as well as gourds for *ye*, the tobacco of the fire god (Furst 1968:35).

Tatusi—Grandfather Deer-Tail—is the second god of fire and the brother and son of Grandfather Fire. He assumes the form of a deer, and he owns the white-tailed hawk. The two other primary male deities are Sun and Elder Brother (Deer Person), the god of deer, peyote, and hunters (Dutton 1962:14).

The main goddess is Tacutsi Nacave—Grandmother Growth, Mother God, Our Grandmother, or Our Great-Grandmother—the mother of the gods. All of the earth and vegetation belongs to her. She is also known as Corn Mother or Earth Mother and is often shown in Huichol yarn paintings smoking a cigarette or cigar and wearing a tobacco gourd (Dutton 1962:16). She is considered the oldest of the deities, the original creator and owner of the world and all its creatures, the first shamanness, "The One Who Came First" (Noble 1989:53–54). Plants and animals were created when she fell from a cliff. She is the embodiment of germination and is necessary for maize cultivation (Bauml 1994:6).

The Huichol worship corn, deer, and peyote, which they consider one and the same. Corn was once deer, and deer were formerly the main food of the Huichol. The deer god left peyote in his tracks the first time he appeared in the country where peyote now grows. Afterward he became a big peyote plant. Corn was also once peyote, so all three are the same: corn is deer, peyote is deer, corn is peyote (Sedlak 1975:21). Tobacco is also sacred, because of its association with deer and its role as a food for the gods.

Because of the importance of the sacred quartet of corn, deer, peyote, and tobacco, each Huichol temple sends pilgrims every winter to the sacred peyote region, where the small cactus grows in the deer god's tracks. Tobacco and corn are essential aspects of the pilgrimage. Indeed, the first pilgrimage was a hunt for deer, and it was during this journey that the tracks became peyote, which the Huichol use to induce dreams and visions, to keep awake during ceremonies and long trips, and as medicine (Grimes and Hinton 1969:811). Tobacco ingestion and offerings are essential elements of the peyote pilgrimage, as well as of the resulting peyote feast and Parching of the Maize feast. Peyote has to be procured each year, in order to avoid drought. In October, parties consisting of 2 to 12 people from each temple district go on the pilgrimage to Viricuta, near Real de Catorce in San Luis Potosí. The peyote seekers carry *Nicotiana rustica* in small gourds with corncob stoppers. Sometimes as many as five gourds may hang from a pilgrim's shoulders, although some are empty.[4]

The pilgrims' tobacco gourds are directly associated with deer. The wartier a gourd, the greater its value, but smooth gourds covered with deer scrotum skin are sometimes used (Schaefer 1996a:154). Both types are also worn in deer hunts and are symbolic of deer in ceremonies. After a man returns from a peyote pilgrimage, he can wear a tobacco gourd anytime. The Huichol believe that the tobacco gourds are mythologically alive. Each tobacco gourd is a serpent—a messenger of fire. After the world was put in shape, the serpent remained as the tobacco gourd, so whenever its stopper is removed, the hiss of a snake can be heard.

Small tobacco gourds are also attached to arrows and chairs and generally express prayers for luck in hunting. A gourd may reflect a woman's desire that her son will become a shaman (Dutton 1962:42–43). Also, children sometimes wear small pouches of tobacco for protection against the dead and bad spirits (Bauml 1994:9).

A special bag woven to hold the first *makuchi* of the year is carried on the peyote pilgrimage. This bag, or *wainuri*, contains the "spiritual essence, the heart-memory, of the Huichol gods. *Makutse* is considered part of Tatewari, Grandfather Fire. According to some Huichols, the tobacco bag is the single most important ritual item carried on the pilgrimage to guide the pilgrims" (Schaefer 1996a:154).[5] Because the tobacco serves as a guide, it is carried in the first line of pilgrims, and it is the first gift to Grandfather Fire at every stopping place.

The leader of each temple's annual peyote pilgrimage also carries the *yakwai*, a ball of native-grown tobacco. After a certain place is passed on the journey, the tobacco is ritually distributed, with ceremonial arrows placed toward the four quarters of the world. The tobacco ball is set on the ground, and the leader then touches it with plumes and prays. Next he wraps small portions of it in corn husks and gives one to each pilgrim, who puts it in his tobacco gourd. This symbolizes the birth of tobacco. From here on in the pilgrimage a strict order of march is followed, and all of the tobacco gourds are handled very carefully. If a Mexican on horseback gets ahead of the party, he and his horse will drop to the ground, owing to the wrath of the sacred tobacco as the arrow of the fire god is aroused.

Because of the power of the *yakwai*, the men generally remain in the temple when they return from the journey. Women must never touch the tobacco or the tobacco gourds, lest they fall ill. At the peyote feast, the little sacred bundles of tobacco are given back to the fire god—they are burned—and the pilgrim ceases to be a prisoner (Lumholtz 1902, 2:130–132).

Tobacco's central role in Huichol religious life was revealed to me by a Huichol shaman as he examined six different specimens of dried and pressed tobacco I had collected. The shaman recognized *Nicotiana rustica* as *makuchi*, which is also the term for tobacco used in the Tarahumara country to the north (Nabhan 1979a: 261; Pennington 1953:68). Then the shaman

told how tobacco was created and how it is used:

*Makuchi* is a very powerful tobacco used in the Deer ceremony. It is also made into amulets and carried in tobacco gourds in the peyote pilgrimage. There was a time when there was no tobacco, when Deer was a person. Deer Person came from the sea and went to the peyote desert with very powerful shaman's objects. He had a bow and arrows, a gourd bowl, bracelets, and other objects. Half-way between the sea and peyote desert, he saw the Kieri Person.

The Deer Person placed all of his shaman's objects on the ground; then he left. The Kieri Person took them and hid them. When the Deer Person returned, he said, "My things were here, you took them."

"No," said the Kieri Person, "I didn't take them. Here they are."

Then the Deer Person saw flowers, clouds, and trees—the Kieri Person had turned his power objects into these things. The good energy came out of the power objects, so the Kieri Person could use it to turn them into beautiful things.

Deer Person went on to the place of origin where Blue Corn was baptized. He saw two beautiful Deer Girls there, and he shot arrows at them. They took the arrows out of their bodies. There was a lake there, so he asked, "Should we take a swim?"

Then the Deer Person and the Deer Girls took off their clothes and went into the lake. The girls said, "If you make love to us, we will give you your arrows back."

Deer Person needed the arrows to take to the peyote desert. Well, you know how people are, they fooled around, and as he made love with them some of his seed fell on the ground. A beautiful plant grew where his seed fell. The plant was *makuchi*.

When the Deer Person looked at the plant, he noticed a little animal eating it. When the animal left, he followed it into its cave, where he saw that it was a toad. When he hit the toad, seeds came out of its skin, which produced a powerful medicine for visions. The seeds grew into gourd plants, with the gourds used to hold tobacco on the peyote pilgrimage.

The Deer Person put some tobacco in a gourd; then he went on to the peyote desert with the gourd and his arrows. At a certain place he came to the home of Grandfather Fire and the Sun, where there was a corn plant and a *comal* [stone griddle]. He cured the tobacco on the *comal*, and he tied some of it in a corn leaf, which he put into his gourd.

Then he went on to the place of the sacred water. He also went to a location where he placed the sacred arrows. More tobacco was put into a corn leaf, which was placed in his gourd.

Finally he arrived at the peyote desert. There he left his power objects—of the eagle, the mother of the sun, the virgin, fire, and the other gods. He placed them out in the peyote desert.

So that is how the Deer Person taught the Huichol people how to use tobacco. It grew from his seed. A toad took it to its cave, where seeds of the tobacco gourd came out of the toad's skin when Deer Person hit him.

Now whenever someone wants to be a shaman, they do the same thing—they travel to the peyote desert with power objects including tobacco gourds, they put tobacco wrapped in corn leaves in the gourds, they leave their arrows at a certain spot, and they place the power objects in the peyote desert. They also feed tobacco to the fire at the end of the peyote feast, after they return from the pilgrimage.

People also put tobacco in a corn leaf in their mouths when they want to hunt deer. When they find a deer, they place the tobacco and corn leaf back in their gourds. They also put their power objects out on the ground.[6]

The shaman went on to say that he puts tobacco in his mouth when he hunts the deer and peyote. He explained that tobacco is a symbol of purity. When you are on the shaman's path, you are very attractive to women, but you must remain faithful and pure.

Shamans use *makuchi* for both good and evil. It can be used in witchcraft. The Huichol grow it by throwing the seeds on the ground where goats have been kept. The goat manure fertilizes the ground so that the tobacco grows well. *N. rustica* also grows wild. The Huichol cut the leaves and put them in a piece of cloth to dry. Then they mix the leaves with the yellow, vision-producing flowers of *Solandra*, the Kieri Person.

With their rich ethnobotanical knowledge, Huichol shamans are at the core of a vast religious and medical system that depends on a wide range of wild and domesticated plants. Tobacco, corn, peyote, *Solandra*, datura, and marigolds are the main plants in this system, but there are many other gifts of the gods that sustain the Huichol and their tobacco-based shamanism.

## Religious Societies Using Tobacco: The Haudenosaunee Company Of False Faces

The Iroquois-speaking Indians of the eastern woodlands are an excellent example of how Native Americans have formed medicine societies composed of ordinary men and women who have been given the power to cure the sick, and how tobacco use is a basic ingredient of the societies' ideologies and methods. Numbering about 20,000 people in New York State, Quebec, and Ontario, the Seneca, Cayuga, Onondaga, Oneida, and Mohawk of the Haudenosaunee, or Five Nations, use native-grown *Nicotiana rustica* in practically every part of their religious, social, and political lives. They also believe that tobacco sprang from the grave of the Earth Mother (fig. 26), who died after giving birth to the twins Good-Minded (the Great Creator) and Evil-Minded (the Great World Rim Dweller). Corn, beans, and squash also grew from her grave. The tobacco (*o-yeh-qua-a-weh*, "the only tobacco" [Tooker 1994:105, 133]) grew from

Figure 26. The first tobacco grew from the grave of Sky Woman's daughter. Illustration by Daniel Burgevin from a story in Bruchac 1985.

her head, so that "it soothes the mind and sobers thought" (A. Parker 1910:36–37).

The Haudenosaunee also have shamans who are called in when all else fails, but the basis of their medical and religious system is the medicine societies, which are composed of all men and women who have been cured by a particular society or who have dreamed about joining one. The powers of the societies and the justification for their existence lie in the compact or covenant agreed upon between man and god, in which humans promised to offer prayers, tobacco, and songs to the supernatural beings in return for the power to cure.

The major society is the Company of False Faces, an organization that traces its origin to the Iroquois creation story, the birth of the twins, and the Great World Rim Dweller's addiction to tobacco. In the beginning, before there was the earth, there was only sky, filled with living plants and animals and manlike beings who were never sick. There was a family with five sons in the sky world. The youngest son was so much in love with a young woman that he became weak. Even after marrying her he was weak, but then he dreamed that his brothers could cure him by pulling up the Tree-That-Is-Called-Tooth. They did so, and the young couple sat beside the hole where the tree used to grow, until she was impregnated by air coming up out of the hole. Then her husband pushed her through the hole in the sky, and she fell, but birds caught her and placed her on the back of a great turtle, which carried her and the birds as they rested. Finally the birds brought mud from the bottom of the sky ocean to create the earth on the turtle's back.

Soon the woman gave birth to a girl, who eventually grew up to become the Earth Mother. When she was young, the girl wanted to play in the water. Her mother forbade her to do so, but she went into the water anyway, thereby conceiving and later giving birth to the twins—the evil twin Tawiskaron and his brother Tarachiawagon, the good spirit. The good spirit filled the earth with men and women, animals, vege-tation, rain, rivers and streams, and all of the rest of the good things of creation, except for corn, squash, beans, and tobacco, which later grew from his mother's grave. When he finished with creation he went on a tour of the world, but his evil twin followed him, making monsters, owls, snakes, waterfalls, corn blight, diseases, storms, and other evil things.

At the end of his tour, far to the west, the good spirit met his twin on the rocky rim of the world. The evil twin was now in the form of a giant—Shagadyoweh—who argued with his brother over who was responsible for creation. Finally they agreed to settle the dispute by a contest of magical power. Each would try to move the Rocky Mountains. The good spirit won, moving the mountains so close that when the giant turned around, he bashed his nose against the side of a mountain.

So the giant submitted, begging his brother to allow him to live. His brother granted the request, so long as the giant agreed to help the Haudenosaunee people by taking them as his grandchildren. The giant responded that if the people would wear masks representing him and burn tobacco for him and give him a little corn mush, he would give them power, through the masks, to drive away diseases, witches, and high winds (Wallace 1972).

There are several types of False Face masks that represent Shagadyoweh, the Great World Rim Dweller, and the other gods standing behind him—including the Four Brothers Who Control the Winds, the Evil Twin, and the Whirlwind Spirit. There are also common masks, which represent a whole legion of quasi-human forest spirits who visit lonely hunters, begging them for tobacco and food. Their appearance brings illness or possession unless the hunter feeds them tobacco and corn, in which case they bring good luck. The False Faces are therefore the many faces of the gods, and tobacco and corn are their only food (Wallace 1972:86–92).

This somewhat detailed summary of the Iroquois creation story demonstrates how a religious society differs from a shaman or other individual practitioner. Both are able to cure, but the individual practitioner's power comes from his personal relationship with the supernatural, or at least from his knowledge of how to contact the supernatural and offer it tobacco, prayers, and other things. The society's collective power, in contrast, comes from a covenant previously reached with a deity, in which the ability to cure is bestowed on the society as a whole in return for tobacco, the use of ritual equipment, and the recitation of special songs and prayers. Both types of curing power—as well as the medical abilities of the more complex priesthoods—rest upon the use of tobacco as a food of the gods.

The Faces of the Gods (the False Faces) perform at the Midwinter and Green Corn ceremonies. They also drive out diseases and witches in the spring and fall, and they cure illness in private at any time of the year. All of their curing ceremonies and public dances begin with a tobacco invocation, during which tobacco is burned as an offering and the faces are asked to protect the people and cure them when necessary:

> Partake of this sacred tobacco, O mighty Shagodyoweh, you who live at the rim of the earth, who stand towering, you who travel everywhere on the earth caring for the people.
>
> And you, too, whose faces are against the trees in the forests, whom we call the company of faces; you also receive tobacco.
> . . .
> So now your mud-turtle rattle receives tobacco.
> (Here the Faces scrape their rattles on the floor in delight.)
> And now another thing receives tobacco, your staff, a tall pine with the branches lopped off at the top. (Wallace 1972:82–83)

The Midwinter ceremony is the major Iroquois festival, held in January or February to mark the beginning of the year, whereas the Green Corn ceremony is held in late August or September. Both include the appearance of the False Faces, who beg and grovel for tobacco, then dance and cure the sick in return for gifts of this precious plant. They also cure the sick and drive away witches, high winds, and ill luck in the spring and fall, when a great company of dancing, cavorting faces moves through the sacred tobacco patches (see fig. 1 in chapter 2) and then from house to house, exorcising evil and illness, imploring the gods behind the faces to protect the people, and receiving in return *Nicotiana rustica*, which is later burned in their longhouse while the tobacco invocation is given. The False Faces can actually smell the sacred tobacco smoke. Many people in the society have the power to lay their hands on the piles of burning tobacco; then they raise their hands to their masks, so that the masks can better smell the smoke (Fenton 1987:315).

The wooden False Face masks are continually anointed with tobacco from the moment of their creation until the time that they are buried. New masks are carved from living basswood or other soft-wooded trees when a new member of the society needs a mask, when a member dreams that he needs another one, or when an exceptional event or a great calamity, such as a plague, threatens the Iroquois and a special Living Mask is carved. The first thing a carver does, after he selects a tree, is to burn tobacco at its base while reciting the Shagodyoweh tobacco invocation. The mask will never break if the tobacco is burned and the tree is asked to give its life.

Then the mask is carved in the tree. The completed mask is a living likeness and deputy of the Great False Face—Shagodyoweh—who is supplicated at the new mask's baptism by the burning of powdered tobacco. The mask is now alive, capable of great good or evil, and supernatural power to cure disease is conferred upon the person wearing it, so long as he fulfills the covenant (Fenton 1937, 1987; Keppler 1941; Wallace 1972).

Tobacco is required to sustain the mask's power throughout its life. A little bag of tobacco is tied inside the mask, because the faces love and crave the native *Nicotiana rustica*. If the mask falls or even if the owner merely dreams of it falling, tobacco must be burned as an offering. If the mask is going to be sold or otherwise transferred to a new owner, it must be assured that the new owner will continue to feed, anoint, and supply it with tobacco. False Faces are rarely neglected, since an unhappy mask will cause illness or even death. Neglected, improperly treated, or mocked masks must have tobacco burned for them, to propitiate the faces and bring back the power of the mask. Also, another small bag of tobacco is tied to it, to ensure its future power and goodwill.

There are several other kinds of sacred Haudenosaunee masks, and other medicine societies that wear them. Husk-Face masks, for example, represent another class of earth-bound supernatural beings who formed a pact with humans and taught them how to hunt and raise crops in return for tobacco. The Husk-Faces are a race of farmers living on the far side of the earth, in a ravine where they till their fields. They are messengers of the three sisters—corn, squash, and beans—with great powers of prophecy, which they bring with them when they visit the Iroquois during the Midwinter ceremony. They also love tobacco and have their own tobacco invocation, medicine song, and curing dance. Two special Husk-Faces appear as doorkeepers of the False Faces during the spring and autumn exorcisms of disease, witchcraft, and stormy weather. No one is supposed to leave the longhouse when the False Faces are burning the tobacco given to them by individual householders, but the two doorkeeper Husk-Faces can be bribed with a pinch of tobacco (Fenton 1937).

There are also Beggar and Thief masks, miniature masks, and Society of Mystic Animal masks. The Beggar and Thief masks are regular False Faces worn by boys who dance comically at public festivals while chanting "hooo hooo hooo" and begging for tobacco. They steal food if tobacco is not given to them (Keppler 1941).

Miniature masks are replicas of all of the larger types of masks—the Great Rim of the World Dweller masks and the common masks. They are kept as personal charms or hung on the larger masks so that they can "ride along" in the ceremony. Society of Mystic Animal members have very special, secret masks (Fenton 1941).

There are also a number of Iroquois medicine societies whose members do not wear masks but who still have tobacco invocations and curing rites. The same general pattern occurs at their public and private ceremonies, with tobacco invocations forming the opening rites. People join different societies depending on their dreams, just as different types of dreams call for different societies' curing rites. Some of these other societies are the Dew Eagle society, the Little Water Company, the Pygmy society, and the Society of Otters.

The Eagle Dance of the Dew Eagle society, for example, is filled with tobacco imagery and actions (Fenton 1953). The society's membership is composed of followers of the Handsome Lake religion. Handsome Lake, a Seneca prophet in the early part of the nineteenth century, sought to eliminate the medicine societies and Iroquois ceremonial system and replace it with a new religion. He claimed to have received a revelation from the Creator, ordering that the various societies should have a final meeting to throw tobacco in their ceremonial fires and then disband. Those who feared Handsome Lake or were friendly to him decided to disband the societies, but they failed to cast tobacco in the fires. Rival leaders—especially Cornplanter and Blacksnake—argued that the old order was still intact, because the tobacco had not been burned as required by the Creator. The societies therefore continued to hold meetings in secret. After tensions subsided, the societies began to appear again at the annual festivals. Then gradually they assimilated the adherents of the new religion, including those who formed the Dew Eagle society.

This society meets whenever anyone who is ill requests its ministrations. The members meet and perform the Eagle Dance, which cures the patient. *Nicotiana rustica* is burned during the invocation, and 12 packages of chewing tobacco are given to the dancers. The native tobacco is offered to the Dew Eagles, who were given the power to heal by the Great Spirit. The Dew Eagles expect that tobacco will be given to them, because the fumes of the burning tobacco carry aloft their prayers and songs (which they taught to the people). Then the dancers perform, speakers tell how the birds can be reached with tobacco, and the patient is cured if he has the proper dreams. Tobacco is burned throughout the ceremony, including no fewer than 13 times in the invocation alone. Tobacco also figures prominently in the society's origin story.

And there are many other Iroquois uses of tobacco and beliefs in its potency and sacred origin. The Seneca's name for tobacco—"the only tobacco"—refers to the fact that they consider it superior to all other types. They use it only for smoking (not chewing), and they mix it with sumac to "diminish its stimulating properties" (Tooker 1994:189). An Onondaga man whom I interviewed believes not only that Iroquois tobacco is superior to all other types but that tobacco was created for the Iroquois and spread from central New York to all other Indian tribes.

The Seneca raise their tobacco from seeds planted in the spring. It ripens early, and then the leaves are picked and dried. The following year it grows spontaneously from the plant's seeds, but it has to be thinned after a few years because it grows too thick and the leaves become small (Tooker 1994:134).

Some Iroquois pick the leaves only when a thunderstorm approaches. Otherwise the tobacco is inferior and less acceptable to the False Faces, Dew Eagles, and other supernatural beings. When properly picked, the tobacco writhes and wriggles when cast on the coals of a fire, as if it is alive, as the smoke swirls upward with its message of thanks.

Native tobacco is an indispensable part of all Iroquois ceremonies. It is much more valuable than commercial tobacco and is highly valued

in gambling. Sometimes it is used in sorcery, as when a False Face society member uses it to make someone's mouth twist up like the face on a mask. Other people use it to make Heno (the thunder being) shoot his bolts of lightning where and when they want him to. If a man's wife leaves him, he can smoke his pipe, puff the smoke in the direction she went, and cause her to return (Skinner 1925a).

Tobacco binds ceremonial friends together. Bear Dancers smoke it, Little Water Medicine society members smoke it, and the Society of Charmed Animals uses it. Tobacco is offered to herbs before they are collected. Later they give tobacco back to the collector, who prays for them (Fenton 1949:235).

William Fenton (1937, 1978, 1987) has presented many other facts about Iroquois uses of tobacco, especially in the False Face society. His 1987 book, *False Faces of the Iroquois*, is an excellent source of information about the relationship of the False Faces to the plant they crave.

## The Crow Tobacco Society

Most Native American medicine societies depend upon tobacco, but some are so dedicated to its growth and worship that their members revere it as a deity whose existence is essential for the survival of the tribe. The Crow, Siksika (Blackfoot), and Tsuu T'ina (Sarsi) still have tobacco societies, the Hidatsa once had one, and the Mandan and Arikara may have had them. For the Crow, *Nicotiana quadrivalvis* var. *multivalvis* ("short tobacco") is so sacred that they do not smoke it—not even in ceremonies—but only dance with it in tobacco society ceremonies and plant and raise it in a seasonal cycle (photo 67). For ceremonial and other smoking, they raise "tall tobacco" (*N. quadrivalvis* var. *quadrivalvis*) or obtain it in trade from the Hidatsa. The Crow used both varieties of this very special tobacco until at least 1931 (Lowie 1920: 274, 1935:xvi), and it is assumed that they still do so today.

Photo 67. Crow Indian tobacco garden with young plants, digging sticks, and fence. The men are members of the Crow tobacco society, and the plants are probably *Nicotiana quadrivalvis* var. *multivalvis*. Courtesy of the Department of Library Services, American Museum of Natural History, negative no. 338432. From Lowie 1920.

Prior to the imposition of farming during the reservation period, the Crow were nomadic buffalo hunters, and their only cultivated crops were their two varieties of sacred tobacco. Originally they roamed over the Yellowstone and Bighorn country, all the way to the Rocky Mountains and the headwaters of the Cheyenne River. They speak a Siouan language, as do the Hidatsa; the languages of the two tribes are so similar that they were probably a single people until about 500 years ago (Lowie 1935:3–4). As explained in the Hidatsa origin story presented in chapter 2, the group that became the Crow took the tobacco society with them when they split off from the Hidatsa, leaving the latter tribe without any tobacco society members.

The basis of both Crow religion and the tobacco society is the individual vision quest. There are a few shamans among the Crow, but most people communicate directly with the supernatural through visions. In response to almost any need—from a major catastrophe to a desire for luck—a Crow will go on a vision quest, fasting and going without water and sometimes cutting off a finger, which is offered to the Sun, the most important supernatural being. The only tobacco that can be grown in the arid high plains is *N. quadrivalvis*, which is very low in nicotine, so self-torture is used to induce hallucinations, which are interpreted as visions. The Sun, Buffalo, snakes, chicken hawks, thunderbirds, tobacco, dwarfs, mystical men and women, and many other supernatural apparitions appear in the visions, to bestow songs, prayers, medicine, and other favors on the visionary. The medicine consists of feathers, rocks, tobacco, weasels, or any other living or inanimate object that can be used for power— even buffalo dung. A few men have such outstanding visionary powers that they become shamans who then use their medicine to cure the sick. Some visionaries can work minor miracles, such as turning bark into tobacco (Lowie 1935:238).[7]

Next to the Sun, Tobacco is the most important supernatural being, and the tobacco plant serves as the most distinctive medicine, one that is mystically identified with the stars. In the Hidatsa creation story, First Creator was alone until he met Lone Man, who carried a pipe but did not know what to do with it. First Creator therefore made Male Buffalo and ordered him to make Tobacco.

In the Crow version of the same story, First Creator (Transformer) walks about the newly made earth with his companions until he notices a man who "is one of the Stars above. He is down here now and standing on the ground. Come on, let us look at him." When they approach him, he turns into Tobacco, the first growing plant. Transformer decrees that the Crow must plant it and dance with it, so that it will be their "means of living." Then the Sun adopts a poor fasting boy and starts the Tobacco Order. The boy adopts novices, who adopt still other novices, right up until the time of the anthropologist Robert Lowie's visits in the 1920s. Only initiates into the *bacu'sua* ("soaking"— tobacco society) were allowed to grow this plant.

Tobacco is always identified with the stars— sometimes with Morning Star, also known as Old Woman's Grandson. Each individual knows a slightly different version of the creation story, but they all involve stars turning into tobacco, the adoption of a novice, and the creation of the tobacco society. Whatever the version, the Crow origin story involves the creation of tobacco, as well as of the tobacco society and its mystical ceremonies, which are essential for the survival of the Crow people. The "short" variety of tobacco, in fact, is so powerful that it cannot be smoked—simply that it exists is enough to sustain the Crow. After the plants are gathered and dried, the seeds are kept for the next year's planting, and the stems and leaves are cast as offerings in the river.

Tobacco and the tobacco society are often identified with warfare and buffalo hunting. As S. C. Simms described it in 1904, the cured meat of a special cow buffalo killed at the beginning of winter is eaten at the tobacco planting, which occurs as soon as the chokecherry trees begin to blossom in late May. Today beef is eaten, but ritualistic references to warfare are still present, or at least they were until 1931, the year of Lowie's final visit.

Visions of tobacco and dreams during the Tobacco ceremony are very important aspects of Crow culture. Success in war, hunting, working, and life in general result from visions, in contrast to failure, which is ascribed to a lack of them. Some men never have visions, but they can still dream. Members of the tobacco society frequently have both visions and dreams about tobacco, hearing it sing and learning its songs. Sleeping in the tobacco patch after its planting is an especially good way to receive new tobacco songs, as well as dreams of an abundant harvest. One man received a new tobacco song in a vision at the garden: "I once lay at the garden for three days and nights. I . . . saw a man singing this song and going through different movements, and I now [1911] dance with it. 'I am Tobacco [I sing]. My body all over is Tobacco'" (Lowie 1920:170).

Examples of other tobacco songs include the following (Lowie 1920:114, 179, 184, 191):

Tobacco I'll take out.
These I'll paint. Tobacco I raise.
Thank you very much, our Tobacco
    grows.
The Planter where is he? The Planter
    am I.
All the Tobacco plants are walking,
    towards the mountains they are
    walking.
I, the Tobacco, am a person, look at
    me. I, I am the Tobacco, I am the
    medicine-rock, look at it.
I am trying to raise Tobacco. It is mine,
    there is plenty, it is said. It is
    growing well, it is said. It is mine,
    there is plenty, it is said.
As it grows, it makes them dance,
    when it has grown it makes them

dance. Now it is glad, it makes them dance.

For the Crow and other Plains tribes with tobacco societies, tobacco is a mystical, sentient being with magical powers. Through dreams and visions, it grants powers of enormous significance. Some visions include *batsira'pe*—mystical animals, plants, or inanimate objects that enter and dwell within a person's body. Later they emerge when properly stimulated, such as at a Tobacco ceremony. Yellow tobacco entered one man in a dream. He was already in the tobacco society, so he started a new chapter. An egg entered another man in a dream and always emerged at a certain song in the Tobacco Dance. After a gray horse entered her stomach in a vision, one woman was able to cure horses with urinary problems by chewing tobacco and then putting it in the horse's mouth.

Tobacco is planted on behalf of the whole tribe. Crow who are not members of the tobacco society cannot plant it, but they nevertheless benefit from it and can fulfill vows by erecting a miniature sweatlodge for the Sun at the garden. Tobacco conferred luck on war parties; as prayers the warriors sang tobacco songs that they had heard. Nonmembers can also have visions and dreams of tobacco, as in the case of one man who saw an old man singing: "Tobacco I am calling; Tobacco is growing; Tobacco is growing stronger" (Lowie 1920:192).

Dreams or visions of tobacco are also signs that nonmembers should join the tobacco society or that members should form new chapters of the society. Each visionary member adopts new members—often husbands and wives serve together as a single member—who participate in the blessings, pay a large initiation fee, and in turn are empowered to have their own tobacco visions, adopt their own novices, and sometimes form their own chapters. Some people ask to join because of a vow or because they or one of their relatives was cured of an illness by the society. Rather than remaining so many individuals enjoying the fruits of membership, the society is a collective whole that is greater than the sum of its parts. It plants and sustains this most sacred of substances for the benefit of everyone in the tribe.

Lowie recorded the names of approximately 30 tobacco society chapters, though relatively few were in existence at any one time. One of the more popular was the Strawberry chapter, founded in the following fashion:

When Medicine-crow was still a young man, he fasted and prayed for four days on the west bank of the Yellowstone, near the Old Agency. He cut off a finger joint and offered it to the Sun. "Sun, look at me, I am poor. I wish to own horses. Make me wealthy. This is why I give you my little finger." The blood poured down. He fell dead. Towards dawn he saw a young man and a young woman coming from the west. They stood before him and said, "We have seen that you are a poor man, and we have come to see what we can do for you." Each held in one hand a hoop, which was decorated with feathers painted red, and in the other hand a hoop of strawberries. Looking more closely, Medicine-crow saw that each also had a Tobacco "cherry" and a strawberry tied to the back of the head, as well as the entire body of a redheaded woodpecker. The woman said, "We have come here to let him hear something." Medicine-crow said to himself, "I wonder what it is that they wish to show me." The young man went to the other side of the ridge, but soon reappeared with a herd of horses. He drove them up to Medicine-crow. The young woman said, "Wait, I will go and bring some too." She went over the hill, and returned with a fairly large herd of horses. She said, "My child, I have shown you a good thing." Both said, "We have shown you twenty head of horses." These two young people were the Tobacco plant itself; they wore wreaths around the head. It said, "I have shown you these horses. I am the Tobacco. I want you to join the Tobacco with these crowns. (Lowie 1920:117)

Another chapter, the Weasels, had only a few members at the time of Lowie's visits. One of them fasted in the mountains until a weasel entered his stomach. It said, "This is what we want to give you," and it sang a song: "The weasels are coming out; Tobacco to come out I shall cause" (Lowie 1920:122).

The various tobacco society chapters differ slightly in dress, songs, and other features. For example, people of the Yellow Tobacco chapter use some different ingredients when mixing the seed for planting, and they used to wear yellow shirts in battle. They also wear yellow clothing while dancing in the Tobacco ceremony and hold sticks with yellow handkerchiefs and small tobacco bags attached to them, with eagle plumes on the bags. One member of the chapter was able to dream about the yellow tobacco in any place, indoors or outdoors, day or night. In his dreams he heard the tobacco sing.

Membership in the society and the right to raise tobacco can be achieved only through adoption by a current member. The adopter forms a parent-child relationship with the novice that is extended to all facets of life and to all other society members (for example, the adopter's "father" becomes the adoptee's "grandfather"). Husbands and wives are usually adopted by the same person at the same time, as a single person. Women play a prominent role throughout the tobacco society.

Some novices are induced to join by large gifts. The initiation fees they pay—such as the fee of 33 horses that one man paid to join a chapter—more than make up for the gifts. Because of the tobacco society's importance, most tribal members in the early part of the twentieth century were members of one or more chapters.

One of the most important aspects of the tobacco society is the cycle of planting ceremonies, which has five stages: mixing of the seeds; procession to the garden; planting the seeds and performing rituals at the garden; inspection of the growing plants; and harvesting the crop. The Mixers are the most important officers of the society, because only they can prepare the seeds for planting by mixing them with eight different kinds of flowers and roots, along with elk, deer, or buffalo dung (cow dung in recent times), water, dirt from a mole hill, and other ingredients called for in dreams. The name of the tobacco society—*bacu'sua*, or soaking—is derived from the soaking of the seeds and other ingredients in water. Usually the mixing privelege is achieved through dreams, along with the location chosen for the garden, but like almost every other facet of the society, both can also be purchased.

When the time for planting approaches, everyone in the tribe moves camp closer to the site of the garden. A feast is held, and a tobacco chant is sung four times (Simms 1904:331–335):

> I am going to plant Tobacco,
> There will be plenty,
> Come and see the Tobacco.

Then the members of the society turn their seeds over to the Mixers in each chapter, who are paid to mix them. Each person's mixture is poured into a section of cow intestine (buffalo in the old days), tobacco smoke is blown into the section, its ends are tied, the sausagelike container is tied to a stick, and the bottom of the stick is driven into the ground inside a large tipi. After all of the seeds and containers have been prepared, there is a nightlong Tobacco Dance in the Mixers' lodge (Lowie 1920: 161–163).

On the following day the members of the various chapters are painted by a Mixer or by a Painter, if there is one. Then they set out for the garden, followed by the rest of the tribe. They are led by the Medicine Bearer, who carries a powerful otter skin along with other sacred emblems. Each member carries his own tobacco container, along with his personal medicine. After 400 yards the leader stops. Her husband fills a pipe with tobacco, lights it, smokes it, says "May the Tobacco grow very tall," and offers the pipe to other society members. At first everyone declines, for the act of smoking the pipe is equivalent to sacrificing one's life—if the tobacco fails to grow, a great calamity will befall the smoker. Eventually someone agrees to smoke, thereby taking on the dangerous responsibility of ensuring the tobacco's growth, as everyone says "Thank you!" The smoker sings his song to the musicians, who chant it four times. Then the procession starts again.

After a short walk, the leader stops a second time, and the procedure is repeated. Two more times it is repeated; by the fourth stop the procession is only a few hundred yards from the garden. Again the smoker sings (Simms 1904: 331–335):

> I am going to plant Tobacco,
> There will be plenty,
> Come and see the Tobacco.

Then the young men of the tribe race to the garden (the winner will have good fortune), followed slowly by the procession. The Mixers lay all of the seed bags on blankets while the chapter members remove all of the vegetation from the garden, spread dry grass and twigs over the surface, and burn them (nowadays the surface is plowed). Each member of each chapter is given a row in the garden, and each Mixer marks the rows until the whole garden is divided up. The Mixers sing four songs (apparently including the "I am going to plant tobacco" song). Then they dig the first holes with sharp sticks.

Women are very important in the tobacco society. The unity of married couples is emphasized throughout the ceremony, and female fertility is one of the possible reasons for the society's existence and for its emphasis on the growth of tobacco. After the four songs, the women dig all of the holes in their rows as their husbands follow behind, planting the seeds and the mixture, which probably acts as fertilizer. After each chapter has finished planting all of its rows, the members dance, sing, and eat. In the evening they perform a Tobacco Dance. Some members spend the night sleeping beside the garden, in order to receive tobacco visions or dreams.

Four visits are made to the garden during the growing season, to inspect the condition of the tobacco. During this period society members make a special motion outward and upward with their pipes when they are smoking the "tall tobacco" obtained from the Hidatsa. The inspectors take experienced scouts with them on their visits, and the scouts treat the inspection as a raid. Only the scouts actually view the tobacco, but they tell the inspectors about its condition. After each inspection the chapter performs another Tobacco Dance.

On the fourth and final inspection the Mixers come along to see if the garden needs weeding. If it does, all the members remove the weeds. Weeding occurs one more time if the Mixers decide it is necessary, and then the harvest begins. During Lowie's visits, all of the members had the right to "take back" (that is, harvest) their own tobacco, but in the past they had to purchase the right from the Mixers. If they didn't have the right, their sponsors would harvest it for them.

The tobacco is so powerful that it is considered poisonous. The pickers rub their hands beforehand with a special root to protect their skin. They also remove the seed cases with little wooden tongs. Later there are separate chapter tobacco dances. Following the last harvest of the season, an adoption lodge is erected and the members dance with their new tobacco. Nonmembers can sometimes purchase a necklace of tobacco for a horse. After the dance the seeds are saved for the next year, while the leaves, roots, and stems are cut up finely, mixed with meat and "tall tobacco," and thrown into a creek or river (Lowie 1920:173–176; Simms 1904:331–335).

The power of the sacred tobacco is reflected by the belief that everyone will die if it fails to grow. At no time should anyone point with his or her hands at either the tobacco or the stars. Sticks are used if someone wants to point at them.

The Crow are inveterate smokers, but as a rule smoking is reserved for ceremonies and other special occasions, when only tobacco society members, Medicine Pipe holders, and other qualified individuals are allowed to smoke. The pipe is offered to the cardinal directions before smoking, and no one is allowed to take more than three puffs at a time. Each man always hands the pipe to the man on his left. Pipes are never smoked if moccasins are hanging in the lodge, and all children are supposed to wear small packages of tobacco around their necks as amulets (Lowie 1935:xiii–xiv; Lowie 1954:29).

Most Crow pipes are imported from the Hidatsa and Dakota (Sioux) (photo 68).[8] Pipe smoking is an important element of all Crow ceremonies, including the Meat Festival, where there is a ritualized offer of tobacco-lighting. When a pipe is empty, the Lighter holds it out to the owner, and then both men hold it together. The Bear Song Dance, another important ceremony, also involves ritual smoking. *Batsira'pe* have been known to emerge at Bear Song dances.

Another ceremony that entails smoking is the Sacred Pipe Dance. In 1910 there were 26 owners of sacred pipes in the Crow tribe. There was no Sacred Pipe society at that time, though the owners of all of the pipes occasionally met to discuss their pipes, the power of their medicines, and related topics. Each owner had a sacred pipe bundle, each containing corncobs, sweetgrass, and two pipe stems decorated with eagle feather fans. A redstone pipe bowl was attached to the stems for smoking. Owning a sacred pipe conferred distinction and luck.

Despite the very low percentages of nicotine in the short and tall varieties of *Nicotiana quadrivalvis*, they are still the most powerful plants used by the Crow—so powerful, in fact, that occasionally the Crow give some to their traditional enemies, the Lakota. Readers interested in learning more about the Crow tobacco society should read Lowie's excellent descriptions.

Photo 68. Both tobacco and the pipes in which it is smoked are extremely powerful medicines for the Crow, Hidatsa, and other Sioux-speaking Indians. In this photograph, Red Eagle (Martha Bad Warrior) holds the White Buffalo Calf Pipe of the Lakota (Sioux). She charged the photographer two packs of cigarettes and eight pounds of beef to take the picture. Courtesy of the Maxwell Museum of Anthropology, University of New Mexico. 92.1.109.

### Priests and Tobacco: The Karok-Yurok-Hupa World Renewal Ceremony

The distinction between individual religious practitioners and priests, or between medicine societies and priesthoods, is often subtle, and many Indians and anthropologists use the terms interchangeably. There is no mistaking the difference between shamans and priests or between societies and priesthoods among the Aztec, since

Aztec priests were elite, full-time religious functionaries who dedicated their entire lives to their gods. To the north, however, the distinctions are less clear; many tribes have shamans and medicine men who are sometimes called "priests." In writing about the Zuni, for example, anthropologists and tribal members alike mention the Kachina society, the Kachina Priests, the Bow Priest society, the Beast Priests, and so on—all of whom smoked tobacco (Ladd 1979: 482; Tedlock 1979:499).

Elsewhere in North America, distinctions between priests and other practitioners and between societies and priesthoods are equally unclear and confusing. Indeed, in some instances, as in the case of the Yurok, Hupa, and Karok of the Trinity and Klamath river valleys in northwest California, the same anthropologist, Alfred Kroeber, called them priests in one sentence and medicine men or shamans in another. What is clear is that certain native North American groups have trained religious functionaries who are responsible for performing regularly scheduled ceremonies that involve tobacco and are essential for the yearly renewal of the world and the continued existence of humanity. These individuals use tobacco in their communications with supernatural beings, but unlike medicine men and doctors in the same tribes, they do not use it in such large quantities that they have visions or enter into trance states.[9] Among the Yurok, Karok, and Hupa, special priests perform a ten-day ceremony aimed at the annual reestablishment and "firming" of the earth, celebrating the first salmon and acorns, lighting the new fire, and preventing calamity and disease for another year.

The Karok, Yurok, and Hupa belong to three separate language families—Hokan, Algonkian, and Athabaskan, respectively—yet they share the same basic culture and religion and the same traditional economic emphasis on salmon fishing, acorn gathering, and deer hunting. They also attend each other's World Renewal ceremonies, which entail the precise recitation of a long narrative formula repeating the words of the supernatural spirits of the prehuman past, who began the rite, accompanied by magical acts symbolizing these ancient actions. White Deerskin, First Salmon, and Jump dances are performed during the ceremonial cycle, but the core of the rite is the sacred formula, which is recited in segments in a fixed order by a single priest or formulist who is purified by prolonged abstenion from water, sexual activity, and other profane actions, as well as by semifasting and bathing in a sweathouse. He also smokes and blows tobacco to the spirits; almost every action in the rite is accompanied by the offering of this sacred plant. The beliefs requiring the ceremony also involve tobacco, and indeed the original process of creating the universe and the first religious ceremonies associated with it are inexorably linked with tobacco in the mythologies of the three tribes (photo 69).

For the Yurok, the deity Pulekukwerek—the supernatural *woge* who grew from a tobacco plant and who first gave it to humans (see the opening paragraph of chapter 5)—was a critical player in the act of creation, along with a nameless boy, Wetskak the smallest dentalium (seashell), Megwomets the Food-Giver, and the Sky-Possessor. The following brief excerpts from a long Yurok myth describe the creation of the universe and the first World Renewal ceremony, along with tobacco's role in it. The story starts at the end of the sky, where the boy grew. There was sickness all about:

[The boy] thought, "I wish to know all the world." . . .
[Then Wetsak, the one who grew first, appeared to the boy and offered to take him with him, as he made the world.] The boy was glad that he was to go all over the world, but thought, "I do not believe I shall be able to walk." That one [Wetsak] said, "No, you need not think that. You can sit on my back, because I want you with me." "What shall we use?" "What for?" "What shall we eat when we travel?" "We shall eat nothing. We shall use tobacco, that is all." "Have you some of that thing? I do not

Photo 69. Captain John, at the Hupa village of Medildin along the Trinity River, about 1892. The plant in the lower right part of the photograph appears to be *Nicotiana quadrivalvis*, which still grows along the river. Photo by A. W. Ericson. Courtesy of Humboldt State University, California.

know it." "It is only a short distance to where one lives (who has tobacco). We will take him along with us." "I do not think he can go. He is an old man." "Oh, he can go. I will tell you his name." "Yes." "He knows. He knows more than I, that old man. He uses only tobacco. His name is Pulekukwerek. That is his name." . . .

[After they joined Pulekukwerek, they went to Kepel, where they saw a man sitting outside a sweathouse.] "Ah! I am glad to see you [said the man]. Sit down." He took out his pipe. "Have a smoke," he said. That old man (Pulekukwerek), this is where he got tobacco. All the way he had seen no one that had tobacco, and now he came to Kepel and an old man had tobacco and a pipe. The old man (of Kepel) said, "Boy, you had better smoke, too. It is nothing bad. All is good and undisturbed and they are making much fun. We will take you down to where they are playing as soon as we have smoked." The boy took the pipe and smoked. Pulekukwerek had already smoked. Then Pulekukwerek thought, "Well, he is a man. He smokes." Then Pulekukwerek gave the old man his own pipe. He said, "You had better smoke this." . . .

[Later, after they visited and made other places] Pulekukwerek took out his pipe and prepared to smoke. There was nothing there, no fire, and the floor was smooth. Pulekukwerek took out his fire drill and turned it. It burned. He lit the pipe and gave it to him [the Sky-Possessor] to draw at. He took it, sucked once, and spoke. "You are the kind of man I like to see. I have never seen one like you." Pulekukwerek said, "I shall live with you if you will do what I wish." "Yes, it is well. Whatever you say I shall do." "I will tell you. I have gone halfway (over the world). I want to make all this world good. Then I thought and looked up, but could see nothing. I wish we had fog close by (above). It would look well." "Well, light another. Then we shall go out and you will tell me what it is that you wish to have." So he gave him another pipeful, for Pulekukwerek had grown with

his hand full of tobacco. It was never gone. He always had it with him. That one smoked and talked. Then he put the pipe into its skin case and handed it back. Pulekukwerek said, "You can keep it if you do what I tell you." "Good. Let us go out."

They went out. Pulekukwerek said, "If you can make that, it will be called sky. If you can make it, in the evening we shall see something good. We shall call that stars." . . .

[Then the Sky-Possessor lit his] pipe, blew, and fog came out and spread. Some are black now and some white. They are clouds. They are tobacco smoke blown out by him. . . .

Then Pulekukwerek lit his pipe to make the stars. He drew long, blew the smoke into his hollow hand, threw it down, blew in his hand again, threw the smoke downward, again and again, and made the stars. (Kroeber 1976:116, 120–121, 126–127)

Because of the ancient supernaturals' use of tobacco in creating the world and then making it right with the ceremony, the World Renewal rite is immersed in tobacco smoke. The ceremony and the associated First Salmon, Jump, and White Deerskin dances are also linked in concept and timing in a sequence that must be completed to properly fix the world. The White Deerskin Dance consists of the ceremonial use of finely decorated hides of albino deer, which symbolize purity and birth, the male principle, and the beneficence of the deer spirit. The ceremony lasts as long as 16 days, ending with a climax of dancing and a display of wealth, where potential power becomes action.

The Jump Dance also lasts several days. The male dancers wear elaborate woodpecker-scalp headbands and carry sacred baskets. Thousands of people attend both dances, thereby integrating the three language groups into one culture and exercising considerable power.

Tobacco is one of the main forms of power in the World Renewal rite and the associated dances. The priest represents the Immortals who created the ceremony along with the rest of the universe. Tobacco smoking and dancing are equivalent to "cooking"—that is, transforming the world into new forms (Bean and Vane 1978:38).

In the Karok and Yurok World Renewal origin myth, Pulekukwerek, Wetskak, and the other supernaturals established the sequence as they traveled up and down the Klamath River, making the ceremony and different parts of creation at certain villages and other locations. The rite can be held only at one or another of these locations, such as the Karok village of Amaikiara, which is associated with many Immortals—including Rat, who obtained venison for his son-in-law Bat by giving him tobacco. During the First Salmon part of the ceremony, the priest's primary activity is to sit in the sacred sweathouse at Amaikiara for nine days, meditating and praying for abundant salmon, acorns, and other food. While doing so, he blows an offering of unburned tobacco on ten sacred stones on top of the sweathouse (Palmer 1980: 11, 21–22).

Katimin, another Karok village, is the Center of the World and one of only three Karok locations where the World Renewal ceremony can be held. For ten days the priest makes offerings of tobacco and prays for salmon and acorns, representing the Immortals' creation of them. Nearby is Pipe Bowl Rock, in the Klamath River, which the Immortals threw into the river and then used in making their pipe bowls. The Karok make the same use of it, but they do not let whites use it, fearing that they will take it away and bring the world to an end (Palmer 1980:37, 42, 48).

The formula of Kitaxrihar medicine, used to protect oneself against enemies, was also developed at Katimin when a savage Kitaxrihar, or Winged One, dwelling at Katimin used tobacco smoke to overcome the Sun, "He Who Travels Above Us." Part of the formula reads:

Then he took out his tobacco pipe. . . . He thought: "I have much smoking tobacco,

and my tobacco is strong." . . . Behold then he started to smoke. And he thought: "I too am a Savage One. I think: He will not kill me, when he smelleth my tobacco smoke." He kept smoking. Then presently the Sun came up. For a little while he looked around, the savage one of the middle of the world Here. He kept smoking. Dimness was entering the deep places (the gulches and canyons) of the earth. He (the Sun) was already high. "Indeed, I said it, in no wise canst thou kill me." Behold the Sun swooned away from the tobacco smoke. (Harrington 1932:256–257)

The *fatawenan* (priest) in the Katimin World Renewal ceremony carries his pipe and tobacco with him wherever he goes, never letting go of them. While he prays and fasts, the people also smoke; "sometimes there are five pipes there, they pass them to each other, they take two or three puffs each. Behold, they all smoke. Then when they are through, they put their pipes away under their belts" (a Karok, quoted in Harrington 1932:243).

One of the ten days of the ceremony at Katimin and the other World Renewal sites is even called "Going Toward Tobacco," because the priest walks toward tobacco stems placed on a rock and prays over them. The rock is called "where they put tobacco on" (Harrington 1932:224). Then, on the last day of the ceremony at Katimin, the priest takes along ten sacks of tobacco, called *tcirixxus*, and carries his pipe to the altar at Inkir, called Ma. "He also throws around tobacco there by the fireplace, the *tcirixxus* sacks of tobacco; he throws the tobacco around. He throws it around a little at a time. He feeds the tobacco mostly to Medicine Mountain; he also feeds to Lower Mountain. He uses up 10 *tcirixxus* sacks of tobacco as he prays" (Harrington 1932:247).

Nearly identical offerings of tobacco are made in the World Renewal ceremony at the Karok village of Panamenik. At the first stopping place on the first day, the priest builds a small fire, smokes tobacco, and performs a ritual to protect acorns. Later, in another place, he digs up ten Immortals who reside there in small stones and feeds them tobacco. Since these Immortals are among the supernaturals who created the world and its institutions, protection of the buried stones is essential for the survival of the world. On the second, third, fifth, and ninth days the priest also smokes and offers tobacco at medicine-making places; on the eighth day he makes tobacco offerings at ten different places (Palmer 1980:58, 60, 85–87, 92). Hundreds of additional details concerning the Karok's religious uses of tobacco can be found in John P. Harrington's 1932 description, as well as in chapter 2 of this book.

Ceremonial tobacco is still smoked by the Yurok, Hupa, and Karok, who are reviving their ceremonies and dances and using the power of tobacco in their fight against the United States government over the preservation of their sacred doctor-training sites in the mountains. As one Karok-Hupa medicine man put it:

> The physical (world) is a battleground. It's within the darkness. We are here at the creator's desire. We are sent into the darkness of the world at the creator's desire with three weapons—the individual prayer pipes, the spiritual dance grounds, and the spiritual places in the mountains, for our guidance and protection and security. . . . There is no higher purpose than following the heart to the spiritual places. . . . Without the spiritual places, the dance grounds, and the prayer pipes, there is no continuation of the spiritual and physical (worlds). (USDA n.d.)

Whereas the World Renewal priests help remake the world each year by reciting prayers and offering tobacco, the prayer doctors of the Yurok, Karok, and Hupa tribes use tobacco to drive out sickness and to ward off evil. By smoking her pipe, dancing, and singing, the Yurok doctor enters a trance in which her guardian spirit shows her the cause of the patient's illness. Not only is she trained with tobacco in the mountains, but she often practices her medicine

in the mountains while smoking her pipe and contemplating a diagnosis (Buckley 1992:123, 127, 160). In this way the doctors of the three tribes walk a spiritual path that links the World Renewal priests and ceremonial dance grounds along the rivers with the use of sacred tobacco in the high mountain prayer seats—the doctors and priests allow all of life to survive and prosper as the individual Indian, the larger community, and the universe as a whole become a "communion of interrelated forces" (Norton 1992:234).

The priests, medicine men, and other traditional members of the three tribes also recognize that the power of tobacco can be used to cause illness and death through cancer, heart disease, and other sickness. In addition, this power can be used malevolently, in witchraft. Some medicine men use it for evil purposes, as do witches, secret poisoners, and "Indian devils," who take a person's feces, hair, clothing, or other personal items and use them to kill him (Bean 1992:60). The same Hupa-Karok medicine man who described how tobacco was used in the battle against darkness also told me how someone in his family was once poisoned when an Indian devil discovered his tobacco patch and urinated on it.

In the 1950s, the Bureau of Indian Affairs attempted to eradicate all the patches of wild tobacco growing along the Trinity and Klamath rivers, because of tobacco's association with traditional Indian religion. As a result, wild tobacco is now relatively rare in the region, and many Indians, such as the Hupa-Karok medicine man, grow their own plants or receive them in payment from patients. It is probable that the priests and medicine men of the tribes also use commercial tobacco and introduced species.

As more is learned about the harmful effects of using commercial tobacco, all three tribes are increasing their efforts to eliminate the smoking, chewing, and snuffing of nontraditional *Nicotiana*. In 1994, representatives of the Hoopa Health Association, the Karok Tribe's Tobacco Control Health Education Outreach Program, and the Yurok Tribe's Education Department presented a Teen Health Educators Training Program in Orleans, California, for the youth of all three tribes. The dangers and negative health effects of commercial tobacco use, as well as the positive, sacred aspects of traditional tobacco use, were emphasized in the daylong program. For all three tribes, the power of tobacco is ultimately traced to the strength of their traditions and religions, which are centered on the World Renewal ceremony villages and dance grounds along the rivers, where their priests recreate the world each year with the aid of tobacco, and the high mountain prayer seats, where their medicine men and doctors are trained and where they use tobacco to diagnose illness and combat the forces of destruction.

## Aztec Tobacco Priests: The Cult of Cihuacoatl

Aztec priests were full-time religious specialists who held public office and who served as intermediaries between the inhabitants of the Aztec empire and the gods of the supernatural world. Typically members of the elite class, they presented tobacco and other sacrificial offerings to the gods, and they were spokespersons and mediators for the gods. In contrast to shamans, they usually did not enter trances, nor were they possessed by spirits. Most Aztec priests, however, did use tobacco, peyote, morning-glory seeds (ololiuhqui), and perhaps even datura to intoxicate themselves so that they could better communicate with their gods. There were also true Aztec shamans who used tobacco and other hallucinogens to cure and to predict the future, and it is likely that some priests also served as shamans. Burr C. Brundage offers the intriguing suggestion that the hundreds and perhaps thousands of years of tobacco and other hallucinogenic plant use might have contributed to the vivid and at times nightmarish quality of Aztec religion (Brundage 1979:184).

There were also Aztec "sorcerers" (shamans) called *ticitl*, who used tobacco and other drugs to tell the future, determine the causes of illness, heal the sick, and otherwise treat patients. The priests' use of tobacco went far beyond this, however, well into the realm of magic and near-madness. Tobacco was the main ingredient of an ointment called "divine meat" that the priests applied not only as an offering to the gods and in healing but also to cause a patient to lose all fear—especially captives who were about to be sacrificed. This divine offering was made of spiders, scorpions, vipers, and salamanders burned in the temple hearth and then mixed with tobacco and ololiuhqui (Dobkin de Rios 1984:147).

Aztec priesthoods served as penitential surrogates for the general population; most priests shed their own blood (as well as that of others) for the gods they served. One of the most common forms of penitential practice was an arduous journey at night up a mountain, when the priest went naked, painted black, chewing tobacco, with his ears and thighs pierced with thorns (Brundage 1979:187).

All Aztec priesthoods used tobacco, but one stood above all others, for it was dedicated to Cihuacoatl (Snake Woman), the goddess whose body was manifested on earth as the tobacco plant (fig. 27). Tobacco was the very embodiment of Cihuacoatl, and she in turn was an aspect of Ilamatecuhtli—the great goddess of the Milky Way. Tobacco was often called the infant of the Star-Skirted One, Creation of the Star-Skirted One, and Human Creation of the Star-Skirted One. Other names and metaphors for tobacco given in Ruiz de Alarcón's seventeenth-century treatise on Aztec sorcery are Nine Pounded, Nine Struck, Turquoise Flyer, Priest Nine Pounded, The Yellow Priest, Nine Rubbed, One of the Land of Medicine, Nine Crackled, Blue-Green Pounded, Blue-Green Crackled, and "the little dog at all weddings." Ruiz de Alarcón (quoted in Coe and Whittaker 1982:36) used the last term because tobacco was universal in all spells, while the epithets

Figure 27. Cihuacoatl, or Snake Woman, the Aztec earth goddess, whose physical manifestation was the tobacco plant. Drawing by Ray Allen Hernandez based on the plate following p. 95 in Duran 1964.

Nine Pounded, Nine Crackled, and the like probably referred to the fact that it was pounded nine times, into powder, then mixed with lime in the ratio of ten parts tobacco and one part lime, to form *tenexyhetl*. A typical Aztec invocation using one or more of these metaphors reads as follows (Coe and Whittaker 1982: 124):

> Please come forth, Nine Pounded,
> Creation of the Star-Skirted One,
> Who knows the Land of the Dead,
> Who knows the Beyond.
> What are you thinking?
> Rejoice that I have finally come,
> I the priest,
> I the Lord of Enchantment,
> I the Plumed Serpent.

This and other invocations recorded by Ruiz de Alarcón clearly demonstrate how tobacco

was considered a powerful, mystical deity, mothered by the Milky Way.

In addition to Ilamatecuhtli, Cihuacoatl was identified with a number of other mother and earth goddesses, such as Coatlicue, Quilaztli, Toci, Teteonin, and Tlazoltcotl (Brundage 1979; Miller and Taube 1993). In one or another of these guises, she was the highest of the goddesses—the mother of most of the other gods and the patroness of childbirth, newborns, and the *cihuateteo*—the warriorlike women who died in childbirth, thereby serving the state (Broda 1983:243; Brundage 1979). The *cihuateteo* descended to earth on certain days to appear at crossroads, where they killed children. One of the reasons that Cihuacoatl's priesthood was so important was that her priests read the horoscopes of the newborn and then gave them their names. She therefore represented the earth in its dual function of creator and destroyer, birth and death. She was the protector of plants and animals, the devourer of bodies, and the drinker of the blood of the dead (Caso 1958: 53–54, 56).

Cihuacoatl also symbolized the regenerative forces of the earth, along with the destructive elements of death. She was a mother goddess related to fertility, warfare, and human sacrifice; sometimes her image cried out at night, desiring human hearts to eat, and she did not calm down so long as she went hungry, nor did she bear fruit or produce tobacco without human blood to irrigate her (Broda 1983:243).

The regenerative face of Cihuacoatl was embodied in one of her other transfigurations—Quilaztli, the Instrument That Generates Plants—who presided over all edible things. In Xochimilco, where Cihuacoatl was regarded as the greatest goddess of all, she was worshiped as the two-headed deer of Mixcoatl, whose bones may have been buried in her temple (Brundage 1979:170).

Because tobacco was her manifestation on earth, it was considered a living, sentient, divine being, to which prayers, human sacrifices, and other gifts were offered. Tobacco was also used to anoint rulers and priests, and it was given to sacrificial victims before they were ritually killed. Adorned with flowers and given cigarettes to comfort them, an endless stream of captive warriors flowed back from the never-ending Aztec wars, only to lose their lives on the hundreds of altars that lined the strees and plazas of Tenochtitlán. Powdered tobacco in special gourds was also the insignia of the priests and of the creative deities who functioned as priests and diviners. Tobacco gourds were worn by women doctors, and all of the females in the Feast of Toci wore them (Brundage 1979:204; Thompson 1970b:112, 118).

No document better describes the use of tobacco by Cihuacoatl's priests and the other priests and inhabitants of the Aztec empire than Fray Bernardino de Sahagún's sixteenth-century *General History of the Things of New Spain*, also known as the Florentine Codex, as translated by Arthur J. O. Anderson and Charles E. Dibble.[10] The Tecuacuitlin and other priests who took care of the various gods "went (out) having put about them only their pouches with cords, which were filled with dyed, powdered tobacco—this tobacco mixed with a black (dye)—which they chewed as they went" (Anderson and Dibble 1954:81). Their beribboned tobacco pouches (*yequachtli*) first and foremost were insignia of high office; even the newly elected Moctezuma II wore one at his installation. The Tlillancalqui (Snake Woman) also wore one, as did the other members of the Council of Four, along with all senior priests and probably many other priests as well (Klein 1983:320–321, 346).[11]

Dibble and Anderson (1963:146) identified the *picietl* of the Florentine Codex as both *Nicotiana rustica* and *N. tabacum*, whereas Michael D. Coe and Gordon Whittaker (1982:36) concluded that the *picietl* in Ruiz de Alarcón's treatise was only *N. rustica*. *N. tabacum*, they claimed, was called *quauhyetl*—*yetl* being the generic term for tobacco. Both species appear to have been used by the Aztec. The following description by Sahagún obviously applies to *N. rustica*:

Its leaves are wide, somewhat long; and its blossoms are yellow. It is pounded with a stone, ground, mixed with lime. He who suffers fatigue rubs himself with it; likewise he who has the gout. And it is chewed. In this manner it is chewed: it is only placed in the lips. It intoxicates one, makes one dizzy, possesses one, and destroys hunger and a desire to eat. He who has a swollen stomach places it on the stomach and there in the navel. (Dibble and Anderson 1963:146)

Sahagún described numerous ceremonies, feasts, and other occasions when tobacco was used for sacrificial as well as profane purposes. When feasts were held for the great war god Huitzilopochtli (Cihuacoatl's son), a ceremony called "the Bathing" was performed, in which captives and slaves were ritually bathed and annointed with tobacco, then sacrificed. After buying male and female slaves in the slave market, merchants dressed them in fine clothes and adorned them with flowers and put tubes (cigarettes) of fine tobacco in their hands. For a while the slaves went around the market sucking on the tubes and smelling the flowers. When the Feast of Bathing occurred, they were continuously given tobacco to smoke and flowers to smell. Later they were ritually killed and their flesh was cooked, salted (without chile), served over maize, and eaten by the host of the feast and his kinsmen (Dibble and Anderson 1959: 45–46, 59, 67).

Another major feast included the killing of all men, women, and children captured in battle. A warrior who took hair from a captive's head merited honor, flowers, tobacco, and capes. At another feast, the offering priests carried tobacco bags on their backs, and little bags filled with powdered tobacco hung from cord necklaces. At still another feast, gifts were given to all of the servers and workers, including those who cared for the tobacco.

Merchants often gave lavish feasts for generals, noblemen, and other elites, with seasoned warriors distributing the tobacco. When someone held a banquet or left on an important trip or returned from one, he made offerings of tobacco and flowers to Huitzilopochtli at the landing of the supreme god's pyramid. Offerings of burning tobacco were also made at the temples of Uitznauc, Pochtlan, Yopico, and Tlamatzinco. At the end of the banquets, as the sun came up, tubes of tobacco were burned as prayers were said: "We put the maguey thorns (and) tubes of tobacco in the earth. Our children (and) grandchildren shall eat; they shall drink; they will not perish forever." Then the departing guests were given tubes of tobacco, as were the poor old men and women. Later in the day there was still another feast, with more tubes of tobacco provided, and still again another feast with tubes of tobacco, if any remained (Dibble and Anderson 1959:41–42).

With all of this feasting and giving away of tobacco tubes taking place almost daily, certain men specialized in selling tobacco. Called "proprietors of tobacco," they "spread out smoking tubes, pipes, cigars, (some) quite resinous and aromatic; and tobacco bowls" (Anderson and Dibble 1954:69). Because of the Aztec's insatiable demand for tobacco, these merchants spent most of their time producing and selling tobacco tubes:

The Smoking Tube Seller, the tobacco (tube) seller, is one who provides a covering (for the tobacco tube)—a maker of reed smoking tubes, a cutter of reeds. He . . . covers (the reeds with moist charcoal dust); he paints them, he colors them, he gilds them. He sells the tobacco (tubes) destined for fondling in the hand—long, of an arm's span, (covered with) a thickness of clay . . . gilded, painted . . . with flowers; (he sells) tobacco tubes in the form of a blow gun, (painted with) fish, eagles, etc. There are made market tobacco (tubes), tobacco (tubes) of little value; they flake off, they crumble. (There are) shredded tobacco, chopped tobacco, scented tobacco, cigars, tobacco tubes. The tobacco burns. (The smoking tubes) are filled with tobacco, the inside is filled, crammed, the opening is

closed, the end is closed. (The seller) prepares tobacco, rubs it in his hands, mixes it with flowers, with *uei nacaztli* (*Cymbopetalum penduliflorum*), with bitumen, with *uacalxochitl* (*Xanathosoma* sp. or *Phyllodendron affine*), with *tlilxochitl* (*Vanilla plantifolia*), with *mecarxochitl* (*Piper amalago*), with mushrooms, with *poyomatli* (unidentified fern or narcotic root), with "obsidian tobacco" (unidentified). (Dibble and Anderson 1961:88)

Tubes of tobacco were also given at wedding feasts, along with food, drink, and flowers. The emperor Moctezuma offered Huitzilopochtli many types of flowers, including yellow and blue(?) tobacco blossoms. And the priests of Cihuacoatl, Huitzilopochtli, and the other gods continuously burned tobacco in bundles, filling the areas before the gods' images with smoke, which "arose, . . . spread a cloud, extended, settled, and lay billowing." It was the priests' responsibility to assemble all of the tobacco and other offerings—for example, at the temple of Toci (an aspect of Cihuacoatl), where the priest was called Cinaquacuilli. The Tlacolquacuilli took care of the temple of Mecaltan; as a high priest, he wore a tobacco gourd (Dibble and Anderson 1969:129, 1957:78; Anderson and Dibble 1981:211–212).

Aztec doctors ordered their patients to inhale green tobacco for headaches. Cysts in the throat were surgically removed, and then powdered tobacco mixed with lime and salt was placed in the incision. Tobacco was inhaled for catarrh and spread on head abcesses (Dibble and Anderson 1961:140, 144–149). Rubbing the patient with tobacco was a rite physicians used to diagnose illness as well as to treat it (Caso 1958:56). Ruiz de Alarcón described how the Aztec used tobacco to treat scorpion bites, earaches, jawbone aches, toothaches, and childbirth (Coe and Whittaker 1982). Sahagún added boils, snake bites, and coughs (Dibble and Anderson 1963).

In essence, tobacco was not only the living body of the earth goddess Cihuacoatl and the subject of veneration by her priests, but it also filled the lives of the Aztec, from the lowest captive and humblest servant to the divine ruler himself. Throughout the Aztec empire and elsewhere in Mesoamerica, tobacco gourds and bags were (and still are) the insignia of shamans, pilgrims, priests, and deities. Even today the fire god and other ancient Aztec deities are worshipped by the Huichol, who continue to offer sacrificial victims (deer and bulls, instead of humans) anointed with the blossoms of tobacco and other sweet-smelling flowers, copal incense, and other fragrant gifts (Winter, field notes).

## Conclusion

From the Navajo Earth Mother to the Aztec Snake Woman, native North Americans and their deities have long been associated with tobacco, which often served an essential role in the very creation of the world and which continues to play a part in the daily, seasonal, and yearly renewal of existence. Tobacco is at the heart of Amerindian religion and at the core of Native American culture. Sometimes a god or spirit itself, always sacred, its use and associated beliefs are shrouded by a smoke-filled mysticism that most non-Indians have difficulty understanding or appreciating. Whether it is the *batsira'pe* that enters into the body of a Crow Indian and then emerges at tobacco ceremonies or the Nine Pounded creation of the Aztec Star-Skirted Milky Way, or even the pollen, jewels, and turquoise pipes of the Navajo Black God, tobacco binds the natural world with its supernatural counterpart, eliminates the boundaries between them, and, as Harrington so aptly put it, serves as a "heritage of the gods, a strange path which juts into this world and leads to the very ends of magic" (Harrington 1932:13).

Clearly tobacco played a critical role in the evolution of increasingly more complex forms of Native American religious organization. Tobacco was a constant, unifying force, a route of direct and immediate communication with the spirit world that linked Native Americans all across North, Central, and South America, regardless of whether their religion was organized around individual medicine men, tobacco shamans, medicine societies, tobacco societies, or even tobacco priesthoods. Almost from the beginning of their presence in North America—and certainly starting with their discovery of wild tobacco—shamans, medicine men, and other individual practitioners recognized the powers inherent in this amazing plant and its ability to create the altered states of consciousness that are so basic to this most elemental form of religion. Then, as more complex forms of Native American religion developed—as individual practitioners were replaced or transformed, first by groups of practitioners in informal medicine societies and eventually by organized priesthoods—tobacco provided the chemical vehicle that tied all of these individuals, groups, and cultures together. It linked them through time and across space; it served as the very core of their existence and the reality of their spirits.

For most traditional Native Americans, the use of tobacco in ritual, mythology, and everyday religious activity is a positive, unifying force that actually serves to limit the amount of nicotine and other chemicals that are ingested, through religious proscriptions which require that relatively small, carefully controlled doses are administered. It is likely that the traditional, low-dosage use of tobacco rarely harms Native Americans, who recognize its extremely powerful, dangerous, and sacred nature and therefore treat it with the respect and awe that it deserves.

This does not mean, however, that Native Americans are immune to the debilitating, long-term effects of regular tobacco use, or even the harmful effects of short-term abuse. Tobacco shamans in South America have been known to die from the immense amounts of nicotine they ingest, and addiction to the nicotine in wild tobacco probably played a role in the domestication of *Nicotiana rustica* and *N. tabacum*. In addition, Native American death rates from tobacco-associated diseases are steadily climbing as more and more Indians (especially teenagers and adolescents) adopt the habit that is so prevalent in non-Indian society. Migrant Indian laborers in the Mexican commercial tobacco fields also suffer from the effects of green tobacco contamination, and many die from the effects of pesticide poisoning. All of these tragic consequences of commercial tobacco use are discussed in detail in the final three chapters of this book.

This dark, deadly side of tobacco is nowhere more evident than in the Aztec use of it to anoint sacrificial victims and to comfort them before they were slaughtered on a scale and by methods that are almost beyond imagination. On one occasion alone, when the Great Temple of the War God was dedicated in Tenochtitlán in 1487, more than 80,000 captives were reportedly sacrificed—so many, in fact, that it took four days to kill them all, using four separate blood-drenched altars (Duran 1964:194). Cihuacoatl, whose earthly manifestation was the tobacco plant, was the most horrifying and powerful of the Aztec goddesses, with a thirst for blood that required near-constant wars in the name of her son, the war god. As shown by figure 27, her image was as frightening as her reputation. The lower part of her face was an exposed jawbone, forming a wide-open, grisly mouth hungry for victims. "She is clothed and painted in chalky white. She was referred to as a horror and a devourer: she brought nothing but misery and toil and death" (Brundage:168).

Perhaps it is no coincidence that the Aztec were also one of the only Native American cultures to have full-time tobacco merchants and cigarette makers who provided the immense amounts of tobacco necessary for the sacrificial rites. In addition, the Aztec used tobacco on a near-constant, casual basis. It was considered good for digestion, and no feast was complete without this "little dog at all weddings." It was given to guests and gods alike, and even the poor received it—albeit in the form of common, cheap cigarettes in plain reeds, in contrast to the liquid-amber-scented, gilded gold beauties consumed in immense numbers by the nobility, warriors, and other wealthy Aztecs.

Tobacco was, in short, almost as popular in ancient Mexico as it is today throughout the Americas. In Mexico hundreds of thousands of victims died each year numbed by its effects. Today they die from the effects of habitual use. Cihuacoatl was and is an apt metaphor and symbol for this dark side of tobacco. Her exposed jawbone and gaunt, chalky appearance are familiar images on cancer wards, while her earthly embodiment continues to bring "misery and toil and death."

## Notes

1. There is also secular, or nonreligious, tobacco use, in all native tribes—the so-called recreational use of tobacco as a drug for pleasure or to satisfy addictive cravings. Probably there have always been some Native Americans in all tribes who have used tobacco in such a self-destructive manner, but previously they may have been in the minority. Today as many as 50 percent of all native North Americans use tobacco as a secular drug (see chapters 15 and 17).

2. Even *N. glauca* is sometimes used, according to Mayes and Rominger 1994 and ". . . Of the Jungle" 1995.

3. Gladys Reichard (1950) described many of the deities' uses of tobacco; see pages xxx, v, 116, 264, 265, 302–303,

4. This description of the Huichol peyote pilgrimage basically follows the detailed observation by Lumholtz, in *Unknown Mexico* (1902), from the late 1800s. There are many more recent descriptions, such as Schaefer 1996a. Some of the details have changed since the time of Lumholtz, but the overall purpose and nature of the pilgrimage remain the same.

5. Lemaistre (1996:315) describes the *wainuri* as a feathered arrow with a small bag containing tobacco attached to it. As discussed

earlier, there are many variations in the literature concerning the details and terms used in the peyote pilgrimage.

6. This story was translated by Susana Valadez as it was being told.

7. Unless otherwise noted, all of the information concerning the Crow tobacco society is from Lowie 1920 and 1935.

8. The pipe in this plate is the most sacred object in the Lakota religion. Presented to the people by White Buffalo Calf Woman—the daughter of the Sun and Moon—the pipe is used only in the Sun Dance and certain other ceremonies. Its current guardian is Arval Looking Horse, who tells the story of White Buffalo Calf Woman and the pipe in "The Sacred Pipe in Modern Life" (1987; also see his Internet site at http://indy4.fdl.cc). Because of the photograph's great sanctity, I was hesitant to include it this in the book. However, since the current Keeper of the Pipe describes and discusses it in his article, which even has a drawing of White Buffalo Calf Woman holding the pipe, I concluded that it was appropriate to do so. (See

note 1, chapter 2, concerning the publication of other sacred, tobacco-related objects in this book.) In addition, other photographs and descriptions of the pipe by Native American as well as non-native authors can be found in several sources, including R. Hall 1997; Lame Deer and Erdoes 1972; Mails 1979; J. L. Smith 1970; and Thomas 1941. Photo 68 shows the great-great grandmother of Arval Lookinghorse holding the pipe when she was the Keeper around 1940.

9. Because it is a powerful psychoactive drug, nicotine in large quantities can cause hallucinations, which are interpreted as visions.

10. There are eleven translated volumes of this codex, including Anderson and Dibble 1954, 1970, 1981; Dibble and Anderson 1957, 1959, 1961, 1963, 1969.

11. The highest priest in her priesthood was also the second most powerful man in the Aztec empire. Named after her, Cihuacoatl, or Snake Woman, was the most distinguished religious functionary in Mexico, second only to the emperor in status and power.

# 14

# Food of the Gods

## Biochemistry, Addiction, and the
## Development of Native American Tobacco Use

### Joseph C. Winter

In our way, there stood a great Stone about the Size of a large Oven, and hollow; this the Indians took great Notice of, putting some Tobacco into the Concavity, and Spitting after it. I ask'd them the Reason of their so doing, but they made me no Answer. . . . Their teeth are yellow with Smoking Tobacco, which both Men and Women are much addicted to.

—John Lawson, *A New Voyage to Carolina,* 1709

When Europeans "discovered" tobacco in 1492, a vast array of tobacco-using tribes stretched all across the North American continent. Most of these groups smoked tobacco, though they also chewed, snuffed, licked, and drank to ingest the psychotrophic chemicals in this powerful, dangerous plant. In many tribes, tobacco was used on an individual basis, not only by shamans and medicine men, who smoked to communicate with the spirits and to heal, but also by ordinary tribal members, who utilized it for offerings and for pleasure. Among some tribes, tobacco shamanism and tobacco societies had evolved, and tobacco had become an essential ingredient in their curing, diagnosing, communicating, and other medico-religious activities. And for some cultures—especially the Aztec and related theocracies in Mexico—nicotine use by tobacco priests, royalty, warriors, and commoners alike became so pervasive that full-time tobacco merchants appeared, as well as cigarette makers who produced gilded, befeathered, tobacco-filled cane tubes that make today's factory-made cigarettes seem plain in comparison. Some Aztec cigarettes even contained chocolate, vanilla, mushrooms, and flowers mixed with tobacco. Many were painted with eagles, fish, flowers, and other gaily colored designs.

Many questions can be asked about Native Americans' ubiquitous use of tobacco and its effects on their health, economies, and religions. When, where, and how did the ingestion of tobacco develop? Did it originate in South America, where two tobacco species were domesticated? Did it then spread north through Mesoamerica to northern Mexico, the southwestern United States, and southern California, where several wild species were added to the complex? Or were there independent centers of exploitation, so that different ways of utilizing tobacco evolved as a result? Was tobacco domesticated before, during, or after the domestication of maize, potatoes, and other food plants? What was the relationship between the domestication of tobacco and the development of agriculture in general? Could the addictive, narcotic, and psychotropic properties of nicotine have been involved in tobacco's domestication? Could addiction or habituation have favored tobacco's cultivation and ultimate domestication? When and how did ritual uses, tobacco societies, and tobacco shamans evolve? How did the use of tobacco affect the health and mortality rates of prehistoric and historic Native American populations? Could ritual use have evolved as a way of avoiding abuse and controlling access to tobacco, or did it lead to addiction? What exactly was the role of ritual addiction in prehistoric North America, and when and how did it develop?

## Pharmacological and Ideological Addiction

There is no question (or should be none) that the nicotine in tobacco is an addictive agent. It not only stimulates the user and creates psychoactive, mood-altering effects but also produces tolerance, craving, withdrawal effects, and other symptoms associated with physical as well as psychological dependency (Fisher, Lichtenstein, and Haire-Joshu 1993:61; Siegel 1989:96). In 1988, U.S. Surgeon General C. Everett Koop reported that nicotine was an addictive agent (USDHHS 1988). Later it was shown to be even more addictive than cocaine. Then in 1990, U.S. Health and Human Services Secretary Louis Sullivan added that not only was nicotine addictive, but the younger a person was when he or she started to smoke tobacco, the more likely that smoking would become a lifetime disease. About 90 percent of adult smokers began their addiction as children or adolescents, and approximately 35 percent of the youngsters and adolescents who expose themselves to tobacco become addicted (USDHHS 1990).

Ronald K. Siegel has defined tobacco addiction as the establishment of a chemical bond between plants and humans (Siegel 1989:11). Fisher and colleagues (1993:61) note that tobacco addiction meets the following criteria, which define chemical addiction: (1) the pattern of drug use is highly controlled or compulsive; (2) psychoactive or mood-altering effects are involved in the pattern of drug taking; and (3) the drug functions as a reinforcer to strengthen the behavior and lead to further drug ingestion. However it is defined, the withdrawal effects of attempting to break this chemical bond can be excruciatingly painful. Typical effects are tension, irritability, restlessness, increased hunger, insomnia, an inability to concentrate, and a

craving for more nicotine. These effects are so pronounced that the ban on smoking in U.S. airliners does not (or did not) apply to pilots, because "the adverse effects of withdrawal on a chronic smoker are deemed potentially significant and may have an adverse effect on flight safety" (NIH 1978).

Although these studies and their conclusions about nicotine addiction are relatively recent, the anthropological literature and historical records contain numerous references indicating that earlier Native Americans were also addicted to tobacco. Not only do we have historic descriptions such as John Lawson's 1709 observation that Carolina Indians were addicted, but there are also many other, often ironic observations. William Wallace (1953:193–199), for example, claimed that tobacco use among the Mohave Indians of Arizona in the early twentieth century did not enter very deeply into their religious or social life. But he went on to note that their tobacco was so strong that they could not smoke it regularly, and that men did not smoke until they were 50 to 60 years old, because they feared they would lose their souls if they smoked earlier. He added that a few individuals would acquire the "habit" and become "devotees" and that "some men would go on an overnight trip just to get a smoke."

The early historic records for the eastern woodlands are filled with references to the Indians' addiction to tobacco, as von Gernet discussed in chapter 3. Even hunting cultures far beyond the range of tobacco cultivation craved it. A Jesuit described an example in 1634:

The fondness they [the Montagnais in Canada] have for this herb is beyond all belief. They go to sleep with their reed pipes in their mouths, they sometimes get up in the night to smoke; they often stop in their journeys for the same purpose, and it is the first thing they do when they reenter their cabins. I have lighted tinder, so as to allow them to smoke while paddling a canoe; I have often seen them gnaw the stems of their pipes when they had no more tobacco,

I have seen them scrape and pulverize a wooden pipe to smoke it. Let us say with compassion that they pass their lives in smoke, and at death fall into the fire. (Thwaites 1896–1901, 7:137–139)

More recent observations from California, Mexico, and elsewhere present the same pattern of addiction. A. L. Kroeber (1960a:245), for example, wrote that some of the older Yurok Indians of early-twentieth-century northern California were "passionately addicted to tobacco." W. W. Elmendorf (1960:246) noted that most Twana shamans were habitual smokers. And Siegel, Collings, and Diaz (1977:17–18) stated that modern Huichol Indians in Mexico sometimes smoked ceremonial tobacco continuously for up to four days. Analysis of samples of Huichol *Nicotiana rustica* revealed that they contained, on average, 1.9 percent to 4.0 percent nicotine, in contrast to U.S. commercial tobacco (*Nicotiana tabacum*), which averages about 1.5 percent. Other Huichol samples have been found to contain 8.6 percent nicotine, and two very special ritual samples analyzed by Siegel and his colleagues contained 12.7 percent and 18.7 percent nicotine, respectively—doses capable of producing catatonia, not to mention hallucinations.

The pattern of prolonged tobacco use resulting in apparent addiction is especially pronounced in the Amazon and Orinoco drainages of South America, where tobacco shamanism is at the core of many tribes' religions. For the Jivaro, Warao, Witoto, and other groups, tobacco is a spirit unto itself, a purifying, mortifying, and revitalizing agent used during rites of passage and life-crisis ceremonies such as male and female puberty rites and the long and arduous initiatory training of neophyte shamans. It is even used to induce narcotic trances that transport shamans into the realm of the supernatural, where they meet the Mother of Tobacco—the principal tobacco spirit—as well as other tobacco wives, daughters, nieces, and related spirits (Wilbert 1975, 1987).

For the Campa of eastern Peru, apprentice and full-fledged shamans obtain their special powers by the near-constant, "heroic" consumption of tobacco syrup and other drugs (Weiss 1973:43, 45):

> "Tobacco, tobacco," they sing, "pure tobacco
> It comes from River's Beginning
> *Koakiti*, the hawk, brings it to you
> Its flowers are flying, tobacco
> Tobacco, tobacco, pure tobacco
> *Koakiti*, the hawk is its owner."

Among the Jivaro of the Ecuadorian Amazon, shamans who believe themselves weak drink large quantities of tobacco juice as an aid against other shamans' witchcraft. Sucking shamans will drink tobacco juice every few hours to feed the spirits hovering over them, and shamans in general will drink the juice almost constantly, at all hours of the day and night, to fight off spirits thrown at them by other shamans. Jivaro shamans will not even take a walk in the forest without carrying green tobacco leaves that can be prepared as a juice to keep their spirit helpers alert (Harner 1973:22, 25).

Among the Yanoama of the upper Orinoco, both sexes, children as well as adults, chew and suck tobacco almost incessantly (Wilbert 1975: 449). And among the Warao of Venezuela, the shamans are so addicted that they become sick without tremendous quantities of potent tobacco. A Warao shaman will smoke up to 30 large cigars until he falls into an intoxicated, hallucinogenic trance. Some Warao shamans have been paralyzed and killed by the hugh amounts of tobacco they ingest; others have been so poisoned that they have become color blind (Siegel 1989:82; Wilbert 1975:455).

There is no question, then, that tobacco ingestion by Native Americans can result in addiction, especially among the tobacco shamans and other religious practitioners who use it frequently and in large doses. Most North American groups, such as the Navajo, do not use it in large enough quantities to induce hallucinations or visions, and its traditional use is generally restricted to small amounts during rituals and social and political occasions.[1] Also, as is discussed in chapters 15 and 17, the Navajo and certain other North American Indian groups have lower rates of lung cancer and other tobacco-related disease than are found in the general United States population. Nevertheless, for tobacco shamans, tobacco society members, tobacco priests, and other regular users, tobacco addiction can be a serious problem, though it may be masked or justified by religious activity.

The effects of addiction are both psychological and physiological. For many groups, they are ideological as well. Not only are humans addicted, but their gods and other spirits are also believed to be dependent on tobacco, and they crave its smoke so intensely that they are unable to resist it. "Just as the tobacco shaman of the Warao requires tobacco smoke with tremendous physiological and psychological urgency, and is literally sick without it, so the gods want their gift of tobacco smoke with the craving of the addict, and will enter into mutually beneficial relationships with man so long as he is able to provide the drug" (Wilbert 1975:455).

We see this pattern of Indians attributing their own addiction to their gods and ancestral spirits throughout parts of South America, Central America, and North America (table 47). The Mundurucu Mother of Tobacco not only created tobacco but also died when she ran out of it. The Supreme Spirits of the Warao require tobacco smoke as nourishment from humans. If neglected, they spread sickness and death. The Akawaio recognize their own addiction as well as that of their gods—once a spirit has drunk tobacco, it can no longer resist it and can thus be enticed with tobacco to help humans. The spirits of the Guyana Indians are "crazy" for smoke and are controlled and manipulated through offerings of tobacco (Wilbert 1975:455).

The Balam, or "smoking gods," of the Maya universe also require enormous amounts of tobacco and are well disposed toward humans so long as they provide it (Robicsek 1978). So, too, are the *manitous* of the Sauk Indians of the Great Lakes area, who desire tobacco above everything else (Callender 1978:643). The southwestern Chippewa spirits can also be placated by tobacco, then manipulated into controlling the weather and warding off catastrophe (Ritzenthaler 1978:754). The section on the Haudenosaunee in the previous chapter described how the False Faces and other spirits crave large quantities of tobacco and cannot live without it. Similarly, the great Monster Destroyers at the beginning of the Yurok world smoked constantly—they never ate, drank, or had sex. The Yurok realize that humans crave tobacco, and they attribute this same craving to the immortal spirits (*woge*), such as Pulekukwerek, who grew from a tobacco plant and always had tobacco sprouting from the palms of his hands, so that he never ran out.

In each of these instances and in similar ones, the addictive, chemical bond between plants and humans has been extended symbolically to plants and gods. Just as men and women depend on plants for the mood-altering, vision-inducing effects of nicotine, many of the gods and other spirits depend on humans to provide them with tobacco for life-giving nourishment. Tobacco, the source of addiction, becomes the bridge between the ordinary and superordinary worlds, and in some instances it becomes a god itself. Humans, plants, and spirits are linked together in a complex chemical and ideological relationship. At the heart of it is a simple pharmacological explanation—a chemical dependency—but it is shrouded in sacred smoke and explained by religious belief.

## Prehistoric Origins

Some authors believe that the link between humans and nicotine in the Americas dates back to paleo-Indian times, when the earliest immigrants brought a "cultural predisposition" for

**Table 47: Examples of How Native North American Spirits Crave or Are Identified with Tobacco**

| Group | Example |
|---|---|
| Haudenosaunee | The spirits represented by the False Faces crave tobacco and need it for life. Tobacco grew from the brain of the Earth Mother goddess. |
| Fox | The *manitous* desire tobacco above all else. |
| Delaware | Grandfather Thunder requires the sacrifice of Grandfather Tobacco to avert thunder. |
| Crow | Morning Star, one of the principal deities, turned into the first tobacco plant. |
| Kickapoo | The creator Kitzihiat used a piece of his heart to create the first tobacco. |
| Sioux (Lakota) | Tobacco is the tangible essence of Wholpe, the daughter of the Sun and the Moon. |
| Haida, Tlingit | Raven and other deities created tobacco and bribed each other with its seeds. |
| Yurok | Tobacco turned into Pulekukewerek, one of the creator *woges*, then continued to grow from the palms of his hands, so that he never ran out. He and the other creators ate only tobacco and did not need food, water, or sex. |
| Cahuilla | The creator Mukat drew the first tobacco and pipe from his heart, then created the sun to light them. |
| Aikmel O'odham | The creation of tobacco is an essential part of their creation story, which is called "Smoking Tobacco." |
| Navajo | First Man and First Woman needed to smoke tobacco to create the universe. |
| Aztec | Tobacco was the earthly embodiment of Cihuacoatl, the most powerful of the goddesses. She needed vast quantities of human blood to irrigate her. |
| Maya | Balam "smoking gods" require enormous amounts of tobacco to survive. |
| Huichol | Tobacco grew from the seed of Deer Person, one of the principal deities. |

the use of psychoactive plants from Asia as part of their shamanistic religion (Dobkin de Rios 1984:6; Furst 1976:5–6; La Barre 1970; von Gernet 1989a:6, 1989b:713; von Gernet and Timmons 1987:41; Wilbert 1975:83). According to this theory, the earliest American Indians and their Asian ancestors already used hallucinogenic plants to communicate with the spirit world and to produce the visions and out-of-body journeys that are so much a part of shamanism. When wild tobacco was encountered and experimented with, its powers were easily recognized, so it was added to the Indians' rich pharmacopeia. Von Gernet (1989b:713) has suggested that the earliest paleo-Indian foragers in South America may have discovered tobacco. Siegel (1989:83) has proposed that tobacco shamanism dates back to 6000 B.C., whereas

Johannes Wilbert (1987:149–150) argued that it first evolved with "Neo-Indian farmers." Regardless of the differences over proposed dates, all three authors agree that tobacco was added to an underlying ideological system in which plants were already used for visions, hallucinations, and other shamanistic journeys. They also agree that Indians have continued to use tobacco for shamanistic and related religious purposes for thousands of years, right up to the present.

What proof have we that prehistoric Indians were addicted to tobacco and that this addiction favored its continued use (and possibly even its domestication)? First, concerning the antiquity of tobacco use, the key region of presumed domestication—the Andes, where it is presumed that the two domesticated species evolved—has received almost no archaeological research that bears on this question. Deborah Pearsall (1992), following Edward Lanning (1967:60, 179), has proposed that tobacco appeared on the coast of Peru between 2500 and 1800 B.C., well after the appearance of squash, cotton, beans, sweet potatoes, and the other crops that were first used between 8000 and 6000 B.C. Tobacco does not seem to have been found at many (or any?) other South American archaeological sites, but this does not necessarily mean that it was absent. It may simply mean that it is extremely difficult to recover and identify tobacco seeds, because they are so tiny, or tobacco pollen, which some researchers even say is impossible to distinguish at the species level. It is highly likely that there are many sites in South America that contain the whole prehistoric sequence of tobacco evolution, but no one appears to have searched for them.

The same can be said about Central America and Mexico, where very little relevant research has been carried out. Fortunately, the opposite is true for the United States and Canada, where well over 100 archaeological sites have yielded tobacco seeds, capsules, possible pollen, and other material. Most of the sites producing domesticated *Nicotiana rustica* are late prehistoric and early historic (that is, they range from about A.D. 1000 to 1600); the earliest well-dated one is a Middle Woodland period site in Illinois dating between A.D. 80 and 240. There are more than a dozen other tobacco-bearing sites in the eastern United States and Canada that date from A.D. 300 to 1000; the rest have post–A.D. 1000 contexts.

In other words, by about A.D. 160 a fully domesticated South American species of tobacco was being grown in the heartland of the upper Mississippi Valley, before the definite appearance of corn but in association with a gardening complex of squash, gourds, May grass, marsh elder, goosefoot, knotweed, and sunflowers (Johannessen 1984a; Johannessen and Whalley 1988). It is likely that *N. rustica* was raised even earlier in the eastern woodlands, since pipes

date to a thousand or more years earlier, but even if it was not (and the pipes were used to smoke other plants), it still had to have been raised much earlier in Central America and even earlier than that in South America, where it originated. This species is essentially unknown in the wild—there is only a single South American wild variety (*pavonii*)—and it is likely that it was under cultivation or at least intense exploitation for thousands of years before it reached Illinois. It had to have been carried north by earlier horticulturists and perhaps even by earlier foragers—certainly it did not spread by itself—and it would not be suprising if eventually archaeologists uncover a trail of tobacco-bearing sites stretching south through Central America and on into western South America, dating perhaps as far back as 6000 or 7000 B.C., if not earlier.

Because it is dependent on human propagation, *N. rustica* must have been taken north more than 7,000 miles, from the slopes of the Andes all the way to southern Canada, perhaps as the seeds were passed from one Indian to another, traveling at the rate of only a mile or less per year. Therefore, it is not unreasonable that it took 6,000 or 7,000 years for humans to spread the range of domesticated tobacco, beginning around 7000 B.C. if not earlier, until it reached the upper Mississippi Valley no later than A.D. 160.

The histories of the wild species are also relevant. In the southwestern United States, definite tobacco seeds that are probably *N. attenuata* have been recovered from a site in Arizona dating to about 300 B.C., and possible tobacco pollen dating to about A.D. 1 has been recovered from a site in New Mexico (see chapter 5). Tobacco seeds have also been found in sites that date between A.D. 300 and 400. All of this material is most likely the local wild *N. attenuata*, however, and not the domesticated *N. rustica*, which may not have appeared in the Southwest until A.D. 720 or later. Prior to that, one or more wild tobaccos were used, as they still are, by a number of indigenous groups.

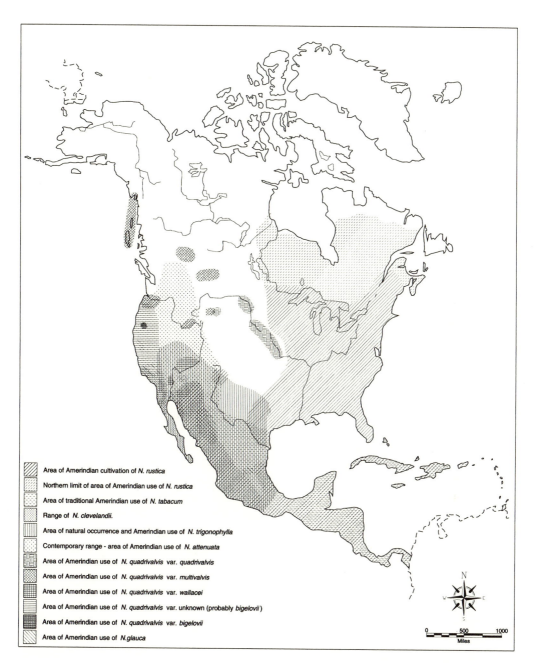

Map 28. Overlapping ranges of wild and domesticated Native American tobaccos in North America.

Map 28 illustrates the overall archaeological, historical, and botanical ranges of the various domesticated and wild tobacco species used by Indians in North America. Several conclusions can be drawn from the patterns shown on this map. First, there are many places on the continent where no tobacco was gathered or raised, undoubtedly because of environmental extremes such as low temperatures, too much or too little moisture, and other factors that forced the local Native Americans to depend on trade and long-distance transport for their tobacco. The Arctic, the southern Great Plains, the high mountain ranges, and the northern boreal forests are such places.

Second, there are other locations where the wild species could not grow but where domesticated *Nicotiana rustica*, the semi-domesticated varieties *multivalvis* and *quadrivalvis* of *N. quadrivalvis*, and even *N. tabacum* could be grown. The eastern woodlands, the Missouri Valley, the northern plains, and the far Northwest Coast are obvious examples.

Third, there are still other areas, such as California, Oregon, and the Great Basin, where the naturally occurring wild species were gathered and often cultivated and where their range was clearly extended by cultivation, as far north as British Columbia.

Fourth, and perhaps most intriguing, are areas such as the Southwest and northern Mexico where not only were the wild and semi-wild species gathered and grown but where *N. rustica* and probably *N. tabacum* were also cultivated, and where five if not more tobacco taxa were utilized. These are the most interesting areas of all, because the domesticated species were not necessary. Equally important, the cultivation of the wild species was not required, since *N. attenuata* and *N. trigonophylla* were and are growing in relative abundance. Yet some groups, such as the Akimel O'odham, Tohono O'odham, and Pueblos, raised and gathered an abundance of tobacco—far more than was necessary for their own use—while developing a highly elaborate ceremonial system that depended to a great extent on tobacco and its symbols. Historical and cultural as well as natural processes were obviously at work in these areas; indeed, it is even possible that the overlapping ranges of the tobacco taxa in these regions are a key to understanding the origins of tobacco use in North America, perhaps even the evolution of the species themselves.

On map 29, the overlapping distributions have been transformed into isotherms that illustrate the number of species used in North America. This idealized map shows a core area

of tobacco use in California, the southwestern U.S., and northern Mexico, with five species used in parts of California and the Southwest and up to three used in northern, central, and southern Mexico. It is proposed that this pattern of multiple taxa use evolved over a considerable period of time. The local wild species served as the first tobacco to have been used in the core areas. The domesticated taxa were added later, followed by the weedy *N. glauca*, which is used primarily in areas where the traditional wild taxa are no longer available (or are no longer known about), such as parts of southern California.

This brings us to the question of the origins of tobacco use in North America and its relationship to other plant use complexes, such as medical plant gathering and food plant agriculture. For some authors, including Richard Ford (1981, 1985:343–344), Richard Yarnell (1964:85), and Harold Driver (1970:106), tobacco use is thought to have appeared relatively late in the sequence of agricultural and medicinal plant developments. Ford and Yarnell each suggest that it was added to already developed farming and medical complexes, and Driver argues that it spread from South America to North America along with other cultivated plants. Ford proposes that the use and cultivation of *N. attenuata* and *N. trigonophylla* outside their native ranges were relatively recent, and that *N. rustica* was added to the eastern agriculture complex in late prehistoric times and to the southwestern agriculture complex only in the historic period. Yarnell suggests that even if *N. rustica* arrived in what is now the United States along with corn, its use was preceded by the smoking of a number of other species of wild plants for medical and religious purposes.

The idea that tobacco use is a relatively recent and nonessential aspect of Native American culture is epitomized by George Carter's conclusion that tobacco is a "useless plant" and that its ingestion was a "strange idea" that spread from South America to North America. During the course of that spread, local wild species were

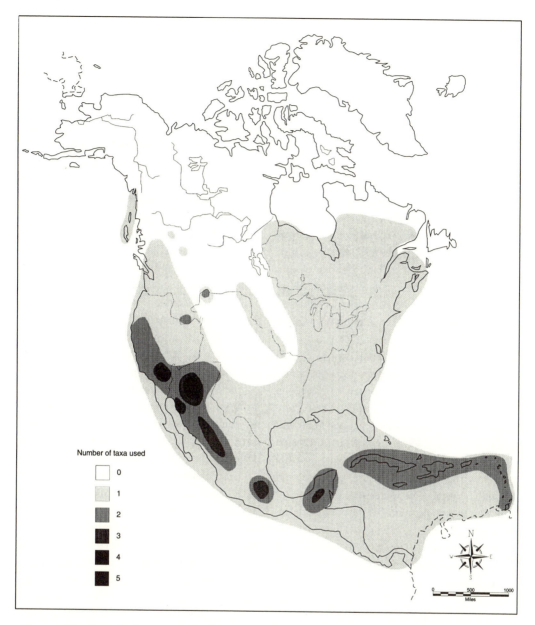

Map 29. Number of tobacco taxa used by native North Americans. Many groups in areas of zero taxa received tobacco through trade.

taken in hand, some becoming fully domesticated, some semi-domesticated, and some tended, and others remaining fully wild and only gathered (Carter 1977:126). Underlying all of this use, according to Carter, was the spread of the "idea" of smoking.

At the opposite end of the continuum are a number of researchers, including me, who propose that tobacco use is a very ancient and far-reaching cultural complex that formed or at least became part of the foundation for other kinds of plant manipulation, perhaps even of agriculture. Siegel (1989:83), for example, believes that tobacco shamanism dates back some 8,000 years and that tobacco was adopted by Paleolithic shamans whose Asian ancestors used mushrooms and other psychotropic plants to induce visions. The use of wild tobacco was added to this shamanistic base, and after the development of slash-and-burn agriculture, tobacco began to be cultivated as a domesticated drug plant.

Charles Heiser (1969:160) proposed that the use of the widely distributed wild tobacco species in the Americas probably extended back to before the beginning of agriculture, and Edgar Anderson (1971 [1952]:135) argued that human use of weedy plants such as tobacco, along with other forms of horticulture, began as far back in time as the Pleistocene. I, too, have suggested that plant husbandry of one form or another was probably practiced by most if not all Native Americans, including those in the Arctic, and that it dates back to the Pleistocene, when the digging of roots, harvesting of seeds, burning of old plant patches to improve the next year's growth, and other intensive gathering techniques began to affect the nature and distribution of plants. In our study of Great Basin Indian use of plants, Pat Hogan and I (Winter and Hogan 1986:120) suggested that the use of tobacco and other manipulated plants by the Shoshone, Paiute, Goshute, and Ute Indians represented a very basic and ancient complex underlying many of the cultural developments in the region. It was only at a relatively recent point in the prehistoric Great Basin archaeological sequence—around A.D. 1—that the Indians added corn farming.

Volney H. Jones and Elizabeth Ann Morris's (1960:117) and Richard Yarnell's (1977:872) proposals that *N. attenuata* was introduced into the Southwest in the prehistoric period is relevant here, particularly in light of Thomas Goodspeed's conclusion (1954:45–46) that the spread of all of the indigenous North American tobaccos throughout the Southwest, California, and the Great Basin was a post-Pleistocene phenomenon. According to Goodspeed, the ancestral indigenous tobaccos probably entered Central America from South America no earlier than the late Pliocene or early Pleistocene, when

desert conditions were pushed southward, linking similar environments on both continents. Prior to this period of dramatic climate change, the arid North American tobacco species could not have survived the more tropical Central American conditions. It probably was not until the early Pleistocene that glacial conditions to the north lowered temperatures and humidity in Central America enough to make the northward migration possible. Goodspeed therefore assumed that the ancestral species of *N. attenuata*, *N. trigonophylla*, and *N. quadrivalvis* entered North America over the Panamanian isthmus during the late Pliocene–early Pleistocene, eventually moving north into southern Mexico. The later replacement of Pleistocene pluvial conditions by post-Pleistocene aridity then allowed them to move north into the Southwest, California, and the Great Basin as the restoration of tropical conditions to the south destroyed their former ranges. *N. attenuata* and *N. quadrivalvis* became restricted to the higher latitudes and elevations as extreme aridity set in, whereas *N. trigonophylla* and *N. clevelandii* were more tolerant of the lower, hotter, and drier elevations and latitudes.

I believe that one more key ingredient should be added to this model: humans. As suggested by Jones and Morris (1960) and by Yarnell (1977), human tobacco gathering and perhaps even tending could have favored this northward movement, as it definitely did with *N. rustica*, *N. tabacum*, and the *N. quadrivalvis* varieties *multivalvis* and *quadrivalvis*. There is no question that these cultivars were taken far from their natural ranges by human cultivation, and there is no question that *N. attenuata* was cultivated well beyond its natural range by the British Columbia Indians. Perhaps all North American tobacco species and their immediate ancestors were affected this way, possibly beginning as far back as the late Pleistocene or early post-Pleistocene, when humans first encountered them.

I propose, then, that when the earliest hunters and gatherers arrived in the New World from

Asia, they already possessed a set of magical and medicinal practices that used plants by drinking, smoking, and otherwise ingesting their chemical powers. As the paleo-Indians slowly moved south through North America, Central America, and eventually South America, they encountered other psychotropic plants, including the various wild species of tobacco, the daturas, and even coca, which they added to this complex. Eventually they began to change the distributions and natures of the tobacco species, first by disturbing the ground around their camp and kill sites, where the tobaccos could grow, then by burning the old plants in the fall to improve the next season's growth, next by pruning and irrigating them, and finally by planting them. Over the next few millenia—as they came increasingly to depend on tobacco—they developed tobacco shamanism and other religious rites organized around the large-scale ingestion of nicotine. They also increased the nicotine content of tobacco through intentional selection, and many of them—and even their gods—became addicted.

The antiquity of this sequence is reflected in the fact that many tribes' origin stories mention the use of tobacco very early in the groups' mythological histories. For some tribes, tobacco was necessary for the very act of creating the universe. Indeed, for certain groups tobacco is the manifestation of the creating god itself, or part of his or her body. Sometimes tobacco is also necessary for existence itself to continue, as well as for the daily, seasonal, and yearly cycles of creation.

This power of tobacco as an absolutely essential food of the gods—at times the creator god itself—is surely a reflection of the antiquity of tobacco use and its pervasive role in the evolution of Native American religion. The use of tobacco can probably be traced back to the earliest proto-Indian cultures as they spread south through what is now northern Mexico and adjacent parts of Arizona, New Mexico, and California, where they first began to harness the coercive, magical powers of this amazing plant.

And while they were doing so, they sometimes found it necessary to manipulate the plant—to burn and water and weed and plant it—so that they could extend its range a little farther as their seasonal movements took them into areas where it did not grow naturally. Thus the ranges of *N. attenuata*, *N. trigonophylla*, and *N. quadrivalvis* were gradually extended far to the north, east, and south as the hunters and gatherers traveled widely throughout their annual cycle. And in the case at least one wild species (*N. quadrivalvis*), the wide-ranging foragers learned that the only way they could continue to have access to this important drug was to carry its seeds with them and plant them far from its natural range, in places such as southern Alaska and the far northern Canadian plains.

They also increased the nicotine content of tobacco and created entirely new species. In California, two species (*N. quadrivalvis* and *N. clevelandii*) may have been created, or at least heavily modified, by human selection. There is no question that the varieties *multivalvis* and *quadrivalvis* of *N. quadrivalvis* were created by human activity. In chapter 6, Julia Hammett described how the two varieties might have been created, then taken far from their natural range to locations where they could survive only through cultivation. Their parent species, as well as the closely related *N. clevelandii*, appear to have evolved in southern California from a now-extinct species that grew in northwestern Mexico, which in turn evolved from one or more South American species. The northwest Mexico species may have combined with one or more of the ancestors of *N. attenuata*, thereby creating the earliest *N. quadrivalvis* and *N. clevelandii* (Goodspeed 1954:48).

Although it is certainly possible that this process occurred before humans arrived on the scene, it is more likely that it was due to (or at least helped by) the activities of the earliest Indians in the region, who began using the ancestral species, expanding their ranges, and even growing them together in southern California.[2] *N. clevelandii* and *N. quadrivalvis*

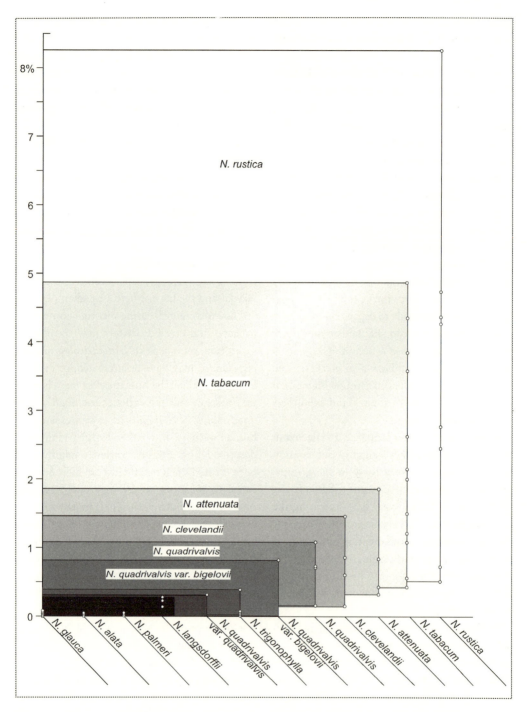

Figure 28. Mean nicotine frequencies of native North American tobacco taxa. See accompanying tables for sources.

differentiated as a result, with *N. clevelandii* remaining along the southern California coast and in adjacent Mexico while *N. quadrivalvis* was taken to slightly higher and moister areas to the north. Eventually the cultivated varieties of *N. quadrivalvis* were taken as far north and east as the Alaska panhandle, the upper Missouri, and the Canadian plains.

*N. attenuata*'s range was also extended (at least in part) by human manipulation, all the way from northern Mexico to southern Canada. Equally important, its nicotine content was probably increased as well. As shown in figure 28 and tables 48–51, *N. attenuata* has the highest mean nicotine content of all of the wild tobaccos used by North American Indians. Indeed, its nicotine content is even higher than that of several strains of the domesticated *N. tabacum* and *N. rustica*. *N. clevelandii*, *N. quadrivalvis*, and *N. trigonophylla* also have a fairly high nicotine content, at least in comparison with the recently introduced and infrequently used *N. glauca*, *N. alata*, and *N. langsdorffii*. In other words, it appears that the more extensive and widespread the use of the wild tobacco species by Native Americans, the higher the nicotine content.

Human selection was also responsible for the domestication of *N. rustica* and *N. tabacum*, as well as for the northward expansion of their ranges in prehistoric times for 7,000 miles or more, and their worldwide expansion more recently. Selection by Native Americans has also produced extremely high nicotine measurements for *N. rustica*; Huichol Indian tobacco in western Mexico ranges up to an astounding 18 percent, with an equally amazing mean nicotine content of 8.26 percent. This same kind of selection for higher nicotine content—which increases the psychotropic qualities of the plant—probably played an important part in the domestication of the two cultivars, and perhaps in their very creation. Several authors have concluded that the manner of origin, selection, and cultivation of the domesticated species must have produced a high alkaloid content, which favored

the formation of nicotine (Smith and Smith 1942:347).[3] It is also likely that the increased alkaloid content enhanced the survival of the species.

These conclusions are supported by the fact that all tobacco species contain nicotine and/or the closely related alkaloids nornicotine and anabasine, which probably reflect some adaptive value to the genus as a whole. The results of comparative studies, such as H. H. Smith and D. V. Abashian's analyses (1963:445), indicate that the kinds and relative amounts of alkaloids in the different species are unrelated to adaptations to specific environmental conditions. Instead, they appear to be the result of human selection: the wild taxa generally contain much lower levels of nicotine and other alkaloids, and the two domesticated species contain higher levels.

Table 48 and figure 28 demonstrate how the domesticated taxa have higher percentages of nicotine and total alkaloids. *N. rustica* has the highest nicotine–total alkaloid frequency by dry leaf weight, followed by *N. tabacum* and then by the wild species used by Native Americans. Of the latter, *N. attenuata* has the highest nicotine content, followed by *N. clevelandii*, *N. quadrivalvis* var. *bigelovii*, *N. trigonophylla*, and *N. quadrivalvis* var. *quadrivalvis*.

The data in these tables and the figure have been taken from many different studies, which varied greatly in their methods of analysis and the manner in which the tobaccos were raised. Also, variations in soil, water, the age of the plants, the position of the leaves on the plants, and other factors have been shown to affect nicotine content in the same species. Nevertheless, the patterns emerging from the analyses are probably accurate, especially in the most recent and well-controlled studies, such as Verne Sisson and R. F. Severson's (1990), with *N. attenuata* representing one of the most preferred of the North American wild species, probably because of its higher nicotine content. *N. clevelandii* is next in nicotine frequency, followed by *N. quadrivalvis* and *N. trigonophylla*,

Table 48: Percentages of Nicotine, Nornicotine, and Anabasine in Tobacco Species Used by Native North Americans

| *Nicotiana* Taxon | % Nicotine | % Nor-nicotine | % Anabasine | % Total Alkaloids[a] | Source |
|---|---|---|---|---|---|
| N. alata | Trace[b] | 0.00 | 0.00 | Trace | Saitoh et al. 1985[c] |
| | Trace | 0.00 | 0.00 | Trace | Sisson and Severson 1990[d] |
| | 0.01 | Trace | Trace | 0.02 | Sisson and Severson 1990[e] |
| N. attenuata | 0.73 | NC | NC | NC | Couch 1927 |
| | 1.86 | 0.14 | 0.00 | 2.0% | Bowen 1945 |
| | 1.45 | 0.00 | 0.00 | 1.45 | Bowen 1945 |
| | 0.41 | 0.01 | Trace | 0.35 | Jeffrey 1959 |
| | 2.18 | 0.02 | Trace | 2.22 | Saitoh et al. 1985[c] |
| | 0.34 | Trace | Trace | 0.37 | Sisson and Severson 1990[d] |
| | 0.86 | Trace | Trace | 0.90 | Sisson and Severson 1990[e] |
| N. quadrivalvis | 0.16 | 0.00 | 0.18 | 0.34 | Bowen 1945 |
| | 0.16 | NC | NC | NC | Smith and Smith 1942 |
| | 0.75 | 0.02 | Trace | 0.78 | Saitoh et al. 1985[c] |
| | 0.73 | Trace | 0.00 | 0.78 | Sisson and Severson 1990[d] |
| | 1.10 | Trace | Trace | 1.24 | Sisson and Severson 1990[e] |
| Var. bigelovii | 0.83 | Trace | 0.02 | 0.87 | Jeffrey 1959 |
| Var. quadrivalvis | 0.32 | Trace | 0.00 | 0.37 | Jeffrey 1959 |
| N. clevelandii | 0.16 | 0.00 | 0.00 | 0.17 | Jeffrey 1959 |
| | 0.88 | Trace | Trace | 0.89 | Saitoh et al. 1985[c] |
| | 0.62 | Trace | 0.00 | 0.64 | Sisson and Severson 1990[d] |
| | 1.48 | Trace | Trace | 1.57 | Sisson and Severson 1990[e] |
| N. glauca | 0.02 | 0.00 | 0.62 | 0.64 | Smith and Smith 1942 |
| | – | 0.00 | 0.33 | 0.33 | Jackson 1940 |
| | – | 0.00 | 0.82 | 0.86 | Jeffrey 1959 |
| | 0.11 | 0.01 | 0.76 | 0.89 | Saitoh et al. 1985[c] |
| | 0.01 | Trace | 0.08 | 0.09 | Sisson and Severson 1990[d] |
| | Trace | Trace | 0.41 | 0.42 | Sisson and Severson 1990[e] |
| N. langsdorffii[f] | 0.25 | Trace | Trace | 0.26 | Saitoh et al. 1985[c] |
| | 0.16 | Trace | 0.00 | 0.17 | Sisson and Severson 1990[d] |
| | 0.30 | Trace | Trace | 0.31 | Sisson and Severson 1990[e] |
| N. palmeri (trigonophylla) | 0.02 | 0.44 | 0.04 | 0.52 | Jeffrey 1959 |
| | 0.03 | 0.41 | Trace | 0.47 | Sisson and Severson 1990[d] |
| | Trace | 0.19 | Trace | 0.21 | Sisson and Severson 1990[e] |
| N. rustica | 0.75 | Trace | Trace | 0.78 | Saitoh et al. 1985[c] |
| | 2.47 | 0.02 | 0.01 | 2.53 | Sisson and Severson 1990[d] |

Table 48: Percentages of Nicotine, Nornicotine, and Anabasine in Tobacco Species Used by Native North Americans (continued)

| *Nicotiana* Taxon | % Nicotine | % Nor-nicotine | % Anabasine | % Total Alkaloids[a] | Source |
|---|---|---|---|---|---|
| | 0.53 | Trace | Trace | 0.54 | Sisson and Severson 1990[e] |
| Tall type | 2.77 | NC | NC | NC | Smith and Bacon 1941 |
| 25 types | 4.27 | NC | NC | NC | Smith and Bacon 1941 |
| Var. *brasilia* | 4.37 | NC | NC | NC | Smith and Bacon 1941 |
| 2 types | 4.74 | NC | NC | NC | Smith and Bacon 1941 |
| Huichol | 8.26 | NC | NC | NC | Siegel et al. 1977 |
| Var. *brasilia* | 3.67 | 0.00 | 0.00 | 4.09 | Jeffrey 1959 |
| *N. sylvestris* | 0.33 | NC | NC | NC | Jeffrey 1959 |
| *N. tabacum* | 0.43 | NC | NC | NC | Jackson 1940 |
| | 3.59 | NC | NC | NC | Bascot 1960 |
| | 1.50 | NC | NC | NC | Siegel et al. 1977 |
| | 3.85 | 0.28 | 0.00 | 4.13+ | Weybrew and Mann 1963 |
| | 2.64 | NC | NC | NC | Lancet 1912, cited in Ortiz 1978 |
| | 4.37 | NC | NC | NC | Wright and Moffat 1958, cited in Ortiz 1978 |
| | 4.88 | NC | NC | NC | Schloesing 1888, cited in Ortiz 1978 |
| | 1.10 | 0.03 | Trace | 1.14 | Saitoh et al. 1985[c] |
| | 2.33 | 0.17 | Trace | 2.53 | Sisson and Saunders 1982 |
| | 1.23 | 0.02 | Trace | 1.30 | Sisson and Severson 1990[d] |
| | 0.58 | Trace | Trace | 0.61 | Sisson and Severson 1990[e] |
| 20 types | 2.02 | NC | NC | NC | Sisson and Saunders 1982 |
| 13 types | 2.15 | NC | NC | NC | Tso 1972 |
| 19 commercial brands | 1.98 | NC | NC | NC | Santa Fe Natural Tobacco Co. 1989 |
| *N. trigonophylla* | 0.03 | 0.20 | 0.00 | 0.23 | Bowen 1945 |
| | – | 0.06 | 0.00 | 0.06 | Smith and Smith 1942 |
| | 0.39 | 0.00 | 0.00 | 0.39 | Marsh et al. 1927 |
| | Trace | 0.10 | Trace | 0.11 | Saitoh et al. 1985[c] |
| | 0.01 | 0.10 | Trace | 0.12 | Sisson and Severson 1990[d] |
| | Trace | 0.11 | Trace | 0.12 | Sisson and Severson 1990[e] |

Note: In some cases ranges of percentages have been averaged. Measurements are by dry leaf weight. NC = not calculated or reported.

a   In certain cases other alkaloids are present.
b   Trace = less than .01%.
c   Leaf measurements only; roots not included.
d   Field-grown plants.
e   Greenhouse-grown plants.
f   Evidence for use of *N. langsdorffii* is very weak.

which also have relatively widespread geographic distributions and are culturally preferred. *N. palmeri* (probably a variety of *N. trigonophylla*), *N. glauca*, and several introductions—which are seldom used—have the smallest amounts of nicotine. In short, with only one exception (*N. clevelandii*), the greater the nicotine (or other alkaloids), the more widespread the use. The very limited distribution of *N. clevelandii* may be due to the fact that it is a diminutive, low desert and coastal version of *N. quadrivalvis*, which has a relatively widespread range.

The nicotine frequencies of four of the six wild North American taxa that were *not* used by Indians support this conclusion (table 49). Two varieties of the introduced *N. accuminata*, the indigenous *N. nudicaulis*, and the introduced *N. longifolia* have some of the lowest nicotine and/or other alkaloid frequencies of any species that have been measured. Two other species, in contrast, do not fit this pattern. One of the nonutilized North American wild species (*N. nesophila*) has almost as high an alkaloid content as *N. attenuata*, and *N. repanda* is also relatively high in nicotine–other alkaloid content for an unused wild species. I suspect that both taxa were actually used by Native Americans, despite their apparent absence from the ethnographic and archaeological records. Also, *N. nesophila* has an extremely restricted distribution (it grows only on a few small islands off the west coast of Mexico), and *N. repanda* is from a region (southeastern Texas and adjacent parts of Mexico) that has received relatively little relevant research.

Although they were not used in North America, the presumed wild ancestors of *N. tabacum* and *N. rustica* also have interesting

Table 49: Percentages of Nicotine and Total Alkaloids in North American Tobacco Species Not Used by Native Americans

| Taxon | % Nicotine | % Total Alkaloids |
|---|---|---|
| N. acuminata | 0.06 | 0.07 |
| | Trace[a] | 0.01 |
| | Trace | 0.02 |
| Var. acuminata | – | 0.04 |
| Var. multiflora | 0.17 | 0.14 |
| N. longifolia | Trace | 0.04 |
| | Trace | Trace |
| | 0.01 | 0.02 |
| | Trace | 0.06 |
| N. nesophila | 0.65 | 1.33 |
| | 0.48 | 1.06 |
| | 0.16 | 1.81 |
| | 0.07 | 0.75 |
| N. nudicaulis | 0.01 | 0.15 |
| | Trace | 0.18 |
| | 0.02 | 0.25 |
| | Trace | 0.10 |
| N. repanda | 0.66 | 0.89 |
| | Trace | 0.33 |
| | 0.11 | 0.56 |
| | 0.01 | 0.18 |

Sources: Jeffrey 1959; Saitoh et al. 1985; Sisson and Severson 1990.
Note:    Measurements are by dry leaf weight. Some taxa are introduced.
a    Trace = less than .01%.

Table 50: Mean Percentages of Alkaloids in Domesticated Tobacco Species and Their Presumed Wild Ancestors

| Nicotiana Taxon | % Nicotine | % Nor-nicotine | % Anabasine | Total Alkaloids |
|---|---|---|---|---|
| N. rustica | 2.47 | 0.02 | 0.01 | 2.56 |
| N. undulata | 1.17 | 0.09 | 0.01 | 1.28 |
| N. paniculata | 0.29 | 0.03 | Trace[a] | 0.95 |
| N. tabacum | 1.23 | 0.02 | Trace | 1.30 |
| N. sylvestris[b] | 1.30 | 0.05 | Trace | 1.42 |
| N. otophora[b] | Trace | 0.08 | Trace | 0.10 |
| N. tomentosiformis[b] | Trace | 0.08 | Trace | 0.06 |

Source:  Sisson and Severson 1990, field-grown data. See other tables for earlier studies, as well as for Sisson and Severson's 1990 greenhouse-grown data.

Note:  Measurements are by dry leaf weight.

a   Trace = less than .01%.

b   Either N. otophora or N. tomentosiformis (or one of its ancestors) is considered one of the ancestral species, along with N. sylvestris (or one of its ancestors).

Table 51: Mean Percentages of Nicotine and Total Alkaloids by Rank for Native North American Tobacco Species Used by American Indians, and Certain Ancestral Tobacco Species

| Taxon | % Nicotine | % Total Alkaloids |
|---|---|---|
| N. rustica | 2.47 | 2.56 |
| N. sylvestris[a] | 1.30 | 1.42 |
| N. tabacum | 1.23 | 1.30 |
| N. undulata[a] | 1.17 | 1.28 |
| N. quadrivalvis | 0.73 | 0.78 |
| N. clevelandii | 0.62 | 0.64 |
| N. attenuata | 0.34 | 0.37 |
| N. paniculata[a] | 0.29 | 0.33 |
| N. langsdorffii | 0.16 | 0.17 |
| N. alata | 0.10 | 0.10 |
| N. palmeri (trigonophylla) | 0.03 | 0.46 |
| N. trigonophylla | 0.01 | 0.12 |
| N. otophora[a] | Trace | 0.10 |
| N. glauca | Trace | 0.09 |
| N. tomentosiformis[a] | Trace | 0.06 |

Note:  Measurements are by dry leaf weight. Only Sisson and Severson's 1990 field-grown data are shown. See other tables for earlier data and references. Evidence for Native American use of N. langsdorffii is very weak.

a   Presumed ancestor of N. tabacum and N. rustica.

nicotine frequencies. Two of the taxa (N. sylvestris and N. undulata) have the highest nicotine-alkaloid contents of any wild tobacco, and N. paniculata is close behind. Both domesticated species therefore have at least one presumed wild ancestor that is extremely high in nicotine (relative to other wild taxa), which indicates that prehistoric Native Americans were almost certainly selecting the seeds of wild tobaccos with high nicotine content, planting them together, and raising the resulting hybrids.

Taken together, the data in the accompanying tables and figure 28 suggest that prehistoric selection for nicotine and/or other alkaloids played an important role in the creation and domestication of the two domesticated tobacco species, as well as in the manipulation of several semi-domesticated wild species. A mutation in the gene that is responsible for nicotine demethylation (which creates nornicotine) also probably played a part in this process (Bohm 1985:13), at least with respect to *N. tabacum*. Since this gene is dominant and unstable with a high mutation frequency, it is entirely possible that the Indians' earliest attempts at selecting for nornicotine and nicotine in *N. sylvestris*, *N. otophora*, and/or *N. tomentosiformis* helped to create an entirely new species with an even higher alkaloid content. Their attempts to enhance the plants' survival by weeding, burning old plants, sowing seeds, irrigating young plants, and other forms of tending may also have contributed to the process.

Nicotine $(C_{10}H_{14}N_2)$ and nornicotine $(C_9H_{12}N_2)$ are closely related, the only difference being that nornicotine is a demethylated form of nicotine. Otherwise, the two highly toxic alkaloids are essentially the same, with identical potency (Volle and Koelle 1970:587; Wilbert 1987:134). Anabasine—the other main alkaloid in most tobacco species—is also very similar to nicotine, with an identical chemical formula $(C_{10}H_{14}N_2)$. Sometimes called neonicotine, anabasine and nicotine have the same physiological effects on humans, including the ways in which they change blood pressure, the manner in which they stimulate and then paralyze the cervical ganglia, and their ability to increase the flow of adrenalin (Budavari 1989; Volle and Koelle 1970). This may help explain why *N. glauca*, the tobacco species with the highest concentration of anabasine (but almost no nicotine), has been readily accepted by the Barona band of the Diegueno in southern California and is sometimes used by other southern California and Mexican tribal groups (see chapters 2 and 5). My informal experiments in smoking very small amounts of *N. glauca*, *N. trigonophylla*, and *N. sylvestris*—all of which have greater amounts of anabasine and/or nornicotine than do the domesticated taxa—also suggest that both alkaloids are capable of producing the same short-term, mildly psycho-

trophic effects as nicotine, and they have a similar taste and smell.[4] This could explain why several of these taxa were and are used by native North Americans despite their lower levels of nicotine.

## Proposed Sequence of Tobacco Evolution

On the basis of all this information, the following hypothetical model of the evolution of the two domesticated species and the various wild species used by indigenous North Americans has been developed (Winter 1991). This proposal takes into account the issues of Native American addiction and the adverse effects of tobacco abuse as well as the relationship of the domestication of tobacco to the domestication of food crops. There are four stages to the sequence; map 30 illustrates it.

### Stage 1: Evolution of the Wild Desert Species of North America

The ancestors of the so-called desert or indigenous species—*N. attenuata*, *N. trigonophylla/palmeri*, *N. quadrivalvis*, and *N. clevelandii*—probably entered Central America from South America during the late Pliocene or early Pleistocene, when the onset of glaciation far to the north reduced temperature and humidity enough that dry conditions were pushed south, linking the deserts in North and South America (Goodspeed 1954:45–46). The desert species could not have survived the more tropical conditions of Central America before or after that period, and indeed it was probably not until the end of the Pleistocene that the ancestral desert species were able to reach northern Mexico as pluvial conditions in those areas were replaced by increasing aridity. The restoration of tropical conditions in Central America at the end of the Pleistocene would have destroyed their range in that region.

The northward migration of these species was favored by climatic change and increasing aridity. The arrival of humans in northern Mexico and

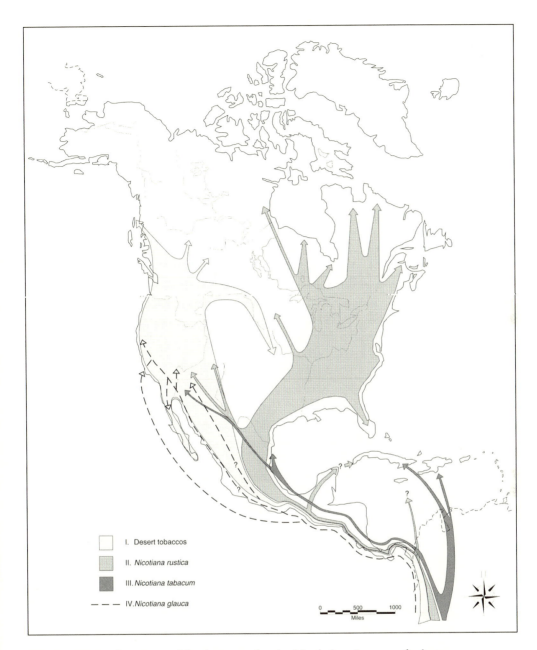

Map 30. Proposed sequence of development of native North American use of tobacco.

Central America during or after the late Pleisto-cene was probably of equal importance, because foraging populations disturbed the landscape with their camps and fires and began to use the wild tobaccos for medicinal, religious, and recreational purposes. Within a short time the Indians were encouraging the ancestral wild species by burning the old plants in the fall and perhaps by broadcast sowing their seeds. Then, as the paleo-Indians pushed south through Central America and into South America, other Indians carried and traded tobacco back to the north.

By 8000 or 9000 B.C., the ancestral North American tobacco species were established in the low deserts of southern California and the Southwest. By 4000 or 5000 B.C., the modern species had probably evolved as a result of natural and cultural selection.

Over the next 5,000 to 6,000 years, Native Americans took *Nicotiana attenuata* throughout the high deserts of the Southwest, California, and the Great Basin and even beyond, into southern Canada. *N. quadrivalvis* was taken even further, all the way to south coastal Alaska and east across the Continental Divide onto the northern plains and down the Missouri, eventually reaching the Dakotas by A.D. 1000. Both of its cultivated varieties (*multivalvis* and *quadrivalvis*) were created by human selection, and even the evolution of the parent species and the extension of its range into nondesert environs were probably the result of human activity. *N. trigonophylla/ palmeri* and *N. clevelandii* remained in Mexico, the Southwest, southern California, and the southern Great Basin, where they were restricted to the low deserts.

One final note about the indigenous *Nicotianas* is that they are essentially the tobaccos of choice of the hunters, gatherers, and fishers. A few of the later farming groups in the Southwest continued to use them, but for the most part they were used by (and sometimes raised by) the foragers of the west, the fishers of the western coast and river valleys, and the hunters of the plains. Even the farmers of the Southwest evolved out of earlier Archaic foraging cultures who probably used and may even have grown *N. attenuata* and *N. trigonophylla*. Anthropologists have traditionally viewed hunters and gatherers as nonfarmers, yet many of these cultures raised tobacco, and others weeded, pruned, and otherwise manipulated it. This pattern of casual horticulture by foragers probably extends back to Archaic if not paleo-Indian times, so we may be seeing the origins of agriculture, not for food but for drugs and medicine.

## Stage 2: Evolution of Domesticated *Nicotiana rustica*

Domesticated tobacco, in contrast, is the tobacco of farmers. The more potent of the two domesticated species may have originated among hunters and gatherers, and in the far north it was used by historic foragers, but otherwise it was raised by farming populations throughout parts of South America, Central America, and North America.

The ancestral species—which may have been *N. paniculata* and *N. undulata* or their progenitors—were probably in existence by the end of the late Pliocene or early Pleistocene in the highlands of South America. It was not until humans arrived on the scene that *N. rustica* was taken north out of the mountains into Central America. This probably did not occur until the species was domesticated, or at least selected for as a weed. Indeed, the very creation of *N. rustica* as a species may have occurred through human manipulation. By 5000 B.C. it could have arrived in Central America and perhaps even Mexico, and by 1000–2000 B.C. (if not earlier) it had reached the Mississippi Valley. It was almost definitely raised there by about A.D. 160, and by A.D. 1000 it was probably raised throughout the eastern woodlands and parts of the Southwest.

The origins of *N. rustica* in South America could date back as far as paleo-Indian times, when the earliest Indians in the Andes began to use the local wild tobaccos. Within a short time this pattern of use might have included the broadcast sowing of seeds of both of the ancestral species, as well as the selection of plants and seeds with greater amounts of nicotine. Tobacco tending and nicotine selection eventually produced a new species (*N. rustica*) that contained even higher levels of nicotine and was basically dependent on human propagation. Within a short time this potent tobacco became a central element in the religious systems of its creators, who used it to induce visions and other forms of communication with the spirit world. It was also carried and/or traded to groups outside of its natural range, who attempted to plant it, tend it, and select for even higher nicotine content. In this way its range was steadily expanded to the north as its nicotine content steadily increased. It probably reached western Mexico by 5000 B.C., if not earlier. There the ancestors of the Huichol Indians continued to increase its nicotine content, eventually producing a variety that contained up to 18 percent nicotine.

In addition to *N. rustica*'s ability to induce visions, its steadily increasing levels of nicotine may have produced addiction, at least among the shamans and other religious practitioners who used it in large doses daily or frequently. Addiction might therefore have been another factor contributing to its domestication and/or northward expansion. As shamans at the very edge of its range began to use it regularly and become addicted to it, they might have shared it with nearby colleagues just outside its range, who also became addicted, while other tribal members traded it to still other shamans even farther away. Lacking direct access to the plant but depending on it not only for its vision-inducing powers but also to satisfy their physiological need (as well as the craving of their gods), perhaps they started to plant its seeds or otherwise tend it or its ancestors, thereby producing a domesticate or at least extending the range of a weedy semi-domesticate. By the time that it reached western Mexico and the prehistoric Huichol Indians it was probably a true domesticate. Then the same processes continued to favor the northward expansion of its range from one garden to another, all the way to what is now Ontario and Quebec.

This set of interrelated processes would not have required prior knowledge of agriculture. Indeed, many historic hunters, gatherers, and fishers in California, the Great Basin, the Northwest Coast, and interior Canada planted or otherwise tended wild tobacco without the use of other cultigens. As discussed previously, it is likely that even the earliest paleo-Indians manipulated wild plants, and their foraging descendants could have manipulated and tended tobacco as soon as they came to depend upon it.

If tobacco was tended, raised, and domesticated before the food crops were, then this knowledge could have been extended to the wild ancestors of potatoes, beans, maize, and other crops, perhaps as the earliest *N. rustica* was carried northward out of the Andes into Central America, Mexico, and eventually the rest of North America. It is also possible that a whole complex of cultigens evolved together as humans learned to manipulate more and more plants, to select for higher levels of nicotine, larger tubers, and softer kernels, and otherwise to modify the plants they encountered.

### Stage 3: Evolution of *Nicotiana tabacum*

The other domesticated tobacco is the weaker (though still potent) *N. tabacum*, with a native North American range that was restricted to Mexico and the rest of Central America, the Caribbean, and the southern parts of Texas and Arizona. It is extremely important in the lowlands of South America, especially in the Amazon basin, where it forms the basis of tobacco shamanism. It also appears that *N. rustica* cannot be grown in the wet, tropical lowlands, which may explain why *N. tabacum* was domesticated. Whereas *N. rustica* was taken north out of the Andes, *N. tabacum* was taken east, down into the jungle. The same processes that were involved in the domestication of the more potent *N. rustica* might also have figured in the domestication of *N. tabacum*—tobacco tending and the sowing together of seeds of the ancestral species at the edges of and just beyond their natural ranges; selection for plants with higher nicotine content; and shamans' addiction to tobacco use.

Because *N. rustica* was stronger and better adapted to conditions in Central America and Mexico, it was probably preferred over *N. tabacum* once the Johnny-come-lately arrived on the scene. Nevertheless, the Indians of the region gradually accepted the less potent species, possibly because of its lower nicotine content and smoother taste, which would have facilitated the development of widespread cigarette manufacture and use for pleasure, feasts, and social occasions as well as for religious events, as reported for the Aztec and other protohistoric, state-level inhabitants of Mexico. Even today the Huichol, Zuni, Navajo, and other traditional groups in North America appear to prefer *N. tabacum* cigarettes for social occasions and "recreational" smoking, whereas *N. rustica, N. attenuata,* and other species are saved for special religious uses.

### Stage 4: Introduction of *N. glauca, N. alata,* and Other Recent Arrivals

The final tobaccos in this sequence of taxa ingested by native North Americans are the newcomers, which may all have been introduced relatively recently from South America. *N. glauca* was probably introduced by boat into one or more of the California ports in the eighteenth or nineteenth centuries, and from there it spread throughout southern California and into southern Arizona. It was also introduced into Mexico, where it grows as far north as Chihuahua City. A number of native groups in southern California and perhaps southern Arizona use it as a traditional tobacco.

*N. alata* and *N. sylvestris* were introduced more recently as ornamentals. They are occasionally grown by Native Americans who recognize them as true tobaccos and use them for religious purposes. Their use, along with that of *N. glauca,* demonstrates how American Indians are opportunistic when it comes to this special plant.

### Discussion

The domestication of tobacco and its widespread use by Native Americans has had profound effects upon the rest of the world. Previously used by Indians primarily as an offering and a way to communicate with the spirit world, tobacco is now ingested as a recreational, addictive drug all around the planet, with enormous economic and medical consequences. According to a former U.S. Department of Health and Human Services Secretary, the costs of health care and lost productivity due to smoking-related illnesses and death amount to $52 billion a year in the United States alone, or about $221 per person per year in medical, insurance, and other costs. "Smoking is perhaps the single most important cause of chronic disease in the world" (Health Research 1990).

For many Native Americans, tobacco is also a food of the gods, at times a god itself. Many thousands of years ago, perhaps before the food plants were domesticated, Native Americans began to collect the leaves of a number of wild tobacco species (including the ancestors of the two domesticated taxa) for use in religious, social, and other activities. Soon they discovered that certain species and particular patches of certain species produced mind-altering effects ranging from short-term, pleasant relaxation to visions and transportation to the supernatural world. The continued selection of plants in these patches, the probable manipulation of them through weeding, burning, and perhaps even irrigating, and the possible sowing together of seeds from two high-nicotine taxa outside of their natural ranges may well have produced the two domesticated species. Over time the domesticated taxa were taken throughout the Americas, and the ranges of a number of the wild species were greatly expanded, resulting in the creation of several cultivated wild varieties.

This long evolutionary process was ultimately caused by two interrelated pharmacological properties of the tobacco plant: the first is that nicotine, nornicotine, and the other alkaloids in tobacco are mind-altering, pyschotropic chemicals, and the second is that they are addictive. These are, of course, the same properties that have resulted in the worldwide use of the domesticated species in the historic period, but they probably had an effect upon Native

Americans for thousands of years prior to the appearance of Europeans in North America—ever since the earliest Indians discovered one or another of the wild taxa.

Nicotine and the other alkaloids are biphasic drugs: in small doses they increase locomoter activity and vigilance and allow more rapid, enhanced learning. They are also stimulants, while at the same time they provide selective calming and relaxing effects, serve as hunger and thirst supressants, and are analgesics. In large doses they produce visions, hallucinations, trances, seizures, color blindness, catatonia, and even death (Siegel 1989:96; Wilbert 1987:19).

Regular use of tobacco, even in small doses as a stimulant, increases tolerance and rapidly leads to habituation and eventually to addiction. As the effects of the regular use of nicotine wear off—be they the pleasant, calming effects of small doses or the intoxicating effects of massive doses—withdrawal symptoms set in, with opposite effects: tension, restlessness, irritability, increased hunger, insomnia, inability to concentrate, and intense craving for more tobacco. The ingestion of more tobacco relieves these symptoms (nicotine reaches the brain within seven seconds of the ingestion of smoke), thereby producing a cycling between satiation and withdrawal, which defines the state of physical addiction (Siegel 1989:96).

It is precisely these properties—the short-term, mind-altering effects of nicotine and the other alkaloids and their ability to create long-term addiction—that might have led shamans and other heavy users to domesticate a number of the wild species and to expand the ranges of others. This does not mean, however, that all Indian users became addicts, or that all shamans are. In the next chapter, Jonathan Samet presents considerable evidence indicating that as a group, traditional native North Americans have historically had lower rates of tobacco-induced lung cancer and heart disease than the rest of the U.S. population. Equally important, Indians in the southwestern United States, who are generally more traditional than Indians in more urban areas, such as parts of California, have lower rates of these diseases than do other Indians. The Southwest is also a region where tobacco shamanism, tobacco societies, and tobacco priesthoods are not present and where even medicine men and priests do not appear to ingest large amounts of tobacco. Rather, they and much of the traditional Indian population as a whole use tobacco in carefully controlled ritual situations, in relatively small amounts, and with great respect for its power and danger. Commercial tobacco use and the rates of tobacco-related diseases are on the increase amoung Native Americans, especially among the youth, but on the whole traditional tobacco use is still fairly ritualized, though extremely important.

It therefore appears that the ritual use of traditional tobacco has a continuum of increasing health effects leading up to addiction and death, depending upon the nicotine concentrations in the species that are used, the dosage ingested, and the frequency of use. For many religious practitioners and other Indians, traditional tobacco use is strictly controlled and limited to sacrificial offerings and rituals. It may be used fairly often, but in tiny amounts, and more often than not its use involves puffing a pipe or corn-husk cigarette a few times without inhaling. These Native Americans have great respect for the dangers inherent in tobacco, and they do not become addicted, nor do they suffer from the long-term health effects associated with addiction.

Other Indians, in contrast, especially tobacco shamans, ingest extremely large quantities of very potent domesticated *N. rustica* and relatively potent *N. tabacum* and certain wild taxa, frequently over long time periods. Not only does this heavy use produce visions, trances, and direct communication with the supernatural world, but it can also lead to addiction, seizures, color blindness, comas, and death. Thousands of years ago in the Andes and adjacent tropics, this heavy use of several wild tobacco species that are fairly high in nicotine (including *N. sylvestris*, which has the highest levels of nicotine of any wild species) probably led to addiction and the creation of the first domesticated tobacco plant.

It is even possible that as soon as the earliest Native Americans encountered wild tobacco, they began using it. Even as early as paleo-Indian times, Native Americans may have discovered not only its pleasurable effects but also the addiction and craving that often accompany these effects. Addiction has probably been associated with the use of tobacco since its first discovery. As a consequence, it has always been a factor in the development of the use complex. Eventually the religions of most Native American groups became organized in one way or another around tobacco, with even the gods of some tribes addicted to it. Thus it was spread throughout the Americas, all the way to southern Alaska and southern Chile, well beyond the natural range of any wild species, by hunters and gatherers who grew it during the earliest stages of agriculture in the New World. Later, Indian farmers also grew it in its domesticated form as they continued (and continue) to ensnare themselves with its potent chemicals. "We touch a part of our being that we share with many other animals who want to steal the powers from plants but so often become their victims" (Siegel 1989:11).

And so the Indians took tobacco with them wherever they went, smoking and chewing and snuffing it, gathering and tending and sometimes raising it, expanding its range northward in small incremental steps until it reached from Hudson's Bay to southern Chile. Tobacco lay at the core of many of their religions, and it was such an important trade item for those who lacked it that several tribes began to specialize in its propagation and trade. When the Spanish, French, and English arrived, they were puzzled by its use, as well as by the ceremonies associated with it. But soon they overcame their aversion, and before long the colonists themselves were using tobacco, as were many of their countrymen in Europe. Thus wrote William Camden, around 1600: "Whilst in a short time many men every-where, some for wantonness, some for health sake, with insatiable desire and greediness sucked in the stinking smoke thereof through an earthen pipe" (West 1934:38).

## Notes

1. Unfortunately, the rates of use of commercial tobacco among Native American youth are on the rise, even among the Navajo, whose frequency of use has been relatively low. See chapters 15 and 17.

2. In her review of a draft of this book, Jan Timbrook added: "Range expansion may not have been entirely deliberate. Tobacco's sticky leaves and minute seeds would easily promote dispersal by adhering to footgear, clothing, baskets and other implements. I think that's how tobacco may have gotten out to the Southern California Channel Islands. It grows best in disturbed soil of middens but that doesn't mean it was planted there."

3. Alkaloids are a class of extremely toxic chemicals that include cocaine, morphine, and curare, as well as nearly 300 compounds secreted by poison-dart frogs. Many alkaloids have proven useful to humans, which probably has favored the survival of the plant and animal species that produce them.

4. All species of tobacco contain toxic alkaloids; readers are urged *not* to smoke them unless they are Native Americans, and then they should use them only for prayers and ceremonies, in very small amounts.

# PART SIX

# The Negative Health Effects of Tobacco Use

## 15
# Health Effects of Tobacco Use by Native Americans
## Past and Present

### Jonathan M. Samet

Tobacco, transported by Columbus from the New World to the Old on his first voyage, is now a well-established cause of disease when used in snuff and other smokeless tobacco products or when smoked in cigarettes, cigars, and pipes. Scientific research conducted largely during the last half of the twentieth century has causally linked the smoking of tobacco to diverse diseases, both acute and chronic, malignant and nonmalignant (USDHHS 1989). Even persons who have never smoked are at increased risk for some diseases through passive or involuntary smoking—that is, the involuntary inhalation of tobacco smoke (USDHHS 1986b; USEPA 1993). Smokeless tobacco use also causes disease (USDHHS 1986a).

The history of documented tobacco use by Native Americans long antedates Columbus's voyages to the New World. As reviewed in this volume, tobacco was (and is) widely used throughout the Americas for magico-religious purposes. Although the historical record documents extensive and widespread use, discussion of the health effects sustained by Native American users of tobacco has been limited. This chapter addresses the health effects that might have been sustained by the original Native American users of tobacco and the burden of morbidity and mortality sustained by current Native American smokers, with emphasis on tribes in the United States. The speculative discussion of consequences of earlier patterns of tobacco use draws on data now available on active and passive smoking. I begin the chapter by summarizing the current status of evidence

on smoking and health, and then I review the available data on the health of Native Americans. I conclude with hypotheses concerning possible health effects produced by the pre-Columbian New World pattern of smoking and offer suggestions for further research.

### Health Effects of Active and Passive Smoking

Tobacco, when burning in the form of manufactured cigarettes, produces a rich chemical mixture containing about 5,000 distinct compounds (USDHHS 1979, 1986b). The smoke, too, is physically complex, comprising both a particulate and a gaseous phase. Smoke from cigarettes is classified as mainstream smoke (MS) or sidestream smoke (SS)—MS is directly inhaled by the smoker, whereas SS is emitted directly into the air by the burning end of the cigarette. Tar is the particulate matter collected by drawing MS through a filter. The components of tobacco smoke include carcinogens, asphyxiating agents, oxidizing agents, and pharmacologically active agents such as nicotine. Some components of tobacco smoke are regulated by the U.S. Environmental Protection Agency as harmful pollutants in outdoor air—nitrogen dioxide, carbon monoxide, benzo-alpha pyrene, radionuclides, and benzene—and some of these agents and others are regulated in the workplace by the Occupational Safety and Health Administration. Nicotine, which is considered responsible for the addiction of smokers, is present in the particulate phase of tobacco smoke (USDHHS 1988).

Although Columbus probably brought tobacco back to Europe on his first voyage,[1] it was principally used in forms other than manufactured cigarettes until the twentieth century (Burns 1994). The invention of the automatic cigarette manufacturing machine and the advent of widespread and aggressive advertising led to increasing cigarette use early in the century, particularly among men; cigarette smoking increased rapidly among men during and immediately after World War I (NCI 1975). Women began smoking somewhat later than men, but World War II accelerated the uptake of smoking in women. By the 1950s, about 60 percent of men and 40 percent of women in the general population were smoking cigarettes. Additionally, a small percentage of men smoked pipes and cigars.

Evidence about smoking's adverse health effects emerged in the twentieth century, with early reports suggesting decreased life span and increased lung cancer risk in smokers (USDHEW 1964). By the late 1940s, an epidemic increase of lung cancer was evident among males, and this previously rare malignancy became an increasingly common cause of death (Samet 1995). About 1950, several epidemiologic studies provided convincing evidence that smoking cigarettes caused lung cancer (Doll 1950; Wynder 1950). These studies compared the smoking habits of persons with lung cancer with those of control subjects who did not have lung cancer, and they showed dramatically increased risks of lung cancer for smokers compared with people who had never smoked—about tenfold overall but increasing to even higher levels for those smoking more than the average of about one pack per day. They were also confirmed by other case-control studies and by cohort studies involving longitudinal observation of large numbers of current and former smokers and of "never smokers" (Samet 1992; Wu-Williams 1994). By 1964, the evidence warranted the now-momentous conclusion by the Advisory Committee to the U.S.

Surgeon General that smoking caused lung cancer and other diseases (Samet 1992).

Subsequent research has linked smoking to numerous diseases and other adverse effects. Smoking causes cancers of the oral cavity and pharynx, the larynx, the lung, the esophagus, the pancreas, the kidney, and the bladder; it is a suspect cause of cancer of the stomach, the cervix, and the liver, and of leukemia (USDHHS 1989). In the United States, cardiovascular diseases are presently the leading cause of death; smoking increases risk of fatal and nonfatal heart attacks, strokes, aortic aneurysms, and peripheral vascular disease (USDHHS 1983). It is the principal cause of chronic obstructive pulmonary disease and is associated with permanent respiratory impairment and chronic bronchitis. It increases the frequency of common respiratory symptoms including cough, phlegm, and wheeze, while reducing the level of lung function (USDHHS 1984). Smokers are at increased risk for respiratory infections such as influenza and pneumonia (USDHHS 1990), as well as peptic ulcer disease. Smoking increases the risk of miscarriage and perinatal mortality, and it reduces birth weight by an average of 200 grams (USDHHS 1990). Overall, smoking reduces life expectancy.

The American Cancer Society has conducted two cohort (that is, longitudinal) studies of smoking and mortality in populations of approximately one million Americans. Follow-up for the first group (the American Cancer Society's Cancer Prevention Study I, or CPS-I) extended from 1962 through 1972; the population for CPS-II was enrolled in 1982, and follow-up continues. Together, these studies provide strong documentation for the marked increases in risk of the principal diseases sustained by cigarette smokers (table 52).

The increased risks for smokers varied among disease categories and between genders and the two time periods covered by the studies. In both studies, however, smoking was associated with increased risks for diverse cancers, respiratory diseases, cardiovascular diseases, and all-cause

Table 52: Summary of Estimated Relative Risks for Current Cigarette Smokers for Major Disease Categories Causally Related to Cigarettes, Males and Females Aged 35 Years and Older, CPS-I (1959–1965) and CPS-II (1982–1986)

| Underlying Cause of Death | Males | | Females | |
|---|---|---|---|---|
| | CPS-I | CPS-II | CPS-I | CPS-II |
| Coronary heart disease, age ≥ 35 years | 1.83 | 1.94 | 1.40 | 1.78 |
| Coronary heart disease, age 35-64 years | 2.25 | 2.81 | 1.81 | 3.00 |
| Cerebrovascular lesions, age ≥ 35 years | 1.37 | 2.24 | 1.19 | 1.84 |
| Cerebrovascular lesions, age 35-64 years | 1.79 | 3.67 | 1.92 | 4.80 |
| Chronic obstructive pulmonary disease | 8.81 | 9.65 | 5.89 | 10.47 |
| Cancer of the lip, oral cavity, and pharynx | 6.33 | 27.48 | 1.96 | 5.59 |
| Cancer of the esophagus | 3.62 | 7.60 | 1.94 | 10.25 |
| Cancer of the pancreas | 2.34 | 2.14 | 1.39 | 2.23 |
| Cancer of the larynx | 10.00 | 10.48 | 3.81 | 17.78 |
| Cancer of the lung | 11.35 | 22.36 | 2.69 | 11.94 |

Source: Report of the U.S. Surgeon General, 1989 (USDHHS 1989).

mortality, for both males and females. The relative risk was particularly high for lung cancer and chronic obstructive pulmonary disease; in the United States, smoking is the predominant causal agent for both. The more modest relative increase in risk for coronary heart diseases translates into a substantial burden of smoking-attributable disease; the number of smoking-caused deaths from coronary heart disease and cancer are approximately equivalent, owing to the former's high background rate. The higher risks in males reflect the earlier age at which men start to smoke and the larger numbers of cigarettes they consume per day. Comparing CPS-I and CPS-II, the increasing risks for many diseases may be the consequence of changing smoking patterns and changes in cigarettes themselves, along with differences in the two studies' methods.

Malignancies associated with smoking generally occur only after a substantial number of years have elapsed since the start of smoking. For example, cases of lung cancer are rare before age 40, whereas the age-specific mortality rates climb exponentially from the middle-aged years onward (Samet 1995). The risk varies with the number of years of smoking and the number of cigarettes smoked daily; mathematical modeling of data from a study of British physicians showed that risk increased by about the fourth or fifth power of the duration of smoking and by a lesser power of the number of cigarettes smoked (Doll 1978). Risk also drops after smoking is stopped (USDHHS 1990). The occurrences of other cancers show a similar dependence on age, although the quantitative relations with smoking pattern are more fully described for lung cancer.

Some tobacco-related diseases develop only with continued regular smoking. The nonmalignant effects of smoking on the lung—that is, increased symptoms and acceleration of the normal age-related decline of lung function (which leads to the development of chronic obstructive pulmonary disease)—lessen with cessation and sustained abstinence (USDHHS 1990). Chronic obstructive pulmonary disease usually develops only after smoking has been maintained from the teenage years through midlife. By contrast, risks for some diseases change quickly with the starting or stopping of smoking; thus the smoking-related risk of heart attack drops quickly after cessation, though some residual increased risk remains for as much as five to ten years after quitting (USDHHS 1990).

Nonsmokers are exposed to environmental tobacco smoke—the mixture of sidestream smoke with exhaled mainstream smoke. Although much more dilute than mainstream smoke, environmental tobacco smoke contains many of the same agents and is sufficiently similar to mainstream smoke to evoke concern about its adverse effects in nonsmokers (USDHHS 1986b; USEPA 1992). These health effects are reviewed in the 1986 report of the U.S. Surgeon General (USDHHS 1986b) and the 1992 risk assessment of the U.S. Environmental Protection Agency (USEPA 1992). A brief summary of this now-extensive literature follows.

Epidemiological studies during the 1970s provided evidence that smoking by mothers increased the risk of more severe types of lower respiratory infection in their infants. Other studies showed increased respiratory symptoms and reduced lung growth in the children of smokers, in comparison with the children of nonsmokers. In 1981, two studies documented increased lung cancer risk in never-smoking women married to smokers (Hirayama 1981; Trichopoulos 1981). Summary analysis of the combined data from these and other studies worldwide demonstrates increase in the risk of lung cancer of about 25 percent in never smokers married to smokers (USEPA 1992). Reviews of the evidence in 1986 by both the U.S. Surgeon General and the National Research Council (NRC 1986; USDHHS 1986b) concluded that passive smoking was a cause of lung cancer in non-smokers. Newer evidence suggests that passive smoking increases risk for ear problems in children, worsens the status of children with asthma, and possibly increases risk of heart attack in never smokers (Samet 1992).

Since the mid-1960s, there has been extensive research on factors that influence both the decision to begin smoking and to maintain smoking once started, although few studies have involved Native American populations. In addition, findings with regard to determinants of smoking by youths in the general population are not necessarily relevant to Native Americans. Nevertheless, extensive investigation of the pharmacologic effects of nicotine has shown that the addictive nature of cigarette smoking can be attributed to the nicotine delivered in tobacco smoke (USDHHS 1988), and that smoking cessation is followed by a craving to smoke, which may be lasting (USDHHS 1990).

Extensive information about the health effects of smoking and evidence of its addictive nature provide a well-documented framework for considering the effects of smoking associated with use of tobacco by pre-Columbian peoples. I use descriptive evidence on the variation of risks with age and pattern of smoking as a basis for speculating about the health risks of smoking among pre-Columbian Native Americans.

## Cigarette Smoking and Health in Present-Day Native Americans

We do not have a good picture of the modern-day use of commercial tobacco by Native Americans. Early studies of selected tribes in the Southwest showed generally low rates of smoking (Archer 1976; Sievers 1968). More recent data from a survey of adult American Indians for the period 1985 to 1988 showed that the prevalence of smoking varied widely among the tribes, and for some tribes it exceeded the overall prevalence of smoking in the United States (Sugarman et al. 1992). Among American Indians in the southwestern states, 18.1 percent of men and 14.7 percent of women reported current smoking, compared with 48.4 percent of Native American men and 57.3 percent of women in the Great Plains states. Data from the National Medical Expenditure Survey of 1987 (Lefkowitz and Underwood 1991) indicated that the overall prevalence of smoking among American Indians and Alaska Natives was slightly higher than that among the general U.S. population (table 53) (CDC 1992b; DeStefano, Coulihan, and Wiant 1979; Gillum, Gillum, and Smith

1984; Lefkowitz and Underwood 1991). This finding was confirmed by the Behavioral Risk Factor Surveillance System, a study conducted from 1987 through 1991. American Indians and Alaska Natives, however, smoked fewer cigarettes than did whites.

The high prevalence of smoking among adult American Indians found in recent surveys has also been found among adolescents. In a study of American Indian school children, R. W. Blum and coworkers found that for every grade level after the seventh, female students were more likely to be daily cigarette smokers than were male students, with prevalence increasing from 8.9 percent in junior high school to 17.8 percent in high school. The increment for male students was found to be from 8.1 percent to 15.0 percent across the same grades (Blum et al. 1992).

Whereas there is extensive evidence on the health effects of smoking in the general population, particularly among whites, the data are far more limited on Native Americans in the United States and elsewhere. The available data do not systematically cover all tribes in the U.S., nor do they provide a clear picture of trends across either past or recent times. The data are most abundant for southwestern tribes. For the purpose of gauging the effects of tobacco use among Native Americans, these data are further limited by being available largely in the form of public health statistics, providing morbidity or mortality rates without linkage to the smoking habits of specific individuals. However, several comprehensive reviews of these data have recently been published (Coultas 1994; USDHHS 1998; T. K. Young

Table 53: Selected Surveys of Cigarette Smoking among American Indians

| Study | American Indian Population | Findings | | | |
|---|---|---|---|---|---|
| Navajo, 1977 (DeStefano et al. 1979) | 640 Navajo adults | Smoking prevalence 13%; 94% of smokers used less than 1 pack per day | | | |
| Minneapolis, 1982 (Gillum et al. 1984) | 242 urban Indians | 70% current smokers; 45% of smokers exceeded 1 pack per day | | | |
| National Medical Expenditure Survey, 1987 (Lefkowitz and Underwood 1991) | Total sample includes about 35,000, with approximately 6,500 American Indians/Alaska Natives (AI/AN) living on or near an Indian reservation | **Sample** | **NS** | **EX** | **S** |
| | | *Male* | | | |
| | | AI/AN | 40% | 19% | 38% |
| | | U.S. | 36% | 27% | 30% |
| | | *Female* | | | |
| | | AI/AN | 54% | 15% | 28% |
| | | U.S. | 52% | 18% | 25% |
| Behavioral Risk Factor Surveillance System, 1987-1991 (CDC 1992b) | 3,102 AI/AN; 297,438 whites from 47 states and the District of Columbia | **Sample** | **% Who Smoked** | **Mean No. Cigarettes** | |
| | | *Male* | | | |
| | | AI/AN | 33.4 | 19.4 | |
| | | Whites | 25.7 | 21.4 | |
| | | *Female* | | | |
| | | AI/AN | 26.6 | 15.5 | |
| | | Whites | 23.0 | 17.7 | |

1994). Chapter 17 of this volume also contains recent comparative data.

In spite of the limitations of the available information, the evidence indicates that tobacco-related diseases are currently less common among Native Americans in the United States than among other groups (table 54).[2] Overall, all-cause mortality rates are lower in Native Americans than in whites and African Americans. To a large extent, the lower rates reflect patterns of mortality from causes of death that are causally linked to cigarette smoking.

Looking specifically at cancer, its low overall occurrence in Native Americans compared with non-Hispanic whites has been documented in a number of studies across the twentieth century (Creagan 1972; Hoffman 1928; Nutting 1993; T. K. Young 1994). In 1926, F. L. Hoffman (1928) surveyed physicians who provided health care to approximately 100,000 Native Americans and identified only 276 cancer deaths in total and not one lung cancer death. Subsequent anecdotal reports from clinicians continued to document that cancer was generally infrequent (Salsbury 1959), while mortality studies showed that

cancer was a relatively uncommon cause of death in comparison with expected numbers based on the general population (Creagan 1972). Autopsy series from the Southwest have confirmed this distinct pattern of disease occurrence (Kravetz 1964).

Lung cancer remains relatively uncommon among Native Americans in the United States, although there is substantial heterogeneity in the occurrence of this malignancy among Native American groups (table 55). Lung cancer mortality rates are now rising in Native Americans in some states, although they remain low in the southwestern tribes. In general, geographic patterns of smoking parallel those of lung cancer. Data from the Behavioral Risk Factor Surveillance System document greater smoking among those living in the Great Plains region (CDC 1992b). Among men, the proportions of current smokers in 1985–1988 were as follows: Southwest, 18.1 percent; Great Plains, 48.4 percent; West, 25.2 percent; and other, 38.0 percent. Among women, the corresponding figures were 14.7 percent, 57.3 percent, 31.6 percent, and 30.7 percent, respectively. To date,

Table 54: Age-Adjusted Mortality Rates per 100,000 for Selected Smoking-Related Causes of Death, by Race and Sex, United States, 1986–1988

| Disease Category (ICD-9 Code) | Males, Non-Hispanic | | | | Females, Non-Hispanic | | | |
|---|---|---|---|---|---|---|---|---|
| | White | Black | AI/AN[a] | Asian/ PI[b] | White | Black | AI/AN[a] | Asian/ PI[b] |
| All Causes | 1,053.8 | 1,439.2 | 969.0 | 619.4 | 676.3 | 890.7 | 631.2 | 398.0 |
| Lung Cancer (162) | 80.7 | 104.6 | 44.1 | 38.2 | 32.1 | 30.3 | 20.9 | 16.7 |
| Ischemic heart disease (410–414, 429.2) | 312.0 | 299.2 | 207.0 | 158.7 | 188.3 | 209.4 | 117.2 | 90.0 |
| Stroke (430–434, 436–438) | 56.7 | 85.1 | 46.7 | 51.4 | 55.9 | 75.9 | 43.8 | 43.4 |
| Chronic obstructive pulmonary disease (491, 492, 496) | 47.8 | 34.1 | 29.7 | 18.8 | 21.0 | 10.2 | 11.1 | 5.6 |

Source: Desenclos and Hahn 1992. Figures for whites and blacks are based on data from 18 states and the District of Columbia.

a   AI/AN = American Indian/Alaska Native.
b   PI = Pacific Islander.

Table 55: Mortality Rates per 100,000 for Selected Respiratory Causes of Death, by Indian Health Service Area, American Indians and Alaska Natives, 1984–1988

| Cause of Death | IHS Total | Aberdeen | Alaska | Albuquerque | Bemidji | Billings | California | Nashville | Navajo | Oklahoma | Phoenix | Portland | Tucson |
|---|---|---|---|---|---|---|---|---|---|---|---|---|---|
| Malignant neoplasm of bronchus and lung | 17.4 | 27.6 | 37.7 | 6.3 | 26.0 | 31.8 | 10.8 | 21.3 | 3.6 | 22.6 | 7.3 | 16.8 | 9.6 |
| Pneumonia, all types | 19.9 | 29.2 | 22.7 | 17.1 | 23.2 | 30.9 | 9.8 | 16.4 | 20.8 | 17.2 | 24.3 | 12.5 | 33.1 |
| Emphysema | 1.3 | 2.4 | 0.8 | 0.4 | 3.2 | 3.2 | 1.6 | 1.6 | – | 1.5 | 0.9 | 2.0 | – |
| Chronic airway obstruction not elsewhere classified | 7.4 | 12.7 | 10.5 | 4.1 | 11.6 | 11.3 | 6.6 | 10.9 | 2.6 | 6.2 | 6.4 | 9.1 | 8.6 |

Source: Coultas et al. 1994.

studies have not been conducted to assess the risks of smoking by Native Americans and to compare the risks with those observed in other racial or ethnic groups.

For cancers of sites other than the lung, available incidence and mortality data also document differing patterns in Native Americans (tables 56–57). These data are derived from Indian Health Service statistics (AANHS 1993; Valway 1991) and from the New Mexico Tumor Registry, a population-based cancer registry that has ascertained incident cancer cases in New Mexico and Arizona with coverage beginning in 1969. For these sites, risk factors other than smoking also have strong effects, and studies have not been undertaken to directly assess the effects of smoking and these other risk factors in Native Americans.

The principal cardiovascular diseases caused by smoking include coronary heart disease and cerebrovascular disease. The occurrence of these broad classes of disease is low among Native Americans in comparison with nationwide data.

As summarized in a report of the U.S. Surgeon General (USDHHS 1998), ratios of the occurrence of coronary heart disease in Native Americans to its occurrence nationwide have ranged from 0.1 to 0.5. The evidence for cerebrovascular disease is more limited but also indicates lower rates, although the gap is smaller.

J. Desenclos and R. A. Hahn (1992) analyzed mortality for the United States for 1986–1988. Overall mortality rates for Native Americans were approximately 90 percent of the rates for non-Hispanic whites, and mortality rates from stroke were about 80 percent. The ratio for coronary heart disease was higher than in earlier time periods.

Respiratory diseases associated with cigarette smoking are less common causes of death among Native Americans than they are among whites and African Americans. Prevalence data are lacking.

In order to develop hypotheses about health effects resulting from past ritualistic uses of tobacco by Native Americans, it would be useful

Table 56: Age-Adjusted Mortality Rates for Cancers of Selected Sites in American Indians and Alaska Natives, All 12 Indian Health Service Areas, 1984–1988[a]

| Site | Males All 12 Areas | | | Females All 12 Areas | | |
|---|---|---|---|---|---|---|
| | N | Rate | US Rate[b] | N | Rate | US Rate[b] |
| Oral cavity and pharynx | 48 | 3.2 | 5.0 | 20 | 1.4 | 1.7 |
| Digestive system | | | | | | |
|   Esophagus | 41 | 3.0 | 5.8 | 16 | 1.2 | 1.5 |
|   Stomach | 129 | 9.1 | 7.3 | 93 | 6.3 | 3.3 |
| Respiratory system | | | | | | |
|   Larynx | 15 | 1.1 | 2.6 | 5 | 0.3 | 0.5 |
|   Lung and bronchus | 562 | 40.1[c] | 74.2 | 296 | 21.4 | 27.3 |
| Female Genital system | | | | | | |
|   Cervix uteri | — | — | — | 126 | 7.6[c] | 3.1 |
| Urinary system | | | | | | |
|   Urinary bladder | 18 | 1.3 | 5.8 | 12 | 0.9 | 1.7 |
|   Kidney and renal pelvis | 80 | 5.6 | 4.8 | 44 | 3.2 | 2.2 |

Source: Valway 1991.

a  Age-adjusted mortality rate 1970 U.S. Standard per 100,000.

b  All races, cancer mortality rates 1984-1988.

c  Rate is significantly different from the U.S. rate.

Table 57: Average Annual Age-Adjusted Cancer Incidence Rates per 100,000 by Primary Site and Racial or Ethnic Group, SEER Program, 1978–1981

| Primary Site | Whites | Blacks | Hispanics[a] | Japanese | Chinese | Filipinos | Native Hawaiians | Native Americans |
|---|---|---|---|---|---|---|---|---|
| All Sites | 335.0 | 372.5 | 246.2 | 247.8 | 252.9 | 222.4 | 357.9 | 164.2 |
| Bladder | 15.4 | 8.6 | 8.2 | 7.7 | 7.7 | 5.1 | 8.2 | 1.1 |
| Cervix uteri | 8.8 | 20.2 | 17.7 | 7.6 | 11.2 | 8.8 | 14.1 | 22.6 |
| Esophagus | 3.0 | 11.5 | 1.6 | 2.4 | 3.4 | 3.6 | 6.4 | 2.4 |
| Larynx | 4.6 | 6.6 | 2.6 | 2.6 | 1.9 | 1.8 | 5.2 | 0.9 |
| Lung, male | 81.0 | 119.0 | 34.3 | 45.1 | 62.6 | 38.1 | 100.9 | 14.6 |
| Lung, female | 28.2 | 30.5 | 13.0 | 14.1 | 31.2 | 18.4 | 38.6 | 3.1 |
| Pancreas | 8.9 | 13.6 | 10.8 | 7.4 | 9.3 | 6.7 | 10.0 | 6.0 |
| Stomach | 8.0 | 13.8 | 15.7 | 27.9 | 9.0 | 7.0 | 32.4 | 19.3 |

Source: Bacquet et al. 1986.

[a] Cancer incidence data for Hispanics come from New Mexico only.

to have data on the health status of present-day Native Americans who use tobacco in this way. The aggregate data for various Native American groups indicate a relatively low occurrence of chronic diseases associated with the sustained smoking of manufactured cigarettes, but these data are not indicators of the potential effects of present-day ritual uses of tobacco.

## Potential Health Effects of Ritualistic Use of Tobacco

We now attribute the addictive potential of tobacco use to the nicotine in tobacco (USDHHS 1988), whereas the identified health effects reflect various toxic and carcinogenic components of tobacco smoke. Nicotine is an amine with potent pharmacological effects; it can be absorbed through both the oral mucosa and the epithelial lining of the lung, depending on the pH of the smoke. It binds to acetylcholine receptors at autonomic ganglia, the adrenal medulla, neuromuscular junctions, and the brain. It thus has widespread effects that follow a complex dose-response curve. Whereas nicotine stimulates ganglia at low doses, it blocks them at higher doses. The physiologic effects of nicotine reflect its stimulatory effects at the doses received

through usual levels of smoking: behavioral arousal, increased cardiac output and tachycardia, and a variety of metabolic effects. Nicotine intoxication produces nausea, vomiting, pallor, weakness, dizziness, sweating, and headache; more extreme degrees of intoxication produce seizures, low blood pressure, and even arrest of breathing. Tolerance can develop with repeated use (USDHHS 1988).

In present societies, social and psychological factors lead people to begin smoking manufactured cigarettes, whereas maintenance of smoking is driven by nicotine addiction and the discomfort associated with cessation. Manufactured cigarettes appear to be particularly effective for delivering nicotine in an addicting fashion. Indeed, many of the chronic diseases associated with smoking are manifested only after many years of sustained smoking.

Published accounts of ritualistic smoking by Native Americans emphasize intense but often brief use by either oral administration of mixtures of tobacco juice or by smoking. The induction of trancelike states implies that severe nicotine intoxication was produced in some uses. For persons not usually exposed to nicotine and given the drug during ceremonies, acute manifestations of nicotine toxicity would be expected—nausea, dizziness, tachycardia, vomiting, and sweating. Greater doses were probably used to produce seizures and respiratory paralysis, with the risk of a lethal overdose.

What are potential adverse consequences of this ritualistic use of tobacco? The possibility, indeed the probability, of addiction seems high. Smoking of manufactured cigarettes begins with experimentation by youths, then typically results in regular smoking after several years. Intermittent contact with tobacco, if associated with controlled access to it, might have eliminated the possibility of addiction by persons other than shamans who had sustained access. Alternatively, pleasurable contact with tobacco or the presumption of magical properties might have led to regular attempts to find and consume tobacco leaf.

Acute effects dominate the array of those that would have been likely. Heavy use of smoke from pipes and cigars might have produced conjunctivitis, pharyngitis, laryngitis, and bronchitis, all reflecting irritation of mucosal surfaces. With continued use, chronic bronchitis might have occurred; it entails chronic cough and sputum production, reflecting increased mucus-producing capacity in the airways of the lung in response to sustained irritation. Even those not actively smoking might have experienced irritant effects during intense exposure.

The present-day chronic effects responsible for most cigarette-related deaths might not have been manifested. Cancer, ischemic heart disease, and chronic obstructive pulmonary disease are rarely manifested before age 40, even in populations placed at higher risk for these diseases by aspects of life-style and the environment other than cigarette smoking. Thus, cardiovascular diseases associated with smoking do not become common among smokers until about the fifth decade, and rates of malignancy increase exponentially beginning at about the same age. For pre-Columbian tribes, it seems reasonable to assume that few persons lived beyond age 40, as is suggested by limited life-table information. I would thus speculate that the chronic diseases now caused by cigarette smoking did not affect early Native American users of tobacco.

## Research Approaches

It is now possible to assess concentrations of tobacco smoke by measuring particles in air or by making measurements of specific tobacco smoke components, such as nicotine, carbon monoxide, and nitrogen dioxide. These measurements can be made with portable equipment that might be brought into current-day ceremonies where tobacco is used or into re-creations of prior use patterns. Measurements of nicotine in air can be linked to measurements of nicotine and of its metabolite cotinine in body fluids. Carbon monoxide can be measured in blood as the level of carboxyhemoglobin, or in exhaled air. These techniques would determine whether nicotine poisoning is induced by ritual uses of tobacco. High levels of carbon monoxide poisoning from intensive and rapid smoking could also be assessed. Such measurements of smoke levels would describe the exposures of non-smokers present as well.

Documenting the disease burden that might have been sustained in pre-Columbian times is more problematic. Mummies could be examined noninvasively using both conventional chest X-rays and newer imaging techniques such as CAT scanning. Lung cancers might be detected if they were sufficiently large and if the lungs were adequately preserved. Detection of other diseases seems implausible. Cotinine concentration can be measured in hair samples, but its stability over long time periods is completely unknown. Other molecular techniques for identifying markers of exposure to tobacco smoke or injury by it are also of unknown utility at this time.

The long historical record of tobacco use is remarkable—society after society incorporated the tobacco leaf into religion and even everyday existence. Its rich array of pharmacological effects has sparked its use and persistence. Unfortunately, pre-Columbian Native Americans did not have a surgeon general's warning.

## Notes

1. Editor's note: While there is no question that some of Columbus's men observed tobacco use by Native Americans during the first voyage, it is unclear whether they brought any tobacco back to Europe. See the opening passage of chapter 1.

2. Editor's note: The evidence also suggests that the gap between Native Americans and non-natives with regard to rates of tobacco-related disease is narrowing. See chapter 17.

# 16

# The Huichol Indians, Tobacco, and Pesticides

## Patricia Díaz-Romo and Samuel Salinas Alvarez

On the basis of an ancient tradition, the Huichol Indians celebrate ceremonies to ask the gods to protect humanity and the planet so that the world may continue to exist. This old tradition—known as *el costumbre* in Spanish—is a set of cultural and community rules that reflects the metaphysical knowledge of this very traditional ethnic group. This chapter describes the paradoxical relationship between the Huichol Indians and tobacco. On the one hand, native tobacco (*makuchi*) is an important part of el costumbre and an essential part of their religion. On the other hand, many Huichols have to work as migrant laborers in commercial tobacco fields, where they are surrounded by poisonous pesticides. *El costumbre* uses sacred tobacco to keep the fire of life burning on the planet. Commercial tobacco is destroying this life, for the Huichols are dying within a circle of industrial poison.

The sacred region inhabited by the Huichols is located between the coast of Nayarit and the desert in the central plateau of northwestern Mexico. It is believed that it is there that the energies of "Our Mother the Ocean," Haramara, and "Our Father the Sun," Tayau, are concentrated (photo 70). The Huichols know that their life commitment is to understand this territory, work it, bless it, and preserve it.

Many miles away from this region, in the management office of a tobacco company, someone writes a document with the rules for tobacco production. In the chapter about "the reasonable use of pesticides," the firm underlines: "Anyone

Photo 70. A Huichol family offering tobacco and prayers at Haramara, "Our Mother the Ocean."

who uses agricultural pesticides is responsible for complying with the regulations set forth by the law and to follow the instructions on the label" (Anonymous 1991:14).

Not far from the sea, on the coastal plain of the state of Nayarit, a Huichol woman drinks water from a bottle that once contained pesticide. She continues with her job, cutting and stringing large tobacco leaves—tobacco poisoned with pesticides. She does not know how to read, nor is she aware that an obscure and ambiguous document exists that would hold her responsible for disobeying a regulation that is totally unknown to her. She cannot read the print on the label and does not know that the little picture of a skull signifies death. She is still there, at the seaside, working, celebrating life. She is unaware that a circle of poison has surrounded her and her people.

In the middle of this circle the Huichol Indians work. They are being contaminated even as they continue to make vows for life on the planet.

## The Huichols and Their Sacred Territory

The Huichol Indians speak a language in the Uto-Aztecan language family, which also includes Nahuatl, Hopi, Shoshone, Comanche, and many other Native American tongues spoken over a vast region stretching from Idaho in the north to central Mexico in the south. The Huichols have survived for thousands of years in Mexico's western mountain range, the Sierra Madre Occidental. During all of this time they have preserved their traditions and followed the rules set forth by *el costumbre*.

Optimistic studies estimate that there are between 15,000 and 20,000 Huichols left in Mexico (AJAGI 1994). Some of us who work in Huichol territory consider that only 7,000 Huichols survive in five principal communities in the Sierra Madre Occidental.

This land was inhabited by the Huichols long before the Spanish conquest in the sixteenth century. Although access to the area is difficult, it was continuously invaded throughout the centuries, most recently by cattlemen and lumber companies. The Huichols' progressive loss of control over the land they inhabit has resulted in the dismantling of much of the communities' social fabric and life-style. For centuries the Huichols depended on a self-sufficient economy based on the production of corn, squash, beans, peppers, and amaranth. Now they are linked to the larger Mexican economy as they breed and sell cattle and work as migrant laborers.

Besides the territory they normally inhabit, the Huichols move throughout the large sacred zone known as Rirrikitá. Five basic sites mark the limits of this area: to the north, Haurra-manaka, located in Cerro Gordo in the state of Durango; to the south, Rapawiyeme, near Lake Chapala in the state of Jalisco; to the east, Pariteke, or Cerro Quemado, and Wirikuta, or the Sacred Desert, both situated in the state of San Luis Potosí; to the west, San Blas, on the coast of Nayarit; and in the center, Te'akata, in Jalisco.

The Huichol deities inhabit each of these sites. Their shamans, or *mara'akames*, communicate with the gods when in deep trance under the effects of peyote (*Lophophora williamsii*), a sacred and powerful hallucinogenic cactus believed to have been used by the Huichols for more than two millenia and known as *hikuri* in Huichol. When in trance, the *mara'akame* becomes the Sacred Deer, or Tamatzi Kauyumarie, who speaks with Our Grandfather Fire, Tatewari. Through Tatewari the sorcerer can communicate with the gods that are incarnate in the sacred sites and pose to them the questions that human beings want to ask them.

In their pilgrimage to Wirikuta, the Sacred Desert, the Huichols purify their hearts by fasting and sexual abstinence. They also carry out public confessions, and they make vows and sacrifices to the gods, following the guidelines set forth by *el costumbre*. When they reach this desert the Huichols find that the tracks left by the Sacred Deer have been transformed into peyote (*hikuri*). As they spear the *hikuri* with their arrows the Huichols are symbolically hunting the Sacred Deer, and by eating the peyote they are taking communion with him.

According to *el costumbre*, the Huichol Indians must travel through their ceremonial territory without any obstacles or difficulties in order to transport their sacred cactus. For a long time, however, this ceremonial land has not been under the control of the Huichol people. They now live in a greatly reduced geographical area, and when they make their pilgrimage, they have to travel over very difficult terrain and are continously exposed to persecution, mistreatment, and arrest by drug enforcement authorities who charge them with possession of narcotics.

## Nicotiana rustica and the Huichols

In their own language, the Huichols refer to traditional tobacco (*Nicotiana rustica*) as *tabaco makuchi* or *ya*. This ethnic group has created many myths and interpretations concerning the origins of the tobacco plant and its role in sacred ceremonies. Indeed, *ya* is an integral part of the search for peyote, the ceremonies associated with it, and its ingestion. According to Carl Lumholtz, tobacco pertains to fire:

> The leader, having prayed much, places the ball of tobacco on the ground; touches it with his plumes, and prays aloud. Then he wraps very small portions of it in pieces of corn-husks so that they look like dimunitive tamales and hands one such little bundle to each member of the party, who places it in a special tobacco gourd tied to the quiver apart from the other ones. To the Huichols this act symbolizes the birth of the tobacco, and those who have the sacred little parcel have to watch it very carefully and are separated from the rest of the world. (Lumholtz 1902, 2:131)

Two stories about the origin of tobacco have been told by Huichol artists José Benítez and Mariano Valadez. The story told by Valadez was confirmed and detailed by Cheria'akame (don Toño), from the community of Santa Catarina in the state of Jalisco. A similar version is reported by Joseph Winter in chapter 13 of this book.

As shown by the yarn painting in photo 71, José Benítez tells the story of the birth of tobacco with images. He also notes that "this is where Our Elder Brother Tamatzi Kauyumarie created tobacco in a seed bed (the dark area at the bottom center). Kauyumarie (lower right), in front of a prayer bowl containing his thoughts, made his hand become tobacco and his vertebrae become the veins of the leaf" (Negrín 1975:94).

The second story was told by Mariano Valadez (personal communication with Díaz-Romo, 1994):

Photo 71. "Our Elder Brother Kauyumarie Created Tobacco." Yarn *tabla* by José Benítez Sánchez and Tutukila Carrillo. From Negrín 1975. Courtesy of Juan Negrín.

Our Elder Brother Tamatzi Kauyumarie had made four trips to Wirikuta. Before the fifth pilgrimage he went to the coast. There he found two young girls who invited him to bathe in the sea. When Tamatzi Kauyumarie was in the water the girls hid his bow and arrow. The girls would return them under the condition that Tamatzi Kauyumarie have sex with them.

When he engaged in the act of love one of them asked that he please not ejaculate. Tamatzi Kauyumarie, thus, deposited his semen in his hand and threw it on the beach, near the sea, the sea where Tatei Haramara, Our Mother the Sea, lives. But when he was ready to continue his trip he was accosted by a pack of K'muki, the Wolfmen.

Tamatzi Kauyumarie was able to release himself after a series of vicissitudes and he returned to the site where he made love to the girls. A *makuchi* [tobacco] plant was growing where he had placed his semen.

Tamatzi Kauyumarie noticed that a toad was eating the tobacco leaves. He became very upset because the tobacco he was eating had grown from his semen and his blood. He then cut the toad in half and pulled out the blood clots and buried them. Five days later he returned to the same place and found that a gourd vine called

Figure 29. Tobacco gourd, a necessary adjunct of the Huichol priest.

*yaari* in the Huichol language had grown. One of the gourds was facing the sun and, like the toad, it had many excrescences on its skin. With this squash he made a tobacco gourd or *ya:kuai* to carry the *makuchi*.

Mariano Valadez explains: "Many people know this story, although everyone tells it differently. I tell it the way it was told to me by my grandmother."

Contemporary ethnographic reports confirm these stories. Indeed, Huichol peyote seekers still use the ceremonial tobacco gourds to carry *makuchi*, which guides and protects them in their pilgrimage to Wirikuta (fig. 29). The use of tobacco gourds was documented by Lumholtz at the beginning of the twentieth century:

And all (*Hikuli*-seekers) carry tobacco gourds, an essential part of the outfit of the *Hikuli*-seeker, who thereby assumes a priestly function. The small, round gourds are raised for the purpose; those with many

natural excrescences being the most highly valued. Each gourd is provided with a string and a stopper, and is worn hanging from the shoulder. A man may have as many as five tobacco gourds rattling against each other as he walks; some of which contain a little tobacco, but most of which are empty. (Lumholtz 1902, 2:127)

According to the brothers Silviano and Jorge Camberos, who work with the Huichols, *makuchi* is an important ethnobotanical resource of the Huichol people and is sacred because it is a representation of Our Grandfather Fire, Tatewari. Occasionally, the Huichols cover the gourds with the skin from a deer scrotum. By uniting tobacco and deer, the object turns into a very powerful item (Camberos and Camberos 1995).

The artist José Benítez (personal communication with Díaz-Romo, 1995) explains how tobacco is a natural complement of corn: "Tobacco arises with corn. Respiration, will, and memory arise with corn. Tobacco arises with the corn leaves." Benítez adds that corn represents food for the body while tobacco represents food for the soul. Proof of this is the Huichol farming practice of cultivating *Nicotiana rustica* plants alongside corn plants (Pacheco 1995).

The Huichols also call the tobacco plant *tabaquito*. Rafael Pateyo López de la Torre, from the Huichol village of Nueva Colonia in the community of Santa Catarina, Jalisco, says that *tabaquito* grows wild on the cliffs during the rainy season, but now every *kawitero* (a medicine man or ceremonial singer) grows his own to be smoked in the ceremonies (personal communication with Díaz-Romo, 1995).

The medicinal use of tobacco has pre-Hispanic origins. In several Aztec codices, tobacco gourds appear as priestly emblems. The Huichol *mara'akame* still uses tobacco to heal spells cast by reptiles such as striped snakes and lizards. The healer exhales the smoke rapidly with his hands around his mouth so that it will easily reach the ailing body. The "enchanted" tobacco, prepared by the shamans, must not be smoked. It must be burned upon returning from the peyote pilgrimage and after the Hikuri Neixa ceremony. Huichols smoke *makuchi* when they are weak. If someone fractures a foot or arm or is bitten by a snake, a *makuchi* leaf is heated and placed on the affected area to relieve the swelling (López de la Torre, personal communication with Díaz-Romo, 1995).

López de la Torre, a Huichol in his forties who is in charge of cultural activities for his people, speaks about *tabaquito* (personal communication with Díaz-Romo, 1995):

> The Huichols hang cloth bags containing *tabaquito* on the necks and wrists of newborn babies to protect them, especially against the reptiles that live alongside the streams and that could attack them while their mothers bathe the babies. When the children are five years old it is considered that they are no longer vulnerable. Thus the little bags with *makuchi* can be removed. Then they are burnt so that they can return to Our Grandfather Fire. The children have become strong because they have followed the tradition, throughout a period of five years, in a ceremony referred to as El Tambor (the drum), or as the Corn Ceremony or Feast of the First Fruits.

The protection provided by *makuchi* reaches human beings by unsuspected means. The Huichols condemn the fact that coyotes eat their hens and leave the family without food. Therefore, Huichol Indians hang little bags containing tobacco, similar to the ones carried by babies, on the necks of their dogs. This way they will be protected from the coyotes' power to outsmart the dogs as they care for the hens (Camberos and Camberos 1995:1).

Culturally, tobacco has two functions in Huichol communities, each very different from the other. Although the Huichols have been able to maintain the symbolism and medicinal benefits of traditional tobacco (*Nicotiana rustica*), Western society has degraded this essential plant by converting the closely related *Nicotiana tabacum*

into an industrialized product with highly toxic substances that make it extremely harmful to human health.

## Pesticides, Commercial Tobacco, and the Huichols as a Migrant Labor Force

Year after year, thousands of Huichols have to leave their homeland in the dry season to seek low-paying, high-risk jobs in the tobacco plantations of Nayarit. There they live, work, and are exposed to strong doses of deadly pesticides that soak the tobacco leaves. The causes of this migration have to do with the Indians' social and economic situation and their calendar of rituals.

During the rainy season, the Huichols traditionally cultivate crops of corn, chili peppers, beans, squash, and amaranth. This combination is an excellent ecological option, because it preserves the earth's nutrients and provides alternative crops if one or more of the others are attacked by insects. For example, the chili is a natural insecticide plant that protects the other plants from pests. The variety of crops also allows the Huichols a broader and healthier diet.

Unfortunately for the Huichols, Mexico's agricultural ministry promotes just the opposite—the single-crop field. It does this by distributing hybrid corn seeds that require the use of synthetic pesticides and fertilizers, thus replacing the seeds that the Huichols have traditionally used to combine their crops. This condition has gradually caused the people's diet to deteriorate.

Single-crop agricultural fields and other modern developments have also weakened indigenous traditions and increased malnutrition and the consumption of liquor and "junk food" alarmingly. The Huichol Indians are exposed to many other negative factors, including continuous invasions by cattlemen and lumber companies that devastate their pastures and forests, and herbicides that poison their soil and dismantle their system of mutual aid by poisoning

Photo 72. Containers of the herbicides Paraquat (GRAMOXONE) and 2,4–D (Esteron 47M) in a Huichol community. The pipe contains drinking water.

the people. The government's promotion of single-crops fields also promotes the use of agro-chemicals. In particular, the use of herbicides such as Paraquat and 2,4-D gradually destroys the ethic of community labor, endangers the health of the *campesinos* and their families, and damages their land, which is normally on hillsides and cliffs (photo 72).

Faced with few opportunities to survive in the mountains, the Huichols are forced to migrate seasonally toward the coastal plains of Nayarit, where they work on tobacco plantations that are severely poisoned by agro-chemicals. The Huichols also migrate for cultural reasons, as the activist Juan Negrín noted during an interview in 1993: "They have a religious need to visit the ocean, life's female ancestor, associated with fertility and the earth. At the same time, once they arrive at the coast they find that if

they don't work in the tobacco plantations they will not be able to return to the mountains."

Native tobacco was grown in the state of Nayarit long before the Spanish conquest. During the twentieth century, especially in the 1940s, the commercial tobacco market grew as a result of World War II, leading to the development of tobacco agro-industry in the state. Currently, Nayarit has a population of 825,000, of which 99,000 people live in the municipality (county) of Santiago Ixcuintla. This is Mexico's tobacco capital, with rich, fertile land that also produces tomatoes, beans, peppers, corn, rice, sorghum, bananas, mangos, cantaloupes, and papayas.

Approximately 3,000 Huichol Indians (about 40 percent of their estimated population) work on the plantations cutting and stringing Burley-type, semi-shade *Nicotiana tabacum* leaves, which represent 40 percent of the state's total tobacco production—some 24,000 tons in 1995. Each year, rural landowners gather in the village public squares to await the arrival of the Huichols, so that they can subcontract them as a cheap labor force. The work done by the Huichols is highly appreciated, especially the stringing of tobacco, because it is practically a handicraft.

To reach the tobacco plantations, the Indians have to make a difficult trip from the mountains. They arrive in pickup trucks, packed and treated like cattle after having traveled for hours, sometimes days. They arrive hungry and thirsty. The "valuable shipments" also include pregnant mothers and sick, weakened babies born to malnourished, tubercular women. Elderly men and even "strong" young men arrive in painful conditions.

Negotiations between the Huichols and landowners and *ejidatarios*—acting as middlemen between the labor force and tobacco companies—usually take place in the village squares, bus stations, or sometimes even in the landowner's home. In some cases, the Huichol Indians will timidly ask for "extra conditions" such as a certain number of tortillas per day for the family, or purified water. Very few, however, are able to obtain these amenities, and those who receive them consider themselves fortunate. The rest are forced to drink water from the Santiago River, one of the most contaminated rivers in Mexico. The irrigation canals and wells in the area are also polluted as a result of the continuous use of pesticides and agro-chemicals that have penetrated the ground.

Many Huichols do not even attempt to negotiate either the "extra conditions" or the fair monetary value of their work. Many do not speak Spanish, and if they do, they are reticent, due to the discrimination against Indians that is rampant throughout Mexico. Most are afraid that they will not be hired if they seem to be "too demanding." Besides, they need the job so desperately that they will end up taking any offer.

When business deals are worked out, they are usually unfair to the Indians. Sometimes, after arguing for hours about prices and working conditions, the boss leaves abruptly, refuses to hire the Indians, and also denies them the opportunity to be hired by another employer. Then there are bosses who fire the workers after one or two weeks, forcing entire families to migrate again in their painful search for a job. After being hired, the Huichols are transported to the tobacco fields. On many occasions they have to confront the bosses upon arrival in order to guarantee payment for their work once the labor contract has been fulfilled.

All the members of a Huichol family have to work in the cutting and stringing of tobacco leaves, since their work is paid for in bulk (photo 73). A mestizo field worker described the process: "The stringing of 20 tobacco lines takes from six to eight hours. Each line with five tobacco needles is sold for two pesos [present currency (1994) is six pesos to the dollar] and each needle is sold at 40 centavos. Picking the tobacco takes about three hours and is done every day, followed by the eight hours of string-

Photo 73. Huichol woman stringing tobacco leaves in lines (*sartas*). Photo courtesy of José Hernández-Claire.

ing." The peasant described with admiration the magical hands of the Huichols: "They work better than we do. They do beautiful strings because their hands are graceful and because they do art work. For them this work is simple. Their hands are very agile. They say God gave them that grace" (Díaz-Romo 1994).

One of the reasons the Huichols prefer to be hired in the picking and stringing of tobacco is because this job is done at dawn or dusk, when the temperature is pleasant compared with the extreme heat at noon. The cutting and stringing of tobacco is performed under the shade of the plants' branches, whereas other farming jobs in the same coastal region, such as the picking of tomatoes, peppers, and beans, take place in direct sun for hours on end.

The apparent advantage of working under shade is actually a health hazard. When the Huichols are picking the wet tobacco leaves, the plants are constantly in contact with their skin, and the Indians are soaked fron head to foot. Humid skin easily absorbs pesticides. In addition, the nicotine in tobacco causes skin irritation and allergies, symptoms that, according to U.S. medical reports, are known as green tobacco sickness, or GTS (CDC 1993). According to a study by the Centers for Disease Control, "nearly one in every 100 tobacco harvesters will get sick from the plant, not because they chew or smoke it but because they pick it" (Schwartzkopff 1993:3). Tobacco experts note that the dimensions of GTS have been largely hidden because it often is misdiagnosed. "Harvesters contract GTS when their skin absorbs dissolved nicotine from wet tobacco leaves. Most vulnerable are harvesters who don't use tobaco—and are therefore less immune to its effects—or those who work without long-sleeved shirts when the crop is wet" (Schwartzkopff 1993:3).

Children who actively participate in the picking chores are particularly susceptible to the hazardous effects of pesticides and nicotine. It is "easier" for them to work on the first phase of the harvest because they pick the leaves in the lower part of the tobacco plant stem and do not have to bend over. They work along the furrows, picking the leaves and becoming smeared by the gummy, sticky resin that impregnates the tobacco. They also inhale and absorb the residues of toxic pesticides applied to the leaves.

To use the term "living conditions" for their camps is totally inappropriate. The families sleep on blankets or plastic sheets placed underneath the tobacco lines. They try to protect themselves from the sun during the day and from the cold at night, but they are constantly exposed to the toxic substances covering the leaves. Water is unpurified, and there is no drainage or latrines. Even food is cooked under the tobacco lines (photo 74). Instead of burying the plastic bottles that contained pesticides, as they are instructed to do (sometimes in English), the Huichols use them as canteens (see photo 65 in chapter 13). Sometimes they even take them back to their communities as "practical souvenirs" from the coast.

For extra pesos, some Huichol harvesters will continue to work at night. When physical exhaustion hits, they fall asleep alongside the contaminated plants.

## The Huichols and Nayarit's Tobacco Production: Contradictions and Lethal Liaisons

The abuse of *Nicotiana tabacum* is in direct opposition to the ceremonial use of *Nicotiana rustica* by the Huichol people. The *makuchi* carried by the *kawiteros* is an organic, cultural, and religious resource, whereas industrialized tobacco is a dangerous drug impreganted with toxic substances. These include methyl bromide, which destroys the ozone layer and is the most toxic gas produced on the planet. Methyl bromide is used to disinfect the soil. Aldicarb is another extremely toxic chemical sprayed by aircraft over the crops and harvesters during the last stage of tobacco picking.

Photo 74. Huichol family cooking in the tobacco fields. Photo courtesy of José Hernández-Claire.

Pesticide is a generic term that includes insecticides, herbicides, fungicides, rodenticides, nematicides, acaricides, molluscicides, pisicides, and avicides, named according to the pest against which they are active. . . . "Fumigant" is a classi-fication based on physical state (gas). The [United States] Federal Insecticide, Fungi-cide and Rodenticide Act [FIFRA] defines pesticides as economic poisons. (Moses 1993:916)

Pesticides are poisons designed to kill. They are toxic chemicals that contaminate and degrade anything they touch. Contrary to what pesticide producers say, there are no remedies or cures against the damage they cause. These chemicals are destroying life cycles, as well as the ecosystem of the planet and its inhabitants.

No one in Mexico has taken the necessary measures to protect the health of the workers who handle these substances. This includes na-tional and transnational pesticide firms, tobacco companies, and Mexico's public health and ecological institutions.

The endemic malnutrition suffered by the Huichol population is further worsened by their increasing rate of alcoholism, and drinking binges occur more often while they live and work on the coast. This aggravates the toxicological problem:

Migrant and seasonal farm workers and their children, who cultivate and harvest crops heavily sprayed with pesticides, are the largest single group exposed. Minorities as a group are most likely to be exposed to pesticides, and yet they have the least control over mitigation of their exposures or over the proper assessment and treat-ment of potential health problems arising from the exposures. (Moses 1993:914–915)

Table 58 lists the pesticides used in the tobacco fields. Based on available medical records, figure 30 shows the number of Huichols treated for acute pesticide intoxication during the first six months of 1995. When migrant harvesters are

## Table 58: Pesticides Used in Mexican Tobacco Fields

| Common Name in Mexico | Commercial Name in Mexico | Manufacturer |
|---|---|---|
| 2,4-D | Esteron 47M, DMA 6m | DOW Elanco, Mexicana |
| Aldicarb | COBOX, Temik 150 | Ortho Basf, Rhone-Poulenc |
| Azinfos metílico | Gusathion-Guthion, Gus-Action | Bayer, Helios SA de CV |
| Bladafume | Sulfotep, BLADAFUM | Bayer |
| Bromuro de metilo | Bromuro de Metilo | VITESA-FAX |
| Carbarilom | SEVIN 80 PH, SEVIN 5G | Rhone-Poulenc |
| Clordano | CLORDANO, CLORDANO Técnico | Anajalsa, Velsimex SA deCV |
| Clorpirifos | Lorsban 480 EM | DOW Elanco |
| Deltametrina | Decis, K-OBIOLCE | HELIOS SA de CV, Roussel UCLAF |
| Diazinon | DIAZINON 25 E | Anajalsa-CIBA, Drexel |
| Isotiosianato de metilo | VORLEX | NOR-AM |
| Metamidofos | TAMARON or Tamaron 600 | Bayer, Du Pont |
| Metidation | SUPRACID 40-E PM | Ciba Geigy |
| Metomilo | LANNATE 90-LV, Nudrin 90 | Du Pont, Shell |
| Monocrotofos | NUVACRON 690, Azodrín 5 | Ciba Geigy, Shell |
| Omethoato | Folimar-Folimat | Bayer |
| Oxamil | VIDATEL | Du Pont |
| Paratión etílico | Folidol, Parathion Etílico | Bayer, ChemiNova-Dinamarca |
| Paration metílico | THIODAN | Hoteh |
| Piridazinonas | ROYAL MH 30 | UniRoyal Chemical |
| Pirimicarb | Pirimor-Pirimicarb | ICI |

Note: In all cases, the medium of lethal dosage is oral.

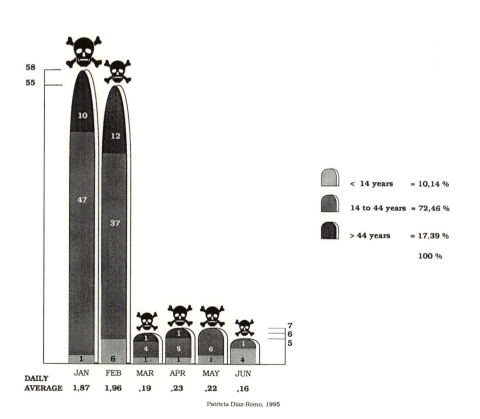

Patricia Diaz-Romo, 1995

Figure 30. Pesticide- and tobacco-intoxicated Huichols in the first six months of 1995, Santiago Ixcuintla, Nayarit, Mexico.

affected by acute intoxication, they are sometimes taken to rural clinics or to the emergency wards at hospitals in nearby towns. In most cases, however, they receive negligent or unfair medical treatment. Rural hospitals often refuse to treat them, arguing that they do not have a "pass"—a proof that they have officially ensured social security benefits. If they are treated, there is often a lack of adequate medicine or antidotes, or they are attended by unqualified medical personnel. "Lack of access to and unavailability of adequate health care contribute significantly to the impact of environmental contamination, and constitute a major problem for farm workers who live in rural areas" (Moses 1993:915).

The World Health Organization reports that around 3 million people are poisoned by pesticides every year. Approximately 20,000 die. Ninety-nine percent of those deaths occur in Mexico and other Third World countries.

The Huichol shamans do not know any chants or rituals to counteract the illnesses that are caused by these chemical substances. It is a paradox and crime that, although the Huichol people have spent thousands of years keeping their ritual candles burning to preserve life on the planet, a circle of industrial poison has been closing in on them for the last 50 years. If nothing is done about it, tobacco will no longer be the food of their gods, since their gods and people will no longer exist.

### Notes

This chapter was prepared with the cooperation of Ramón Salaberria and was translated by Kim Lopez. We thank them both.

# 17

# Native Americans and Tobacco

## Deer Person's Gift or Columbus's Curse?

Joseph C. Winter, Glenn W. Solomon, Robert F. Hill,
Christina M. Pego, and Suzanne E. Victoria

For thousands of years, Native Americans have had a unique relationship with tobacco. Their ancestors domesticated two tobacco species, *Nicotiana rustica* and *N. tabacum*, many millenia ago in the Andes of South America and one species, *N. quadrivalvis*, in North America.[1] Today the natives of North, Central, and South America continue to use these taxa, along with at least four wild tobacco species, for ceremonies, prayers, offerings, invocations, and other traditional religious purposes (photos 75–76). This pattern of use contrasts with that of the other inhabitants of the two continents, who ingest tobacco only for so-called recreational purposes.

Until relatively recently, this important relationship between the original inhabitants of the Americas and a very powerful and dangerous

Photo 75. Navajo herbalist collecting mountain tobacco (*Nicotiana attenuata*) for use in a ceremony. Photo by Joseph Winter

Photo 76. Kuna Indian ritual haircutter smoking tobacco during a girl's puberty ceremony. See Salvador 1997 for other photographs of the ritual use of tobacco by the Kuna Indians. Courtesy of Mari Lyn Salvador.

plant was generally positive, and tobacco formed a core element in their religious systems. With only an occasional exception, there were probably few adverse health effects, because traditional tobacco was used with great care, in very small amounts, and only in strictly controlled religious contexts. For the most part, traditional tobacco was considered a positive source of the highest form of religious power, so long as it was ingested appropriately and not misused. Abuse did occur, especially among tobacco shamans and other Indians who ingested huge amounts of nicotine to induce visions so that they could communicate directly with the spirits. Addiction was probably an important factor in the domestication and spread of tobacco, as was proposed in chapter 14. Nevertheless, most Native Americans probably used tobacco infrequently and in small amounts, mainly because of religious proscriptions concerning its dangerous spiritual power.

Today, many Native Americans continue to use traditional tobacco for rituals and other religious purposes. About half of the First Nations inhabitants of Canada and the United States abstain from commercial tobacco. The others, unfortunately, have adopted the Euro-American pattern of hedonistic, secular use, which involves the frequent ingestion of relatively large doses of nicotine in the form of cigarettes, snuff, and other commercially prepared delivery devices (photos 77–78). The positive relationship between Native Americans and the ancient plant they domesticated is breaking down, and a number of serious health problems are occurring as a result, including major increases in the use of cigarettes and smokeless tobacco (SLT) and a corresponding increase in premature deaths from lung cancer, heart disease, chronic obstructive pulmonary disease, and other tobacco-associated illnesses. No fewer than 55 percent of the indigenous people of Canada regularly use commercial tobacco, in contrast with 20 percent of the overall Canadian population (figs. 31–32). Estimates of the number of adult Native Americans in the United States

Photo 77. California Indian smoking a commercial cigarette. Photo by Frank Leonhardy, 1976.

Photo 78. Inuit woman smoking a commercial cigarette at a wedding near Angmangsslik, Greenland, 1979. Photo by George Duck. Courtesy of George Duck and the Maxwell Museum of Anthropology, University of New Mexico. 92.11.55.

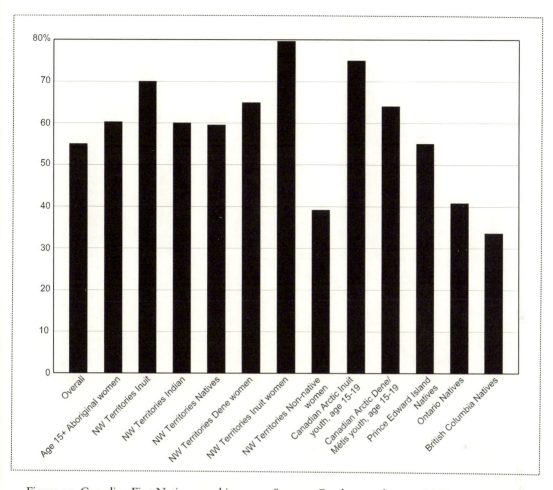

Figure 31. Canadian First Nations smoking rates. Sources: Gandette at al. 1993; McKenzie 1995; Millar 1990; CHSF n.d.

who regularly smoke or ingest smokeless tobacco range from about 27 percent to 45 percent, depending on age and sex of the sample population. Less than 26 percent of the general U.S. population as a whole regularly ingests commercial tobacco (figs. 33–34).

This chapter explores the possibility that centuries of aboriginal sacred use of tobacco, combined with increasing commercial use after the arrival of Europeans, created a residual base of susceptibility for later secular use—an old form with a new meaning. Because of its high rate of use at most American Indian social gatherings, commercial tobacco is probably the greatest threat to the health of Native Amer-

icans today. Its addictive qualities place it on a par with alcohol as a source of physical and psychological dependency, a fact not always recognized in American Indian social contexts.

## A Brief Review of Native American Use of Traditional and Commercial Tobacco

As discussed elsewhere in this book, the tradition of ingesting nicotine may have started as long ago as 10,000 to 12,000 B.C., when the earliest Indians to reach the low deserts of what is now northern Mexico encountered *Nicotiana attenuata* (mountain tobacco), *N. trigonophylla*

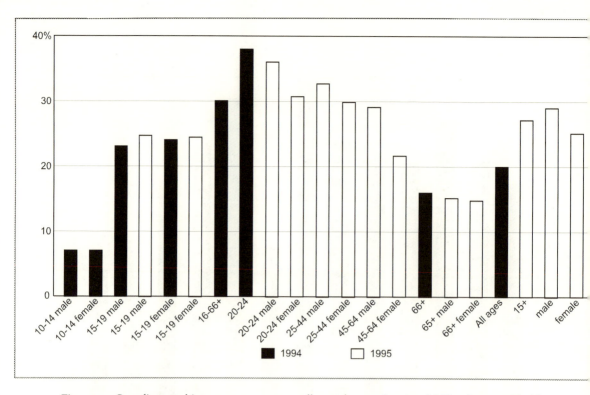

Figure 32. Canadian smoking rates, 1994–1995, all races by age. Sources: McKenzie 1995; Health Canada 1994, 1995.

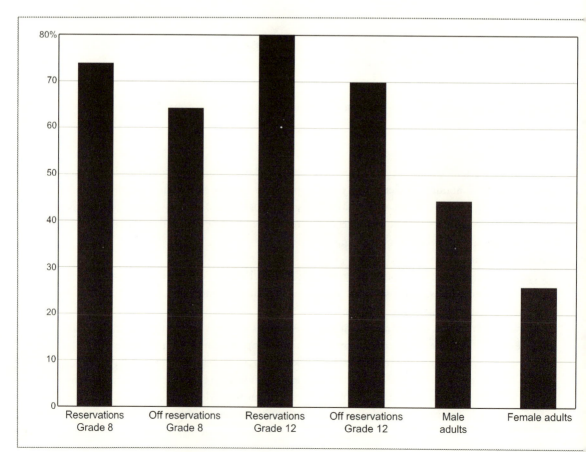

Figure 33. Overall Native American smoking rates in the United States. Sources: CDC 1992b; Beauvais 1992.

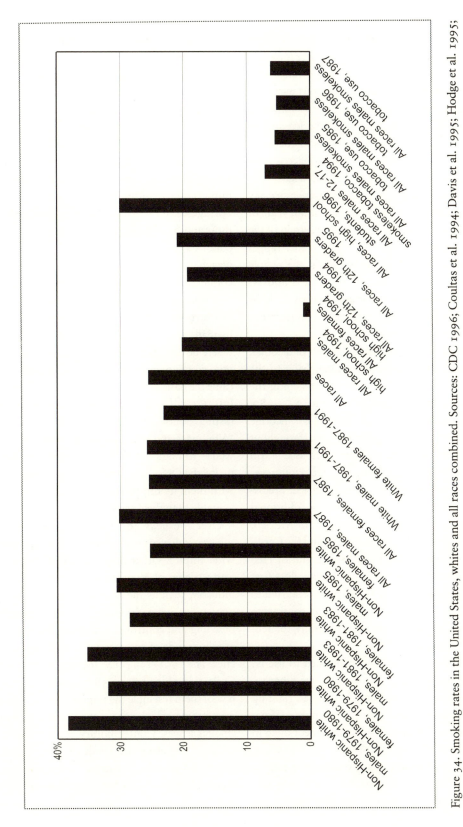

Figure 34. Smoking rates in the United States, whites and all races combined. Sources: CDC 1996; Coultas et al. 1994; Davis et al. 1995; Hodge et al. 1995; Severson 1993.

(Coyote's tobacco), and several other wild tobacco species. It probably did not take long for these Native Americans to discover tobacco's psychoactive as well as addictive powers and to begin using these powers for religious purposes. Then, as their descendants migrated southward through Mexico and Central America and on into South America, the earliest Americans continued to use the local wild tobaccos until they reached the Andes of Peru, where they discovered four wild species that were especially high in nicotine. After several thousand years of harvesting the leaves and planting certain of the species together at the edges of the plants' ranges and even beyond, in the lowlands, the people created two new species, N. *rustica* and N. *tabacum*. These "domesticated" species could be grown in a variety of different environments, but only with human help.

Owing to their much higher levels of nicotine, the new species were then taken back to the north, with N. *rustica* probably reaching the upper Mississippi Valley around A.D. 180. Within a few hundred years this high-nicotine species was most likely being grown throughout the eastern woodlands as far north as Ontario and Quebec. And although N. *tabacum* never made it beyond the Mexican border in prehistoric times, it was (and is) used for traditional purposes throughout the lowlands of Mexico, Central America, South America, and the Caribbean. It was on the Caribbean island of Hispaniola that several of Columbus's sailors first "discovered" tobacco and may have started to use it for "recreational" smoking, in contrast to the local Indians, who used it mainly for religious ceremonies.

Native Americans have continued to use N. *tabacum*, N. *rustica*, and at least five other tobacco species for traditional purposes, right up to the present. Beginning on November 9, 1492, however, when tobacco was first mentioned in Columbus's log book (Brooks 1937–1952, 1: 243), Euro-Americans took tobacco in an entirely different direction by creating a completely secular, commercial commodity that formed the economic backbone of a number of early colonies and continues to be an extremely important economic resource for the United States, Canada, China, England, Turkey, and many other countries. The first commercial tobacco plantation may have been planted as early as Columbus's second voyage, when he established the first permanent European colony in the "New World," on Hispaniola. Throughout the next century, tobacco evolved into an extremely important agricultural product for the Spanish, Portugese, and French colonies as hundreds of thousands of Europeans, Africans, Asians, and colonists themselves became addicted to it. It was therefore only natural that the first English colonists at Jamestown tried to grow commercial tobacco, but they found the local N. *rustica* too strong and harsh for European tastes. Instead, they sent John Rolfe to Venezuela, where he acquired some seeds of a variety of N. *tabacum* known as "Orinoco," which soon became the basis of the Virginia economy (Tobacco Institute n.d.). Within a short time this mild-tasting South American tobacco was called "Virginia," and wherever the English colonists went—to Plimouth Colony, Connecticut, Kentucky, the Ohio Valley, and Ontario—they took with them its tiny seeds, which were far more valuable than their weight in gold.

Over the next 400 years, the commercial tobacco industry evolved into a colossal, world-wide empire. Other traditional Native American varieties of N. *tabacum* were added to the industry, such as the dark tobaccos, but most new types were developed by experimental breeding and controlled selection. Today there are thousands of commercial N. *tabacum* varieties. The 1993–1994 U.S. Tobacco Germplasm Collection alone has 2,358 varieties, and very few of them resemble the original Native American strains, which are much shorter and have smaller leaves. Contemporary commercial tobacco is therefore the result of 500 years of controlled selection for larger leaves and standardized levels of nicotine, experimental breeding, recent genetic engineering, and the use of immense quantities of chemical fertilizers, insecticides, and additives. As a consequence, the commercial varieties of N. tabacum are very different from the smaller, traditional varieties still grown by Native Americans. The uses to which they are put are also quite different, though many Indians do ingest commercial tobacco for secular purposes and even for ceremonies when they have no other choice.

Native American use of commercial N. tabacum appears to have started early in the contact period. Trade tobacco and the sale of commercial tobacco have long been key aspects of Euro-American economic domination of the First Nations—as in Greenland, where Danish settlers paid Inuit workers with tobacco; in Canada, where French and later Hudson's Bay Company traders began every trading session with gifts of tobacco; and in the United States, where the structure of the tax system and the history of treaty relations have fostered the development of reservation "smoke shops." Trade in particular was an important source of N. tabacum. By the end of the sixteenth century, the European penetration of North America was well under way from all directions, and with it came a new era of tobacco distribution and use. Tobacco, the gift of Deer Person to American Indians and the gift of Indians to the rest of the world, now came back to them in a new and much more abundant form. Most of this reverse diffusion of tobacco came by way of the fur trade.

Table 59 shows the approximate chronology of the arrival of trade tobacco to selected American Indian tribes from east to west. Most if not all of the trade tobacco was N. tabacum imported from commercial fields in Brazil. The Native Americans' new dependence on manufactured trade goods, dried corn, cornmeal, cloth, knives, axes, kettles, awls, beads, and brandy (known as "Ononthio's milk" after the Huron word for the king of France) established early the situational climate for a dual or parallel tobacco classification system. Aboriginal tobacco was in relatively short supply and was sacred. Trade tobacco was more plentiful in exchange for furs, but it belonged symbolically in the secular, European realm, like Ononthio's milk.

The distribution of imported tobacco to Indians has a long and doleful history. By 1600, the French empire had devised a way to harvest a trade item that everyone accepted wholeheartedly: furs. The method was to induce Native Americans to replace with metal pots, traps,

Table 59: Diffusion of "Trade Tobacco" to Selected North American Tribes, 1603–1743

| Tribe | Area | Year |
|---|---|---|
| Abenaki | Maine | 1608 |
| Huron, Wyandotte | Ontario | 1608 |
| Pequot | New England | 1609 |
| Kickapoo | Wisconsin | 1634 |
| Cheyenne | Minnesota | 1650 |
| Salish Confederacy | Oregon and Washington | 1656 |
| Chickasaw, Choctaw, Osage | Louisiana and Mississipi | 1659 |
| Kansa, Ponca, Osage, Omaha, Quapaw | Illinois Confederacy | 1680 |
| Caddoan et al. (52 tribes) | Texas | 1685 |
| Taos and Picuris Pueblos | New Mexico | 1695 |
| Pawnee | Kansas | Before 1700 |
| Comanche et al. | Louisiana, Texas and Oklahoma | 1719 |
| Mandan, Cree, Sioux, et al. | Minnesota, Montana, and Dakotas | 1724–1743 |
| Sauk and Fox, Menominee, Ojibway | Wisconsin | 1731 |

Source: Pego et al. 1995.

hatchets, and other trade goods those indigenous items whose manufacture would keep an entire village from participating in the fur harvest. From Maine to Washington and from Canada to Louisiana, this practice spread across the continent in about 50 years. The French imported millions of tons of nicotine-saturated Brazilian tobacco to trade right along with the whiskey, iron cooking utensils, axes, and blankets—commercial goods that replaced items that had to be gleaned from nature.

Native Americans also favored trade tobacco for its smoother taste and aroma. Even the Haudenosaunee (Iroquois), who grew (and continue to grow) relatively large quantities of their own powerful, high-quality *N. rustica*, frequently received large amounts of trade tobacco from the Dutch and British, as did the Mahican, Warrenacockse, Catskill, Schagticoke, and other eastern groups. Examples of how Europeans provided vast quantities of commercial tobacco are listed in table 60, which also illustrates the Haudenosaunee's taste for commercial Virginia tobacco, obtained during raids.

As trade tobacco became an important aspect of Native American culture, it began to serve as a substitute for traditional tobacco in ceremonies, rituals, and similar activities. Traditional domesticated tobacco was and is relatively difficult to grow, especially in the germination and post-germination stages, when the seedlings are extremely small and fragile. Wild tobacco, too, is difficult to grow, and in many parts of its former range it is no longer available, or American Indians have stopped collecting it because of the ready availability of commercial tobacco. Melvin Gilmore (1919:113) observed, for example, that "since the advent of the Europeans tobacco is one of the crops whose culture has been abandoned by the tribes [in the central and southern plains] and they have all lost the seeds of it, so that the oldest living Omaha has never seen it growing." More recently, the senior author of this chapter received numerous statements about the lack of traditional tobacco in response to his offers of free seeds and leaves to Native

Americans.[2] Following are a few examples, which also indicate how new Native American ceremonies are being developed that require the use of tobacco.

We have been using other [store-bought] tobacco for prayers, offerings, and ceremonies. Since I have not grown tobacco before, if you could give me some instruction on when to plant, harvest, etc. . . . This means a great deal to me and the others in my tribe [Cowlitz] who still practice tradition.

I am a member of the Confederated Salish and Kootenai Tribes of Montana. . . . Many years ago the Kootenai tribe used to plant and harvest tobacco at a place called Tobacco Plains just north of the Canadian border in British Columbia. . . . I have sort of been elected as the pipemaker for the elders in our community. . . . Tobacco was given to our people centuries ago by a spirit who also told them how to grow and harvest the plant. I have often thought that I should have our own traditional tobacco to give along with the pipes that I make (and the elders agree). The problem is that nobody in the Tobacco Plains area has any of the plant left nor do they remember how to grow and harvest it. Sadly enough Tobacco Plains is only a name any more.

Thank you so much for the . . . tobacco seeds and the leaves. . . . I shall give them to our Chaplain/Medicine Man . . . who lives in the Gila River Indian Community. He says that he can grow them. Then we can use them in our ceremonies.

My husband is Paiute Indian, and he . . . would be very interested in obtaining seeds of tobacco used by his tribe. He is active in the American Indian Student Association here at UC Santa Barbara and would have much use for the tobacco during ceremonies.

Our native intertribal support group in Nashville has been looking for seeds to grow tobacco to use in repatriation

Table 60: Examples of Native Americans' Obtaining Tobacco by Trading, Raiding, and Gift-Giving in the Eastern Woodlands

| Group | Description |
|---|---|
| Mahican | Received "good smelling tobacco" from the Dutch at Albany in 1674. |
| Mahican, Warrenacockse, and Catskill | Obtained three rolls of tobacco and other gifts at a conference in Albany in 1682. Rolls were thick ropes of spun tobacco leaves weighing from 1 to 30 lb., probably similar to (if not the same as) the Hudson's Bay Company's tobacco "carrots." |
| Schaghticoke | Traded 159 lb. of deerskins for 20 lb. of tobacco and other goods in 1685. |
| Schaghticoke | British gave them permission to join the Mohawk, where "both you and the Mohawk may be able to and will freely smoke tobacco there." |
| Schaghticoke | Along with some Canadian Indians, were given four rolls of tobacco in 1685. |
| Mohawk | Col. William Kendall of Virginia complained at a conference in Albany in 1679 about Mohawk raids in his colony. He warned them to stop, then gave them "florins, 150 in Sewant, 11 ells duffels, 3 vatts of rum, three rolls of tobacco, 25 wheat and 10 brown loaves." |
| Mohawk | Received tobacco and other goods at a meeting in Albany in 1690. |
| Mohawk | Given three rolls of tobacco along with other gifts in 1691. |
| Mohawk | Obtained 100 lb. of tobacco and other goods in Albany in 1693. |
| Oneida | Given tobacco and other goods in 1678 or 1679, in return for several whites captured during a raid in Virginia. |
| Haudenosaunee (Iroquois) | Representatives of the Five Nations received three rolls of tobacco at a 1682 Albany conference concerning their repeated incursions into Virginia. High-quality tobacco was frequently looted during the Virginia raids. After one such raid, the governor general of the colony ordered them to stop, then gave them one roll of tobacco and other gifts. |
| Haudenosaunee (Iroquois) | In 1685, representatives of the Five Nations were again at Albany, responding to more charges of Virginia raids. They were presented with many items, including 60 twists of tobacco. The tobacco given to the Indians on these occasions was usually damaged, low-quality leaves unfit to ship to England. As a consequence, they often brought their own, better-quality tobacco with them, as they did at a 1688 meeting. |
| Haudenosaunee (Iroquois) | The Five Nations were given 579 lb. of tobacco, 15 guns, 500 lbs of lead, and many other gifts in 1691, when a French raid was expected against Albany. |

Source: McCashion 1994.

ceremonies for several years. We would very much appreciate your sending Cherokee, Choctaw, and Lakota seeds to our group.

I am Sarcee/Blackfoot tribal affiliation and wish to request some of your tobacco seeds for ceremonial use. Since I moved from the plains, I have run out of my supply from home and have been unable to find any here in Halifax that would be suitable for offerings or for ceremonial use.

Native Americans in prisons, rehabilitation programs, AIDS treatment centers, and other organizations are also in need of seeds and leaf for ceremonies (fig. 35):

We are but a few who desire to find our path to spiritual healing. I speak for myself and my brothers who are incarcerated behind the great walls of cold steel. We seek help from those willing to reach out . . . by sending tobacco for our smudging ceremonies.

Over the past year I have been supplied your tobacco through the Native American AIDS Project in San Francisco. I used this tobacco in my faith to help me heal and I am doing well. I've gone from a full blown AIDS diagnosis to an HIV diagnosis. . . . If you could send me one packet of tobacco monthly I know this helps me in my prayer to my ancestors and the four winds.

The acceptance of commercial tobacco as a ceremonial substitute for traditional tobacco can be seen in the case of the Sun Dance, at least as it was performed during the 1970s by the Lakota at the Rosebud and Pine Ridge Indian reservations in South Dakota. The Sun Dance leader responded to an anthropologist's question about fasting: "They [the participants] can smoke but they are not able to take water or food. Men smoke because the act is associated in the Indian mind with ceremonies, and the spirits have never told me to deny the men commercial cigarettes" (Mails 1978:208).

The ceremonies of the Native American Church also include the use of commercial tobacco, along with peyote. In several branches of the church it has become institutionalized and traditionalized, with certain types, such as Bull Durham, preferred for use in corn-husk and maple-leaf-wrapped cigarettes. As Weston La Barre (1989 [1960]) described it several decades ago, Bull Durham or unspecified commercial tobacco was smoked after the first peyote plant was found on a collecting trip, and it figured prominently throughout the peyote ceremony.[3]

As these examples show, the line between the use of sacred traditional tobacco and commercial tobacco has become blurred in contemporary Native American culture. Indeed, many Native Americans use commercial tobacco for both religious and secular purposes.

## Native American Health Problems and Commercial Tobacco Use

One of the greatest health threats that Native Americans currently face is that of commercial tobacco use. With long-term use, tobacco has specifically been associated with conditions such as cardiovascular disease and cancers of the lung, larynx, bronchus, trachea, and pancreas, and with fetal and infant morbidity and mortality. Recent studies suggest that substantial dangers are also associated with "second-hand" tobacco smoke, resulting in considerable costs to both families and the national health care system. Smoking, by itself, is responsible for approximately 419,000 deaths in the United States each year (Horgan 1993:32). Lung cancer rates continue to rise for both men and women and have surpassed the rates of death caused by other common forms of cancer, including prostate and breast cancer.

Information concerning the tobacco-related health problems of the First Nations of North America is extremely heterogeneous and uneven and often contradictory. Nevertheless, four

Figure 35. The use of traditional tobacco is an important ceremonial activity for many Native American prison inmates. Drawing by Ronnie Silas (1988), a Native American inmate. Reprinted with permission of the artist and the American Indian Science and Engineering Society.

general patterns are present in the data, as illustrated by figures 37–48 in the appendix to this chapter. Most references for the data that follow are provided in the figure captions.

First, lung cancer mortality rates among Native Americans are steadily rising (see fig. 37). With 80 percent to 90 percent of lung cancer deaths due to long-term smoking, increases in the rate of this disease are probably due to increases in the rate of tobacco use during the preceding 20 to 40 years. In 1926, not a single lung cancer death was identified in a study of approximately 100,000 Native American deaths (Hoffman 1928). Since then, lung cancer mortality rates have increased to 5 per 100,000 deaths among New Mexico indigenous males in the 1958–1962 period and then to 44.1 per 100,000 among Native American males throughout the United States in the 1986–1988 period. Native American females in the United States had a lung cancer death rate of 20.9 per 100,000 in 1986–1988. The rates for First Nations males and females are still lower than those for whites and African Americans, but they nevertheless represent sharp increases over time—a doubling of the lung cancer death rates for indigenous males and a tripling for females between the 1980–1986 and 1986–1988 periods. There is also considerable variation in death rates from region to region, from a low of 3.6–9.6 per 100,000 for the four southwestern U.S. Indian Health Service areas to highs of 31.8 for Billings, Montana, and 37.7 per 100,000 for Alaska. In general, these geographic rates of lung cancer deaths parallel the Native American rates for commercial tobacco use.

Second, the available incidence and mortality data for other tobacco-induced diseases also indicate lower rates for American Indians than for whites and blacks, but with recent rate increases and considerable geographic variation. Heart disease death rates, for example, were approximately 80 per 100,000 for Native American males in New Mexico in the 1973–1982 period and greater than 200 per 100,000 for Native American males in the United States in 1986–1988. Part of the difference is probably due to a lower incidence of commercial tobacco use among Indians of the Southwest, but it may also represent actual increases in the death rates, regardless of geographic location.

Death rates from strokes and chronic obstructive pulmonary disease are also lower for Native Americans, but again they appear to be on the rise. Overall, death rates due to all smoking-related causes are still slightly lower for Native Americans than for whites and blacks. The situation will undoubtedly change, however, because of sharp increases in the last few years in Native American commercial tobacco use.

Third, there is considerable heterogeneity in the rates of commercial tobacco use among Native Americans throughout the United States and Canada. Canadian First Nations rates vary from 33.7 percent in British Columbia to 59.3 percent in the Northwest Territories. Rates in general are much higher than for the general population; 55 percent of Canada's indigenous people regularly use commercial tobacco, compared with 20 percent of the general population. In the United States, the overall Native American rate of regular tobacco use is probably around 45 percent, compared with 25.7 percent for the general population. Use is lowest in the Southwest, where 18.1 percent of Native American men and 14.7 percent of women smoked in 1985–1988, and highest in the Great Plains, where 48.4 percent of men and 57.3 percent of women regularly used tobacco. Within each region there is also considerable variation, though not as much as between regions. Urban Native Americans also smoked at higher rates in 1985–1988. For example, in California, 56 percent of the Indians in San Francisco used tobacco, versus 32 percent of the Yurok in rural northwestern California. We suspect that these variations are due, at least in part, to variations in access to and the presence of traditional tobacco use systems.

Recent reports of prevalence rates for the use of smokeless tobacco reflect a similar epidemiological pattern; for example, the highest rates are among American Indians in the Northwest (Brueld 1990; Glover, Gillum, and Smith 1989: 81; Halland and Dexter 1988:1586; Royd 1987:402). Suprisingly, American Indian prevalence rates are also substantially higher than those for whites, even among Indians with a college education, according to one listing—a large, national, random telephone survey conducted by the Centers for Disease Control (CDC 1992a:861). This contrasts with substantial research over the years that has shown a higher prevalence of use associated with less-educated whites. Native American women also have higher rates of SLT use than white women.

Finally, the available evidence indicates that rates of tobacco use are rising rapidly among Native American youths, even in the Southwest, where they are lower than elsewhere. A study by Sally M. Davis and colleagues (1995) of Navajo and Pueblo children, for example, indicated that 11 percent of fifth-grade boys and 1.2 percent of fifth-grade girls smoked cigarettes at least once a week. Of the seventh-grade boys, 27.2 percent smoked regularly or occasionally, as did 19.3 percent of seventh-grade girls. These rates compare with data from D. B. Coultas and colleagues (1994), which indicate that 18.1 percent of adult Native American men in the Southwest and 14.7 percent of women smoke tobacco on a regular basis.

Smoking and SLT use rates among native youths in other parts of North America are even more disturbing. In California, 37.0 percent of indigenous youths aged 19 or younger are current smokers. In Washington State, approximately 28 percent of sixth-, ninth-, and eleventh-grade Indian females regularly smoke, as do 40 percent of pregnant native females. In the south-central United States, 38.1 percent of Cherokee youths in grades 9–12 smoke. In Minneapolis, 70 percent of Native Americans smoke, and in the Canadian Arctic, 64.0 percent of Dene-Métis 15- to 19-year-olds and 75.0 percent of Inuit of the same age regularly use tobacco. It has been estimated that from one-fifth to one-half of these Canadian teenagers will die pre-maturely from tobacco-related disease (Ashley 1995; Marleau 1995; Shannon and McCall Consulting 1992).

Even more startling is the sharp rise and regional variation in SLT use. In the Southwest, 11.0 percent of seventh-grade Native American boys and 7.5 percent of girls use SLT at least once a week. In Washington State, approximately 34 percent of sixth-, ninth-, and eleventh-grade indigenous males and about 24 percent of females use SLT. On the Montana Blackfoot Reservation, nearly 60 percent of 15- to 24-year-olds use SLT. And in one Alaskan study, 10 percent of native kindergartners reportedly used SLT.

The implications of these patterns are extremely disturbing. Unless something is done to curb the increase in smoking and SLT use among Native American youths and even reduce it, the future for the First Nations in North America is bleak. Some groups are especially at risk, such as the Inuit in certain parts of Canada, whose females have the highest rates of lung cancer ever recorded (Gandette et al. 1993) and whose 15- to 19-year-olds have a 75 percent smoking rate. Native American women in other areas are also at risk, including pregnant females in Washington State, who have a smoking rate of 40 percent, and females in Oregon, Idaho, and Washington, who have a smoking rate of about 55 percent. First Nations children everywhere are at risk, and if the many Native American communities and cultures are going to survive relatively intact beyond the next 20 to 40 years, these rates have to be reduced.

## Conclusion

Tobacco is an extremely dangerous, powerful, addictive drug. Many of the beliefs and practices associated with traditional use may actually serve to limit its use; without them, young indigenous people are especially vulnerable to tobacco's coercive power, owing to peer pressure and manipulation by the tobacco industry and its massive campaign of sophisticated media advertising. The commercial development of tobacco as a drug and the manufacture and sale of cheap delivery devices (pipes, snuff, chewing tobacco, and, most recently, machine-made cigarettes) began during the sixteenth century. Later, during the seventeenth and eighteenth centuries, commercial tobacco was introduced into Native American culture on a widespread basis, primarily in the form of trade tobacco. This "rediffusion" of tobacco back into Indian populations began with the fur traders, continued with the free cigarettes given to soldiers in World War II, and is perpetuated with the slick advertising campaigns for Camel, Marlboro, and other popular cigarette brands. As a consequence, there are now two types of Indian use of tobacco: sacred (in which tobacco is mostly acquired and used for religious and ceremonial purposes in the old, traditional way) and secular (in which commercial tobacco is used for individual, hedonistic purposes, in the modern Euro-American way).

During the past half-century, the distinction between sacred and secular tobacco has become blurred. Traditional sacred tobacco is seldom grown or collected and thus is unavailable for many religious ceremonies. More and more American Indians clearly have become addicted to commercial Euro-American tobacco, especially cigarettes. Moreover, tribal governments or their affiliates in many parts of North America have become modern traders of commercial tobacco in Indian-country establishments called "smoke shops." The "Indians' revenge" against Europeans for the loss of life, land, and livelihood has been turned into a revenge against their own people for profit. What began many centuries ago as a way to control the gods now symbolizes a loss of control to the power of addiction and tobacco corporations.

Contemporary examples of the blurred distinction between sacred tobacco and commercial tobacco are (1) the preference for Bull Durham in peyote ceremonies of the Native American Church; (2) the use of commercial cigarette tobacco (with paper removed) at a 1993 Sun Dance organized by members of the Oklahoma Cheyenne tribe, observed by one of the authors (Solomon); (3) an American Indian's passionate stuffing of a pack of Camel cigarettes through a wire fence holding the sacred white buffalo calf in Wisconsin, also observed by one of the authors (Hill) during a 1994 broadcast of the Cable News Network; and (4) the use of commercial pipe or cigarette tobacco (without the paper) as invocations at several meetings of native tobacco health-care workers and educators in 1994 and 1995, as observed by another author (Winter). These ethnographic vignettes suggest a fairly wide distribution of this trend, although further ethnographic and other empirical substantiation is clearly called for.

On the basis of information presented in this book, we recommend a return to the sharp distinction between sacred and secular tobacco in American Indian communities, especially with regard to substance-abuse prevention programs. Symbols are important. Sacred tobacco should again be defined as *only* that cultivated or collected in the wild by members of each tribe, specifically for ceremonial use. Secular tobacco, cultivated and manufactured by Euro-Americans for commercial profit, should be avoided *for any reason*, including ceremonies. Like Ononthio's milk, commercial tobacco is a threat to the health and well-being of all Native Americans exposed to its toxins. Because of the harmful effects of secondhand smoke on family members, especially children and the elderly, tobacco addiction has more in common with alcohol addiction than has generally been recognized. Both alcohol (in the form of sacramental wine) and tobacco (in the form of a sacred substance) can be used for positive purposes, in very small amounts. Both, however, also have negative health and economic consequences for individuals and families, especially those at the lower end of the economic

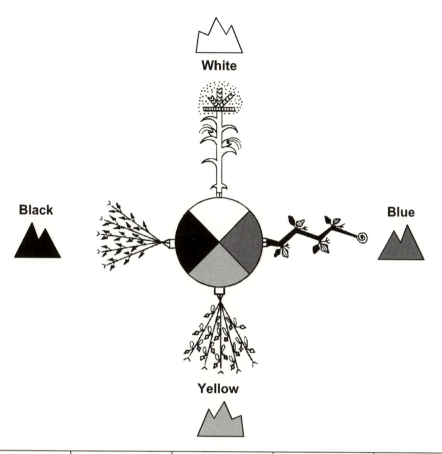

**White**

**Black**

**Blue**

**Yellow**

| Direction | Ha'a'aah, East | Shádi'ááh, South | E'e'aah, West | Náhookás, North |
|---|---|---|---|---|
| *Color* | White | Blue | Yellow | Black |
| *Mountain* | Blanca Peak | Mount Taylor | San Francisco Peaks | Hesperus Peak |
| *Gem* | White Shell | Turquoise | Abalone Shell | Jet |
| *Time of Day* | Dawn | Mid-Day/Noon | Dusk/Evening | Mid-Night |
| *Stage of Life* | Birth | Childhood | Adulthood | Old Age |
| *Philosophy* | Ntsékees, Thinking | Nahat'á, Planning | Iiná, Life | Síí hasin, Hope |
| *Plant* | Corn | Squash | Beans | Tobacco |
| *Season* | Spring | Summer | Fall | Winter |

Figure 36. When used properly in ceremonies and prayers, tobacco helps maintain the balance of life. In the Navajo religion, each direction is balanced by its own color, mountain, gem, sacred plant, and other attributes.

spectrum. Both additionally have negative effects on vocational performance and productivity at work, owing to increased use of health services and increased absenteeism. Moreover, the use of one is highly predictive of the use of the other. In a recent study of Cherokee adolescents, four of the authors of this chapter found that the "any use" congruence of alcohol and tobacco was greater than 80 percent (Pego et al. 1995).

Tobacco is a sacred substance that kills when used inappropriately. Given to Native Americans by Deer Person and the other deities, tobacco is a food of the spirits, at times a god itself. When used properly, tobacco is part of the balance of life and helps one walk the Beauty Road or Red Road (fig. 36). Throughout the past 500 years, however, more and more of the tobacco ingested by Native Americans has been nontraditional commercial tobacco, which is associated with the dominant culture's economic orientation and value system. Commercial tobacco is a deadly killer that threatens the very fabric and survival of Native American life. The same power that provides traditional tobacco with its life-affirming, positive spiritual role has been turned back against the people who discovered and domesticated it and who continue to depend upon it as a core element in their many cultures and religions, all the way from the Amazon basin in South America to Hudson's Bay in North America.

Because of the importance of this power and the danger that it represents, we end this book with two recommendations. First, the use of *any* commercial tobacco, no matter how infrequent or "light" the product, is detrimental to the physical, mental, and spiritual health of Native Americans. Even when traditional tobacco is unavailable, commercial tobacco should never be ingested in ceremonies or rituals, because its use in these contexts legitimates it and opens the possibility for use in other contexts. Moreover, commercial tobacco is a totally non-native, merchandized product associated with a value system and

code of conduct that is detrimental to the long-term survival of traditional American Indian cultures.

The growth, sale, and use of commercial tobacco has evolved over a 500-year-period into a multinational cartel of tobacco companies and associated corporations (for example, RJR Nabisco). From the very start, European colonizers stole tobacco from Native Americans, who used it primarily for ceremonies, and turned it into a commercial product. At the same time, many other Native American plants, ideas, and symbols were appropriated by the dominant Euro-American culture. Commercial tobacco represents everything that is wrong with Euro-American culture, including greed, dishonesty, theft, drug addiction, and a hedonistic value system at its worst.

Equally important, commercial tobacco still retains the sacred power of traditional tobacco, but in a corrupt, poisoned, and debased form that leads rapidly to addiction, illness, and death when it is used without respect. Even when it is used with respect in ceremonies, it is still extremely dangerous and better left alone. If Native Americans need traditional tobacco for ceremonies but lack it, seeds and leaves of the types normally collected or grown by their cultures can be obtained at no cost from the Native American Plant Cooperative (NAPC) in Albuquerque, New Mexico.[4]

Second, all tobacco (including traditional varieties) has the ability to produce both short- and long-term adverse health effects. Even *Nicotiana trigonophylla* and the other wild species contain levels of nicotine or other alkaloids high enough to produce debilitating psychoactive as well as adverse physical effects, and they are potentially addictive. Therefore, traditional tobacco should *never* be used for recreational smoking or other nontraditional purposes. It should be used only in very small amounts, at infrequent intervals, and in carefully controlled Native American contexts. Tobacco is a gift of choice. Please use it wisely, or don't use it at all.

## Appendix:
## Additional Data on Health and Rates of
## Tobacco Use by Native Americans

The following illustrations (figs. 37–49) provide details that augment this chapter's summaries of data on Native American use of tobacco and its adverse health. Readers who want to learn more should consult the original referenced sources. Especially good, comprehensive overviews can be found in recent publications by Burhansstipanov and Dresser (1994), Miller et al. (1996), and Valway (1991). The CDC (U.S. Centers for Disease Control) also has a tremendous amount of information about ethnic smoking patterns available through its Tobacco Information and Prevention Sourcepage on the World Wide Web (http://www/cdc/gov/nccdphp/osh/search.htm).

## Notes

Portions of this chapter appeared previously in Pego et al. 1995, 1997.

1. Chapter 5 of this book discusses how *Nicotiana quadrivalvis* has several varieties that are for all practical purposes "domesticated" (that is, dependent upon humans for survival), as well as others that are wild.

2. The Native American Plant Cooperative (NAPC) in Albuquerque, New Mexico, offers free tobacco seeds to any Native American requesting them, so long as they agree to use the resulting tobacco only in small amounts for prayers, offerings, and ceremonies, and not for recreation or pleasure.

3. Bull Durham is no longer made or sold commercially and has become difficult to obtain in recent years. At one point, NAPC was asked to supply traditional tobacco in its place for the ceremonies of a branch of the Native American Church, but when the church's elders saw the traditional tobacco, they felt that it was too powerful to use in their services. As one of them put it, "Nothing new should be brought into the tipi, and nothing old should be taken out."

4. NAPC can be reached by contacting Joseph Winter at P.O. Box 36749, Albuquerque, NM, 87176.

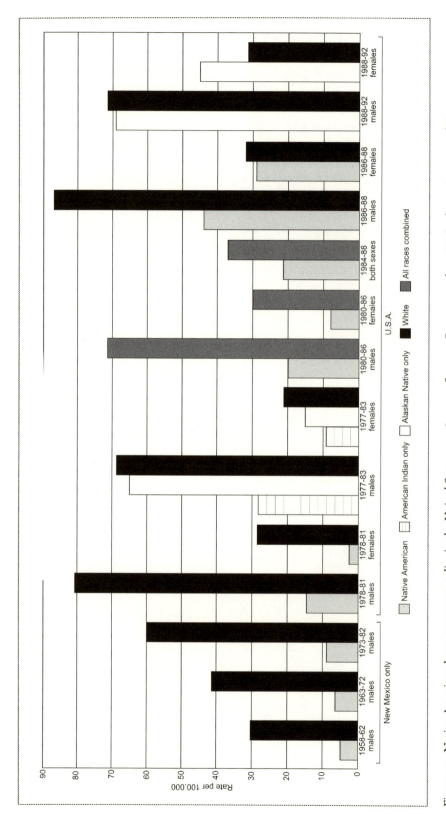

Figure 37. Native American lung cancer mortality in the United States, 1958–1992. Sources: Bacquet et al. 1986; Burhansstipanov and Dresser 1994; Coultas et al. 1994; Rhoades 1990; Samet 1990; Samet et al. 1988; Samet and Winter 1991.

| Tribal Group: | Aleut | Apache | Athapaskan | Eastern Cherokee | Eskimo | Navajo | Oklahoma Cherokee | Sioux | Tohono O'odham/Pima | Seer Whites |
|---|---|---|---|---|---|---|---|---|---|---|
| Male | 92.3 | 6.1 | 88.4 | 26.8 | 106.1 | 13.1 | 35.0 | 46.2 | 10.5 | 82.5 |
| Female | 101.7 | 8.3 | 111.3 | 35.2 | 53.2 | 4.6 | 16.4 | 34.1 | 17.9 | 36.3 |

Figure 38. Male and female age-adjusted lung cancer incidence rates per 100,000 population (1970 U.S. population). Source: Burhansstipanov and Dresser 1994.

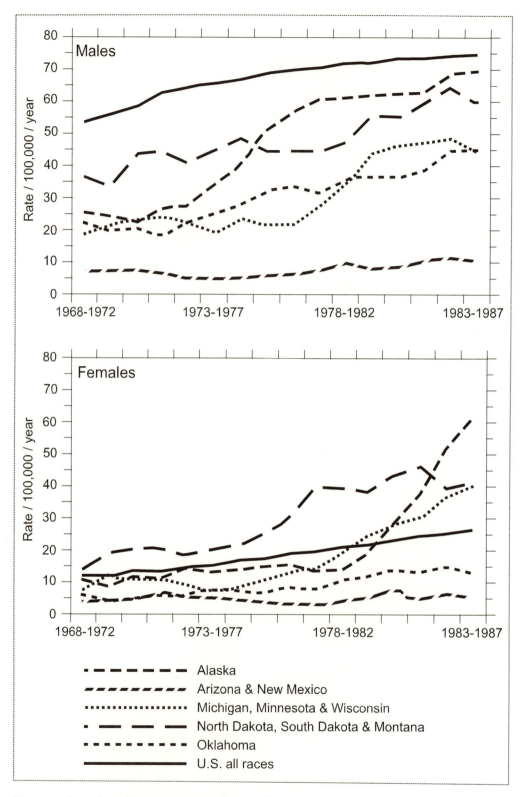

Figure 39. Age-adjusted lung cancer mortality rates for Native Americans in selected states, compared with all races in the United States, 1968–1987. Source: Valway 1991.

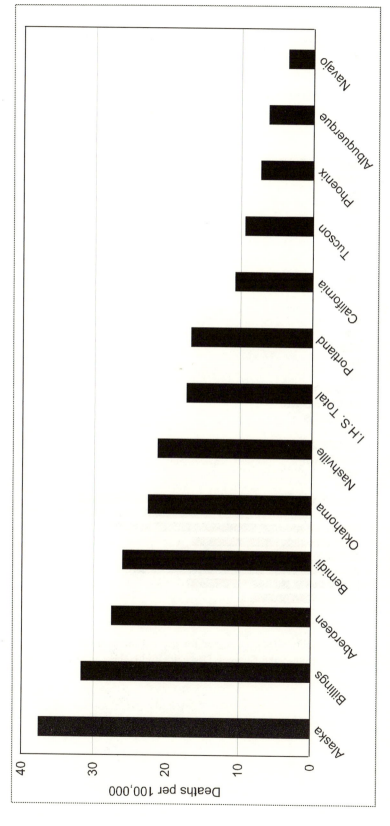

Figure 40. Native American mortality rates from lung cancer, 1984–1988, by Indian Health Service area. Source: Coultas et al. 1994.

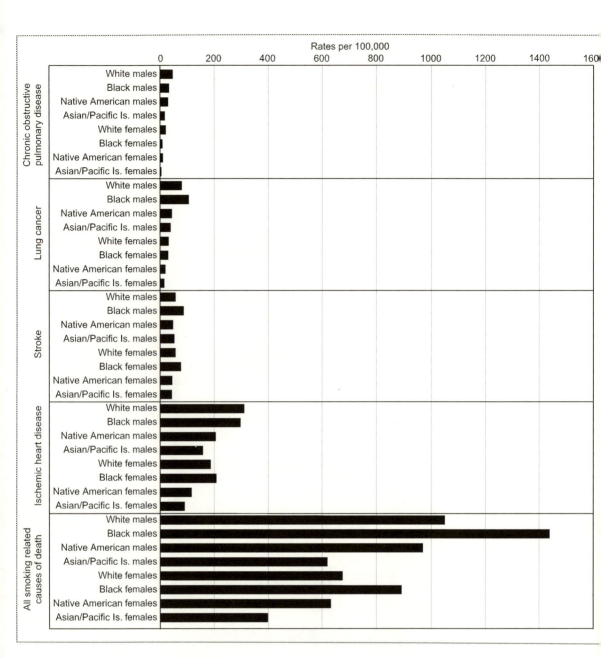

Figure 41. Age-adjusted mortality rates per 100,000 for selected smoking-related causes of death, by race and sex, United States, 1986–1988. Sources: Desenclos and Hahn 1992; Samet, this volume.

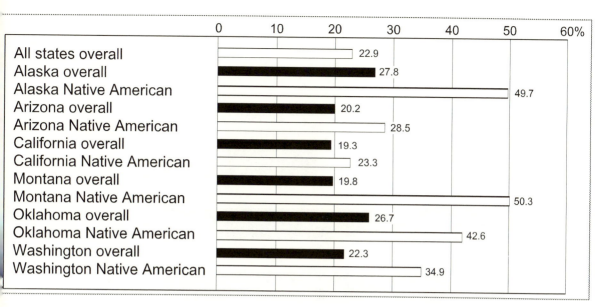

| | 0 | 10 | 20 | 30 | 40 | 50 | 60% |
|---|---|---|---|---|---|---|---|
| All states overall | | | 22.9 | | | | |
| Alaska overall | | | 27.8 | | | | |
| Alaska Native American | | | | | | 49.7 | |
| Arizona overall | | | 20.2 | | | | |
| Arizona Native American | | | | 28.5 | | | |
| California overall | | 19.3 | | | | | |
| California Native American | | | 23.3 | | | | |
| Montana overall | | 19.8 | | | | | |
| Montana Native American | | | | | | 50.3 | |
| Oklahoma overall | | | 26.7 | | | | |
| Oklahoma Native American | | | | | 42.6 | | |
| Washington overall | | | 22.3 | | | | |
| Washington Native American | | | | 34.9 | | | |

Figure 42. Native American cigarette smoking among adults (18 and older) in selected states.

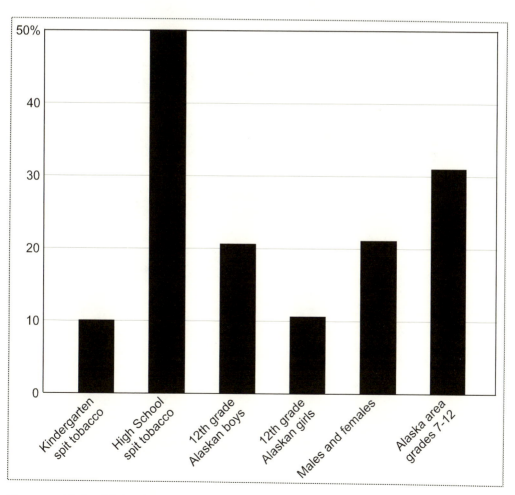

Figure 43. Alaskan Native American smoking rates. Sources: Blum et al. 1992; IHS n.d.

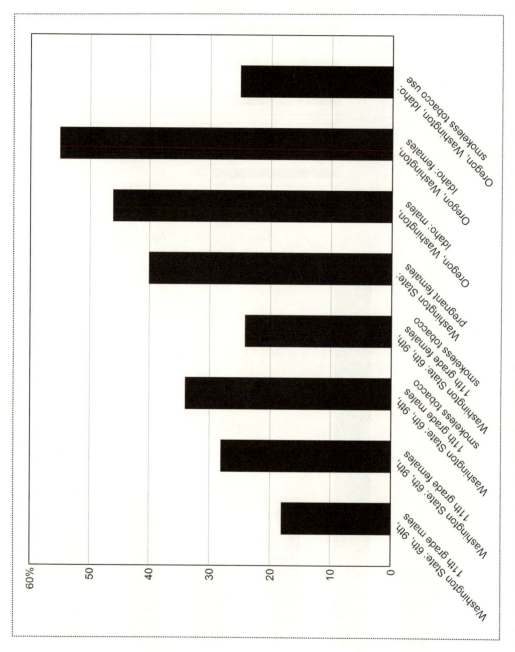

Figure 44. Smoking rates of Native Americans in Washington, Oregon, and Idaho. Source: IHS n.d.

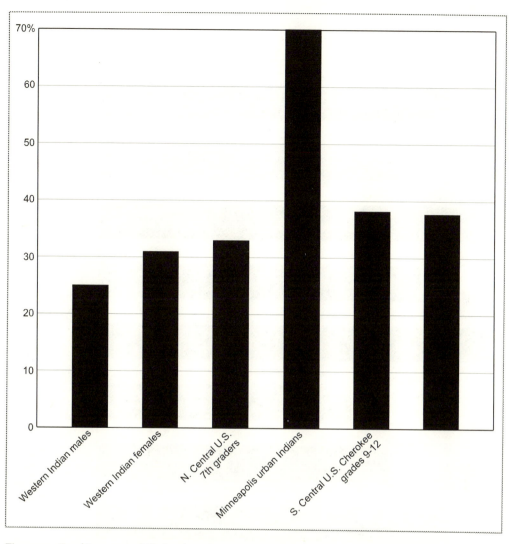

Figure 45. Smoking rates of Native Americans in the western, north-central, and south-central United States. Sources: CDC 1992b; Burhansstipanov and Dresser 1994; Gilllum, Gillum, and Smith 1984; Hill et al. 1994; Murray, Perry, and Oafs 1987; Pego et al. 1995.

Figure 46. Smoking rates for Native Americans in Montana, the Great Plains, and the northern Great Plains. Sources: CDC 1992b;

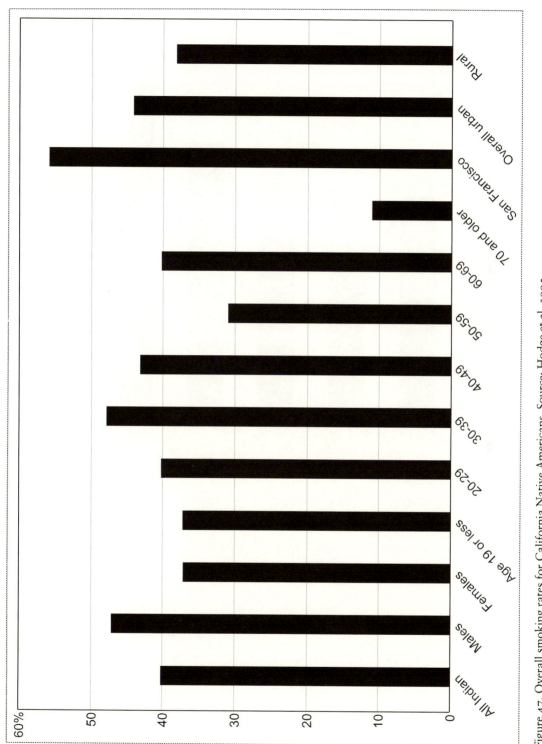

Figure 47. Overall smoking rates for California Native Americans. Source: Hodge et al. 1995.

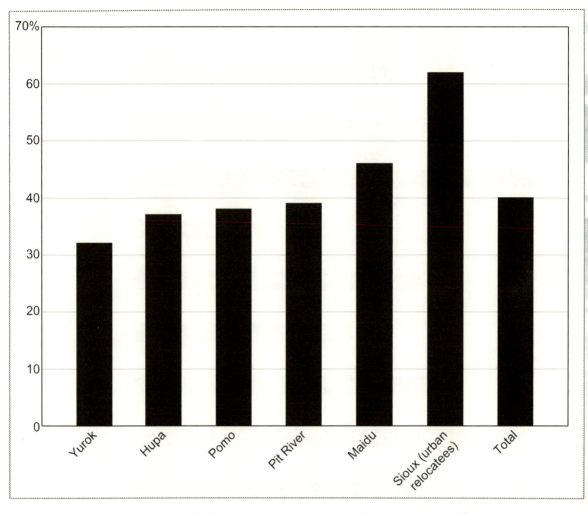

Figure 48. Smoking rates for California Native Americans by tribe, 1991. Source: Hodge et al. 1995.

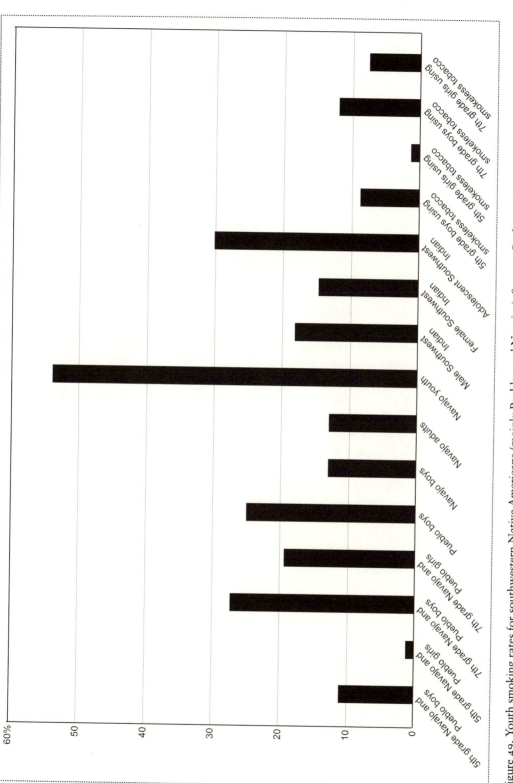

Figure 49. Youth smoking rates for southwestern Native Americans (mainly Pueblos and Navajos). Sources: Burhanstipanov and Dresser 1994; Davis et al. 1995; De Stefano, Coulihan, and Wiant 1979; IHS n.d.; Samet, this volume; Samet and Winter 1991; Sugarman et al. 1992; Wolfe and Carlos 1987.

# 18

## *Tricky Tokes, Those Coyote Smokes*

### How Coyote Learned the True Power of Tobacco

Lawrence A. Shorty

### Editor's Introduction

This story is told to Native American children to help them understand the difference between the positive effects of traditional tobacco use for prayers and ceremonies and the terrible health effects of tobacco when it is used as a recreational drug. The story was first told by Mr. Shorty at a week-long tobacco health education program I organized at the Tyendinaga Mohawk Reserve in Ontario, Canada. The story is based on the Navajo understanding that everything has its place and should have *hozho*—it should be in balance. Each of the different animals, as well as humans, was given its own special tobacco smoke medicine, which helps to define who and what it is. What may be good for one group in a particular situation can be very bad for another. While the author tells this story, he acts out the events, thereby engaging the children's attention.

### Coyote's Mischief

One day Coyote was out running his games of mischief when he spied what looked to be a cloud merrily dancing from peak to peak, high up in the mountains. When he squinted he could see that it was not a cloud but Mountain Sheep. This was, after all, Dibe Ntsaa, the sacred mountain of the north!

Oh, how Coyote wished he could leap from peak to peak like that sheep! How Coyote wished he had the grace and balance of that nimble-footed mountain walker. How Coyote wished he could have dominion over everything he could see from that mountaintop.

You see, Coyote, being so sly and cunning, believed he already had control over all that roamed the desert floor. Never satisfied, Coyote also wanted control over everything he could see from Dibe Ntsaa. He wanted the power that kept Mountain Sheep in balance, because often he was out of balance. Often he lacked *hozho*. He wanted the power that made Mountain Sheep so powerful and beautiful. Yes, he wanted the power that today would be defined as being "cool." But it was not "coolness" that made Mountain Sheep so powerful. Mountain Sheep was merely himself. Mountain Sheep was in balance—he was defined and refined by his respectful use of his special tobacco medicine, *dibe binatoh*.

Animals, as well as native people, have something in common. They each have a *nat'oh*, or tobacco, an herb that is sacred to them as a medicine, that is used in ceremonies and prayers to communicate with the Creator. The Creator gave man and each of the different animals their own tobaccos so they could pray, so they could be true to themselves and to others. The Creator also showed them how to harvest and use their special tobacco. If tobacco is treated with respect, the plant can be very helpful. If treated with disrespect, the plant is very deadly. Coyote is often disrespectful. This is what gets him into trouble.

Now, being ever so busy causing mischief, Coyote didn't have time to find out what made

Mountain Sheep so strong. So he asked his friend Red Ant for a favor. Coyote asked him to climb to the top of Dibe Ntsaa and spy on Mountain Sheep. Red Ant was reluctant until Coyote promised him that he would reward him with some delicious honey for the winter months. He also threatened to squeeze the life out of him if he didn't help. That did it! Off went Red Ant!

Being so small, with tiny legs, it took Red Ant two full months to climb the mountain. Boy, was he tired! Thankfully, Red Ant didn't have long to wait long for Mountain Sheep to appear.

Mountain Sheep was beautiful as he leapt from peak to peak, stopping momentarily to nibble greens. Mountain Sheep had terrific balance and strength.

Red Ant crouched behind a small rock. He watched Mountain Sheep's behavior intently. Red Ant saw Mountain Sheep pick a plant, drop an offering, make a prayer, and then roll a smoke in a corn-husk cigarette. Then Mountain Sheep bounded away, gliding powerfully from peak to peak.

Amazed, Red Ant left his hiding place, took a leaf of the plant that Mountain Sheep had used, and began his trip back down. It took another two months to get to the desert floor.

Coyote Steals Mountain Sheep's Tobacco

Coyote was lying under the hot sun, taking a nap, when Red Ant approached. Sleepily, Coyote received Red Ant. In triumph, Red Ant held up the leaf and began to tell the story of his lengthy trip. But Coyote couldn't wait—he leapt from his resting place, snatched away the trophy, and ran hurriedly toward the mountain. Again, Coyote was being disrespectful.

Coyote had not thanked Red Ant. He did not wait to hear how to make an offering; he did not know how to pray; he did not know much at all.

Coyote ran up Dibe Ntsaa. By the time he got to the top he was tired and sweaty. His wet paw had reduced the leaf to a dark, unrecognizable mess. But he was undeterred—he knew that each of the other animals had a *nat'oh* that gave it strength. So he rudely began to pull up all the plants he could find! He greedily stuffed his magic sack full. Coyote did not make an offering; he did not make a prayer. He was about to make trouble for himself and everyone else. What you do always affects others.

Then Coyote used his magic to quickly grow a stalk of corn of extraordinary size. The ear was four times as big around as he, and at least twice as tall. He took a huge husk and filled it with the leaves of the plants. Next he rolled an immense cigarette, and then he started a big fire and lit the end of his giant smoke (fig. 50). He inhaled deeply. He wished for the strength and grace of Mountain Sheep. Coyote wished for everything! But he did not make an offering; he did not pray; he was not respectful. He was out of balance. He lacked *hozho*. The plant did not become real tobacco for Coyote.

Coyote did feel something, however. At first he felt strong and powerful! He challenged Mountain Sheep to a race, a race for the mountains, from one side of Dibe Ntsaa to the other.

Coyote limbered up. The animal spectators were tense because they knew he could be very tricky. Sometimes his fate would be theirs.

Mountain Sheep and Coyote began at the east end of the mountain, running west. The two were neck and neck for a while. Coyote thought he truly had the strength of Mountain Sheep and the power of all of the other animals. But then he began to cough and wheeze as they ran higher up the mountain. By the time Mountain Sheep and Coyote were at the peak, Coyote was spitting putrid-smelling phlegm and coughing great clouds of smoke. His hacking was so loud and the smoke so thick that many animals thought it was an approaching thunderstorm.

Coughing, hacking, and spitting, Coyote began to falter. He lost his balance. He tried desperately to keep up with the powerful Mountain Sheep, but he could not. Finally he fell from

Figure 50. Coyote stole Mountain Sheep's tobacco and made it into a huge corn-husk cigarette. The other animals were dismayed when he smoked it without respect. Drawing by Daniel Burgevin.

the peak to the desert floor, breaking into many bits.

### Coyote Restores Himself to Life

Despite their anger at him for stealing Mountain Sheep's *nat'oh*, the other animals felt sorry for Coyote. What a horrible way to die, they said to one another. Look at the pieces of those diseased, black lungs, others said.

For a while the many parts of Coyote lay strewn across the desert floor. But Coyote has an amazing capacity to revive himself. He hides his heart in a secret place so that he can restore himself. And restore himself he did: he pulled all of his pieces back together again, except for the lungs, which were too worn and holey to be of any use to him.

So the animals agreed that they should make a prayer and heal him. But with what medicine? Coyote had already pulled up all the plants from their mountain and smoked them. Red Ant figured he could help. He crawled up Coyote's nose, down through his throat, and into the place where his lungs used to be. There he found many small pieces of *nat'oh*. The animals used them to pray by offering smoke. They healed Coyote. Then they supplied him with new lungs fashioned from the pads of a prickly pear cactus.

Coyote needed to learn why he failed. All the animals gathered to share how and why they made smoke. This discussion helped to rees-tablish *nat'oh* as their sacred plant. But soon Coyote was back to his old mischief.

### Coyote's Lesson

Coyote was able to revive himself. He is like a cat with multiple lives. People, however, are not able to do that so easily. Remember the lesson Coyote learned about tobacco. Unless you acknowledge its power, its sacredness, the plant can never become "real." It will only cause harm. Learn the name of your sacred plant.

As native people we must change our environment and what we do within it. We are beginning to understand that commercial tobacco is very harmful. We understand that there are risks associated with smoking cigarettes. But do we acknowledge that learning occurs through example? Then why do people smoke in front of their children? By doing so, we are teaching them how to smoke. How else would nonsmokers know how to smoke if it wasn't taught by others? What you do affects others. For native people, the stories need to be remembered and shared. A Navajo belief is that to undo an illness, one must return to the beginning. The beginning means going back to the era of creation to relearn what was not understood the first time. It is through this process that our well-being—our physical, emotional, and spiritual health—can be preserved.

# References

AANHS (Alaska Area Native Health Service). 1993. *Cancer in the Alaska Native Population: Eskimo, Aleut, and Indian Incidence and Trends*. Washington, D.C.: U.S. Government Printing Office.

Adair, Mary J. 1988. *Prehistoric Agriculture in the Central Plains*. University of Kansas Publications in Anthropology, no. 16. Lawrence.

———. 1989. "Floral Remains." In *1986 Investigations at 14MN328, a Great Bend Aspect Site along U.S. Highway 56, Marion County, Kansas*, by William B. Lees et al. Report prepared for the Kansas Department of Transportation, Topeka.

———. 1992. "Plant Remains from El Quartelejo: Subsistence Change or Continuity during the Protohistoric Period." Paper presented at the 50th Plains Conference, Lincoln, Nebraska.

Adams, Karen R. 1990a. "Prehistoric Reedgrass (*Phragmites*) 'Cigarettes' with Tobacco (*Nicotiana*) Contents: A Case Study from Red Bow Cliff Dwelling, Arizona." *Journal of Ethnobiology* 10(2):123–139.

———. 1990b. "A Review of Ancient Tobacco (*Nicotiana*) Use in the Prehistoric Southwestern United States." Paper presented at the 13th Annual Ethnobiology Conference, Tempe, Arizona.

———. 1991. "Annual Report. Mesa Verde Fire Effects: An Ecological and Ethnobotanical Study of Vegetation Recovery after the Long Mesa Fire of July 1989." Manuscript on file, Mesa Verde National Park.

———. 1993a. "Second Annual Report. Mesa Verde Fire Effects: An Ecological and Ethnobotanical Study of Vegetation Recovery after the Long Mesa Fire of July 1989." Manuscript on file, Mesa Verde National Park.

———. 1993b. "Description of Some Uncharred Plant Remains from Red Cave." In "Red Cave: A Prehistoric Cave Shrine in Southeastern Arizona," by Alan Ferg and Jim I. Mead. *Arizona Archaeologist* 26:22–25.

Ager, Thomas A., and Lynn Price. 1980. "Ethnobotany of the Eskimos of Nelson Island, Alaska." *Arctic Anthropology* 27:26–48.

AJAGI (Asociación Jalisciense de Apoyo a Grupos Indígenas). 1994. "Wixaritari: Los Huicholes. Su modo de vida: Resistir para sobrevivir." *Ce Acatl* 58. México, D.F.

Akehurst, B. C. 1981. *Tobacco*. 2d ed. London: Longman.

Albee, Beverly J., Leila M. Shultz, and Sherel Goodrich. 1988. *Atlas of the Vascular Plants of Utah*. Salt Lake City: Utah Museum of Natural History.

Alcorn, Janis B. 1984. *Huastec Mayan Ethnobotany*. Austin: University of Texas Press.

Alexander, Michael, ed. 1976. *Discovering the New World Based on the Works of Theodore de Bry*. New York: Harper and Row.

Anderson, Arthur J. O., and Charles E. Dibble, trans. 1954. *General History of the Things of New Spain*, by Fr. Bernadino de Sahagun. Book 8, Kings and Lords. Salt Lake City: University of Utah Press.

———, trans. 1970. *General History of the Things of New Spain*, by Fr. Bernadino de Sahagun. Book 1, The Gods. Salt Lake City: University of Utah Press.

———, trans. 1981. *General History of the Things of New Spain*, by Fr. Bernadino de Sahagun. Book 2, The Ceremonies. Salt Lake City: University of Utah Press.

Anderson, Edgar A. 1971 [1952]. *Plants, Man, and Life*. Berkeley: University of California Press.

Anderson, G. J., and P. G. Gensel. 1976. "Pollen Morphology and the Systematics of Solanum Section Basarthrum." *Pollen et Spores* 4:533–552.

Anonymous. 1991. "Normas de producció." Manuscript on file with Patricia Díaz-Romo. México, D.F.

Applegate, Richard B. 1978. *Atishwin: The Dream Helper in South-Central California*. Socorro, New Mexico: Ballena Press.

Arber, Edward, ed. 1910. *Travels and Works of Captain John Smith*. 2 vols. Edinburgh: John Grant.

Archer, V. E. 1976. "Respiratory Disease Mortality among Uranium Miners." *Annals of the New York Academy of Sciences* 271:280–293.

Arévalo Valera, Guillermo. 1994. *Medicina indígena: Los plantas medicinales y su beneficio en la salud Shipibo-Conibo*. Lima: Associación Interétnica de Desarrollo de Selva Peruana.

Arima, Eugene Y. 1984. "Caribou Eskimo." In *Handbook of North American Indians*, vol. 5: Arctic, edited by D. Damas, 447–462. Washington, D.C.: Smithsonian Institution.

Arzigian, Constance M. 1987. "The Emergence of Horticultural Economies in Southwestern Wisconsin." In *Emergent Horticultural Economies of the Eastern Woodlands*, edited by William F. Keegan, 217–242. Center for Archaeological Investigations, Occasional Paper no. 7. Carbondale: Southern Illinois University.

———. 1989. "The Pammel Creek Site Floral Remains." In *Human Adaptation in the Upper Mississippi Valley: A Study of the Pammel Creek Oneota Site (47Lc61), La Crosse, Wisconsin*, by Constance Arzigian et al., 111–156. *Wisconsin Archeologist* 70.

———. 1990. "Floral Remains." In *The Farley Village Site, 21Hu2: An Oneota/Ioway Site in Houston County, Minnesota*, by James Gallagher, 52–54. Mississippi Valley Archaeology Center, Reports of Investigations no. 117. La Crosse: University of Wisconsin.

———. 1994. "Charred Plant Remains." In *The Gunderson Site: An Oneota Village and Cemetery in La Crosse, Wisconsin*, by Constance Arzigian et al., 52–58. *Journal of the Iowa Archeological Society* 41.

Asch, David L. 1991. *Tobacco Seeds in the Archeobotanical Collections of the Center for American Archeology*. Center for American Archeology Archeobotanical Laboratory Report no. 82. Kampsville, Illinois: Center for American Archeology.

———. 1995. "Aboriginal Specialty-Plant Propagation: Illinois Prehistory and an Eastern North American Post-Contact Perspective." Ph.D. diss., Department of Anthropology, University of Michigan.

Asch, David L., and Nancy B. Asch. 1985a. "Prehistoric Plant Cultivation in West-Central Illinois." In *Prehistoric Food Production In North America*, edited by R. I. Ford, 149–203. Anthropology Papers 75. Ann Arbor: Museum of Anthropology, University of Michigan.

———. 1985b. "Archeobotany." In *Smiling Dan: Structure and Function at a Middle Woodland Settlement in the Lower Illinois Valley*, edited by Barbara D. Stafford and Mark B. Sant, 327–401. Research Series vol. 2. Kampsville, Illinois: Center for American Archeology.

———. 1987. "Middle Woodland and Historic Indian Archeobotany of the Naples-Abbott Site (Tabbycat and Smith Areas), Scott County, Illinois." In *Archaeological Testing of the Naples-Abbott Site: Smith and Tabbycat Areas, Scott County, Illinois*, by Barbara D. Stafford, 87–107. Historic Properties Management Report 35. St. Louis: U.S. Army Corps of Engineers.

Asch, David, and William Green. 1992. *Crops of Ancient Iowa: Native Plant Use and Farming Systems*. Iowa City: Office of the State Archaeologist, University of Iowa.

Asch, Nancy B., and David L. Asch. 1985. "Archeobotany." In *The Hill Creek Homestead and the Late Mississippian Settlement in the Lower Illinois Valley*, edited by Michael D. Conner, 115–170. Research Series vol. 1. Kampsville, Illinois: Center for American Archeology.

Ashley, Mary Jane. 1995. *Health Effects of Tobacco Use*. National Clearinghouse on Tobacco and Health, Canadian Council on Smoking and Health.

Bacquet, C. R., K. Ringen, E. S. Pollack, et al. 1986. *Cancer among Blacks and Other Minorities: Statistical Profiles*. Bethesda, Maryland: U.S. Government Printing Office.

Bahadur, Bir, and S. M. Farooqui. 1986. "Seed and Seed Coat Characters in Australian *Nicotiana*." In *Solanaceae: Biology and Systematics*, edited by William G. D'Arcy, 114–137. New York: Columbia University Press.

Baker, Marigold H. 1984. "An Analysis of Four Late Woodland Pits in Eastern Cole County, Missouri." M.A. thesis, Department of Anthropology, University of Missouri.

Baker, Mark A. 1981. "The Ethnobotany of the Yurok, Tolowa, and Karok Indians of Northwest California." M.A. thesis, Humboldt State University, Arcata, California.

Balls, Edward K. 1972. *Early Uses of California Plants*. Berkeley: University of California.

Bandelier, Adolf. 1890. *The Delight Makers*. New York: Dodd, Mead.

Barbour, Philip L., ed. 1969. *The Jamestown Voyages under the First Charter 1606–1609*. 2 vols. Cambridge: Cambridge University Press.

———. 1986. *The Complete Works of Captain John Smith (1580–1631)*. 3 vols. Chapel Hill: University of North Carolina Press.

Barrett, Samuel A. 1952. *Material Aspects of Pomo Culture*. Bulletin of the Milwaukee Public Museum 2, no. 4.

Barrows, David P. 1900. *The Ethno-Botany of the Cahuilla Indians of Southern California*. Chicago: University of Chicago Press. Reprint, 1967. Malki Museum Press, Morongo California.

Bartlett, Erwin. 1998. "Sweating in Perspective." *Big House Bulletin* 4(2):3, 9. New Mexico Penitentiary, Santa Fe, New Mexico.

Bascot, A. M. 1960. *The Chemical Composition of Representative Grades of the 1952 and 1954 Crops of Flue-Cured Tobacco*. U.S. Department of Agriculture Technical Bulletin 1225. Washington, D.C.

Bates, Craig D. 1992. "Sierra Miwok Shamans, 1900–1990." In *California Indian Shamanism*, edited by L. J. Bean, 97–116. Ballena Press Anthropology Papers no. 39. Menlo Park, California: Ballena Press.

Bauml, James A. 1989. "A Review of Huichol Indian Ethnobotany." In *Mirrors of the Gods: Proceedings of a Symposium on the Huichol Indians*, edited by Susan Bernstein, 1–10. San Diego Museum Papers no. 25. San Diego: San Diego Museum of Man.

———. 1994. "Ethnobotany of the Huichol People of Mexico." Ph.D. diss., Claremont Graduate School, California.

Beals, Ralph L. 1973 [1945]. *Ethnology of the Western Mixe*. New York: Cooper Square.

Bean, Lowell J. 1992. "Power and Its Application in Native California." In *California Indian Shamanism*, edited by L. J. Bean, 21–32. Ballena Press Anthropology Papers no. 39. Menlo Park, California: Ballena Press.

Bean, Lowell J., and Harry Lawton. 1976. "Some Explanations for the Rise of Cultural Complexity in Native California with Comments on Proto-Agriculture and Agriculture." In *Native Californians: A Theoretical Perspective*, edited by L. J. Bean and T. C. Blackburn, 19–48. Ramona, California: Ballena Press.

———. 1993. "Some Explanations of the Rise of Cultural Complexity in Native California with Comments on Proto-Agriculture and Agriculture." In *Before the Wilderness: Environmental Management by Native Californians*, edited by T. C. Blackburn and K. Anderson, 27–54. Menlo Park, California: Ballena Press.

Bean, Lowell J., and Katherine Siva Saubel. 1972. *Temalpakh: Cahuilla Indian Knowledge and Usage of Plants*. Morongo Indian Reservation: Malke Museum Press.

Bean, Lowell J., and Florence Shipek. 1978. "Luiseño." In *Handbook of North American Indians, vol. 8: California*, edited by R. F. Heizer, 550–563. Washington, D.C.: Smithsonian Institution.

Bean, Lowell J., and Sylvia Brakke Vane. 1978. "Cults and Their Transformation." In *Handbook of North American Indians, vol. 8: California*, edited by R. F. Heizer, 662–672. Washington, D.C.: Smithsonian Institution.

Beardsley, Gretchen. 1941. "Notes on Cree Medicine, Based on Collections Made by I. Cowie in 1892." *Papers of the Michigan Academy of Science, Arts, and Letters* 28:483–496.

Beauvais, Fred. 1992. "Comparison of Drug Use Rates for Reservation Indian, Non-Reservation Indian, and Anglo Youth." *American Indian and Alaska Native Mental Health Research* 5:13.

Becklake, M. R. 1990. "The 'Healthy Smoker': A Phenomenon of Health Selection?" *Respiration* 57(3):137–144.

Beinhart, E. G. 1941. "Nicotiana rustica in New Mexico." *Science* 94(2449):538–539.

Benn, David W. 1974. "Seed Analysis and Its Implications for an Initial Middle Missouri Site in South Dakota." *Plains Anthropologist* 19:55–72.

———. 1981a. "The Paleoethnobotany of the M.A.D. Sites (13CF101 and 13CF102) and Relationships with Other Prairie Peninsula Sites." In *Archaeology of the M.A.D. Sites at Denison, Iowa*, edited by David W. Benn. Iowa City: Iowa State Historical Department.

———. 1981b. "Paleobotany." In *Archaeological Investigations at the Rainbow Site, Plymouth County Iowa*, edited by David Benn. Decorah, Iowa: Luther College Archaeological Research Center.

———. 1990. "Paleobotany." In *Woodland Cultures of the Western Prairies: The Rainbow Site Investigations*, edited by David W. Benn, 193–209. Office of the State Archaeologist, University of Iowa, Report 1. Iowa City.

Bennett, Wendell C., and Robert M. Zingg. 1935. *The Tarahumara: An Indian Tribe of Northern Mexico*. Chicago: University of Chicago Press.

Benz, Bruce F., and Meredith H. Matthews. 1982. "Macrobotanical Remains from Prairie Dog Hamlet." In *Excavations at Prairie Dog Hamlet (Site 5MT4614), a Basketmaker III–Pueblo I Habitation Site*, by Richard W. Yarnell, 192–207. Dolores Archaeological Program Technical Reports DAP-029. Salt Lake City: Bureau of Reclamation.

Berlin, Alfred F. 1905. "Early Smoking Pipes of the North American Aborigines." *Proceedings and Collections of the Wyoming Historical and Geological Society* 9:107–136.

Berlin, Brent, Dennis E. Breedlove, and Peter H. Raven. 1974. *Principles of Tzeltal Plant Classification*. New York: Academic Press.

Betts, Edwin Morris. 1985. *Thomas Jefferson's Garden Book*. Philadelphia: American Philosophical Society.

Biggar, H. P., ed. 1922–1936. *The Works of Samuel de Champlain*. 6 vols. Toronto: Champlain Society.

———. 1924. *The Voyages of Jacques Cartier*. Publications of the Public Archives of Canada, no. 11. Ottawa: F. A. Acland.

Birks, H. J. B., and S. M. Peglar. 1980. "Identification of *Picea* Pollen of Late Quaternary Age in Eastern North America: A Numerical Approach." *Canadian Journal of Botany* 58:2043–2058.

Blackburn, Thomas C. 1975. *December's Child: A Book of Chumash Oral Narratives*. Berkeley: University of California Press.

Blackburn, Thomas C., and Lowell J. Bean. 1978. "Kitanemek." In *Handbook of North American Indians, vol. 8: California*, edited by R. F. Heizer, 564–569. Washington D.C.: Smithsonian Institution.

Blaffer, Sarah C. 1972. *The Black-Man of Zinacantán: A Central American Legend*. Austin: University of Texas Press.

Blakeslee, Donald J. 1975. "The Plains Interband Trade System: An Ethnohistoric and Archaeological Investigation." Ph.D. diss., Department of Anthropology, University of Wisconsin, Milwaukee.

———. 1981. "The Origin and Spread of the Calumet Ceremony." *American Antiquity* 46:759–768.

Blankenship, J. W. 1905. *Native Economic Plants of Montana*. Bozeman: Montana Agriculture College Experimental Station, Bulletin 56.

Blum, R. W., B. Harmon, L. Harris, L. Bergeisen, and M. D. Resnick. 1992. "American Indian–Alaska Native Youth Health." *Journal of the American Medical Association* 267:1637–1644.

Boas, Franz. 1888. *The Central Eskimo*. Sixth Annual Report of the Bureau of American Ethnology. Washington, D.C. Reprint, 1965. Lincoln: University of Nebraska Press.

———. 1928. *Keresan Texts*. Publications of the American Ethnological Society, vol. 8. New York.

Bocek, Barbara R. 1984. "Ethnobotany of the Costanoan Indians, California, Based on Collections by John P. Harrington." *Economic Botany* 38(2):240–255.

Bock, Philip K. 1978. "Micmac." In *Handbook of North American Indians, vol. 15: Northeast*, edited by Bruce G. Trigger, 109–122. Washington, D.C.: Smithsonian Institution.

Bodner, Connie Cox. 1989. "The Ethnobotany of Tobacco." Paper presented at the Smoking Pipe Conference sponsored by the Arthur C. Parker Fund for Iroquois Research and the RMSC Research Division. Rochester, New York: Rochester Museum and Science Center.

Bohm, H. 1985. "The Biochemical Genetics of Alkaloids." In *Biochemistry of Alkaloids*, edited by K. Mothes, H. R. Schutte, and M. Luckner. Berlin: VEB Deutsche. Verlag der Wissenschaften.

Bohrer, Vorsila L. 1962. "Nature and Interpretation of Ethnobotanical Materials from Tonto National Monument." In *Archaeological Studies at Tonto National Monument, Arizona*, by Charlie R. Steen et al., 75–114. Southwestern Monuments Association Technical Series 2. Globe, Arizona.

———. 1986. "The Ethnobotanical Pollen Record at Arroyo Hondo Pueblo." In *Food, Diet, and Population at Prehistoric Arroyo Hondo Pueblo, New Mexico*, by Wilma Wetterstrom, 187–250. Santa Fe: School of American Research Press.

———. 1989. *Ethnobotanical Remains from Michael's Land Exchange in the El Morro Valley of New Mexico*. Southwestern Ethnobotanical Enterprises Report 10. Portales, New Mexico.

Bolton, Herbert E., ed. 1908. *Spanish Exploration in the Southwest 1542–1706*. New York: Barnes and Noble.

———, ed. 1914. *Spain in the West: Athanase de Mézèires and the LouisianaTexas Frontier, 1768–1780*. 2 vols. Cleveland: Arthur H. Clark.

Bolton, Reginald P. 1920. "New York City in Indian Possession." *Indian Notes and Monographs* 2(7):223–395. New York: Museum of the American Indian, Heye Foundation.

Boucher, Pierre. 1883. *Canada in the Seventeenth Century*. Translated by Edward L. Montizambert. Montreal: George E. Desbarats.

Bowen, C. Verne. 1945. "Alkaloids in *Nicotiana attenuata* and *Nicotiana trigonophylla*." *Journal of the American Pharmaceutical Association* 34:199.

Bowen, Willis H. 1938. "The Earliest Treatise on Tobacco: Jacques Gohory's 'Instruction sur l'herbe Petum.'" *Isis* 28:349–363.

Bowers, Alfred W. 1965. *Hidatsa Social and Ceremonial Organization*. Bureau of American Ethnology Bulletin 194. Washington, D.C.: Smithsonian Institution.

Boyd, C. Clifford, Jr., Donna C. Boyd, Paul S. Gardner, and Michael B. Barber. 1992. "The Bonham Site (44SM7): A Late Woodland Village Complex in Southwest Virginia." Paper presented at Southeastern Archaeological Conference, Little Rock, Arkansas.

Bozell, John R., and James V. Winfrey. 1994. "A Review of Middle Woodland Archaeology in Nebraska." *Plains Anthropologist* 39(148):125–144.

Bradbury, John. 1819. *Travels in the Interior of America, in the Years 1809, 1810, and 1811*. 2d ed. London: Sherwood, Neely and Jones.

Brandt, Carol B. 1990a. *Analysis of Archaeobotanical Remains from Three Sites near the Rio Grande Valley, Bernalillo County, New Mexico*. Ethnobiological Technical Series 90-2. Zuni Pueblo, New Mexico: Zuni Archaeology Program.

———. 1990b. "Analysis of Archaeobotanical Remains from the N-2007 Discoveries." Manuscript on file. Zuni Pueblo, New Mexico: Zuni Archaeology Program.

———. 1990c. "Archaeobotanical Analysis of Flotation Samples from Vogt Ranch, Ramah, New Mexico." In *Excavations at a Thirteenth-Century Pueblo near El Morro Valley, West-Central New Mexico*, edited by Mark B. Sant and Edward M. Kotyk. Report 274. Zuni Pueblo, New Mexico: Zuni Archaeology Program.

———. 1991a. *Early Agriculture in Montezuma Valley: Analysis of Archaeobotanical Remains from the Towaoc Canal Reach II Project*. Ethnobiological Technical Series 91-1. Zuni Pueblo, New Mexico: Zuni Archaeology Program.

———. 1991b. *The River's Edge Archaeobotanical Analysis: Patterns in Plant Refuse*. Ethnobiological Technical Series 91-2. Zuni Pueblo, New Mexico: Zuni Archaeology Program.

————. 1991c. "Analysis of Archaeobotanical Remains." In *Duration, Tempo, and the Archaeological Record: Excavations at Site AZ:P:60:31*, by William R. Latady, Jr., 169–186. Report 316. Zuni Pueblo, New Mexico: Zuni Archaeology Program.

————. 1992a. *Prehistoric Plant Utilization in Anasazi Communities near Towaoc, Southwestern Colorado: Analysis of Plant Macro-Remains for the Towaoc Canal Reach III Project*. Ethnobiological Technical Series 92-6. Zuni Pueblo, New Mexico: Zuni Archaeology Program.

————. 1992b. "Analysis of Macrobotanical Remains from the N30/31 Project, Mexican Springs, New Mexico." Manuscript in the possession of Carol Brandt.

————. 1993a. *Analysis of Plant Macro-Remains from the Arkansas Loop Pipeline Corridor, San Juan County, New Mexico*. Ethnobiological Technical Series 93-2. Zuni Pueblo, New Mexico: Zuni Archaeology Program.

————. 1993b. "Unpublished Data from the 1992 Field Season of the Fruitland Archaeology Project." Manuscript on file. Dolores, Colorado: La Plata Archaeological Consultants, Inc.

Brisbin, Joel M. 1985. *Excavations at Poco Tiempo Hamlet (Site 5MT2378), a Basketmaker III Habitation*. Dolores Archaeological Program Technical Reports DAP-182. Salt Lake City: Bureau of Reclamation.

Broda, Johnna. 1983. "The Provenience of the Offerings: Tribute and Cosmovision." In *The Aztec Templo Mayor: A Symposium at Dumbarton Oaks*, edited by E. H. Boone, 211–256. Washington, D.C.: Dumbarton Oaks.

Brooks, Jerome E., ed. 1937–1952. *Tobacco: Its History Illustrated by the Books, Manuscripts and Engravings in the Library of George Arents, Jr.* 5 vols. New York: Rosenbach.

Brown, Ian W. 1989. "The Calumet Ceremony in the Southeast and Its Archaeological Manifestations." *American Antiquity* 54:311–331.

Brown, Joseph Epes, ed. 1953. *The Sacred Pipe: Black Elk's Account of the Seven Rites of the Oglala Sioux*. Norman: University of Oklahoma Press.

Brown, Kenneth L. 1984. "Pomona: A Plains Village Variant in Eastern Kansas and Western Missouri." Ph.D. diss., Department of Anthropology, University of Kansas, Lawrence.

Bruchac, Joseph. 1985. *Iroquois Stories*. Freedom, California: Crossing Press.

Bruerd, B. 1990. "Smokeless Tobacco Use among Native School Children." *Public Health Reports* 105:196.

Brugge, David, and Charlotte Frisbie. 1982. *Navajo Religion and Culture: Selected Views. Papers in Honor of Leland C. Wyman*. Papers in Anthropology, no. 17. Santa Fe: Museum of New Mexico.

Brundage, Burr C. 1979. *The Fifth Sun: Aztec Gods, Aztec World*. Austin: University of Texas Press.

Buckley, Thomas. 1992. "Yurok Doctors and the Concept of 'Shamanism.'" In *California Indian Shamanism*, edited by L. J. Bean, 117–162. Ballena Press Anthropology Papers no. 39. Menlo Park, California: Ballena Press.

Buckskin, Floyd. 1992. "Ajumawi Doctoring." In *California Indian Shamanism*, edited by L. J. Bean, 237–248. Menlo Park, California: Ballena Press.

Budavari, Susan, editor. 1989. *The Merck Index: An Encyclopedia of Chemicals, Drugs, and Biologicals*. 11th ed. Rahway, New Jersey: Merck.

Burhansstipanov, L., and C. Dresser. 1994. *Documentation of the Cancer Research Needs of American Indians and Alaskan Natives*. Native American Monograph no. 1. Bethesda, Maryland: Department of Health and Human Services, National Cancer Institute.

Burns, D. M. 1994. "Tobacco Smoking." In *Epidemiology of Lung Cancer*, edited by J. M. Samet, 15–49. New York: Marcel Dekker.

Burpee, Lawrence J., ed. 1927. *Journals and Letters of Pierre Gaultier de Varennes de La Vérendrye and His Sons*. Toronto: Champlain Society.

Burrage, Henry S., ed. 1906. *Early English and French Voyages Chiefly from Hakluyt, 1534–1608*. New York: Charles Scribner's Sons.

Busby, A. M. 1979. *The Pipeline Site: A Component of the Late Ontario Iroquois Stage*.

Report no. 10. London, Ontario: Museum of Indian Archaeology, University of Western Ontario.

Bushnell, David I., Jr. 1911. "New England Names." *American Anthropologist* 13:235–237.

———. 1935. *The Manahoac Tribes in Virginia, 1608.* Smithsonian Miscellaneous Collections 94, no. 8. Washington, D.C.: Smithsonian Institution.

Butterfield, Consul W. 1898. *History of Brulé's Discoveries and Explorations, 1610–1626.* Cleveland: Helman-Taylor.

Bye, Robert A., Jr. 1972. "Ethnobotany of the Southern Paiute Indians in the 1870s: With a Note on the Early Ethnobotanical Contributions of Dr. Edward Palmer." *Desert Research Institute Publications in the Social Sciences* 8:87–104. Reno, Nevada.

———. 1979 and various other dates. Harvard University Botanical Museum herbarium voucher specimens no. 3989 (*Nicotiana rustica* "makuchi"), 3345 (*N. rustica* "wiuraka"), 3589 (*N. tabacum* "wipaka"), and 5733 (*N. tabacum* "wipanto"). Collected by Robert Bye from Tarahumara Indians.

Cabeza de Vaca, Alvar Núñez. 1966. *Relation of Núñez Cabeza de Vaca.* Ann Arbor, Michigan: University Microfilms.

Calabrese, F. A. 1969. "Doniphan Phase Origins." M.A. thesis, Department of Anthropology, University of Missouri, Columbia.

Callaghan, Catherine A. 1978. "Lake Miwok." In *Handbook of North American Indians, vol. 8: California,* edited by R. F. Heizer, 264–273. Washington, D.C.: Smithsonian Institution.

Callaway, Donald, Joel Janetski, and Omer C. Stewart. 1986. "Ute." In *Handbook of North American Indians, vol. 11: Great Basin,* edited by Warren L. D'Azevedo, 336–367. Washington, D.C.: Smithsonian Institution.

Callender, Charles. 1978. "Fox." In *Handbook of North American Indians, vol. 15: Northeast,* edited by Bruce G. Trigger. Washington, D.C.: Smithsonian Institution.

Camberos, Silviano, and Jorge Camberos. 1995. "Tabaco Macuchi." Manuscript on file with Patricia Díaz-Romo.

Carlson, Gustav G., and Volney H. Jones. 1940. "Some Notes on Uses of Plants by the Comanche Indians." *Papers of the Michigan Academy of Science, Arts, and Letters* 25:517–542.

Carr, Lloyd G., and Carlos Westey. 1945. "Surviving Folk Tales and Herbal Lore among the Shinnecock Indians." *Journal of American Folklore* 58:113–123.

Carrier Linguistic Committee. 1973. *Plants of Carrier Country.* Fort St. James, British Columbia: Carrier Linguistic Committee.

Carter, George F. 1977. "A Hypothesis Suggesting a Single Origin of Agriculture." In *Origins of Agriculture,* edited by Charles A. Reed, 89–134. Paris: Mouton.

Caso, Alfonso. 1958. *The Aztecs: People of the Sun.* Norman: University of Oklahoma Press.

Castetter, Edward F. 1943. "Early Tobacco Utilization and Cultivation in the American Southwest." *American Anthropologist* 45:320–325.

———. 1944. "The Domain of Ethnobiology." *American Naturalist* 78:158–170.

Castetter, Edward F., and Willis H. Bell. 1942. *Pima and Papago Indian Agriculture.* Inter-Americana Studies 1. Albuquerque: University of New Mexico Press.

———. 1951. *Yuman Indian Agriculture: Primitive Subsistence in the Lower Colorado and Gila Rivers.* Albuquerque: University of New Mexico Press.

Castetter, Edward F., and M. E. Opler. 1936. *The Ethnobiology of the Chiricahua and Mescalero Apaches and the Use of Plants for Foods, Beverages, and Narcotics.* University of New Mexico Bulletin, Biological Series 4, no. 5. Albuquerque.

Castetter, Edward F., and Ruth M. Underhill. 1935. *The Ethnobiology of the Papago Indians.* Ethnobiological Studies in the American Southwest 2. University of New Mexico Bulletin 275, Biological Series 4, no. 3. Albuquerque.

Castillo, Edward D. 1978. "The Impact of Euro-American Exploration and Settlement." In *Handbook of North American Indians, vol. 8: California,* edited by R. F. Heizer, 99–127. Washington, D.C.: Smithsonian Institution.

CDC (Centers for Disease Control). 1992a. "Cigarette Smoking among Adults, United States 1990. *Morbidity and Mortality Weekly Report* 41:354–362. Atlanta: U.S. Centers for Disease Control and Prevention.

———. 1992b. "Cigarette Smoking among American Indians, Alaska Natives: Behavioral Risk Factor Surveillance System, 1987–1991." *Morbidity and Mortality Weekly Report* 41:861–863. Atlanta: U.S. Centers for Disease Control and Prevention.

———. 1993. "Green Tobacco Sickness in Tobacco Harvesters: Kentucky 1992." *Morbidity and Mortality Weekly Report*, Synopsis, April 9. Atlanta: U.S. Centers for Disease Control and Prevention.

———. 1996. *State Tobacco Control Highlights—1996*. Atlanta: U.S. Centers for Disease Control and Prevention.

Chamberlin, Ralph V. 1911. "The Ethno-botany of the Gosiute Indians of Utah." *Memoirs of the American Anthropological Association* 2(5):331–405.

Chance, Norman A. 1966. *The Eskimo of North Alaska*. New York: Holt, Rinehart, and Winston.

Chandler, R. Frank, Lois Freeman, and Shirley N. Hooper. 1979. "Herbal Remedies of the Maritime Indians." *Journal of Ethnopharmacology* 1:49–68.

Chesnut, V. K. 1902. *Plants Used by the Indians of Mendocino County, California*. Contributions from the United States National Herbarium, vol. 8. Reprint, 1974. Mendocino County Historical Society.

Chissoe, William F., Edward L. Vezey, and John J. Skvarla. 1994. "Hexamethyldisilazane as a Drying Agent for Pollen Scanning Electron Microscopy." *Biotechnic and Histochemistry* 69(4):192–198.

CHSF (Canadian Heart and Stroke Foundation). n.d. *Women and Tobacco Fact Sheet*. Handout produced in cooperation with Canadian Council on Smoking and Health.

Clemmer, Richard O., and Omer C. Stewart. 1986. "Treaties, Reservations, and Claims." In *Handbook of North American Indians, vol. 11: Great Basin*, edited by Warren L. D'Azevedo, 525–557. Washington, D.C.: Smithsonian Institution.

Coe, Michael D., and Gordon Whittaker. 1982. *Aztec Sorcerers in Seventeenth-Century Mexico: The Treatise on Superstitions by Hernando Ruiz de Alarcón*. Institute for American Studies, Publication no. 7. Albany: State University of New York.

Collins, James M. 1990. *The Archaeology of the Cahokia Mounds ICT-II: Site Structure*. Illinois Cultural Resources Study no. 10. Springfield: Illinois Historic Preservation Agency.

Colton, Harold S. 1974. "Hopi History and Ethnobotany." In *Hopi Indians*, edited by D. A. Horr. New York: Garland.

Colville, Frederick V. 1897. "Notes on the Plants Used by the Klamath Indians of Oregon." *Contributions from the United States National Herbarium* 5(2):87–110.

Compton, Brian D. 1993. "Upper North Wakashan and Southern Tsimshian Ethnobotany: The Knowledge and Usage of Plants." Ph.D. diss., University of British Columbia.

Conzemius, Edward. 1932. *Ethnographical Survey of the Miskito and Sumu Indians of Honduras and Nicaragua*. Bureau of American Ethnology Bulletin 106. Washington, D.C.: Smithsonian Institution.

Cook, Sarah L. 1930. "The Ethnobotany of the Jemez Indians." M.A. thesis, University of New Mexico.

Cooper, M. S. 1982. "A Preliminary Report on the Carbonized Plant Remains from the Dymock Villages (AeHj-2)." *Kewa* 4:2–10. London, Ontario.

Cooper, John M. 1949. "Stimulants and Narcotics." In *Handbook of South American Indians, vol. 5: The Comparative Ethnology of South American Indians*, edited by Julian H. Steward, 525–558. Washington, D.C.: Smithsonian Institution.

Correll, Donovan S., and Marshall C. Johnston. 1970. *Manual of the Vascular Plants of Texas*. Renner: Texas Research Foundation.

Cosgrove, C. B. 1947. *Caves of the Upper Gila and Hueco Areas in New Mexico and Texas*. Papers of the Peabody Museum of American Archaeology and Ethnology 24, no. 2. Cambridge, Massachusetts: Harvard University.

Couch, James F. 1927. "Isolation of Nicotine from *Nicotiana attenuata*, Torr." *American Journal of Pharmacy* 99:519–523.

Coultas, D. B. 1994. "Other Occupational Carcinogens." In *Epidemiology of Lung*

*Cancer*, edited by J. M. Samet, 299–333. New York: Marcel Dekker.

Coultas, D. B., H. Gong, Jr., R. Grad, A. Sandler, S. A. McCurdy, R. Player, E. R. Rhoades, J. M. Samet, A. Thomas, and M. Westley. 1994. "Respiratory Diseases in Minorities of the United States." *American Journal of Respiratory Critical Care Medicine* 149:S93–S131.

Crawford, Gary W. 1981. "Plant Remains from the Haag Site." In *A Linear Programming Model of Prehistoric Subsistence: A Southeastern Indiana Example*, by Van A. Reidhead, 236–247. Prehistory Research Series, vol. 6, no. 1. Indianapolis: Indiana Historical Society.

Creagan, E. T. 1972. "Cancer Mortality among American Indians, 1950–67." *Journal of the National Cancer Institute* 49:959–967.

Cronquist, A., A. H. Holmgren, N. H. Holmgren, J. L. Reveal, and P. K. Holmgren. 1984. *The Intermountain Flora: Vascular Plants of the Intermountain West, USA*, vol. 4. Bronx: New York Botanical Garden.

Curtis, Edward S. 1909. *The North American Indian*, vol. 5. Cambridge.

Cushing, Frank H. 1920. *Zuñi Breadstuff*. Indian Notes and Monographs 8. New York: Museum of American Indian, Heye Foundation.

Cutler, Hugh C., and Leonard W. Blake. 1973. *Plants from Archaeological Sites East of the Rockies*. St. Louis: Missouri Botanical Gardens.

———. 1976. *Plants from Archeological Sites East of the Rockies*. American Archaeology Reports, no. 1. Columbia: University of Missouri.

Cutright, Paul Russell. 1989. *Lewis and Clark: Pioneering Naturalists*. Lincoln: University of Nebraska Press.

D'Anglure, Bernard Saladin. 1984. "Inuit of Quebec." In *Handbook of North American Indians, vol. 5: Arctic*, edited by D. Damas, 476–507. Washington, D.C.: Smithsonian Institution.

D'Arcy, William G. 1991. "The Solanaceae since 1976, with a Review of Its Biogeography." In *Solanaceae III: Taxonomy, Chemistry, Evolution*, edited by J. G. Hawkes et al., 75–138. Richmond, UK: Royal Botanic Gardens, Kew.

Davis, James T. 1974. *Trade Routes and Economic Exchange among the Indians of California*. Ballena Press Publications in Archaeology, Ethnology, and History 3. Ramona, California: Ballena Press.

Davis, Sally M., Lori C. Lambert, Leslie Cunningham-Sabo, and Betty J. Skipper. 1995. "Tobacco Use: Baseline Results from 'Pathways to Health,' a School-Based Project for Southwestern American Indian Youth." *Preventive Medicine* 24:454–460.

Day, Gordon M. 1978. "Western Abenaki." In *Handbook of North American Indians, vol. 15: Northeast*, edited by Bruce G. Trigger, 148–159. Washington, D.C.: Smithsonian Institution.

Day, Gordon M., and Bruce G. Trigger. 1978. "Algonquin." In *Handbook of North American Indians, vol. 15: Northeast*, edited by Bruce G. Trigger, 792–797. Washington, D.C.: Smithsonian Institution.

D'Azevedo, Warren L. 1986. "Washoe." In *Handbook of North American Indians, vol. 11: Great Basin*, edited by Warren L. D'Azevedo, 466–498. Washington, D.C.: Smithsonian Institution.

de Bry, Theodore. 1591. *Brevis Narratio Eorum Quae in Florida Americae Provincia Gallis Acciderunt*. Part 2 of *Grands Voyages Comprising Jacques Le Moyne de Morques' Account*. Frankfurt-on-the-Main.

———. 1966 [1590]. *Thomas Hariot's Virginia*. Readex Microprint. Reprint of the English edition of 1590.

De Laguna, Frederica. 1990. "Tlingit." In *Handbook of North American Indians, vol. 7: Northwest Coast*, edited by Wayne Suttles, 203–228. Washington, D.C.: Smithsonian Institution.

Delorit, Richard J. 1970. *An Illustrated Taxonomy Manual of Weed Seeds*. River Falls, Wisconsin: Agronomy Publications.

Densmore, Frances. 1928. *Uses of Plants by the Chippewa Indians*. Forty-fourth Annual Report of the Bureau of American Ethnology. Washington, D.C.: U. S. Government Printing Office.

Denys, Nicolas. 1908. *The Description and Natural History of the Coasts of North America (Acadia)*. Edited by William F. Ganong. Toronto: Champlain Society.

Desenclos, J., and R. A. Hahn. 1992. "Years of Potential Life Lost before Age 65, by Race, Hispanic Origin, and Sex—United States, 1986–1988." *Morbidity and Mortality Weekly Report* 41/SS6:13–23. Atlanta: U.S. Centers for Disease Control.

DeStefano, F., J. L. Coulihan, and M. K. Wiant. 1979. "Blood Pressure Survey on the Navajo Indian Reservation." *American Journal of Epidemiology* 109:335–345.

DeWolf, Gordon P. 1957. Review of The Genus Nicotiana, by T. H. Goodspeed. *Southwestern Naturalist* 2(4):177–179.

Díaz-Romo, Patricia. 1994. *Huicholes y plaquicidas*. Video. México, D.F.

Dibble, Charles E., and Arthur J. O. Anderson, trans. 1957. *General History of the Things of New Spain*, by Fr. Bernadino de Sahagun. Book 4, *The Soothsayers*. Salt Lake City: University of Utah Press.

———, trans. 1959. *General History of the Things of New Spain*, by Fr. Bernadino de Sahagun. Book 9, *The Merchants*. Salt Lake City: University of Utah Press.

———, trans. 1961. *General History of the Things of New Spain*, by Fr. Bernadino de Sahagun. Book 10, *The People*. Salt Lake City: University of Utah Press.

———, trans. 1963. *General History of the Things of New Spain*, by Fr. Bernadino de Sahagun. Book 11, *Earthly Things*. Salt Lake City: University of Utah Press.

———, trans. 1969. *General History of the Things of New Spain*, by Fr. Bernadino de Sahagun. Book 6, *Rhetoric and Moral Philosophy*. Salt Lake City: University of Utah Press.

Dickson, Sarah A. 1954. *Panacea or Precious Bane: Tobacco in Sixteenth-Century Literature*. Arents Tobacco Collection Publication no. 5. New York: New York Public Library.

Dixon, Roland B. 1921. "Words for Tobacco in American Indian Languages." *American Anthropologist* 23:19–49.

Dixon, Roland B., and John B. Stetson, Jr. 1922. "Analysis of Pre-Columbian Pipe Dottles." *American Anthropologist* 24:245–246.

Dobkin de Rios, Marlene. 1984. *Hallucinogens: Cross-Cultural Perspectives*. Albuquerque: University of New Mexico Press.

Dohm, Karen M., and Melissa Gould. 1985. *Excavations at Kin Tl'iish (Site 5MT2336), a Multiple-Occupation Site*. Dolores Archaeological Program Technical Reports DAP-166. Salt Lake City: Bureau of Reclamation.

Doll, R. 1950. "Smoking and Carcinoma of the Lung." *British Medical Journal* 2:739–748.

———. 1978. "Cigarette Smoking and Bronchial Carcinoma: Dose and Time Relationships among Regular Smokers and Life-Long Non-Smokers." *Journal of Epidemiology and Community Health* 32:303–313.

Donaldson, Marcia, and Mollie S. Toll. 1982. "Prehistoric Subsistence in the Bis sa'ani Community Area: Evidence from Flotation, Macrobotanical Remains, and Wood Identification." In *Bis sa'ani: A Late Bonito Phase Community on Escavada Wash, Northwest New Mexico*, vol. 3, by Cory D. Breternitz, David E. Doyel, and Michael P. Marshall, 1099–1180. Papers in Anthropology 14. Window Rock, Arizona: Navajo Nation Cultural Resources Management Program.

Doub, Albert, Jr., and Larry Crabtree. 1973. *Tobacco in the United States*. USDA, Agricultural Marketing Service. Washington, D.C.: U.S. Government Printing Office.

Douglas, David. 1904–1905. "Sketch of a Journey to the Northwestern part of the Continent during the Years 1824–1827." *Oregon Historic Quarterly* 5–6.

Downs, James H. 1966. "The Significance of Environmental Manipulation in Great Basin Cultural Developments." In *The Current Status of Anthropological Research in the Great Basin: 1964*. Technical Report Series S-H, Social Science and Humanities, Publication 1. Reno, Nevada: Desert Research Institute.

Dozier, Edward P. 1966. *Hano: A Tewa Indian Community in Arizona*. New York: Holt, Rinehart, and Winston.

Drass, Richard R. 1995. "Prehistoric Cultivation of Marshelder on the Southern Plains." Paper presented at the 53d Annual Plains Conference, Laramie, Wyoming.

Driver, Harold E. 1970. *Indians of North America*. Chicago: University of Chicago Press.

Drucker, Philip. 1941. *Culture Element Distributions: Yuman-Piman 17*. Anthropological Records 6. Berkeley: University of California.

———. 1955. *Indians of the Northwest Coast.* Garden City, New York: Natural History Press.

Drucker, Susana, Roberto Escalante, and Roberto J. Weitlaner. 1969. "The Cuitlatec." In *Handbook of Middle American Indians, vol. 7: Ethnology,* edited by E. Z. Vogt, part 1, 565–576. Austin: University of Texas.

Duby, Gertrude, and Frans Blom. 1969. "The Lacandon." In *Handbook of Middle American Indians, vol. 7: Ethnology,* edited by E. Z. Vogt, part 1, 276–297. Austin: University of Texas.

Du Creux, François. 1951–1952. *The History of Canada or New France.* Edited and translated by Percy J. Robinson and James B. Conacher. 2 vols. Toronto: Champlain Society.

Duke, James A. 1975. "Ethnobotanical Observations on the Cuna Indians." *Economic Botany* 29(3):278–293.

Dunavan, Sandra. 1990. "Floral Remains." In *Selected Early Mississippian Household Sites in the American Bottom, part 5: The Olszewski Site (11–S-465),* by Ned H. Hanenberger, 389–403. American Bottom Archaeology FAI-270 Site Reports, vol. 22. Urbana: University of Illinois Press.

———. n.d. "Plants and People." In *Recent Research at the Madisonville Village Site, Hamilton County, Ohio,* edited by C. Wesley Cowan. Occasional Papers in Anthropology, no. 1. Cincinnati: Cincinnati Museum of Natural History. In press.

Dunbar, John. 1910. "The Presbyterian Mission among the Pawnee Indians in Nebraska, 1834 to 1846." *Kansas Historical Collections* 11:323–332.

Duran, Fr. Diego. 1964. *The Aztecs: The History of the Indies of New Spain.* Translated by Doris Heyden and Fernando Horcasitas. New York: Orion Press.

Dutton, Bertha P. 1962. *Happy People: The Huichol Indians.* Santa Fe: Museum of New Mexico Press.

Eastwood, Alice. 1938. "The Tobacco Collected by Archibald Menzies on the Northwest Coast of America." *Leaflets of Western Botany* 2(6):92–95.

Eggan, Fred. "Pueblos: Introduction." 1979. In *Handbook of North American Indians, vol. 9: Southwest,* edited by Alfonso Ortiz, 224–235. Washington, D.C.: Smithsonian Institution.

Elferink, Jan G. 1983. "The Narcotic and Hallucinogenic Use of Tobacco in Pre-Columbian Central America." *Journal of Ethnopharmacology* 7:111–122.

Elmendorf, W. W. 1960. *The Structure of Twana Culture.* Research Studies 28, no. 3. Pullman: Washington State University.

Elmore, Francis H. 1944. *Ethnobotany of the Navajo.* University of New Mexico Bulletin 392. Albuquerque.

Elsasser, Albert B. 1978a. "Wiyot." In *Handbook of North American Indians, vol. 8: California,* edited by R. F. Heizer, 155–163. Washington, D.C.: Smithsonian Institution.

———. 1978b. "Mattole, Nongatl, Sinkyone, Lassik, Wailaki." In *Handbook of North American Indians, vol. 8: California,* edited by R. F. Heizer, 190–294. Washington, D.C.: Smithsonian Institution.

Erdtman, G. 1943. *An Introduction to Pollen Analysis.* New York: Ronald Press.

———. 1952. *Pollen Morphology and Plant Taxonomy: An Introduction to Palynology. I. Angiosperms.* Waltham, Massachusetts: Chronica Botanica.

———. 1960. "The Acetolysis Method: A Revised Description." *Svensk. Botanisk Tidskrift Bd.* 54:561–564.

Esquivel, M., and K. Hammer. 1991. "The Cultivated Species of the Family Solanaceae in Cuba." In *Solanaceae III: Taxonomy, Chemistry, Evolution,* edited by J. G. Hawkes et al., 357–364. Richmond, UK: Royal Botanic Gardens, Kew.

Ewers, John C. 1968. *Indian Life on the Upper Missouri.* Norman: University of Oklahoma Press.

Faegri, K., and J. Iversen. 1975. *Textbook of Pollen Analysis.* New York: Munksgaard Press.

Fair, Susan W. 1985. "Alaska Native Arts and Crafts." *Alaska Geographic* 12(3):133.

Faris, James C. 1990. *The Nightway: A History and a History of Documentation of a Navajo Ceremonial.* Albuquerque: University of New Mexico Press.

Farooqui, S. M., and Bir Bahadur. 1985. "Studies on Seed Morphology (LM and SEM) of American *Nicotiana* L. (Solanaceae)." *Indian Journal of Botany* 8(2):191–197.

Fecteau, Rudolph. 1978. *A Preliminary Report on Seed Remains from Longhouse Features at the Draper Site*. University of Western Ontario, Research Report no. 4. London, Ontario: Museum of Indian Archaeology.

———. 1979. "A Preliminary Report on the Archaeobotanical Remains from the Kelly Site (AfHi-20), Caradoc Township, Middlesex County, Ontario." Manuscript in possession of Gail Wagner, University of South Carolina.

———. 1980. "Archaeobotanical Remains from the Robin Hood Site." Manuscript in possession of Gail Wagner, University of South Carolina.

———. 1981a. "Archaeobotany of the Steward Site (BfKt-2), Williamsburg Township, Dundas County, Ontario." Manuscript on file. Ottawa: Archaeology Unit, Heritage Branch, Ontario Ministry of Citizenship and Culture.

———. 1981b. "Archaeobotany of the Wolf Creek Site (AcHm-3), Kent County, Chatham Township, Ontario." Manuscript in possession of Gail Wagner, University of South Carolina.

———. 1983a. "A Preliminary Report on Plant Remains from Three Early Iroquoian Sites in Southwestern Ontario." Report submitted to Archaeology Unit, Heritage Branch, Ontario Ministry of Citizenship and Culture, London, Ontario.

———. 1983b. "An Initial Report on Carbonized Plant Remains from the Harrietsville Earthworks Site (AfHf-10), Midden I, in North Dorchester Township, Middlesex County." *Kewa* 83(3):13–17. London, Ontario.

Feest, Christian F. 1978a. "Virginia Algonquians." In *Handbook of North American Indians, vol. 15: Northeast*, edited by Bruce G. Trigger, 253–270. Washington, D.C.: Smithsonian Institution.

———. 1978b. "North Carolina Algonquians." In *Handbook of North American Indians, vol. 15: Northeast*, edited by Bruce G. Trigger, 271–281. Washington, D.C.: Smithsonian Institution.

Feinhandler, Sherwin J., Harold C. Fleming, and Joan M. Monahon. 1979. "Pre-Columbian Tobaccos in the Pacific." *Economic Botany* 33(2):213–226.

Felger, Richard S., and Mary B. Moser. 1985. *People of the Desert and Sea: Ethnobotany of the Seri Indians*. Tucson: University of Arizona Press.

Fenton, William N. 1937. "The Seneca Society of Faces." *Scientific Monthly* 44:215–238.

———. 1941. "Masked Medicine Societies of the Iroquois." *Smithsonian Institution Annual Report for 1940*, 397–429. Washington, D.C.: U.S. Government Printing Office.

———. 1949. "Medicinal Plant Lore of the Iroquois: Chauncey Johnny John and James Crow Instruct He-lost-a-bet in the Use of Native Plants." *Bulletin to the Schools* 35:233–237. Albany: University of the State of New York.

———. 1953. *The Iroquois Eagle Dance: An Offshoot of the Calumet Dance*. Bureau of American Ethnology Bulletin 156. Washington, D.C.: Smithsonian Institution. Reprint, 1991. Syracuse, New York: Syracuse University Press.

———. 1978. "Northern Iroquoian Culture Patterns." In *Handbook of North American Indians, vol. 15: Northeast*, edited by Bruce G. Trigger, 296–321. Washington, D.C.: Smithsonian Institution.

———. 1987. *The False Faces of the Iroquois*. Norman: University of Oklahoma Press.

Fewkes, J. Walter. 1896. "A Contribution to Ethnobotany." *American Anthropologist* 9:14–21.

———. 1912. *Casa Grande, Arizona*. Twenty-eighth Annual Report of the Bureau of American Ethnology, 1906–1907. Washington, D.C.: Smithsonian Institution.

Fikes, Jay C. 1985. "Huichol Indian Identity and Adaptation." Ph.D. diss., University of Michigan, Ann Arbor.

Finlayson, W. D. 1975. *The 1975 Rescue Excavations at the Draper Site: A Preliminary Report*. Canadian Archaeological Association Bulletin no. 7. Ottawa.

Finlayson, W. D., D. G. Smith, M. W. Spence, and P. Timmins. 1985. "The 1985 Salvage Excavations at the Keffer Site: A Field Report." *Kewa* 8:2–10. London, Ontario.

Finlayson, W. D., D. G. Smith, and B. Wheeler. 1987. *What Columbus Missed!* St. George Press.

Fisher, Edwin B., Jr., Edward Lichtenstein, and Debra Haire-Joshu. 1993. "Multiple Determinants of Tobacco Use and Cessation." In *Nicotine Addiction: Principles and Management*, edited by C. Tracy Orleans and John Slade. Oxford: Oxford University Press.

Flannery, Kent V., Joyce Marcus, and Stephen A. Kowalewski. 1981. "The Preceramic and Formative in the Valley of Oaxaca." In *Handbook of Middle American Indians, vol. 1: Supplement to Handbook*, edited by J. A. Sabloff, 48–93. Austin: University of Texas Press.

Fleisher, Mark S. 1980. "The Ethnobotany of the Clallam Indians of Western Washington." *Northwest Anthropological Research Notes* 14(2):192–210.

Fletcher, Alice C. 1904. "The Hako: A Pawnee Ceremony." *Twenty-second Annual Report of the Bureau of American Ethnology*, part 2, 5–368. Washington, D.C.: U.S. Government Printing Office.

Ford, Richard I. 1981. "Gardening and Farming before A.D. 1000: Pattern of Prehistoric Cultivation North of Mexico." *Journal of Ethnobiology* 1(1):6–27.

———. 1983. "Inter-Indian Exchange in the Southwest." In *Handbook of North American Indians, vol. 10: Southwest*, edited by Alfonso Ortiz, 711–722. Washington, D.C.: Smithsonian Institution.

———. 1985. "Patterns of Prehistoric Food Production in North America." In *Prehistoric Food Production in North America*, edited by R. I. Ford, 341–364. Anthropological Papers 75. Ann Arbor: Museum of Anthropology, University of Michigan.

Fortier, Andrew C. 1992a. "Features." In *The Sponemann Site 2: The Mississippian and Oneota Occupations (11-Ms-517)*, by D. K. Jackson, A. C. Fortier, and J. A. Williams, 335–337. American Bottom Archaeology FAI-270 Site Reports, vol. 24. Urbana: University of Illinois Press.

———. 1992b. "Radiocarbon Dates." In *The Sponemann Site 2: The Mississippian and Oneota Occupations (11-Ms-517)*, by D. K. Jackson, A. C. Fortier, and J. A. Williams, 335–337. American Bottom Archaeology FAI-270 Site Reports, vol. 24. Urbana: University of Illinois Press.

Fortuna, Luis. 1978. "Análisis polénico de Sanate Abajo." *Boletín del Museo del Hombre Dominicana* 7(10):125–130.

Foster, Gary. 1990. *The Wolfe Creek Site, AcHm-3: A Prehistoric Neutral Frontier Community in Southwestern Ontario*. Monographs in Ontario Archaeology, no. 3. Publisher unknown.

Foster, George M. 1969. "The Mixe, Zoque, and Popluca." In *Handbook of Middle American Indians, vol. 7: Ethnology*, edited by E. Z. Vogt, part 1, 448–477. Austin: University of Texas Press.

Foster, Steven, and James A. Duke. 1990. *A Field Guide to Medicinal Plants: Eastern and Central North America*. Boston: Houghton Mifflin.

Fowler, Catherine S. 1986. "Subsistence." In *Handbook of North American Indians, vol. 11: Great Basin*, edited by Warren L. D'Azevedo, 64–97. Washington, D.C.: Smithsonian Institution.

———. 1989. *Willard Z. Park's Ethnographic Notes on the Northern Paiute of Western Nevada, 1933–1940*. Salt Lake City: University of Utah Press.

———. 1994. "Historical Perspectives on Timbisha Shoshone Land Management Practices, Death Valley, California." Paper presented at the annual Ethnobiology Conference, Victoria, B.C.

Franciscan Fathers. 1910. *An Ethnologic Dictionary of the Navaho Language*. Saint Michaels, Arizona.

Fried, Jacob. 1969. "The Tarahumara." In *Handbook of Middle American Indians, vol. 8: Ethnology*, edited by E. Z. Vogt, part 2, 846–870. Austin: University of Texas Press.

Fritz, Gayle. 1986a. "Paleoethnobotanical Analysis." In *Phase III Archaeological Investigations at the Chapius (23PI176) and Bundy (23PI177) Sites, Pike County, Missouri*, by C. M. Niquette and T. K. Donham, 108–118. Jefferson City: Missouri State Highway and Transportation Department.

———. 1986b. "Prehistoric Ozark Agriculture: The University of Arkansas Rockshelter Collections." Ph.D. diss., Department of Anthropology, University of North Carolina.

———. 1990. "Multiple Pathways to Farming in Precontact Eastern North America." *Journal of World Prehistory* 4(4):387–435.

Fritz, Gayle, and Tristram R. Kidder. 1993. "Recent Investigations into Prehistoric Agriculture in the Lower Mississippi Valley." *Southeastern Archaeology* 12(1):1–14.

Fuentes y Guzmán, F. A. 1882. *Historia de Guatemala y recordación de Florida.* Reprint, 1932. Guatemala City: Sociedad de Geografía y Historia Guatemala.

Furst, Peter T. 1968. "The Parching of the Maize: An Essay on the Survival of Huichol Ritual." *Acta Ethnologica et Linguistica* 14. Vienna.

———. 1972. *Flesh of the Gods: The Ritual Use of Hallucinogens.* New York: Praeger.

———. 1976. *Hallucinogens and Culture.* Novato, California: Chandler and Sharp.

Gad, Finn. 1984. "History of Colonial Greenland." In *Handbook of North American Indians, vol. 5: Arctic*, edited by D. Damas, 556–576. Washington, D.C.: Smithsonian Institution.

———. 1988. "Danish Greenland Policies." In *Handbook of North American Indians, vol. 4: History of Indian-White Relations*, edited by W. E. Washburn, 110–118. Washington, D.C.: Smithsonian Institution.

Gager, Forrest L., Jr., Virginia Johnson, and Joseph C. Holmes. 1960. "Ancient Tobacco Smokers." *Science* 132:1021.

Gandette, L. A., et al. 1993. "Cancer Incidence by Ethnic Group in the Northwest Territories, 1969–1988. *Health Report* 5:23.

Garber, Emily. 1980. "Analysis of Plant Remains." In *Tijeras Canyon: Analyses of the Past*, edited by Linda Cordell, 71–87. Albuquerque: University of New Mexico Press.

Gardner, Paul W. 1992a. "Carbonized Plant Remains from the Late Prehistoric Bonham Site (44SM7), Smyth County, Virginia." Report submitted to Cliff Boyd, Department of Sociology and Anthropology, Radford University, Radford, Virginia.

———. 1992b. "Economic Optimization Models and Prehistoric Subsistence Change in the Southern Appalachians." Ph.D. diss., Department of Anthropology, University of North Carolina.

Garrad, Charles, and Conrad E. Heidenreich. 1978. "Khionontaternon (Petun)." In *Handbook of North American Indians, vol. 15: Northeast*, edited by Bruce G. Trigger, 394–397. Washington, D.C.: Smithsonian Institution.

Garth, T. R. 1978. "Atsugewi." In *Handbook of North American Indians, vol. 8: California*, edited by R. F. Heizer, 236–243. Washington, D.C.: Smithsonian Institution.

Gayton, Anna H. 1976a. "Culture-Environment Integration: External References on Yokuts Life." In *Native Californians: A Theoretical Perspective*, edited by L. J. Bean and T. C. Blackburn, 79–98. Ramona, California: Ballena Press.

———. 1976b. "Yokuts-Mono Chiefs and Shamans." In *Native Californians: A Theoretical Perspective*, edited by L. J. Bean and T. C. Blackburn, 175–224. Ramona, California: Ballena Press.

Gayton, A. H., and S. S. Newman. 1940. *Yokuts and Western Mono Myths.* Anthropological Records 5, no. 1. Berkeley: University of California.

Gehring, Charles T., and William A. Starna, eds. 1988. *A Journey into Mohawk and Oneida Country, 1634–1635: The Journal of Harmen Meyndertsz van den Bogaert.* Syracuse: Syracuse University Press.

Gentry, Howard S. 1942. *Rio Mayo Plants: A Study of the Flora and Vegetation of the Valley of the Rio Mayo, Sonora.* Publication 527. Washington, D.C.: Carnegie Institution of Washington.

Gerstel, D. U. 1961. "Essay on the Origin of Tobacco." *Tobacco Science* 5:15–17.

———. 1976. "Tobacco *Nicotiana tabacum* (Solanaceae)." In *Evolution of Crop Plants*, edited by N. W. Simmonds, 273–277. London: Longman.

Gibson, James R. 1988. "The Maritime Trade of the North Pacific Coast." In *Handbook of North American Indians, vol. 4: History of Indian-White Relations*, edited by Wayne Suttles, 375–390. Washington, D.C.: Smithsonian Institution.

Gifford, E. W. 1936. "Northeastern and Western Yavapai." *University of California Publications in American Archaeology and Ethnology* 34:247–354.

———. 1940. *Culture Element Distributions 12: Apache-Pueblo*. Anthropological Records 4, no. 1. Berkeley: University of California.

Gifford, E. W., and A. L. Kroeber. 1937. "Culture Element Distributions 4: Pomo." *University of California Publications in American Archaeology and Ethnology* 37(4):117–254.

Gifford, James C. 1980. *Archaeological Explorations in Caves of the Point of Pines Region, Arizona*. Anthropological Papers 36. Tucson: University of Arizona.

Gillespie, Beryl C. 1981. "Yellowknife." In *Handbook of North American Indians, vol. 6: Subarctic*, edited by J. Helm, 285–290. Washington, D.C.: Smithsonian Institution.

Gillum, R. F., B. S. Gillum, and N. Smith. 1984. "Cardiovascular Risk Factors among Urban American Indians: Blood Pressure, Serum Lipids, Smoking, Diabetes, Health Knowledge and Behavior." *American Heart Journal* 107:765–76.

Gilmore, Melvin R. 1913. "A Study in the Ethnobotany of the Omaha Indians." *Collections of the Nebraska State Historical Society* 17:314–357.

———. 1919. "Uses of Plants by the Indians of the Missouri River Region." *Thirty-third Annual Report of the Bureau of American Ethnology, 1911–1912*, 43–154. Washington, D.C.: U.S. Government Printing Office. Reprint, 1977. Lincoln: University of Nebraska Press.

———. 1922. "Some Comments on 'Aboriginal Tobaccos.'" *American Anthropologist* 24:480–481.

Giraud, David M. 1958. "Etienne Veniard de Bourgmont's 'Exact Description of Louisiana.'" *Missouri Historical Society Bulletin* 15(1):3–19.

Gish, Jannifer W. 1993. "Morphologic Distinctiveness of *Nicotiana* Pollen and the Potential for Identifying Prehistoric Southwest Tobacco." In *Across the Colorado Plateau: Anthropological Studies for the Transwestern Pipeline Expansion Project, vol. 15: Subsistence and Environment*, by Jannifer W. Gish et al., 211–266. Albuquerque: Office of Contract Archeology and Maxwell Museum of Anthropology, University of New Mexico.

Gish, Jannifer W., Julia E. Hammett, Marie E. Brown, Pamela McBride, Joseph C. Winter, Kenneth L. Brown, John J. Ponczynski, and Jeanne L. Delanois. 1993. *Across the Colorado Plateau: Anthropological Studies for the Transwestern Pipeline Expansion Project, vol. 15: Subsistence and Environment*. Albuquerque: Office of Contract Archaeology and Maxwell Museum of Anthropology, University of New Mexico.

Glover, E. D., B. S. Gillum, and N. Smith. 1989. "Smokeless Tobacco Use among American College Students." *Journal of American College Health* 38:81.

Goddard, Ives. 1978. "Delaware." In *Handbook of North American Indians, vol. 15: Northeast*, edited by Bruce G. Trigger, 213–239. Washington, D.C.: Smithsonian Institution.

Goddard, Pliny Earle. 1903. "Life and Culture of the Hupa." *University of California Publications in American Archaeology and Ethnology* 1(1):36–37.

Goggin, John M. 1938. "A Note on Cheyenne Peyote." *New Mexico Anthropologist* 3, no. 2.

Goldberg, H. I., et al. 1991. "Prevalence of Behavioral Risk Factors in Two American Indian Populations in Montana." *Preventive Medicine* 7:155.

Goldschmidt, Walter. 1978. "Nomlaki." In *Handbook of North American Indians, vol. 8: California*, edited by R. F. Heizer, 341–349. Washington, D.C.: Smithsonian Institution.

Goodman, Jordan. 1993. *Tobacco in History: The Cultures of Dependence*. London: Routledge.

Goodrich, Jennie, and Claudia Lawson. 1980. *Kashaya Pomo Plants*. Los Angeles: American Indian Studies Center, University of California.

Goodspeed, Thomas Harper. 1913. "Notes on the Germination of Tobacco Seed, part 1." *University of California Publications in Botany* 5(5):199–222.

———. 1915. "Notes on the Germination of Tobacco Seed, part 2." *University of California Publications in Botany* 5(5):233–248.

———. 1945. "Studies in Nicotiana III: A Taxonomic Organization of the Genus." *University of California Publications in Botany* 18:335–343.

———. 1954. *The Genus Nicotiana: Origins, Relationships, and Evolution of Its Species in the Light of Their Distribution, Morphology, and Cytogenetics*. Waltham, Massachusetts: Chronica Botanica, vol. 16.

Goodwin, Guy. 1969. "Wise Man of Algonquins Sees Tobacco Tranquilizer." *Bright Leaf*, April–May, 35, 45.

Gorenstein, Shirley, and Helen P. Pollard. 1983. *The Tarascan Civilization: A Late Prehispanic Cultural System*. Publications in Anthropology, no. 28. Nashville, Tennessee: Vanderbilt University.

Gould, Richard A. 1978. "Tolowa." In *Handbook of North American Indians, vol. 8: California*, edited by R. F. Heizer, 128–136. Washington, D.C.: Smithsonian Institution.

Grange, Roger. 1952. "Wooden Artifacts." In *Mogollon Cultural Continuity and Change: The Stratigraphic Analysis of Tularosa and Cordova Caves*, 331–451. Fieldiana: Anthropology 40. Chicago: Chicago Natural History Museum.

Grant, Campbell. 1978. "Eastern Coastal Chumash." In *Handbook of North American Indians, vol. 8: California*, edited by R. F. Heizer, 509–519. Washington, D.C.: Smithsonian Institution.

Great Plains Flora Association. 1986. *Flora of the Great Plains*. Topeka: University Press of Kansas.

Green, William, and William T. Billeck. 1993. "Plant Use at the Millipede Site (13ML361), a Central Plains Earthlodge in Southwestern Iowa." Paper presented at the 51st Plains Anthropological Conference, Saskatoon, Canada.

Gremillion, Kristen J. 1995. "Comparative Paleoethnobotany of Three Native Southeastern Communities of the Historic Period." *Southeastern Archaeology* 14(1):1–16.

Griffin, James B. 1952. "Radiocarbon Dates for the Eastern United States." In *Archeology of Eastern United States*, ed. by James B. Griffin, 365–370. Chicago: University of Chicago Press.

Grimes, Joseph E., and Thomas B. Hinton. 1969. "The Huichol and Cora." In *Handbook of Middle American Indians, vol. 8: Ethnology*, edited by E. Z. Vogt, part 2, 792–813. Austin: University of Texas Press.

Grinnell, George B. 1924. *The Cheyenne Indians: Their History and Ways of Life*. 2 vols. New Haven: Yale University Press. Reprint, 1972, in 1 vol. Lincoln: University of Nebraska Press.

Gullick, C. J. M. R. 1985. *Myths of a Minority: The Changing Tradition of the Vincentian Caribs*. Assen, Netherlands: Van Gorcum.

Gundersen, James N. 1993. "'Catlinite' and the Spread of the Calumet Ceremony." *American Antiquity* 58(3):560–562.

Gunn, Charles R., and Frederick B. Gaffney. 1974. *Seed Characteristics of 42 Economically Important Species of Solanaceae in the United States*. USDA Technical Bulletin 1471. Washington, D.C.: U.S. Government Printing Office.

Gunnerson, James H., and Dolores A. Gunnerson. 1971. "Apachean Culture: A Study in Unity and Diversity." In *Apachean Culture History and Ethnology*, edited by Keith H. Basso and Morris E. Opler, 7–27. Anthropological Papers, no. 21. Tucson: University of Arizona.

Gunther, Erna. 1973. *Ethnobotany of Western Washington*. Seattle: University of Washington Press.

Haberman, Thomas W. 1982. "Carbonized Seeds from the Extended Middle Missouri Component at the Travis I Site (39CO213)." *South Dakota Archaeology* 6:47–67.

———. 1984. "Evidence for Aboriginal Tobaccos in Eastern North America." *American Antiquity* 49:269–287.

Hack, John T. 1942. *The Changing Physical Environment of the Hopi Indians of Arizona*. Papers of the Peabody Museum of American Archaeology and Ethnology, Harvard University, 35, no. 1. Cambridge, Massachusetts.

Hafner, Gertrude. 1962. "Das Calumet Und Seine Beziehungen Zum Nordamerikanischen Südwesten." In *Proceedings of the 34th International Congress of Americanists, 1960*, 564–568. Vienna: Ferdinand Berger, Horn.

Hair, J. F., R. E. Anderson, and R. L. Tatham. 1987. *Multivariate Data Analysis*. New York: Macmillan.

Hall, Clayton C., ed. 1910. *Narratives of Early Maryland 1633–1684*. New York: Charles Scribner's Sons.

Hall, Pat. 1984. "Fossil Tobacco Pollen in Pipe: Direct Evidence of Prehistoric Tobacco Pipe Smoking in California." Manuscript on file with Joseph Winter.

———. 1985. "Climatic Factors That Influenced the Initiation of Tobacco-Related Cultivation Practices among Prehistoric California Indians." M.A. thesis, Sonoma State University, California.

Hall, Robert L. 1983. "The Evolution of the Calumet-Pipe." In *Prairie Archaeology: Papers in Honor of David A. Baerris*, edited by Guy E. Gibbon, 37–52. University of Minnesota Publications in Anthropology 3.

———. 1997. "The Gift of White Buffalo Calf Maiden." In *An Archaeology of the Soul: North American Indian Belief and Ritual*. Urbana: University of Illinois Press.

Halland, R. J., and D. Dexter. 1988. "Smokeless Tobacco Use and Attitudes Towards Smokeless Tobacco among Native Americans and Other Adolescents in the Northwest." *American Journal of Public Health* 78:1586.

Hamel, Paula B., and Mary U. Chiltoskey. 1975. *Cherokee Plants and Their Uses: A 400-Year History*. Sylva, North Carolina: Herald Publishing.

Hammett, Julia E. 1993. "Paleoethnobotanical Evidence of Tobacco Use along the Transwestern Pipeline." In *Across the Colorado Plateau: Anthropological Studies for the Transwestern Pipeline Expansion Project, vol. 15: Subsistence and Environment*, by Jannifer W. Gish et al., 509–518. Albuquerque: Office of Contract Archeology and Maxwell Museum of Anthropology, University of New Mexico.

Hammond, George P., and Agapito Rey. 1940. *Narratives of the Coronado Expedition 1540–1542*. Albuquerque: University of New Mexico Press.

———. 1953. *Don Juan de Onate: Colonizer of New Mexico, 1595–1628*, parts 1–2. Coronado Historical Series, vols. 5–6. Albuquerque: University of New Mexico Press.

———. 1966. *The Rediscovery of New Mexico, 1580–1594: The Explorations of Chamuscado, Espejo, Castaño de Sosa, Morlete, and Leyva de Bonilla and Humaña*. Albuquerque: University of New Mexico Press.

Handelman, Don. 1976. "The Development of a Washo Shaman." In *Native Calfornians: A Theoretical Perspective*, edited by L. J. Bean and T. C. Blackburn, 379–406. Ramona, California: Ballena Press.

Hann, John T. 1986. "The Use and Processing of Plants by the Indians of Spanish Florida." *Southeastern Archaeology* 5(2):1–102.

Harlan, J. R., J. M. J. de Wet, and E. G. Price. 1973. "Comparative Evolution of Cereals." *Evolution* 27:311–325.

Harner, Michael J. 1973. "The Sound of Rushing Water." In *Hallucinogens and Shamanism*, edited by Michael J. Harner. New York: Oxford University Press.

Harrick, Royal B. 1964. *The Sioux: Life and Customs of a Warrior Society*. Norman: University of Oklahoma Press.

Harrington, H. D. 1964. *Manual of the Plants of Colorado*. Chicago: Sage Books.

Harrington, John P. 1932. *Tobacco among the Karuk Indians of California*. Bureau of American Ethnology Bulletin 94. Washington, D.C.: Smithsonian Institution.

———. 1942. *Cultural Element Distributions 14: Central California Coast*. University of California Anthropological Records 7, no. 1.

Harrison, Kathleen. 1998. "The Saints of Tobacco in Mazatec Prayer." Paper presented at the 21st annual conference of the Society of Ethnobiology, Reno, Nevada.

Harshberger, John W. 1906. "Phytogeographic Influences in the Arts and Industries of American Aborigines." *Geographical Society of Philadelphia Bulletin* 4(6):25–41.

Hart, Jeffrey A. 1981. *The Ethnobotany of the Early Peoples*. Helena: Montana Historical Society Press.

———. 1992. "Montana Native Plants and Northern Cheyenne Indians of Montana." *Journal of Ethnopharmacology* 4:1–55.

Harvey, H. R., and Isabel Kelly. 1969. "The Totonac." In *Handbook of Middle American Indians, vol. 8: Ethnology*, edited by E. Z. Vogt, part 2, 638–681. Austin: University of Texas.

Haury, Emil W. 1945. *The Excavation of Los Muertos and Neighboring Ruins in the Salt River Valley, Southern Arizona*. Papers of the Peabody Museum of American Archaeology and Ethnology 24, no. 1. Cambridge, Massachusetts: Harvard University.

Hawkes, J. G., R. N. Lester, and A. D. Skelding. 1979. *The Biology and Taxonomy of the Solanaceae*. London: Academic Press.

Health Canada. 1994. *Youth Smoking Survey*. Toronto: Minister of National Health and Welfare.

———. 1995. *Survey on Smoking in Canada*. Toronto: Minister of National Health and Welfare.

Health Research. 1990. *Health Research: Essential Link to Equity in Development*. Oxford: Oxford University Press.

Hedges, Ken. 1986. *Santa Ysabel Ethnobotany*. San Diego Museum of Man Ethnic Technology Notes, no. 20. San Diego.

Heidenreich, Conrad E. 1978. "Huron." In *Handbook of North American Indians, vol. 15: Northeast*, edited by Bruce G. Trigger, 368–388. Washington, D.C.: Smithsonian Institution.

Heiser, Charles B., Jr. 1969. *Nightshades: The Paradoxical Plants*. San Francisco: W. H. Freeman.

———. 1992. "On Possible Sources of the Tobacco of Prehistoric Eastern North America." *Current Anthropology* 33(1):54–56.

———. 1988. "Aspects of Unconscious Selection in the Evolution of Domesticated Plants." *Euphytica* 37:77–81.

Heizer, Robert F. 1940. "The Botanical Identification of Northwest Coast Tobacco." *American Anthropologist* 42:704–706.

———. 1947. *Francis Drake and the California Indians, 1579*. Berkeley: University of California Press.

———. 1974. *The Costanoan Indians*. Local History Studies, vol. 18. Cupertino, California: California History Center, De Anza College.

Hellson, John C., and Morgan Gadd. 1974. *Ethnobotany of the Blackfoot Indians*. Canadian Ethnology Service Paper no. 19. Ottawa: National Museums of Canada.

Helm, June, Edward S. Rogers, and James E. G. Smith. 1981. "Intercultural Relations and Cultural Change in the Shield and Mackenzie Borderlands." In *Handbook of North American Indians, vol. 6: Subarctic*, edited by J. Helm, 140–157. Washington, D.C.: Smithsonian Institution.

Hendron, J. W. 1946. "We Found America's Oldest Tobacco." *New Mexico Magazine* 24(11):11–13, 33–37.

Henning, Dale R. 1970. "Development and Interrelationships of Oneota Culture in the Lower Missouri River Valley." *Missouri Archaeologist* 32:1–180.

Herrick, James W. 1977. "Iroquois Medical Botany." Ph.D. diss., State University of New York, Albany.

Heusser, Calvin J. 1971. *Pollen and Spores of Chile*. Tucson: University of Arizona Press.

Hickerson, Harold. 1970. *The Chippewa and Their Neighbors: A Study in Ethnohistory*. New York: Holt, Rinehart, Winston.

Hill, Robert F., et al. 1994. "Cultural Correlates of Health among Oklahoma Cherokees." Unpublished paper. Center for Substance Abuse Program.

Hill, W. W. 1938. "Navajo Use of Jimson Weed." *New Mexico Anthropologist* 3:19–21.

Hirayama, T. 1981. "Nonsmoking Wives of Heavy Smokers Have a Higher Rate of Lung Cancer." Letter. *British Medical Journal* 283:916–917.

Hocking, George M. 1956. "Some Plant Materials Used Medicinally and Otherwise by the Navaho Indians in the Chaco Canyon, New Mexico." *El Palacio* 56:146–165.

———. 1949. "From Polkroot to Penicillin." *Rocky Mountain Druggist*, November, 12–13.

Hodge, Felicia S., S. Cummings, L. Fredericks, P. Kipinis, Melody Williams, and Kevin Teehee. 1995. "Prevalence of Smoking among Adult American Indian Clinic Users in Northern California." *Preventive Medicine* 24:441–446.

Hoebel, E. Adamson. 1960. *The Cheyennes: Indians of the Great Plains*. New York: Holt, Rinehart, and Winston.

Hoffman, F. L. 1928. *Cancer among North American Indians*. Newark: Prudential Press.

Hogan, Patrick. 1989. "Dinetah: A Re-Evaluation of Pre-Revolt Navajo Occupation of Northwest New Mexico." *Journal of Anthropological Research* 45:53–66.

Holloway, Richard G., and Glenna Dean. 1990. *New Mexico Solanaceae Pollen*. Castetter Laboratory for Ethnobotanical Studies, Technical Series, Report 290. Albuquerque: University of New Mexico.

Holm, Thomas C. 1834 [1702]. *Description of the Province of New Sweden. Now Called, by the English, Pennsylvania, In America*. Edited and translated by Peter S. Du Ponceau. Philadelphia: M'Carty and Davis.

Honigmann, John J. 1981. "West Main Cree." In *Handbook of North American Indians, vol. 6: Subarctic*, edited by J. Helm, 217–230. Washington, D.C.: Smithsonian Institution.

Hoppe, Walter A., Andres Medina, and Roberto J. Weitlaner. 1969. "The Popolaca." In *Handbook of Middle American Indians, vol. 7: Ethnology*, edited by E. Z. Vogt, part 1, 489–498. Austin: University of Texas.

Hoppe, Walter A., and Roberto J. Weitlaner. 1969a. "The Chocho." In *Handbook of Middle American Indians, vol. 7: Ethnology*, edited by E. Z. Vogt, part 1, 506–515. Austin: University of Texas Press.

———. 1969b. "The Ichacatic." In *Handbook of Middle American Indians, vol. 7: Ethnology*, edited by E. Z. Vogt, part 1, 499–505. Austin: University of Texas Press.

Horgan, C. 1993. *Substance Abuse, the Nation's Number One Health Problem: Key Indicators for Policy*. Waltham, Massachusetts: Brandeis University, Institute For Health Policy.

Hosmer, James K., ed. 1959. *Winthrop's Journal "History of New England" 1630–1649*. 2 vols. New York: Barnes and Noble.

Hough, Walter. 1897. "The Hopi in Relation to Their Plant Environment." *American Anthropologist* 10(2):33–44.

Howard, James. 1965. *The Ponca Tribe*. Bureau of American Ethnology Bulletin 195. Washington D.C.: Smithsonian Institution.

Huckell, Lisa. 1995. "Macrobotanical Remains." In *Archaeological Investigations of Early Village Sites in the Middle Santa Cruz Valley, Arizona: Analyses and Synthesis*, edited by Johnathan Mabry, part 1, 57–148. Anthropological Papers no. 19. Tucson: Center for Desert Archaeology.

Huckell, Lisa, and Mollie S. Toll. 1995. "Botanical Data from Henderson Pueblo (LA 1549) near Roswell, New Mexico." Manuscript on file. University of Michigan Museum of Anthropology.

Hughes, Charles C. 1984a. "Saint Lawrence Island Eskimo." In *Handbook of North American Indians, vol. 5: Arctic*, edited by D. Damas, 262–277. Washington, D.C.: Smithsonian Institution.

———. 1984b. "Siberian Eskimos." In *Handbook of North American Indians, vol. 5: Arctic*, edited by D. Damas, 247–261. Washington, D.C.: Smithsonian Institution.

Hulton, Paul. 1984. *America 1585: The Complete Drawings of John White*. Chapel Hill: University of North Carolina Press.

Hulton, Paul, and David B. Quinn. 1964. *The American Drawings of John White 1577–1590, with Drawings of European and Oriental Subjects*. 2 vols. Chapel Hill: University of North Carolina Press.

IHS (Indian Health Service). n.d. *Tobacco in Indian Country*. Albuquerque: Indian Health Service, Cancer Prevention and Control Program.

Jackson, Kirby E. 1940. "Alkaloids of Tobacco." *Chemical Reviews* 29:124–125.

Jameson, J. Franklin, ed. 1909. *Narratives of New Netherland 1609–1664*. New York: Charles Scribner's Sons.

Jeffrey, R. N. 1959. "Alkaloid Composition of Species of *Nicotiana*." *Tobacco Science* 3:89–93.

Jepson, W. L. 1993. *The Jepson Manual: Higher Plants of California*. Berkeley: University of California Press.

Johannessen, Sissel. 1983. "Plant Remains from the Mund Phase." In *The Mund Site (11-S-435)*, by A. C. Fortier, F. A. Finney, and R. B. Lacampagne, 299–318. American Bottom Archaeology FAI-270 Site Reports, vol. 5. Urbana: University of Illinois Press.

———. 1984a. "Paleoethnobotany." In *American Bottom Archaeology*, by Charles J. Bareis and James W. Porter. Urbana: University of Illinois Press .

———. 1984b. "Plant Remains." In *The Fish Lake Site (11-Mo-608)*, by A. C. Fortier, R. B. Lacampagne, and F. A. Finney, 189–199. American Bottom Archaeology FAI-270 Site Reports, vol. 8. Urbana: University of Illinois Press.

———. 1984c. "Plant Remains from the Edelhardt Phase." In *The BBB Motor Site (11-Ms-595)*, by Thomas E. Emerson and Douglas K. Jackson, 169–189. American Bottom Archaeology FAI-270 Site Reports, vol. 6. Urbana: University of Illinois Press.

———. 1985a. "Plant Remains." In *The Dohack Site*, by Anne Brower Stahl. Urbana: University of Illinois Press.

———. 1985b. "Mississippian Plant Remains." In *The Carbon Dioxide Site (11-Mo-594) and the Robert Schneider Site (11Ms-1177)*, by Fred A. Finney and Andrew C. Fortier, 259–263. American Bottom Archaeology FAI-270 Site Reports, vol. 11. Urbana: University of Illinois Press.

———. 1987a. "Plant Remains." In *The George Reeves Site (11-S-650)*, by Dale L. McElrath and Fred Finney, 349–356. Urbana: University of Illinois Press.

———. 1987b. "Patrick Phase Plant Remains." In *The Range Site: Archaic through Late Woodland Occupations*, by John E. Kelly et al., 404–416. Urbana: University of Chicago Press.

Johannessen, Sissel, and Lucy A. Whalley. 1988. "Floral Analysis." In *Late Woodland Sites in the American Bottom Uplands*, by Charles Benz et al., 265–288. American Bottom Archaeology FAI-270 Site Reports, vol. 18. Urbana: University of Illinois Press.

John, Elizabeth A. H. 1975. *Storms Brewed in Other Men's Worlds: A Confrontation of Indians, Spanish, and French in the Southwest, 1540–1795*. College Station: Texas A&M University Press.

Johnson, Alfred E. 1979. "Kansas City Hopewell." In *Hopewell Archaeology: The Chilicothe Conference*, edited by David S. Brose and N'omi Greber, 86–93. Kent, Ohio: Kent State University Press.

———. 1994. "A SteedKisker Effigy Pipe." *Plains Anthropologist* 39(148):185–194.

———. n.d. "Plains Woodland." Manuscript on file, Museum of Anthropology, University of Kansas, Lawrence.

Johnson, Amandus, ed. 1925. *Geographia Americae with an Account of the Delaware Indians, Based on Surveys and Notes Made in 1654–1656 by Peter Lindeström*. Philadelphia: Swedish Colonial Society.

Johnson, Jerald J. 1978. "Yana." In *Handbook of North American Indians, vol. 8: California*, edited by R. F. Heizer, 361–369. Washington, D.C.: Smithsonian Institution.

Johnson, Patti J. 1978. "Patwin." In *Handbook of North American Indians, vol. 8: California*, edited by R. F. Heizer, 350–360. Washington, D.C.: Smithsonian Institution.

Johnson, V. C., F. L. Gager, and J. C. Holmes. 1959. "A Study of the History of the Use of Tobacco." Paper presented at the 13th Tobacco Chemists Research Conference, Lexington, Kentucky.

Johnston, Alex. 1970. "Blackfoot Indian Utilization of the Flora of the Northwestern Great Plains." *Economic Botany* 25(3):301–303.

———. 1987. *Plants and the Blackfoot*. Lethbridge Historical Society 23. Lethbridge, Alberta, Canada.

Jones, Volney H. 1930. "Ethnobotany of Isleta." M.A. thesis, Department of Anthropology, University of New Mexico, Albuquerque.

———. 1935. "Ceremonial Cigarettes." *Southwestern Monuments Monthly Report*, October, 287–292.

———. 1936. "The Vegetal Remains of Newt Kash Hollow Shelter." In *Rock Shelters in Menifee County, Kentucky*, by W. S. Webb and W. D. Funkhouser, 147–167. Reports of Archaeology and Anthropology 3, no. 4. Lexington: University of Kentucky.

———. 1944. "Was Tobacco Smoked in the Pueblo Region in Pre-Spanish Times?" *American Antiquity* 9(4):451–456.

Jones, Volney H., and Sandra L. Dunavan. n.d. "Tobacco." In *Handbook of North American Indians, vol. 3: Environment, Origins, and Population*, edited by Richard I. Ford. Washington, D.C.: Smithsonian Institution Press. In press.

Jones, Volney H., and Elizabeth Ann Morris. 1960. "A Seventh-Century Record of Tobacco Utilization in Arizona." *El Palacio* 67:115–117.

Jorgenson, Joseph G. 1983. "Comparative Traditional Economics and Ecological Adaptations." In *Handbook of North American Indians, vol. 10: Southwest*, edited by Alfonso Ortiz, 684–710. Washington, D.C.: Smithsonian Institution.

Josselyn, John. 1865. *An Account of Two Voyages to NewEngland, Made during the Years 1638, 1663*. Boston: William Veazie.

Kapp, Ronald O. 1969. *How to Know Pollen and Spores*. Dubuque, Iowa: William C. Brown.

Kari, Priscilla Russe. 1985. *Upper Tanana Ethnobotany*. Anchorage: Alaska Historical Commission.

Kartesz, John T. 1994. *A Synonymized Checklist of the Vascular Flora of the United States, Canada, and Greenland*. 2d ed. Portland, Oregon: Timber Press.

Kartesz, John T., and Rosemarie Kartesz. 1980. *A Synonymized Checklist of the Vascular Flora of the United States, Canada, and Greenland*. Chapel Hill: University of North Carolina Press.

Kearney, Thomas H., and Robert H. Peebles. 1960. *Arizona Flora*. 2d ed. Berkeley: University of California Press.

Kelley, Klara B., and Harris Francis. 1994. *Navajo Sacred Places*. Bloomington: Indiana University Press.

Kelly, Isabel. 1978. "Coast Miwok." In *Handbook of North American Indians, vol. 8: California*, edited by R. F. Heizer, 414–425. Washington, D.C.: Smithsonian Institution.

Kelly, Isabel, and Catherine S. Fowler. 1986. "Southern Paiute." In *Handbook of North American Indians, vol. 11: Great Basin*, edited by Warren L. D'Azevedo, 368–397. Washington, D.C.: Smithsonian Institution.

Kendall, Daythal L. 1990. "Takelma." In *Handbook of North American Indians, vol. 7: Northwest Coast*, edited by Wayne Suttles, 589–592. Washington, D.C.: Smithsonian Institution.

Keppler, Joseph. 1941. *Comments on Certain Iroquois Masks*. Contributions from the Museum of the American Indian, Heye Foundation, vol. 12, no. 4.

Kidder, Tristram R., and Gayle J. Fritz. 1993. "Subsistence and Social Change in the Lower Mississippi Valley: The Reno Brake and Osceola Sites, Louisiana." *Journal of Field Archaeology* 20:281–297.

King, L., and Gary Crawford. 1974. "Paleoethnobotany of the Draper and White Sites." Report on file. Botany Department, Royal Ontario Museum.

Kivett, Marvin F. 1952. *Woodland Sites in Nebraska*. Publications in Anthropology, no. 1. Lincoln: Nebraska State Historical Society.

Klein, Cecilia F. 1983. "The Ideology of Auto-sacrifice at the Templo Mayor." In *The Aztec Templo Mayor: A Symposium at Dumbarton Oaks*, edited by E. H. Boone, 293–370. Washington D.C.: Dumbarton Oaks.

Kleivan, Inge. 1984. "West Greenland before 1950." In *Handbook of North American Indians, vol. 5: Arctic*, edited by D. Damas, 595–621. Washington, D.C.: Smithsonian Institution.

Kluckhohn, Clyde, and Leland C. Wyman. 1940. *An Introduction To Navaho Chant Practice*. Memoirs of the American Anthropological Association, no. 53. Reprint, 1969. Germantown, New York: Krause Reprint Company.

Knight, Paul J. 1982. "Ethnobotany and Agriculture on the McKinley Mine Lease." In *Anasazi and Navajo Land Use in the McKinley Mine Area near Gallup, New Mexico, vol. 1: Archeology*, edited by C. G. Allen and B. A. Nelson, 668–711. Albuquerque: Office of Contract Archeology, University of New Mexico.

Knight, Vernon J., Jr. 1975. "Some Observations concerning Plant Materials and Aboriginal Smoking in Eastern North America." *Journal of Alabama Archaeology* 21(2):120–144.

Kraft, Shelly K. 1990. "Recent Changes in the Ethnobotany of Standing Rock Reservation." M.A. thesis, University of North Dakota.

Krause, Aurel. 1956 [1885]. *The Tlingit Indians: Results of a Trip to the Northwest Coast of America and the Bering Straits*. Translated by Erna Gunther. Seattle: University of Washington Press.

Kravetz, R. E. 1964. "Disease Distribution in Southwestern American Indians: Analysis of 211 Autopsies." *Arizona Medicine* 21:628–634.

Kroeber, A. L. 1925. *Handbook of the Indians of California*. Bureau of American Ethnology Bulletin 78. Washington, D.C.: Smithsonian Institution. Reprint, 1976. New York: Dover.

————. 1941. *Culture Element Distributions 15: Salt, Dogs, Tobacco*. Anthropological Records 6, no. 1. Berkeley: University of California.

————. 1960a. "Comparative Notes on the Structure of Yurok Culture." In *The Structure of Twana Culture*, by W. W. Elmendorf, 245–247. Research Studies 28, no. 3. Pullman: Washington State University.

————. 1960b [1922]. "Elements of Culture in Native California." In *The California Indians: A Source Book*, edited by R. F. Heizer and M. A. Whipple, 3–65. Berkeley: University of California Press.

————. 1973 [1932]. "Principal Local Types of the Kuksu Cult." In *The California Indians: A Source Book*, 2d ed., compiled and edited by R. F. Heizer and M. A. Whipple, 485–495. Berkeley: University of California Press.

————. 1976. *Yurok Myths*. Berkeley: University of California Press.

Kwiatkowski, Scott. 1994. "Flotation and Macrobotanical Results for Dutch Canal Ruins." In *Early Desert Farming and Irrigation Settlements: Archaeological Investigations in the Phoenix Sky Harbor Center*, vol. 2, edited by David H. Greenwald, M. Zyniecki, and Dawn M. Greenwald, 275–292. SWCA Anthropological Research Paper 4. Flagstaff, Arizona.

Kwiatkowski, Scott, and Robert E. Gasser. 1988. "Hohokam Archaeology along Phase B of the Tucson Aquaduct, Central Arizona Project." In *Excavations at Fastimes AZ:AA:12:384, a Rillito Phase Site in the Aura Valley*, vol. 2, edited by John S. Zaplicki and John C. Ravesloot, 277–302. Archaeological Series 178, no. 2. Tucson: Arizona State Museum.

La Barre, Weston. 1970. "Old and New World Narcotics: Statistical Question and an Ethnological Reply." *Economic Botany* 24:73–80.

————. 1989 [1960]. *The Peyote Cult*. Norman: University of Oklahoma Press.

Ladd, Edmund J. 1979. "Zuni Social and Political Organization." In *Handbook of North American Indians, vol. 9: Southwest*, edited by Alfonso Ortiz, 482–498. Washington, D.C.: Smithsonian Institution.

Laird, Carobeth. 1976. *The Chemehuevis*. Banning, California: Malki Museum, Morongo Indian Reservation.

Lame Deer (John Fire), and Richard Erdoes. 1972. *Lame Deer, Seeker of Visions: The Life of a Sioux Medicine Man*. New York: Simon and Schuster.

Lamphere, Louise. 1983. "Southwestern Ceremonialism." In *Handbook of North American Indians, vol. 10: Southwest*, edited by Alfonso Ortiz, 743–763. Washington, D.C.: Smithsonian Institution.

Lang, Julian. 1996. "Indian Tobacco in Northwestern California." *News from Native California*, Spring, 27–36. Berkeley, California.

————. 1997. "The Divine Origin of Tobacco." *Winds of Change*, Summer. Boulder, Colorado: American Indian Science and Engineering Society.

Lange, Charles H. 1968. *Cochiti: A New Mexico Pueblo, Past and Present*. Carbondale: Southern Illinois University Press.

Lanning, Edward P. 1967. *Peru before the Incas*. Englewood Cliffs, New Jersey: Prentice-Hall.

Lantis, Margaret. 1984. "Nunivok Eskimo." In *Handbook of North American Indians, vol. 5: Arctic*, edited by D. Damas, 209–223. Washington, D.C.: Smithsonian Institution.

Lapena, Frank R. 1978. "Wintu." In *Handbook of North American Indians, vol. 8: California*, edited by R. F. Heizer, 324–340. Washington, D.C.: Smithsonian Institution.

Lathrap, Donald W. 1987. "The Introduction of Maize in Prehistoric Eastern North America: The View from Amazonia and the Santa Elena Peninsula." In *Emergent Horticultural Economies of the Eastern Woodlands*, edited by William F. Keegan. Occasional Papers no. 7. Carbondale: Center for Archaeological Investigations, Southern Illinois University.

Latorre, Felipe A., and Dolores L. Latorre. 1976. *The Mexican Kickapoo Indians*. Austin: University of Texas Press.

Laughlin, Robert M. 1969a. "The Huastec." In *Handbook of Middle American Indians, vol. 7: Ethnology*, edited by E. Z. Vogt, part 1, 298–315. Austin: University of Texas Press.

———. 1969b. "The Tzotzil." In *Handbook of Middle American Indians, vol. 7: Ethnology*, edited by E. Z. Vogt, part 1, 152–194. Austin: University of Texas Press.

Lavender, David, ed. 1972. *The Oregon Journals of David Douglas, of His Travels and Adventures among the Traders and Indians in the Columbia, Willamette and Snake River Regions during the Years 1825, 1826, and 1827*. 2 vols. Ashland: Oregon Book Society.

La Vérendrye, Pierre Gaultier de Varennes de. 1941. "The Journal of La Vérendrye, 1738–1739." *North Dakota Historic Quarterly* 8:242–271.

Lawson, John. 1967 [1709]. *A New Voyage to Carolina*. Edited by Hugh T. Leffer. Chapel Hill: University of North Carolina Press.

Le Clercq, Chrestien. 1881 [1691]. *First Establishment of the Faith in New France*. Edited by John G. Shea. 2 vols. New York: J. G. Shea.

Lees, William B. 1990. "Evidence for Early European Contact with the Wichita in Kansas." Paper presented at the Conference on Historical and Underwater Archaeology, Tucson.

Lees, William B., John Reynolds, Terrance J. Martin, Mary J. Adair, and Steven Bozarth. 1989. *Summary Report, 1986 Archaeological Investigations at 14MN328, a Great Bend Aspect Site along U.S. Highway 56, Marion, Kansas*. Archaeology Department, Kansas State Historical Society.

Lefkowitz, D., and C. Underwood. 1991. *Personal Health Practices: Findings from the Survey of American Indians and Alaska Natives*. National Medical Expenditure Survey Research Findings 10, Agency for Health Care Policy and Research. AHCPR Publication no. 91-00. Rockville, Maryland: Public Health Service.

Lehmer, Donald J. 1971. *Introduction to Middle Missouri Archeology*. Anthropological Papers 1. Washington D.C.: National Park Service.

Leighton, Anna L. 1985. *Wild Plant Use by the Woods Cree (Nihithawak) of East-Central Saskatchawan*. Ottawa: National Museums of Canada.

Lemaistre, Denis. 1996. "The Deer That Is Peyote and the Deer That Is Maize: The Hunt in the Huichol Trinity." Translated by Karen Simoneau. In *People of the Peyote*, edited by Stacy B. Schaefer and Peter T. Furst, 306–329. Albuquerque: University of New Mexico Press.

Lennox, P. A., C. F. Dodd, and C. R. Murphy. 1986. "The Wiacek Site: A Late Middleport Component in Simcoe County, Ontario." Report on file. London, Ontario: Ontario Ministry of Transportation and Communications, Environmental Unit, Planning Design Section.

Lentz, David L. 1986. "Ethnobotany of the Jicaque of Honduras." *Economic Botany* 40(2):210–219.

Lescarbot, Marc. 1907–1914 [1618]. *The History of New France*. Edited and translated by W. L. Grant. 3 vols. Toronto: Champlain Society.

Le Sueur, Jacques. 1952 [1744]. "History of the Calumet and of the Dance." *Contributions from the Museum of the American Indian, Heye Foundation* 12(5):1–22.

Letts, John B. 1990. "The Paleoethnobotany of a Terminal Woodland Period Iroquoian Community in Ontario, Canada: The Wallace Site (AkGx-1)." M.A.Sc. thesis, Department of the Environment, Institute of Archaeology, University College, London, Ontario.

Levermore, Charles H., ed. 1912. *Forerunners and Competitors of the Pilgrims and Puritans 1601–1625*. 2 vols. Brooklyn, New York: New England Society.

Levy, Richard. 1978a. "Eastern Miwok." In *Handbook of North American Indians, vol. 8: California*, edited by R. F. Heizer, 398–413. Washington, D.C.: Smithsonian Institution.

———. 1978b. "Costanoan." In *Handbook of North American Indians, vol. 8: California*, edited by R. F. Heizer, 485–495. Washington, D.C.: Smithsonian Institution.

Lewis, Henry T. 1993. "Patterns of Burning in California: Ecology and Ethnohistory." In *Before the Wilderness: Environmental Management by Native Californians*, edited by T. C. Blackburn and K. Anderson, 55–116. Menlo Park, California: Ballena Press.

Lewis, Oscar. 1960. *Tepoztlan: A Village in Mexico*. New York: Holt, Rinehart, and Winston.

Libermann, Gisèle, and Conrad Libermann. 1975. "Les civilisations du tabac: Signification rituelle et sociale chez les Indiens d'Amérique." *Flammes et Fumées* 73(1):1–72.

Liljeblad, Sven. 1986. "Oral Tradition: Content and Style of Verbal Arts." In *Handbook of North American Indians, vol. 11: Great Basin,* edited by Warren L. D'Azevedo, 641–659. Washington, D.C.: Smithsonian Institution.

Lindley, John. 1827. "*Nicotiana multivalvis:* White Columbia Tobacco." *Edward's Botanical Register* 13:1057.

Linton, R. 1924. *Use of Tobacco among North American Indians.* Anthropology Leaflet 15. Chicago: Field Museum of Natural History.

Loewe, Walter. 1988. *In Golden Boxes.* Translated by Roger Tanner. Boras, Sweden: Norma Publishing House.

Logan, Brad. 1990. *Archaeological Investigations in the Plains Village Frontier, Northeastern Kansas.* Project Report Series, no. 70. Lawrence: University of Kansas, Museum of Anthropology.

Looking Horse, Arval. 1987. "The Sacred Pipe in Modern Life." In *Sioux Indian Religion: Tradition and Innovation,* edited by R. J. DeMallie and D. R. Parks. Norman: University of Oklahoma Press.

Lopez, Barry Holstun. 1977. *Giving Birth to Thunder, Sleeping with His Daughter: Coyote Builds North America.* New York: Avon.

Lopinot, Neal. 1989. "Archaeobotany." In *Archaeological Investigations Relating to the Glen Carbon Interceptor Sewer Line, Divisions 3 through 7, Madison County, Illinois,* by G. R. Holley and A. J. Brown, 99–111. Archaeology Program Research Report 1. Edwardsville: Southern Illinois University.

———. 1990a. "Archaeobotany." In *Archaeological Investigations at the Hays Site (RL-179), Franklin County, Illinois,* by Michael L. Hargrave et al, 136–148. St. Louis District Historic Properties Management Report no. 38. U.S. Army Corps of Engineers.

———. 1990b. *Archaeology of the Little Hills Expressway Site (23C572), St. Charles County, Missouri.* Archaeology Program Research Report no. 6. Edwardsville, Illinois: Southern Illinois University.

———. 1991. "Archaeobotanical Remains." In *Archaeology of the Cahokia Mounds ICT-II: Biological Remains,* by Neal H. Lopinot et al, 1–268. Illinois Cultural Resources Study no. 13. Springfield: Illinois Historic Preservation Agency.

———. 1992. "Archaeobotany." In *The Petitt Site: An Emergent Mississippian Occupation in the Thebes Gap Area of Southern Illinois,* edited by Paul A. Webb, 261–293. Center for Archaeological Investigations Research Paper 58. Carbondale: Southern Illinois University.

Lopinot, Neal H., Alan J. Brown, and George R. Holley. 1989. *Archaeological Investigations on the Western Periphery of the Cahokia Site, St. Clair and Madison Counties, Illinois.* Archaeology Program Research Report no. 4. Edwardsville: Southern Illinois University.

Lorant, Stefan, ed. 1946. *The New World: The First Pictures of America Made by John White and Jacques Le Moyne, and Engraved by Theodore de Bry.* New York: Duell, Sloan and Pearce.

Loven, Sven. 1935. *Origins of the Tainan Culture, West Indies.* English edition. Goteborg, Sweden: Elanders Boktrycheri Aktiebolag.

Lowell, E. S. 1970. "A Comparison of Mexican and Seri Indian Versions of the Legend of Lola Casanova." *Kiva* 35(4):144–158.

Lowery, Woodbury. 1911. *The Spanish Settlements within the Present Limits of the United States, 1513–1561.* New York: G. P. Putnam's Sons.

Lowie, Robert H. 1920. *The Tobacco Society of the Crow Indians.* Anthropological Papers of the American Museum of Natural History, vol. 21, part 2. New York.

———. 1935. *The Crow Indians.* New York: Farrar and Rinehart.

———. 1954. *Indians of the Plains.* Garden City, New York: Natural History Press.

Ludwickson, John. 1978. "Central Plains Tradition Settlements in the Loup River Basin: The Loup River Phase." In *The Central Plains Tradition: Internal Developments and External Relationships,* edited by Donald J. Blakeslee, 94–108. Report 11. Iowa City: Office of the State Archaeologist, University of Iowa.

Lumholtz, Carl. 1902. *Unknown Mexico: A Record of Five Years' Exploration among the Tribes of the Western Sierra Madres; in the Tierra Caliente of Tepic and Jalisco; and among the Tarascans of Michoacan.* 2 vols. New York: Charles Scribner's Sons.

Luomala, Katherine. 1978. "Tipai-Ipai." In *Handbook of North American Indians, vol. 8: California,* edited by R. F. Heizer, 592–609. Washington, D.C.: Smithsonian Institution.

Macaulay, Jane Katherine. 1990. "The Palaeoethnobotany of the Hine Village Site, a Fort Ancient Component in the Middle Ohio River Valley." M.A. thesis, Department of Anthropology, University of Toronto.

MacDonald, R. I. 1986. "The Coleman Site (AiHd-7): A Late Prehistoric Iroquoian Village in the Waterloo Region." M.A. thesis, Department of Anthropology, Trent University.

MacLachlan, Bruce B. 1981. "Tahltan." In *Handbook of North American Indians, vol. 6: Subarctic,* edited by J. Helm, 458–468. Washington, D.C.: Smithsonian Institution.

MacNutt, Francis A. 1912. *De Orbe Novo: The Eight Decades of Peter Martyr D'Anghera.* 2 vols. New York: G. P. Putnam's Sons.

Mahar, James Michael. 1953. "Ethnobotany of the Oregon Paiutes of the Warm Springs Indian Reservation." B.A. thesis, Reed College.

Mails, T. E. 1978. *Sundancing at Rosebud and Pine Ridge.* Sioux Falls, South Dakota: Center for Western Studies.

———. 1979. *Fools Crow.* Lincoln: University of Nebraska Press.

Malefijt, Annemarie deWall. 1974. *Images of Man: A History of Anthropological Thought.* New York: Alfred A. Knopf.

Mangelsdorf, Paul C., Richard S. MacNeish, and Gordon R. Willey. 1964. "Origins of Agriculture in Middle America." In *Handbook of Middle American Indians, vol. 1,* 427–444. Austin: University of Texas Press.

Manrique, Leonard C. 1969. "The Otomí." In *Handbook of Middle American Indians, vol. 8: Ethnology,* edited by Evon Z. Vogt, part 2, 682–724. Austin: University of Texas.

Margry, Pierre. 1875–1878. *Decouvertes et establissements des Francais dans l'ouest et dans le sud de l'Amerique Septentrionale (1614–1754).* 6 parts. Paris.

Marleau, Diane. 1995. *Tobacco Control: A Blueprint to Protect the Health of Canadians.* Toronto: Minister of National Health and Welfare, Health Canada.

Marsh, C. D., A. B. Clawson, and C. G. Roe. 1927. *Technical Bulletin* 22. Washington, D.C.: U.S. Department of Agriculture.

Martin, P. C., and C. R. Hutchins. 1980. *A Flora of New Mexico.* 2 vols. Vaduz: J. Cramer der A. R. Ganter Verlag.

Martin, Paul S., John B. Rinaldo, E. Bluhm, H. C. Cutler, and R. Grange, Jr. 1952. *Mogollon Cultural Continuity and Change: The Stratigraphic Analysis of Tularosa and Cordova Caves.* Fieldiana: Anthropology, vol. 40. Chicago: Field Museum of Natural History.

Martínez, Maximino. 1991. *Catálogo de nombres vulgares y científicos de plantas mexicanas.* México, D.F.: Fondo de Cultura Económica.

Mary-Rousseliere, Guy. 1984. "Igulik." In *Handbook of North American Indians, vol. 5: Arctic,* edited by D. Damas, 431–446. Washington, D.C.: Smithsonian Institution.

Mathews, Zena P. 1976. "Huron Pipes and Iroquoian Shamanism." *Man in the Northeast* 12:15–31.

Matthews, Meredith H. 1983a. "The Macrobotanical Assemblage from Prince Hamlet." In *Excavations at Prince Hamlet (Site 5MT2161), a Pueblo I Habitation Site,* by Lynne Sebastian, 279–304. Dolores Archaeological Program Technical Reports DAP-082. Salt Lake City: Bureau of Reclamation.

———. 1983b. "The Macrobotanical Assemblage from LeMoc Shelter." In *Excavations at LeMoc Shelter (Site 5MT215), a Multiple-Occupation Anasazi Site,* by Patrick Hogan, 309–339. Dolores Archaeological Program Technical Reports DAP-083. Salt Lake City: Bureau of Reclamation.

———. 1983c. "Macrobotanical Remains from Area 4, Grass Mesa Village." In *Archaeological Investigations on Grass Mesa: Area 4, 1979,* by Richard V. N. Ahlstrom and Karen Dohm, 115–127. Dolores Archaeological Program Technical Reports DAP-086. Salt Lake City: Bureau of Reclamation.

———. 1983d. "Macrobotanical Remains from Periman Hamlet, Area 1." In *Excavations at Periman Hamlet (Site 5MT4671), a Pueblo I Habitation*, by Richard H. Wilshusen, 340–356. Dolores Archaeological Program Technical Reports DAP-090. Salt Lake City: Bureau of Reclamation.

———. 1983e. "Macrobotanical Remains from Aldea Sierritas." In *Excavations at Aldea Sierritas (Site 5MT2854), a Basketmaker III Habitation*, by Kristin A. Kuckelman, 229–245. Dolores Archaeological Program Technical Reports DAP-107. Salt Lake City: Bureau of Reclamation.

———. 1984. "Information Retrieval on a Micro-Level of Inquiry: Bulk Soil Analysis from Food Processing Activity Areas in Two Habitation Units." In *Dolores Archaeological Program: Synthetic Report 1978–1981*, prepared under supervision of D. A. Breternitz, 165–184. Salt Lake City: Bureau of Reclamation.

———. 1985. "The Macrobotanical Assemblage from Singing Shelter." In *Excavations at Singing Shelter (Site 5MT4683), a Multicomponent Site*, by G. Charles Nelson and Allen E. Kane, 296–334. Dolores Archaeological Program Technical Reports DAP-180. Salt Lake City: Bureau of Reclamation.

———. 1986a. "Macrobotanical Remains from Windy Wheat Hamlet." In *Dolores Archaeological Program: Anasazi Communities at Dolores. Early Anasazi Sites in the Sagehen Flats Area*. Salt Lake City: Bureau of Reclamation.

———. 1986b. "Macrobotanical Remains from Periman Hamlet Area l." In *Dolores Archaeological Program: Anasazi Communities at Dolores. Middle Canyon Area*, Book 1 of 2, compiled by A. E. Kane and C. K. Robinson, 199–208. Salt Lake City: Bureau of Reclamation.

———. 1986c. "The Dolores Archaeological Program Macrobotanical Data Base: Resource Availability and Mix." In *Dolores Archaeological Program: Final Synthetic Report*, compiled by D. A. Breternitz, C. K. Robinson, and G. T. Gross, 151–183. Denver: U.S. Department of Interior, Bureau of Reclamation.

———. 1988a. "Macrobotanical Remains." In *Bodo Canyon*, edited by Steve Fuller. Cortez, Colorado: CASA, Inc.

———. 1988b. "Results of Macrobotanical Analysis of Remains from Eight Sites Excavated within the South Canal Right-of-Way." In *Archaeological Investigations on South Canal*, vol. 2, compiled by Kristin A. Kuckelman and James N. Morris. Cortez, Colorado: CASA, Inc.

Matthews, Washington. 1886. "Navajo Names for Plants." *American Naturalist* 20:767–777.

———. 1902. *The Night Chant: A Navaho Ceremony*. Memoirs of the American Museum of Natural History, vol. 6. New York.

Mayes, Vernon O., and James M. Rominger. 1994. *Navajoland Plant Catalogue*. Lake Ann, Michigan: National Woodlands Publishing.

McBride, Pamela J. 1994. "Archaeobotanical Analysis." In "Results of the 1993 Excavations at the Chama Alcove Site, AR-03-10-01-374," by Bradley J. Vierra. Manuscript on file. Office of Contract Archeology, University of New Mexico, Albuquerque.

———. 1996a. "Archaeobotanical Analysis Results." In *Phase I and II Data Recovery at Four Sites near the Sanders Rural Community High School, Sanders, Arizona*, prepared by Brian Billman and Patricia Ruppe. Zuni Cultural Resource Enterprise Report 442. Zuni Pueblo, New Mexico.

———. 1996b. "Flotation and Charcoal Analysis." Letter report from which data are presented in *Survey and Excavation in the Hidden Mountain Area: The Tri-Sect Landfill Road Project*, by William H. Doleman. Albuquerque: Office of Contract Archaeology, University of New Mexico.

McBride, Pamela J., and Kenneth L. Brown. 1997. "Archeobotanical Analysis." In *Data Recovery along the Alameda Boulevard Improvement Project, Bernalillo County, New Mexico*, by Marie Brown, 261–272. Office of Contract Archeology Report 185-468. Albuquerque: Office of Contract Archeology, University of New Mexico.

McCashion, John H. 1994. *The Clay Pipes of New York State, part 5: An Analysis of the*

*Clay Tobacco Pipes from the White Orchard Mohawk Site (CNJ-3)*. New York State Archaeological Association Bulletin 6, no. 1.

McClellan, Catherine. 1981a. "Tagish." In *Handbook of North American Indians, vol. 6: Subarctic*, edited by J. Helm, 481–492. Washington, D.C.: Smithsonian Institution.

———. 1981b. "Intercultural Relations and Cultural Change in the Cordillera." In *Handbook of North American Indians, vol. 6: Subarctic*, edited by J. Helm. Washington, D.C.: Smithsonian Institution.

McClintock, Walter. 1909. "Medizinal-Und Nutzflanzer der Schwarzfuss Indianer." *Zeitschriff fur Ethnologie* 41:273–279.

McDougall, Walter B. 1973. *Seed Plants of Northern Arizona*. Flagstaff: Museum of Northern Arizona.

McGuire, Joseph D. 1897. "Pipes and Smoking Customs of the American Aborigines, Based on Material in the U.S. National Museum." *Report of the U.S. National Museum*, 351–641. Washington, D.C.

———. 1910. "Tobacco." In *Handbook of American Indians North of Mexico*, edited by F. W. Hodge, 767–769. Washington D.C.: Smithsonian Institution.

McKenzie, Diane. 1995. *Alcohol, Tobacco, and Other Drugs*. Canadian Profile 1995, Aboriginal People. Ottawa: Canadian Centre on Substance Abuse.

McLendon, Sally, and Michael J. Lowy. 1978. "Eastern Pomo and Southeastern Pomo." In *Handbook of North American Indians, vol. 8: California*, edited by R. F. Heizer, 306–323. Washington, D.C.: Smithsonian Institution.

McMurtrey, J. E. 1981. "Tobacco Production." *The New Encyclopaedia Britannica* 18:464–467. Chicago: Encyclopaedia Britannica.

McNulty, Gerard E., and Louis Gilbert. 1981. "Attikamek (Tête de Boule)." In *Handbook of North American Indians, vol. 6: Subarctic*, edited by J. Helm, 208–216. Washington, D.C.: Smithsonian Institution.

McVickar, Janet. 1995. "Archaeobotanical Analysis." In *Pipeline Archaeology: El Paso North System Expansion Project, New Mexico and Arizona, vol. 12: Supporting Studies*, complied by T. M. Kearns and J. L. McVickar. Farmington, New Mexico: Western Cultural Resource Management, Inc.

Meilleur, Brien A. 1979. "Speculations on the Diffusion of *Nicotiana quadrivalvis* Pursh to the Queen Charlotte Islands and Adjacent Alaskan Mainland." *Syesis* 12:101–104.

Merkur, Dan. 1992. *Becoming Half Hidden: Shamanism and Initiation among the Inuit*. New York: Garland Press.

Merriam, C. Hart. 1966. *Ethnographic Notes on California Indian Tribes*. Berkeley: University of California Archaeological Research Facility.

Merxmüller, H., and K. P. Buttler. 1975. "*Nicotiana* in der Afrikanischen Namibein Pflanzengeographisches und Phylo-Genetisches Ratsel." *Mitteilungen der Botanischen Staatssammlung Muenchen* 12:91–104.

Miksicek, Charles H. 1983a. "Plant Remains from Agricultural Features." In *Hohokam Archaeology along the Salt-Gila Aqueduct, Central Arizona Project, vol. 3: Specialized Activity Sites*, edited by L. S. Teague and P. L. Crown, part 4, 605–620. Archaeological Series 150. Tucson: Arizona State Museum.

———. 1983b. "Plant Remains from Smiley's Well (AZ:U:14:73, Locus A)." In *Hohokam Archeology along the Gila-Salt Aqueduct, Central Arizona Project, vol. 5: Small Habitation Sites on the Queen Creek*, edited by L. S. Teague and P. L. Crown, parts 1–2, 87–98. Archaeological Series 150. Tucson: Arizona State Museum.

———. 1983c. "Archaeobotanical Aspects of Las Fosas: A Statistical Approach to Prehistoric Plant Remains." In *Hohokam Archaeology along the Gila-Salt Aqueduct, Central Arizona Project, vol. 6: Habitation Sites on the Gila River*, edited by L. S. Teague and P. L. Crown, parts 5–6, 671–700. Archaeological Series 150. Tucson: Arizona State Museum.

———. 1983d. "Flotation Results from AZ:U:15:84." In *Hohokam Archaeology along the Gila-Salt Aqueduct, Central Arizona Project, vol. 6: Habitation Sites on the Gila River*, edited by L. S. Teague and P. L. Crown, parts 5–6, 741–744. Archaeological Series 150. Tucson: Arizona State Museum.

———. 1984a. "Historic Desertification, Prehistoric Vegetation Change, and Hohokam Subsistence in the Salt-Gila Basin." In

*Hohokam Archaeology along the Salt-Gila Aqueduct Central Arizona Project, vol. 7: Environment and Subsistence,* edited by L. S. Teague and P. L. Crown, 53–80. Archeological Series 150. Tucson: Arizona State Museum.

———. 1984b. "Archeobotanical Remains from Frogtown." In *Hohokam Archeology along the Salt-Gila Aqueduct, Central Arizona Project, vol. 4: Prehistoric Occupation of the Queen Creek Delta,* edited by L. S. Teague and P. L. Crown, 563–590. Archaeoloical Series 150. Tucson: Arizona State Museum.

———. 1984c. "Macrofloral Remains from the Siphon Draw Site." In *Hohokam Archeology along the Salt-Gila Aqueduct, Central Arizona Project, vol. 4: Prehistoric Occupation of the Queen Creek Delta,* edited by L. S. Teague and P. L. Crown, 179–204. Archaeological Series 150. Tucson: Arizona State Museum.

———. 1986. "Plant Remains." In *Archaeological Investigations at the West Branch Site, Early and Middle Rincon Occupation in the Southern Tucson Basin,* by Frederick W. Huntington, 289–313. Anthropological Papers 5. Tucson, Arizona: Institute for American Research.

Miksicek, Charles H., and Robert E. Gasser. 1989. "Hohokam Plant Use at Las Colinas: The Flotation Evidence." In *The 1982–1984 Excavations at Las Colinas: Environment and Subsistence,* by Donald A. Graybill et al., 95–115. Archaeological Series 162, no. 5. Tucson: Arizona State Museum.

Millar, W. J. 1990. "Smokeless Tobacco Use by Youth in the Canadian Arctic." *Arctic Medical Research* 49:39.

Miller, Jay, and William R. Seaburg. 1990. "Athapaskans of Southwestern Oregon." In *Handbook of North American Indians, vol. 7: Northwest Coast,* edited by Wayne Suttles, 580–588. Washington, D.C.: Smithsonian Institution.

Miller, Joanne. 1994. "Pueblo Grande Flotation, Macrobotanical, and Wood Charcoal Analysis." In *The Pueblo Grande Project, vol. 5: Environment and Subsistence,* edited by Scott Kwiatkowski, 127–204. Phoenix: Soil Systems Publications in Archaeology 24.

———. 1995. "Preliminary Ute Mountain Flotation Report." Manuscript on file. Soil Systems, Inc. Phoenix.

Miller, Mary, and Karl Taube. 1993. *The Gods and Symbols of Ancient Mexico and Maya.* London: Thames and Hudson.

Miller, Virginia P. 1978. "Yuki, Huchinom, and Coast Yuki." In *Handbook of North American Indians, vol. 8: California,* edited by R. F. Heizer, 249–255. Washington, D.C.: Smithsonian Institution.

Minnis, Paul E. 1981. "Seeds in Archaeological Sites: Sources and Some Interpretive Problems." *American Antiquity* 48(1):143–152.

Moerman, Daniel E. 1986. *Medicinal Plants of Native America.* Research Reports in Ethnobotany, contribution 2, vol. 1. Technical Reports no. 19. Ann Arbor: University of Michigan, Museum of Anthropology.

Monardes, Nicolas. 1577. *Joyfull Newes Out of the Newe Founde Worlde.* Translated from the 1574 edition by John Frampton. London.

Monckton, Stephen G. 1988. "Norton (AfHh-58) Site Plant Remains." Manuscript on file. Archaeological Services, Inc.

———. 1989. "Myer's Road Site Plant Remains." Manuscript on file. Archaeological Services, Inc.

———. 1990a. "Huron Paleoethnobotany." Ph.D. diss., University of Toronto.

———. 1990b. "Parson (AkGv-8) Site Plant Remains." Manuscript on file. Archaeological Services, Inc.

———. 1990c. "Plant Remains from the Dunsmore (BcBw-10) Site." Manuscript on file. Archaeological Services, Inc.

———. 1990d. "Plant Remains from the Finch (AeHg-58) Site." Manuscript on file. Archaeological Services, Inc.

Moore, Michael. 1979. *Medicinal Plants of the Mountain West.* Santa Fe: Museum of New Mexico Press.

Morris, Elizabeth Ann. 1980. *Basketmaker Caves in the Prayer Rock District, Northeastern Arizona.* Anthropological Papers 35. Tucson: University of Arizona.

Moses, Marion. 1993. *Environmental Equity and Pesticide Exposure.* Princeton, New Jersey: Princeton Scientific Publishing.

Moulton, Gary E., ed. 1987. *The Journals of the Lewis and Clark Expedition, vol. 3: August 25, 1804–April 6, 1805.* Lincoln: University of Nebraska Press.

Mowat, Farley. 1975. *People of the Deer.* Toronto: Seal Books.

Munn, Henry. 1973. "The Mushrooms of Language." In *Hallucinogens and Shamanism,* edited by Michael J. Harner. New York: Oxford University Press.

Munz, Philip A., and David D. Keck. 1968. *A California Flora.* Berkeley: University of California Press.

Murphey, Edith Van Allen. 1959. *Indian Uses of Native Plants.* Palm Desert, California: Desert Printers.

Murray, Charles A. 1839. *Travels in North America during the Years 1834, 1835, and 1836.* 2 vols. New York: Harper and Bros.

Murray, D. M., C. L. Perry, and C. Oafs. 1987. "Seventh-Grade Cigarette, Alcohol, and Marijuana Use: Distribution in a North-Central vs. Metropolitan Population." *International Journal of Addictions* 22:356.

Murry, L. E., and W. H. Eshbaugh. 1971. "A Palynological Study of the Solaninae (Solanaceae). *Grana* 11:65–78.

Mydans, Seth. 1990. "Ban on Smoking in Airliners Doesn't Apply to the Cockpit." *New York Times,* March 10, p. 7.

Myers, Albert C., ed. 1912. *Narratives of Early Pennsylvania, West New Jersey, and Delaware, 1630–1707.* New York: Charles Scribner's Sons.

Myers, James E. 1978. "Cahto." *In Handbook of North American Indians, vol. 8: California,* edited by R. F. Heizer, 244–248. Washington, D.C.: Smithsonian Institution.

Nabhan, Gary. 1979a. "Cultivation and Culture." *The Ecologist* 9(8–9):259–263.

———. 1979b. "The Ecology of Floodwater Farming in Southwestern North America." *Agro-Ecosystems* 5:245–255.

Nader, Laura. 1969. "The Zapotec of Oaxaca." In *Handbook of Middle American Indians, vol. 7: Ethnology,* edited by E. Z. Vogt, part 1, 329–359. Austin: University of Texas Press.

Native Seeds/SEARCH. 1994. *1994 Seedlisting.* Tucson: Native Seeds/SEARCH.

NCI (National Cancer Institute). 1975. *Third National Cancer Survey: Incidence Data.* National Cancer Institute Monograph 41. Washington, D.C.: U.S. Government Printing Office.

Negrín, Juan. 1975. *The Huichol Creation of the World: Yarn Tablas by José Benítez Sánchez and Tutukila Carrillo.* Sacramento: E. B. Crocker Art Gallery.

Nelson, G. Charles. 1985. *Dovetail Hamlet (Site 5MT2226), a Pueblo I Habitation.* Dolores Archaeological Program Technical Reports DAP-165. Salt Lake City: Bureau of Reclamation.

Nelson, N. C. 1917. "Contributions to the Archaeology of Mammoth Cave and Vicinity, Kentucky." *American Museum of National History Anthropological Papers* 22(1):1–73. New York.

Nelson, Richard K. 1983. *The Athabaskans: People of the Boreal Forest.* Alaska Historical Commission Studies in History, no. 27. Fairbanks: University of Alaska Museum.

Newcombe, W. W., Jr., and W. T. Field. 1967. "An Ethnohistoric Investigation of the Wichita Indians in the Southern Plains." In *A Pilot Study of Wichita Indian Archaeology and Ethnohistory, Final Report,* compiled by R. E. Bell, E. B. Jelks and W. W. Newcombe, 240–354. Washington D.C.: National Science Foundation.

Newsom, Lee. 1993. "Native West Indian Plant Use." Ph.D. diss., Department of Anthropology, University of Florida.

Nicholson, Henry P. 1971. "Religion in Pre-Hispanic Central Mexico." In *Handbook of Middle American Indians, vol. 10: Archaeology of Northern Mesoamerica,* edited by Gordon F. Ekholm and Ignacio Bernal, part 1, 395–446. Austin: University of Texas Press.

NIH (National Institutes of Health). 1978. *National Institutes of Health Study on Effect of Smoking on Airline Pilots.* Washington, D.C.

Noble, Vicki. 1989. "The Matriarchal Backbone of Huichol Shamanic Culture." In *Mirrors of the Gods: Proceedings of a Symposium on the Huichol Indians,* edited by Susan Bernstein, 51–57. San Diego Museum Papers no. 25. San Diego: San Diego Museum of Man.

Norton, Jack. 1992. "Ridge Walkers of North-western California: Paths towards Spiritual Balance." In *California Indian Shamanism,* edited by L. J. Bean, 227–236. Menlo Park, California: Ballena Press.

NRC (National Research Council). 1986. *Environmental Tobacco Smoke: Measuring Exposures and Assessing Health Effects.* Washington, D.C.: National Academy Press.

Nuttall, Thomas. 1818. *The Genera of North American Plants, and a Catalogue of the Species to the Year 1817.* 2 vols. Philadelphia: D. Heartt.

Nutting, P. A. 1993. "Cancer Incidence among American Indians and Alaska Natives, 1980 through 1987." *American Journal of Public Health* 83(11):1589–1598.

O'Callaghan, Edmund B., ed. 1856–1887. *Documents Relative to the Colonial History of the State of New York; Procured in Holland, England and France, by John R. Brodhead.* 15 vols. Albany, New York: Weed, Parsons.

O'Connell, James F., Peter K. Latz, and Peggy Barnett. 1983. "Traditional and Modern Plant Use among the Alyawara of Central Australia." *Economic Botany* 37(1):80–109.

. . . Of the Jungle. 1993. *Exotic Botanicals Catalog.* Sebastopol, California: . . . Of the Jungle.

———. 1994. *Catalog Supplement, Spring Equinox 1994.* Sebastopol, California: . . . Of the Jungle.

———. 1995. *Exotic Botanicals Catalog.* Sebastopol, California: . . . Of the Jungle.

Oliver, Billy L. 1986. "Dottle Research in North Carolina." Paper presented to the Archaeological Society of North Carolina, Fayetteville.

Olmstead, Richard, and Jeffrey D. Palmer. 1991. "Chloroplast DNA and Systematics of the Solanaceae." In *Solanaceae III: Taxonomy, Chemistry, Evolution,* edited by J. G. Hawkes et al., 161–168. Richmond, UK: Royal Botanic Gardens, Kew.

Olmsted, D. L. 1969. "The Teguestlatec and Tlapanec." In *Handbook of Middle American Indians, vol. 7: Ethnology,* edited by E. Z. Vogt, part 1, 553–564. Austin: University of Texas Press.

Olmsted, D. L., and Omer C. Stewart. 1978. "Achumawi." In *Handbook of North American Indians, vol. 8: California,* edited by R. F. Heizer, 225–235. Washington, D.C.: Smithsonian Institution.

Orellana, Sandra L. 1987. *Indian Medicine in Highland Guatamala: The Pre-Hispanic and Colonial Periods.* Albuquerque: University of New Mexico Press.

Ortiz, Fernando. 1978. *Contrapunto cubano del tabaco y el azucar.* Caracas: Biblíoteca Ayacucho.

Ott, Jonathan. 1993. *Pharmacotheon Entheogenic Drugs: Their Plant Sources and History.* Kennewick, Washington: Natural Products.

Ounjian, Glenna L. 1986. "Subsistence Patterns of the Ontario Indian: The Paleoethnobotany of the Glen Meyer-Neutral. A Preliminary Report." Manuscript on file with Gail Wagner, University of South Carolina.

Pacheco, Lourdes. 1995. "Huicholes: El tabaco es la enspiración de los dioses." Manuscript on file with Patricia Díaz-Romo.

Palmer, Gary B. 1975. "Shuswap Indian Ethnobotany." *Syesis* 8:29–51.

———. 1980. "Karok World Renewal and Village Sites: A Cultural and Historical District." Manuscript prepared for Klamath National Forest, Yreka, California.

Panet, Lisa. 1987. "The Archaeobotany of Mortland Island." Manuscript on file. Archeobotany Laboratory, Center for American Archeology, Kampsville, Illinois.

Paper, Jordan. 1988. *Offering Smoke: The Sacred Pipe and Native American Religion.* Moscow, Idaho: University of Idaho Press.

Parker, Arthur C. 1909. "Secret Medicine Societies of the Seneca." *American Anthropologist* 11(2):161–185.

———. 1910. *Iroquois Uses of Maize and Other Food Plants.* Museum Bulletin 144. Albany: New York State Museum.

Parker, Kathryn E. 1987. "Plant Remains." In *Emergent Mississippian and Mississippian Communities at the Radic Site (11-Ms-584),* by Dale L. McElrath et al., 221–245. American Bottom Archaeology FAI-270 Site Reports, vol. 17. Urbana: University of Illinois.

———. 1988. "Plant Remains from Three Prehistoric Sites in the Edelhardt Lake Locality." Paper presented at the Midwest Archaeological Conference, Urbana-Champaign, Illinois.

———. 1990. "Oneota Botanical Remains." In *Archaeological Data Recovery at Five Prehistoric Sites, Lake Red Rock, Marion County, Iowa*. Cultural Resources Management Report no. 133. Carbondale, Illinois: American Resources Group, Ltd.

———. 1991. "Sponemann Phase Archaeobotany." In *The Sponemann Site: The Formative Emergent Mississippian Sponemann Phase Occupations (11-Ms-517)*, by A. D. Fortier, T. O. Maher, and J. A. Williams, 377–420. American Bottom Archaeology FAI-270 Site Reports, vol. 22. Urbana: University of Illinois Press.

———. 1992a. "Archaeobotany." In *The Sponemann Site 2: The Mississippian and Oneota Occupations (11-Ms-517)*, by D. K. Jackson, A. C. Fortier, and J. A. Williams, 305–324. American Bottom Archaeology FAI-270 Site Reports, vol. 24. Urbana: University of Illinois Press.

———. 1992b. "Plant Remains from Archaeologial Excavations at the Walmart Site (11-MS-1369)." Report submitted to Charles L. Rohrbaugh, Archaeological Consultants, Normal, Illinois.

———. n.d. "Three Corn Kernels and a Hill of Beans: The Evidence for Prehistoric Horticulture in Michigan." In *Investigating the Archaeological Record of the Great Lakes States: Essays in Honor of Elizabeth Baldwin Garland*, edited by M. B. Holman, J. G. Brashler, and K. E. Parker. Kalamazoo: Western Michigan University, New Issues Press. In press.

Parkman, E. B. 1992. "Dancing on the Brink of the World: Deprivation and the Ghost Dance Religion." In *California Indian Shamanism*, edited by Lowell J. Bean, 163–184. Ballena Press Anthropological Papers no. 39. Menlo Park, California: Ballena Press.

Pearsall, Deborah M. 1992. "The Origins of Plant Cultivation in South America." In *The Origins of Agriculture: An International Perspective*, edited by C. Wesley Cowan and Patty Jo Watson, 173–205. Washington, D.C.: Smithsonian Institution Press.

Pego, Christine M., Robert F. Hill, Glenn W. Solomon, Robert M. Chisholm, and Suzanne E. Ivey. 1995. "Tobacco, Culture, and Health among American Indians: A Historical Review." *American Indian Culture and Research Journal* 19(2):143–164.

Pego, Christine M., Robert F. Hill, Glenn W. Solomon, Robert M. Chisholm, Suzanne E. Ivey, and Joseph C. Winter. 1997. "Tobacco: Deer Person's Gift or Columbus's Curse?" *Winds of Change*, Summer, 62–66. Boulder, Colorado: American Indian Science and Engineering Society.

Pennington, Campbell W. 1963. *The Tarahumara of Mexico: Their Environment and Material Culture*. Salt Lake City: University of Utah Press.

———. 1969. *The Tepehuan of Chihuahua: Their Material Culture*. Salt Lake City: University of Utah Press.

———. 1980. *The Pima Bajo of Central Sonora, Mexico, vol. 1: The Material Culture*. Salt Lake City: University of Utah Press.

———. 1983a. "Tarahumara." In *Handbook of North American Indians, vol. 10: Southwest*, edited by Alfonso Ortiz, 276–289. Washington, D.C.: Smithsonian Institution.

———. 1983b. "Northern Tepehuan." In *Handbook of North American Indians, vol. 10: Southwest*, edited by Alfonso Ortiz, 306–314. Washington, D.C.: Smithsonian Institution.

Perry, F. 1952. "Ethno-Botany of the Indians in the Interior of British Columbia." *Museum and Arts Notes* 2(2):36–43.

Pierce, Richard A. 1988. "Russian and Soviet Eskimo and Indian Policies." In *Handbook of North American Indians, vol. 4: History of Indian-White Relations*, edited by W. E. Washburn, 119–127. Washington, D.C.: Smithsonian Institution.

Piperno, Dolores R. 1988. *Phytolith Analysis: An Archaeological and Geological Perspective*. New York: Academic Press.

Porter, H. C. 1979. *The Inconstant Savage: England and the North American Indian 1500–1660*. London: Duckworth.

Porter, Muriel N. 1948. *Pipas precortesianas*. Acta Antropológica 3, no. 2. Mexico.

Powell, Gina. n.d. "Flotation Results from Five Sites on the McKinley Mine." In *Population Dynamics on the McKinley Mine South Lease*, edited by Cherie L. Scheick. Santa

Fe, New Mexico: Southwest Archaeological Consultants. In preparation.

Powers, Stephen. 1877. *Tribes of California.* Contributions to North American Ethnology, vol. 3. Washington, D.C.: Department of the Interior. Reprint, 1976. Berkeley: University of California Press.

Preuss, Konrad Theodore. 1996. "Konrad Theodore Preuss (1869–1938) on the Huichols." Translated by Peter T. Furst. In *People of the Peyote*, edited by Stacy B. Schaefer and Peter T. Furst, 88–135. Albuquerque: University of New Mexico Press.

Pulliam, Christopher B. 1987. "Middle and Late Woodland Horticultural Practices in the Western Margin of the Mississippi River Valley." In *Emergent Horticultural Economies of the Eastern Woodlands*, edited by William F. Keegan, 185–199. Occasional Paper no. 7. Carbondale: Center for Archaeological Investigations, Southern Illinois University.

———. 1988. "Analysis of Archaeobotanical Remains from 23SC609: The Boschert Site, St. Charles County, Missouri." In *The Boschert Site (23SC609): A Late Woodland Extraction Site in the Uplands of St. Charles County, Missouri*, by J. Elaine Hardy Geller and David B. Crampton, 134–152. Jefferson City: Missouri Highway and Transportation Department, Archaeology Section, Surveys and Plans Division.

———. 1989. "Tobacco Use at the Burkemper 2 Site (23LN104): A Middle and Late Woodland Occupation in Eastern Missouri." *Missouri Archaeologist* 47:233–239.

Punt, W., S. Blackmore, S. Nilsson, and A. L. Thomas. 1994. *Glossary of Pollen and Spore Terminology*. Utrecht, Netherlands: Laboratory of Paleobotany and Palynology, University of Utrecht.

Purseglove, J. W. 1968. "Nicotiana." In *Tropical Crops: Dicotyledons*, by J. W. Purseglove, 538–555. London: Longman.

Pursh, Fredrick. 1814. *Flora Americae Septentrionalis*, vol. 1. London: James, Black and Sons.

Quaife, Milo M. 1925. *The Southwestern Expedition of Zebulon M. Pike.* New York: Books for Libraries Press.

Quinn, David B., ed. 1955. *The Roanoke Voyages, 1584–1590.* 2 vols. Cambridge: Hakluyt Society.

———. 1977. *North America from Earliest Discovery to First Settlements: The Norse Voyages to 1612.* New York: Harper and Row.

———. 1979. *New American World: A Documentary History of North America to 1612.* 5 vols. New York: Arno and Hector Bye.

Quinn, David B., and Alison M. Quinn, eds. 1983. *The English New England Voyages 1602–1608.* Hakluyt Society Works, 2d Series, no. 161. London: Hakluyt Society.

Radin, P. 1970. *The Winnebago Tribe.* Lincoln: University of Nebraska Press.

Ravicz, Robert, and A. Kimball Romney. 1969a. "The Mixtec." In *Handbook of Middle American Indians, vol. 7: Ethnology*, edited by E. Z. Vogt, part 1, 367–399. Austin: University of Texas.

———. 1969b. "The Amuzgo." In *Handbook of Middle American Indians, vol. 7: Ethnology*, edited by E. Z. Vogt, part 1, 417–433. Austin: University of Texas.

Ray, Arthur J. 1988. "The Hudson's Bay Company and Native People." In *Handbook of North American Indians, vol. 4: History of Indian-White Relations*, edited by W. E. Washburn, 335–350. Washington, D.C.: Smithsonian Institution.

Rea, Amadeo M. 1997. *At the Desert's Green Edge: An Ethnobotany of the Gila Pima.* Tucson: University of Arizona Press.

Reagan, Albert B. 1928. "Plants Used by the Bois Fort Chippewa (Ojibwa) Indians of Minnesota." *Wisconsin Archaeologist* 7:230–248.

———. 1929. "Plants Used by the White Mountain Apache Indians of Arizona." *Wisconsin Archaeologist* 8:143–161.

Redding, George H. H. 1960 [1880]. "Fire-Making of the Wintu Indians." In *The California Indians: A Source Book*, edited by R. F. Heizer and M. A. Whipple, 341–345. Berkeley: University of California Press.

Redfield, Robert, and Alfonso Villa Rojas. 1962. *Chan Kom: A Maya Village.* Chicago: University of Chicago Press.

Reichard, Gladys A. 1950. *Navaho Religion: A Study of Symbolism*. Bollinger Series 18. Princeton, New Jersey: Princeton University Press.

Reina, Ruben E. 1969. "Eastern Guatamala Highlands: The Pokomames and Chorti." In *Handbook of Middle American Indians, vol. 7: Ethnology*, edited by E. Z. Vogt, part 1, 101–132. Austin: University of Texas Press.

Rhoades, E. R. 1990. "The Major Respiratory Diseases of American Indians." *American Review of Respiratory Disease* 141:595–600.

Richter, Elise. 1928. "Zu Leo Wiener's Africa and the Discovery of America." *Anthropos* 23:436–447.

Rico-Gray, Victor, José G. García-Franco, Alexander Chemos, Armando Puch, and Paulino Sima. 1990. "Species Composition, Similarity, and Structure of Mayan Home-gardens in Tixpenal and Tixcacltuyub, Yucatán, Mexico." *Economic Botany* 44(4):470–487.

Riddell, Francis A. 1978. "Maidu and Konkow." In *Handbook of North American Indians, vol. 8: California*, edited by R. F. Heizer, 370–386. Washington, D.C.: Smithsonian Institution.

Riley, Thomas J., Richard Edging, and Jack Rossen. 1990. "Cultigens in Prehistoric Eastern North America." *Current Anthropology* 31(5):525–541.

Rindos, David. 1984. *The Origins of Agriculture: An Evolutionary Perspective*. Orlando, Florida: Academic Press.

Ritzenthaler, Robert E. 1978. "Southwestern Chippewa." In *Handbook of North American Indians, vol. 15: Northeast*, edited by Bruce G. Trigger, 743–759. Washington, D.C.: Smithsonian Institution.

Robbins, Wilfred William, John Peabody Harrington, and Barbara Freire-Marreco. 1916. "Ethnobotany of the Tewa Indians." *Bureau of American Ethnology Bulletin* 53. Washington, D.C.: Smithsonian Institution.

Roberts, Alexa, Richard M. Begay, and Klara B. Kelley. 1995. *Bits' iis Nineezi (The River of Neverending Life): Navajo History and Cultural Resources of the Grand Canyon and the Colorado River*. Window Rock, Arizona: Navajo Nation Historic Preservation Department.

Robicsek, Francis. 1978. *The Smoking Gods: Tobacco in Maya Art, History and Religion*. Norman: University of Oklahoma Press.

Robinson, Christine K., and Joel M. Brisbin. 1984. *Excavations at House Creek Village (Site 5MT2320), a Pueblo I Habitation*. Dolores Archaeological Program Technical Reports DAP-181. Salt Lake City: Bureau of Reclamation.

Rogers, Brant S., and Alex G. Ogg, Jr. 1981. *Biology of Weeds in the Solanum nigrum Complex (Solanum Section Solanum) in North America*. USDA Agricultural Reviews and Manuals, ARM-W-23. Washington, D.C.: U.S. Government Printing Office.

Rogers, Dilwyn. 1980. *Lakota Names and Traditional Uses of Plants by Sicangu (Brule) People in the Rosebud Area, South Dakota*. St. Francis, South Dakota: Rosebud Educational Society.

Rogers, Edward S., and Eleanor Leacock. 1981. "Montagnais-Naskapi." In *Handbook of North American Indians, vol. 6: Subarctic*, edited by J. Helm, 169–189. Washington, D.C.: Smithsonian Institution.

Rojas, Alfonso Villa. 1969. "The Maya of Yucatan." In *Handbook of Middle American Indians, vol. 7: Ethnology*, edited by E. Z. Vogt, part 1, 244–275. Austin: University of Texas Press.

Ronda, James P. 1984. *Lewis and Clark among the Indians*. Lincoln: University of Nebraska Press.

Rossen, Jack. 1987. "Botanical Remains: Environmental Reconstruction and Plant Subsistence." In *Chambers (15ML109): An Upland Mississippian Village in Western Kentucky*, by David Pollack and Jimmy A. Railey, 61–73. Frankfort, Kentucky: Kentucky Heritage Council.

Rouse, Irving. 1992. *The Tainos: Rise and Decline of the People Who Greeted Columbus*. New Haven, Connecticut: Yale University Press.

Rousseau, Jacques. 1945. "Le folklore botanique de Caughnawaga." *Contributions de L'Institut de Montreal* 55:7–72.

Royd, G. 1987. "Use of Smokeless Tobacco among Children and Adolescents in the United States." *Preventive Medicine* 16:402.

Roys, Ralph L. 1967. *The Book of the Chilam Balam of Chumayel*. Norman: University of Oklahoma Press.

Rozel, R. J. 1979. "The Gunby Site and Late Pickering Manifestations." M.A. thesis, Department of Archaeology, McMaster University, Hamilton, Ontario.

Russell, Frank. 1975 [1908]. *The Pima Indians*. Tucson: University of Arizona Press.

Rutter, Richard A. 1990. *Catálogo de plantas útiles de la amazonia peruana*. Yarinacocha, Pucallpa, Peru: Summer Institute of Linguistics.

Safford William E. 1916a. "Identity of Cohoba, the Narcotic Snuff of Ancient Haiti." *Journal of the Washington Academy of Science* 6(15):547–562.

———. 1916b. "Narcotic Plants and Stimulants of the Ancient Americans." *Smithsonian Institution Annual Report*, 387–424.

———. 1924. "The Isolation of Ancient America as Established by the Cultivated Plants and Languages of Its Aborigines." *Proceedings of the 20th International Congress of Americanists*, 1:167–171. Rio de Janeiro.

Sagard, Gabriel. 1865. *Le grand voyage du pays des Hurons situé en l'Amérique vers la mer douce, es derniers confins de la Nouvelle France dite Canada. Avec un dictionnaire de la langue Huronne*. New edition. Paris: Librairie Tross.

———. 1866. *Histoire du Canada et voyages que les Frères Mineurs recollects y ont faicts pour la conversion des infidèles depuis l'an 1615. . . . Avec un dictionnaire de la langue Huronne*. New edition, 4 vols. Paris: Edwin Tross.

———. 1939. *The Long Journey to the Country of the Hurons*. Edited by George M. Wrong. Toronto: Champlain Society.

Saitoh, Fumiyo, Masana Noma, and Nobumaro Kawashima. 1985. "The Alkaloid Contents of Sixty *Nicotiana* Species." *Phytochemistry* 24(3):477–480.

Salsbury, L. G. 1959. "A Cancer Detection Survey of Carcinoma of the Lung and Female Pelvis among Navajos on the Navajo Indian Reservation. *Surgery Gynecology Obstetrics* 108:257–266.

Salvador, Mari Lyn, ed. 1997. *The Art of Being Kuna: Layers of Meaning among the Kuna of Panama*. Los Angeles: Fowler Museum of Culture History, University of California.

Salwen, Bert. 1978. "Indians of Southern New England and Long Island: Early Period." In *Handbook of North American Indians, vol. 15: Northeast*, edited by Bruce G. Trigger, 160–176. Washington, D.C.: Smithsonian Institution.

Samet, J. M. 1992. "Environmental Tobacco Smoke." In *Environmental Toxicants: Human Exposures and Their Health Effects*, edited by M. Lippmann, 231–265. New York: Van Nostrand Reinhold.

———. 1995. "Lung Cancer." In *Cancer Prevention and Control*, edited by P. Greenwald, 561–584. New York: Marcel Dekker.

Samet, J. M., C. L. Wiggins, C. R. Key, and T. M. Becker. 1988. "Mortality from Lung Cancer and Chronic Obstructive Pulmonary Disease in New Mexico, 1958–1982." *American Journal of Public Health* 78:1182–1186.

Samet, J. M., and J. C. Winter. 1991. "Health Effects of Tobacco Use by Native Americans: Past and Present." Paper presented at the annual meeting of the Society for American Archaeology, New Orleans.

Santa Fe Natural Tobacco Company. 1989. "Chemical Analysis Reveals American Spirit Ranks Lowest in Combined Tar and Nicotine Compared to Top 18 Cigarette Brands." Prepared for customers and others. Santa Fe, New Mexico.

———. 1993. "Bearboy Finds the Sacred Herb, Tobacco (Navajo Legend)." Prepared for customers, partly on the basis of a story in Reichard 1950. Santa Fe, New Mexico.

Savinsky, Joel S., and Hiroko S. Hara. 1981. "Hare." In *Handbook of North American Indians, vol. 6: Subarctic*, edited by J. Helm, 314–325. Washington, D.C.: Smithsonian Institution.

Schaaf, Jeanne M. 1981. "A Method for Reliable and Quantifiable Subsampling of Archaeological Features for Flotation." *Midcontinental Journal of Archaeology* 6(2):219–248.

Schaefer, Stacy B. 1996a. "The Crossing of the Souls: Peyote, Perception, and Meaning among the Huichol Indians." In *People of the Peyote, edited by Stacy B. Schaefer and Peter T. Furst, 136–168. Albuquerque: University of New Mexico Press.

———. 1996b. "The Cosmos Contained: The Temple Where Sun and Moon Meet." In People of the Peyote, edited by Stacy B. Schaefer and Peter T. Furst, 330–376. Albuquerque: University of New Mexico Press.

Schaefer, Stacy B., and Peter T. Furst, eds. 1996. People of the Peyote. Albuquerque: University of New Mexico Press.

Schenck, Sara M., and E. A. Gifford. 1952. "Karok Ethnobotany." Anthropological Records 13(6):377–392.

Schleiffer, Hedwig, ed. 1979. Narcotic Plants of the Old World Used in Rituals and Everyday Life: An Anthology of Texts from Ancient times to the Present. Monticello, New York: Lubrecht and Cramer.

Schlesinger, Roger, and Arthur P. Stabler. 1986. André Thevet's North America: A SixteenthCentury View. Montreal: McGill-Queen's University Press.

Schloesing, T. 1888. "Investigaciones acerca del tabaco." In Documentos relativos al cultivo del tabaco, by Alvaro Reynoso. Havana.

Scholes, Frances V., and Dave Warren. 1965. "The Olmec Region at Spanish Contact." In Handbook of Middle American Indians, vol. 3: Archaeology of Southern Mesoamerica, edited by G. R. Willey, part 2, 776–787. Austin: University of Texas Press.

Schoolcraft, Henry. 1853. Information Respecting the History, Condition, and Prospects of the Indian Tribes of the United States, Collected and Prepared under the Direction of Bureau of Indian Affairs per Act of Congress of March 3rd, 1847, part 1. Philadelphia: Lippincott, Grambo.

Schroeder, Albert H. 1979. "Pueblos Abandoned in Historic Times." In Handbook of North American Indians, vol. 9: Southwest, edited by Alfonso Ortiz, 236–254. Washington D.C.: Smithsonian Institution.

Schroeder, Marjorie B. 1989. Lundy Site Archaeobotany. Quaternary Studies Program, Technical Report no. 89-365-23. Springfield: Illinois State Museum.

Schultes, Richard E. 1945. "El uso del tabaco entre los Huitotos." Agricultura Tropical, October, 19–22. Bogota.

———. 1979. "Solanaceous Hallucinogens and Their Role in the Development of the New World Cultures." In The Biology and Taxonomy of the Solanaceae, edited by J. G. Hawkes, R. N. Lester, and A. D. Skelding, 137–160. London: Academic Press.

Schultes, Richard E., and William A. Davis. 1992. The Glass Flowers at Harvard. Cambridge, Massachusetts: Botanical Museum of Harvard University.

Schultes, Richard E., and Albert Hofmann. 1979. Plants of the Gods: Origins of Hallucinogenic Use. New York: McGraw-Hill.

Schultes, Richard E., and Robert F. Raffauf. 1990. The Healing Forest: Medicinal and Toxic Plants of the Northwest Amazon. Portland, Oregon: Dioscorides Press.

Schwartzkopff, Frances. 1993. "Sickness strikes. The other victims: Tobacco crews risk health in fields of nicotine." Atlanta Journal and Constitution, April 9, A3.

Scott, Linda J. 1983. "A Model for the Interpretation of Pitstructure Activity Areas at Anasazi Sites (Basketmaker III–Pueblo III) through Pollen Analysis." M.A. thesis, Department of Anthropology, University of Colorado, Boulder.

———. 1986. "The Pollen Record at Windy Wheat Hamlet." In Dolores Archaeological Program: Anasazi Communities at Dolores. Early Anasazi Sites in the Sageheun Flats Area, compiled by Allen Kane and Timothy Gross, 773–804. Salt Lake City: U.S. Bureau of Reclamation.

Sebastian, Lynne. 1985. Archeological Excavations along the Turquoise Trail: The Mitigation Program. Albuquerque: Office of Contract Archeology, University of New Mexico.

Sedlak, Lynn. 1975. "Cultural Patterns in Huichol Art." Ph.D. diss., Columbia University. Ann Arbor, Michigan: University Microfilms.

Seeds of Change. n.d. (Acquired by Joseph Winter in 1994.) Seeds of Change Plant List. Santa Fe, New Mexico.

Seig, Louis. 1971. Tobacco, Peace Pipes, and Indians. Palmer Lake, Colorado: Filter Press.

Setchell, William Albert. 1912. "Studies in Nicotiana, part 1." University of California Publications in Botany 5(1):1–86. Berkeley: University of California.

———. 1921. "Aboriginal Tobaccos." *American Anthropologist* 23:397–414.

Severson, Herbert H. 1993. "Smokeless Tobacco: Risks, Epidemiology, and Cessation." In *Nicotine Addiction: Principles and Management*, edited by C. T. Orleans. New York: Oxford University Press.

Shannon and McCall Consulting. 1992. In *Brief: Smoke-Free Schools for Healthier Students*. Shannon and McCall Consulting, Ltd.

Shepard, Alice. 1992. "Notes on the Wintu Shamanic Jargon." In *California Indian Shamanism*, edited by L. J. Bean, 185–210. Menlo Park, California: Ballena Press.

Sherman, Glen. 1972. "Tobacco Pipes of the Western Eskimos." *The Beaver* 303:49–51.

Shimkin, Demitri B. 1986. "Eastern Shoshone." In *Handbook of North American Indians, vol. 11: Great Basin*, edited by Warren L. D'Azevedo, 308–335. Washington, D.C.: Smithsonian Institution.

Shipek, Florence. 1992. "The Shaman: Priest, Doctor, Scientist." In *California Indian Shamanism*, edited by L. J. Bean, 89–96. Menlo Park, California: Ballena Press.

Shippee, J. Mett. 1972. *Archaeological Remains in the Kansas City Area: The Mississippian Occupation*. Missouri Archaeological Society, Research Series no. 9. Columbia.

Shreve, Forrest, and Ira L. Wiggins. 1964. *Vegetation and Flora of the Sonoran Desert*. Palo Alto, California: Stanford University Press.

Sibley, John. 1832. "Historical Sketches of the Several Indian Tribes in Louisiana, South of the Arkansas River, and Between the Mississippi and River Grande." *American State Papers, Indian Affairs* 1:721–728. Washington, D.C.

Siegel, Ronald K. 1989. *Intoxication: Life in Pursuit of Artificial Paradise*. New York: E. P. Dutton.

Siegel, Ronald K., P. R. Collings, and J. L. Diaz. 1977. "On the Use of *Tagetes lucida* and *Nicotiana rustica* as a Huichol Smoking Mixture." *Economic Botany* 31:16–23.

Sievers, M. L. 1968. "Cigarette and Alcohol Usage by Southwestern American Indians." *American Journal of Public Health* 58:74–83.

Silas, Ronnie. 1998. "Memories of What Could Have Been." *Winds of Change*, Winter.

Boulder, Colorado: American Indian Science and Engineering Society.

Silver, Shirley. 1978a. "Chimariko." In *Handbook of North American Indians, vol. 8: California*, edited by R. F. Heizer, 205–210. Washington, D.C.: Smithsonian Institution.

———. 1978b. "Shastan Peoples." In *Handbook of North American Indians, vol. 8: California*, edited by R. F. Heizer, 211–224. Washington, D.C.: Smithsonian Institution.

Silverstein, Michael. 1990. "Chinookans of the Lower Columbia." In *Handbook of North American Indians, vol. 7: Northwest Coast*, edited by Wayne Suttles, 533–546. Washington, D.C.: Smithsonian Institution.

Simms, S. C. 1904. "Cultivation of 'Medicine Tobacco' by the Crows: A Preliminary Paper." *American Anthropologist* 6:331–335.

Simon, Mary. 1994. "Floral Remains." In *The Holdener Site: Late Woodland, Emergent Mississippian, and Mississippian Occupations in the American Bottom Uplands (11-S-685)*, by Warren L. Wittry et al., 71–98. American Bottom Archaeology FAI-270 Site Reports, vol. 26. Urbana: University of Illinois Press.

Sisk-Franco, Caleen. 1996. "Use or Abuse: Indian Tradition and Tobacco Education." *News from Native California*, Spring, 37–38. Berkeley, California.

Sisson, Verne, and James A. Saunders. 1982. "Alkaloid Composition of the USDA Tobacco (*Nicotiana tabacum* L) Introduction Collection." *Tobacco Science* 26:117–120.

Sisson, Verne A., and R. F. Severson. 1990. *Alkaloid Composition of the Nicotiana Species*. Beitrage Zun Tabakforschung International, vol. 14, no. 6.

Skinner, Alanson. 1925a. "Some Seneca Tobacco Customs." *Indian Notes* 2:127–130. New York: Museum of the American Indian, Heye Foundation.

———. 1925b. "Observations on the Ethnobotany of the Sauk Indians, part 3: Notes on Material Culture." *Bulletin of the Public Museum of the City of Milwaukee* 5(3):119–180.

———. 1926. "The Mascoutens or Prairie Potawatomi Indians, part 3: Notes on the Material Culture." *Bulletin of the Public Museum of the City of Milwaukee* 6(2):263–326.

Smith, Bruce D. 1992. "Prehistoric Plant Husbandry in Eastern North America." In *The Origins of Agriculture: An International Perspective*, edited by C. W. Cowan and P. J. Watson, 101–119. Washington D.C.: Smithsonian Institution Press.

Smith, Bruce D., and C. Wesley Cowan. 1987. "Domesticated *Chenopodium* in Prehistoric Eastern North America: New Accelerator Dates from Eastern Kentucky." *American Antiquity* 52:355–357.

Smith, Charles R. 1978. "Tubatulabal." In *Handbook of North American Indians, vol. 8: California*, edited by R. F. Heizer, 437–445. Washington, D.C.: Smithsonian Institution.

Smith, Derek G. 1984. "Mackenzie Delta Eskimo." In *Handbook of North American Indians, vol. 5: Arctic*, edited by D. Damas, 347–358. Washington, D.C.: Smithsonian Institution.

Smith, H. H. 1979. "The Genus as a Genetic Resource." In *Nicotiana: Procedures for Experimental Use*, 1–16. Technical Bulletin no. 1586. Washington, D.C.: Science and Education Administration, United States Department of Agriculture.

Smith, H. H., and D. V. Abashian. 1963. "Chromatographic Investigations on the Alkaloid Content of *Nicotiana* Species and Interspecific Combinations." *American Journal of Botany* 50:435–447.

Smith, Harold H., and Charles W. Bacon. 1941. "Increased Size and Nicotine Production in Selections from Intraspecific Hybrids of *Nicotiana rustica*." *Journal of Agricultural Research* 63(8):457–467.

Smith, Harold H., and Claude R. Smith. 1942. "Alkaloids in Certain Species and Interspecific Hybrids of *Nicotiana*." *Journal of Agricultural Research* 65(7):347–360.

Smith, Huron H. 1923. *Ethnobotany of the Menomini Indians*. Bulletin of the Public Museum of the City of Milwaukee 4:1–174.

———. 1928. *Ethnobotany of the Miskwaki Indians*. Bulletin of the Public Museum of the City of Milwaukee 4:175–326.

———. 1932. *Ethnobotany of the Ojibwe Indians*. Bulletin of the Public Museum of the City of Milwaukee 4:327–525.

———. 1933. *Ethnobotany of the Forest Potawatomi Indians*. Bulletin of the Public Museum of the City of Milwaukee 7:1–230.

Smith, J. L. 1970. "The Sacred Calf Pipe Bundle: Its Effect on the Present Teton Dakota." *Plains Anthropologist* 15(48):87–93.

Smith, Nicholas N. 1957. "Smoking Habits of the Wabanaki." *Bulletin of the Massachusetts Archaeological Society* 18(4):76–77.

Snake, Reuben. 1996. *Reuben Snake: Your Humble Serpent*. As told to Jay Fikes. Santa Fe: Clear Light Publishers.

Sparkman, Philip S. 1908. "The Culture of the Luiseño Indians." *University of California Publications in American Archaeology and Ethnology* 8(4):187–234.

Speck, Frank G. 1917. "Medicine Practices of the Northeastern Algonquians." *Proceedings of the 19th International Congress of Americanists*, 303–321.

———. 1937. *Oklahoma Delaware Ceremonies, Feasts, and Dances*. Memoirs of the American Philosophical Society, vol. 2. Philadelphia.

———. 1977 [1935]. *Naskapi: The Savage Hunters of the Labrador Peninsula*. Norman: University of Oklahoma Press.

Speck, Frank G., and R. W. Dexter. 1951. "Utilization of Animals and Plants by the Micmac Indians of New Brunswick." *Journal of the Washington Academy of Sciences* 41:250–259.

Spencer, Robert F., Jesse D. Jennings, et al. 1965. *The Native Americans*. New York: Harper and Row.

Spicer, Edward H. 1980. *The Yaquis: A Cultural History*. Tucson: University of Arizona Press.

Spier, Leslie. 1928. *Havasupai Ethnography*. Anthropological Papers of the American Museum of Natural History 29, part 3. New York: American Museum of Natural History.

———. 1933. *Yuman Tribes of the Gila River*. Chicago: University of Chicago Press.

Spinden, Herbert J. 1950. *Tobacco Is American: The Story of Tobacco before the Coming of the White Man*. Arents Tobacco Collection Publication no. 2. New York: New York Public Library.

Spores, Ronald. 1965. "The Zapotec and Mixtec at Spanish Contact." In *Handbook of Middle American Indians, vol. 3: Archaeology of Southern Mesoamerica*, edited by G. R. Willey, part 2, 962–990. Austin: University of Texas.

Springer, James W. 1981. "An Ethnohistoric Study of the Smoking Complex in Eastern North America." *Ethnohistory* 28(3):217–235.

Stains, Donna Jean. 1972. "Seed Analysis: Brewster Site (13CK15), Western Iowa." M.A. thesis, Department of Anthropology, University of Wisconsin, Madison.

Steedman, E. V. 1928. "The Ethnobotany of the Thompson Indians of British Columbia." *Bureau of American Ethnology Annual Report* 45:441–522. Washington, D.C.: Smithsonian Institution.

Steinbring, Jack H. 1981. "Saulteaux of Lake Winnipeg." In *Handbook of North American Indians, vol. 6: Subarctic*, edited by J. Helm, 244–255. Washington, D.C.: Smithsonian Institution.

Stephen, Alexander M. 1936. *Hopi Journal of Alexander M. Stephen*. Edited by Elsie C. Parsons. 2 vols. Columbia University Contributions to Anthropology 23. New York.

Stevens-Arroyo, Antonio M. 1988. *Cave of the Jaqua: The Mythological World of the Tainos*. Albuquerque: University of New Mexico Press.

Stevenson, Katherine P. 1985a. "Floral Remains." In *Prehistoric Ridged Field Agriculture in the Upper Mississippi Valley*, by Robert F. Sasso et al., 147–158. Mississippi Valley Archaeology Center, Reports of Investigations no. 38. La Crosse, Wisconsin: University of Wisconsin.

———. 1985b. "Oneota Subsistence-Related Behavior in the Driftless Area: A Study of the Valley View Site near La Crosse, Wisconsin." Ph.D. diss., Department of Anthropology, University of Wisconsin.

Stevenson, Matilda Cox. 1915. *Ethnobotany of the Zuni Indians*. Thirtieth Annual Report of the Bureau of American Ethnology. Washington, D.C.: Smithsonian Institution.

Steward, Julian H. 1933. "Ethnography of the Owens Valley Paiute." *University of California Publications in American Archaeology and Ethnology* 33(3):233–250.

———. 1938. *Basin-Plateau Aboriginal Socio-Political Groups*. Bureau of American Ethnology Bulletin 120. Washington, D.C.: Smithsonian Institution.

Stewart, Omer C. 1941. *Cultural Element Distributions, 14: Northern Paiute*. University of California Anthropological Records 4, no. 3.

———. 1942. "Cultural Element Distributions: Ute-Southern Paiute." *University of California Anthropological Records* 6:231–355.

Stone, Doris. 1949. *The Boruca of Costa Rica*. Papers of the Peabody Museum of American Archaeology and Ethnology 25, no. 2. Cambridge, Massachusetts: Harvard University.

———. 1966. "Synthesis of Lower Central American Ethnohistory." In *Handbook of Middle American Indians, vol. 4: Archaeological Frontiers and External Connections*, edited by Gordon F. Ekholm and Gordon R. Willey, 209–233. Austin: University of Texas Press.

Strachey, William. 1953 [1612, based on manuscript in Princeton Library]. *The Historie of Travell into Virginia Britania*. Edited by Louis B. Wright and Virginia Freund. Hakluyt Society, 2d Series, no. 103. London: Hakluyt Society.

Strike, Sandra S. 1994. *Ethnobotany of the California Indians, vol. 2: Aboriginal Uses of California's Indigenous Plants*. Champaign, Illinois: Koeltz Scientific.

Struever, Mollie. 1980. "Botanical Materials from Sevilleta Shelter." In *The Excavation of Sevilleta Shelter (LA 20896)*, by Joseph C. Winter, 119–124. Albuquerque: Office of Contract Archeology, University of New Mexico.

Struever, Mollie, and Paul J. Knight. 1979. "Analysis of Flotation Samples and Macrobotanical Remains: Block III Mitigation, Navajo Indian Irrigation Project." Manuscript on file. Window Rock, Arizona: Navajo Nation Cultural Resource Management Program.

Sturtevant, William. 1954. "The Mikasuki Seminole: Medical Beliefs and Practices." Ph.D. diss., Yale University.

Sugarman, J. R., C. W. Warren, L. L. Oge, and S. D. Helgerson. 1992. "Using the Behavioral Risk Factor Surveillance System to Monitor Year 2000 Objectives among American Indians." Public Health Reports 107(4):449–456.

Sullivan, Louis. 1990. *Smoking and Health: A National Status Report.* A report to Congress. Washington, D.C.: U.S. Health and Human Services Department.

Sullivan, Lynne P., Sarah W. Neusius, and Phillip D. Neusius. 1995. "Earthworks and Mortuary Sites on Lake Erie: Believe It or Not at the Ripley Site." *Midcontinental Journal of Archaeology* 20(2):115–142.

Suttles, Wayne, and Barbara Lane. 1990. "Southern Coast Salish." In *Handbook of North American Indians, vol. 7: Northwest Coast,* edited by Wayne Suttles, 485–502. Washington, D.C.: Smithsonian Institution.

Swagerty, William R. 1988. "Indian Trade in the Trans-Mississippi West to 1870." In *Handbook of North American Indians, vol. 4: History of Indian-White Relations,* edited by W. E. Washburn. Washington, D.C.: Smithsonian Institution.

Swank, George R. 1932. "The Ethnobotany of the Acoma and Laguna Indians." M.A. thesis, University of New Mexico.

Swanton, John R. 1905. *Haida Texts and Myths, Skidigate Dialect.* Bureau of American Ethnology Bulletin 29. Washington, D.C.: Smithsonian Institution.

———. 1909. *Tlingit Myths and Texts.* Bureau of American Ethnology Bulletin 39. Washington, D.C.: Smithsonian Institution.

———. 1928. "Religious Beliefs and Practices of the Creek Indians." *Bureau of American Ethnology Annual Report* 42:473–672. Washington, D.C.: Smithsonian Institution.

Switzer, Ronald R. 1969. *Tobacco, Pipes, and Cigarettes of the Prehistoric Southwest.* Special Report no. 8. El Paso, Texas: El Paso Archaeological Society.

Symon, D. E. 1991. "Gondwanan Elements of the Solanaceae." In *Solanaceae III: Taxonomy, Chemistry, Evolution,* edited by J. G. Hawkes et al., 139–150. Richmond, UK: Royal Botanic Gardens, Kew.

TABAMEX. 1989. *Atlas del Tabaco en Mexico.* Mexico, D.F.: TABAMEX and the Instituto Nacional de Estadística Geografía e Enfomática.

Tantaquidgeon, Gladys. 1995. *Folk Medicine of the Delaware and Related Algonkian Indians.* Anthropological Series no. 3. Harrisburg: Pennsylvania Historical and Museum Commission.

Taylor, J. Garth. 1984. "Historical Ethnography of the Labrador Eskimo." In *Handbook of the North American Indians, vol. 5: Arctic,* edited by D. Damas, 508–521. Washington, D.C.: Smithsonian Institution.

Taylor, Linda Averill. 1940. *Plants Used as Curatives by Certain Southeastern Tribes.* Cambridge, Massachusetts: Botanical Museum of Harvard University.

Tedlock, Dennis. 1979. "Zuni Religion and World View." In *Handbook of North American Indians, vol. 9: Southwest,* edited by Alfonso Ortiz, 499–508. Washington, D.C.: Smithsonian Institution.

Teit, James A. 1928. "The Salishan Tribes of the Western Plateau." *Bureau of American Ethnology Annual Report* 45:23–396. Washington, D.C.: Smithsonian Institution.

Terrell, John Upton. 1975. *The Plains Apache.* New York: Thomas Y. Crowell.

Theodoratus, Robert J. 1989. "Loss, Transfer, and Reintroduction in the Use of Wild Plant Foods in the Upper Skagit Valley." *Northwest Anthropological Research Notes* 23(1):35–52.

Thomas, Alfred B. 1935. *After Coronado: Spanish Exploration Northeast of New Mexico, 1696–1727.* Norman: University of Oklahoma Press.

Thomas, Sidney J. 1941. "A Sioux Medicine Bundle." *American Anthropologist* 48:606–609.

Thompson, J. Eric S. 1970a. *Maya History and Religion.* Norman: University of Oklahoma Press.

———. 1970b. "Tobacco among the Maya and Their Neighbors." In *Maya History and Religion,* by J. Eric S. Thompson, 103–123. Norman: University of Oklahoma Press.

Thwaites, Reuben G., ed. 1896–1901. *The Jesuit Relations and Allied Documents.* 73 vols. Cleveland, Ohio: Burrows Brothers.

———. 1904. "Bradbury's Travels in the Interior of America: 1809–1811." In *Early Western Travels, 1748–1846,* vol. 5. Cleveland, Ohio: Arthur H. Clark.

———. 1905a. "Edwin James' Account of the Steven H. Long Expedition, 1819–1820." In *Early Western Travels, 1748–1846,* vol. 14. Cleveland, Ohio: Arthur H. Clark.

———. 1905b. "Prince Maximilian of Weid's Travels, 1932–1834." In *Early Western Travels, 1748–1846*, vol. 23. Cleveland, Ohio: Arthur H. Clark.

Tiffany, Joseph A. 1981. "A Compendium of Radiocarbon Dates for Iowa Archaeological Sites." *Plains Anthropologist* 26:55–73.

Timbrook, Jan. 1987. "Virtuous Herbs: Plants in Chumash Medicine." *Journal of Ethnobiology* 7(2):171–180.

———. 1990. "Ethnobotany of the Chumash Indians, California, Based on Collections by John P. Harrington." *Economic Botany* 44(2):236–253.

Tobacco Institute. n.d. "Tobacco Deeply Rooted in America's Heritage." Twenty-page history of the U.S. tobacco industry, provided to Joseph Winter by the Tobacco Institute, Washington, D.C.

Toll, H. Wolcott. 1995. *An Analysis of Variability and Condition of Cavate Structures in Bandelier National Monument.* National Park Service, Bandelier Archeological Survey, Contribution 3. Intermountain Cultural Resources Center, Professional Paper 53. Santa Fe, New Mexico.

Toll, Mollie S. 1985a. "An Overview of Chaco Canyon Macrobotanical Materials and Analysis to Date." In *Environment and Subsistence of Chaco Canyon, New Mexico*, edited by Frances Joan Mathien. National Park Service Publications in Archaeology 18E. Albuquerque.

———. 1985b. "Flotation and Macrobotanical Remains." In *Archeological Excavation along the Turquoise Trail: The Mitigation Program*, by Lynne Sebastian, 158–170. Albuquerque: Office of Contract Archeology, University of New Mexico.

———. 1985c. "Flotation, Macrobotanical, and Charcoal Analyses." In *The Excavation of the Cortez Co2 Pipeline Project Sites, 1982–1983*, by Michael P. Marshall, 219–234. Albuquerque: Office of Contract Archeology, University of New Mexico.

———. 1989. *Plant Materials from Two Historic Sites near Abiquiu, New Mexico: La Puente (LA 54313) and the Trujillo House (LA 59658).* Castetter Laboratory for Ethnobotanical Studies, Technical Series 240. Albuquerque: University of New Mexico.

———. 1993a. "Botanical Indicators of Early Life in Chaco Canyon: Flotation Samples and Other Plant Materials from Basketmaker and Early Pueblo Occupations." Manuscript on file, Division of Cultural Research, National Park Service, Southwest Regional Office, Santa Fe.

———. 1993b. "Flotation and Macrobotanical Analysis at 29SJ629." In *The Spadefoot Toad Site: Investigations at 29SJ629 in Marcia's Rincon and the Fajada Gap Pueblo II Community, Chaco Canyon, New Mexico*, vol. 2, by Thomas C. Windes. Reports of the Chaco Center 12. Santa Fe, New Mexico: National Park Service, Branch of Cultural Research, Division of Anthropology.

———. 1993c. "Flotation and Macrobotanical Evidence of Plant Use." In *The Excavation of a Multicomponent Anasazi Site (LA 50337) in the La Plata River Valley, Northwestern New Mexico*, by Bradley J. Vierra, 247–280. Archaeology Notes 49. Santa Fe: Museum of New Mexico, Office of Archaeological Studies.

———. 1993d. *Plant Utilization at a Thirteenth-Century Pithouse Village (the Fox Place, LA 68188) on the Edge of New Mexico's Eastern Plains.* Ethnobotany Lab Technical Series 11. Santa Fe: Museum of New Mexico, Office of Archaeological Studies.

———. 1994a. *Plant Remains from Two Late Basketmaker/Early Pueblo Sites in Central New Mexico: LA 70163 and LA 3558.* Ethnobotany Lab Technical Series 16. Santa Fe: Museum of New Mexico, Office of Archaeological Studies.

———. 1994b. "Plant Remains." In *Studying the Taos Frontier: The Pot Creek Data Recovery Project, vol. 1: Excavation*, by J. L. Boyer et al.. Archaeology Notes 68. Santa Fe: Museum of New Mexico, Office of Archaeological Studies.

———. 1995a. "Unpublished Botanical Data from Basketmaker and Anasazi Occupations of the La Plata Valley, Northwest New Mexico." Manuscript on file. Santa Fe: Museum of New Mexico, Office of Archaeological Studies.

———. 1995b. "Botanical Materials Retrieved by Flotation and Dry-Screening from a Three-Room Suite at San Lazaro Pueblo,

New Mexico." Manuscript on file. Santa Fe: Museum of New Mexico, Office of Archaeological Studies.

———. 1995c. *Plant parts Found in Adobe Bricks at an Eighteenth-Century Spanish Mission, Pecos, New Mexico: III.* Ethnobotany Lab Technical Series 24. Santa Fe: Museum of New Mexico, Office of Archaeological Studies.

———. 1995d. "Unpublished Botanical Data from LA 3333, a Large Pithouse Village in the Galisteo Basin, New Mexico." Manuscript on file. Santa Fe: Museum of New Mexico, Office of Archaeological Studies.

———. 1995e. "Botanical Study." In *The Belen Bridge Site and the Late Elmendorf Phase of Central New Mexico*, by Regge N. Wiseman, 139–165. Archaeology Notes 137. Santa Fe: Museum of New Mexico, Office of Archaeological Studies.

———. 1996. "Picacho: A Record of Diverse Plant Use in a Diverse Ecological Setting." In *The Land In Between: Archaic and Formative Occupations along the Upper Rio Hondo of Southeastern New Mexico*, by Regge N. Wiseman, 125–156. Archaeology Notes 125. Santa Fe: Museum of New Mexico, Office of Archaeological Studies.

———. 1997a. *Plant Remains from San Antonio (LA 24): A Late Coalition/Early Classic Pueblo with Hispanic Occupation in Tijeras Canyon, New Mexico.* Ethnobotany Lab Technical Series 52. Santa Fe: Museum of New Mexico, Office of Archaeological Studies.

———. 1997b. "Plant Use and Subsistence at Rowe Pueblo." Part 3 in *Before Pecos: Settlement Aggregation at Rowe, New Mexico*, by Linda C. Cordell. Anthropological Papers 6. Albuquerque: Maxwell Museum of Anthropology, University of New Mexico.

———. 1997c. "Analysis of Botanical Remains." In *Excavation of a Jornada Pithouse along U.S. 380, Socorro County, New Mexico*, by Daisy F. Levine, 95–107. Archaeology Notes 138. Santa Fe: Museum of New Mexico, Office of Archaeological Studies.

Toll, Mollie S., and Marcia L. Donaldson. 1982. "Flotation and Macro-Botanical Analyses of Archaeological Sites on the McKinley Mine Lease: A Regional Study of Plant Manipulation and Natural Seed Dispersal Over Time." In *Anasazi and Navajo Land Use in the McKinley Mine Area near Gallup New Mexico*, vol. 1, edited by Christine G. Allen and Ben A. Nelson, 712–786. Albuquerque: Office of Contract Archeology, University of New Mexico.

Toll, Mollie S., and Pamela McBride. 1996. *Flotation and Macrobotanical Materials from Early Pithouse and Early Pueblo Period Sites of the Quemado Area, New Mexico: The Gallo Mountain Project.* Ethnobotany Lab Technical Series 37. Santa Fe: Museum of New Mexico, Office of Archaeological Studies.

———. 1998a. *Botanical Analysis from Archaic to Athabaskan Sites in the Luna and Pinelawn Valleys, West-Central New Mexico.* Ethnobotany Lab Technical Series 55. Santa Fe: Museum of New Mexico, Office of Archaeological Studies.

———. 1998b. *Botanical Expressions of Cultural and Economic Diversity at Three Sites along the Old Santa Fe Trail, New Mexico.* Ethnobotany Lab Technical Series 57. Santa Fe: Museum of New Mexico, Office of Archaeological Studies.

Tooker, Elisabeth. 1994. *Lewis H. Morgan on Iroquois Material Culture.* Tucson: University of Arizona Press.

Tootill, Elizabeth, and Stephen Blackmore, eds. 1984. *The Facts on File Dictionary of Botany.* New York: Facts on File.

Tozzer, A. M. 1907. *A Comparative Study of the Mayas and Lacondones.* New York.

Train, Perry, James R. Henricks, and W. Andrew Archer. 1941. *Medicinal Uses of Plants by the Indian Tribes of Nevada.* Washington, D.C.: U.S. Department of Agriculture.

Trichopoulos, D. 1981. "Lung Cancer and Passive Smoking." *International Journal of Cancer* 27:1–4.

Trigger, Bruce G. 1969. *The Huron: Farmers of the North.* New York: Holt, Reinhart and Winston.

Tschopic, Harry. 1941. *Navaho Pottery Making: An Inquiry into the Affinities of Navaho Painted Pottery.* Papers of the Peabody Museum of American Archaeology and Ethnology, vol. 17, no. 1. Cambridge, Massachusetts: Harvard University.

Tso, T. C. 1972. *Physiology and Biochemistry of Tobacco Plants*. Stroudsburg, Pennsylvania: Dowden, Hutchinson and Ross.

Turnbaugh, William A. 1975. "Tobacco, Pipes, Smoking, and Rituals among the Indians of the Northeast." *Quarterly Bulletin of the Archaeological Society of Virginia* 30(2):59–71.

———. 1979. "Calumet Ceremonialism as a Nativistic Response." *American Antiquity* 44:685–691.

———. 1984. "Cloudblowers and Calumets." In *Plains Indian Seminar in Honor of Dr. John C. Ewers*, edited by George P. Horse Capture and Gene Ball, 54–72. Cody, Wyoming: Buffalo Bill Historical Center.

Turner, Nancy, and Marcus A. M. Bell. 1971. "The Ethnobotany of the Coast Salish Indians of Vancouver Island." *Economic Botany* 25(3):257–310.

———. 1973. "Ethnobotany of the Southern Kwakiutl Indians of British Colombia." *Economic Botany* 27(3):257–310.

Turner, Nancy, R. Bouchard, and D. D. Kennedy. 1980. *Ethnobotany of the Okanagan-Colville Indians of British Columbia and Washington*. Occasional Paper no. 21. Vancouver: British Columbia Provincial Museum.

Turner, Nancy, and B. S. Efrat. 1982. *Ethnobotany of the Hesquiat Indians of Vancouver Island*. Culture Recovery Report no. 2. Victoria: British Columbia Provincial Museum.

Turner, Nancy, and Roy L. Taylor. 1972. "A Review of the Northwest Coast Tobacco Mystery." *Syesis* 5:249–257.

Turner, Nancy J., Laurence C. Thompson, M. Terry Thompson, and Annie Z. York. 1990. *Thompson Ethnobotany: Knowledge and Usage of Plants by the Thompson Indians of British Columbia*. Memoir no. 3. Victoria: Royal British Columbia Museum.

Tyler, Hamilton A. 1991. *Pueblo Birds and Myths*. Flagstaff, Arizona: Northland Press.

Tyler, Lyon G., ed. 1930. *Narratives of Early Virginia 1606–1625*. New York: Charles Scribner's Sons.

Udden, Johan August. 1900. *An Old Indian Village*. Lutheran Augustana Book Concern.

Underhill, Ruth. 1953. *Here Come the Navaho*. Washington, D.C.: Bureau of Indian Affairs.

University of New Mexico. Various dates. Herbarium records: tobacco voucher specimens no. 756/1169, 3599, 13997, and 67365. Also, unnumbered Edward Castetter Seed Collection: Mandan and Crow tobacco. Albuquerque: University of New Mexico, Biology Department.

Unrau, William E. 1965. *The Kansa Indians*. Norman: University of Oklahoma Press.

USBC (United States Bureau of Census). 1993. *Statistical Abstracts of the United States: 1993*. Washington, D.C.

USDA (United States Department of Agriculture). n.d. *Nin-A-Saan: "Set Here for You."* Videotape produced by Shenandoah Film Production for Six Rivers National Forest, Eureka California.

USDHEW (United States Department of Health, Education, and Welfare). 1964. *Smoking and Health: Report of the Advisory Committee to the Surgeon General of the Public Health Service*. Washington, D.C.: U.S. Government Printing Office.

USDHHS (United States Department of Health and Human Services). 1979. *A Report of the Surgeon General: Smoking and Health*. Atlanta, Georgia: U.S. Government Printing Office.

———. 1983. *A Report of the Surgeon General: The Health Consequences of Smoking—Cardiovascular Disease*. Washington, D.C.: U.S. Government Printing Office.

———. 1984. *A Report of the Surgeon General: The Health Consequences of Smoking—Chronic Obstructive Lung Disease*. Washington, D.C.: U.S. Government Printing Office.

———. 1986a. *A Report of the Advisory Committee to the Surgeon General: The Health Consequences of Using Smokeless Tobacco*. Washington, D.C.: U.S. Government Printing Office.

———. 1986b. *A Report of the Surgeon General: The Health Consequences of Involuntary Smoking*. Washington, D.C.: U.S. Government Printing Office.

———. 1988. *A Report of the Surgeon General: The Health Consequences of Smoking: Nicotine Addiction*. Washington, D.C.: U.S. Government Printing Office.

———. 1989. *A Report of the Surgeon General: Reducing the Health Consequences of*

*Smoking. 25 Years of Progress*. Washington, D.C.: U.S. Government Printing Office.

———. 1990. *A Report of the Surgeon General: The Health Benefits of Smoking Cessation.* Washington, D.C.: U.S. Government Printing Office.

———. 1998. *A Report of the Surgeon General: Tobacco Use among U.S. Racial/Ethnic Minority Groups: African Americans, American Indians, Alaska Natives, Asian Americans, Pacific Islanders, and Hispanics.* Washington, D.C.: U.S. Government Printing Office.

USEPA (United States Environmental Protection Agency). 1992. *Current Federal Indoor Air Quality Activities.* Washington, D.C.: U.S. Government Printing Office.

———. 1993. *Respiratory Health Effects of Passive Smoking: Lung Cancer and Other Disorders.* Monograph 4. Washington, D.C.: U.S. Government Printing Office.

Usner, Daniel H. Jr. 1988. "Economic Relations in the Southeast until 1783." In *Handbook of North American Indians, vol. 4: History of Indian-White Relations*, edited by Wilcomb E. Washburn, 391–395. Washington, D.C.: Smithsonian Institution.

U.S. Tobacco Germplasm Catalog. 1993–1994. *Catalog of the U.S. Tobacco Germplasm Collection (8/19/93–5/5/94).* Maintained by and available through the Crops Research Laboratory, North Carolina State University, Oxford, North Carolina.

Valadez, Mariano, and Susana Valadez. 1992. *Huichol Indian Sacred Rituals.* Paintings by Mariano Valadez and text by Susana Valadez. Oakland, California: Dharma Enterprises.

———. 1995. *Huichol Indian Ceremonies 1995.* Calendar. Paintings by M. Valadez and text by S. Valadez. Oakland, California: Amber Lotus.

Valadez, Susana E. 1989. "Problem Solving in a Threatened Culture: The Practice of Humanthropology among the Huichols." In *Mirrors of the Gods: Proceedings of a Symposium on the Huichol Indians*, edited by Susan Bernstein, 17–32. Museum Papers no. 25. San Diego: San Diego Museum of Man.

Valway, Sarah. 1991. *Cancer Mortality among Native Americans in the United States: Regional Differences in Indian Health, 1984–1988, and Trends over Time, 1968–1987.* Rockville, Maryland: U.S. Indian Health Service.

Vehik, Susan C. 1992. "Wichita Culture History." *Plains Anthropologist* 37(141): 311–332.

Vestal, Paul A. 1940. "Notes on a Collection of Plants from the Hopi Indian Region of Arizona Made by J. G. Owens in 1891." *Botanical Museum Leaflets* 8(8):153–168. Cambridge, Massachusetts: Harvard University.

———. 1952. *Ethnobotany of the Ramah Navajo.* Papers of the Peabody Museum of American Archaeology and Ethnology 40, no. 4. Cambridge, Massachusetts: Harvard University.

Vestal, Paul A., and Richard E. Schultes. 1939. *The Economic Botany of the Kiowa Indians.* Cambridge, Massachusetts: Botanical Museum, Harvard University.

Viereck, Phillip, comp. and ed. 1967. *The New Land.* New York: John Day.

Voegelin, Erminie W. 1938. *Tubatulabal Ethnography.* Anthropological Records 2, no. 1. Berkeley: University of California.

Vogel, V. 1969. *American Indian Medicines.* Norman: University of Oklahoma Press.

Voges, Ernst, comp. and ed. 1984. *Tobacco Encyclopedia.* London: Tobacco Journal International.

Vogt, Evon Z. 1969. *Zinacantan: A Maya Community in the Highlands of Chiapas.* Cambridge, Massachusetts: Belknap Press of Harvard University.

Volle, Robert L., and George B. Koelle. 1970. "Ganglionic Stimulating and Blocking Agents." In *The Pharmacological Basis of Therapeutics*, edited by Louis S. Goodmand and Alfred Gilman, 585–600. London: Macmillan.

von Gernet, Alexander. 1982. "Interpreting Intrasite Spatial Distribution of Artifacts: The Draper Site Pipe Fragments." *Man in the Northeast* 23:49–60.

———. 1985. *Analysis of Intrasite Artifact Spatial Distributions: The Draper Site Smoking Pipes.* Museum of Indian Archaeology Research Report no. 16. London, Ontario: University of Western Ontario.

———. 1988. "The Transculturation of the Amerindian Pipe/Tobacco/Smoking Complex and Its Impact on the Intellectual Boundaries between 'Savagery' and 'Civilization,' 1535–1935." Ph.D. diss., Anthropology, McGill University, Montreal.

———. 1989a. "Some Observations on the Hallucinogenic Origins of the Iroquoian Pipe/Tobacco/Smoking Complex." Paper presented at the Smoking Pipe Conference, Rochester Museum and Science Center, Rochester, New York.

———. 1989b. Review of *Tobacco and Shamanism in South America*, by Johannes Wilbert. Man 24(4):713.

———. 1989c. "'Gens de Petun': A Case Study in Exegesis and the Deconstruction of Images in Ethnohistory." Manuscript on file with author.

———. 1990. Review of *Offering Smoke: The Sacred Pipe and Native American Religion*, by Jordan Paper. American Anthropologist 92:1040–1041.

———. 1992a. "Hallucinogens and the Origins of the Iroquoian Pipe/Tobacco/Smoking Complex." In *Proceedings of the 1989 Smoking Pipe Conference*, edited by Charles F. Hayes III, 171–185. Research Records no. 22. Rochester, New York: Rochester Museum and Science Center.

———. 1992b. "A Possible Matouweskarini Hunting Camp: Excavations at the Highland Lake Site, Renfrew County." In *Annual Archaeological Report Ontario 1991* (new series), edited by Peter L. Storck, 120–124. Toronto: Ontario Heritage Foundation.

———. 1992c. "New Directions in the Construction of Prehistoric Amerindian Belief Systems." In *Ancient Images, Ancient Thought: The Archaeology of Ideology*, edited by S. Goldsmith et al., 133–140. Calgary, Alberta: Archaeological Association, University of Calgary.

———. 1993a. "The Construction of Prehistoric Ideation: Exploring the Universality-Idiosyncrasy Continuum." *Cambridge Archaeological Journal* 3:67–81.

———. 1993b. "Archaeological Investigations at Highland Lake: 1991 Field Season." In *Annual Archaeological Report Ontario 1992* (new series), edited by Peter L. Storck,

74–79. Toronto: Ontario Heritage Foundation.

———. 1995. "*Nicotiana* Dreams: The Prehistory and Early History of Tobacco in Eastern North America." In *Consuming Habits: Drugs in History and Anthropology*, edited by J. Goodman, P. E. Lovejoy, and A. Sherratt, 67–87. London: Routledge.

von Gernet, Alexander, and Peter Timmins. 1987. "Pipes and Parakeets: Constructing Meaning in an Early Iroquoian Context." In *Archaeology as Long-Term History*, edited by Ian Hodder, 31–42. Cambridge: Cambridge University Press.

Wagner, Gail E. 1985a. *Botanical Remains from the Island Creek Village (33AD25), a Fort Ancient Site in Adams County, Ohio*. Report submitted to U.S. Army Corps of Engineers, Huntington District, West Virginia.

———. 1985b. "Botanical Remains from the Stop Sign Site and the Doctor's Island Site." In "The Mississippian Occupation of the Upper Kaskaskia Valley: Problems in Culture History and Economic Organization," by Charles R. Moffat (Ph.D. diss., Department of Anthropology, University of Illinois, Urbana-Champaign), 388–407. Ann Arbor, Michigan: University Microfilms.

———. 1987. "Uses of Plants by the Fort Ancient Indians." Ph.D. diss., Department of Anthropology, Washington University, St. Louis.

———. 1995. "Botanizing along Green River." In *Of Caves and Shell Mounds*, edited by Kenneth C. Carstens and Patty Jo Watson, 145–152. Tuscaloosa: University of Alabama Press.

Wallace, Anthony F. C. 1972. *The Death and Rebirth of the Seneca*. New York: Vintage Books.

Wallace, Henry D., and Charles Miksicek. 1995. "Plant Remains." In *Archaeological Investigations at Los Morteros (AZ:AA:12:57), a Prehistoric Settlement in the Northern Tucson Basin*, part 1, edited by Henry D. Wallace. Anthropological Papers 17. Tucson: Center for Desert Archaeology.

Wallace, William J. 1953. "Tobacco and Its Use among the Mohave Indians." *Masterkey* 27(6):193–202.

————. 1978a. "Hupa, Chilula, and Whilkut." In *Handbook of North American Indians, vol. 8: California*, edited by R. F. Heizer, 164–179. Washington, D.C.: Smithsonian Institution.

————. 1978b. "Southern Valley Yokuts." In *Handbook of North American Indians, vol. 8: California*, edited by R. F. Heizer, 448–461. Washington, D.C.: Smithsonian Institution.

Wasson, R. Gordon. 1973. *The Role of "Flowers" in Nahuatl Culture: A Suggested Interpretation*. Botanical Museum Leaflets 23, no. 8. Cambridge, Massachusetts: Harvard University.

Watahomigie, Lucille. 1982. *Hualapai Ethnobotany*. Peach Springs, Arizona: Hualapai Bilingual Program, Peach Springs School District 8.

Waugh, F. W. 1916. *Iroquois Foods and Food Preparation*. Ottawa: Canada Department of Mines.

Weber, Steven A., and P. David Seaman. 1985. *Havasupai Habitat: A. F. Whiting's Ethnography of a Traditional Indian Culture*. Tucson: University of Arizona Press.

Wedel, Mildred Mott. 1982. "The Wichita Indians in the Arkansas River Basin." In *Plains Indian Studies: A Collection of Essays in Honor of John C. Ewers and Waldo R. Wedel*, edited by Douglas H. Ubelaker and Herman J. Viola, 118–134. Smithsonian Contributions to Anthropology, no. 30. Washington, D.C.

————. 1988 [1971]. "J. B. Bénard, Sieur de la Harpe: Visitor to the Wichita in 1719." *J&L Reprints in Anthropology* 38:131–163. Lincoln, Nebraska.

Wedel, Waldo R. 1943. *Archaeological Investigations in Platte and Clay Counties, Missouri*. United States National Museum, Bulletin 183. Washington, D.C.: Smithsonian Institution.

————. 1959. *An Introduction to Kansas Archeology*. Bureau of American Ethnology Bulletin 174. Washington, D.C.: Smithsonian Institution.

————. 1986. *Central Plains Prehistory*. Lincoln: University of Nebraska Press.

Wegner, Steven A. 1979. "Analysis of Seed Remains from the ChanYaTa Site (13BV1), a Mill Creek Village in Northwestern Iowa." *South Dakota Archaeology* 3:1–80.

Weigand, Phil C. 1972. *Co-operative Labor Groups in Subsistence Activities among the Huichol Indians of the Gubernancia of Mezquitic, Jalisco, Mexico*. Research Records of University Museum, Mesoamerican Studies no. 7. Carbondale: Southern Illinois University.

————. 1978. "Contemporary Social and Economic Structure." In *Art of the Huichol Indians*, edited by K. Berrin, 101–116. New York: Abrams.

Weinstein-Farson, Laurie. 1989. *The Wampanoag*. New York: Chelsea House Publishers.

Weiss, Gerald. 1973. "Shamanism and Priesthood in the Light of the Campa Ayahuasca Ceremony." In *Hallucinogens and Shamanism*, edited by Michael J. Harner. Oxford: Oxford University Press.

Weitlaner, Roberto J. 1969. "The Cuicatec." In *Handbook of Middle American Indians, vol. 7: Ethnology*, edited by E. Z. Vogt, part 1, 434–447. Austin: University of Texas.

Weitlaner, Roberto J., and Howard F. Cline. 1969. "The Chinantec." In *Handbook of Middle American Indians, vol. 7: Ethnology*, edited by E. Z. Vogt, part 1, 523–552. Austin: University of Texas Press.

Weitlaner, Roberto J., and Walter A. Hoppe. 1969. "The Mazatec." In *Handbook of Middle American Indians, vol. 7: Ethnology*, edited by E. Z. Vogt, part 1, 516–522. Austin: University of Texas Press.

Weitzner, Bella. 1979. *Notes on the Hidatsa Indians Based on Data Recovered by the Late Gilbert L. Wilson*. Anthropological Papers 56, no. 2. New York: American Museum of Natural History.

Wells, Phillip V. 1959. "An Ecological Investigation of Two Desert Tobaccos." *Ecology* 40(4):626–644.

Welsh, Stanley L., N. Duane Atwood, Sherel Goodrich, and Larry C. Higgins, eds. 1987. *A Utah Flora*. Great Basin Naturalist Memoirs 9. Provo, Utah: Brigham Young University.

Welsh, Stanley L., and James A. Erdman. 1964. "Annotated Checklist of the Plants of Mesa Verde, Colorado." *Brigham Young University Science Bulletin, Biological Series* 4(2):1–32.

Weltfish, Gene. 1965. *The Lost Universe: Pawnee Life and Culture*. Lincoln: University of Nebraska Press.

West, George A. 1934. *Tobacco, Pipes, and Smoking Customs of the American Indians*, part 1. Bulletin of the Public Museum of the City of Milwaukee 17.

Weybrew, J. A., and T. J. Mann. 1963. "Comparative Composition of Certain *Nicotiana* Species and Their F1 Hybrids with *Nicotiana tabacum*." *Tobacco Science* 7:28–36.

Whalley, Lucy. 1983. "Plant Remains from the Turner Site." In *The Turner and DeMange Sites (11-S-50)(11-S-447)*, by George R. Milner, 213–233. American Bottom Archaeology FAI-270 Site Reports, vol. 4. Urbana: University of Illinois Press.

———. 1984. "Plant Remains from the Stirling Phase." In *The BBB Motor Site*, by Thomas E. Emerson and Douglas K. Jackson, 321–335. American Bottom Archaeology FAI-270 Site Reports, vol. 6. Urbana: University of Illinois Press.

———. 1990a. "Dohack Phase Floral Remains." In *The Range Site 2: The Emergent Mississippian Dohack and Range Phase Occupations (11-S-47)*, by J. E. Kelly, S. J. Ozuk, and J. A. Williams, 269–280. American Bottom Archaeology FAI-270 Site Reports, vol. 20. Urbana: University of Illinois Press.

———. 1990b. "Range Phase Floral Remains." In *The Range Site 2: The Emergent Mississippian Dohack and Range Phase Occupations (11-S-47)*, by J. E. Kelly, S. J. Ozuk, and J. A. Williams, 515–530. American Bottom Archaeology FAI-270 Site Reports, vol. 20. Urbana: University of Illinois Press.

Wheeler, George M. 1871. *Report upon United States Geographical Surveys West of the One-Hundredth Meridian, vol. 6: Botany*. Washington, D.C.: U.S. Government Printing Office.

White, Leslie A. 1941. "*Nicotiana rustica* Cultivated by Pueblo Indians." *Science* 94:64–65.

———. 1942. "Further Data on the Cultivation of Tobacco among the Pueblo Indians." *Science* 96:59–60.

———. 1943. "Punche: Tobacco in New Mexico History." *New Mexico Historical Review* 18:386–393.

———. 1945. "Notes on the Ethnobotany of the Keres." *Papers of the Michigan Academy of Arts, Sciences, and Letters* 30:557–568.

Whiting, Alfred H. 1939. *Ethnobotany of the Hopi*. Bulletin 15. Flagstaff: Museum of Northern Arizona.

Wiggins, Ira L. 1980. *Flora of Baja California*. Palo Alto, California: Stanford University Press.

Wilbert, Johannes. 1975. "Magico-Religious Use of Tobacco among South American Indians." In *Cannabis and Culture*, edited by V. Rubin, 439–461. Paris: Mouton.

———. 1987. *Tobacco and Shamanism in South America*. New Haven, Connecticut: Yale University Press.

Will, George F., and George E. Hyde. 1917. *Corn among the Indians of the Upper Missouri*. Lincoln: University of Nebraska Press.

Williams, Roger. 1973. *A Key into the Language of America*. Edited by John J. Teunissen and Evelyn J. Hinz. Detroit: Wayne State University Press.

Williamson, R. F. 1983. *The Robin Hood Site: A Study in Functional Variability in Late Iroquian Settlement Patterns*. Monographs in Ontario Archaeology no. 1.

Wilshusen, Richard H., comp. 1985. *Excavations at Rio Vista Village (Site 5MT2182), a Multicomponent Pueblo I Village Site*. Dolores Archaeological Program Technical Reports DAP-160. Salt Lake City: Bureau of Reclamation.

Wilson, Gilbert Livingstone. 1977 [1917]. *Agriculture of the Hidatsa Indians: An Indian Interpretation*. J&L Reprints in Anthropology, vol. 5. Lincoln, Nebraska.

———. 1987 [1917]. *Buffalo Bird Woman's Garden: Agriculture of the Hidatsa Indians*. St. Paul: Minnesota Historical Society Press.

Wilson, Michael R. 1978. "Notes on Ethnobotany in Inuktitut." *Western Canadian Journal of Anthropology* 8:180–196.

Winter, Joseph C. 1986. "New Evidence on the Arrival of the Athabaskans in the Southwest and the Western High Plains." Paper presented at the first Navajo Studies Conference, Albuquerque.

———. 1990a. "The Tobaccos of America." Paper presented at the Society of Ethnobiology Conference, Tempe, Arizona.

———. 1990b. "Prehistoric Use of Tobacco: A Pathway to Plant Domestication?" Paper presented at second International Ethnobiology Conference, Kunming, China.

———. 1991. "Prehistoric and Historic Native American Tobacco Use: An Overview." Paper presented at the annual meeting of the Society for American Archaeology, New Orleans.

———. 1994a. Field notes, tobacco voucher specimens and seeds, and other material collected from various California Native American tribes. In author's possession.

———. 1994b. Field notes, tobacco voucher specimens and seeds, and other material collected from the Nageezi Navajo and various Pueblo groups in New Mexico. In author's possession.

———. 1995a. Field notes, tobacco voucher specimens and seeds, and other material collected from various Native American tribes in New York, Massachusetts, Maine, New Brunswick, Quebec, and Ontario. In author's possession.

———. 1995b. Field notes, tobacco voucher specimens and seeds, and other material collected from the Huichol Indians and nearby mestizos, Nayarit and Jalisco, Mexico. Also later trips in 1996, 1997 and 1998. In author's possession.

———. 1995c. Field notes, tobacco voucher specimens and seeds, and other material collected from the Shipibo, Capa Nahua, and Yagua Indians and nearby mestizos, Peruvian Amazon. In author's possession.

———. 1996. Information on the Kootenai provided by a Kootenai recipient of seeds from the Traditional Native American Tobacco Seed Bank and Education Program, University of New Mexico, Albuquerque. In author's possession.

Winter, Joseph C., and Patrick F. Hogan. 1986. "Plant Husbandry in the Great Basin and Adjacent Northern Colorado Plateau." In *Anthropology of the Desert West: Essays in Honor of Jesse D. Jennings*, edited by C. J. Condie and D. D. Fowler, 117–144. University of Utah Anthropological Papers 110. Salt Lake City.

Wolfe, M. D., and J. T. Carlos. 1987. "Health Effects of Smokeless Tobacco Use in Navaho Indian Adolescents." *Community Dentistry Oral Epidemiology* 15:230.

Wood, W. Raymond. 1967. *An Interpretation of Mandan Culture History*. River Basin Survey Papers no. 39. Bureau of American Ethnology Bulletin 198. Washington D.C.: Smithsonian Institution.

———. 1980. "Plains Trade in Prehistoric and Protohistoric Intertribal Relations." In *Anthropology on the Great Plains*, edited by W. R. Wood and M. Liberty, 98–109. Lincoln: University of Nebraska Press.

Wood, William. 1898 [1634]. *New Englands Prospect*. Boston: E. M. Boynton.

Woosley, Anne I. 1977. "Farm Field Location through Palynology." In *Hovenweep 1976*, by Joseph C. Winter. Archeological Report 3, San Jose State University, California.

Wright, J. Leitch, Jr. 1986. *Creeks and Seminoles: The Destruction and Regeneration of the Muscogula People*. Lincoln: University of Nebraska Press.

Wright, Louis B., ed. 1965. *The Elizabethans' America: A Collection of Early Reports by Englishmen on the New World*. London: Edward Arnold.

Wright, Louis B., and Virginia Freund, eds. 1953. *The Historie of Travell into Virginia Britania (1612) by William Strachey*. London: Hakluyt Society.

Wright, Patti. 1990. "Archaeobotanical Data." In *Data Recovery and Archaeological Investigations at the Prehistoric Riverside Site, 23SL481, in Southern St. Louis County, Missouri*, by Neal H. Lopinot and Joseph M. Nixon, 205–221. Archaeological Survey, Research Report 52. St. Louis: University of Missouri.

Wroth, Lawrence C. 1970. *The Voyages of Giovanni da Verrazzano, 1524–1528*. New Haven, Connecticut: Yale University Press.

Wu-Williams, A. H. 1994. "Lung Cancer and Cigarette Smoking." In *Epidemiology of Lung Cancer*, edited by J. M. Samet, 71–108. New York: Marcel Dekker.

Wyman, Leland C. 1987. *Blessingway*. Tucson: University of Arizona Press.

Wyman, Leland C., and Stuart K. Harris. 1941. *Navajo Indian Medical Ethnobotany*. University of New Mexico Bulletin no. 366, Anthropological Series, vol. 3, no. 5. Albuquerque.

———. 1951. *The Ethnobotany of the Kayenta Navajo*. University of New Mexico Publication in Biology no. 5. Albuquerque.

Wymer, Dee Anne. 1990. "Archaeobotany." In *Childers and Woods: Two Late Woodland*

Sites in the Upper Ohio Valley, Mason County, West Virginia, edited by Michael J. Shott, 402–535. University of Kentucky Cultural Resource Assessment, Archaeological Report 200. Lexington: University of Kentucky.

Wynder, E. L. 1950. "Tobacco Smoking as a Possible Etiologic Factor in Bronchiogenic Carcinoma: A Study of 684 Proved Cases." *Journal of the American Medical Association* 143:329–346.

Yarnell, Richard A. 1964. *Aboriginal Relationships between Culture and Plant Life in the Upper Great Lakes Region*. Anthropological Papers of the Museum of Anthropology 3. Ann Arbor: University of Michigan.

———. 1977. "Native Plant Husbandry North of Mexico." In *Origins of Agriculture*, edited by Charles A. Redd, 861–878. Paris: Mouton.

———. 1989. "A Survey of Prehistoric Crop Plants in Eastern North America." In *New World Paleoethnobotany: Collected Papers in Honor of Leonard W. Blake*, edited by E. E. Voight and D. M. Pearsall, 47–59. *Missouri Archaeologist* 47.

Young, Alexander. 1844. *Chronicles of the Pilgrim Fathers of the Colony of Plymouth, from 1602 to 1625*. Boston: Charles C. Little and James Brown.

Young, Bennett R. 1910. *The Prehistoric Men of Kentucky*. Filson Club Publications 25. Louisville, Kentucky.

Young, Robert W., and William Morgan, Sr. 1987. *The Navajo Language*. Albuquerque: University of New Mexico Press.

Young, T. K. 1994. *The Health of Native Americans: Toward a Biocultural Epidemiology*. New York: Oxford University Press.

Zenk, Henry A. 1990a. "Kalapuyans." In *Handbook of North American Indians, vol. 7: Northwest Coast*, edited by Wayne Suttles, 547–553. Washington, D.C.: Smithsonian Institution.

———. 1990b. "Suislawans and Coosans." In *Handbook of North American Indians, vol. 7: Northwest Coast*, edited by Wayne Suttles, 572–579. Washington, D.C.: Smithsonian Institution.

Zigmond, Maurice L. 1981. *Kawaiisu Ethnobotany*. Salt Lake City: University of Utah Press.

———. "Kawaiisu." 1986. In *Handbook of North American Indians, vol. 11: Great Basin*, edited by Warren L. D'Azevedo, 398–411. Washington, D.C.: Smithsonian Institution.

# Contributors

❦

Mary J. Adair is associate curator at the Museum of Anthropology of the University of Kansas. Her research interests are primarily in central Great Plains paleo-ethnobotany, and she has worked over the years to establish the recognition of early agriculture and wild plant use in the prehistoric central plains.

Karen R. Adams, an archaeobotanist specializing in the prehistoric American Southwest, is a staff researcher for Crow Canyon Archaeological Center in Cortez, Colorado, and director of environmental studies for the Gila River Indian Community in Sacaton, Arizona. She is also an adjunct professor in anthropology at Lakehead University in Ontario, Canada, and a visiting scholar at the Arizona State Museum in Tucson.

Carol B. Brandt holds an M.S. in botany from Colorado State University and is a doctoral student in education at the University of New Mexico. She is exploring the use of ethnobiology as a vehicle for teaching math and science education.

Linda Scott Cummings is the director of Paleo Research in Golden, Colorado, and an adjunct professor in the Department of Anthropology at Colorado State University. Her primary research interest is the interpretation of prehistoric and historic subsistence activities, dietary patterns, and paleonutrition from archaeobotanical remains.

Glenna Dean is the New Mexico State Archaeologist with the Historic Preservation Division in Santa Fe. Her research interests range from prehistoric diet and archaeological pollen analysis to experimental archaeology and the technical analysis of textiles and other perishable artifacts.

Patricia Díaz-Romo has worked as a graphic and craft designer with nongovernmental organizations in Mexico, Guatamala, Nicaragua, and Africa on projects relating to cultural diversity and natural resource management and conservation. A founding member of the Research, Training, and Aid Association for the Wixarika (Huichol) people, she has been researching pesticide-associated health problems among the Huichol since 1986.

Jannifer W. Gish is a doctoral candidate in anthropology at the University of New Mexico. Since 1993 she has been the owner and director of Quaternary Palynology Research.

Julia E. Hammett, an anthropology instructor at Truckee Meadows Community College in Nevada, is also a research associate with the Stanford University Campus Archaeology Program and works for the Ohlone Indian Tribe in California. Her research specialties include paleoethnobotany, historical ecology, and environmental archaeology.

*Robert F. Hill* is a professor of pediatrics at the University of Oklahoma Health Science Center and director of evaluation at the Center on Child Abuse and Neglect at the Children's Hospital of Oklahoma. In 1993 he received the Governor's Commendation from the State of Oklahoma for his service to Oklahoma's youth on the Child and Adolescent Health Issues Committee of the Oklahoma Commission on Children and Youth.

*Richard G. Holloway*, a botanist, is the proprietor of Quaternary Service in Flagstaff, Arizona. He has more than 25 years of experience in pollen analysis, primarily in the U.S. Southwest and the Northwest Coast.

*Christina M. Pego* is a medical student at the University of Oklahoma. She is a member of the Saginaw Chippewa Indian Tribe and has been active in the Association of Native American Medical Students.

*Samuel Salinas Alvarez* is a sociologist and educator who has worked with indigenous groups as well as with urban and rural groups in Mexico in training projects, handicraft production, the recovery of oral tradition, and the traditional management of natural resources. He is a founding member of the Asociación Mexicana de Arte y Cultura Popular.

*Jonathan M. Samet, M.D.,* is a professor and chairman of the Department of Epidemiology of the Johns Hopkins University School of Hygiene and Public Health, where he is also director of the Institute for Global Tobacco Control. He has served on the science advisory board for the U.S. Environmental Protection Agency and as editor for reports of the U.S. Surgeon General on smoking and health.

*Lawrence A. Shorty*, of Diné (Navajo) and Mississippi Choctaw descent, is a graduate of the University of New Mexico Master's in Public Health Program. He was a founding member of the Traditional Native American Tobacco Seed Bank and Education Program at the University of New Mexico, and he maintains his own ceremonial tobacco growing program.

*Glenn W. Solomon* is the clinical epidemiologist for the Adolescent Medicine Section and the Pediatric Rhuematology Section of Children's Hospital in Oklahoma City. A Cherokee-Delaware from Ochelata, Oklahoma, he was one of the founders of the American Indian Historical Society and of WASSAJA, the national Indian newspaper, in 1970.

*Mollie S. Toll*, an archaeobotanist at the Museum of New Mexico in Santa Fe, was trained in both anthropology and plant ecology. She has worked on many archaeological projects and vegetation surveys in the American Southwest.

*Suzanne E. Victoria* is a computer programmer of Cherokee descent. She contributed to a chapter in this book while participating in a mentoring program with Robert Hill and Glenn Solomon during their Culture and Health Study at the Children's Hospital of Oklahoma.

*Alexander von Gernet* is an assistant professor of anthropology at the University of Toronto and editor-in-chief of *Ontario Archaeology*. He is often called to testify as an expert witness on ethnohistorical methodology in jurisdictions across Canada and the United States.

*Gail E. Wagner*, an associate professor of anthropology at the University of South Carolina, has worked as a paleoethnobotanist in India, Israel, the American Southwest, and eastern North America. She co-directs an archaeological project that studies the social and landscape dynamics of the late prehistoric chiefdom that controlled central South Carolina.

*Joseph C. Winter* is retired as professor of anthropology, director of the Traditional Native American Tobacco Seed Bank and Education Program, and director of the Office of Contract Archeology, all at the University of New Mexico. Currently he is the director of the Native American Plant Coalition in Albuquerque, New Mexico. Of mixed ancestry with white, Narragansett, Wampanoag, Pequot, and Mohegan blood, he spends most of his free time supplying Native American prison inmates with tobacco, sage, cedar, and other medicinal plants.

# Index

Page references to illustrations are in *italic* type.

Abashian, D. V., 317
Abenaki, 64
Achumawii, 32
Acoma Pueblo, 102, 150
Adair, Mary J., 171
Adams, Karen R., 143
Addiction, 74–78, 80, 283, 355, 358, 366;
    nicotine as source of, 305–308, 315, 325,
    326–27, 331–32, 334, 339–40, 368; role in
    domestication of tobacco, 4, 302, 305–306,
    309, 325, 327–28, 354
Adena peoples, 73
Africa, 3, 90, 186, 358
Akawaio, 308
Akehurst, B. C., 186
Akimel O'odham (Pima), 41, 44, 47, 94, 125,
    312. *See also* Hohokam
Alabama, 191
Alaska, 6, 9, 11–12, 12, 13, 92, 269;
    commercial tobacco use by Native
    Americans in, 334, 335, 336, 338, 365,
    375; *N. quadrivalvis* in, 6, 130, 315, 317,
    324. *See also* Haida; Tlingit
Alcohol use, 355, 366, 368
Aleut, 9, 266
Algoa site, 194
Algonkians, 60, 74, 75; in New England, 17; in
    North Carolina, 18, 62, 66, 67–68, 69, 72;
    in Virginia, 18, 63–64, 70, 71, 72, 78
Alkaloids, 8, 126, 168, 196, 317, 321–22,
    326–27, 328n.3, 328n.4, 368. *See also*
    Nicotine
Alvarez, Samuel Salinas, 342
American Bottom, 196, 197, 198
American Cancer Society, 332
American Indian Tobacco Education Network
    (AITEN), 37
Anabasine, 8, 126, 317, 321, 322

Anasazi, 108, 114, 153, 156–63, 168, 169, 227,
    259. *See also* Pueblos
Anderson, Arthur J. O., 300
Anderson, Edgar, 314
Anderson, R. E., 213–14
Animism, 72, 74
Anishinabe (Ojibway), 17, 108, 127
Apache, 44, 46, 177–78
Apalachee, 18
Apiaceae (Umbelliferae), 206
Arawak, 56–57, 93, 97
Archaeobotany, methods of, 4, 8n.1, 114, 115,
    152, 171, 185, 195, 200. *See also* Pollen;
    Seeds
Archaic period, 114, 153–55, 153, 195, 324
Arctic, 9, 11–12, 265, 266, 311–12, 365
Argentina, 104, 109, 127
Arikara, 20, 22, 23, 26, 173, 267, 286; *N.
    quadrivalvis* among the, 39, 117, 120, 129,
    136, 176–77, 182
Arizona, 110, 306, 338; archaeological sites in,
    108, 114, 143, 150, 152–53, 153, 155,
    156, 158, 159, 162–64, 164, 165, 166,
    168, 169, 223, 310; *N. attenuata* in, 108,
    114, 115, 140n.1, 144, 145, 315; *N.
    clevelandii* in, 144; *N. glauca* in, 144,
    170n.2, 326; *N. palmeri* in, 144; *N.
    rustica* in, 108; *N. tabacum* in, 93, 94, 95,
    325; *N. trigonophylla* in, 7, 124–25, 126,
    144, 164; Solanaceae in, 224–27, 257,
    258, 259. *See also* Pima (Akimel
    O'odham); Pueblos
Arkansas, 191, 195
Arroyo Hondo site, 222
Asch, David, 174
Asia, 11, 79, 93, 96, 186, 358; shamans in, 309,
    313–14, 315
Assiniboin, 176
Asteraceae, 208, 208
*Atlas del Tabaco en Mexico*, 55–56

*Atropa* (belladonna), 89
Atsugewi, 32
Attikamek (Tête de Boule), 13
Australia, 90, 93
Aztec, 53, 150, 265, 277; cigarettes among the, 300–301, 303, 305, 326; tobacco priests among the, 54, 267, 268, 292–93, 298–302, 299, 304n.11, 305, 345

Bahadur, Bir, 188
Baja California, 36, 122, 143, 144, 227
Bandelier National Monument, 168
Barrows, David, 36
Bartlett, S. A., 140n.4
Basketmaker period sites, 114, 152, 153–55, 153, 168, 169
Bauml, James, 277
BBB Motor site, 196
Bean, Lowell, 36
Beinhart, E. G., 108
Benítez Sánchez, José, 344, 344, 345
Benn, David, 179
Birds, 73, 80
Birks, H. J. B., 222
Blackfoot (Siksika), 9, 13, 26, 173, 267, 286, 362; commercial tobacco use among the, 365; *N. quadrivalvis* among the, 20, 22, 24–25, 120, 121, 177, 182
Blake, Leonard W., 177
Blum, R. W., 335
Bole-Maru cult, 32–33
Boley site, 181
Bolivia, 99
Boruca, 54
Boschert site, 194
Bourgmont, Etienne de, 175, 178
Bradbury, John, 176
Brandt, Carol, 45, 81
Brazil, 14, 66, 73, 110, 127, 186, 359, 360
Brewster site, 180
*Brickellia oblongifolia*, 273
British Columbia, 115, 134, 312, 314, 364
Bronchitis, chronic, 332, 340
Brooks, Jerome, 56
Brundage, Burr C., 298
*Buffalo Bird Woman's Garden*, 24
Bull Durham, 24, 362, 366, 369n.3
Bureau of Indian Affairs, 297
Burkemper 2 site, 190
Bye, Robert, 50

Caddo, 24
*Cahoba*, 56, 57
Cahokia ICT-II site, 196

Cahuilla, 6, 8, 36, 37, 41, 106, 110, 115, 120, 124
California, 28–37, 47, 65, 73, 138, 151, 153, 223, 271, 305, 312, 325, 327, 354; commercial tobacco use in, 364, 365, 379–80; Hoopa Valley in, 107, 130, 135, 136; *N. acuminata* in, 133; *N. attenuata* in, 30, 31–36, 92, 115, 132, 145, 314, 315, 324; *N. clevelandii* in, 8, 30, 36, 122, 128, 144, 315, 317, 324; *N. glauca* in, 7, 8, 30, 36, 106, 110, 133, 170n.2, 322, 326; *N. quadrivalvis* in, 6, 6, 30, 31–37, 106, 117, 118–20, 130, 132, 133, 134–35, 137–38, 172, 314, 315, 317, 324; *N. trigonophylla* in, 7, 30, 36, 106, 123, 124, 128, 314; Solanaceae in, 224–27. *See also* Hupa; Karok; Miwok; Pomo; Yurok
Calumet ceremony, 22, 59, 171, 174, 175, 176–77, 181–82. *See also* Pipes
Camden, William, 328
Campa, 307
Canada, 10, 269, 310, 325; commercial tobacco use in, 9, 354–55, 356, 358, 359, 364, 365; Hudson's Bay Company in, 12, 13, 14, 21–22, 359; *N. attenuata* in, 92, 113, 143, 324; *N. quadrivalvis* in, 22, 24–26, 121, 138, 315, 317; *N. rustica* in, 103, 172; *N. sylvestris* in, 126–27. *See also* Blackfoot (Siksika); Cree; Crow; Eastern Woodlands; Inuit (Eskimo); Montagnais; *and under specific regions and provinces*
Cancers, 265, 308, 332–33, 334, 336, 338, 339, 340, 354, 362, 364, 365, 370–74
*Capsicum*, 89; *Capsicum annuum*, 211–22, 212, 231, 255, 256; *Capsicum baccatum*, 231–32, 255
Capsules, 64, 139; in archaeological sites, 149–50, 151, 152, 166, 169, 195, 198–99, 310; dehiscent types, 104–105, 120; indehiscent types, 118, 120, 121, 129, 137, 138, 143, 149, 152, 199; of *N. attenuata*, 112, 149; of *N clevelandii*, 121, 150, 322; of *N. glauca*, 109, 150; of *N. quadrivalvis*, 116, 118, 119, 120, 175; of *N. rustica*, 98, 150, 198–99; of *N. tabacum*, 92, 150; of *N. trigonophylla*, 123, 149
ß-carbolines, 183
Carbon monoxide, 340
Cardiovascular diseases, 332–33, 334, 336, 338, 340, 362
Caribbean, 4–5, 9, 20, 56–57, 93, 95, 128, 325, 358
Caribs, 57
Carrillo, Tutukila, 344

Carter, George, 312

Cartier, Jacques, 59, 73

Casa Grande Pueblo, 152

Castetter, Edward, 102, 103, 108, 150

Catskill, 360

Cayuga, 16, 65, 69, 103, 281

Central America, 4, 18, 26, 31, 310, 314, 323, 325, 358. *See also* Huichol; Mesoamerica; Mexico

Cerebrovascular disease, 333, 338

Ceremonies and rituals: among the Aztec, 300–301, 303; calumet ceremony, 22, 171, 174, 175, 176–77, 181; among the Huichol, 32, 342–46, 342, 352; among the Iroquois (Haudenosaunee), 284; among the Navajo (Diné), 46, 269, 270–73, 275, 353; tobacco used in, 11, 13, 16, 17, 18, 19, 21, 22, 24, 26, 32–36, 39–40, 41, 44–45, 46, 49–50, 54–55, 57, 59, 79–80, 83, 114, 126–27, 151, 171, 175–76, 177–78, 182, 183, 198, 199, 200, 206, 265–66, 267, 290–92, 293, 305–306, 308, 312, 315, 326, 327, 339–40, 354, 359, 360, 362, 363, 366, 368, 369n.2; *toloache* cults, 34, 35, 36, 37, 44; World Renewal Ceremony, 31, 37, 265, 268, 292–93, 295–98

*Cestrum flavescens*, 236, 255, 256, 257

Chaco Canyon, 159

*Chamaesaracha*, 89, 89, 255, 256; *Chamaesaracha conioides*, 211–22, 212, 234; *Chamaesaracha coronopus*, 234–35, 255, 256

Champlain, Samuel de, 65

Chan-Ya-Ta site, 180

Chemehuevi, 39–40

Cherokee (Tsalagi), 18, 94, 108, 362, 365, 368

Cheyenne, 14, 21–22, 24, 172–73, 176, 366

Chihuahua, 143, 227, 326

Chilcotin, 13, 26, 115

Childers site, 195

Chile, 104

Chilula, 31

Chimariko, 31

China, 3, 186, 358

Chinook, 26, 28

Chippewa, 17, 308

Chloroplast DNA, 87, 88, 89, 90, 95

Chocho, 55

Choctaw, 18, 362

Chontal, 110

Chorti Maya, 55

Chronic obstructive pulmonary disease, 332–33, 336, 340, 354, 364

Chumash, 35–36, 110, 122, 127n.4

Cigarettes, 3, 5, 50, 54, 55, 128, 269; in archaeological sites, 150, 156, 164, 168, 169; among the Aztec, 300–301, 303, 305, 326; cane cigarettes, 7, 34, 40, 97, 151, 156; commercial manufacture of, 9, 35, 95, 108, 114–15, 208, 209, 277–78, 327, 331, 332, 333, 334–39, 354, 362, 365, 366, 375–81, 385; corn-husk cigarettes, 4, 7, 21, 24, 44, 206–207, 270, 273, 276, 327, 383, 384; among the Zuni, 81–83, 82

Cigars, 3, 5, 47, 47, 53, 55, 56, 57, 73, 95, 128, 207, 209, 331, 332, 340

Cihuacoatl, 268, 298–302, 299, 303, 304n.11, 309

*Cleome* (Rocky Mountain beeweed) pollen, 205, 206, 206

Cluster analyses, 219–21

Coalescent Indian School site, 181

Coca, 315

Cochiti Pueblo, 44, 99, 101, 102, 103, 108, 150

Cocopa, 36

Coe, Michael D., 300

Collings, P. R., 277, 307

Colombia, 105, 127

Colorado, 114, 177; archaeological sites in, 143, 144, 153, 153, 154, 156, 156, 157, 159, 159, 160, 164, 166, 168, 169, 205–10, 222, 223; Solanaceae in, 224–27, 257–58, 258, 259

Colorado River valley, 122

Columbus, Christopher, 3, 4–5, 56, 331, 332, 341n.1, 358

Comanche, 20, 21, 172–73

Connecticut, 14, 65

Conoy, 73

Coosan, 28

Cora, 54

*Cornus amomum* (red dogwood), 175

Coronado, Francisco Vázquez de, 173–74

Coronary heart diseases, 332–33, 334, 336, 338

Costanoan, 33–34

Costa Rica, 52, 267

*Costumbre*, 342, 343

Coultas, D. B., 365

Cowlitz, 360

Coyote's tobacco. *See Nicotiana trigonophylla*

Craddock Shelter site, 195

Cree, 13, 14, 105, 173, 176, 177

Creek, 18

Cronquist, A., 129

Crow, 26, 79, 176, 183, 292; *N. quadrivalvis* among the, 6, 20, 25, 118, 138, 140n.4, 182, 286, 287, 287, 291; tobacco-related myths among the, 288, 289, 309; tobacco-related trade among the, 176, 177, 286; tobacco societies among the, 22, 24, 120, 136, 137, 177, 267–68, 286–92, 287, 302

Cuartelejo, 177–78

Cuba, 56, 186

Cuicatec, 54

Cummings, Linda Scott, 114, 115–16, 205, 222

Cuna, 52–53, 265, 267, 353

Cunningham site, 194

Cushing, Frank H., 81

Cutler, Hugh C., 177

Dance for the Dead, 35

D'Arcy, William, 87, 88, 89, 90

Datura, 31, 39–40, 50, 57, 89, 196, 227, 254, 256, 266, 281, 298, 315; *Datura innoxia*, 228–29, 255; *Datura meteloides*, 211–22, 212, 229, 255; *Datura quercifolia*, 228–29, 255; and tobacco, 3, 34, 35, 36, 114; *toloache* cults, 34, 35, 36, 37, 44

Davis, Sally M., 365

Davis, William, 110

Dean, Glenna, 211, 227, 256

De Bry, Theodore, 64, 66

Delaware (Leni Lenape), 18, 60, 67, 71, 172–73

Delaware (state), 18, 186

De Mézèires, Athanase, 174, 175

Dene-Métis, 365

Denmark, 12, 359

Desenclos, J., 338

Dew Eagle society, 285–86

DeWolf, Gordon, 6, 117

Diaz, J. L., 277, 307

Díaz-Romo, Patricia, 342

Dibble, Charles E., 300

Diegueño (Kumeyaay), 36, 106, 110, 115, 124, 126, 322

Diné (Navajo), 44, 46, 110, 112, 115, 166, 267, 268–75, 272, 307–308, 326, 381, 385; balance among the, 367, 382, 383; ceremonies using tobacco among the, 46, 126, 269, 270–73, 275, 353; commercial tobacco use among the, 328n.1, 335, 365; myths among the, 269–70, 269, 273, 275, 302, 309

Discriminant analyses, 213–19, 222

Diseases, tobacco-related, 37, 297–98, 305, 326, 328n.4, 331–41; cancers, 265, 332–33, 334, 336, 338, 339, 340, 354, 362, 364, 365, 370–74; cardiovascular diseases, 332–33, 334, 336, 338, 340, 362; cerebrovascular diseases, 333, 338; chronic bronchitis, 332, 340; chronic obstructive pulmonary disease, 332–33, 336, 340, 354,

364; coronary heart diseases, 332–33, 334, 336, 338; green tobacco sickness, 349, 351; ischemic heart diseases, 336, 340; lung cancer, 308, 332–33, 334, 336, 340, 354, 362, 364, 365, 370–74; among Native Americans, 4, 24, 254, 302–303, 305, 308, 327, 334–41, 341n.2, 349, 362, 364–66, 368, 370–76, 385; respiratory diseases, 332–33, 336, 337, 338, 340, 354, 364

Dodoens, Rembert, 64, 186

Dolores Archaeological Project, 114–15, 205–10, 222

Dominican Republic, 195, 222

Double Butte Cave site, 96–97, 168

Douglas, David, 25, 107, 117, 120, 129, 130, 136, 140n.4

Downs, James, 39

Drake, Sir Francis, 34, 65

Driver, Harold, 312

Dunbar, John, 175, 183

Eastern Woodlands, 9, 14–20, 189, 281, 283–86, 306–307, 312; *N. rustica* in, 4, 18, 47, 98–99, 104, 105, 108, 128, 172, 182, 185–86, 189–200, 310, 324, 358, 360; tobacco-related trade in, 360, 361

Ecuador, 99, 104, 105, 307

Egypt, 3

Elmendorf, W. W., 307

El Salvador, 110

England, 3, 14, 59, 64, 65, 69, 70, 93, 186, 358

Equatorial diameter, 211

Erdtman, G., 211, 227

Eshbaugh, W. H., 211, 221, 227, 256

Eskimo (Inuit), 9, 11–12, 12, 13, 79, 265, 266, 354, 359, 365

Espejo, Antonio de, 66

Esselen, 33–34

Europe, tobacco use in, 2, 3, 59, 65, 69, 70, 93, 96, 99, 128, 144, 186, 328, 332, 341n.1, 358

Faegri, K., 211, 212

*False Faces of the Iroquois*, 286

False Face society, 14, 14, 16, 57n.1, 267, 281, 283–86, 308

Farooqui, S. M., 188

Felger, Richard, 53

Fenton, William, 286

Fewkes, Jesse Walter, 152

Field, W. T., 175

Fisher, Edwin B, Jr., 306

Fish Lake site, 194, 198

Florentine Codex, 300

Florida, 14, 73, 186
Ford, Richard, 108, 144, 169, 312
Fortier, Andrew, 196
Fortuna, Luis, 222
Fowler, Catherine, 39, 40–41
Fox (tribe), 17, 108, 308
Freire-Marreco, Barbara, 206–207
Fritz, Gayle, 198
Furst, Peter T., 79
Fur trade, 359–60, 366

Gabrielino, 35–36, 110
Gadd, Morgan, 138
Gaffney, Frederick, 188, 189
Galice, 28
*General History of the Things of New Spain*, 300
Gerard, John, 64, 69
Germany, 3
Ghost Dance, 33, 34, 40
Gila River Cave, 168
*Gilia longifolia*, 273
Gilmore, Melvin, 129, 138, 140n.4, 360; on *N. quadrivalvis*, 136, 137, 174, 175, 176–77
Gish, Jannifer, 140nn.2,4, 223
Goddard, Pliny Earle, 137
Goggin, John, 24
Goodspeed, Thomas, 99, 101, 120, 122, 123, 127, 129, 132, 135, 255; on distribution of tobacco species, 90, 91, 92, 110, 151, 314; on tobacco phylogeny, 87, 88, 89, 117, 118–19, 126
Gosiute, 37, 115, 314
Gourds, tobacco, 53, 54, 278, 279, 344–45, 345
Great Basin, 9, 28, 37–41, 47, 312, 314, 325; *N. attenuata* in, 6, 41, 92, 114, 115, 128, 138, 143, 172, 314, 324; *N. quadrivalvis* in, 41, 117, 119, 138, 314, 324
Great Bend aspect, 173, 174, 181
Great Lakes region, 183, 308
Great Plains, 9, 13, 20–24, 39, 113, 171–84, 267, 312; archaeological tobacco on, 178–82, 178, 195; commercial tobacco use on, 334, 336, 364, 378; *N. attenuata* on, 172, 177, 182, 186; *N. quadrivalvis* on, 20, 22, 24, 117, 120, 137, 138, 172, 174, 175, 176–77, 180, 182–83, 186; *N. rustica* on, 172, 176, 177, 179, 180–81, 182, 183
Green, William, 174
Greenland, 11, 12, 359
Green tobacco sickness, 349, 350
Ground cherry. *See Physalis*
Guarijio (Waijio), 49, 50
Guatemala, 93. *See also* Mesoamerica

Gullick, C. J. M. R., 57
Gunby site, 198
Gunn, Charles, 188, 189
Guyana Indians, 308
Gwich'in, 13, 14, 269

Habenapo Pomo, 33
Haberman, Thomas, 108, 120, 180, 181, 183, 189
Hahn, R. A., 338
Haida, 6, 13, 24–27, 120, 121, 137
Hair, J. F., 213–14
Haire–Joshu, Debra, 306
Hall, Elihu, 130, 132
Hall, Pat, 110, 115, 118, 120, 122, 223
Hamilton, William, 129
Hammett, Julia E., 105, 108, 117, 118, 128, 315
Handelman, Don, 41
Handsome Lake, 285
Hare, 14
Hariot, Thomas, 69, 186
Harrington, H. D., 258
Harrington, John P., 31, 118–19, 136, 206–207, 297, 302
Harrison, William, 59
Haudenosaunee (Iroquois), 9, 13, 59, 65, 68, 71, 73, 74, 78, 79, 102, 103, 103, 107, 108, 360, 361; False Face society among, 14, 14, 16, 57n.1, 267, 281, 283–86, 308; myths among the, 16, 282, 283; shamans among the, 16
Havasupai, 115, 124, 125, 126, 145
Hawkes, J. G., 255
Hays site, 194
Health risks. *See* Diseases, tobacco-related
Heiser, Charles, 314
Hellson, John, 138
Henbane. *See Hyoscyamus*
Heterosis, 143, 151
Hidatsa, 22–24, 26, 108, 173, 174, 181, 183, 267, 287, 288, 292; *N. quadrivalvis* among the, 6, 20, 22, 39, 120, 136, 176–77, 182; tobacco-related trade among the, 286, 291, 292
Hill, Robert F., 353
Hispaniola, 97, 358
Hogan, Patrick, 39, 314
Hohokam, 96–97, 108, 115, 125, 164, 165, 168, 169, 227. *See also* Pima (Akimel O'odham)
Holloway, Richard G., 211, 227, 256
Holmgren, A. H., 129
Holmgren, N. H., 129
Holmgren, P. K., 129

Hoopa Valley, *107*, 130, 135, 136
Hopewell peoples, 73, 181
Hopi, 44, 45, 114, 115, 125–26, 269, 270
Hovenweep site, 114, 222
Huastec, 53–54
Hudson's Bay Company, 12, *13*, 14, 21–22, 359
Huichol, 108, 110, 127, 302, 307, 317, 325,
    326, 342–52; ceremonies among the, 32,
    342–46, *342*, *352*; as migrant laborers, 4, 6,
    94, 276, 303, 342, 346–52, *348*, *350*;
    myths among the, 278–79, *278*, 280–81,
    309, 343, 344–45, *344*; and pesticides, 276,
    342–43, 347, 348, 349, 350–52; peyote
    among the, 276, 277, 278, 279–80, 281,
    343; tobacco shamanism among the, 50,
    52, 267, 275–81, 343. *See also*
    Mesoamerica; Mexico
Huitzilopchtli, 300, 301
Hulton, Paul, 64
Hupa, 31, 118, 136, 137, 268, 292–93, 294,
    295–98
Huron, 9, 61, 67, 69, 70, 71, 72, 75–76, 78,
    105, 108, 126–27; tobacco-related trade
    among the, 13, 16–17
Hybridization, 143, 151
*Hyoscyamus*, 89; *Hyoscyamus luteus*, 64; *Hyo-*
    *scyamus niger*, 211–12, *212*, 230, 255, 256

Ichcatec, 54
Idaho, 6, 365, 376
Illinois (state), 65, 105, 108, 182, 185, 191, 194,
    196, 197, 310
Illinois (tribe), 17, 22, 108
Imperial Tobacco Company, 14
India, 3
Indiana, 108, 192
*Inipi*, 40
*The Intermountain Flora*, 129
Inuit (Eskimo), 9, 11–12, *12*, *13*, 79, 265, 266,
    354, 359, 365
Inyeri, 57
Iowa, 108, 179, 180, 181, 182, 192
Iroquois (Haudenosaunee), 9, 13, 59, 65, 68, 71,
    73, 74, 78, 79, 102, 103, *103*, *107*, 108,
    360, 361; False Face society among, 14, *14*,
    16, 57n.1, 267, 281, 283–86, 308; myths
    among the, 16, 282, 283; shamans among
    the, 16
Isleta Pueblo, 101, 102, 103, 115, 124, 150
Itiba Cahubaba, 57
Iversen, J., 211, 212

Jalisco, 275
Jamestown, Va., 93, 99, 186, 358

Japan, 3, 186
Jefferson, Thomas, 129
Jemez Pueblo, 99, 102, 150, 269
Jepson, W. L., 110, 124
*The Jepson Manual: Higher Plants of California*,
    124
Jicaque, 54
Jimsonweed. *See* Datura
Jivaro, 307
Johannessen, Sissel, 198
Jones, Volney, 66, 108, 126, 152, 314
Josselyn, John, 65

Kachina cults, 267, 293
Kalapuya, 26, 28
Kamia, 36
Kansa, 175, 178
Kansas, 172, 173, 175, 177–78, 181, 192
Kapp, Ronald, 227
Karok, 31, 32, 73, 136–37, 268, 292–93,
    295–98
Kartesz, John, 223–24
Kartesz, Rosemarie, 223–24
Kawaiisu, 37, 40–41, 115
Kentucky, 192, 195
Khionontaternon, 16–17, 67, 72, 108
Kickapoo, 18–20, 24
Kiowa, 20–21, 24
Kitanemuk, 34, 35
Kitzihiat, 19–20
Koop, C. Everett, 306
Kootenay, 26, 27–28, 115, 360
Kroeber, A. L., 137–38, 267, 293, 307
Kuksu, 33, 267
Kumeyaay (Diegueño), 36, 106, 110, 115, 124,
    126, 322
Kutenai, 26, 27–28, 115, 360
Kwakiutl, 27

La Barre, Weston, 362
Lacandon Maya, 46, 55
La Harpe, J. B. Bénard, Sieur de, 174
Lakota (Sioux), 9, 20, 22, 173, 176, 292, *292*,
    304n.8, 362
Lalemant, Jérôme, 78
Lanning, Edward, 310
Las Casas, Bartolomé de, 3, 56
Lassik, 31
La Vérendrye, Sieur de, 176
Lawson, John, 305, 306
Leingang site, 194
Le Jeune, Paul, 78
Leni Lenape (Delaware), 18, 60, 67, 71, 172–73
Lescarbot, Marc, 65, 70

Lesser Antilles, 57
Lester, R. N., 255
Lewis, Henry, 31
Lewis and Clark Expedition, 22, 24, 39, 120, 129, *129*, 176
Lichtenstein, Edward, 306
Light microscope (LM) photography, 227, 228, 254, 255–56
Lillooet, 26, 27, 115
Linnaeus, Carolus, 65
Linton, Ralph, 151
Little Hills site, 194
Long Island, 17
López de la Torre, Rafael Pateyo, 345, 346
*Lophophora williamsii. See* Peyote
Louisiana, 192, 198
Lower Loup (Itskari), 175
Lowie, Robert H., 137, 138, 288, 290, 291
Luiseño, 35, 36, 122
Lumholtz, Carl, 344, 345
Lung cancer, 308, 332–33, 334, 336, 340, 354, 362, 364, 365, 370–74
*Lycium*, 89, *89*, 145; *Lycium andersonii*, 237, 255–57, 258; *Lycium barbarum*, 259; *Lycium berlandieri*, 258–59; *Lycium pallidum*, 211–22, *212*, 237–38, 255–57, 258, 259; *Lycium torreyi*, 237–39, *238*; vs. tobacco, 205, 228, 255–61
*Lycopersicon* (tomato), 89

Machu Picchu, 97
M.A.D. site, 179, 190
Maha (Omaha), 176–77
Mahhaha site, 177, 181
Mahigan, 61, 108, 360
Maidu, 32, 115
Maine, 14, 20
Mandan, 26, 173, 183, 267, 286; *N. quadrivalvis* among the, 6, 20, 22, 39, 117, 120, 136, 176–77, 182
*Mandragora* (mandrake), 89
*Manitous*, 17, 18, 19–20, 308
*Margaranthus*, 89, *89*; *Margaranthus purpurascens*, 211–22, *212*; *Margaranthus solanaceus*, 235, 255, 256, 257
Marigold, 277, 281
Marquette, Père Jacques, 22
Martínez, Fray Alonso, 174
Maryland, 186
Mascouten, 17
Massachusett, 17
Matthews, Meredith, 114, 126
Mattole, 31–32
Maximilian of Weid, 176

Maya, 46–47, 53, 54, 93, *93*, 94, 268, 308. *See also* Huichol
Mayes, Vernon, 110
*Mayflower*, 64
Mazatec, 54
Medicine societies, tobacco use by, 265, 267, 281, 283–86, 292, 302
Meilleur, Brien, 26, 117, 136
Mems site, 174, 181
Menominee, 17
Meridian Hills site, 190
Mescal, 266
Mesoamerica, 9, 10, 46–56, *47*, *53*, 74, 93, *93*, 95, 99, 267, 271, 305. *See also* Central America; Huichol; Mexico
Mexico, *10*, 26, 28, 31, 36, 90, 126, 127, 143, 310, 322–23; migrant Indian laborers in, 4, 276, 303, 342, 346–52, 348, *350*; *N. attenuata* in, 5, 6, 315, 317, 355, 358; *N. clevelandii* in, 5, 8, 122, 144, 324; *N. glauca* in, 5, 8, 110, 322, 326; *N. rustica* in, 4, 5, 41, 45, 103, 104, *106*, *107*, 108, 128, 135, 172, 185, 200, 312, 325, 344–46; *N. tabacum* in, 5, 6, 19, 20, 41, 53, 94, 312, 325–26, 346–52, 358; *N. trigonophylla* in, 5, 123, 124, 324, 355, 358; Solanaceae in, 224–27; tobacco priests in, 268, 292–93, 298–302, *299*, 305; tobacco shamanism in, 267, 275–81. *See also* Huichol; Mesoamerica
Mézèires, Athanase de, 174, 175
Miami, 17
Michigan, 192, 198, 199
Micmac, 61, 65, 67, 70, 71, 72, 74, 76, 79
Middle Missouri period, 108
Midewiwin, 267
Midwest, 108, 267
Migrant Indian laborers, 4, 6, 94, 276, 303, 342, 346–52, 348, *350*
Miksicek, Charles, 108
Mill Creek sites, 179, 180
Millipede site, 180
Minnesota, 65, 192, 365
Miskito, 52, 267
Mississippian period, 108, 180, 182, 191, 192; George Reeves phase, 194, 197; Lindemann phase, 197; Lohmann phase, 196, 197; Stirling phase, 196–97, 198
Mississippi River valley, 108, 201n.4, 310, 324, 358
Missouri (state), 179, 180, 182, 190, 192, 194, 196, 198
Missouri River valley, 26, 178, 201n.4; *N. quadrivalvis* in, 6, 20, 22, 117, 120, 121,

129, 136, 139, 172, 176, 312, 317, 324.
   *See also* Arikara; Crow; Hidatsa; Mandan
Mitchell site, 179, 180
Miwok, 33, 34, 39, 65, 115, 140n.4, 267
Mixe, 55
Mixtec, 55
Moctezuma, 301
Mogollon, 227
Mohave (tribe), 44, 115, 125, 306
Mohawk, 16, 61–62, 77–78, 103, 281, 382
Mohegan, 18
Monardes, Nicolás, 66
Monckton, Stephen, 198
Mono, 39
Montagnais, 13, 62, 69–70, 72, 76–77, 78,
   306–07
Montana, 27–28, 79, 140n.4, 172, 360, 364,
   365, 378
Montauk, 17
Moore, Michael, 110
Mopan Maya, 93, 94
Morgues, Jacques Le Moyne de, 73
Morning-glory seeds, 266, 298
Morris, Elizabeth Ann, 314
Mortland Island site, 194
Moser, Mary, 53
Mountain tobacco. *See Nicotiana attenuata*
Mukat, 36
Mund site, 194
Mundurucu, 308
Murray, Charles, 175
Murry, L. E., 211, 221, 227, 256
Myer's Road site, 198
Myths, 22–24, 26–27, 34–35, 44, 46–47, 53,
   57, 328, 382–83, 384, 385; among the
   Crow, 288, 289, 309; among the Huichol,
   278–79, 278, 280–81, 309, 343, 344–45,
   344; among the Iroquois (Haudenosaunee),
   16, 282, 283, 309; among the Karok,
   136–37; among the Kickapoo, 19–20, 309;
   among the Navajo (Diné), 269–70, 269,
   273, 275, 302, 309; among the Yurok, 31,
   87, 293, 295–96, 308, 309

Nanticoke, 18
Naples-Abbot site, 190
Narragansett, 17, 63, 67, 70, 78
Naskapi, 74
Natchez, 18
Native American Church, 24, 362, 366, 369n.3
Native American Plant Cooperative (NAPC),
   58n.2, 94, 95, 368, 369n.2; *N. attenuata*
   examples at, 116; *N. quadrivalvis* examples
   at, 117; *N. trigonophylla* examples at, 126

Native Americans: altered states of consciousness desired by, 39, 73, 74, 79, 99, 183,
   265–66, 302, 324–25, 326, 340–41, 354;
   commercial tobacco used by, 9, 24, 26, 27,
   35, 46, 53, 81–82, 83, 108, 126, 138, 151,
   266, 271, 273, 276–77, 297–98, 303n.1,
   327, 328n.1, 334–39, 354–57, *354*,
   359–60, 361, 362, 364–66, 368, 375–81,
   385; tobacco-related diseases among, 4, 24,
   254, 302–303, 305, 308, 327, 334–41,
   341n.2, 349, 362, 364–66, 368, 370–76,
   385. *See also under specific regions and
   groups/tribes*
Navajo (Diné), 44, 46, 110, 112, 115, 166, 267,
   268–75, 272, 307–308, 326, 381, 385;
   balance among the, 367, 382, 383;
   ceremonies using tobacco among the, 46,
   126, 269, 270–73, 275, 353; commercial
   tobacco use among the, 328n.1, 335, 365;
   myths among the, 269–70, 269, 273, 275,
   302, 309
Nayarit, 275, 276, *276*, 342, 346, 347, 351
Nebraska, 172, 175–76, 177, 179, 180
Negrín, Juan, 347
Nelson, Nels C., 105, 108
Neutral, 16–17, 62, 67, 108
Nevada, 33, *107*, 114, 115, 124, 144;
   Solanaceae in, 224–27
New Brunswick, 20, 70
Newcomb, W. W., 175
New England, 17–18, 64, 65
New Mexico, 315, 338; archaeological sites in,
   114, 115, 143, 150, 152, 153, *153*, 154–55,
   156, 157–58, 159, *159*, 160–62, 164, *164*,
   165, 166, 167, 168, 169, 223, 310;
   commercial tobacco use in, 364; *N.
   attenuata* in, 7, 106, 108, 114, 115, 140n.1;
   *N. rustica* in, 5, 45, 46, 66, 102–103, 108;
   *N. trigonophylla* in, 7, 7, 124–25, *124*,
   140n.1; Solanaceae in, 211–22, 224–27,
   258, 259, *259*. *See also* Apache; Navajo
   (Diné); Pueblos
Newsom, Lee, 195
New York State, 14, 20, 65, 103, 108, 192, 281
New Zealand, 93
*Nicandra physalodes*, 229–30, 255, 256
Nicaragua, 52, 267
*Nicotiana acuminata*, 135, 251–52, 255–57; var.
   *multiflora*, 133, 320
*Nicotiana alata*, 8, 127, 254, 316, 317, 318,
   321, 326
*Nicotiana attenuata*, 24, 26, 27–28, 31, 32, 33,
   35, 36, 41, 81–83, 88, 110, 116, 127, 177,
   182, 269, 271, 272–73, 326, 355, 358;

archeological sites related to, 108, 114–15,
150, 152, 164, 168, 205–10, 222, 258, 310;
capsules, 112, 149; cultivation, 39, 45,
113–14, 119–20, 134, 140n.3, 150, 151,
172, 312; description, 6–7, 7, 46, 106,
110–12, 112, 272, 353; and fire, 39, 138,
144–45, 315; nicotine content, 126, 315,
316, 317; pollen, 205–10, 228, 239, 240,
255–61; range, 5, 6, 13, 30, 43, 90, 92, 96,
112–13, 113, 132, 133, 140n.1, 143, 144,
172, 173, 258, 311, 312, 314–15, 317, 324;
seeds, 107, 108, 112, 114, 115, 120, 145,
146, 147, 147, 148, 149, 186, 187, 189,
205, 210

Nicotiana benavidesii, 105

Nicotiana bigelovii. See Nicotiana quadrivalvis,
var. bigelovii

Nicotiana clevelandii, 30, 36, 53, 88, 90, 126,
128; capsules, 121, 150, 322; description,
121–22, 122; nicotine content, 315, 316,
317, 318, 320, 321; pollen, 252, 255–61;
range, 5, 8, 50, 51, 122, 123, 132, 134,
144, 311, 314, 315, 317, 324; seeds, 146,
147, 147, 148

Nicotiana glauca, 7, 33, 35, 36, 49–50, 53, 88,
105, 127, 127n.4; archeological sites related
to, 110; capsules, 109, 150; description, 8,
106, 108–109, 109; nicotine content, 316,
317, 318, 320, 321, 322; pollen, 211–22,
212, 250–51, 255–61; range, 5, 7–8, 30,
43, 50, 51, 109–10, 111, 133–34, 135, 144,
311, 312, 322, 323, 326; seeds, 109, 110,
145, 146, 147, 148, 148, 149

Nicotiana glutinosa, 95

Nicotiana knightiana, 105

Nicotiana langsdorffii, 127, 316, 317, 318, 321

Nicotiana longifolia, 320

Nicotiana multivalvis. See Nicotiana
quadrivalvis, var. multivalvis

Nicotiana nesophilia, 320

Nicotiana nudicaulis, 320

Nicotiana obtusifolia. See Nicotiana
trigonophylla

Nicotiana otophora, 95, 321, 322

Nicotiana palmeri, 170n.1, 269, 271; capsules,
149–50; nicotine content, 316, 318, 320;
pollen, 252–53, 255–61; range, 126, 128,
132, 143, 144, 322, 324; seeds, 146, 147,
147, 148

Nicotiana paniculata, 103, 105, 321, 324

Nicotiana pulmonariodies, 105

Nicotiana quadrivalvis, 34, 37, 88, 110, 115–22,
128–32, 201n.4; archeological sites related
to, 118, 119, 120, 182; capsules, 116, 118,

119, 120, 175; among the Crow, 6, 20, 25,
118, 138, 140n.4, 182, 286, 287, 287, 291;
cultivation, 20, 28, 31, 32, 39, 118, 120,
129, 131, 132, 134–39, 140nn.3,4, 174,
175, 176–77, 182–83, 287, 290–91, 312,
317, 324; description, 6, 115–17, 118, 119,
120, 121, 129, 130, 132, 287, 294;
domestication, 129, 132, 134, 139, 324,
353, 369n.1; nicotine content, 183, 287,
292, 315, 316, 318, 321; pollen, 246–50,
255–61; range, 5, 6, 8, 24–25, 30, 43, 90,
96, 118, 119, 120, 132, 140n.1, 172, 173,
182–84, 311, 314–15, 316, 317, 322, 324;
seeds, 107, 108, 116, 117, 118–19, 118,
120–21, 121, 129–30, 137, 138, 139, 182,
186, 187, 189, 199; var. bigelovii, 5, 6, 25,
30, 31, 33, 117, 118–19, 118, 119, 120,
128–29, 132, 132, 134–35, 137, 140n.4,
246–48, 255–57, 261n.1, 311, 316, 317,
318; var. multivalvis, 5, 6, 22, 24–27, 117,
118, 119, 120–21, 121, 128–30, 129, 130,
132, 134–36, 138–39, 140n.4, 172, 173,
177, 182, 247–49, 255–57, 286, 287, 311,
312, 314, 317, 324; var. quadrivalvis, 5, 6,
22, 24, 25–26, 108, 117, 118, 119, 120,
128–30, 134–36, 138–39, 172, 173, 177,
180, 182, 286, 291, 311, 312, 314, 316,
317, 318, 324; var. wallacei, 5, 6, 6, 30, 35,
36, 41, 106, 119, 119, 120, 128–29, 132,
132, 246–47, 255–57, 311

Nicotiana repanda, 54, 320

Nicotiana rustica, 3, 54, 88, 127, 279, 280–81,
282, 284, 285, 286, 300; archeological sites
related to, 105, 108, 144, 152, 177, 179,
180–81, 182, 183, 201, 258; capsules, 98,
150, 198–99; cultivation, 14, 14, 16–17,
18, 20, 35, 41, 45, 46, 46, 49, 66–70, 79,
93, 96, 98–103, 104, 144, 150, 181, 199,
276–77, 312, 324–26; description, 4, 5, 17,
97–98, 99, 101, 102, 103, 106; domestication, 4, 14, 20, 90, 98–99, 104, 105, 152,
169, 254, 261, 265, 302, 305, 309–10, 317,
324–26, 353, 358; among the Huichol,
344–46; nicotine content, 99, 183, 277,
302, 307, 316, 317, 318–19, 320–21,
324–26, 327, 358; vs. N. tabacum, 99, 105,
108, 144, 185–86, 277, 325, 346, 349, 360;
origins, 103–104, 144; pollen, 228, 241–44,
254, 255–61; preparation, 70–71;
psychoactive effects of, 74, 99; punche de
Mexicano, 5, 45, 102–103, 103; range, 5,
43, 50, 51–52, 56, 65–66, 91, 98–99, 104,
104, 144, 172, 173, 182–84, 258, 310, 311,
312, 314–15, 317, 323, 324–26; seeds, 98,

101, *107*, 108, 118, 120, 130, 145, *146*,
147, *148*, 149, 169, 182, 186–89, 198–99;
var. *brasilia*, 99, *99*; var. *pavonii*, 99, *102*,
*102*, 103, 104–105, *192*, 310; var. *pumila*,
99, *103*; var. *texana*, 103

*Nicotiana sylvestris*, 95, 96, 252–53, 255–57,
326; nicotine content, 319, 321, 322, 327;
range, 8, 126–27

*Nicotiana tabacum*, 3, 53, 54, 88, 92–97, 300;
archeological sites related to, 96–97, *98*;
capsules, 92, *150*; as commercial tobacco,
4, 6, 27, 46, 65, 92–95, *93*, 151, 186, 271,
346–52, 358–60, 361; cultivation, 18–19,
20, 41, 46, 49, 53, 57, 92–93, 95–96, *96*,
*98*, 144, 150, 174–75, 277, 312, 325–26,
346–52; description, 5, 6, *53*, 92, *92*, *93*,
*94*, *106*; domestication, 4–5, 20, 90, 152,
254, 261, 265, 302, 305, 309–10, 317,
325–26, 353, 358; nicotine content, 277,
302, 307, 316, 317, 319, 320–21, 322,
325–26, 327, 358, 360; vs. *N. rustica*, 99,
105, 108, 144, 185–86, 277, 325, 346, 349,
360; pollen, *195*, 222, 244–46, 254,
255–61; range, 5, 14, 43, 50, 52, 56, 65,
91, 93, 95, *96*, 98, 99, 128, 144, 186, 311,
314, 317, 323, 325–26, 358; seeds, 92, *118*,
*146*, 148, *148*, 149, 186, *187*, 199; var.
*havanensis*, 56; var. *Orinoco*, *93*, 186, 358

*Nicotiana tomentosiformis*, 95, 321, 322

*Nicotiana trigonophylla*, 36, 41, 45, 49, 53, 88,
110, 122–26; archeological sites related to,
108, 124, *168*; capsules, *123*, *149*;
cultivation, 124, 150, 312; description, 7, *7*,
*106*, 122–23, *124*; nicotine content, 126,
316, 317, 319, 320, 321, 322, 368; pollen,
228, 240–41, 255–61; range, 5, 7, 30, 43,
50, 52, 90, 96, 123–24, *125*, 134, 140n.1,
143, 144, 258, 311, 312, 314–15, 324, 355,
358; seeds, 145, 146, *147*, 148, 149,
149–50; var. *palmeri*, 126, 128, 132, 143,
144, *146*, 147, *147*, *148*, 149–50, 170n.1,
252–53, 255–57, 269, 271, 316, 318, 320,
324; var. *trigonophylla*, 128, 132

*Nicotiana undulata*, 103, 105, 321, 324

Nicotine, 8, 52, 95, 150, 151, 168, 169, 195,
317–22; as addictive, 305–308, 315, 325,
326–27, 331–32, 334, 339–40, 368; in *N.
alata*, 316, 317, 318, 321; in *N. attenuata*,
126, 315, 316, 317; in *N. clevelandii*, 315,
316, 317, 318, 320, 321; in *N. glauca*, 316,
317, 318, 320, 321, 322; in *N. langsdorffii*,
316, 317, 318, 321; in *N. otophora*, 321,
322; in *N. palmeri*, 316, 318, 320; in *N.
quadrivalvis*, 183, 287, 292, 315, 316, 317,
318, 321; in *N. rustica*, 99, 183, 277, 302,
307, 316, 317, 318–19, 320–21, 324–26,
327, 358; in *N. sylvestris*, 319, 321, 322,
327; in *N. tabacum*, 277, 302, 307, 316,
317, 319, 320–21, 322, 325–26, 327, 358,
360; in *N. tomentosiformis*, 321, 322; in *N.
trigonophylla*, 126, 316, 317, 319, 320,
321, 322, 368; in *N. undulata*, 321;
psychoactive effects of, 74, 99, 126, 183,
265–66, 277, 304n.9, 305, 306, 308, 317,
325, 326, 334, 339, 340–41, 368

Nightshade. *See* Solanum

Nipmuck, 17

Nlaka'pamux (Thompson), 134

Nomlaki, 32–33

Nongatl, 31, 32, 132

Nornicotine, 126, 317, 321, 322, 326

North Carolina, 14, 64, 69, 192, 195;
Algonkians in, 18, 62, 66, 67–68, 69, 72

North Dakota, 108, 118, 172, 176, 177, 181,
192, 324

Northwest Coast, 117, 130–31, 176, 183, 267,
312, 325; Haida/Tlingit on, 6, 9, 13, 24–27,
27, 120, 121, 137

Northwest Interior Plateau, 9, 24–28

Northwest Territories, 364

Nova Scotia, 70

Nuttall, Thomas, 172, 176

Offerings, tobacco. *See* Tobacco, as offering

Ohio, 108, 188, 192, 196

Ojibway (Anishinabe), 17, 108, 127

Okanagan, 26, 27, 115

Oklahoma, 18, 174, 177, 179, 180

Olmstead, Richard, 87, 88, 90, 95

*Ololiuhqui*, 266, 298

Olszewski site, 197

Omaha, 20, 26, 176–77

Oñate, Juan de, 173–74

Oneida, 16, 103, 281

Oneota, 178, 180

Onondaga, 16, 65, 103, 281, 286

Ontario, 18, 20, 65–66, 281; archaeological sites
in, 190, 193–94, 195, 196, 198, 200; *N.
rustica* in, 108, 325, 358; *N. sylvestris* in, 8,
127

Oregon, 26, 144, 312; commercial tobacco use
in, 365, 376; *N. quadrivalvis* in, 6, 25, 28,
117, 120, 129, 130, 132, 135, 139, 140n.4,
172

Osage, 24, 175

Oseola site, 198

Oto, 24

Otomí, 55

Ott, Jonathan, 105
*Oxytropis*, 273

Pacific Coast, 6, 13, 24–28, 53, 176, 183
Paipai, 36
Paiute, 33, 37, 39, 40, 115, 145, 314, 360
Palmer, Edward, 150
Palmer, Gary, 31
Palmer, Jeffrey, 87, 88, 90, 95
Paloma, 177–78
Palynology. *See* Pollen
Panama, 31, 52–53, 90, 265, 267
Papago (Tohono O'odham), 41, 47, 94, 115, 125, 312
Paper, Jordan, 73–74
Paraguay, 127
Parish, S. B., 110
Parker, Kathryn E., 180, 198, 199
Paspahegh, 69
Passamoquoddy, 14
Patterson site, 180
Patuxent, 73
Paugusset, 17
Pawnee, 20, 22, 26, 121, 138, 173, 175–76, 182, 183
Pearsall, Deborah, 310
Peglar, S. M., 222
Pego, Christina M., 353
Pennsylvania, 18, 192
Penobscot, 14, 70, 71, 78
Percy, George, 69
Peru, 99, 104, 110, 307, 310, 358
Pesticides, 276, 342–43, 347, 348, 349, 350–52
Petun, 16–17, 67, 108
*Petunia*, 89; *Petunia parviflora*, 211, 212, 236–37, 255, 256
*Petunioides*, 88, 90, 91; *See also under individual species*
Peyote, 266, 298; among the Huichol, 276, 277, 278, 279–80, 281, 343; and tobacco, 21, 24, 50, 277, 279–80, 344–45, 362, 366
Philippines, 3
*Physalis*, 89, 89, 145; *Physalis acutifolia*, 231–32, 255, 256; *Physalis hederaefolia*, 232–33, 255, 256; *Physalis heterophylla*, 211, 212
*Piciete*, 66
Picuris Pueblo, 102, 150
Pike, Zebulon, 175
Pima (Akimel O'odham), 41, 44, 47, 94, 125, 312. *See also* Hohokam
Pima Bajo, 47, 49, 110
Pipeline site, 198

Pipes, 3, 4, 5, 11–12, *12*, 13, 21, 23, 27, 32, 33, 34, 36, 40, *40*, 44, 53, 60–64, 73–74, 80, 209, 270, 290–91, 292, *292*, 296, 297, 306–307, 327, 331, 332, 340, 360; in archaeological sites, 114, 128, 151, 152–53, 159, 310; calumet ceremony, 22, 59, 171, 174, 175, 177–78, 181–82; dottles from, 150, 152, 166, 169, 178, 180, *180*, 182, 195, 200; as sacred, 22, 58n.5, 304n.8
Plains. *See* Great Plains
Pleistocene, 90, 314, 322–23
Pokanoket (Wampanoag), 17–18, 63, 64, 71
Polar area index (PAI), 211, 212, 213, 218, 221
Polar axis, 211, 213, 227
Polar-equatorial index (P/E), 212, 213, 216, 227
Pollen, 97, 120, 150, 310; in archaeological sites, 4, 114–15, 166, 205–10, 207, 223; of *Cleome* (Rocky Mountain beeweed), 205, 206, 206; cluster analysis of, 219–21; discriminant analysis of, 213–19, 222; modern contamination of archaeological sites, 114–15, 207–10; of *N. attenuata*, 205–10, 228, 239, 240, 255–61; of *N. glauca*, 211–22, 212, 250–51, 255–61; of *N. quadrivalvis*, 246–50, 255–61; of *N. rustica*, 228, 241–44, 254, 255–61; of *N. tabacum*, 195, 222, 244–46, 254, 255–61; of *N. trigonophylla*, 228, 240–41, 255–61; of Solanaceae, 211–22, 223–28, 229–53, 253–61; transverse furrow of, 213, 221, 227, 256; vestibulum of, 213, 221, 227, 255; of *Zea mays* (maize), 205, 206, 206, 207
Polydiploidy, 143, 151
Polynesia, 90
Pomo, 33, 110, 118, 267
Ponca, 20, 26
Popoluca, 55
Portugal, 3, 186
Potawatomi, 17, 173
Powers, Stephen, 35
Powhatan, 18, 64, 68, 108
Prayer Rock site, 114, 153–54, 168
Priests, tobacco. *See* Tobacco priests
*Psoralea tenuiflora*, 273
Puduca, 177–78
Pueblo I sites, 114, 115, 156, 157–58, 169
Pueblo II sites, 114, 115, 159, 160–63, 169
Pueblo III sites, 115, 159, 160–63, 169
Pueblo IV sites, 115, 164, 165, 169
Pueblos, 20, 42–43, 44–45, 66, 68, 99, 101–103, 127, 150–51, 177, 206, 267, 268, 312, 365, 381. *See also* Anasazi; Hopi; Zuni

Pulekukwerek, 31, 87, 293, 294, 295, 296, 308, 309
*Punche de mexicano*, 5, 45, 102–103
Punt, W., 227
Putumayo, 127

Quebec, 20, 65, 69–70, 72, 281, 325, 358
Queen Charlotte Islands, 118, 130, 135, 136, 139
Quiché Maya, 55
Quids, yucca, 150, 153, 168, 169
Quinn, David, 64

Raffauf, Robert, 95–96
Rainbow site, 179, 190
Range site, 194, 197
Red Bow Cliff Dwelling site, 164, 168
Red Cave site, 168
Red cedar, eastern (Juniperus virginiana), 196, 197, 198, 199
Red dogwood (Cornus amomum), 175
Red willow bark, 22, 151
Renewal of Sacred Arrows, 22
Respiratory diseases, 332–33, 336, 337, 338, 340, 354, 364
Reveal, J. L., 129
Rio Grande valley, 102–103, 155, 158, 161, 165, 167
Rituals. *See* Ceremonies and rituals
Robbins, W. W., 206–207
Robicsek, Francis, 54
Rolfe, John, 93, 186, 358
Rominger, James, 110
Rosier, James, 64–65, 70, 186
Ruiz de Alarcón, Hernando, 298–99, 300, 301
Russia, 11, 13, 93, 138

Safford, William, 56
Sahagún, Fray Bernardino de, 66, 300, 301
Salinan, 33–34
Salish, 26, 27–28, 115, 360
*Salpichroa organifolia*, 235–36, 255, 256
Salts Cave site, 105
Samet, Jonathan M., 327, 331
Sanate Abajo site, 195
Sandia Pueblo, 124
San Juan Pueblo, 44, 45–46, 46, 101, 103
Santa Ana Pueblo, 101, 102, 103, 108, 115, 150
Santa Clara Pueblo, 206–207
Santa Fe Natural Tobacco Company, 46, 101
Santo Domingo Pueblo, 99, 101, 102, 103, 150
Saracha procumbens, 230–31, 255, 256
Sarsi (Tsuu T'ina), 13, 20, 22, 24, 25, 26, 120, 121, 267, 286, 362

Saubel, Katherine, 36
Sauk-Fox, 17, 108, 308
Saulteaux, 13
Say, Thomas, 178
Scanning electron microscope (SEM), 227, 228, 254, 255–56
Schagticoke, 360
Schroeder, Albert, 66
Schultes, Richard, 95–96, 110, 183
Secotan, 18
Seeds: in archaeological sites, 4, 7, 69, 97, 105, 108, 115, 120, 122, 145, 147, 149, 151–52, 154–55, 166, 168, 169, 171, 174, 177, 178, 179, 180–81, 182, 185, 188, 194–200, 205, 223, 310; with dehiscent capsules, 104–105, 120; description, 64; and domestication, 147; with indehiscent capsules, 118, 120, 121, 129, 137, 138, 143, 152, 199; of *N. attenuata*, 107, 108, 112, 114, 115, 120, 145, 146, 147, 147, 148, 149, 186, 187, 189; of *N. glauca*, 109, 110, 145, 146, 147, 148, 148, 149; of *N. quadrivalvis*, 107, 108, 116, 117, 118–19, 118, 120–21, 121, 129–30, 137, 138, 139, 186, 187, 189, 199; of *N. quadrivalvis* var. *bigelovii*, 118–19, 118; of *N. quadrivalvis* var. *multivalvis*, 107, 120–21, 121, 129–30, 138, 139; of *N. quadrivalvis* var. *quadrivalvis*, 107, 108, 120–21, 129–30, 138, 139; of *N. rustica*, 98, 101, 107, 108, 118, 120, 130, 145, 146, 147, 148, 149, 169, 182, 186–89, 198–99; of *N. tabacum*, 92, 118, 146, 148, 148, 149, 186, 187, 199; of *N. trigonophylla*, 145, 146, 147, 148, 149, 149–50; reticulations, 145, 149, 188, 189
Seminole, 14, 18
Seneca, 16, 17, 69, 103, 107, 281, 285, 286
Seri, 8, 53, 110, 122, 126
Serra, Fr. Junípero, 34
Serrano, 35, 36, 37
Setchell, William A., 65, 93, 118, 122, 129, 132, 135–36, 177; on distribution of tobacco species, 66, 151, 172, 173
Severson, R. F., 126, 317
Shamans, 17, 345; in Asia, 309, 313–14, 315; light-to-moderate use of tobacco by, 11, 28, 31–33, 37, 39–40, 41, 44, 46, 50, 54, 56–57, 73, 78, 99, 182, 183, 266–67, 298; vs. priests, 298; tobacco shamanism, 11, 12, 14, 52–53, 57, 59, 79–80, 80n.1, 265, 302, 305, 307–308, 309, 315, 325, 327, 354
Shasta, 32, 118
Shepard, Alice, 32

Shinnecok, 17
Shipibo, 94
Shorty, Lawrence A., 382
Shoshone, 28, 37, 39, 115, 136, 183, 314
Shuswap, 26, 27, 115
Siberia, 11, 13
Sibley, John, 174
Siegel, Ronald K., 277, 306, 307, 309, 313–14
Sierra Madre Occidental, 343
Siksika (Blackfoot), 9, 13, 26, 173, 267, 286, 362; commercial tobacco use among the, 365; *N. quadrivalvis* among the, 20, 22, 24–25, 120, 121, 177, 182
Simms, S. C., 288
Sinagua, 115, 169
Sinkyone, 31
Sioux (Lakota), 9, 20, 22, 173, 176, 292, 292, 304n.8, 362
Sisson, Verne, 126, 317
Skelding, A. D., 255
Skinner, Alanson, 69
Smiling Dan site, 105, 190
Smith, H. H., 317
Smoke, tobacco, 44, 72–73, 284, 295, 296, 340; components of, 331, 339; as medicine, 3, 18, 53, 266, 272, 277–78, 345; as secondhand, 4, 334, 362, 366. *See also* Cigarettes; Cigars; Pipes
Smokeless tobacco, 331, 354, 355, 364–65, 365. *See also* Snuff; Tobacco, as chewed; Tobacco, as eaten
*The Smoking Gods*, 54
Snake Indians, 39, 136
Snuff: commercial manufacture of, 108, 114–15, 207–208, 209, 297, 331, 354, 366; traditional use of, 3, 5, 7, 9, 12, 27, 35, 56, 57, 305
Societies. *See* Medicine societies; Tobacco societies
Solanaceae, 4, 88, 89, 89, 90, 145, 149, 188; pollen, 211–22, 223–28, 229–53, 253–61. *See also* Datura; *Lycium*; *Solanum*; Tobacco
*Solandra*, 281
*Solanum*, 89, 89, 145, 188, 195, 196, 197; *Solanum americanum*, 180, 187, 198–99; *Solanum douglasii*, 232–33, 255, 256; *Solanum eleagnifolium*, 211, 212; *Solanum fendleri*, 233–34, 255, 256; *Solanum jamesii*, 233, 255, 256; *Solanum nigrum*, 187
Solomon, Glenn W., 353
Sonora, 143, 227
South America, 28, 31, 47, 53, 56, 73, 79, 90, 126, 305, 322; *N. alata* in, 127, 326; *N. glauca* in, 7, 109–110, 133, 144, 170n.2, 326; *N. rustica* in, 4, 14, 74, 99, 103, 104–105, 128, 172, 185, 200, 223, 265, 310, 310–11, 312, 324, 353, 358; *N. sylvestris* in, 8; *N. tabacum* in, 4–5, 20, 93, 95, 96, 97, 105, 106, 128, 223, 265, 310–11, 312, 325, 353, 358; tobacco shamanism in, 57, 267, 307
South Carolina, 14, 18
South Dakota, 108, 118, 120, 176, 179, 180, 181, 193, 198, 324, 362
Southeast, 108, 183
Southwest, 9, 28, 41–46, 143–69; archaeological sites in, 7, 145, 152–69, 153, 159, 164, 166, 205–210; commercial tobacco use in, 327, 334, 336, 364, 365, 381; *N. attenuata* in, 6–7, 7, 41, 43, 45, 46, 92, 104, 108, 112, 113–14, 115, 143, 144, 148–49, 150, 152, 164, 168, 172, 310, 314, 324; *N. clevelandii* in, 143, 144, 147, 148–49, 150, 324; *N. glauca* in, 43, 144, 145, 147, 148–49, 150; *N. palmeri* in, 144, 147, 148–49; *N. quadrivalvis* in, 41, 43, 117, 314; *N. rustica* in, 4, 5, 41, 43, 45, 45, 46, 47, 66, 99, 102–103, 108, 143, 144, 145, 147, 148–49, 150, 169, 312, 324; *N. tabacum* in, 41, 43, 47, 143, 144, 145, 148–49, 312; *N. trigonophylla* in, 7, 7, 41, 43, 45, 123, 124, 143, 144, 145, 148–49, 150, 164, 168, 314, 324; Solanaceae in, 223–28, 229–53, 253–61; tobacco pollen in, 205–10, 211–22, 223–61. *See also* Apache; Arizona; California; Colorado; Navajo (Diné); Nevada; New Mexico; Pima (Akimel O'odham); Pueblos; Utah
Spain, 3, 5
*Sphaeralcea*, 206
Sponemann site, 194, 196, 197, 198
Stains, Donna Jean, 180
Stems, tobacco, 145, 150, 151, 156, 166, 168, 169, 175, 199, 296
Steward site, 198
Stone Pipe site, 153, 168
Strachey, William, 65, 70, 185
Stratford Flats site, 194
Strokes, 336, 338, 364
Subarctic, 9, 12–14, 266
Suislaw, 26, 28
Sullivan, Louis, 306
Sumu, 52, 267
Sun Dance, 362
Switzer, Ronald, 108
Symon, D. E., 90

Tacutsi Nacave, 279
*Tagetes lucida* (marigold), 277, 281
Tahltan, 13
Taino Arawak, 56–57, 93, 97
Takelma, 118
Talamanca, 52, 267
Tantaquidgeon, Gladys, 18
Taos Pueblo, 102, 150
Taovaya, 174
Tarahumara, 8, 47, 49–50, 53, 108, 110, 280
Tarascans, 268
Tars, 331
Tatevari, 278–79, 278, 280, 343, 345
Tatham, R. L., 213–14
Tawakoni, 174, 175
Taylor, Roy, 26
Tciplitcu, 34
Temaiyawit, 36
Tepecano, 54
Tepehuan, 47, 110
Tequistlatec, 55
Terrell, John Upton, 177
*Tesquino*, 266
Tesuque Pueblo, 101, 103
Tête de Boule (Attikamek), 13
Tewa Pueblo, 115, 206–207
Texas, 18, 20, 65, 93, 95, 108, 124, 177, 185, 325; Solanaceae in, 224–27
Thevet, Jean André, 59, 73, 186
Thompson (Nlaka'pamux), 134
Three Affiliated Tribes. *See* Arikara; Hidatsa; Mandan
Tiffany, Joseph, 180
Tijeras Pueblo, 125
Tillamook, 26, 28
Timbrook, Jan, 36, 127n.4
Timucua, 14, 18
Tipai-Ipai, 36
Tlingit, 6, 9, 13, 24–27, 27, 120, 121
Tobacco: and birds, 73, 80; as chewed, 3, 5, 7, 12, 26, 27, 28, 35, 36, 53, 54, 55, 56, 57, 150, 153, 168, 169, 207–209, 208, 209, 286, 297, 300, 305, 307, 354, 366; chloroplast DNA of, 87, 88, 89, 90, 95; and datura, 3, 34, 35, 36, 114; diffusion of, 4, 18, 65–66, 79, 90, 91, 92, 93, 96, 99, 103, 103–104, 108, 110, 121, 126–27, 128, 133, 135–36, 144, 174–75, 182–83, 185–86, 189–90, 199–200, 305, 310–17, 322–28, 323, 331, 332, 355, 358–59, 365, 366, 368; as eaten, 3, 34, 35, 36, 37, 72, 120, 271, 305, 308, 339; as food of the gods, 3, 16, 17, 18, 19, 72, 266, 269, 278, 283–84, 308, 309, 315, 325, 326, 328, 368; as a god, 3,

11, 12, 18, 19, 37, 52, 55, 266, 267, 286, 288, 289, 302, 308, 309, 315, 326, 368; vs. *Lycium*, 205, 228, 255–61; as medicine, 3, 17, 31–32, 34, 36, 40, 41, 44, 54, 57, 99, 266–67, 271, 272, 277–78, 288, 297, 298, 301, 305, 345–46; as offering, 3, 13, 17, 18, 19, 21, 33, 34, 35, 40, 44, 54, 72, 80, 266, 270, 283, 285, 286, 297, 301, 308, 342, 385; and peyote, 21, 24, 50, 277, 279–80, 344–45, 362, 366; phylogeny of, 87, 88, 89, 89; psychoactive effects of, 3, 32, 64, 74, 99, 126, 183, 265–66, 277, 304n.9, 305, 306, 313–14, 317, 324–25, 325, 326, 334, 339, 340–41, 368; as recreational drug, 3–4, 9, 24, 28, 37, 126, 266, 273, 277, 303n.1, 326, 353, 358, 382; as sacred plant, 3–4, 9, 37, 41, 52, 54, 55, 72–73, 120, 137, 138, 266, 293, 298, 302, 303, 328, 344–46, 358, 366. *See also* Addiction; Nicotine; Tobacco use; *and under individual species*
Tobacco carrots, *13*, 14
Tobacco Nation, 16–17, 67, 108
Tobacco priests, 57, 80n.1, 265, 267, 308, 327; among the Aztec, 54, 268, 292–93, 298–302, 299, 304n.11, 305, 345
Tobacco shamanism, 11, 12, 52–53, 59, 79–80, 80n.1, 265, 305, 327, 354; in the Caribbean, 57; in Eastern Woodlands, 14; among the Huichol, 50, 52, 267, 275–81, 343; in South America, 267, 302, 307, 307–308, 309, 315, 325. *See also* Shamans
*Tobacco and Shamanism in South America*, 53, 79
Tobacco societies, 14, 33, 37, 57, 80n.1, 265, 292–93, 302, 305, 308, 327; among the Crow, 22, 24, 120, 136, 137, 177, 267–68, 286–92, 287, 302
Tobacco use: vs. alcohol use, 355, 366, 368; documentary evidence for, 2, 59–80; in Europe, 2, 3, 59, 65, 69, 70, 93, 96, 99, 128, 144, 186, 328, 332, 341n.1, 358; and other cultivated plants, 4, 312–14, 324, 325; in United States, 4, 5, 10, 326, 331, 362, 364. *See also* Cigarettes; Cigars; Medicine societies; Shamans; Snuff; Tobacco; Tobacco priests; Tobacco shamanism; Tobacco societies; *and under individual tobacco species*
Tohono O'odham (Papago), 41, 47, 94, 115, 125, 312
*Toloache. See* Datura
Toll, Mollie S., 143
Tolowa, 26, 28, 136

Toltec, 267, 268
Tonkawa, 20, 108
Totonac, 54, 55
Towaoc Canal project, 156
Trade, tobacco-related, 9, 20, 22, 26, 39, 70, 79,
    93, 96, 128, 139, 150, 174–75, 182–83,
    201n.4, 311–12, 313, 323, 325, 328,
    359–60, 366; in the Arctic/Subarctic,
    11–14; among the Crow, 176, 177, 286; in
    Eastern Woodlands, 16–17, 360, 361;
    among the Hidatsa, 286, 291, 292; among
    the Huron, 13, 16–17
Transverse furrow, 213, 221, 227, 256
Travis I site, 179, 180, 198
Tree tobacco. See Nicotiana glauca
Tribulus maximus, 273, 275
Trichomes, 150, 195
Trinidad, 57, 93, 99, 185
Tsalagi (Cherokee), 18, 94, 108, 362, 365, 368
Tsimshian, 25, 26
Tsuu T'ina (Sarsi), 13, 20, 22, 24, 25, 26, 120,
    121, 267, 286, 362
Tubatulabal, 35, 115, 119–20
Tularosa Cave site, 153, 156, 168
Turkey, 3, 99, 358
Turner, Nancy, 26
Tuscarora, 103
Tutuni, 28
Twana, 307
Tzeltal Maya, 55
Tzotzil Maya, 54–55

United States, tobacco use in, 4, 5, 10, 326, 331,
    354–55, 356, 357, 358, 362, 364. See also
    under specific regions and states
Upper Coquille Athapaskans, 28
Utah, 115, 126; archaeological sites in, 143,
    144, 153, 156, 159, 164, 166, 168, 222;
    Solanaceae in, 224–27, 258, 259, 260
Ute, 37, 39, 40, 115, 270, 314

Valadez, Mariano, 344–45
Venezuela, 93, 99, 110, 186, 307, 358
Vestibulum, 213, 221, 227
Victoria, Suzanne E., 353
Village period, 179–80, 181, 182
Virginia, 193, 195; Algonkians in, 18, 63–64,
    70, 71, 72, 78; N. tabacum in, 3, 14, 65,
    93, 99, 144, 174–75, 186, 358, 360
Von Gernet, Alexander, 59, 309

Wagner, Gail E., 185
Wailaki, 31
Wallace, William, 306

Walnut River valley, 174
Wampanoag (Pokanoket), 17–18, 63, 64, 71
Warao, 307, 308
Warijio (Guarijio), 49, 50
Warrenacockse, 360
Washington State, 6, 25, 26, 28, 139, 365, 376
Washo, 37, 41, 115
Wegner, Steven, 180
Wells, Phillip, 126, 144, 151
Weltfish, Gene, 175–76
West Indies, 110, 144, 186
West Virginia, 193, 194
Whalen site, 195
Whilkut, 31
White, John, 66–67
White, Leslie, 102, 108
Whittaker, Gordon, 300
Wiacek site, 198
Wichita, 173–75, 177, 182, 187
Wilbert, Johannes, 53, 79, 80n.1, 95–96, 267,
    309
Wilkes, Charles, 130
Wilson, Gilbert L., 24, 176
Windy Wheat Hamlet site, 222
Winnebago, 17, 20, 65, 108, 137
Winter, Joseph, 138, 172
Wintu, 32
Wisconsin, 65, 193, 196, 366
Wissler, Clark, 66
Witoto, 307
Wiyot, 31
Wolfberry. See Lycium
Wolfe Creek site, 198
Woodland period, 59, 73, 105, 108, 181, 182,
    185, 190–95, 198, 199, 310; Boyer phase,
    178–79; Hill Lake phase, 190; Mund phase,
    194; Rosewood phase, 190, 194
Woosley, Anne, 114, 222
World Renewal Ceremony, 31, 37, 265, 268,
    292–93, 295–98

Xochipilli, 150

Yana, 32
Yanoama, 307
Yaqui, 54, 94
Yarnell, Richard, 108, 201n.4, 312, 314
Yavapai, 44, 115
Yaviza, 53
Yellowknife, 14
Yokia Pomo, 33
Yokuts, 8, 34–35, 37, 39, 110
Young, Bennett, 105
Yucatec, 46–47, 54

Yuki, 33
Yuma, 36, 44, 125
Yumbo, 94
Yurok, 26, 28, 136, 137–38, 307; commercial tobacco use among the, 264; myths among the, 31, 87, 293, 295–96, 308, 309; World Renewal ceremonies among the, 268, 292–93, 295–98

Zacatecas, 275
Zapotec, 54, 94, 268
*Zea mays* (maize) pollen, 205, 206, 206, 207
Zigmond, Maurice, 40–41
Zuni, 44, 45, 81–83, 82, 115, 268, 269, 293, 326
*Zuni Breadstuff*, 81